The Youth of Vichy France

THE YOUTH OF VICHY FRANCE

BY
W. D. HALLS

CLARENDON PRESS · OXFORD
1981

Oxford University Press, Walton Street, Oxford OX2 6DP

OXFORD LONDON GLASGOW
NEW YORK TORONTO MELBOURNE WELLINGTON
KUALA LUMPUR SINGAPORE HONG KONG TOKYO
DELHI BOMBAY CALCUTTA MADRAS KARACHI
NAIROBI DAR ES SALAAM CAPE TOWN

Published in the United States by Oxford University Press, New York

British Library Cataloguing in Publication Data

Halls, Wilfred Douglas
The youth of Vichy France.
1. Children – France – History – 20th Century
2. Youth – France – History – 20th Century
3. World War, 1939–1945 – Children
4. World War, 1939–1945 – France
I. Title
301.43'15'0944 HQ792.G7 80-41065

ISBN 0–19–822577–6

Typeset by Express Litho Service (Oxford).
Printed in Great Britain at the University Press, Oxford
by Eric Buckley
Printer to the University

Preface

"17 juin 1940
Voilà, c'est fini. Un vieil homme qui n'a même plus la voix d'un homme, mais parle comme une vieille femme, nous a signifié à midi trente que cette nuit il avait demandé la paix. Je pense à toute la jeunesse. Il était cruel de la voir partir à la guerre. Mais est-il moins cruel de la contraindre à vivre dans un pays déshonoré?"[1]

Who was to be responsible for shaping anew the destinies of youth in France from the Armistice to the Liberation? What principles, what ideas governed their actions as they set about the task of controlling, educating, and training children and young people? What means did they have at their disposal, with what success did they meet? These are some of the questions that must be answered regarding the 'mentors' of youth from 1940 to 1944 in Vichy France.

There was firstly the new 'Establishment' which took over after the collapse of France, headed by Marshal Pétain. He led a motley crew with very diverse views: Maurrassians, traditionally-minded and more liberally inclined Catholics, his military colleagues, and former Parliamentarians. Beyond his reach there quickly grew up a band of collaborationists in Paris. In the schools there were the teachers, accused of much of the misfortune that had befallen their country, yet indispensable if ever Vichy were to implement its policies for youth. There was also, immediate or in threatening proximity, the brooding presence of the Germans, who in the final analysis held the whip hand. And, lurking off stage, loomed the portents of the future, the 'dissident' Frenchmen in London and the as yet embryonic Resistance in France. It was these six groups who remained to the end the dominant actors in the destiny of the 'generation of 1940', if such a term may be used to embrace all those who were not yet masters of their own lives, from the very young to those that came to early adulthood during the four long years of Occupation.

The present study aims to depict and analyse the world in which these young people lived, the circumstances that surrounded their daily existence. It can lay no claim to completeness. The public files on the Vichy period, save for those that the writer was allowed to consult,[2] and most of the private archives, are at present still closed to researchers, so close to the surface are still the passions that the events of four dramatic years arouse among Frenchmen.[3]

The book has been planned as follows. The first two chapters sketch an outline of the whole period, situating in context events and institutions treated more fully later, dealing briefly with the principal strictly educational changes that occurred, which are not the central concern of the work. Next there is examined in detail the history of two important groups which affected the lives of young people closely, the Church and the school teachers. Lack of available primary sources precludes for the time being a study of the very important youth movements which continued to flourish within the Church. Some idea is then given of the policies that were followed to regiment young people. The moral and physical conditions and the national and cultural factors that determined their daily life are then dealt with, before turning to the various institutions for youth that Vichy, as part of its campaign for national 'revival', created, or which flourished with official encouragement, or, particularly if they were collaborationist and political, with German approval. The study concludes with an account of other dangers that hung over young people, such as their transportation as cheap labour or as cannon-fodder to Germany, and their plight at the downfall of the Vichy regime.

Just as it was not possible to deal, save incidentally, with the Catholic and Protestant youth movements, so it has not proved feasible to treat systematically the role played by students. As for the Resistance and the Gaullist movement, apart from the question of sources, to describe and analyse the part played by young people in them would require another book. Another omission concerns the unhappy fate of young Jews, although this is soon to be remedied by others.[4]

The author extends his warmest thanks across the Channel to the following:

M. Cézard, Conservateur en chef de la section contemporaine, Archives Nationales; those responsible for the various Archives Départementales visited, and in particular M. Robinet, Conservateur en chef of the archives of the Département du Nord; M. Henri Michel, Director of the Comité d'histoire de la Deuxième Guerre Mondiale, for permission to consult material held at the committee's headquarters in Paris; the Centre de Documentation Juive, Paris; the Bibliothèque de Documentation Internationale Contemporaine, Nanterre; the staff of the Bibliothèque Nationale and of many municipal libraries scattered throughout France; and the many Frenchmen who were kind enough to recount their personal experiences of the Vichy period. In the academic sphere the author wishes particularly to thank M. Hilaire, of the history department at the University of Lille III, who has kindly corrected some solecisms; and M. Jean Auba, Director of the Centre International d'Études Pédagogiques, Sèvres, whose institution has given me hospitality on my visits to Paris.

Across the Atlantic I have to thank the Hoover Institution for permission to quote from a speech made by Laval.[5]

In England, my thanks go principally to Professor Richard Cobb, of Worcester College, Oxford, who criticized the manuscript of this book and encouraged me to continue; and to Dr Roderick Kedward, of the University of Sussex, who likewise read the manuscript. I am most grateful for their comments. My gratitude also goes to Dr Theodore Zeldin, who was good enough to read a chapter in draft; to the librarians and their staffs at St. Antony's College, the Taylorian and Bodleian Libraries, Oxford. I must also thank the Leverhulme Trust, who generously awarded me a research fellowship to assist my research. And nearest home, as usual, I owe a special debt to Pamela, my wife. They have all improved this book; its errors remain my own.

November 1980 W.D.H.

NOTES

1. J. Guéhenno (Cévennes), *Dans la prison,* Éditions de Minuit, 1944, 9.
2. Cf. Bibliographical Note, p. 411.
3. For this reason it has been deemed appropriate, when referring to private individuals who played little or no official part in the period, to preserve their anonymity.
4. Cf. M. Marrus and R. Paxton, *Vichy et les Juifs,* Calmann-Lévy, Paris. (Forthcoming).
5. Hoover Institute, De Chambon Collection, No. 221. Speech made by Laval at a dinner for primary teachers on September 3, 1942.

Contents

Reproduced by kind permission of the Presses Universitaires de France

Preliminary Note and List of Abbreviations

The term 'Vichy' or 'Vichy regime' is used indifferently to designate the administration that ruled in France during the German Occupation from 1940–4, although many of its ministries were transferred, wholly or in part, from Vichy back to Paris. Pétain, of course, was officially installed at Vichy throughout. Likewise the term 'ministry of education' is used regardless of the various titles under which it functioned: until the appointment of Bonnard in 1942 it ranked as a 'secretariat of state for education'.

In the notes to chapters the place of books published in France during the Occupation is given, save when they were published in Paris. Elsewhere, where no place of publication is stated, the place is also Paris.

The following are the principal abbreviations used in the text or in the chapter notes:

A	Arrêté (regulation)
ACA	Assemblée des Cardinaux et Archevêques
ACJF	Association Catholique de la Jeunesse Française
AD	Archives Départementales
ADAC	Association des Anciens des Chantiers
AN	Archives Nationales
APEL	Association des Parents de l'Enseignement Libre
BDM	Bund Deutscher Mädchen
C	Circulaire
CDJC	Centre de Documentation Juive Contemporaine.
CIMADE	Comité Inter-mouvements d'aide aux évacués
D	Décret
DEPP	Diplôme des Études Primaires Préparatoires
HJ	Hitler-Jugend

IPN	Institut Pédagogique National
JEC	Jeunesse Étudiante Chrétienne (member of movement: 'Jéciste')
JFOM	Jeunesse de France et d'Outremer
JNP	Jeunesses Nationales Populaires
JO	Journal Officiel
JOC	Jeunesse Ouvrière Chrétienne (member of movement: 'Jociste')
JOFTA	Jeunes Ouvriers Français travaillant en Allemagne
JPF	Jeunesses Populaires Françaises
L	Loi
LVF	Légion des Volontaires Français contre le Bolchévisme
MSR	Mouvement Social Revolutionnaire
PPF	Parti Populaire Français
PSF	Parti Social Français
RHDGM	Revue d'Histoire de la Deuxième Guerre Mondiale
RNP	Rassemblement National Populaire
SGJ	Secrétariat (or: Secrétaire) Général à la Jeunesse
SNI	Syndicat National des Instituteurs
SOL	Service d'Ordre Légionnaire
STO	Service du Travail Obligatoire
UNEF	Union Nationale des Étudiants de France
VERDINASO	Verbond van Diestchen Nationalisten. Solidariteit voor geheel Nederland
VNV	Vlaams(ch) Nationaal Verbond

Part I

The Young and their Mentors

Chapter I

New Beginnings

The defeat that overwhelmed the French in 1940 came with devastating swiftness. After months of an artificial war on land, on May 10 the German armies invaded the Low Countries. From then on the pace of events was unrelenting: the breakthrough into France at Sedan, the British retreat from the Continent, the German entry into Paris. Within six weeks the French abandoned the struggle. At the head of a new government, Marshal Pétain, the hero of Verdun regarded as the saviour of his country in the First World War, signed an armistice, by which the Germans occupied two-thirds of France, including all the Channel and Atlantic seaboard. They had captured more than a million and half prisoners of war. A host of civilians had taken flight before the advancing armies. At Vichy the National Assembly wound up the Third Republic and voted full powers to Pétain. The 'Constitutional Acts' that followed made him a virtual dictator, although any declaration of war had to be approved by the legislature now placed in abeyance. No one knew how the Marshal would use his powers. How, in particular, would the man whose interest in education had been lifelong, regenerate youth so as to accomplish a national revival?

After the armistice perhaps a fifth of the population – soldiers and civilians, including young people and children – were left wandering aimlessly along the roads of France, seeking escape from the Germans. Children had become separated from their parents. Pathetic notices began to be inserted in provincial newspapers, such as one that appeared on July 4 in *Le Courrier du Centre:*[1] 'Le Mans family seeks: Madeleine Dorée, aged six months, Jean Dorée, aged nine, and Francine Dorée, aged ten, who boarded a tanker lorry on the road from Poitiers to Limoges.' Some 90,000 children were temporarily lost in this way. Through the authorities and the Red Cross most were eventually reunited with their parents, although some were still missing years after the war ended.[2]

Although contingency plans had been made for an orderly evacuation of the northern and eastern departments, none had allowed for the speed of the German advance. Little practical preparation could be made, since local authorities were ordered to keep secret as long as possible the ultimate destination of evacuees, so as not to alarm the population. Thus the mayor of Nouvion-sur-Meuse had only one municipal councillor to assist him in moving six hundred pupils to the south.[3] In the larger cities and the greater part of Alsace the removal of children to safe areas had occurred at the outbreak of war. A large number had left Paris in October 1939 for the so-called 'colonies de refuge'. The false start to hostilities had resulted in many returning to the capital, but the bombings of May 13, 1940 stimulated a fresh exodus to the department of the Nièvre.[4] At this time also many parents left Paris to bring back their children from the western departments to which they had been evacuated. Apart from the areas of possible invasion or air attack, however, the number of young people moved to safety was comparatively small.

In the North evacuation after the German onslaught began quickly became a rout. Becquart, the Fédération Républicaine deputy for the Nord department, took a month to cross France from North to South, finally arriving on June 13 at Lourdes with his wife and ten children.[5] By the end of May it was reckoned that only one-tenth of the total population of 400,000 living in the Lille–Roubaix–Tourcoing industrial 'triangle' had 'stayed put'. That there was muddle and confusion is illustrated by the case of Lille University. On May 18, Hardy, the Rector, instructed it to transfer to Le Touquet.[6] He then decided to move, with the rest of the education staff of the academy of Lille, to Cayeux-sur-Mer, just south of the Somme estuary. On May 21 his deputy at Le Touquet received orders to move south to the University of Rennes, but by then all crossings across the Somme had been cut. Meanwhile a blanket instruction from General Gamelin, the French commander in chief, for the population of the Northern towns not to leave had clearly been disregarded.[7]

During the débâcle, farther south the evacuation of more schoolchildren from large cities was improvised. On June 6 another contingent left from Paris by coach.[8] Liaison between the military and civilian authorities had clearly broken down, for on June 9 General Weygand, Gamelin's successor, seemingly unaware that steps had already been taken, recommended to Reynaud, the prime minister, that all children under 16 should leave the capital,[9] which fell to the Germans on June 14. The next day it was the turn of the pupils of Lyons, who were dispatched to the Ardèche, accompanied if possible by their parents.[10] The tidal wave of refugees was stemmed in part by the request for a cease-fire on June 17 but between May 15 and June 20 some six to eight million people had taken to the road;[11] it is likely that a quarter to a third of these were children and young people. The dislocation of families, which in the case of those from the Ardennes and Alsace-Lorraine sometimes lasted for years, took their toll of youngsters' nerves perhaps even more than the concentrated bombing that ensued later: the evidence is that air attack may heighten morale; the opposite is probably true of an ignominious rout.

Afterwards deeper meanings were sought in the headlong flight of 1940: 'Those ten [*sic*] million refugees who so seriously hampered army communications, do they not, for their part, bear witness to the extent that the education of courage had been overwhelmingly neglected, if not sabotaged and obliterated at all levels from the educational system and the nation? The school has too often been a school of cowardice. . .'[12] On the other hand the Catholic professor and literary critic, Pierre-Henri Simon, thought this too simplistic an explanation, at least for the behaviour of the troops. Anti-secularists might point to the fact that the army routed in 1940 was the product of the secular school, but their courageous comrades of the First World War had sat on the same benches: 'Clearly if it could be proved that the war was lost on the benches of the primary school it would be very convenient. It would, for instance, relieve us of the need for investigating whether, on the benches of the École de Guerre, they as well had always worked hard.'[13]

Nevertheless, after the collapse the disarray of young people was absolute. 'La grande peur' had gripped them and there was a collective psychosis abroad. Young men of an age to bear arms feared that they would all be rounded up by the Germans;[14] young women were beset with similar apprehensions. In the event, the invaders were initially 'correct'. But for a long while the movement of young Frenchmen homewards was blocked. The demarcation line divided the country and in the occupied zone the Germans imposed further divisions. The civil authorities had to spend the summer re-establishing communications. The centralization of education was a hindrance to getting the schools working again. Since the abrupt end of the last school year school buildings had been bombed or requisitioned. Yet by the autumn vast transformations were occurring in the national life, so that the defeat signified a sudden discontinuity. But in educating the young no such sea-change was possible: schools reopened after the holidays with mostly the same teachers, the same programmes, and the same textbooks.

If educational change could only be gradual, those that assumed power were nevertheless determined that change there would be: since all else had failed it was youth that held the strongest promise for the future. Upbringing would be different, declared the Catholics, the followers of Maurras's Action Française and other right-wing politicians assembled at Vichy. Yet there was little novel in what was now proposed as educational wisdom. Becquart, the right-wing deputy who had fled before the Germans, typifies a certain ideology current in the 1930s. In 1936, when giving away the prizes at the École Saint Joseph at Lille, he had warned his audience that a revolution was on its way, that they were witnessing 'the collapse of a society' engulfed by 'a wave of materialism'. The community had taken second place to individualism, but, he told the pupils: 'You will have to restore for yourselves those great traditions that God himself has placed at the basis of every human society: *Family,* Authority in the State, Liberty and Dignity of the individual, *Work,* Charity, *Country.*'[15] (Becquart's capitals and underlining.)

'Travail, Famille, Patrie'. The Right in French politics, particularly the Maurrassians, were now close to the centre of power and able to influence education. During the 1930s the educational focus for them had been the Cercle Fustel de Coulanges.[16] This right-wing pressure group had been founded by a secondary teacher of classics, Henri Boegner, who, from being a Protestant had turned Catholic, and, from being a Socialist, had turned towards the Action Française.[17] The group commemorated Fustel de Coulanges because the nineteenth-century historian had been both a good patriot and a man of intellectual probity. Before the war the Cercle had attracted the interest of many whose names came to be associated with young people and with education during the Vichy era, either through attendance at its dinners or through its bimestrial publication, the *Cahiers*. Among them were Marshal Lyautey, held up as the great exemplar of a life of service; Pétain himself, no less a paragon; General Weygand, who after the armistice lost no time in advocating intellectual and moral reform; two future ministers of education, Rivaud, who was appointed by Pétain as the last 'grand maître' of the Third Republic, and Bonnard, who was the last and longest-serving Vichy minister of education; Bérard, the education minister in the early 1920s who had proposed some of the reforms now to be mooted; René Gillouin, who drew up Pétain's first outline of educational reform; Bernard Faÿ, who became a zealous persecutor of freemasons and in December 1940 supplanted Julien Caïn as the head of the Bibliothèque Nationale; and Serge Jeanneret, a primary teacher who for a while became a member of Bonnard's ministerial 'cabinet'. All believed that the education system was racked by a crisis that heralded the general break-up of society in the Third Republic. They believed that the egalitarian dream of an 'école unique', a single school that all would attend, was a delusion, because intellectual cultivation accorded ill with a democratic form of society.

Weygand, Foch's lieutenant in the First World War, who had hurriedly been brought back from Syria in 1940 and, first as supreme commander and then as defence minister, had failed to avert defeat, had published in 1937 *Comment élever nos fils*, a book that reflected many of the Cercle's preoccupations. He had deplored the lack of moral training and character building, the omission of 'éducation' in the broadest sense of the term, and the emphasis on 'instruction', too often mere 'cramming' of facts. He stigmatized the products of the primary school as semi-literate and physically unfit, ignorant of what true patriotism was,[18] a fault that could be remedied only by teaching a new kind of history. Their teachers, particularly their leaders in the Syndicat National des Instituteurs (SNI), needed to shed their rabid, secularizing Republicanism. Parents must also be persuaded to interest themselves more in their children's schooling. The Cercle Fustel de Coulanges suggested how these tares might be remedied. Thus the school books must be pruned of Republican bias and due regard paid to the achievements of the pre-Revolutionary monarchy. Children must be steeped in the values of classical civilization, which meant that all secondary pupils should learn Latin. Future primary teachers should be educated, not in a closed institution such as the 'école normale', but along with other professions in the *lycée* – a suggestion that was violently rejected by SNI. For the majority of children education should be practical and technical, an idea much favoured by Bonnard when he became minister. Foreshadowing the corporatist approach to national life later adopted by Vichy, the Cercle favoured a Corporation de l'Enseignement, headed by a 'grand maître' rather than a minister, who would be advised by a Conseil National de l'Éducation, in which would be grouped teachers' unions, employers, local education authorities, and parents. Links between teachers and the home would be strengthened. In a national hierarchy of committees all branches and levels of education would be represented. Serge Jeanneret, who was secretary of the small Union Corporative des Instituteurs, regarded his union as the prototype for such a corporation, which would be able to rid education of its political overtones. On the basis of such ideas, some traditionalist, some Maurrassian, the education policy of the new regime was to be elaborated.

Pétain had his own ideas on educational reform. Appointed minister of war in 1934, he had volunteered to take on the education portfolio as well, declaring, 'I would deal with the

Communist primary teachers.'[19] The link between the school and the army was a constant in his thinking. For the conscript the army should be 'the last stage of education', 'the prolongation of school', itself 'a school of tradition, honour and high moral training'.[20] The Marshal was in good company. For civilians turned soldiers, wrote in 1902 Georges Duruy, himself the son of a minister of education, the army must be 'a great school of moral and physical hygiene as well as of honour, valour, discipline and patriotism'.[21] He was echoing a sentence of Eugène, son of Napoleon III, 'The army will be the keystone of the social edifice, the great school of the nation.'[22] Since in 1940 no military leader would admit that the army had failed the nation, the fault must lie elsewhere. The generals looked towards the education system. They alleged a need to purge the teaching body and refurbish curricula, textbooks, and methods. Since conscription would no longer be able to complete the education begun in school, they sought a surrogate in youth organizations.

Pétain's unfeigned interest in young people is reflected in his writings and speeches. In the 1941 collection of these pronouncements pride of place is given to a talk he delivered entitled 'The education of French youth'. A linguistic analysis of the corpus of his 'Messages et écrits' reveals that, of the 116 most common lexicological items, in a frequency list headed by 'France' (170 times), 'jeunesse' occupies the tenth place (53 times).[23] There is indeed a remarkable consistency in Pétain's ideas,[24] which are summarized in the article on education which he wrote (or which he allowed to be published under his name) in the *Revue des deux mondes* on August 15, 1940 – the right-wing periodical had published a number of such articles on education before the war. Pétain's article declared that the school, which in the past had unduly exalted the individual, must now educate him to function within the family, society, and nation, for, 'above all, the school will be national'. Christian values must be inculcated: neutrality is impossible when the sole choice lies between 'good and evil, order and disorder, France and anti-France'. Youth's watchword must be 'discipline, obedience, service'. Moral education is inextricably linked to training in patriotism, because modern warfare requires 'strong moral preparation'. School and army share a common task: 'to develop physical strength, temper the heart and forge the will'.[25] Striking a firmly anti-intellectual note, the Marshal pronounced against 'the fatal prestige of a pseudo-culture that is merely bookish.'[26] Training solely the mind does not produce a moral being. Another task of schooling is to prepare for a future occupation. Manual work, learnt in school, has social and moral value. In unconscious agreement with Rousseau, Goethe, and Marx, Pétain reiterated that to work with one's hands was not degrading and 'It is no less profitable to the mind to wield a tool as to hold a pen, and to know thoroughly a trade than to have superficial views on everything.'[27] Élites must acquire in school a taste for initiative, adventure, and leadership. The dream of an 'école unique', conceived in the trenches of the First World War by the reforming group that styled itself the 'Compagnons de l'Université nouvelle', was a chimera that was a formula for division and social strife. His own vision of the school, in contrast, was hierarchical, one of an institution 'which will put all Frenchmen in their place, in the service of France'.[28] In the 'Principles of the Community', a series of thoughts and maxims that the Marshal drew up, the twelfth principle ran:

> The school is the extension of the family. It must make the child understand the benefits of the human order which protects and sustains him. It must make him sensitive to the beauty, the greatness and continuity of his country. It must teach him respect for moral and religious beliefs, particularly those that France has professed since the origins of its national existence.[29]

Such views were strongly supported by General Weygand. Whilst still defence minister the general, harking back to his pre-war ideas, circulated to his colleagues a general statement in which he laid the prime blame for the disaster upon 'the former order of things, that is to say a political regime of masonic, capitalist and international compromises'. The class struggle had riven the nation in two. Now a new nation must arise based on co-operation between employers and workers. The paramount position of the family must be restored: a population in decline had meant that colonial troops and foreigners had had to be called upon to defend the country, which had also been undermined by the naturalization of too many immigrants. The cause of national weakness was a philosophy of materialism. Hence his conclusion: 'We must return to the cult and practice of an ideal, summed up in these few words: God, Country, Family. The education of the young must be reformed.'[30] Other defeated generals – Huntziger, de Lattre de Tassigny, de La Porte du Theil, even Gamelin, dismissed for incompetence – agreed that a new kind of education was necessary to save France.

Politicians and top-ranking officials were of the same mind. Laval, the architect of the new regime, demanding on July 10, 1940 from the National Assembly full powers for Pétain, had stressed the high priority that in future must be given to education and youth.[31] Particularly influential at this time was Paul Baudouin, Pétain's foreign minister, whose interest in youth, like the Marshal's, had been unfailing. An air ace of the First World War, an ex-Polytechnicien and then successively an Inspecteur des Finances and a director of the Banque d'Indochine, he had spoken out in 1938 against totalitarian regimes but had praised their efficiency. Now his hopes, he said, were fixed firmly on the rising generation. In his diary for June 25, 1940[32] he noted that, having reread Renan's post-1870 plea for intellectual and social reform, he wanted Pétain to follow a similar policy, thereby moving towards 'a stronger and purer political order'. Maurrassians such as Raphael Alibert spoke in similar vein. Also a one-time higher official – he had been a Conseiller d'État – this right-wing doctrinaire has been described as Pétain's 'evil genius' until he was dismissed from his post as minister of justice in January 1941. Asked by the Marshal in the summer of 1940 to produce post-haste a plan for educational reform, he had delegated the task to another ex-civil servant, René Gillouin. A Protestant of the moderate Right, Gillouin had worked in the Prefecture of the Seine until 1931, when he had resigned to devote himself to literature; he had been a Paris municipal councillor, and his one claim to expertise in education was that he had been associated with the Cercle Fustel de Coulanges. The plan he drew up contained a condemnation of individualism, rationalism, and mere 'instruction'.[33] Gillouin continued to be close to Pétain, until the return to power of Laval in 1942, when he fled to Switzerland. Against this Protestant influence in the early days of Vichy must be balanced that of a small group of social Catholics, mainly Personalists, who responded to the 'community' aspect of Pétain's ideas: for them the school's task was to create an organic community.[34]

A discordant note among the unison at Vichy was struck by Marcel Déat, the author of the sensational leading article that appeared in the spring of 1939 in his newspaper, *L'Œuvre,* entitled, 'Mourir pour Dantzig?' This intellectual turned politician had made his way by his own efforts from a village school to the École Normale Supérieure and had been a philosophy teacher at the Lycée of Reims before being elected to the Chamber of Deputies. He had passed from Socialism to a neo-Socialism strongly tinged with authoritarianism. On July 27, 1940 he had submitted to Pétain a project for a single-party state which included proposals for the complete regimentation of youth.[35] When his plan had been rejected he had taken himself off to Paris. The Rassemblement National Populaire (RNP), a movement which bore the stamp of National-Socialism, which he founded in early 1941, kept up a continual sniping at Vichy's educational policy until Bonnard, an overt collaborationist, was appointed minister of education. Déatistes wanted their 'total doctrine' to be reflected in an 'école unique'. Since this would mean the closure of the confessional schools,[36] the movement clashed with the Catholics. Déat's policy for youth was in conformity with his idea of a totalitarian state, a necessary step, he considered, to ensure France's future in the new, German-dominated Europe.

Déat apart, Maurrassian and Catholic views on young people converged in the early days at Vichy. They were given substance in the concept of the so-called Révolution Nationale, a term borrowed from the vocabulary of the pre-war Jeunesses Patriotes, a party headed by Pierre Taittinger which, from a youth movement, had developed into a right-wing organization for all ages. The Révolution Nationale – Pétain preferred the word 'redressement' – was not of course exclusively concerned with youth. It lacked any manifesto save the pronouncements of the Marshal, but an indication of how education and youth were to be treated may be gathered from its general principles.[37] The regime was to be 'mon-archic', in the sense that Maurras and the Action Française gave to the term, founded upon authority, 'hierarchical in internal policy . . . above all, social in spirit'. Christian values, the sanctity of the family, and the dignity of labour would be upheld. There would be a return to the land, which 'does not lie'. Naive faith in liberalism, capitalism, Marxism, and rationalism were all equally to be condemned. Corporatism was to be the basis for the organization of agriculture and industry. For this new social order youth would be moulded in a narrow nationalism and undergo 'intellectual and moral renewal'. However, the educational corollary to these ideas was never fully worked out and certainly never realized. The Révolution Nationale was largely a spent force by mid-1942, blown off course by more pressing priorities and the changing circumstances of war. The one idea that survived the war, that 'éducation' was more important than mere 'instruction', had been perennial in all reform proposals. How Vichy, through successive ministers of education, attempted none the less to implement its 'doctrine' must now be considered.

First, however, came the cult of the national hero, the leader, which expressed itself in the near adoration of Pétain fostered among schoolchildren. Books were written about the Marshal almost in the style of fairy stories, and the descriptions were almost lyrical: 'Il est un beau vieillard, solide et droit comme l'arbre des Druides, un clair regard illumine son visage impassible, clair comme l'eau calme de son pays quand elle reflète un coin du ciel.'[38] The woodcraft image was carried even further by the dedication to the Marshal of a magnificent oak tree – 'le chêne Pétain' – in the forest of Tronçais, not far from Vichy, on the occasion of the first youth movement created by Vichy. The oak had been planted in Colbert's time to provide bottoms for the French fleet. When the old man was shown it he modestly remarked: 'Two hundred and seventy years old. I'm overwhelmed. I'll never catch up with it!' Later the oak was solemnly 'shot' by the Resistance because of its Vichy associations.[39]

The childless head of state had a genuine affection for children. Dr Ménétrel, his personal secretary and physician, wielded great influence because he had two small daughters with whom Pétain loved to play.[40] He also enjoyed descending upon village schools in the department of the Allier and, in fatherly fashion, adjuring the pupils to work hard. At the opening of the new school year he broadcast an appeal to children to stick at their lessons and not to cheat. The father-image was sedulously built up by propagandists, and adults as well as children were taken in by it. In schools the pupils were taught 'the Marshal's song', 'Maréchal, nous voilà', composed by André Montagard (who also numbered among his successes 'Un pastis bien frais'!):

All children who love you and venerate your age
To your supreme appeal have answered 'Present!'
Marshal, here we are before you, the saviour of France.
We swear to you, we your men, to serve you and follow
In your footsteps. . . For Pétain is France, and France is Pétain.

This side of idolatry, adulation could go no further. At Christmas children wrote letters to him from school; in 1940 some 200 post-bags arrived, accompanied by a million drawings on the theme of France.[41] Ten thousand of the best efforts went on display at Vichy. One consisted of a map of France inscribed with Pétain's memorable phrase, 'I make the gift of my person to France to mitigate its misfortunes', to which the girl artist had added, 'For this magnificent gift, our thanks'.[42] Indeed, thanks-offerings of all kinds – sheaves of corn, lambs suitably beribboned, albums of drawings on the theme of 'The France we love' – flowed in. Pamphlets containing Pétain's 'messages' were sold to pupils for use in civics lessons.[43] His picture was displayed in the class-room. Jean Guéhenno, a teacher as well as a writer, referred scathingly to the portrait: 'There was this horrible coloured print. That man with seven stars [the insignia of the Marshal's rank], sometimes covered with paper pellets, who, like God the Father, presided over our work.'[44] But by November 1941, the ministry announced, sales of portraits, posters, and calendars bearing the Marshal's picture amounted to seventeen million francs.[45] The profits went to the Secours National, for which children collected assiduously. Those who collected most travelled to Vichy, where they would be entertained in the Grand Casino in the Marshal's presence. Teachers to accompany their charges on this expedition were sometimes hard to find; for one group from Rouen bearing New Year greetings there was only one teacher volunteer.[46] The young were encouraged to write freely to Pétain. After the overnight bombing of her Dunkirk school one little girl confided proudly that her class had cleared away the debris in a few hours.[47] This personality cult, fostered round wartime leaders everywhere, gratified an old man's vanity, satisfying his real love of children. It was also thought to promote national solidarity.

A sardonic postscript to this came after the Liberation. Recalling the yearly epistle that had to be written to Pétain, a young Communist commented: 'Your memory disappears from all our schools, where your portrait will serve to light the stoves as soon as the weather requires it. Each year the "scribblers" at Vichy "required" from us a letter that we used to "write" spontaneously. This school year [1944] this tradition has not been renewed.'[48] Bitterly the writer reminds Pétain that another marshal of great age, de Bono, had been shot in the back and that this could be his fate also, 'for the nation cannot acknowledge all the good that you have done for it, particularly for the children and the prisoners, your two main concerns, nor for the family: homes have never been more divided or broken up than under your government.' He 'fears' that the Maquis will seek out Pétain in Germany and for the last time require of him 'the gift of his person'. Such an indictment illustrates admirably the extreme volatility and malleability of the young, as well as the ephemeral effect of all propaganda, and perhaps of much education.

Patriotism and solidarity were encouraged by a 'colours ceremony'. Once a week pupils were paraded to witness the hoisting of the national flag. In the Hautes-Alpes it was decreed[49] that on the first occasion local dignitaries, parents, and members of the Légion des Combattants would attend. Teachers who failed to put in an appearance would be reported. A colours party of pupils would act as guard of honour. The mayor of Sennecy-le-Grand in Burgundy justified the ceremony on the grounds that 'patriotism had not been taught adequately in the school'; it was the teaching of 'internationalism' – a term of opprobrium in both France and Germany during the war – that had brought about their present sufferings.[50] In Ardèche, at a Catholic school, a prayer terminated the ceremony: 'Under the eyes of God. . . Obeying the instructions of Marshal Pétain, our leader, children of France, for family and country. . . To work!'[51] Occasionally the ceremony was used for fraternization between State and Catholic schoolchildren, who paraded together. On at least one occasion the local State inspector and the Catholic diocesan inspector symbolically raised the colours together. Admiral Darlan, versed in naval practices, issued instructions as to the correct way of hoisting and lowering the flag. The symbolism of such ceremonies was not lost upon anyone, least of all upon the Germans. In the Seine-et-Oise they forbade it 'once and for all'[52] but later relented, leaving the matter to the discretion of the local commander.[53]

If most could accept the imperative for national unity, expressed in the cult of the leader and of the Tricolour, there was less consensus on the educational measures that Pétain should take to realize the Révolution Nationale and the sum of doctrines elaborated before the war. In the space of six months he ran through three different ministers of education, Rivaud, Mireaux, and Ripert. These, together with Chevalier, who succeeded Ripert, may be characterized as 'intellectual reactionaries'[54] of Catholic and right-wing persuasion. Rivaud, a Sorbonne professor, was appointed on June 17, 1940, just before the Armistice. Planté, a high official of the ministry, has recounted how he first met his new chief during the retreat, wandering uncertainly along a corridor. Planté had taken him for a parent wanting to complain about the baccalaureate – the trait is significant. Having identified himself as Delbos's successor the new minister remarked, 'Some primary teachers will have to answer for having given up to the enemy the roads from the frontier.' Rivaud persuaded Planté to issue him with a certificate saying that he was the minister and that Mme Rivaud was his wife![55] But he lasted only twenty-six days in office: he was notorious for his anti-Nazism and was thus an embarrassment to the new regime. In 1938 he had published a strongly condemnatory book, *Le Relèvement de l'Allemagne,* and in 1938 an article, 'L'Âme du Nazi', in the *Revue des deux mondes,* in which he had misguidedly predicted: 'Tomorrow this lunatic Germany is perhaps going to crumble, but not without having encompassed unspeakable devastation. Hitler and his creatures will return to nothingness.' But 'tomorrow' was five years away and it was Rivaud who returned more quickly to anonymity. After the war he was accused, like all his successors in ministerial office, of endangering State security. Proceedings against him, as against the others, with the exception of Chevalier and Bonnard, were dropped because he had assisted the Resistance.

His successor was Mireaux, who took over on July 12. Mireaux was an ex-Normalien, a senator who was co-director of *Le Temps,* a member of the Institut, an *agrégé* with expertise in economics. He was closely linked to Laval and probably owed his appointment to his skilful pleading in the final session of the National Assembly in 1940, when he had argued that a simple majority of the members voting, rather than an absolute majority of members, including those not present, as was prescribed in the constitutional law of 1875, was sufficient in order to revise the laws relating to the Constitution. Having done Laval this good turn, he was rewarded with the education portfolio, but held it for only fifty-five days.[56] During that time a number of general measures that affected education indirectly were promulgated. The law of July 17 empowered the State to dismiss or suspend for any reason whatsoever all civil servants, including teachers. Another law laid down that neither foreigners nor those naturalized since 1927 could normally be State employees. On July 23 those public servants who had fled abroad were dismissed their post. Finally, the law of August 13 forced freemasons to declare their membership; a later law dismissed those who had held office in a lodge.[57] Mireaux himself initiated a number of more narrowly educational measures. He restored formally to religious orders the right to teach, although in practice this prohibition had not been enforced since 1914. The minister was relieved of the obligation of having to consult his advisory bodies and, in particular, the Conseil Supérieur de l'Instruction Publique. He initiated sanctions not only against freemason teachers, but also against those whose conduct was deemed to have been disloyal or who had abandoned their posts during the débâcle. He introduced a tighter control over primary teachers by reorganizing the departmental committees for primary education on which they sat. His abrupt dismissal was probably because Pétain did not like Parliamentarians and as a senator he was too closely associated with the defunct Republican regime. His departure was welcomed by the Déatistes in Paris, who accused him of representing the interests of the Comité des Forges.

His successor, appointed on September 6, was Ripert, dean of the Paris law faculty, where he passed for being 'the most anti-democratic of the whole establishment'.[58] His policy statement, characterized by that 'langue musclée' which gives the tone of many official pronouncements from now on, announced that his prime concern would be 'to restore authority, which has disappeared. Young people . . . must be disciplined. They must indeed – why not say so boldly? – grow accustomed to obedience.'[59] Thus student demonstrations would be stamped upon, 'politicking' in education would be eradicated, moral education reinforced, primary education 'cleansed' ('assaini'), insubordinate teachers punished. Root and branch reforms indeed followed. Primary-teacher-training colleges were abolished. Teachers' unions, politically powerful in the 1930s, were disbanded; they were to be replaced by State-controlled professional associations. Sanctions taken against teachers who had offended in the past were implemented. By a general measure, the Statut des Juifs, Jews were excluded from teaching. On the more narrowly educational front, in secondary education the so-called 'modern' option – 'Section B' – was to be progressively phased out, so that once again all *lycée* pupils would learn Latin. In primary schools the ethics and civics programme was revised to include the controversial 'devoirs envers Dieu', whilst the programme for the higher elementary school ('école primaire supérieure') prescribed: 'the moral ideal, the appeal of the hero and the saint. God'. Ethical teaching should be centred round 'travail, famille, patrie'. (It is probable that Chevalier, the next minister of education, who was then secretary-general to Ripert, was the real initiator of these programme changes.) A list of banned books was issued and procedures for vetting new texts for school use and for pruning school libraries were introduced. The State charitable fund for needy pupils, the Caisse des Écoles, was thrown open to Catholic schools. Educational charities, many of which were left wing, were banned and replaced by a new body, the Fédération des Œuvres de l'Enseignement Public. The Conseils Départementaux for education which, like the consultative committees for primary education, had been open to political manipulation through the left-wing teachers' unions in the past, were reformed. Henceforth appointments of teachers to them would be made by the minister. The post of cantonal delegate for education, whose task had been to liaise between families and the school, was abolished because it was alleged that delegates had used their position for political manœuvring and personal ends. Finally, primary-school inspectors would no longer be appointed by open competition but directly by the minister. The purpose of both Ripert's and Mireaux's measures is clear: it was to inaugurate a more authoritarian style in education, to emphasize moral and Christian values, to tighten the rein upon the secular, left-wing primary teachers, to favour the confessional schools more. The impact of the measures upon teachers and young people is discussed later. Their implementation required time and in the first six months the Vichy regime was much preoccupied with overcoming the practical difficulties of getting the educational machine to function again.

By the end of the year Ripert had been ousted. Various reasons have been given for his somewhat dramatic departure. On December 13, 1940 Pétain accomplished a 'palace revolution' which greatly aroused German wrath. In order to force out Laval, the Marshal followed a procedure that he had followed before when he had reshuffled his government. He required all ministers to sign a letter of resignation. Not feeling at risk in any way, Laval cheerfully signed and was flabbergasted when the Marshal announced that his resignation and that of Ripert – but none of the others' – had been accepted. Pétain suspected that Laval was negotiating with the Germans behind his back. But why Ripert, it must be asked? The education minister had come under fire from the Paris collaborationist press as a reactionary and had incurred German displeasure for not having forestalled an anti-German student demonstration on Armistice Day.[60] By sacrificing Ripert whilst ridding himself of Laval Pétain had offered 'satisfaction to the "conspirators" of Paris just as he "beheads" them, as if in this way the operation was balanced.'[61] Du Moulin de Labarthète, probably the best informed of the Marshal's immediate entourage, noted: 'Doubtless M. Ripert will never have understood the reasons for his departure, nor why his destiny was associated with that of Laval. There is always one innocent person in the best-prepared tumbrils. . .'[62] Others asserted that Ripert was anxious to resign because he had quarrelled with Chevalier, his secretary-general, and had become increasingly opposed to the Révolution Nationale,[63] a supposition confirmed by Laval.[64] On the other hand Pétain may have required his post in order to give ministerial rank to Chevalier, who needed some standing in order to negotiate (if negotiate he did) with Lord Halifax, whom he had met at Oxford, in an attempt to improve Franco-British relations and gain some material advantages for France.

Jacques Chevalier, whose tenure of the ministry was also short – seventy-two days – is one of the more interesting characters thrown up by the Vichy regime. Like Mireaux, Déat, Carcopino, Pucheu, and many others who came to the fore during the period, he was a graduate of the École Normale Supérieure. His father had been a general and a friend of Pétain, who was Chevalier's godfather. By training a philosopher, after graduating Chevalier had spent a year or so in Oxford,[65] working, curiously enough, with the professor of mineralogy on crystallography and at the same time preparing a thesis on the religious revival in nineteenth-century Wales, an academic exercise that was later rejected. He and Lord Halifax, who was then a fellow of All Souls, had become friends. During the First World War he had been attached to the British army and claimed to have won a

British military decoration. After the war he had taught philosophy and had become the friend and disciple of Bergson. By 1938 he was dean of the Faculty of Letters at Grenoble. His appointment as minister was not likely to commend itself to the Germans, who associated it with the departure of Laval and were deeply suspicious of his British connections and his devout Catholicism.

As a staunch believer, he saw his prime task as being to reinstate religion in education. His measures to restore the power of the Church by reintroducing religious instruction into State schools and by giving subsidies and other benefits to the confessional schools are discussed in detail later. His part in the replacing of the 'duties towards God' in State-school syllabuses has already been mentioned. Now, by two laws of January 6, 1941 religious instruction was made an optional subject in State schools and communes were authorized, if they so wished, to subsidize Catholic schools to a limited extent. State scholarships were also thrown open to Catholic pupils. It was even envisaged that communes should subsidize the fees of children attending Catholic schools. This help was to be channelled through the Caisse des Écoles. This abrupt reversal of half a century of secularist policies in education stirred up a hornet's nest.

It soon became obvious that Chevalier would have to go, since most of those employed in the State education system and all the collaborationists, now beginning to make their views heard in Paris, were opposed to him. Moderate opinion, which included some Catholics, at Vichy thought he had overreached himself. The Germans were particularly incensed. Their ambassador in Paris, Otto Abetz, knew France well and was well able to sense the mood. Abetz, a former art teacher at the Gymnasium of Karlsruhe, had always favoured Franco-German rapprochement. (In 1931 he had met Jean Luchaire, the journalist, at a youth congress, and had eventually married a Frenchwoman, Luchaire's secretary. In 1939 Abetz had been expelled from France by Daladier.) Thus Admiral Darlan, appointed Vice-Président du Conseil on February 25, 1941, was summoned to attend upon Abetz[66] to hear a condemnation of Chevalier at a time when France was already in Germany's bad books because of the sacking of

Laval two months previously. Chevalier was reproached not only with having reintroduced religion into education but also because he had sent a telegram of sympathy to Bergson's widow when the great Jewish philosopher had died a few weeks earlier. Darlan could only counter by saying that Chevalier was the friend of Pétain and that he would instruct the minister to change his policy. The marked German mistrust of Catholicism evident here is a constant throughout the Occupation. Pétain himself may have thought that his protégé had outlived his usefulness but nevertheless got Darlan to move the 'great believer', the 'predestined being', as Planté referred to Chevalier, sideways to the less conspicuous post of minister of family and health. In August 1941 he fell ill and also relinquished this post and ultimately resumed his university functions at Grenoble. He remained a fanatical devotee of Pétain to the end. Although later in the Occupation he tried to prevent the shipping of students to Germany for forced labour, he aided and abetted the actions of the pro-German Milice in suppressing 'terrorism' towards the end. For this he was tried and imprisoned at the Liberation. He died in comparative obscurity.

In February 1941 a new minister of education, Jérôme Carcopino, took over. Pétain favoured André Bellessort, secretary of the French Academy, for the post. Abetz had wanted Abel Bonnard (who was later to succeed Carcopino), known for his collaborationist views, and Darlan would not have opposed the appointment.[67] Carcopino was therefore a compromise appointment. He accepted office on condition that he could rescind the religious measures of his predecessor, maintain the 'traditional freedoms' of the university, in particular its right to appoint whom it willed to certain high-level posts, and revert, after his term of office was over, to his position as Director of the École Normale Supérieure.[68]

Carcopino had entered the École Normale Supérieure as a student in 1901, the same year as Chevalier. After a spell as a history teacher at the Lycée of Le Havre, in 1912 he had secured a professorship at the university of Algiers. Service in the First World War had been followed by his appointment to a chair of Roman history at the Sorbonne. In 1930 he had become the Director of the École de Rome. Returning from

Italy, he had accepted in July 1940 Mireaux's invitation to become the Director of the École Normale Supérieure. When Roussy, the Rector of the University of Paris, had been dismissed after the student demonstration on Armistice Day, Carcopino had temporarily assumed the functions of Rector. His contact with Pétain dated from 1934, when they had met at the 'déjeuners Hervieu', a lunching club founded by Paul Hervieu. The Germans did not oppose Carcopino's appointment as minister: their evaluation was that he had worked 'completely fairly' with them and had even, so they believed, come out 'more or less openly for collaboration'.[69] The truth, however, was a little more intricate. Carcopino was one who accepted the limitations of a situation and, whilst remaining uncommitted, worked to obtain the maximum advantage from it. Opportunist and 'attentiste', he was a seeker after compromises and accommodation, shunning extremes with Roman moderation – he was after all a great classical scholar. His ambiguous attitude was misinterpreted. Frenchmen of the Resistance held him to be 'the Gauleiter of the University, the Ferdonnet of the school, the eye of Berlin, the delegate of the German Military Commander, a sneak, lackey and traitor', a man 'skilful in hypocrisy and cynicism', aiming at a seat in the French Academy.[70] The judgement is inaccurate. Many Frenchmen approved of him as minister, recognizing that he was playing the game skilfully against extremism at Vichy and against German interference. Post-war opinion largely vindicated him for his efforts to preserve the high standards of French education and yet effect moderate changes.

All this, however, was in the future. The new minister began his tenure with a broadcast (March 16, 1941)[71] in which he set out his initial policy, disclaiming any desire to proceed precipitately, but wanting gradual reforms. In higher education he sought to preserve the internal autonomy of its institutions. In implementing sanctions against teachers he would not act weakly, but he would punish acts and not opinions. Chevalier had punished about one hundred teachers during his time as minister. Carcopino proclaimed his intention of winding up all punitive action by the end of March 1941, either confirming or revoking the penalties imposed provisionally by his predecessors for a three-month period. After that date only exceptional cases would be judged. He opposed reprisals for their own sake, because 'I esteem it impossible to rebuild a post-war France that excludes a section of pre-war Frenchmen.'[72] He had immediately changed the primary-school syllabus for ethics, replacing the 'duties towards God' by: 'spiritual values: our country; Christian civilization'. He had done this, he said, because primary teachers had not been trained to teach religion. Religious instruction must not normally be given in school buildings. Expressed in peasant language, what he wanted was, he said, 'The primary teacher in his school, the parish priest in his church, and the teacher the priest's friend'. The reversal of policy was not well received by Catholics, who claimed that '. . . his plea, very welcome to minds who "play upon the sophistry of neutrality", has nonetheless not convinced the immense majority of French people who believe in God' or even those who might not practise their religion but still had 'Christianity in their bones'.[73]

For the time being the law allowing communes to grant aid to Catholic schools was maintained. This did not go far enough for the Catholic hierarchy, who pressed for larger subsidies. Eventually, after negotiations which are discussed elsewhere, subsidies were channelled to the confessional schools through the ministry of the interior (law of November 2, 1941), although Carcopino stressed that the additional aid was a temporary and exceptional measure to assist only private primary schools. The global sum allocated was at first estimated at about 400 million francs. A parallel measure established, as a quid pro quo, a right of supervision of private schools. At the same time aid from the communes was stopped. The compromise arrived at suited neither Catholics nor secularists.

During the spring of 1941 Carcopino was much concerned at the lack of information regarding education in German-occupied territory, particularly in the Nord and the Pas-de-Calais, both of which departments were administered not from Paris but by the German High Command in Brussels. Thus he dispatched two officials concerned with primary education, F——— and P———, on an inspection tour. In

June they delivered their report to him.[74] It was brutally frank. In the two northernmost departments they found that many Vichy measures were countered by a German veto. Inter-city telephone and telegraph facilities were often non-existent and even the ministry's official telegrams took five days to arrive. At first no radios and not even the Paris collaborationist newspapers had been allowed, so that only news permitted by the Germans filtered through. Conditions were particularly precarious in the coastal strip facing England, where, despite a food shortage, the inhabitants were not allowed to forage for black-market supplies outside the area. There the bombing was so severe that older teachers requested that they be replaced for a time by younger colleagues or at least be allowed to spend their holidays in a quieter region. The population felt abandoned by the Vichy government, so much so that even Pétain was criticized. Yet, despite German 'correctness', the people were opposed to any Franco-German *rapprochement* and in some towns maintained secret lists of collaborators. Here and there traditional pro-British sentiments reinforced hostility to the Germans who, it was feared, might well carve out an enlarged Flemish or Lotharingian satellite state from French territory.

The two officials were careful to point out that such 'negative' attitudes were not stirred up by the teachers. Indeed, 'It would be dangerous to let there arise. . . a slanderous legend according to which the education system, which some have wished to make responsible for the military defeat, was now held to be comporting itself in such a way as to make us lose the peace and to favour a national schism from which French unity would suffer grievously.' On the contrary, teachers, pupils, and school staff in general were on the whole commended. More than half the teachers had returned to their posts. Since the Germans had largely refrained from interference in the schools, the teachers observed a strict neutrality. Even temporary appointees were enthusiastic and self-sacrificing. Somewhat ingenuously, the officials remarked that there was much curiosity about the new type of 'general education' being introduced into the schools and anxiety to learn how the new physical-training programme could be adapted for pupils that were undernourished. Salaries were a sore point. Many teachers had lost all their belongings in the looting that had gone on in 1940 or in subsequent bombing. They bitterly resented that those of their colleagues who had not yet returned from the southern zone continued to receive an extra indemnity for living away from home. Head teachers complained that the number of pupils had fallen partly because of the lack of boarding facilities, partly because, through force of circumstances, some schools had become mixed, which parents disliked. Catholic schools, where such difficulties did not exist, were envied. Pupils generally were commended for the admirable discipline they had shown, although isolated demonstrations of hostility towards the Germans had led to some massive expulsions. Carcopino took note of the report of the two officials, but there was little he could do about the matters raised, even though dissatisfaction about salaries was felt by all teachers.

In setting about reform, the minister's efforts were directed towards internal changes within the education system, and it was for these that he was praised after the war. The 'réforme Carcopino', as it became known, had as its main purpose the re-establishment of the primacy of 'culture générale'. Proposals for change had been circulating even before he came to power, but Carcopino finalized them in a few months: in the *Journal Officiel* for September 2, 1941 there appeared no less than thirty laws and regulations regarding education.

Till then *lycées* and colleges had been the only truly secondary institutions. Now, with the aim of upgrading their status, technical schools and higher elementary schools ('écoles primaires supérieures'), which were both general and vocational and stood half-way between primary and secondary education proper, all became colleges of secondary rank. According to the minister, the higher elementary schools, in particular, had become associated with 'simplism, narrowness, intolerance and credulity'. The general education they had dispensed was far inferior to that of the *lycée*, just as their vocational training was inferior to that of the technical school.[75] Amalgamation and upgrading would help realize '[Pétain's] intention of fusing together social classes hostile to each other, within a State in which Frenchmen, reconciled one with another, serve, each at his post, their country. It is this conception that I have followed, by abolishing the separations which would inevitably revive divisive antagonisms.' Moreover, Carcopino said, he had also followed the Marshal in another important respect: 'The Marshal said one day that he would keep all promises, even those of others. The one that the 'école unique' held out but did not realize will henceforth become true, and in town and countryside not a single Frenchman will remain who does not receive from the State the means of developing his abilities to the utmost.' Nevertheless, Carcopino was careful not to offend the bourgeoisie by abolishing the special fee-paying primary classes given within the *lycée* to younger pupils, a system which enabled them to transfer without difficulty to the main school at eleven. Theoretically these classes, if not filled by fee-payers, were open free to State primary pupils,[76] but in practice this had not happened. Equalization of opportunity was therefore only partial. In another way also the gap between the *lycée* and other schools remained as wide, because it alone would offer a full classical syllabus. It alone would have classes preparing for the competitive examinations for the 'grandes écoles'.

The quarrel about the place of Latin in education has deep roots in French history. Ripert had abolished the so-called 'modern' section – the option without Latin – in the *lycées*. Now that new institutions had been added to secondary education Carcopino was urged to ensure that all pupils learnt Latin. But, despite his own classical scholarship, the minister set his face against this, observing that '. . .if I have the cult of the humanities I have no superstition about them'. Nevertheless, the Latin lobby remained strong. Before becoming minister Chevalier had canvassed the educational ideas of his master, Bergson. In the early 1920s the eminent philosopher had also proposed a two-track system: an élitist school, the *lycée*, dispensing classical culture and training the future leaders in society, would run parallel to a 'modern' type of school, preparing pupils for responsible posts in the armed forces, industry, and agriculture. In 1923 Léon Bérard, when minister of education, had forced through a measure making Latin compulsory for all *lycée* pupils, but his decree was repealed by the incoming Cartel des Gauches administration almost immediately. Since Bérard was much in evidence at Vichy before being appointed ambassador to the Vatican in late 1940, there can be little doubt that he formed part of the classics pressure group. Moreover, another of Bergson's associates, Le Roy, a member of the senatorial commission on education who had previously advised Jean Zay, the reforming education minister of the Third Republic, was invited to draw up a new plan for the structure of education. He also postulated a dual system of secondary education, but came out in favour of Latin for both types of secondary education when he presented his project to the Académie des Sciences Morales et Politiques in March 1941. This intense interest vouchsafed in a classical education was paralleled in West Germany in 1945, after the defeat of Nazism. Defeated nations, looking for a new basis for their societies, tend to dwell upon the past, and on the virtues of Antiquity. Carcopino took careful note of such advocacy, but in the event refused to generalize the teaching of Latin in all secondary schools. Pragmatism rather than ideological considerations characterized his reforms.

He also reformed the method of entry to secondary education, establishing a system that was to function in part almost up to 1965. Access to secondary schools would be on merit, after a new qualification, the diploma of primary preparatory studies ('diplôme des études primaires préparatoires : DEPP), had been obtained at eleven. After the war this examination became known as the 'examen d'entrée en sixième'. In the minister's view this diploma ensured selection on merit alone,[77] a view that was held also of the similar eleven-plus examination that evolved from the English Education Act of 1944. But clandestine Communist propaganda protested against the early age of selection and claimed that examiners for the DEPP had been instructed to cut down the pass-rate.[78] For their part, the *lycées* objected that they were inundated with ill-prepared pupils and that the strict age stipulation that had been imposed prevented bright young pupils coming up through their own internal primary classes from making an early start on their secondary course.[79] The new examination was criticized as being too factual as compared with the old selection system, which relied in part on tests administered in the primary school and on the over-all record of schooling. Since there was still no entrance examination for Catholic secondary schools, a loophole existed for rich pupils: those who failed the DEPP could enrol in them and after a while transfer without difficulty to the State *lycée*. Another unforeseen effect was the much higher pass-rate – at least in Paris – for girls (59.4 per cent) as compared with boys (40.9 per cent).[80] Moreover, a certain imbalance arose regarding both numbers and choice of course: in 1942, as compared with 1941, there were 12.7 per cent more pupils wanting to opt for the classical course, and 28.6 per cent more wanting to opt for a modern one.[81] Academy inspectors would have preferred what they regarded as a more refined selection procedure: the 'orientation' process that Zay had introduced experimentally just before the war. When Bonnard became minister he wanted to revert to this, but was opposed by his top officials, whom he accused of being two-faced. He concluded, 'I understand why M. Carcopino consulted nobody.'[82]

Carcopino summed up these aspects of his reforms as trying 'to open up on all floors of the house, not a ready to wear outfitters, in which all minds would be uniformly clad, but a number of workshops the variety of which, to some extent made to measure, would be in conformity with abilities and aptitudes'.[83] However, having tried to broaden the path to secondary education, he then narrowed the possibility for a pupil to pass successfully through the school to the baccalaureate by reintroducing fees for upper secondary education.[84] His pretext for doing so was the alleged lowering of standards at this top level, because of the presence of 'parasitic elements' in the classes. These senior pupils, realizing that their own failure was inevitable, disrupted teaching. In any case, the minister argued, since many *lycées* were necessarily boarding institutions, even when tuition had been free many poorer children had had to drop out before reaching the top classes because their parents could not afford the boarding charges. Consequently, to provide free upper secondary education could operate unjustly, since pupils in towns, where boarding was unnecessary, had an advantage over those in rural areas. By abolishing all free education beyond the age of fourteen 'every trace of injustice between countryfolk and town-dwellers disappears'. Rich families should in any case pay fees because their children constituted the bulk of *lycée* pupils and therefore free education for them was unfair. To ensure that the poor but clever child did not suffer, generous scholarships, gradated according to parental means, would be awarded to all those who obtained a mark of 60 per cent in the year before entering upper secondary classes. (But rich pupils, although they would receive no financial help, required a mark of only 50 per cent.) Disabled parents keeping their child on at school would receive compensation for the income forgone. Such financial aid would have no ceiling placed upon it, because Bouthillier, the minister of finance, had given his ministry a blank cheque. In such circumstances Carcopino considered that to continue free upper secondary education was 'legally untenable, financially burdensome, intellectually unreasonable, pedagogically pernicious'. The educationalist notes here a rationalization of opportunity and allegedly a step towards the realization of what came later to be known as 'positive discrimination' for the poor.

The bulk of children, however, would still remain in the primary school after the age of eleven. Carcopino put back the age for taking the primary certificate from twelve to fourteen, thus making it possible to organize a coherent three-year course from eleven, building on the basic skills. At fourteen some children would be able to enter a technical school or stay on in classes, known as 'cours complémentaires', for a further two years of general education. These were annexes of primary schools and were mainly located in rural areas. From them some pupils were recruited for training as primary teachers. Those that left school at fourteen would have compulsory part-time schooling: for boys, training in agriculture; for girls, homecraft. One hundred hours per year for a period of three years were envisaged. For those whose education terminated in the primary school – the bulk of rural children – care should be taken not to alienate them from their environment: 'l'étude du milieu', as it later became known in the 'classes nouvelles' experiments of the 1950s, should be encouraged by local studies of all kinds.

Changes in the content of education are discussed in greater detail in subsequent chapters. Here one may note that their general effect was to counteract the tendency to intellectualism that has always characterized French education. Not that Carcopino belittled 'instruction' unduly. But he did not accept Jean Zay's reforms, because 'one talked of "orientation" and in this way claimed to "observe" the pupils, but one forgot to instruct them'. His aim was to produce pupils more intellectually alert, physically robust, morally tempered to face the future. His gradualist approach to reform meant that if all his measures had been implemented they would not have been completed until 1948 at the earliest. Moderate opinion today concurs with Maillard's view that his reforms were 'felicitous and lasting'.[85]

Carcopino's main aim in higher education was to preserve the comparative autonomy that universities enjoyed.[86] In this he got his way. Trouble nevertheless blew up between him and Pétain's 'cabinet' regarding appointments to the prestigious Collège de France, which stood outside the system of higher education proper. The Collège had the right to elect its own professors. Commenting on this, an internal note circulating within the Marshal's entourage claimed that over the previous decade eight Jews and six Communists had been appointed and that the professorial body had largely supported the Front Populaire. Indeed, 'It [the Collège] has not ceased to be Anglophile, pro-Jewish and Germanophile. [*sic:* the writer *may* have meant "Germanophobic", although Pétain's "cabinet" were hardly pro-German at this time.] Now it wished to elect to its number Dhorme, an unfrocked Dominican married to a Jewess, and Gabriel, a Communist. Gabriel would certainly reinforce the masonic majority of "fellow-travellers" ["communisante"] whose leader is M. Wallon, a Party member, the recognised propagandist for Moscow in educational matters, who had retained his professorial chair in the Collège.'[87]

Pétain wanted all elections to the Collège to be suspended until after the war. Some elections nevertheless took place and the head of the Marshal's 'cabinet civil' wrote to

Carcopino expressing Pétain's astonishment.[88] Carcopino must have been aware of the Marshal's wishes long before, but replied[89] that although elections had indeed been postponed indefinitely by a decree of February 22, 1941, because it was difficult to muster a quorum of professors, another decree signed by Pétain on March 4, 1941 had authorized immediate elections. (It was said that the Marshal, in his less lucid moments, did not read what he had to sign.) The minister smugly added that 'in this matter I limited myself to applying strictly the laws of the État Français'. The 'cabinet civil' could only reiterate Pétain's displeasure: the appointment of Dhorme, the lapsed religious, was considered 'more than inopportune'. This minor affair demonstrates how far the legalistic Carcopino was prepared to go when what he considered the 'liberties' of higher education were at stake.

With the return of Laval to power in April 1942 Carcopino's rule was over and he returned to his permanent post as Director of the École Normale Supérieure. On August 22, 1944 he was suspended by the provisional government and beaten and imprisoned before being brought to trial as an ex-minister of Vichy. As an ex-minister of Vichy his arrest had been automatic, but proceedings were dropped. Indeed the court spoke on his behalf. Regarding the educational changes he had made, 'Whatever may have been the criticisms, the reform undertaken by Carcopino, on the admission even of those who opposed him, succeeded in remedying certain deficiencies in our educational system.'[90] He had defended educational liberty. The rescinding of the pro-clerical measures of Chevalier was counted in his favour. With regard to religious education he had afforded the same facilities to rabbis and Catholic priests alike. Teachers had been penalized for their past actions and not for their opinions. He had interpreted the political neutrality of the school very strictly, not even allowing the wearing of the 'francisque' – the Marshal's emblem. He had not promoted the persecution of the Jews or the measures against freemasonry. He had closed down the foreign section of the École Normale Supérieure so that the Germans should not be able to enrol students in it. He had assisted the Resistance. In fact, he was totally exonerated. There is no doubt that this judgement was the only appropriate verdict, but he had nevertheless to wait until 1950 before getting back his chair at the Sorbonne.

Carcopino's departure marks a watershed in the history of education and young people under Vichy. The good faith with which the Révolution Nationale had been pursued largely disappears, constructive reform is virtually abandoned, and the reign of hypocrisy, subservience to Nazism and its abhorrent ideals begins. The period that heralds the ministry of Abel Bonnard ends with the flight of the minister to the frontier in August 1944.

Chapter II

Decline and Fall of the 'New Order'

Abel Bonnard finally became minister of education in April 1942, when Laval again assumed the reins of government. This time the rival contender had been Bernard Faÿ,[1] who had, however, stood little chance because of Abetz's advocacy of Bonnard.

The new 'Grand Maître' was a curious and complex character. A man of letters – essayist, poet, and journalist – whose works never enjoyed great popular acclaim, he was a 'saloniste' more at home in the world of art, the theatre, and literature than in politics. It was said that during his stay at the Rue de Grenelle never were ministerial circulars so brilliantly written. He had published his first work, a book of verse, in 1906. During the First World War he had won the Croix de Guerre. Afterwards he had returned to his writing, winning an Academy essay prize in 1924. For a while he had written articles for a Fascist daily controlled by Georges Valois. He had then begun to evince some interest in education. His *Éloge de l'ignorance* (1926) railed against the primary teacher, who dispensed an education for the masses which lacked technical and practical content; he also deplored the blue-stocking, the female intellectual who might have acquired learning but had, in so doing, betrayed her sex. Elected to the French Academy in 1932, by 1940 he had become its Chancellor. Politically his views were anti-Republican; his book, *Les Modérés,* which dwelt on the need for authoritarian policies, had attracted some attention. The PPF had persuaded him to speak in Doriot's own fief of St. Denis and, to everybody's surprise, including his own, he had proved to be a successful political orator. For a while he was a Paris city councillor. In 1937 he had met Hitler. In 1940 he had come out strongly in favour of collaboration. Through the Cercle Fustel de Coulanges he had continued to interest himself in youth and education. In the autumn of 1940, in an article entitled 'Des Jeunes Gens ou une

Jeunesse?' (reprinted in: *Pensées dans l'Action* (1941)), he joined in the chorus of those who wanted the young to be diligent, respectful, and obedient. In January 1941 Pétain had invited him to become a Conseiller National, the élite group charged with elaborating a new constitution for France. A series of articles in Drieu La Rochelle's collaborationist journal, *Je suis partout,* earned him, together with Drieu and Brasillach, another collaborationist writer, a trip to Berlin in October 1941. The flood of congratulatory letters he received from Doriotistes, the pro-German clique in Paris, and even a few churchmen showed clearly what line they thought he should follow as minister of education. (He also received congratulatory letters from his artistic friends who plainly hoped that he, as minister also responsible for the arts, would shower largesse upon them.) On the whole his cronies were not disappointed.

A small, white-haired man already touching sixty in 1942, Bonnard had an unsavoury personal reputation. Robert Aron describes him as 'the type of intellectual dilettante, inverted and masochistic'.[2] As a pederast he was hardly a model for the new 'moral order'. Pétain, it seems, was ignorant of his new minister's sexual proclivities until he was informed by Mme Jacques Bainville, the widow of the monarchist and anti-German writer.[3] Collaborationist as well as homosexual, he was known as 'Abetz-Bonnard, L'Ami des Hommes'. To describe him the Marshal coined the portmanteau word 'Gestapette' (from 'Gestapo and 'tapette' – homosexual) and remarked to Terracher, the secretary-general of the ministry: 'Eh bien, vous devez être content? On vous a donné un bel ['Abel'] éducateur de la jeunesse.'[4] Jean Zay, the former minister of education, imprisoned by Vichy, noted at the time: 'The personal morality of M. Bonnard is known in the university; his appointment will cause a sensation. But he had wished for the post too long not to obtain it.'[5] But, although backed by the Germans, Laval had had to ask Pétain twice before the Marshal gave way and appointed Bonnard.[6] Although in 1943 Pétain tried to procure his dismissal and replacement by General de La Porte du Theil, he was saddled with this most singular minister of education to the very end. Towards Laval, his patron, Bonnard's attitude was ambivalent: in private he derided him as 'le zéro de la collaboration' and 'le plus attentiste des collaborationistes'.[7] At the ceremony of handing over his office Carcopino, according to Planté, who was present, delicately hinted that he was displeased that his successor should be Bonnard. Planté, with an eye for detail, also records that one of the new minister's staff was dressed 'fancily'.[8] Communists characterized Bonnard as 'the Nuremberg pilgrim' because of the trip he had made to Germany.[9] The sole endearing trait of his character was perhaps his affection for his aged mother and his brother, with whom he lived in Paris. Du Moulin de Labarthète terms him 'a malodorous spirit' and contrasts him with Carcopino, 'admirable' for his 'authority', 'enthusiasm', and 'culture'.[10] The mercurial, arrogant, self-opinionated, and flattery-prone Bonnard was soon to cause educationists to distance themselves from Vichy's policies.

There was no doubt that Bonnard was of a different breed from his predecessors as minister of education. Their style had been in the Republican tradition, the 'cabinets' they had appointed had comprised inspectors and the like. The new minister's entourage was of a different kind: it included Bousquet, a *lycée* teacher of decidedly Nazi tendencies, Jeanneret, the right-wing primary teacher, and Lavenir, another primary teacher who had been active in the former SNI, as well as a rather nebulous figure, Néret, described merely as 'homme de lettres', but noted more for writing school textbooks.

Despite the fact that his very appointment contradicted the Vichy drive to reinforce moral education in the schools, Bonnard was adamant that he regarded this educational plank in the Révolution Nationale as essential. He also wasted no time in outlining the aims of an education that would 'correspond to the New Order'. The goal was to effect a fusion of the social classes, to turn out men, and to impart a practical training.[11] He postulated a new type of young Frenchman who would readily accept discipline, knew his country's past, appreciated sport and nature, was not solely pleasure-seeking, ranged himself with German youth and the youth of other European nations and lacked class-consciousness, because 'the reign of the French bourgeoisie is over'. But Bonnard, who lasted longest as Vichy minister of education, spoke much but did little. He believed that politics and education were inextricably linked. This belief was not of course new, but he was the first minister since public education began who was frank enough to admit openly an intention to politicize the class-room in order to reshape France.

As Langevin and Wallon did after the war – but with totally different goals and using totally different methods – Bonnard wanted to bring education closer to life. He did not deny the value of a classical education for the few but wanted to develop modern, technical, and agricultural courses. Thus he sought to revivify the 'cours complémentaires', the rural schools for children above the leaving age, by turning them into practical institutions. Although he did not accomplish much in the field of technical education, this is where his interest principally lay.

The state of technical education was indeed a parlous one. Before Bonnard took up office an unsigned and undated report (probably compiled in mid-1941) slated the technical schools and those responsible for them. Although some of the manual training given in them was excellent, the academic subjects lacked the appropriate bias. The mathematics syllabus was based upon the traditional secondary programme; the sciences were taught *ex cathedra,* with no experimental work. Luc, the director of technical education in the ministry, together with his chief inspector, was incompetent, displaying 'false energy', playing to the gallery, and manipulating his political masters. What was needed was reform and compression of the syllabuses and a review of all personnel.[12] That little was done may be divined from the fact that over two years later, Néret, of Bonnard's 'cabinet', sent Luc, who was still in his post, a note saying that the minister required him, within twenty-four hours, to propose cuts in the syllabuses for technical education.[13]

Another neglected field was part-time technical education. Carcopino had decreed the extension of part-time schooling beyond the compulsory leaving age. The Astier Law of 1919 and a decree-law of 1938 had in fact already imposed a partial obligation but because of resistance from employers the laws had not been enforced. In January 1942, before the arrival on the scene of Bonnard, instructions had been given to prefects[14] to make a census of the young people involved and set up courses, beginning with the unemployed and prescribing that, even for the employed, courses must be on a day-release basis.

As regards the unemployed, some progress had been made. One difficulty was that responsibility for youth employment and post-compulsory education had oscillated between the secretariat-general for youth and the directorate of technical education within the ministry. The youth secretariat had established centres used by young people for leisure activities and, if unemployed, to acquire skills. Conditions in the training centres were not at all bad, as tools and equipment became available. At Lons-le-Saunier, for example, a centre was opened in 1941 for unemployed aged between fourteen and seventeen. Attenders were given free meals and received 'pay' of 5–8 francs a day. Those that did well on the course, which lasted one year, were eligible for scholarships to schools with longer courses.[15] In the best centres attendance for forty-five hours a week was required. A pre-apprenticeship year was followed by two years of apprenticeship training proper. Approximately one-third of the time was spent on general education. Between 1942 and 1944 numbers attending the courses soared, from 53,925 young people rising to 85,000.[16] It would seem that recruitment was often from young people from unsatisfactory or broken homes. In the occupied zone the Germans did not look too favourably upon the centres, objecting, it seemed, to their management committees, which were often closely linked to Catholic or Protestant churches. At the end of 1942 their reconstitution on purely secular lines was mooted, because the SS, who from mid-1942 undertook the surveillance of youth activities, objected so strongly to them.[17]

Another interesting development was the suggestion that incentives should be given for the brightest pupils to enter technical education at a higher level. Requests came for the creation of a technical *lycée,* with an appropriate baccalaureate which would include such unusual subjects

– for the time – as technical drawing and workshop practice.[18] The idea foreshadowed the present technological baccalaureate in France, which is on a par with, and occasionally more difficult to pass than the other options that give access to higher education. The Catholics, whose stake in technical education was large, went one step further. They proposed a 'baccalaureate of vocational education', of three kinds – technical, commercial, and (for girls) domestic crafts.[19] This suggestion prefigured the present gamut of more specialized technical baccalaureates (not to be confused with the technological baccalaureate just mentioned), which relate to industry and commerce.

There was also an urgent need to put apprenticeship on a firmer footing. The Charte du Travail (October 4, 1941) had laid down general guide-lines on how it should be organized. However, squabbles between the various ministries involved prevented anything being accomplished. A law of July 27, 1942 had established a Commission Interministérielle, for both apprenticeship and domestic crafts, on which were represented the ministries of education, industrial production, and the family. This was a committee very much at war within itself. In December 1942 Luc warned Bonnard[20] that the labour ministry wanted to chair the commission and usurp the training function of the ministry of education; the ministry of industrial production wanted to arrogate to itself the training of artisans; and the ministry of the family, which had secured 'lottery funds', wanted to take over 'enseignement ménager'. In 1944 discussions regarding a full-blown statute of apprenticeship were still proceeding, with Bonnard and the ministry of labour, now headed by Déat, still jockeying for position. In July 1944 Laval wrote to Bonnard again requesting him to work out with other ministries and the representatives of the 'familles professionnelles' (the various industries) concerned a proper statute.[21] As late as July 29, 1944, within three weeks of the Liberation, Bonnard was still arguing with Déat as to the limitation of responsibilities.[22]

In technical education, therefore, some credit must be given to Bonnard. In other fields, despite some perception – although with the wrong motives – of what could be done to change the education system, he accomplished little. He lacked the necessary administrative skill to put his ideas into practical form. Thus what he wrote about his achievements after the war[23] must be taken with a grain of salt. He had seen, he said, his main task as preparing pupils to earn their living – hence his enthusiasm for technical education – whilst developing them as individuals; in short, as he elegantly expressed it, to provide for them 'a pillar of utility crowned by a capital of culture'. For the primary pupil this meant mainly preparation for agricultural work but also an appreciation of the rural environment, through local studies embracing botany, geology, folklore, and local history. At the secondary level he had tried to dissuade parents from opting for a classical education for their children for reasons of social snobbery. He had wanted to upgrade to the level of the classics course one stressing modern languages and knowledge of the contemporary world. If the means had been available he would have liked – and here his ideas become a flight of fancy – to provide a complete agricultural education in which the study of modern farming techniques would have been accompanied by the reading of the poets of rural life, such as Virgil and Mistral; likewise he had wanted to encourage the study of modern industrial techniques. He had effected a reform of medical education and provided facilities for prisoners of war to continue their studies. And, he added rather pathetically, he had introduced modern teaching aids (he had in mind magic lanterns!) to the primary classroom. If to the outside observer it seems that little was done and that his reforms were, as one critic put it, 'a tissue of banalities borrowed from Vichy's arsenal of publicity',[24] it must be remembered that innovation became increasingly more difficult as the situation deteriorated.

Indeed much of Bonnard's effort was concentrated in education on helping the Germans win the war. Teachers were exhorted 'to fight the propaganda of the Anglo-Gaullist radio'. In August 1942 what became known as the 'sneaking circular' was published: teachers were ordered to report any incidents relating to Communism or Gaullism. In 1943 Bonnard inplacably enforced the laws regarding forced labour in Germany, even for school pupils. A convinced anti-Semite, he established a chair of Jewish history at the Sorbonne after

Carcopino had refused to do so. He had plans for a Franco-German *lycée* 'for the fostering of the European spirit' in young people. He authorized the wearing of the 'francisque' in schools. He revived the 'purge' of unacceptable teachers. All in all, this rather nebulous and unlikely 'socialist' proved himself, as Laval is rumoured to have maintained, more German than the Germans.

What assessment may be made of the strictly educational reforms that Vichy's four ministers of education undertook? The lasting character of some of Carcopino's structural reforms has already been touched upon. Chevalier's efforts to assist Catholic schools, sensibly modified by Carcopino, were a precedent for the 1959 Debré Law granting them subsidies. Some innovations in technical education were the forerunner of the post-war apprenticeship centres which blossomed into the present colleges (and *lycées*) of technical education. The attempt to expand the character of education to include greater stress upon the physical, social, and moral aspects must also be duly credited. But it must not be forgotten that there was some continuity with the reforms introduced just before the war by Jean Zay. The jailed ex-minister, however, pronounced a hostile judgement on the Vichy reforms, characterizing them as 'hasty upsets, a hotch-potch of measures borrowed from the most contradictory projects, shot through with political considerations'.[25] The major educational reconstruction of which all three authorities who had some claim to speak for France dreamed – Pétain, de Gaulle, and the Resistance – had to await the post-war era.

The Gaullists in London accepted the need for educational reform but understandably at first ascribed a low priority to it. Nevertheless, four commissions for the movement were set up – for general affairs, for economic, social, and financial questions, for reform of the State – the fourth was concerned with education.[26] In the Comité National Français René Cassin became commissioner for justice and education. After the North-African landings the Free French also participated in the conference of Allied ministers of education presided over by R. A. Butler (now Lord Butler) to consider how educational systems could be quickly restarted after the Liberation. In 1946, René Capitant, who had become the first post-war minister of education, published the Algiers Plan of educational reform.

Within France the various factions within the Resistance also elaborated plans. The Communists were the most explicit: they sought to abolish private schools and to withdraw from religious orders the right to teach; a curriculum more oriented to science; and apprenticeship schools, with a ladder of opportunity for the workman to better himself.[27] The Socialists were less specific but did want greater equality of opportunity, a sentiment echoed by the Conseil National de la Résistance. At its last plenary session before the Liberation, held on March 15, 1944, the Conseil prescribed a programme for action; among its social measures was one that read: '... the real possibility for French children to benefit from education and have access to the highest forms of culture, regardless of their parents' financial situation'.[28] Thus a meritocracy would replace status élites. Sadly, it was not until the coming to power of de Gaulle in 1959 that equality of opportunity, which Carcopino and Bonnard both professed to desire, could begin to be realized. Meanwhile the Resistance criticized reforms introduced by Vichy that were considered to favour the bourgeoisie at the expense of the working class. The issue was raised in an open letter to Bonnard: 'The so-called Révolution Nationale aims solely at degrading education, at lowering the cultural level of the mass of the people. To the masses you say: let us teach the techniques of various trades. Let their intelligence be applied to techniques, let them play at sport and amuse themselves and, for the rest, place themselves in the hands of their venerable leader.'[29] They also grumbled about aid to Catholic schools, but as Catholics became more numerous in the Resistance the 'religious question' was quietly shelved for the duration.

Behind the laws promulgated embodying the reforms what was the reality of education for children and young people under Vichy? One may begin by considering the position of half the school population: girls. Although their Resistance exploits eventually contributed to a radical revision of ideas on the education of women, Vichy took the traditional and Catholic line. The academically gifted girl should be steered towards a classical rather than a scientific training. Girls should be educated to become wives and mothers, the 'organisers and preservers of the home'. Courses should be provided for them in housecraft, child care, and family legislation; there should also be some artistic education; all subjects should have strong moral overtones. By contrast, as the 'providers', men should have an education based upon the cult of the will and the reason. Such views were held even by otherwise enlightened Catholics,[30] although we are not far removed from the Nazi ideology of 'Kinder, Kirche und Küche'.

Co-education was banned; where a primary school was of necessity mixed, from the age of eight the sexes were to sit separately.[31] The older girl engrossed in study for the baccalaureate was gently mocked, for one day, in the bosom of her own family, she will be pleased that knitting ('le tricot') has supplanted the baccalaureate ('le bachot').[32] Housecraft courses were made compulsory: in secondary schools one hour a week for seven years; in technical schools, one hundred hours a year for three years. They were necessary, maintained *La Croix* (April 14, 1942), because of the 'slovenliness, ignorance or indifference of some women' in running a home. In practice Vichy, as in so much else it contracted to do, was unable to run the courses. Extra rations for cookery and coupons for dressmaking could not be made available, specialist teachers were lacking.[33] Yet as late as June 1944 Bonnard was writing to Renaudin, Commissioner General for the Family, enthusing over the new programmes devised, which, 'in contrast to the teaching of yesterday, grown so abstract and undifferentiated that it could apply equally to girls and boys without really being suitable for either. . . , will become that preparation for a function and life which all real teaching should be.'[34] This lesson in sex roles, from Bonnard, is surely surprising.

What was school in wartime France like for the young? In Amiens, at least, one primary-school child thought it 'neither jolly nor pleasant'.[35] In the capital of Picardy, out of

27,740 buildings standing in 1939, by the end of the war 4,750, including seven schools, had been destroyed and 12,440 seriously damaged. Classes, held often in makeshift huts, were frequently interrupted by air raids; if the shelter could not be reached in time the pupils lay on the floor for protection. Hungry children grew thin and shivered in ragged clothes. One child had red flea-bites on his face and most of his companions suffered from dermatitis. To feed the class-room stove in winter they sawed up fittings from a ruined church nearby. The teacher noted, 'From time to time they found an angel's wing, still gilded, or a fragment of neo-Gothic carving, and I believe – honni soit qui mal y pense! – that like the English at Rouen, we even burnt a saint – God forgave us.' Children collected eagerly the strips of silver foil dropped by the Allied bombers to confuse German radar. On the whole, the youngsters were uncomplaining and accepted their lot.

In 1943 a study was made of the effects of the war upon nursery-school toddlers in Arles and Marseilles, with some surprising results.[36] As was to be expected, they had adapted their play to the war. Whereas they had formerly persuaded their companions to play 'mothers and fathers' by chanting, Qui veut jouer à papa-maman?' they now played 'bombing' instead and chorused, 'Qui veut jouer au bombardement, -ment, -ment, -ment?' One child simulated the air-raid siren and the rest had to dive for cover. Because at the time they had had little experience of bombing they had little fear of it. They also played 'police raid', with one child going round asking for identity papers. They were divided as to which side would win the war, although united in fear of the Germans and scorn for the Italians. They were motivated by curiosity rather than apprehension. Their drawings, however, reflected the sadder side of their life: scenes of battle and of the absent father, depicted behind barbed wire in the prisoner of war camp. Despite their extreme youth, they already had a good idea of what the black market stood for and of the value of ration tickets. Put up to it by their parents, they would say that the ration ticket for their mid-day meal had been lost. They bartered and were light-fingered with property, but were generous in sharing their toys; they were more self-reliant, more willing to help each other, more careful and economical. Not all was on the debit side.

In a remarkable diary an adolescent schoolgirl described her school life at the Lycée Racine in Paris,[37] where she noted with satisfaction the pro-English sentiments of the headmistress, Mme Hatinguais, later to become one of the most eminent of post-war French educationists. Interested in foreign languages, the girl had adorned her English exercise-book with the Union Jack and the Tricolour. She detested her German teacher – 'une Bochesse'. After the recital in class of the moving German poem, 'Ich hatt' einen Kameraden', mourning the death of a soldier in battle, one pupil cried out, 'So much the better – that's one less.' The diarist noted the current definition of collaboration: 'Give me your watch and I'll give you the time.' Yet, such is the complexity of adolescence, by the age of sixteen she was 'dating' her first German soldier, whilst continuing to be pro-Allied. When on November 1, 1941, de Gaulle from London had ordered five minutes' silence to be observed, she recorded with satisfaction that most pupils obeyed the instruction. She noted an attack on the German-controlled bookshop on the Boul' Mich', located at the former Café d'Harcourt. Students smashed the shop front and decamped with the police in hot pursuit. Meanwhile others arrived on the scene, perceived that the premises had been left unguarded, promptly planted two bombs, and blew up the shop.

On the other hand, from elsewhere come reports of a few pro-German incidents. At the Lycée Janson de Sailly a pupil denounced a teacher who had set for translation an extract from a Schiller text on liberty, but, fearing the ostracism of his class-mates, the informer had not dared to come to school afterwards.[38] At another school a little girl arrived wearing a black ribbon in her hair on the anniversary of the German entry into Paris – on that day many men were wearing black ties – and was promptly suspended for lack of 'social sense'.[39] Jean Guéhenno records that in his school, despite a few Doriotist informers, when boys were called up for compulsory labour service not one obeyed.[40]

There were occasional minor demonstrations of pro-British sentiments. In Northern France, where the tie with

Britain had always been strong, on All Saints' Day, 1940, the children bedecked Allied war graves with red, white, and blue flowers, but these were promptly removed by the Germans.[41] 'God Save the King', if all reports are to be credited, suddenly became a very popular tune in schools: teachers of English played it on records,[42] pupils practised it in class,[43] on one occasion even when the Germans were drilling in the playground outside.[44] Armistice Day – for the First World War – was always a difficult anniversary. After the student demonstration in 1940 the Germans banned all commemoration of it in public in 1941. A simple act of remembrance was permitted inside schools two days previously, provided that not more than ten teachers and pupils were present.[45] A complete break with the recent past was impossible. Nor could present concerns be entirely obliterated. Required in the DEPP examination to write on a hero, one twelve-year-old chose de Gaulle. Bonnard rebuked the academy inspector for not excluding her from the examination immediately, adding that similar cases had occurred.[46]

Vichy did its best to promote activities within schools that were more exclusively French. Joan of Arc Day was celebrated with particular enthusiasm, sometimes with anti-English fervour. May 1941 was declared to be a 'youth month, under the sign of the Marshal'. The Secours National organized theatrical entertainments in Paris for needy children. They were enacted against high backcloths of Pétain bearing slogans such as 'Lead an upright life like the Marshal'.[47] Tremendous self-help drives were carried out in schools. In October 1941 it was announced[48] that children's efforts had resulted in the following:

Sales of portraits, plaquettes, and calendars of Pétain	16,846,000 f.
Collection of old clothes	3,785,000 kgs.
Collection for prisoners of war	207,000 Books
	69,925 Parcels
Collection of acorns and chestnuts	1,900,000 kgs.
Collection of scrap iron	3,292,000 kgs.

Schools proudly announced the results in their annual reports.[49]

The campaign for 'national revival' took many forms.

There were propaganda drives in schools in favour of a larger population. Ever since 1935 there had been an excess of deaths over births. A pre-war policy of easy naturalization had been adopted in part to counter the threat posed by a declining population. In July 1939 the Code de la Famille had extended family benefits. The study of demographic problems in schools had been mandatory ever since a decree-law of July 29, 1939, which was now enforced by Vichy. Carcopino asserted bluntly that 'a depopulated country, left without strength and without defence, far from avoiding wars, attracts invasions'.[50] The absence of over a million and a half of the male population in prison camps did not help the situation. Instruction in population problems should not be confined to the rather derisory number of hours allocated to study them, but should spill over into history and geography and extend to other subjects, such as mathematics, where demographic statistics could be used, or handicraft, where exercises could be related to the creation of a future home. F. Boverat's work, *La Race blanche en danger de mort* (1933), became a recommended text.[51]

Also in the interest of 'national revival', children were exhorted to learn more about the French Empire. In 1942 the Commission on General Information of the Conseil National recommended intensive study in school of France's imperial possessions and the creation of chairs of colonial affairs in the principal universities.[52] In May a Quinzaine Impériale, a fortnight of propaganda to promote the Empire, was held and schools were involved, for the Empire, declared the ministry of education with tragic irony, 'constitutes at present the strength of our political position'.[53]

Schoolchildren were encouraged to be altruistic. In the autumn of 1943 schools ran a 'good deeds' fortnight in which pupils worked for the less fortunate. Boys refurbished cradles, which girls relined with rabbit skins tanned and sewn together. Old toys were repaired for the poor. Wood was collected for old people's fires. Children sacrificed their bread ration to give to those in need. War orphans and children of prisoners of war were invited to the homes of better-off children. Sick people were visited. Today such actions are commonplace, but in schools before the war they were rare. War breeds self-sacrifice as well as selfishness.

From 1942 onwards conditions grew progressively more difficult. A pre-war decree was invoked to ensure that lessons on air-raid precautions were given,[54] school shelters were dug, and evacuation centres designated. Keeping warm became a problem: in cold weather one class-room was kept heated after school, for use by children from poor homes.[55] Health education was stepped up – the dangers of alcohol were especially mentioned. Children were exhorted to help in the growing of food: 'Sow, harvest as much as possible. . . Not an inch of ground, not an hour of leisure lost!'[56] Footwear was so scarce that teachers were asked to urge their pupils to wear clogs,[57] although these were disliked even by peasants. Writing-paper was rationed: pupils received ration cards for paper for school use according to their age.[58] To boost morale the ministry of information wanted to install radio sets in school canteens, a proposal that Bonnard rejected because he feared it would 'give too many facilities for certain people to listen to the very stations that your action is combatting so effectively'.[59]

The all-prevailing presence of the Germans, particularly after mid-1942, overshadowed education as it did all other activities. The German military commander in France, established in Paris at the Hotel Majestic, dealt officially with Vichy through a Délégation Générale of the regime, headed by de Brinon. This ex-journalist, who had struck up an acquaintanceship with Ribbentrop when the future Nazi foreign minister was still peddling champagne, was a committed collaborationist notorious for reporting everything to his German masters. His educational representative, Roy, originally an inspector general for German, was a man of a different stamp. He liaised with a special group, 'Kultur und Schule' (Gruppe IV), at the Hotel Majestic.[60] Part of the German administrative staff, this group dealt with education and cultural affairs. Its two principal members, originally Dr Rilke and Dr Reiprich, exerted a tight control so far as possible on French education and youth affairs. They supervised any measure that appeared in the *Journal officiel*, occasionally delaying publication for months when it suited the German book, commented on drafts of official documents, scrutinized textbooks, syllabuses, and educational journals, dealt with requests concerning the derequisitioning of school buildings and with incidents involving the Germans and schools or the arrest of education personnel. For arrests, however, they also liaised with a 'police' group consisting of Drs Ernst, Jähnig, and Kübler. 'Kultur und Schule' bombarded the ministry of education also with peremptory demands, sometimes to be complied with within a day, on the most abstruse matters concerning French education. Similar demands and orders likewise emanated from the local German Feldkommandanturen, which displayed a fine interest in education. Towards the end no educational appointment of any consequence could be made without German consent, at national and local level. In addition to the group at the Majestic the ministry had also to work with the German Institute, whose director, Dr Epting, very closely linked to Abetz and the German Embassy, worked indefatigably to promote German language and culture all over France, setting up new institutes at Rennes, Angers, Nantes, Dijon, and Besançon. Thus, one way or another, thorough surveillance was maintained by the Germans over every aspect of education and youth affairs.

The most immediate impact of the Occupation was felt in requisitioning schools for billets and offices for German troops.[61] This often occurred at short notice. A few days' grace might be given for the evacuation of a school that might have to rehouse a hundred boarders. All protests were met with the laconic reply that the move was necessary 'on military grounds'. Universities were also not spared – in fact, they and the secondary schools were hardest hit. Even in 1942, when the situation was more stabilized, some 30 per cent of university and some 40 per cent of secondary premises were still requisitioned, as compared with only 6 per cent of primary schools.[62] Even flats attached to schools had to be turned over to the Germans. Occasionally there was joint occupation of a school by soldiers and pupils, which gave rise to incidents. A favourite German ploy was to move out of a school, wait for the French to renovate it for school use, and then move back in.

The Germans were constantly assessing the attitudes of those connected with education, from the minister downwards.[63] Carcopino, as has been seen, was held by them to be willing and compliant, although the judgement they passed on him on another occasion as a 'clerical' was wildly inaccurate. Of Lamirand, secretary-general for youth, they noted warily that 'to a special degree he enjoys the immediate confidence of Marshal Pétain'. Luc, the ministry's director of technical education, was regarded with suspicion because he was allegedly associated with *L'Université Libre,* which had reappeared as a Resistance broadsheet issued by some Paris teachers in November 1940. After the students' demonstration on Armistice Day 1940, they went closely into the background of Roussy, rector of the University of Paris, to see whether he had instigated the demonstration in any way. They noted that he had been appointed by Jean Zay, a Jew, and was married to a half-Jewess; under the naturalization law he had lost his French citizenship – he was Swiss by origin – but he had later regained this. They characterized Mme Hatinguais, the headmistress of the Lycée Racine previously mentioned, who had meanwhile been appointed to the post of director of the École Normale Supérieure for girls at Sèvres, as being 'the promoter of Jews and freemasons'. They vetted past appointments even at local level: in Rennes the Propaganda-Abteilung required the Rector to provide a list of all changes in educational personnel since January 1941, as well as notification of future changes. The Rector appealed to the ministry, in view of 'the very grave problem of German control which is now posed for academies'.[64] Although de Brinon had persuaded the Germans to accept that only the appointment of prefects and civil servants of equivalent rank should be referred to them,[65] not only did Bonnard discuss appointments with them, but even deferred to their suggestions, promoting, for example, a provincial headmaster to one of the prestigious *lycées* in Paris, despite his blatant lack of qualifications.[66] In one important respect the Germans had the whip hand: appointments in the occupied zone could be blocked by simply refusing a *laisser-passer* to cross the demarcation line.

The ever present oversight of the Germans on all educational activities manifested itself in many other ways. German teachers serving in the occupation forces wanted to visit Paris *lycées* to study, as they put it, 'comparative pedagogy', but Carcopino succeeded in nipping this in the bud.[67] They made surprise visits to see whether banned books were still stocked in the school library,[68] to track down the authors of Resistance tracts, and to control the teaching. At a *lycée* in Douai they were furious to find written on the blackboard, 'I love you, England, in spite of all your faults, because you are my country.'[69] This was explained away as the title of a dictation, the complete text of which had already been rubbed off. At Evreux the Kommandant instituted an inquiry to see whether schools had received specific instructions to co-operate with his forces and warned that his officers would carry out lightning inspections.[70] Orders were issued that German propaganda posters should be displayed in classrooms. Reports that held them up to ridicule made them incensed.[71] Thus they learnt that pupils in Nantes, when asked to write about the present state of affairs, had produced essays which stated, 'Pétain is an idiot', and , 'We don't want anything to do with collaboration'. The local École des Beaux-Arts had displayed pictures of aerial dogfights in which only German planes were being shot down. Justifiably the Germans concluded that 'there is no more detailed proof of the attitude and patent machination of French teachers against Germany'. Occasionally they may have been over-sensitive, as when they complained that in a university history examination at Rennes the following extract had allegedly been set for comment: 'The Athenian Republic is a democracy under the heel of a hostile people. But the friends of the Athenians are powerful because of their war fleet; it is democracy that will triumph in the end.'[72] Upon enquiry, it transpired that no such passage had been set. They were irritated by the 'V-campaign', which reached its peak in schools in 1941. At Nevers the 'V-sign' was even painted inside the school. From Bordeaux it was reported that 'V-tracts' were being distributed and younger children, egged on by their teachers, were shouting, 'Vive de Gaulle!' In Dijon the daubing of the 'V-sign' had been accompanied by the singing – yet again! – of the British national anthem.[73] Anti-German propaganda even penetrated the private schools. In 1941 the good nuns of the Pensionnat Notre Dame de

Sion in Paris enlivened Joan of Arc Day by teaching their pupils a sacred song which contained the egregious lines: 'Joan of Arc, Maid of France/Pray for us, you see our suffering/Pray for us, be our deliverance/ O model of valour.' In 1942 they put on a repeat performance which came to the ears of the Germans. The religious, who were punished by their bishop and on whose behalf Bonnard ate humble pie to pacify the Germans, claimed in mitigation that they had omitted such more offensive lines as, 'Let us chase the barbarian/Over the Rhine.'[74]

A wall of hostility was quickly raised between teachers and pupils on the one hand, and the Germans on the other. The exploits of the Resistance lie outside the scope of this study, but there were many premeditated or spontaneous gestures of defiance. Over-frequent rehearsal of the 'Marseillaise', a song prescribed for the certificate of primary education, caused the Germans at Dijon to ban it completely.[75] At the Lycée Buffon, when the Germans came to arrest a pupil, his fellows intoned the song right under their noses.[76] Nor was intractability all one-sided. At a school in Morbihan the Germans carried out live hand-grenade exercises and blandly dismissed the French protest on the grounds that such drill did not constitute 'a serious inconvenience'.[77] In 1943 candidates for the baccalaureate examination were waiting outside a university building in Lille when they were set upon by fifty German soldiers who wished to make their way through them. Forty pupils were wounded, six seriously. Although the soldiers were clearly in the wrong, the riot act was read to the candidates warning them against further incidents.[78] Such examples of mutual perverseness were very frequent towards the end of the Occupation, when 'correctness' on both sides had been abandoned.

The Germans were at first at a loss to know how to deal with hostile acts committed by young people, but eventually worked out a procedure. Dr Dahnke, of the group 'Kultur und Schule', laid down that, since it was unwise to create martyrs among the young – or heroes out of their mentors –, so far as possible the French should punish miscreants, but under German supervision. Only as a last resort should a German court-martial be mounted. The most effective sanctions were those that involved parents as well as the young offenders. In cases in which teachers were also embroiled or which might entail the closure of an educational institution, Dahnke himself should be consulted.[79] A circular of guidance, entitled 'Gaullist propaganda', was also sent out to all German military commands. As for teachers, if they were mixed up with Communist propaganda the French police should deal with them; for Gaullist propaganda, matters should be referred to the German security police (Geheimfeldpolizei). Teachers should be automatically dismissed if found guilty.

The wide range of the 'offences' actually committed by pupils or teachers against the Germans can be appreciated from the following random sample of crimes committed, extending from the trivial to those which carried the death penalty:

spitting at Germans – shouting 'down with Germany' – chalking the V-sign on military vehicles – distributing photographs of de Gaulle – passing Communist propaganda – sticking the Cross of Lorraine on a classroom door – distributing tracts – 'dealings with the enemy' – 'assisting the English' – smuggling letters across the demarcation line – crossing the line illegally – adopting an anti-German attitude – wearing the British and American colours – using secret codes in internal correspondence – writing offensive anonymous letters – espionage – emitting 'cries hostile to the Occupation forces' – possessing offensive books (e.g., Remarque's *All Quiet on the Western Front*) – stealing German equipment – wearing the star of David 'illicitly' – being British or American – carrying a false identity card – putting maps in prisoner of war parcels – practising scouting (in the occupied zone) – as a teacher, calling a pupil 'a Boche' – possessing or trafficking in arms and ammunition – failing to guard railway lines efficiently – not protecting installations against sabotage – taking part in acts of 'terrorism' – ringing the doorbell of the Feldgendarmerie (German military police) without reason – not replying quickly enough to a high-ranking German official – being Jewish – jostling German officers – carrying two fishing rods ('de[ux] gaules' = de Gaulle) – carrying caricatures of German soldiers – hoisting the French flag without permission – listening to foreign radio stations – adopting an incorrect attitude to a German sentry – insulting a girl accompanied by a member of the German army – singing 'La Marche Lorraine'.

These were some of the crimes reported by de Brinon in Paris.[80] The list shows clearly that the young had lost nothing of their inventiveness, although some of their exploits had tragic endings. In addition to such offences there was always the 'catch-22' crime of 'showing antipathy towards the German authorities'.

Total numbers of those indicted are not available, but partial figures give some indication of how widespread defiance was. Between July 25 and August 25, 1943 no less than 61 arrests of pupils, teachers, and students were notified by the Germans to the ministry of education.[81] The breakdown of these figures is as follows: 'Pupils 23; students 4; primary teachers 20, secondary teachers 7, teachers in higher education 5, others 2.' Another statistic shows that in the Charente-Maritime[82] alone during the Occupation there were 1,120 deportees to Germany, 69 of whom were young people under eighteen. Of these 69, 47 did not return, 30 were aged between six and fourteen, and 27 were girls, of whom 24 did not return. If such figures are typical of France as a whole, it can be seen how greatly young people suffered in German hands.

In the occupied zone German measures of suppression and control were stricter.[83] The ban on meetings of organizations with distinctive uniforms or badges meant that in theory such movements as the Scouts or those run by the Catholics for young people were forbidden. Scouts often got round the prohibition by meeting privately and not wearing uniform, although the Germans were aware of this ruse and did not always enforce their ban rigidly. Catholic movements avoided trouble so far as possible by stressing the religious character of their meetings, holding them in churches, although there were nevertheless many brushes with the German authorities. Within the occupied zone the only other German ordinances which directly affected young people concerned the censorship of school-books and a prohibition on the training of wireless operators, which lasted only for a few months. The movement of children was restricted in the same way as for adults: to cross the demarcation line or enter various areas within the occupied zone a *laisser-passer* was required for those over 15; under 15, children had to be entered on the pass of the adult accompanying them.[84]

The Germans discouraged or sabotaged Vichy's efforts to effect a Révolution Nationale. Thus, for example, they refused requests to release certain categories of prisoners of war. Scapini, a former deputy and a lawyer, a 'grand blessé' of the First World War, had been charged by Pétain with the task of looking after the interests of the prisoners. He wrote to Abetz asking the Germans to release prisoners who were students at the 'grandes écoles' so that, as he put it, this élite could help in the building of the new European order. He made a similar request for the release of physical-education teachers. Their release was desirable because 'the need for the renewal of French youth is imperative' and 'the example given by Germany in this field carried lessons the fruit of which is precious'.[85] In November 1940 both demands were turned down. Abetz was on his guard against any attempt to set France on its feet. He was particularly wary after the dismissal of Laval in December 1940, which he saw as a move by the Action Française to assume the key posts in government and administration – he particularly mentioned education.[86] Once again the question of educational posts was raised: already by February 1941 the Germans favoured the appointment of left-wing teachers, to combat the clericalism of Vichy and win over the disaffected to the German side.[87] But in both teachers and young people the Germans discovered obstacles to manipulating the French for their advantage.

One aspect of the education system merits special mention: the remarkable persistence of the baccalaureate, the secondary leaving-certificate which also qualified the holder for university entrance, has often been commented upon. This 'sacred cow' of French education continued to preoccupy ministers throughout the Occupation. In 1940 one of the first acts of the Vichy ministry had been to institute new sessions of the examination for those who had been prevented from sitting it in June.[88] The question of its reform was constantly raised, although, as one writer observed, 'it resists the conflagration of a universe'.[89] Carcopino thought that it attracted too many incompetents and thus felt justified in making access to it more difficult by introducing fee-paying for the upper classes of the *lycée:* in 1941, for example, the percentage of candidates passing ranged, depending on the option, from only 26 per cent to 39 per cent.[90] In 1942 a leading article in *Le Temps* supported Ripert's contention that the examination should be reserved only for those intending to go to universities.[91] This view would not seem to have been shared by Bonnard, who in 1943 sent out a circular alluding to the growing difficulties of schooling and reminding all concerned of 'the spirit of indulgence that should reign this year in the various examinations'. He set the example himself by dispensing the candidates from the traditional oral examination. He was particularly incensed when one academy set for Latin a difficult translation from Quintilian, at a time, he said, when 'French youth finds itself in especially deplorable material and moral conditions', administering an official rebuke to the examiner responsible, the dean of the faculty of letters at Lille.[92] Even in June 1944 he was still addressing his mind to the examination, referring to complaints made by parents the previous year and saying that he wanted it to be 'an obstacle but not a trap', with less 'padding' and 'parrotting' of the textbook in the anwers.[93] One can but marvel at the perennial nature of a debate that transcends the vicissitudes of war and the alternance of regimes.

The academic year that culminated in the Liberation was one in which the baccalaureate should surely have been the least of the minister's preoccupations. By September 1943 the call-up of teachers for forced labour in Germany was beginning to take its toll. He had to deal with the disruption wrought by bombing as well as the successes scored by the Maquis in fighting the Germans. Summer holidays were extended to allow children to bring in the harvest. In the coastal strip opposite England boarders were not allowed to return to their schools.[94] In Nantes the severe air raids of September 16 and 23 were followed by the evacuation of all children, although adults working in the city had to remain.[95] In November Bonnard ordered the suspension of all homework and teachers, because of the risk of air raids, were instructed to 'simplify their teaching', an instruction that was never elucidated further.[96] By February 1944 the total evacuation of all mothers and children from the Somme coastal zone had been ordered.[97] In May the ministry of labour announced to the education authorities that in the evacuation centres some children 'have never opened a book for a year'.[98] By now Resistance bands were operating openly, raiding country schools and taking away with them, so one despairing headmaster maintained, younger staff of the classes of 1939–45 on the grounds that they were 'mobilized' – although doubtless many went of their own free will. He reported that five such incursions had occurred in a fortnight and that because of what he dubbed this 'terrorist' activity, he had had no alternative but to send his charges home.[99] Clearly the educational system was on the point of collapse.

The Germans became very conscious of the danger of allowing large bodies of young people to be concentrated in the five universities – Caen, Lille, Bordeaux, Aix–Marseille, and Rennes – located in the coastal areas. Although, through call-up of students for compulsory labour service and the fear of bombing and invasion, in the eight months up to March 1944 student numbers in these five universities had dropped from 29,089 to 19,279, a decrease of 34 per cent, the risk remained.[100] German opinion was divided: some argued for keeping the students at their studies, where they could be conveniently watched, others were in favour of dispersal.[101] Eventually the Germans decided against closure everywhere, but resolved that the Mediterranean area required special measures. Thus Montpellier was ordered to close by March 1, 1944, despite a plea by the ministry that it should be allowed a month's grace,[102] and Aix–Marseille was closed about the same time.

A draft agenda in Bonnard's hand for a meeting – probably the last – which he had with his rectors dealt mainly with higher education.[103] Rectors were to be free to decide when the universities were to reopen in the autumn of 1944. Valuable equipment was to be evacuated to Dijon. General Stülpnagel's order for the closure of Aix–Marseille was to be discussed. Bonnard wanted to complain that his instructions regarding compulsory labour service were being circumvented. All in all, it was, for the collaborationist that he was, a very depressing list of topics.

As regards the schools, Bonnard had been advised by the Commissioner General for the Family not to end the school year prematurely because, in the circumstances of 1944, this could only lead to idleness and 'vagabondage'. Town children should not be evacuated[104] – although in May 1944 the minister thought differently and recommended that those parents who could should send their children away from the most dangerous areas. Secondary and technical schools should close on June 14, but primary schools should continue to July 12, because their pupils came from poorer homes where both parents were working and the chances of the children being evacuated were slim. It was therefore best to keep them occupied for as long as possible and even arrange correspondence courses for the summer holidays.[105]

Bonnard himself remained optimistic about a German victory. It is perhaps revealing of his character that preserved in the ministry files, in his own handwriting, are the predictions of a fortune-teller, merely designated as 'Madame L.', dated April 20, 1944. The good lady was convinced that there would be no Allied invasion, but that renewed bombing and 'terrorist' attacks would be followed in June by a diplomatic offensive. The period between June 20–30 would be the most extraordinary of the war: in all countries, but especially in Britain and the United States, fighting would break out between the capitalists and the socialist masses. It would be a time of revolution, signalled by Neptune entering the same phase for the first time since 1789.[106] Alas for the crystal-ballgazing of 'Madame L', the threatened landing took place. On June 29, 1944 B____, the academy inspector in Caen, got through a message to Bonnard[107] saying that a battle was raging near the Lycée Malherbe, where he had set up his headquarters. The school was housing 2,000 refugees and, using other centres nearby, 6,000 meals a day were being served. He was communicating with the rest of the department by sending out as messengers young primary teachers on bicycles, but they were coming under fire. And, he added, – *in cauda venenum* – 'Many illusions have evaporated, dissipated like the smoke from the fires.' On July 5 Bonnard ordered the rector, Mercier, to withdraw with his staff, adding with superb aplomb, 'It is undoubtedly very desirable that you bring back with you the baccalaureate scripts that have been concentrated at Caen.'[108]

Indeed, examinations remained a major preoccupation to the very end. In late May the postponement was announced of all national competitive examinations ('concours'). Candidates who had already arrived in Paris should return home. These instructions were imposed by the Germans, who alleged not only food and transport difficulties but also the danger of political demonstrations. In vain the ministry argued that since the bulk of the candidates were already in Paris to send them away would also burden transport facilities. As for demonstrations, these were traditional, but were better described as 'rags' than rallies with political overtones. Postponement might mean that malcontents might demonstrate in earnest. But the Germans refused to budge from their position.[109]

In the spring instructions had been issued regarding school examinations. Given the situation, no mark in any subject would be eliminatory.[110] Elaborate precautions were taken to see that no cheating took place if an air-raid alert occurred.[111] A Catholic schools association suggested that all examinations should be over for the day by ten o'clock.[112] However, in vulnerable areas such as the Somme, at the end of May it was announced that all examinations had been indefinitely postponed.[113] Communications were difficult, even in the Paris area. Gidel, the rector, complained just after the invasion that the Germans had forbidden all telephone calls and telegrams going outside Paris, which effectively cut him off from many of his staff.[114] But as late as August 5 it was announced that baccalaureate candidates whose scripts had been lost – as, finally, had been those from the academy of Caen – could take a special examination to be held on August 17 and 18 in Paris or at centres elsewhere, including, incidentally, centres in Normandy![115] On August 19, in almost its last issue, *Le Progrès de la Somme* announced as front-page news that the postponed examinations would be held at the end of August. Side by side with this announcement it informed its readers that fighting was going on round Dreux, Chartres, and Orleans.[116] Such an obsession with examinations at so critical a juncture reveals something of the strength of French educational bureaucracy and even of national character.

Bonnard's time as minister was rapidly drawing to a close. His engagement diary for 1944 shows few morning appointments before 10 a.m. and none before 3 p.m. in the afternoon.[117] On August 8 he was due to meet Carcopino. Three days later he was to receive the various directors of the ministry, presumably to give his final instructions. In the week beginning August 7 he had appointments, among others, with Cortot, the concert pianist, Guitry, the actor, Bucard, the leader of the Franciste movement, and Gaït, in charge of youth affairs.[118] For the following week there was only one engagement marked, with a certain Sureau, for August 16 at 4 p.m. It is deleted. On the same day an attendance count at the ministry showed that of a staff of 357 no less than 232 turned up for work and there were 56 authorized absences.[119] It is not known whether the minister himself was already numbered among the defaulters. A final irony of the ministerial diary is that, inscribed as it is in the minister's own hand, 'Agenda d'Abel Bonnard, A.B.', it is rubber-stamped with the old seal of the ministry of education, bearing the superscription, 'République Française' – and not, as other seals were, 'État Français'.

By August 19 Bonnard had laid his plans for flight. On the point of leaving to join his colleagues at Belfort, the minister found that his car, his personal baggage, including a sum of six million francs, jewellery, and manuscripts, were all missing. The thief may have been his private secretary, Georges, the rather enigmatic figure who was a one-time employee of the Renseignements Généraux at Vichy, the branch of police concerned with State security. There is some evidence that Georges was a double agent working for the Resistance,[120] and that he had been entrusted with the task of drugging Bonnard to prevent his escape. Nevertheless, Bonnard eventually left for Eastern France in a German vehicle, arriving after the others, elegantly dressed in a lilac-coloured suit with a loud red tie,[121] and enthusing over his handsome German driver. He claimed to have lost everything, including a specially perfumed cream that was 'introuvable'. On September 7, with the rump of the Vichy government, he crossed the Rhine and settled down eventually to inactivity at Sigmaringen.[122] Even in those dark days, however, the colourful minister bubbled over with witticisms. He dubbed Laval 'the Auvergnat of the Danube' and Pétain, who withdrew into privacy, 'the invisible man'. On May 2, 1945 he took off for Spain with Laval in a Junkers 88. Before doing so he exercised his last prerogative as a minister of the defunct regime: he had Hérold-Paquis, the former commentator of Radio-Paris, turned off the plane to make room for his brother. Condemned to death *in absentia* in 1946, he eventually returned to France and stood trial in 1960. In the more clement atmosphere that by then prevailed he received a nominal sentence of ten years' banishment as from 1945, which meant his immediate release. His unbending rigour in sending off young men to Germany for forced labour was reproached him more than his strictly educational activities.

The 'New Order' in education and for youth lasted barely four years. Inspired at first by strongly meliorist, although mistaken ambitions, diminished by desires to take petty vengeance on those held responsible for French misfortunes, the guiding light of reform quickly fell into wrong hands. In the end idealism was soon swept away by reality. What held good for the schools was also valid, as will be seen, for the youth organizations that Vichy created or sponsored.

Chapter III

The Church and Education

For Charles Maurras Pétain's assumption of power had been a 'divine surprise'. It was equally so for the Church which, despite the interludes of the Ralliement and the 'union sacrée', had never been completely reconciled to the Republic. The causes of conflict dated back to before 1914: Ferry's secular laws on education; clerical attacks on Republicanism during the Dreyfus Affair; Waldeck-Rousseau's assertion of civil supremacy; Combes's measures against the religious orders and their schools, followed by the Separation of Church and State. The identification at first of the Action Française with the Church, with which it shared a disapproval of democracy, freemasonry, individualism, and rationalism – all abominations later of Vichy also – did not help relations with the State. Condemning the Action Française in 1926 and urging a new Ralliement, Pius XI had tried to bring reconciliation, but his successor had removed the ban on the movement in 1939. Meanwhile Frenchmen, especially the industrial masses, had gradually become dechristianized. Clerical antagonism to the Popular Front and opposition to the Republicans in the Spanish Civil War had polarized the situation further. By 1939 the hierarchy regarded France as a 'pays de mission', a territory to reconquer for the faith. In 1940 it regarded the defeat as divine punishment for the godlessness of France, and Pétain – who, it was recalled, had attended a Catholic school – almost as a reincarnated Joan of Arc. In the reconversion for which the bishops now hoped, the key lay in conquering anew the hearts and minds of the young. Two instruments were to hand: the first, the confessional schools, run by the parish priest under the diocesan, epitomized the traditional culture of Catholicism; the second was the Association Catholique de la Jeunesse Française (ACJF), the Church's youth movements. The change of regime offered the Church a golden opportunity to strengthen both – although the youth movements functioned freely only in the southern zone. It might even penetrate the State school and the new, secular youth movements that were being created. The Church, therefore, sought to improve the shining hour.

Much, however, depended upon its leaders. The slight *détente* in Church–State relationships immediately before the war owed much to the character of Cardinal Verdier, Archbishop of Paris. But Verdier had died in the spring of 1940. In any case, he had not much hope that the Daladier government would help Catholic schools, so strongly was the ministry of education the bastion of extreme secularism ('le laïcisme', as opposed to the more neutral term, 'la laïcité'). Of the four French cardinals remaining, the one who was to be most concerned with education and youth was Liénart, Bishop of Lille. Cardinal Liénart had spent all his pastoral life in Northern France. In 1929 his championing of the trade unions against the local textile manufacturers had won him respect even in anti-clerical circles. Despite Verdier's pessimism he had approached the government in early 1940 with a request for aid for the Church schools and had received a sympathetic hearing. The invasion had halted further overtures. Liénart, widely regarded as the protagonist of the 'evangelising Church', hoped for an even more attentive audience with Pétain, whom he had known in the First World War and to whom he gave immediate loyalty.[1] Liénart's colleague, Cardinal Suhard, translated from Reims to become Archbishop of Paris in succession to Verdier, was a prelate with little political experience, although credited with being a 'prudent negotiator',[2] much exercised by the spread of irreligion, which he linked with the growth of Communism. For him the re-education of the young was the prime question.[3] At Lyons, Cardinal Gerlier, Primate of the Gauls, was a former lawyer; as an ex-president of the ACJF he had maintained his interest in youth affairs. Despite being anti-German he boldly declared: 'Victorious, we would probably have remained the prisoner of our errors. Through becoming secularized France ran the risk of dying.'[4] It took the anti-Jewish measures of Vichy and the Germans for him to perceive that France then also ran the risk of 'losing its soul'. The remaining cardinal, Baudrillart, did not hold episcopal office but was the director of the Institut Catholique in Paris, the parallel Catholic institution to the Sorbonne. Already in his dotage, he was so fanatically anti-Communist that he saw the redemption of France in an alliance with Germany in the 'crusade against Bolshevism'. Thus in 1941, under the chairmanship of Bonnard, he served on the committee which organized the Légion des Volontaires Français to fight on the Eastern Front. The stance of the cardinals in 1940, however, was not monolithic. With their fellow-bishops they showed a certain political naivety, tinctured with anti-Communism, submitting themselves, as did indeed most Frenchmen, to Pétain and acknowledging him at least as the 'established power' ('le pouvoir établi'), if not as the 'legitimate authority' ('l'autorité légitime'). To the Marshal and his regime they adjured their flock to give obedience but offered varying degrees of devotion as the war progressed. It was a position from which the most eminent Catholics, clerical and lay, hardly wavered to the end. Their support was invaluable.

The Protestant attitude to Vichy was much more reserved, although much less important. The Fédération Protestante de France, which comprised both Reformed and Lutheran Protestants, had a system of Church governance which was democratic, as opposed to the hierarchism of Catholicism. It was thus far less in tune with the new authoritarian regime. Ecumenical, it had closer ties with Britain than Germany, despite its German religious roots. It was a small minority group, including only 2 per cent of the population.[5] During the war, however, it became more widely known. Members of its youth movements made up almost entirely a committee for relief work, CIMADE (Comité inter-mouvements d'aide aux évacués), which, originally formed to assist evacuees in 1939, transferred its activities to refugees in 1940 and then to all those fleeing from the Nazis, which gained it great respect.

The head of the Fédération Protestante was Pastor Marc Boegner, who figured prominently in the ecumenical movement both before and after the war. Boegner got on well with Pétain and the Catholic dignitaries. Because the strongholds of Protestantism lay mainly in unoccupied France, particularly in the Cévennes, he exerted more influence than he would normally have done. The son of a prefect, he had at one time been the head of the Protestant student movement, the Fédération Chrétienne des Étudiants.[6] In 1936 he had published *L'Éducation et l'idée de la patrie.* In 1941 Pétain made him a member of the Conseil National. Although he was the official spokesman of Protestantism, other Protestants, such as André Siegfried, who at first accepted and then resigned his membership of the Conseil National, and the Monod family, much esteemed in educational circles, were also influential. Boegner later became more distant in his relations with Vichy, speaking out against the extradition of anti-Nazi Germans and against the persecution of the Jews. Protestant families saved many Jewish families from deportation. The Protestants had an interest in subsidies to confessional schools, since they ran a few schools themselves.

In return for their loyalty the Catholics, in particular, expected some material reward in the form of State subsidies. Between the wars what was known as the 'schools question' had made little progress. In 1918 the educational reform group, the Compagnons de l'Université Nouvelle, had at first favoured subsidies to Catholic schools, but had abandoned this support in 1920. A year later the Chamber of Deputies rejected a request for aid. Indeed the acid test of Republicanism for Radicals and Socialists alike remained the principle of secularism. Bodies such as the Ligue de l'Enseignement and the Ligue des Droits de l'Homme, both closely linked to the teaching profession, campaigned vigorously against subsidizing Catholic education throughout the 1920s, a campaign to which the Assembly of Cardinals and Archbishops reacted strongly in 1925: 'In every domain and all over the country, open and unanimous war is declared on secularism and its principles until the iniquitous laws which have arisen from it have been abolished. The school law misleads the intelligence of children, perverts their will and falsifies their conscience.'[7] Catholics wanted 'la répartition proportionnelle scolaire', a system whereby the national school budget was divided between State schools and their own in proportion to the number of pupils respectively in each. But by the end of the decade the Catholic campaign had run out of steam. It was revivified in 1931 by a group of Catholic intellectuals in Lille, backed by Cardinal Liénart. They linked their demand for subsidies to the question of broadening access to secondary education,[8] arguing that Catholic secondary schools (which ten years later catered for some 48 per cent of all secondary pupils),[9] if assisted, would be able to admit poor working-class children then excluded solely through lack of funds. But such a move to a more democratic system of Catholic education was opposed by traditionalists like General de Castelnau, president of the influential Fédération Catholique de France.

The indictment of the secular laws on education was renewed in 1940: bishops declared bluntly that France's misfortunes arose from its error in having expelled God from the school.[10] The defeat arose from moral decadence, which sprang from an irreligious education system. A few Catholics nevertheless saw that extreme anti-secularism might break the fragile unity that Pétain had succeeded in imposing. On July 17, 1940 Baudouin recorded in his diary how much he deplored the activities of clerics seeking the outright abolition of the secular laws: 'I told the Cardinal [Gerlier] that I considered this attitude to be dangerous; the present situation should not at all costs be seen to be a revenge taken by the Church or Churchmen. I added that I was Catholic but anticlerical and Cardinal Gerlier assured me that he was as anticlerical as I.'[11] Nevertheless the hue and cry continued. On August 24, 1940 *La Croix* tersely summed up the course of Republican history: by 1914 the effects of 'total secularism' had not been felt; by 1940 they had.

What impact did the revival of the 'schools question' make at Vichy? Pétain's views, as expressed in the *Revue des deux mondes,* had been interpreted as sympathetic to Catholic aspirations. As regards the school in general he came out strongly in favour of commitment: 'The French school will no longer lay claim to neutrality. Life is not neutral. The school must teach respect for moral and religious beliefs and particularly for those that France has professed from the origins of its existence as a nation.'[12] Although not a fervent Catholic the Marshal is alleged to have remarked that a good mass did no harm to anyone.[13] On June 25, 1940, with Lebrun and other members of the last Republican government, he had attended a service at which Feltin, Archbishop of Bordeaux, had preached in his cathedral on the theme of a new social order to be erected on the foundations of 'God, our country and the family'.[14] On Bastille Day the Marshal had again attended divine service and bowed the knee at the elevation, a gesture which prompted Baudouin to remark that it had been a long while since a head of State had assumed that posture.[15] This outward observance of Catholicism continued throughout the war. General Weygand, a more committed Christian, declared that France had merited its defeat because for half a century its governments had driven God from the school.[16] Some of the Marshal's entourage, such as René Benjamin, the Vichy 'court writer' much in evidence in the early days, had campaigned before the war for Catholic education.[17] Chevalier, who was responsible for the first laws favouring Catholic schools, was 'a sort of Templar, a Leaguing monk', convinced that the débâcle of 1940 had spiritual origins and that Buisson's 'école sans Dieu' must bear a heavy share of the blame for France's downfall.[18] Appointed by Darlan, who is perhaps best described as a Voltairean deist, Carcopino, Chevalier's successor at the ministry of education, was a more moderate Catholic. By contrast, Bonnard, minister until the Liberation, an atheist or at the most an agnostic, was a firm anti-clerical. The peak of Catholic influence was therefore reached by the end of 1940.

The Church was aware that it must strike while the iron was hot. Meanwhile adulation of Pétain soon became the order of the day, the mood was for superlatives, and Catholics were not exempt. Gerlier made his famous declaration, which he lived to regret, that 'Pétain is France, and France today is Pétain'.[19] By Christmas 1940 the Marshal had received a further accolade: an ode by the Catholic poet, Claudel (who later, evenhandedly, also wrote one for de Gaulle). By then the new 'court' at Vichy was well established and the Jesuits and Dominicans who frequented it, noting that the Marshal liked the company of ecclesiastics at table, saw that he was well served. Curiously, however, the highest Church dignitaries appeared only rarely at Vichy, despite their professed 'sincere and total loyalty to the established power'.[20] For Liénart, living at Lille in the 'forbidden zone', the journey was of course difficult and he only travelled to Vichy once (April 10, 1942); Suhard went only twice, but Gerlier, close by at Lyons, was a more frequent visitor.

The question of the Catholic schools was raised when Gerlier and Suhard met in Paris on July 9, 1940.[21] A week later Gerlier saw Pétain and discussed it. Finally Liénart came to Paris to see Suhard. Gerlier, nailed the Catholic colours to the mast in a statement reported in *La Croix:* in a France freed from materialism and rebuilt by spiritual forces the Church would play a full part. First, however, the fetters that bound it must be broken, particularly regarding education, for '. . . in clarity and justice, the school question must be settled. The State school must care scrupulously for the child's soul. The confessional school must be made really available to those Christian families who so desire, through the fairer distribution of school subsidies.'[22] The concrete proposals the cardinals made to Pétain included aid to Catholic schools, the lifting of the teaching ban on religious orders, a right of entry for the parish priest to State schools, the teaching in them of the catechism as part of the regular timetable, and the banning of all parties and organizations hostile to religious education. Matching their professions of loyalty to Vichy, they also presented an address to the Pope in which they expressed their resolve to 'pursue the laborious and heroic effort undertaken for so many years to ensure the maintenance and development of Catholic schools.' Two declarations of intent and a draft programme which reversed half a century of French history had quickly emerged from the confusion of defeat.

The most radical suggestion was that religion should once again be taught in State schools. How far could those schools be regained for Catholicism? The affair of the crucifix is perhaps symbolic of the struggle that now began. Despite the secularist laws of the 1880s in many areas, at least until the Combes ministry the crucifix continued to hang in State classrooms. In the strongly Catholic West the practice continued in schools and 'mairies', even after the Separation of Church and State. After the defeat of 1940 the custom became even more widespread. This aroused indignation in some quarters. Thus the prefect of the Pas-de-Calais wanted clarification of the rules, he said, because in some places the crucifix had been reinstated 'in an ostentatious manner against State teachers'.[23] In April 1941 Darlan circularized the prefects pointing out that this reinstallation of a religious symbol infringed the principle of State 'neutrality'. Canon Polimann, the former deputy for Meuse, sprang to the defence of the practice in a letter to Pétain in which he asserted that before the war a portrait of Stalin had even graced some class-rooms.[24] Darlan had to climb down. In a circular of July 1941 he claimed that he had been misinterpreted. His object was mutual toleration, but he did not forbid the display of the crucifix where the custom had been hallowed by tradition and met with the approval of the local community.[25] It was pointed out that for it to be hung in the class-room the teacher's agreement was not essential.[26] This was a gratuitous snub to the teachers. By November 1942 it was reported that the emblem occupied the place of honour in five hundred schools of the Verdun diocese. But incidents continued to occur and in early 1943, after academy inspectors reported that they were at a loss to know what action to take, Bonnard decided to enforce uniformity.[27] The result is not known, but the emotive power of this comparatively trivial affair illustrates the tension that continued to exist between primary teacher and parish priest.

A more substantial controversy exploded when 'duties towards God' were reintroduced into the State-primary ethics syllabus. It is true that the orthodox Republican view regarding the State school's strict neutrality in religious matters had never been absolute. This neutrality rested upon Ferry's organic law of 1882 on education. During the debate upon the bill Jules Simon had proposed an amendment prescribing that 'teachers will teach their pupils their duties towards God'. Despite Ferry's opposition this got through the Senate but was then thrown out by the Chamber of Deputies, as it was by the Senate when the bill came back to that body. Nevertheless, in the applicatory 'arrêté' of the law, duly endorsed officially, Simon's addition appeared in the programme for primary schools.[28] In 1940 and 1941 many interpretations had been given as to what had been intended. In March 1941, M. Lefas, a member of the Senate commission on education, delivered a paper to the Académie des Sciences Morales et Politiques,[29] in which he affirmed that the controversial 'duties towards God' had eventually been prescribed with Ferry's approval. Ferry had specifically denied the charge of wishing to institute a 'Godless school' and had sought a common religious denominator which would satisfy Catholics, Protestants, and Jews alike. In the 1880s it was often the State-primary teacher whom parents approached and asked whether he would hear their child recite the catechism, although the recitation took place off the school premises and the teacher would sedulously abstain from commenting on the text. Lefas accordingly argued that the 'neutrality' desired was patently deist and postulated an ethical code based upon Christianity. Only later had the concept of neutrality so evolved that the very name of God had disappeared from school textbooks and even those fables of La Fontaine which alluded to the Deity were either not prescribed in the school syllabus or were bowdlerized:

> Petit poisson deviendra grand,
> Pourvu qu'*on lui donne la vie.*

However, the 'duties towards God' were not dropped until new, abridged programmes had been introduced in 1923,[30] and even then the omission had occurred through inadvertence. Paul Lapie, the anticlerical director of primary education, had deliberately left them out and Bérard, the minister, a staunch Catholic, had signed the decree authorizing the new programme without perceiving this significant change. It was an oversight that he rectified by circular (June 20, 1923) a few months later, but the amendment to the programmes had not been made. What part Bérard, who was certainly often at Vichy before being appointed in late 1940 to the embassy at the Vatican, played in the reintroduction of the topic is not known. A further anomaly was that the Instructions for teaching the pre-1923 programmes had never been abrogated. A much used commentary on these Instructions, referring to the 'duties towards God',[31] specified that teachers had not to prove God's existence or expound His attributes, because children were well aware of them But they must impress upon their charges not to take God's name lightly; pupils must learn that 'the first homage owed to the Godhead is obedience to the laws of God as revealed by . . . conscience and reason'. The Instructions and the gloss put upon them, although not wholly acceptable to Catholics and certainly unpalatable to the ultra-secularists ('laïcisants'), were still nominally in force at the demise of the Third Republic, although fallen into disuse.

All the greater, therefore, was the shock when an 'arrêté' of November 23, 1940 reintroduced into the programmes a topic which, since 1923, had been authorized only by circular. Chevalier, the instigator of the change, subsequently argued that he had merely rectified an anomaly, despite the fact that this was undoubtedly an assault upon secularism and particularly upon the secularist primary teachers.[32] Bérard's circular and the Instructions had been conveniently forgotten because the teachers had become atheists, following the anti-religious tendencies of some trade unions, or because they had 'obeyed the injunctions of the masonic lodges'.[33] To redress the balance was not only a matter of faith but also of reason. In an interview with the Agence Havas Chevalier justified himself in this way:

> Need I cite to you that passage in the Fourth Book of the *Laws* in which Plato, the Greek philosopher, puts forward this maxim to the governors of the City: 'It is not Man, but much rather God who must be considered the measure of all things.' . . . The State, by putting into its programmes the duties towards God and thus admitting the divine idea into its teaching, does not favour one Church at the expense of another. It merely recognises – and, after all, it is in its own interest to do so – one of the permanent acquisitions of reason, that which human thought has in all ages propounded as the sole possible basis of morality.

And, he adds somewhat smugly: 'This is exactly what I wrote in 1927. I need not go back in any way on what I wrote then. On the contrary, I am in fact remaining faithful to myself . . .'[34] He held the sincere belief that the fate of France was linked to the persistence of the religious idea. In a preamble to the applicatory 'arrêté' of November 23, 1940 we are reminded that '. . . teachers must reinstall in the place of honour sentiments and ideas whose disappearance or even dilution in hearts and minds may be held to be dangerous for the State or the country.' On December 12, 1940 *La Croix,* harking back to the parliamentary battles of the 1880s, tersely summed up the situation: 'L'École sans Dieu a vécu.'

The other, even more drastic measure, was the introduction of religious instruction into the State school. This may have been implemented by a subterfuge. It was one element in a law of January 6, 1941, but one for which Flandin had forbidden Chevalier to issue the applicatory 'arrêté'. In the interregnum between the resignation of Flandin and the assumption of power by Darlan Chevalier seized the opportunity to publish the necessary authorization to implement the measure.[35] By it religious instruction became an integral part of the school timetable, as an optional subject for the children of parents who so desired. Demolishing one of the pillars of the law of 1882, it meant that Thursday, traditionally a holiday so that pupils who so wished could attend catechism classes outside the school, was no longer reserved for this purpose. From now on one and a half hours a week, preferably at the beginning of the school day, could be allocated for it on the school timetable. Chevalier weakly justified the measure by saying that in future Thursday could be a real holiday for the children. It was decreed that in exceptional cases the final logical step could be taken: not only must it be shown on the timetable, but religious instruction could even take place on school premises, at the discretion of the academy inspector and on the advice of the mayor. In allowing the priest to get his foot inside the school door Chevalier advanced another far-fetched justification: he had in mind a case where a church in the mountains had been destroyed by an avalanche.[36]

The Paris collaborationist press, already angered by the public tribute Chevalier had paid to Bergson, his friend and master, born a Jew but close to conversion to Catholicism, when the great philosopher had died a few days before, accused the minister of wishing to return all education to the bosom of the Church (*L'Œuvre,* January 9, 1941). Socialist collaborators, writing in *L'Effort,* saw the fabric of the secular State under threat. *Le Cri du peuple* (January 7 and 9, 1941) charged the minister with 'solicitude for the Jews' and with 'democratic ideology'. Nor were all Catholics pleased with the strategy that Chevalier was following. Cardinal Suhard perceptively remarked that measures to introduce religion into State schools diverted attention from the real problem, the financial plight of the Catholic schools. Father Dillard, the well-known Jesuit, complained to Pétain: the Church knew how much clericalism France could stand, and 'Your secretary of state for education is busy compromising the good Lord and us with him. Once the clergy foolishly threw itself into the Moral Order of Marshal MacMahon. It ought not to start over again by paying court to your Révolution Nationale.'[37] Such prudence on the part of Catholics was exceptional. Strongly Catholic areas took their cue from the local bishops, who viewed Chevalier's measures as an act of reparation and even an occasion for vengeance.

However, the high tide of Catholic interference into State education quickly began to ebb. Chevalier was removed from office to become minister for health and the family, and immediately afterwards the Vichy censors forbade publication of his previous utterances on religious instruction.[38] This policy had found little sympathy with his ministerial colleagues and even less among the top educational civil servants. His move sideways to a new ministry was seen as a partial retreat by Pétain from his former strongly pro-Catholic position. As such it gave some heart to the primary teachers, who, as one indignant cleric later expressed it, remained faithful to their masonic beliefs and discouraged their pupils from attending the catechism.[39]

Carcopino, the new minister, tried – not unsuccessfully, as it turned out – to be all things to all men. Describing himself as 'secular in so far as he was liberal',[40] he told the Council of Ministers, whose meeting he attended on March 7, 1941 – as, nominally only a secretary of state, he did not attend the Council meetings by right – that he preferred the contribution of Christianity to the world to be taught through history, and proposed that the time allocation for that subject be increased accordingly. A few days later, on March 10, the religious measures were abrogated. From now onwards religious instruction would be a voluntary and additional subject given off the school premises by the parish priest at times fixed by mutual arrangement between the academy inspector and the diocesan authorities. It would, however, remain part of the school timetable and be scheduled for two periods weekly, to be fixed for the beginning or the end of the school day. In a letter to Pétain Carcopino alluded to the fears aroused by his predecessor that the State primary-school might become wholly confessional. The retention of religious instruction on the timetable safeguarded Church rights (although in practice what occurred was a reversion to the status quo), and, he hoped 'that the primary teachers will attend Church in ever-increasing numbers, but I am certain my expectations would be disappointed if the priest, in God's name, entered the school building.'

How many parents availed themselves of the facility for their children to attend religious instruction in school time is not known. In some areas the authorities canvassed parents. Thus at Villeurbanne, a suburb of Lyons, the municipality asked them by letter: 'Do you wish your child to receive religious instruction, Catholic, Protestant or Jewish (*sic*) or not?' Of the 7,779 who replied only 1,489 (19 per cent) declared themselves as of no religion and did not desire any religious instruction for their children. Of the remainder, 6,086 Catholics (78 per cent of the total), 162 Protestants (2 per cent), and 42 Jews (0.53 per cent) signified their willingness for their children to attend. Such a result may reflect a fear of not conforming or be interpreted as a genuine revival of religious sentiment.[41]

At the same time the 'duties towards God' were removed from the school programmes.[42] Instead pupils were to study ethics, which would include 'informal discussions and readings on the principal duties we owe to ourselves and to our fellow-men (respect for the family groupings of our country, for the views of others and for religious beliefs)'. The syllabus would include the study of Christian civilization and spiritual values. This reformulation may have been too feeble for Pétain: he wanted explicit reference to the points covered in the former Instructions regarding reverence for God's name and the duty of obedience to His law.[43] This wish the minister managed to evade. The preamble to his 'arrêté', already published on March 10, 1941, dealt with the substitution of the study of God by the study of spiritual values. For committed Christians, he declared, the mere study of God was a vague notion, evoking only a deistic religiosity. In any case the primary teacher lacked the philosophical competence to teach what it meant. On the other hand, he *was* well equipped to talk about Christian values, as exemplified, for instance, in the life of St. Joan of Arc or St. Vincent de Paul. Carcopino concluded, 'Better not to talk of God in the classroom at all than to do so ineptly.' After the war he put a further gloss upon this reasoning: 'By what teachers, with such qualifications, could theology be taught in the 36,000 communes of France?'[44] This subtle reasoning seems exaggerated: teaching about God to thirteen-year-olds could only be interpreted as teaching theology in the narrowest sense.

Although the minister averred that his modifications were designed to avoid sectarianism, recriminations were not spared him. Osservatore Romano (March 20–1, 1941) voiced what was probably the Vatican view, that he was propounding a 'headless morality', namely, one without God, a criticism that *La Croix* was not allowed by the Vichy censors to reprint.[45] Maurrassians, hinting that Carcopino had masonic connections, saw in his changes the hidden hand of the lodges.[46] Pétain's 'cabinet militaire' received twenty-six letters, all condemnatory.[47] One correspondent noted that the minister had not a French name and enquired pointedly where his grandfather was born – a reference to the anti-Jewish laws. Another wrote, 'M. Carcopino gives me the impression of being something of a Pilate,' perhaps a judgement not too wide of the mark. General de Castelnau, as president of the Fédération Nationale Catholique, registered his protest directly with Pétain.[48] German sources reported that Gerlier and the Lyons Jesuits disliked the new turn of events but that the hierarchy in the occupied zone agreed that Chevalier had tried to force the pace unduly. Carcopino was, after all, a Catholic, and, so the Germans unjustly alleged, enjoyed a 'father and son' relationship with Baudrillart, that most reactionary of all French cardinals.[49] Mgr

Guerry, auxiliary to the Archbishop of Cambrai and secretary-general of the Standing Committee of the Assembly of Cardinals and Archbishops, ascribed the measures to pressure from Déat and the Paris press.[50] Politicians' views were mixed. Henri Lémery, senator for Martinique, asked sardonically, 'What is this way of inviting God into the school in the autumn only to show Him the door in winter?' On the other hand, Pucheu, the minister of the interior, testifying later to the youth commission of the Conseil National, praised Carcopino, who, he said, had 'already rectified the monstrous errors of his predecessor, errors which threatened the country with a terrible wave of anti-clericalism'.[51] Carcopino claimed to have the support of such diverse personalities as Maurras, Mgr Feltin, of Bordeaux, Gaston Martin, the president of the Société des Agrégés, Paul Hazard, the literary critic, and Leon Brunschvicg, the editor of Pascal.[52]

The independent Catholic review, *Esprit,* welcomed the rescinding of Chevalier's measures. 'A notable step has been taken towards the pacification of the school', wrote Emmanuel Mounier, its editor. The review, which had started up in the free zone after the collapse, had been critical of Chevalier from the outset. In February 1941 it had published an enquiry into 'Dieu à l'école', demolishing Chevalier's arguments, which seemed to imply that the idea of God depended on the reason. Mounier caustically remarked that he and others had thought 'God wears a cassock.' Pierre Ganne, a priest posed the question: Which God, who, in Chevalier's terms, 'relates to the reason', is to be taught? That of Voltaire? That of the Vicaire Savoyard? Surely if one is going to teach about God, why should it not be the God of Abraham, Isaac, or Jacob, or even of Jesus Christ? Henri Chatreix, a State primary teacher, reflected that to have to present to pupils the arguments for the existence of God, as could well be the case, might be counter-productive: 'What sad consequences, and what inroads perhaps on the faith of the child!' The most eminent contributor to the enquiry, Gabriel Marcel, postulated the case of the atheist teacher. It would be wrong to remove him from the classroom for his unbelief: 'Is it not something deeply shocking to the mind to impose as a condition of suitability the ability to teach adherence to a certain philosophical creed?'[53] For the State school to have an official philosophy about God was as odious as the official atheism displayed in the closing years of the Third Republic. Such 'dictatorial procedures' were to be condemned. The epithet aroused anger in Rome and among certain French bishops.

To the privacy of his *Entretiens*, not intended for immediate publication, Mounier confided his own view at the time of Chevalier, whose protégé and pupil he had once been, and of the deleterious effect of the measures the one-time minister had initiated. 'In proclaiming in enraged fashion: "The Godless school is no more", the captain of gendarmerie who has been raised up for a time to become minister of education makes the arrangements appear as an act of revenge on the part of the parish priest, in spite of his philosophical assertions. . . ' Indeed '. . . the parish priest has lifted his head once more: in the pulpit and to the children at catechism he declares that the war was lost through the primary teachers, and has opened up guerilla warfare.'[54] Secularism and clericalism had renewed their perennial quarrel.

Three groups of Catholics could therefore be distinguished. There were those, like Mounier, who condemned Chevalier and applauded Carcopino. Their evolution away from Vichy had already begun. A second group gave qualified approval to Carcopino on tactical grounds. And there were some who abominated him. At local level, as Mounier had assumed, the traditional hostility between parish priest and village schoolteacher was stirred up once more. Nevertheless, it is perhaps worth noting that Carcopino's measures brought them into contact, since mutually convenient times for religious instruction had to be arranged. It was a situation, which, declared the ACA in July 1941, 'leads us to desire earnestly a rapprochement between the clergy and the State teachers'.[55]

The very idea that the parish priest should ever be permitted to set foot inside the State school had particularly incensed the secularists. Carcopino had come out against this, although, like Chevalier, he did admit exceptions. Priests who served outlying hamlets in the Limoges diocese were given permission to teach on school premises.[56] The mayor of Doubs sought the same concession, maintaining that it would obviate rural children having to trudge long distances in leaky shoes, in inclement weather, to undergo instruction in unheated churches.[57] Whereas hamlets attached to a commune had often each their own school, there was only one church to serve the commune and the parish. From Bonnard the indefatigable bishop of Limoges later won a further privilege: the work-load on the parish priest being heavy, where a parish extended over several hamlets permission was given for seminarists to give religious instruction on the school premises.[58]

An unexpected effect of the Chevalier–Carcopino measures, ironically enough, was that for the first time in State primary education the name of God was completely eliminated, for Carcopino's law annulled both Chevalier's programmes and those previous Instructions in which the name of God had been specifically mentioned.[59] After the Liberation Carcopino's programmes were provisionally replaced by those of 1923 (C. of September 12, 1944). Later, on October 17, 1945, a new programme included the phrase, 'duties towards one's family and one's country'. By mid-1941 the bid to re-establish Christianity in State schools had failed; the chance was not to come again.

The Catholics ran many secondary schools, but in the State schools the issues took a different form. The Catholics succeeded in obtaining the appointment of chaplains, although priests had occasionally been allowed into residential *lycées* even before the war. By an *arrêté* of February 23, 1941 Chevalier officially sanctioned such appointments. Chaplains were eventually paid: those that worked at least sixteen hours a week received the basic salary of a graduate teacher – 27,000F a year – although Carcopino astutely reduced this to 20,000F. (C. of May 6 1941). Those that worked fewer hours were paid in proportion. This move to chaplaincies was general: they were also authorized in the Chantiers de la Jeunesse (L. of March 18, 1941) and in children's holiday camps ('colonies de vacances') by a decree of March 25, 1942. It was even argued that they should be installed in the new institutes of professional training for primary teachers, because this might win over 'certain members of the Church who still maintain a reserved attitude towards the Révolution Nationale', a rather convoluted form of reasoning.[60] Religious orders were banned from chaplaincies. One Jesuit, who was nevertheless appointed, was removed from his school at Nice for having voiced anti-government sentiments.[61] Permanent officials at the ministry may have been less than diligent in securing the appointment of chaplains. In the very Catholic area of Saint-Brieuc the bishop complained that, having designated priests for service in State schools he was informed by the academy inspector that they could not be appointed until head teachers asked for them.[62] The bishop of Autun, Chalon, and Mâcon pointed out the anomalous position of technical institutions, where chaplains were not officially sanctioned. Bonnard's officials advised the minister that in at least one technical institution within the good bishop's diocese religious instruction was already being given by a private arrangement between pupils, their families, and the local priest. Since the priest was being paid by the parents, what the bishop was really asking for was that the State should pay. This would create a precedent for all other technical establishments: the six Écoles Nationales d'Arts et Métiers, 25 Écoles Nationales, and 170 technical schools.[63] The bishop's request was rejected.

In education legislation and reality rarely correspond. How far the Vichy measures regarding religion had any real impact is difficult to say. A reputable local historian in the Nantes area, Fernand Guériff, a primary teacher working during the war in a school evacuated outside the town, stated that he had never heard of the new programmes stipulating the 'duties towards God', and as regards religious instruction,

> The priest or his curate came in on Thursday morning to hear the catechism in a room above the Orangery which served also as a chapel on Sundays (*sic*). Thursdays being a free day, non-practising Catholic pupils (*sic*) remained in the recreation room where we kept them busy at various occupations (music, art, reading, sport, games). This situation lasted throughout the war without any difficulties. Some of our pupils made their solemn communion.[64]

In fact, as Suhard had pointed out, the debate on religion in State schools masked a more fundamental problem, that of aid to the private – overwhelmingly Catholic – schools.

This dispute between State and Catholic school was of long standing. 'The mayor against the priest, or the mayor and the priest against the schoolmaster, that's the situation in every rural area of France', wrote one contemporary observer describing what was termed 'the war in the village'.[65] The universality of such hostilities may have been exaggerated, but acrimony which continually manifested itself there certainly was. In a village of Western France, the Catholic mayor might refuse to authorize urgent repairs to the State school, hoping to provoke the resignation of the teacher and thus have a pretext to close the school. On the other hand, children elsewhere attending the State school would be forbidden to attend the celebrations on Mother's Day, because these were organized by the Catholic school. Conversely, Catholic children who had attended a Christmas party organized in the State school might be obliged by their own teachers to say a novena for penance. Pressures to attend the one school or the other were particularly strong. In the Dunkirk area a patently secularist primary-school inspector reported in the spring of 1941 several instances of Catholic coercion.[66] Employers were blackmailing their workers into sending their children to the confessional school. Local shopkeepers and artisans not enrolling their children in the Catholic institution were finding their business falling away. When in 1940 a high-ranking customs officer withdrew his daughter from the State school some of his subordinates felt constrained to follow suit. At Loon-Plage the priest was alleged to be bribing parents to switch schools. Help from the Secours National, often run by Catholics, was made conditional on children abandoning the State school. Pressure was particularly brought to bear upon children at the age of eleven if they wished to attend the preparation classes for their first communion. State-school pupils attending the catechism were posed the hardest questions to answer and sometimes not allowed to participate fully in religious ceremonies. They were also instructed by the priest not to work hard at their books until their parents agreed to transfer them to a Catholic school. When the Germans requisitioned a State school the local mayor would make no effort to find alternative accommodation so that the school would be forced to close. 'Against this unleashing of hostile forces', notes this primary inspector dramatically, 'our teachers are almost completely disarmed'. For the first time in half a century Catholics, both locally and nationally, felt powerful enough to reassert their right to educate all Catholic pupils.

The most pressing need, however, was State aid for Catholic schools, if this ambition was to be realized. The historical background to this claim has already been outlined. Catholics, or at least the hierarchy, laboured under a grievance because many parents could not afford to use the fee-paying confessional schools. They cited the more fortunate experience of other places and religions where schools were subsidized: in Alsace, where the former German regime of aid to confessional schools had appertained; in North Africa, where the Islamic schools and those of the Alliance Israélite were assisted.[67] In 1940 the Catholic bishops believed that what was at stake was the very survival of their education system. 'Black France', the rich bourgeoisie, had been in the past a most generous supporter, but as conditions worsened its financial aid dried up. In Northern France, a battlefield once more, Catholic schools had suffered from damage and occupation – but State schools had suffered even more. Rationing and shortages excluded traditional fund-raising activities such as fêtes and bazaars. In particular the plight of the Catholic primary teacher, often underqualified but even more underpaid, was desperate. In June 1940, after the Nord department had been cut off from the rest of France, Cardinal Liénart informed the prefect that the Church coffers were empty and requested an immediate subsidy to pay teachers' salaries. Otherwise, he added, the Catholic schools of the diocese would close and 70,000 pupils would be seeking admission to State schools. On his own authority the prefect advanced one million francs to meet the immediate crisis.[68] But a second request that the cardinal made in August, after communications had been restored, was merely passed on by the prefect to the Délégation Générale in Paris and it is not known whether it was approved.[69] Some two years later Bonnard wrote to the minister of finance insisting that the original loan made in 1940 should be deducted from the subsidies that by then Catholic schools were receiving.[70] Nevertheless, the shortage of Catholic funds for education was undoubtedly genuine.

The measures that Vichy took to favour the Catholics doubtless encouraged them to hope for substantial financial help. The lifting of the ban on teaching by members of religious orders (L. of September 3, 1940) did not make much practical difference as it had not been rigorously applied since 1914, but it was seen as a straw in the wind. The relaxation was ascribed to Alibert, minister of justice, a convert who 'burned with the ardour of a neophyte'. Catholics viewed the rescinding of this 'most iniquitous of all' the secular laws as 'a formal reparation'.[71] There had been periodic reminders that the legislation had remained on the statute book, as when in 1928 Poincaré had not even been successful in procuring the missionary orders nominal exemption from its operation.[72] Others interpreted the repeal of the law differently. Jeanneney, president of the Senate, noted in his diary that although it effected no significant change, 'the desire to take legal revenge on the past was apparent'.[73] Mornet, de Gaulle's future public prosecutor, agreed with the lifting of the ban but held that it was unjustifiable at the same time to harry the freemasons, because this offended the principle of equity, 'But they wished to pay off scores and, whilst striking against the Left, they furnished proof of their friendship for the Right.'[74] Later, Vichy took the final step: religious teaching orders were released from the requirement of 'authorisation' that had been imposed upon them in 1901. As regards their educational activities, the orders were to enjoy privileges similar to those enjoyed by other associations, including tax exemptions (L. of April 8, 1942). Nevertheless, at the Liberation lay teachers still outnumbered religious by two to one in Catholic primary schools, although in their secondary schools religious and lay teachers were roughly equal in numbers.

The first tangible financial assistance came on October 15, 1940 when (as briefly mentioned already) Catholic schools were allowed to participate in the benefits of the Caisse des Écoles. This charitable fund, locally run, relied on private gifts and communal subsidies and helped poor children with free clothing, meals, books, and financial grants. Established in 1867, by a decision of the Conseil d'État of 1903 the Caisse des Écoles had had to exclude Catholic schools from its benefits. A proposal to reverse this decision in 1920 had been rejected by the Senate. The law of October 15, 1940, the prime mover of which was Chevalier, had nevertheless given rise to bad feeling in some areas, since it was argued that Catholics had charitable funds of their own, from which State pupils were rigorously excluded, upon which they could draw. Private benefactors to the Caisse were loath to contribute when they learnt that in future their gifts would also assist Catholic pupils.[76] It was left to Carcopino to restore the situation by limiting the fund once again to State pupils (L. of November 2, 1941). This reversal of policy displeased Pétain, who later pressed Bonnard to re-establish the common fund. The Marshal's 'cabinet civil' wrote to the minister: 'Nothing is more worthy of approval, nothing more in conformity with the views of the Marshal, than this union of the primary teacher, the parish priest and the mayor, a union of which a single Caisse des Écoles, where it is possible, is the symbol.'[77] Bonnard dragged his feet for four months before sending back a veiled refusal. The incident illustrates the striking decline of the Marshal's power and influence that had occurred by September 1942.

Such minor palliatives were in any case no substitute for more massive aid. Chevalier continued to believe that financial assistance could best be channelled to Catholic schools at local level. Isolated local initiatives had already taken place,[78] when on January 6, 1941 the law was promulgated allowing communes to subsidize private schools for lighting, heating, equipment, and school canteens, although such help could only be given if the unit cost per pupil fell below that in the corresponding State school. How many communes availed themselves of this permissive legislation is not known; in the Seine-Inférieure it was reported that only one commune, Yvetot, had refused to grant a subsidy.[79] This law represented a break with a long-standing tradition and gave rise to considerable local resentment. Yet Carcopino, when he took over from Chevalier, was careful not to dispute the principle of such aid, but merely questioned the manner in which it was given. He was in favour of funds being made available through the central government, but not through the ministry of education.[80]

Other small privileges that have already been touched upon were only grudgingly accepted by Catholics. Although Catholic pupils were now allowed to compete for national scholarships to secondary schools (D. of February 25, 1941) and in the Concours Général (D. of March 11, 1941), they were suspicious that the dice were loaded against them, if only because candidates had to make declarations in advance whether they were applying for a State or a Catholic secondary school.[81] Another concession badly wanted by Catholic schools was the right to employ State teachers. Several prestigious Catholic secondary institutions already employed one or two State 'agrégés' on a part-time basis. They now wanted to restore a right a century old, and employ them permanently. In 1821 Louis XVIII had permitted the Collège Stanislas to employ State teachers. This privilege had later been extended to other private schools, secular, Protestant, and Catholic: the Cours Secondaires of Vincennes and Neuilly; the École Alsacienne; the Collège Sévigné and the Collège Sainte-Barbe. The privilege had lasted till 1902 and was now restored by a law of May 30, 1941. This allowed State teachers to take posts in private schools without loss of pension rights and with the option of returning later to the State system.[82] But the effect of the law was partly nullified by a new statute for civil servants (September 15, 1941). Nevertheless, as late as July 1944 the Collège Stanislas was pressing Bonnard to allow it to recruit nine State teachers.[83]

There were many stories circulating about the difficulties being experienced by Catholic schools. The schools at Ducey (Manche) educated 147 boys and 120 girls. One school had been occupied by German units who had caused 27,000F worth of damage.[84] They employed eight teachers between them, the salary bill for whom in 1940–1 amounted to 48,500F. By November 1940 the parish priest had scraped together only 18,750F to foot the salary bill for the school year. From another small town, in Western France, it was reported that 244 pupils attended the Catholic schools and only *two* pupils the State one, yet the latter cost 28,000–30,000F per year to maintain. The local population urged that money be saved by abolishing the *State* school.[85] It was cases such as these that caused Bouthillier, the minister of finance, to urge that clear-cut decisions be made. This ex-Inspecteur des Finances, who clung to power until the return of Laval in 1942, argued that either a State monopoly in education should be established, as Déat wished, or adequate help must be given to the private sector.[86] Pétain's own inclination was to support the private schools, both on grounds of principle and of expediency, because if Catholic schools had to close the State system would be swamped.

His conviction was strengthened after Carcopino and he had received an emissary from Cardinal Liénart in May 1941. Toulemonde was an important textile manufacturer, president of the Association Roubaisienne d'Éducation et d'Enseignement, sent as the representative of the Comité des Écoles Libres de Roubaix. He received a sympathetic hearing from Pétain, always ready to listen to the 'grande bourgeoisie'. At the Marshal's request Toulemonde followed up his visit by setting down a memorandum embodying Catholic demands. Its main point was the familiar one that Catholics paid twice over for the education of their children. In 1938 there were just under one million children in Catholic primary schools. If they had been in the State system they would each have cost the State at least 1,300F a year. Thus Catholic parents were in effect subsidizing the State every year to the tune of some 1.3 billion francs, receiving nothing in return. Equity demanded that this sum should be paid over to Catholic schools by way of subsidy. Realizing that this was too much to expect, Toulemonde proposed instead a voucher system: a 'bon scolaire', valued at 50F per month per pupil – 600F a year – should be handed over to the Catholic school. Such an idea was of course not new: the concept of the educational voucher had been floated by Ernoul in 1872. Nevertheless the industrialist reminded Pétain that when they had met the Marshal had agreed to back this idea. The suggestion was countersigned by Liénart.[87] In his own account Carcopino places the suggested value of the voucher at the slightly higher figure of 700F a year. He also refers to another plan[88] put forward by Maître Blateau, a Paris lawyer: if a private school taught at least 20 per cent of the local school population it should be eligible for a gradated subsidy; if it catered for 70 per cent or more the subsidy should be automatic. In return Catholic schools would concede to the State the right to oversee the competence of their teaching staff.

The Marshal was slow to react to proposals, but in July he asked Carcopino to prepare, at a few days' notice, a subsidies plan for consideration at the next meeting of the Council of Ministers, which would grant aid 'either by means of proportional distribution by school or by other means'.[89] Pétain's request was framed in such a way that it looked as if his intention was not only to subsidize existing private schools but also to support the creation of new ones. Carcopino, already disconcerted by the short notice he had been given, regarded the apparent extension of aid to new schools as being contrary to the terms on which he had accepted office and offered his resignation. This was refused[90] but Pétain constituted a small committee, under the minister's chairmanship, to clarify the whole question. Meanwhile in July 1941 the ACA came out in favour of a voucher system and at a further meeting urged that any law should clearly state 'that financial aid is granted so as to respect the right of the father as the head of the family to send his children to the school of his choice'.[91]

Carcopino could not accept this statement of principle without qualification. He was not willing to go further than saying that existing Catholic schools were in need of assistance; the time was not appropriate to go into the right of choice of school. A moderate, he favoured the 'neutrality' of the school but did not consider this conflicted with the demand for 'freedom in education' ('la liberté d'enseignement'), within certain limits. His policy was one of opportunism: he did not wish, he said, to antagonize 'the army of 130,000 [state] primary teachers'.[92] He therefore proposed to the committee that any aid should be given to Catholic schools obliquely, and then only to those in proven need, through the ministry of the interior rather than the ministry of education. Pucheu agreed that a temporary solution was the most viable one: the substantive problem could be settled only after the war. With this reassurance, in September 1941 Carcopino opened negotiations with Cardinal Suhard in

Paris. To have dealt with Liénart in Lille would have required special permission to travel to and from the forbidden zone and might have entailed German interference. To his relief Suhard showed himself willing to compromise on aid being given only to existing schools. A subsidy of 400–500 million francs a year would be distributed through the prefects, who would work in conjunction with the local bishops. Since department boundaries coincided with diocese boundaries liaison between prefects and bishops would be easy, and it would be possible to proportion the size of the subsidy according to the density of Catholic education within the department.

The law of November 2, 1941 implementing these arrangements did not concede the principle of right that Catholics had sought but described the subsidies as 'an exceptional aid adapted to the circumstances'.[93] Furthermore, it was limited to private schools already in existence and 'regularly declared in conformity with the law of October 30, 1886'. Sufficient pupils had to be on the roll and the schools had to be in such financial straits that they ran the risk of closure. Another law of the same date granted certain State officials the right to inspect the schools: rectors, inspectors (general, academy, departmental, and medical), and – an innovation – the local mayor. Their right of entry was subject to their being accompanied by the school principal or his representative and inspection, save for medical purposes, was to be restricted to the nature and quality of the teaching being given. Any deficiencies were to be reported to the prefect. The schools were free to arrange their own timetable, select their own programmes, and use their own teaching methods, but might not use textbooks forbidden in State schools. Their pupils must sit the primary-leaving-certificate examination, which had just been made compulsory for State pupils as well. As from October 1, 1947 new teachers entering Catholic schools must have at least passed the baccalaureate. At the same time the law of January 1941 which permitted communes to contribute to the costs of running Catholic schools was abrogated.

This last provision was a disappointment for Suhard and the hierarchy, who had wanted such subsidies to continue, side by side with the new State subsidies.[94] But Carcopino was adamant that he was coping with a temporary situation rather than solving a perennial problem. Pucheu, who seconded his efforts, thought that eventually progress should result in the unification of the State and private systems, if children of widely differing social background were to get to know each other, 'the prime condition for mutual respect and tolerance'.[95] Liénart was quick to seize upon the practical advantages of the new legislation: at last the Catholic teacher would earn a living wage – up to 60 per cent that of his State counterpart – and access to Catholic schools would be made easier for the poor.[96] Other reactions were predictable. Gironde Catholics were gratified, like Liénart, that parents would be granted a 'real' as opposed to a theoretical choice.[97] Some bishops would have preferred a straight voucher scheme. But from the anticlerical, collaborationist Paris press came cries of outrage. Even in 1944 Albertini, secretary-general of Déat's Rassemblement National Populaire, was still expostulating that 'In France there must be a single State-run school. There is no place for the private school in this country.'[98] A secularist of a different stripe, Albert Bayet, influential in the former Ligue de l'Enseignement, saw the grant of subsidies as signifying the abandonment to their fate of 80,000 State pupils in Western France, where Catholic schools would take over completely.[99] From London Maurice Schumann, despite his own Catholic beliefs, declared his opposition.[100] Later, non-Catholic elements in the Resistance voiced disapproval: the clandestine Résistance Ouvrière (No. 6 of February 15, 1944), summing up the Occupation years, declared that the secular school had been 'neglected to the advantage of the school that is not the national one'. On the whole the hierarchy avoided giving the impression that the Church had scored off the State system, but some parish priests galumphed and chortled over the local State primary teacher.

The laws undoubtedly exacerbated hostility between clericals and secularists. Even before the settlement of November 1941 the prefect of the Aube reported that Catholics, frantically trying to recover the position they had lost under the Republic, had stirred up enmity: some municipalities, such as Romilly-sur-Seine, would not even grant a communal subsidy.[101] The prefect of the Côte d'Or also reported that Catholic and State schools were again at loggerheads, adding incidentally that the 'bien-pensants' in his department not only preferred Catholic schools because they were a sign of social superiority but also because they found reflected in them their own anti-government attitude[102] – an indication that although Catholics had rallied to Pétain, they were now beginning to distinguish between him and his administration. In Brittany the situation became more tense. At the end of 1942 one report stated that in Morbihan and Finistère 'the ecclesiastical authorities openly refuse the sacrament to those parents who do not send their children to the private school; they will intervene half a dozen times to threaten families'. The Catholics were backed by officials of the Secours National, the new mayors installed by Vichy, and the prefect. The upshot was that in 1941 some 5,000 children had left the State school, and where the State schools had had in consequence to be closed, the clergy were pressing to take over the vacated premises.[103] Some State teachers feared that the whole educational system might become confessional.[104] One such wrote to Déat asking him to procure the release of her prisoner husband, also a primary teacher, because 'in our locality of 1,100 inhabitants, where by his efforts my husband has caused the State school to gain the upper hand, the private school has already made a strong recovery'.[105]

Some Catholics were discontented with the new arrangements. The parents' organization, the Association des Parents de l'Enseignement Libre (APEL), complained that the concessions did not go far enough. On April 17, 1941 they had submitted a draft law to the ministry which had proposed a voucher system allowing free education in either a State or a confessional primary school; it had also proposed that all secondary education, both public and private, should be fee-paying, with generous scholarships for bright pupils and those coming from large families.[106] In November 1941, immediately after the laws had been published, their president, Jean Tournassus, had called a meeting in Lyons; delegates were unanimous that the measures did not constitute the definitive 'statute' for private education which was their ultimate goal. They condemned the repeal of the law of January 1941, because it had not only given communal aid to private primary schools but had been stretched to include primary classes in secondary schools, in 'patronages-garderies', and in 'colonies de vacances'. (In fact a 'rectificatif' to the November laws, dated January 8, 1942, re-authorized subsidies to nursery schools, where these had been enjoyed previously.) Above all, the parents were unhappy that new schools would not be eligible for subsidies; that a certain size of school was stipulated, thus ruling out many Catholic rural schools; that financial need had to be proven, no easy task; that mayors as well as inspectors now had a right of inspection of private schools (but Carcopino asserts that in effect all inspection of Catholic schools ceased after his resignation); and that subsidies would be an annual 'dole' rather than a permanent right. Thus APEL continued to press for a statute to deal comprehensively with what it saw as the three facets of the problem: the material one (buildings and equipment), the social one (teachers' salaries), and the family one (school fees). Grasset, the new minister of health in the Laval government, interested himself in the question and prepared two further versions of a draft statute, in November 1942 and July 1943. These were dispatched for comment to Mgr Aubry, of the Comité National de l'Enseignement Libre, but neither was acceptable. In November 1943 Catholics were still negotiating; they were particularly concerned at this time about the conditions of their secondary teachers, a concern that Pétain shared.[107] Grasset's drafts had mistakenly assumed that Catholic school principals had great autonomy and that the diocesan role was simply to oversee the doctrinal and moral aspects of education. In a final bid the Catholics were therefore prompted to draw up a 'Statut du personnel de l'Enseignement Libre' to achieve better conditions for their teachers. Dated February 9, 1944, this document was presented to Pétain through Mgr Chappoulie, the official Church representative at Vichy, but was shelved.

The case for a definitive statute had been made in *La Croix* (October 10, 1941) by Mgr Beaussart, the Church's Paris representative with the ministry of education. This wish had not been satisfied, but on the whole moderate Catholic opinion concurred with the view expressed in the *Semaine religieuse* for the Paris diocese that Carcopino had shown 'great courage in going beyond prejudices [which were] possibly more deep-seated, rather than serious reasons'.[108]

The applicatory decree did not appear until January 7, 1942. This three-month delay caused serious difficulties. Liénart, again worrying where he was to find the money to pay the Catholic teachers, had already complained in November to the regional prefect when no advance had been forthcoming, after his request for subsidies had gone forward to the ministry of the interior. The supporting statistics are as follows for the diocese of Lille:[109]

No. of schools	339
No. of teachers	1,474
No. of pupils	48,756
Annual salaries' bill	18,707,778F
Other annual expenses	5,856,580F
Total expenses	24,564,358F
LESS Annual receipts	6,087,165F
Deficit (i.e., subsidy required)	18,477,193F

Thus the subsidy request amounted to just over 75 per cent of the total expenses incurred, and was almost equal to the total bill for salaries. It would therefore appear that teachers were working for an average salary of about 12,700F a year. This figure is low, although of course teaching staff who were members of religious orders did not receive a salary as such. The unit cost per pupil is 504F, as compared with the figure of 600F put forward by M. Toulemonde, but this does not include diocesan administrative expenses, for which later special allowance was made in the subsidy. The pupil:teacher ratio of 33:1 does not look very bad but one must recall that many village schools would probably not have more than a dozen or so pupils on the roll, which means that classes in urban areas must have been considerably larger than the average. Figures for the Cambrai diocese were similar. A subsidy of 75 per cent of the total was to become the norm. The prefect of the Morbihan reported in February 1942 that parish priests were clearly expecting to receive about this proportion, since they were urging their flocks to contribute up to one-quarter of school expenses; for the Morbihan this entailed a State subsidy of fourteen million francs,[110] a figure which had risen by the end of the year to 19½ millions.[111] Schools denied a subsidy did not always let the matter rest: from Montier-en-Der (Haute-Marne) one headmistress appealed indignantly to the prefect (January 8, 1942): 'The reason invoked for the rejection of my request hardly seems to be in conformity with the new spirit that imbues our leaders. Why should Frenchmen not have the right to choose their school without being obliged to incur additional expense?'[112] To this rhetoric it was plain that the State had not yet provided a definitive answer.

The scheme did not function at all smoothly, perhaps because some officials did not wish it to succeed. They were suspicious of Catholic claims and particularly disliked the automatic ten per cent, authorized by an interministerial circular of February 26, 1942, which could be added to the claim to cover diocesan expenses, including the cost of additional training for teachers, because it was incapable of verification. Hence perhaps the delays, about which not only Liénart protested: in June 1942 Gerlier was still complaining that unless the subsidies for his diocese were paid before the then imminent end of the school year many teachers would be forced to seek employment elsewhere.[113] Dilatoriness continued, because almost a year later, in April 1943, protests poured in from dioceses that nothing had been received for the current school-year or that salaries were being paid many months in arrears.[114] For their part, academy inspectors complained that the law was being circumvented: subventions were not always being used to pay teachers but were being employed to start up new schools or help Catholic 'patronages'.[115] There may have been some substance in this. Mgr Aubry, of the Comité National de l'Enseignement Libre, pressed Pétain in September 1943 to extend subsidies to all new primary schools and nursery classes after they had been functioning one year. No doubt also other inaccurate claims were made. The ministry had to issue a circular (March 18, 1942) emphasizing that subsidies were available only for primary schools and not for other types of Catholic school which passed for elementary institutions. Another circular (November 17, 1942) reminded prefects that neither new buildings nor alterations to existing ones attracted a subsidy. Mgr Aubry drew the ministry's attention to special circumstances, such as when a school already receiving a subsidy was forced to move because of the danger of military operations. He also protested that schools were being declared ineligible for subsidies, on grounds of insufficient pupils; this was unfair, because, as single-sex institutions they were being compared in size to mixed or 'twinned' State schools in the same locality.[116]

Carcopino probably shared his officials' suspicion that exaggerated claims were being made. He instructed prefects to check carefully all requests and see that the law was observed to the letter.[117] Departmental treasurers, charged with seeing that the instruction was carried out, objected that they lacked adequate means of verification. They had to rely on the primary-school inspectors, who had to be very alert in regard to the pupil:teacher ratio. This had to be 35–40:1, as in State schools, but there were allegations that this was being disregarded. To compile budgets aimed at securing the maximum 75 per cent subsidy schools omitted receipts from boarders and building costs were concealed under current expenses. The duality of the control system was unsatisfactory: the academy inspector could merely certify that the pedagogical conditions for a subsidy were being fulfilled, but the final power of decision lay with the prefect and, ultimately, the ministry of the interior.

The scale of the demand for subsidies could not be ascertained until the spring of 1942, when the first round of claims was completed. For eighty-three departments the total for 1941–2 amounted to 400,436,594F[118] to which had to be added the 'administrative' ten per cent. The departments with the highest and lowest claims were as follows:

Highest		*Lowest*	
Seine	*c.*30 million F	Basses-Alpes	79,551F
Loire-Inférieure	20,515,322F	Hautes-Alpes	284,500F
Ille-et-Vilaine	*c.*20 million F	La Creuse	441,604F
Pas-de-Calais	19,774,000F		

Whereas six departments exceeded eighteen million francs, twelve claimed under one million. Although the law covered all primary schools, most claims were for Catholic schools. Thus Protestant schools claimed only 156,537F in all, 0.04 per cent of the total; other independent schools claimed 419,112F, about one per cent. (Carcopino states that the figure actually paid out for 1941–2 was 386,248,968F.) The report from which the detailed figures are taken drew attention to the anomalies arising from the different methods of computation of claims. One result was that subsidies per head varied widely from one department to another: Orne, 597.50F; Alpes-Maritimes, 307F; Nièvre, 674F; Calvados, 617; Eure, 730.82F; Manche, 718F. In some departments the maximum 75 per cent subsidy was automatically endorsed; in others the prefect insisted that every centime be justified. Similar divergences existed in the claims for teachers' salaries. The law prescribed that the Catholic teacher's salary should not exceed 60 per cent of the average salary of the State teacher, then 16,500F, 60 per cent of which was 9,900F. But in some areas, such as the Loiret, where the average salary of Catholic teachers was already 16,340F, this proportion was greatly exceeded, and yet the full 75 per cent subsidy was still being claimed. The genuineness of claims is therefore open to question. This is confirmed when the claim for the following year, 1942–3, rose to a total of 471,093,321F, an increase over the previous year of 18 per cent, which cannot be justified even if the rather modest rise that by then had occurred in State teachers' salaries is taken into account.[119] In short, the new arrangements led to anomalies and resentment rather than that general pacification of Church–State relationships for which Carcopino had hoped.

What effect had subsidies upon the growth of Catholic education?[120] In some areas, they had started from a position of strength as regards primary schools. In 1939 Catholic schools in the Breton departments of Finistère, Ille-et-Vilaine, Morbihan, and Loire-Inférieure, as well as in Vendée, Mayenne, and Maine-et-Loire, educated at least 40 per cent of all pupils, and in most parts of this area of Western France over 50 per cent. In the South the strongest Catholic area was spread over the five adjacent departments of Aveyron,

Lozère, Ardèche, Haute-Loire, and Loire, where the proportion reached at least 30 per cent. On the other hand, before the war, with the exception of the Nord and the Pas-de-Calais in the north-west and the departments of Alsace-Lorraine in the north-east, under 10 per cent of children attended Catholic primary schools north of a line running roughly from Le Havre to Geneva. This low percentage applied also in most of the departments of Burgundy, the Limousin, and Aquitaine, and in the three most south-westerly departments. The over-all national proportion was 17.7 per cent.

By the beginning of 1944 Catholic primary education had made great strides. In only one department, the Somme, had its share of pupils marginally decreased, from 5.6 per cent in 1939 to 5.3 per cent in 1943. Of the seven Western departments previously mentioned four now educated over 60 per cent and one, the Loire-Inférieure, over 70 per cent of all primary pupils. If the circumstances had not changed, simple extrapolation would show that by the end of the century State education might have died out in Western France. In the southern zone, and particularly in the three most southerly departments, the proportion had risen to at least 40 per cent. In 1943 only in 24 out of the 87 departments – the three 'annexed' departments of Alsace-Lorraine are excluded – did the proportion fall below ten per cent, as compared with 39 departments in 1939. The national figure for Catholic pupils had risen to 22.6 per cent. The heartland of resistance to Catholic education still lay in the North.

Looking at the percentage gains, rather than totals, the largest gains occurred in the southern zone, always excepting Western France, where increases of seven per cent and over had been registered by December 1943. The other exception was the Paris area, where conditions were probably in any case atypical. In 12 out of 33 departments lying entirely in the former unoccupied zone, gains of at least 5 per cent had been recorded, and in the Rhône, which included Lyons, the increase was 11 per cent. (Nevertheless, the highest gain was registered in the occupied zone – the Loire-Inférieure, where the increase was 18.7 per cent.) Nationally the average increase was 4.9 per cent. If the popularity of Catholic schools is any indicator of Church influence, it is apparent that it was strongest where German restrictions were the least in evidence.[121]

As regards Catholic secondary education, already in 1941–2 its share in the total number of pupils was as high as 48 per cent.[122] It will be recalled that there were no subsidies for Catholic secondary education. It may be assumed that by 1950 the wartime pattern of secondary education may not have varied very much. Thus the statistics for 1950 show that north-west of a line drawn from La Rochelle to Givet in the Ardennes all departments had still at least 30 per cent of pupils in Catholic secondary schools. In the Breton and Norman departments the proportion was over half, as also in the Loire, the Rhône, and the Ardèche, and – surprisingly because of their Protestant enclaves – the Haute-Loire and the Lozère. This 1950 pattern probably was almost the same as in wartime, for which statistics are not available. In some academies during the war Catholic secondary schools were so sited that they enjoyed a local monopoly. In the Lille Academy, for example, there were 64 State and 71 Catholic secondary schools, but each category had its schools sited in different areas so that there was no competition between them.[123]

One final word regarding subsidies is necessary. How the scheme was working on the eve of the Liberation may be gathered from a special report[124] for 1943–4, made by Garrone, then inspector general for private education, dispatched from Pallay, Eure ('coupé absolument de Paris – remis à une personne de passage') on June 6, 1944. Garrone summarized 54 department files that he had collected by May 1, 1944. Department treasurers reported that Catholic schools were running into increasing financial difficulties, but Garrone believed that they should be forced to make greater efforts to finance themselves, so that subsidies could be reduced. Some Catholic schools, for example, were no longer charging any fees at all, and the State was keeping them alive. Subsidies, calculated only for 55 departments from which estimates had been obtained, in 1943–4 would run at 380,739,493F. For three departments, Maine-et-Loire,

Morbihan, and Ardèche, the bill over the previous year had risen by 15 per cent. To the total should be added the ten per cent administrative costs. The inflated sum was due to the general rise in the cost of living and the increase in the number of pupils which, for the fifty-five departments, was of the order of 12.27 per cent. Garrone's survey included 5,715 schools, including eighteen that were either Protestant or non-confessional; the rest were Catholic.

The report went on to say that it had been impossible to say whether the private schools were educationally effective, because academy inspectors had received no instructions to carry out the inspections prescribed by law. (It will be recalled that Carcopino had affirmed that all such inspections ceased after he left office.) The requests for subsidies could not possibly be verified, and the accounting remained amateurish. Surprisingly – for Garrone was a devout Catholic, – the report stated that compared with State education 'private education appears not only privileged, but even abusing the temporary favour of the public authorities'. As it was, '. . . the social peace that was the chief concern of the legislator. . .is at the moment seriously threatened'. Garrone goes on to describe the deep malaise felt in State education at the anomalous position of Catholic schools: 'The absence of any control maintains among those in the State education system a state of uneasiness and anxiety. The private school, whose real existence remains unknown . . . appears as a rival. Moreover, State education personnel interpret the benevolent policy of the State towards private education as a sign of challenge to themselves, and in the minds of some, the hope of revenge has taken root.' He points out that there is no equity of treatment: confessional schools can spend money on equipment for any and every individual pupil, but the State schools have to rely on the Caisse des Écoles, which is only open to poor pupils. The inspector *may* be writing to please Bonnard, whose hostility to subsidies was well known, but the criticisms made appear well-founded.

In 1944 also another official of the ministry, anonymous this time, evaluated the effect of subsidies on the Catholic Church in general and concluded that 'it had not brought the Catholic Church as a whole to adopting a political position favourable to the regime and to European collaboration'.[125] This confirms that after the return of Laval in 1942, the round-up of Jews in that summer, and the introduction of compulsory labour service in 1943, the Church had definitely cooled towards the regime.

How did the Catholics fare in other levels of education in which they had a stake? Given the position they had acquired in primary education and the secure foothold they had already in secondary education, it was a disagreeable surprise to them to find that in technical education their position was actually undermined by the regime. The Charte du Travail, the new labour legislation promulgated on October 4, 1941, deprived Catholics of the legal right to open new technical and vocational schools, since this privilege was now reserved to properly constituted 'corporations' (Art. 59). From mid-1942 private firms were obliged to join together to provide their own apprenticeship centres, instead of handing over, as in the past, the training of their young employees to private technical institutions, many of which were Catholic. Another law of August 4, 1942 dealt Catholic technical institutions a further blow, perhaps deliberately, because Bonnard was minister: excepting engineering schools, no private technical schools were allowed to award their own qualifications or even issue attendance certificates. 'Such an insult', one Catholic wrote, 'was never proffered to Christian education by the Popular Front government'.[126] Ostensibly enacted on grounds of equity, the measure sought in reality, 'to put an end to the traffic in diplomas which, it is alleged, goes on in certain unscrupulous institutions'.[127] In return the State examinations for technical qualifications, which in any case were more acceptable to employers, were thrown open to all. On the face of it, the arrangement looked fair, but this was not really the case. Only pupils on recognized courses could take State examinations, but part-time evening schools, many of which were Catholic, ran technical courses that had not achieved State recognition. The net result was to debar part-time students from obtaining any qualifications at all. Liénart wrote to Luc, the ministry's director of technical education, protesting against the new restrictions, but obtained no satisfaction.[128] Doubtless Bonnard's prejudices account for his inflexibility when such anomalies were drawn to his attention.

Moreover, recognized technical schools became eligible for aid but Catholic schools, largely unrecognized, received no assistance. Nevertheless in 1943 Liénart requested from Bonnard a special subsidy of three million francs for the eight Catholic technical schools in his diocese, comprising 1,840 pupils, which had suffered badly in the 1940 campaign. Bonnard merely contented himself with passing on the request to the ministry of finance. When post-school compulsory classes in agriculture or housecraft were instituted for young people aged between 14 and 17, by the law of July 5 1941, Catholics were at first debarred from running them. Likewise, when housecraft classes were made compulsory for girls of school age, by the law of March 18, 1942, teachers with specialist qualifications, but no general teaching certificate, were forbidden to teach the new courses. This hit Catholics hardest.

In higher education the Catholics fared better. The question of aid to their 'free' faculties arose by chance.[129] Suhard and Gerlier, meeting with Pétain, Laval, and Bonnard on October 29, 1942, pointed out that, of the 500 million francs allocated for Catholic primary education in 1942–3, some 15 millions had not been taken up. They wanted to use this sum to benefit Catholic and Protestant institutions of higher education. Pétain proved agreeable. Seminaries were excluded from receiving subsidies by the law of 1905, but eventually the sum of five million francs was allocated to the Institut Catholique in Paris, four millions to the Catholic faculty of Lille, three millions to that of Lyons, and one million each to those of Angers and Toulouse.[130] This unexpected windfall provoked profuse thanks from the Institut Catholique[131] and the faculty at Angers. The rector of Angers wrote to Bonnard assuring him that, despite the Allied invasion of North Africa, the 'université' remained loyal, continuing 'its work of spiritual uplift and moral regeneration'.[132] The distribution of the remaining one million francs, eventually reduced to 800,000F, gave rise to problems. Pastor Boegner, as spiritual leader of 95 per cent of all French

Protestants, controlled the Protestant faculties of Paris (which in 1941–2 had some eighty students) and Montpellier (with some fifty students). But there was also a Protestant faculty at Aix-en-Provence run by the much smaller group of the Églises Réformées Évangéliques de France, more nationalist and less open to radical and liberal theology than the Fédération headed by Boegner. By late 1942 Boegner had fallen into Laval's bad books because he had spoken out against the deportations of the Jews. Laval was more in favour of granting a subsidy to the much smaller independent faculty at Aix rather than to those headed by Boegner. Pétain, who had great esteem for Boegner, objected, one of his staff noting at the time that 'it would be inopportune and dangerous to embitter the pastor by an unexpected disappointment and throw him into opposition, since, although he is obliged to take into account the political ideology which still pervades the majority of French Protestants, he is still their legitimate head'.[133] The incident illustrates yet again the diversity of the Vichy regime: on the one hand, Laval, committed to collaboration, on the other Boegner, supporting Pétain but speaking out against the excesses of the regime, with Pétain and his entourage sitting uneasily between the two extremes.

The liberality of the grant to private higher education was not repeated in 1943–4, when the subsidy was cut to between five and six million francs in all. The largest institution, the Institut Catholique, which received only 1.3 million francs, protested at the cut in vain.[134]

Despite the adulation he received from certain clerics, Bonnard's dislike of the Church was well known at the time. His aversion was shared not only by his entourage but doubtless also by some of his permanent officials at the ministry, bred in the old secularist tradition. Two incidents illustrate this anti-clericalism within the ministry. In 1943 the Catholic faculty of Lille raised the question of scholarships for private higher education. Bonnard was informed that credits had been set aside for this purpose ever since 1941 but that Carcopino had blocked them 'for reasons of opportuneness'. The official responsible urged the minister to release money for scholarships only to private institutions preparing for

State qualifications or to the École Libre des Sciences Politiques.[135] The second episode concerned degree examinations. In late July 1944 Bonnard noted that the examiners for the Catholic law students at Angers had been drawn entirely from the private sector. Despite the difficulties at the time, after consulting Gidel and Ripert, of the Paris law faculty, he ordered the scripts to be sent to Paris for correction by State examiners: the State right to award degrees must remain inviolable.[136] That such an attempt to usurp the State monopoly should occur nevertheless shows how much the concept of 'la liberté d'enseignement' had been enlarged by Catholics. Of course the minister may well have thought it prudent at that stage of the war to make sure that his secularist sentiments were widely known. It was said in any case that Gaullist elements, 'numerous among the clergy', made great play of the minister's anticlericalism, with certain highly placed churchmen using it as a pretext for dissociating themselves from the Révolution Nationale, which rendered the task of those such as Suhard, who remained loyal to the regime, more difficult.[137] Other clerics must have been sorely disappointed in one in whom they had placed such high hopes in 1942, when the Bishop of Chartres, for example, had seen in the appointment of the new minister a guarantee against sectarianism as well as against 'democratic weakness'.[138]

Opportunism and pragmatism characterized both secularists and clericals during the Occupation. The collaborationist writer Robert Brasillach deprecated strongly, however, the Church tightening its grip upon young people, because, he said, it contained many 'democratic Christians' in its ranks: 'The Révolution Nationale has two enemies: one is Monsieur Homais [the Flaubertian prototype of bourgeois self-satisfaction], the other is Tartuffe. Let us not entrust youth to either.'[139] But most Frenchmen would certainly trust it even less to Brasillach and his ilk, among whom Bonnard must be lumped.

The sequel to the Vichy measures concerning religion and education is not uninteresting. Five days after the invasion, Maurice Schumann, sent by de Gaulle from London, attended a luncheon at Bayeux in honour of the Resistance. For the first time the members of the various movements discovered that they included Catholics, atheists, freemasons, and even priests. By the end of the meal the assembled company were already quarrelling over subsidies to the confessional schools.[140] On February 28, 1945 the ACA asked for an assurance that an equitable solution would be found for the 'schools question', obviously apprehensive that subsidies would cease.[141] The Association des Parents de l'Enseignement Libre launched a campaign to preserve the advantages that it had gained during the war. It was in vain. On March 28, 1945, by a vote of 128 to 48, the Consultative Assembly decided that all funds would cease as from the end of July. A Communist source estimated that if subsidies had been renewed for a further year they would have totalled over 716 million francs.[142] The question of whether they should be renewed continued to be canvassed, with a number of solutions being proposed. Organisation Civile et Militaire, the Resistance movement headed by Maxime Blocq-Mascart, wanted a unified education system, in which no confessional schools would be allowed, although the Church would have the right to mount religious courses in State schools. The Christian Democrats wanted optional religious instruction in the primary school and, subject to guarantees, subsidies for Catholic schools. Albert Bayet, of the secularist Ligue de l'Enseignment, put forward the idea of a three-year truce on all discussion.[143] In Western France the matter aroused great passion: meeting in November 1945, the Conseil-Général of the Loire-Inférieure, passed a motion that all parents should receive educational vouchers and invited the prefect to convey their request to the government.[144] In the Maine-et-Loire the Conseil-Général, also meeting in November, deplored the fact that a ministry circular of November 18 had stipulated that children in private schools were not eligible for free school meals or maintenance grants.[145] In the end the Church had failed to improve substantially upon its pre-war financial position. But the precedent for subsidies had been set, and the demand was successfully revived in 1959.

Chapter IV

The School Teachers

Links between the school teachers and the military date back to when Napoleon's 'corps professoral' had been given the task of educating future officers for his armies. After 1870 relations became strained when the myth arose that France had been defeated by the Prussian schoolmaster and, by implication, that the French schoolmaster had failed the nation. Likewise the military men that foregathered at Vichy in 1940 reflected bitterly on the inter-war period, when the primary teacher, in particular, had acquired the reputation of being 'internationalist', which, because of its overtones of the Third International, had become almost synonymous with 'anti-patriotic', and, above all, of being pacifist, so much so that the 'impregnable stronghold' of pacifism had been the primary-teachers' union, the Syndicat National des Instituteurs (SNI).[1] At its national congresses that body had vociferated the slogan, 'servitude rather than death'. From 1936 onwards the 'Vigilance Committee of Anti-Fascist Intellectuals', dominated by those who were for peace at any price, included André Delmas, the secretary-general of SNI[2] and Georges Lapierre, director of the union's journal, *L'École libératrice*. Although the union recognized that the dictators threatened democracy, as late as 1939 at its national congress Delmas had proposed disarmament and a general strike if war broke out.[3] Teachers were prominent in their support of Déat's tract, *Paix Immédiate*. Pétain had viewed these developments with alarm. As early as 1934, speaking at a dinner of the *Revue des deux mondes*, he had flatly accused teachers of not inculcating patriotism in their charges, although later he qualified this blanket assertion.[4] In 1938 he had interested himself in the anti-syndicalist periodical, *L'Instituteur national*, whose proclaimed purpose was to insulate teachers from 'pernicious ideologies'.[5] Condemnation of the teachers came also from elsewhere within their ranks: the writer and teacher Jean

Giono, later an associate of Déat, summed up the 'desert years' before the war as those when 'the teaching profession which had directed and guided human souls from the end of the Renaissance era had set its feet upon false paths'.[6]

In the First World War many primary teachers had served in the front line as reserve officers and had won general commendation for their courage and example. After the collapse in 1940 their repute was otherwise. Even before 1939 military leaders had begun to question their worth as officers. In 1936 General Mittelhauser, alluding to the 143rd Infantry Regiment, in which primary teachers constituted half the total officer war establishment, viewed the situation with apprehension, 'given the state of mind of the primary teachers'. General Dufieux instanced three army corps where half the officers drawn from the conscript 'classes' of 1926–31 were primary teachers. (Nationally the proportion had increased from 10 per cent in 1914 to 48.7 per cent in the mid-1930s.) The general noted that during their service these officers made a good impression but he 'feared that their attitude is modified afterwards through propaganda'.[7] In 1940 the charge against them was not only that they had mistaught their pupils but also that they had let down the men they had commanded. On the day the Germans reached the Somme Weygand, remarking that France was paying for twenty years of blunders, declared it unthinkable to censure the generals without first indicting the teachers, who had failed to instil in young Frenchmen the spirit of sacrifice.[8] Gamelin made a similar observation before relinquishing his command.[9] When the final rout began a corps commander acidly remarked, 'If I were in the government I would begin by wringing the primary teachers' neck,' to which his second in command, turning to a group of primary teachers mobilized as reserve officers, added, 'This is your doing.'[10] Pétain harboured the same sentiments. To Spears, the British liaison officer, he bluntly asserted that schoolmasters and politicians, rather than generals, had brought France to her knees.[11] To Bullitt, the American ambassador, he made a similar remark, this time inculpating the teachers alone.[12] Laval, himself a one-time teaching assistant ('répétiteur'), added his own condemnation of 'certain primary teachers' who had not taught their pupils the love of country.[13] How far the generals sought excuses for their own incompetence, how sincerely they believed their accusations, is difficult to judge. In the distress of the hour the most palpable feature was the failure of the Army; the teacher, however, conveniently failed on both counts – lack of military prowess and want of patriotism.

The chorus of recriminations against the teachers mounted, because they were ready-made scapegoats, already unpopular in many social circles. Jeanneret, himself a primary teacher, drew up an indictment of his own colleagues: conservative elements in society felt only disdain for them; the middle class considered them second-raters; the worker envied them their ostensibly leisured existence; the nationalist resented their 'peace at any price philosophy' and their internationalism. If for anticlericals they passed as 'the parish priests of modern times', Catholic opinion was distinctly less charitable.[14] To the Church their fierce secularism was repugnant. On this issue the recruit to primary teaching was even vetted beforehand: the local academy inspector made discreet enquiries before he was allowed to enter teacher-training college.[15] Once there, pressure was put on him to join the anticlerical SNI. When he began teaching he joined the monstrous army of 'politickers in a pedagogical frock-coat'. Since teachers often were appointed as secretary to the local mayor, they were able to 'infect' adults with their views, whilst in class their '. . .devilish talent attacked the souls of children. . . the words of many schoolteachers, dregs of the masonic lodges or paid disciples of the Kremlin, gnawed at the children's hearts. . . [they were] pioneers of immorality, anarchy and Communism.'[16] The provincial and national press joined in the hue and cry. Within three weeks of the Armistice the *Petit Dauphinois* (15.7.40) was proclaiming that the State school had 'become the closed domain for divisions, forgotten the idea of country and family, and dishonoured labour'. The *République du Sud-Est* (28.6.40) accused teachers of having betrayed their mission.[17] By the autumn the spate of obloquy was in full flood. *Le Temps* (18.11.40) taxed the teachers with having been too free in expressing their opinions, preaching anti-patriotism and the class struggle, when their duty was to inculcate the opposite.[18] Curiously enough, a few days previously (14.11.40) the same newspaper had published an article characterizing the teaching body as 'most honourable'.[19] Ripert's policy was 'to clean up primary education and protect the teachers against subversive propaganda' by punishing mercilessly past ringleaders.[20] Sanctions were particularly urged against those teachers who had joined in the lightning general strike of 1938, called by the Left as a protest against the cancelling of the forty-hour week. Their opponents urged that this was an especially damaging action at a time when Germany was preparing for war and operating, with overtime, a sixty-hour working week. The highest estimate of the number of primary teachers supporting the strike was given as 20,000, but Daladier, after a much lower estimate, had finally given the number of teachers participating as only 3,000. This was a remarkably small percentage of the total, but Ripert intended his action to be dissuasive and exemplary, rather than merely retributive.[21]

After the recriminations had died down many supporters of the regime admitted that disloyal and unpatriotic teachers had been a small minority. Lamirand, secretary-general for youth, speaking in his native Toulouse on December 29, 1940, expressed his desire to 'pay homage to the teaching body. . . whose reputation must not suffer from the lack of understanding some had shown in the past'.[22] Carcopino, who, it will be recalled, intended to punish teachers for acts and not for opinions, was not unsympathetic to the teaching body. Inaugurating a Book of Honour to commemorate those teachers who had served their country well in 1940, he solemnly declared: 'In the test in which no man lies – that of war and fire – the spirit of the teachers manifested its permanent and true nature, national and healthy.'[23] Crouzet, a retired inspector general who had been advisor to Bérard when the latter had been minister in 1923 and who was favourable to the regime, wrote a year or two later that responsibility for the defeat lay with society as a whole and that the ministers of education since 1940 had judged teachers too harshly.[24] Dexmier, a primary teacher who stood in Pétain's good books and was a prime mover in the creation of new professional associations that replaced the former teachers' unions, defended his colleagues with facts and figures. Out of 26,100 primary teachers mobilized, more than half were reserve officers; about 500 – 2 per cent of the total – had been killed; just over half – 13,139 – had been taken prisoner.[25] (Of these only 2,245 had been released by July 1943.) Casualties were as heavy as in any other occupational group. Dexmier argued that if any blame attached to teachers, it was because they had been too loyal to the former regime. He did not hesitate to add that the military machine had also had its defects. He defended the teachers against the charge of having taught schoolchildren 'red revolution'; on the contrary, he asserted, they had followed faithfully the principle laid down in Bérard's 1923 programmes, that 'character training must take precedence over the training of the mind'.[26]

Others took the opposite view. Gidel, rector of the University of Paris, inaugurating the new academic year in 1941, asserted that teachers 'in the happy years' had neglected the moral education of their pupils. Crouzet developed this theme in detail.[27] Ferry's belief that civics, with its moral overtones, was just as much a vital component of primary education as the classical ideal of 'l'honnête homme' was of secondary education, had been superseded in the years leading up to the war by an absolute faith that science was the panacea. 'Disinterested education', which had once meant merely non-utilitarian education, had come to signify a schooling without ethical content. Encyclopedic syllabuses had left no room for moral education, so much so that by 1917 already moral education and civics had been dropped from the primary school leaving examination. Likewise freer discipline and what might be described as 'play way' methods had not emphasized the need for effort. In the secondary school the classical ethos, the study of the values of 'eternal man', had been replaced by a modern relativist approach. Precept counted for more than practice and the inculcation of personal morals had been in any case neglected. Even topics relating to social responsibility, such as depopulation and alcoholism, which Crouzet had tried to introduce into the syllabus for the 'classe de philosophie' in

1923, were not accepted. The ex-inspector general implied that blame must lie for the inadequate primary programmes for ethics upon Durkheim's disciple, Paul Lapie, director of primary education in 1920, who had substituted sociology for moral instruction.[28] When Bérard in 1923 had tried to amend the 1920 programmes with Bergson's support, he had been overruled by the Conseil Supérieur de l'Instruction Publique, the statutory body appointed to advise the minister. By 1940 two generations of schoolchildren had passed through the schools without the benefit of an adequate moral teaching.

In 1940 this crystallized into an attack upon the 'écoles normales primaires', in which primary teachers had been trained. These teacher-training colleges had been the educational bulwark of the Republican regime. In them, so it was charged, pupils aged between 15 and 18 had been indoctrinated with anticlericalism and Durkheimian morality. The colleges had been a vital link in a vicious circle: controlled by the directorate of primary education, staffed by ex-primary teachers, they recruited their intake from primary schools, trained them, and then sent them out to teach in the self-same type of school. It was a closed world in which young teachers became imbued with 'l'espirit primaire', an ethos not permeated by the high culture, intellectually narrow, and undermined politically by republicanism. Given this extreme evaluation of the colleges, their closure by Ripert was inevitable. In future teachers would enter the *lycée* and pass the baccalaureate before embarking on primary training. Thus they would benefit from what Vichy considered a more liberal form of education, dispensed in a more open institution than the former monastic-like, monotechnic 'evil seminaries of democracy'. Studying side by side with the rest of the nation's élite they would no longer, in Maurras's view, be isolated in 'a hothouse where budding plants vegetated and wilted'. The impoverished diet of Rousseau, the Encyclopedists, and Hugo which had hitherto been their intellectual staple would be replaced by the reputedly more wholesome pabulum, because more nationalist and Catholic, provided by writers such as Maistre, Bonald, and Barrès.[29]

The crisis of moral values in 1940 – if crisis there was – was particularly ascribed to the kind of ethical training dispensed in the teacher-training college. The paramount influence of Durkheim was anathematized by Vichy.[30] He was accused of vesting the schoolmaster with the latter-day mantle of the priest and entrusting him with being the main communicator of moral ideas to children. Since for Durkheim moral and social interest coincided, any transcendental basis for morality was automatically excluded; so, argued the sociologist's denigrators, was individual responsibility. The result was that the schoolmaster had become the mere inculcator of the norms of the collective. What was forgotten at the time was that Durkheim had also reacted against excessive individualism, wanting the child to be alive to the various social circumstances in which morality was important – in the family, the corporation, and the national community. *Mutatis mutandis,* the distance between this view and Vichy's 'Travail, Famille, Patrie' does not appear so great. But Durkheim was also reviled for his conception that patriotism did not exclude in a democracy more universal, supranational loyalties. Mistakenly, it was argued, Durkheim had even expounded his ideas in a course he had given for intending primary teachers.[31] Paul Lapie, after the First World War, had not only introduced a 'sociological morality' into the primary-school syllabuses but had also incorporated his master's ideas into the primary teacher training course, thus establishing a kind of counter-theology for 'lay seminaries'.[32]

Incidentally, Durkheim's views on secondary education were just as unacceptable in 1940. His *Évolution pédagogique en France,* published posthumously in 1938, had concluded that, although literature must be ready to illumine the development of civilization, education should be neither literary nor classical, because humanism was outmoded. Instead the secondary pupil should study science, because of the invaluable training imparted by the scientific method. This ran directly counter to the fashionable Vichy wisdom that science should be downgraded in favour of literary classicism. Maurrassians such as Massis, who had known 'the master of the Sorbonne' in his heyday, were particularly hostile to Durkheim's ideas.

In 1940 the accusation was therefore freely bandied about that training-college students had acquired only a morality based upon sociology and pedagogy, taught by a principal who frequented the masonic lodge. Likewise the crude notions of experimental psychology they had been taught led them to embrace materialism. Destined to become reserve officers, they had had antimilitarism preached to them. The colleges, it was said, had been hotbeds of Communism – although this form of political 'colonization' was vigorously denied.[33]

Another charge made against the colleges was that they were antireligious and not just 'neutral'. It was true that in the era of anticlericalism that had preceded the First World War the then director of primary education, Ferdinand Buisson, had regarded the primary teacher as the chosen instrument of a secular faith. The Church had held the teacher to be a prime agent in the dechristianizing of France. Certainly it was unwise for the training-college student or young teacher to display any religious tendencies. This led to some strange accusations after 1940. Thus Terracher, Chevalier's successor as secretary-general of the ministry of education, and Jolly, then director of primary education, the one a former academy rector, the other an inspector, were denounced to Pétain for having expelled from training college students who 'possessed in their personal cupboard, locked, a Bible and certain documents whose religious character was decreed to be contrary to the principles of holy secularism'.[34] To have attended a Catholic school, if only for a few months, to be caught wearing a religious medallion, to admit to reading Pascal, were aberrations that could lead to dismissal from a teacher-training course.[35] Young female teachers who attended mass would be scornfully nicknamed 'Davidées' by their secularist colleagues, a reference to a group of Catholic teachers formed immediately after the First World War. The effect of such antireligious propaganda upon the majority of primary teachers was to turn them into 'bad shepherds' (*La Croix*, January 1–2, 1942), who ostentatiously flaunted their unbelief. Allied to secularism, another hidden hand was also at work: 'The obscure power of freemasonry, by enslaving the schoolteachers, had worked against the Church and against France.'[36] In strongly Catholic areas the hour of revenge had now come and secularist teachers were sent packing.[37] But there were moderates in the Church who hoped that, under a new teacher-training system, because future priest and primary teacher would sit side by side in the *lycée*, a greater understanding would arise.

Although the reform had political and social reasons, the proposal was by no means new and had been put forward as a means of raising the intellectual standards of future primary teachers. Anatole de Monzie, a former minister, had put forward a similar proposal in the reform plans he had drawn up in 1925–6.[38] Laval had a similar plan in 1935. Jean Zay wanted future teachers, whilst still based on the 'école normale', to attend the classes in the *lycée* and pass the baccalaureate before embarking on two years of professional training. He argued that, by remaining as boarders in their own institution, they would not lose their distinctive ethos nor forget their humble origins, so that they would feel at ease when eventually they returned to teach in the rural or working-class industrial environment from which they sprang.[39]

Carcopino completed Ripert's reform by setting up post-baccalaureate institutes of professional training where the teachers would learn the practicalities of teaching. To break the vicious circle of 'l'esprit primaire', high-calibre teachers trained in the 'écoles normales supérieures' of Fontenay-aux-Roses and Saint-Cloud would be responsible for their training.[40] Even 'agrégés' and university teachers might be taken on to the staff of the new institutes. Sixty-six of these were to be set up, located close to university towns so that students might attend university courses. The actual training course lasted eighteen months, the first ten of which were devoted to the study of education, followed first by a term's practice teaching and then by courses in an agricultural, industrial, or housecrafts institution, with a final month devoted to physical training – all subjects that the government wished to foster in primary schools. The weakness of the scheme was that much time was necessarily spent away from the new institutes. In the event the over-all reform was not very successful, because many would-be teachers, having passed the baccalaureate, were lured away to more lucrative occupations. Moreover, the feeling of 'apartheid' remained. Entering the *lycée* only at fifteen, future primary teachers were placed in special classes, thus remaining isolated from pupils who had entered the school at eleven. They felt inferior because of their more lowly social origins.[41] On the other hand, their wealthier schoolmates were sometimes jealous because these late entrants to secondary education often proved to be more intelligent. In *lycées* where boarding places were not available, living away from home and often unaccustomed to town life, the teacher trainee often became distracted from his work. The 'esprit de corps' of the old teacher-training college was lacking.[42]

The reform sparked off interest in the much-neglected training also of the future secondary teacher. Newly qualified 'agrégés' were now obliged to undergo a month's training, mainly practical (A. of March 25, 1942). At Lyons an 'institute of psychology and pedagogy' was set up. Its first director, M. Isambert, stressing the new 'social significance of the role that had fallen to the educator', wanted courses in psychology, sociology, and pedagogy to complement the longer spell of practice teaching in the *lycée*.[43] However, teacher education remained a contentious matter. The old system, for the future primary teacher, had comprised too much professional, too little academic, training. The academically well-qualified secondary teacher had had too little practical training. The interest of the reform is that an attempt was made to redress the balance.

Meanwhile, in 1940 the priority was seen as curbing the influence of the primary teachers, who educated the bulk of children. The indefinite suspension of parliamentary institutions, in which teachers had been well represented, and the disbandment of their unions, had deprived them of political power. Already in 1923 Bérard had tried unsuccessfully to limit their influence. In 1940 their sole remaining effective political voice was in the departmental committees for primary education. The committees advised on local building grants and on decisions to open new schools, both State and private. In particular they had an important voice in the promotion, transfer, and disciplining of teachers. Proposals made for the promotion of teachers could be based on either seniority or merit. It was this criterion of 'merit', it was alleged, that teacher members had abused in the past, interpreting it politically. Membership of the committee comprised the prefect, education officials, the heads of the two department training colleges, nominees of the teachers' unions, and appointees of the Conseil Général of the department. When union and training-college representatives were of the same political persuasion as the members of the Conseil Général they could and did control decisions, acquiring especially large powers of patronage. Now the departmental committees were reconstituted, and teacher representatives were nominated by the ministry. *La Croix* (December 29, 1940) rejoiced that power had been removed from 'irresponsible groups', but the teachers saw it as a further authoritarian act of disfavour towards them.

Because of the disruptive end to the previous school year primary schools reopened earlier than usual and a solemn ceremony was held to mark the occasion. One minute's silence was observed for the dead and extracts were read from Pétain's 'messages', particularly from his armistice broadcast: 'Our flag remains unsullied – I hate the lies that have done you so much harm – we shall draw the lessons from the battles lost – we wanted to spare ourselves effort, and today we encounter misfortune.' Head teachers delivered an exhortation to national revival in which key words and phrases recurred: 'obey' – 'serve' – 'begin again' – 'think of others'.[44] Their homily to the young was often accusatory, although at a similar ceremony in secondary schools at least one headmaster, at the Lycée de Laval, had the grace to acknowledge that it was their elders who had let them down.[45] Teachers who boycotted the ceremony or ridiculed it were threatened with sanctions by Ripert.

By then, however, the witch-hunt of teachers was already under way. The law of July 17, 1940 empowered the authorities to dismiss any teacher who was likely to prove 'an element of disorder, an inveterate politicizer, or incompetent'.[46] In August Mireaux initiated enquiries as to the comportment of teachers during the military campaign.

Department inspectors and school heads who had abandoned their post without instructions were liable to dismissal; even where permission had been given rectors should weigh up whether the moral authority of those who had decamped was too diminished for them to continue in their post.[47] Rank-and-file teachers who had fled without permission were to be demoted or temporarily suspended. The minister also required rectors to report on teachers' past political activities. As a result Communists, former rabid supporters of the Popular Front, or 'agitators' were dismissed or appointed to another post, either outside or elsewhere within the department.[48] Under the law of July 17, 1940 redefining French nationality, rectors had to report the names of all teachers who were foreigners, recently naturalized, or who had not been born of a French father, unless they had previously served in the Foreign Legion or a fighting unit. On October 10, 1940 a law called upon all Jews, defined even more strictly than by the Nuremberg Laws, to resign their teaching posts. This gratified the Germans but alienated many liberal-minded teachers who up to then had not opposed Pétain.

The measures against freemasons affected teachers closely because freemasonry, linked to secularism, had had close connections with education since the 1880s. The Ferry reforms had been planned in conjunction with the masonic lodges and Macé's strongly secularist Ligue de l'Enseignement.[49] The Grand Orient, in particular, had frequently debated educational matters at its annual congresses. It had supported the concept of the 'école unique' and in 1924, in order to eliminate confessional schools, had proposed a State monopoly in education.[50] In 1938 fourteen members, out of a total of sixty-four making up the Council of the Grand Orient Order and the Great College of Rites, had educational connections: two were university professors, six were secondary and four primary teachers, one was an inspector, and one an official.[51] Like Ferry, Jean Zay was a freemason; so, surprisingly, was Peyrouton, for a time Vichy's minister of the interior.[52] For a while no sanctions were taken against those who had been freemasons, provided that they had renounced their membership. All teachers were made to sign a declaration to this effect. They meekly complied. Simone de Beauvoir, then teaching in Paris at the Lycée Camille-Sée, claimed 'there was no alternative'.[53] Jean Guéhenno, another writer also teaching in Paris but later demoted because of his hostile attitude to the regime, likewise complied but confided to his diary, 'Oh, the stupidity of it all!'[54] In May 1941 fresh declarations were required and those who had held masonic office were forced to resign. Some cases were very petty. One primary-school headmaster was dismissed because in 1928, for one year only, he had been the lodge treasurer. Another headmaster, sacked because he had made a false declaration, claimed that he had resigned from his lodge in 1927 and had not attended a masonic function since 1921.[55] Through the diligence of Bernard Faÿ, who, as well as running the Bibliothèque Nationale, had set up a 'service des sociétés secrètes', eventually 60,000 freemasons or ex-freemasons were identified as being public officials and 14,000, named as dignitaries in the movement, were dismissed.[56] Among those dismissed were 1,328 teachers.[57] Appeals against dismissal went to a special commission sitting at Vichy, where each case was judged on its merits. In June 1942 180 such cases concerned teachers; to date none had been allowed but eleven had been definitively rejected.[58]

How many teachers were punished or penalized because of the other measures is difficult to ascertain. In Lille, one of the larger academies, a breakdown of figures showed the following number of dismissals: fourteen teachers (eight primary, five secondary, and one technical) had been sacked for professional incompetence; dismissals for political agitation, for having engaged in rabid left-wing activities, or participated in the pre-war strike, accounted for another thirty-eight (twelve primary, seven secondary, and nineteen technical teachers).[59] These totals, arrived at when the first round of 'purges' was over, seem relatively modest, but it must not be forgotten that they continued throughout, particularly under Bonnard. In higher education the number of Jews and 'foreigners' obliged to resign would appear to have been only two or three per academy and among them the number of titular professors was small. It would also seem that locally the authorities did their best for those so arbitrarily deprived of their livelihood and that at least whilst

Carcopino was in office they were protected.[60] At the beginning the impression is that Ripert, who viewed the primary teachers as a pack of dangerous anarchists, penalized the small fry but let the big fish go scot-free. It was even asserted that the inspector heading the commission to 'purge' school textbooks was a freemason.[61]

Chevalier stoked up the fires again by calling for further names of 'undesirable' teachers (C. of January 13, 1941). In ten weeks of office he took action against about one hundred education personnel.[62] One official claimed to have received 'long lists' of *lycée* teachers proposed for dismissal.[63] The minister would seem to have been somewhat obsessive, since he punished a department inspector solely for having attended a Radical party dinner in the 1920s.[64] Hearing that in the Lycée du Parc at Lyons – the *lycée* in which Georges Bidault taught for a while – anti-Vichy sentiments were being voiced, he forced all teachers to sign a declaration exculpating themselves personally. When, as was inevitable, all cheerfully did so, Chevalier stigmatized them as cowards! The minister repeated this curious procedure in a number of *lycées* in the southern zone.[65]

In the short interval before Carcopino took over the reins ministry officials seized the opportunity to dispose of the files of some suspect teachers. Carcopino announced on March 16, 1941 his intention of winding up the 'purge' by the end of the month. In the fortnight that remained the victims included Albert Bayet, of the Ligue de l'Enseignement, Paul Rivet, the Sorbonne professor, and Paul Langevin, the eminent physicist. The minister explained away the latter's removal by saying that Langevin was almost seventy and due to retire anyway, and that by removing him he had procured his release from German detention. In all, Carcopino claimed that he had only taken action against 46 secondary teachers, out of some 12,000, had suspended action against freemason teachers who were prisoners of war, and had protected Communists, provided that they had forsworn their previous beliefs.[66] He had shielded teachers in othe ways. When Pétain's entourage had floated the idea of an enquiry, to be conducted by General Watteau, into the part that had been played by teachers in the collapse of France, he had nipped the idea in the bud. One high official has testified that Carcopino's period of office marked a 'détente'.[67]

Bonnard restarted the 'purge', concentrating mainly upon Jews and 'Communists', a term widely interpreted. For the rest, he adopted a more conciliatory policy. He appointed specially to his staff a primary teacher, André Lavenir, a one-time pacifist but now a staunch anti-Communist who had formerly been a very active member of the Rhône section of SNI. Lavenir's task was to rehabilitate some four hundred of his ex-union colleagues. It was even claimed at Bonnard's trial that he had sought to reinstate six hundred freemason primary teachers, but this is highly improbable.[68] A committed anti-Bolshevik, he bore down hardest on teachers that offended in this respect.

As a mark of official disapproval primary teachers had been denied any salary increase, despite the rise in the cost of living. By early 1942 the plight of young teachers was desperate. At Orleans several were sleeping in a youth hostel and eating in the restaurant of the Secours National.[69] In areas where the Germans offered high rates of pay to local labour living costs were exorbitant: at Bisacarrosse (Landes) the case was reported of a young teacher earning a mere 39F.70 a day, a sum insufficient, in that area of occupied France, even to cover his board and lodging.[70] The prefect of the Loiret estimated that a bachelor teacher aged twenty-five, not fully qualified, earned only 1173F a month, a salary unchanged since 1939. His monthly expenses exceeded this amount by 852F, whereas before the war he could have met these and still have had 323F over for pocket money.[71] The prefect of the Gers reported that two primary teachers who had resigned to join the police were already earning exactly double as temporary inspectors.[72] Teaching posts in the colonies were over-subscribed; five hundred teachers were seeking posts as youth leaders in the Chantiers de la Jeunesse; others were looking for work on the railways or as customs officers, all of which offered better pay. As employment prospects, stimulated by the war economy, began to improve, a teacher shortage developed in certain areas, manifested initially in a shortfall in recruitment to teacher-training institutions. In 1942 in the Calvados a mere 14 candidates competed for 27 places and were of so poor quality that finally only 8 were accepted. In the Marne there were 26 candidates for 30 places and only 17 passed.[73] But it does not seem that overall the shortage was acute. The 1942 figures showed that there were 1,808 posts vacant for men, that 4875 candidates competed for them, and that 1,679 passed the written examination; for women the corresponding figures were more favourable: 1,934 posts competed for by 8,139 candidates, of whom 2,282 passed the written examination.[74] In certain areas the situation was aggravated by the number of male teachers who were prisoners of war and further exacerbated by a law, issued in 1940 when the employment prospects looked forbidding, which stipulated that women primary teachers must retire at the age of fifty. Nevertheless, the salary problem remained.

Before resigning, and despite some opposition within the government, Carcopino did succeed in raising teachers' salaries as from April 1942. The maximum for primary teachers was raised to 23,500F, although the lowest category still only received a little more than half this amount. Secondary teachers fared better: an 'agrégé' teaching in the provinces received between 30,000 – 50,000F, plus a ten per cent addition. The salary of an inspector general was raised to 90,000F, plus a supplement of 15,000F. By the autumn fresh rumblings of discontent were heard from the primary teachers, complaining that the effect of the increase had been merely to give just under half their number a rise of 100F a month and just over half one of 267F.[75] Some were able to earn more by organizing local sport, or post-school agricultural and adult-education courses. Theoretically they enjoyed free housing or, in lieu, received a housing allowance. If they lived in the few towns of over 100,000 inhabitants this amounted to the princely sum of 900F, an allowance fixed as long ago as 1922. Grumbling continued into 1944, particularly when the supplement of 3,000 – 6,000F a year some had been paid for their sports activities was stopped.[76] Since it was then almost impossible to survive in towns without buying on the black market, the urban teacher was poverty-stricken.

Nevertheless, more and more chores were heaped upon the

luckless teacher. 'He is the donkey of the Arab proverb. He prepares and teaches his class in his spare time.' Thus one writer summed up his wartime duties.[77] Where the primary teacher had continued to be the mayor's secretary, his official tasks had become very arduous. He was involved in a host of activities, from air-raid precautions to acting as local treasurer for the Secours National. He was expected to play a leading part in such celebrations as Mother's Day. In school he had to arrange the collection of old paper, rags, non-ferrous metal, wool, crockery for the homeless, medicinal plants, chestnuts, acorns, and other material that might be used as ersatz, for recycling, or for food. He acted as salesman for Pétain's portrait to pupils and organized for them the 'Marshal's Christmas party'. So many bodies encroached upon his time that in 1944 Bonnard called a halt.

The Occupation forces also made demands. The primary teacher became for them the agent against what they termed 'Public Enemy No. 1', the Colorado beetle. The Germans became so obsessed about this potato pest that their soldiers earned themselves the nickname of 'les doryphores'. Hence the popular 'double entendre' that went the rounds: 'Luttez contre le doryphore'. For some teachers, however, the joke turned sour as they were impressed into special duties. In 1941 the Feldkommandant of Vienne ordered all teachers and pupils to spend three hours on four afternoons a week, in or outside school hours and continuing throughout the holidays, hunting down and destroying the pest in the fields.[78] No excuses were brooked and five teachers earned themselves a few days in prison for failing to obey the order.[79]

Teachers clearly had many grievances. There was substance in the complaint made to Bonnard by a group at Lyons that they were not only 'the least well-paid in Europe and even in the world', but also that they were 'the least held in esteem'.[80] From January 1941 in communes of over a certain size they were forbidden to act as mayor's secretary, on the grounds that they were already overburdened. The ban had been forecast by *Le Temps* a few weeks earlier and the real reason indicated: in the past it had meant 'the almost fatal hand of the schoolmaster on the small town'.[81] For the teacher it signified not only a loss of remuneration but also a diminution of his status and prestige in the community. Women teachers felt aggrieved at having to retire at fifty. The law of October 11, 1940 theoretically applied to all civil servants but had been applied more rigorously to primary – and not even secondary – teachers.[82] Eventually concessions were made, granting exemption to women teachers supporting aged parents or bringing up young children. Finally Bonnard, in a bid to achieve popularity, postponed (C. of May 19, 1942) full application of the law until after the war, although those who had already retired prematurely were not compensated. Resentment also built up over teachers who were prisoners of war, since often man and wife were both teachers. Despite frequent requests made to the Armistice Commission at Wiesbaden, teachers were not released on 'captivity leave'[83] unless they fulfilled the normal German stipulation that they had served in both World Wars or were fathers of large families. Nor were teachers in the relevant age categories exempt later from compulsory labour service in Germany. In principle the quota of primary teachers per department was fixed at about one-third of those eligible, but this fraction was not respected. The Loire academy inspector protested that if the number required from his department were not reduced some three-quarters would have to leave for Germany. Initially it had been decided that only bachelor teachers would be called up, and then not if they ran a one-class school, but this decision was not implemented.[84] By March 1944 the Secretariat General for the Labour Force had decreed that 16,500 civil servants, among whom were 2,806 teachers, would be conscripted.[85] The clandestine L'Université Libre claimed in April that the final figure would reach 4,000 and that eventually all teachers under 35 with less than four children would be obliged to leave for Germany. This statement may well have not been an exaggeration because Bonnard, in his eagerness for a German victory, at the end pressed any and everybody into service, regardless of legal niceties. The prominent position that the teacher occupied in the local small community made it difficult for him to avoid this obligation. There is indeed some justification for the view that teachers were subject to unfair discrimination.

Another means by which Vichy had sought to break

the teachers' power and prestige was by the dissolution in October 1940 of their unions. Theoretically all trade unions for civil servants had been illegal, but in practice the teachers' unions had wielded great power under the Republic. The charge was that they had abused this power. *Le Temps* (October 17, 1940) recalled an incident at one pre-war congress of SNI, where André Delmas, its secretary-general, had even called upon the minister to 'submit or resign' ('se soumettre ou se démettre'). Their assets forfeit to the State, the unions went underground. In their place the regime set up in 1941 six types of new education associations, in which teachers and administrators were segregated according to their grade. Certain grades of the inspectorate were forbidden to join any association. These new bodies were organized at department level and were forbidden to federate and function nationally. Based, like other creations of Vichy, on the principles of hierarchy and authority, they were nominally non-political, but in practice their role was to secure the collective adherence of teachers to the regime. Since membership remained voluntary, few joined this new kind of educational gendarmerie.

The flaws in the constitution of the associations were analysed at the time. It was argued that the veto on a national federation destroyed professional solidarity, as did the rigorous distinctions drawn between various categories of teachers: 'such compartmentalization results in the disintegration of any corporative movement'. Conditions were over-restrictive: elected officials had to be confirmed in office by the ministry; they could be required to resign at any time, without any reason being given; to provide against the permanency of officials, office was limited to a period of five years and re-election was ruled out.[86]

The lack of success of the new associations caused Bonnard, as part of a campaign to win the support of primary teachers, to try a new tack, by linking the associations with the old unions. The Germans were not unsympathetic to this initiative. Already in 1941 Dr Dahnke, of the 'Kultur und Schule' group attached to the German High Command, had made his view known that the SNI had not been anti-German, but merely pacifist and anticlerical – both attitudes of which the Germans approved. Indeed, declared Dahnke, SNI's former secretary-general, Delmas, had shown some sympathy for the Germans, so much so that the German Embassy was anxious for him to become involved in the new associations.[87] Thus it was with German approval that Bonnard announced (C. of June 12, 1942) that former union officials would no longer be excluded from membership and, as a concession, gave the associations the right to make representations directly to the prefect on matters relating to 'their legitimate aspirations'. The minister went even further: he began recruiting former union leaders into his ministry.[88] The cases of Jeanneret, former secretary of the Union Corporative des Instituteurs, and Lavenir, of the Rhône section of SNI, have already been mentioned. Lavenir, apart from his other duties, was charged with re-establishing contact with the former local secretaries of SNI. This he did by sending out fraternal letters beginning 'mon cher camarade', a rather singular form of address for 1942. Recruited also from the Rhône section of SNI was Louis Blain, who was assigned to the ministry of information to deal with teacher propaganda. But by far the most formidable recruit was Léon Eméry, a training-college teacher from Lyons, a former president of the Fédération of the Ligue des Droits de l'Homme and a left-wing 'theorist of pacifism'[89] for SNI who had influenced a whole generation of primary-school teachers. Now, through his book, *La Troisième République* (1943), and articles he published in a new bulletin for primary teachers started by Bonnard, he urged collaboration with the Germans. Despite these recruits from the old 'syndicats', the new associations did not become more popular: by 1943 in only ten departments had they over one hundred members – in the Drôme, for example, their members numbered only eighty in all.[90]

Pétain's entourage were in any case backing different horses. They suspected that Lavenir, far from building up the new associations, wished to scuttle them, supplanting them by an organization similar to the Conseils Syndicaux of the Front Populaire.[91] Pétain had originally invited Sivé, a primary teacher who before the war had been the secretary of a small teachers' union, to play a part in setting up the new associations. He had been assisted by Dexmier, a headmaster from the Loire-Inférieure. Pétain had even received Dexmier in April 1943 at Vichy, where teacher representatives of thirty-two departments, all connected with the new associations, had been presented to him.[92] Sivé and Dexmier likewise suspected Bonnard's collaborators of seeking to reconstitute the SNI in a different guise. Sivé referred bitterly to the fact that his own efforts had met with 'a scornful indifference or scarcely veiled hostility on the part of certain administrators'.[93] This ill will undoubtedly sprang in part from those who opposed the new associations in principle, but also came from Bonnard's office. Eventually Bonnard and Dexmier patched up their differences.[94] The affair exemplifies how loath the minister was to let control of the primary teachers pass into the hands of Pétain's staff, whom he regarded as reactionary, proclerical, and 'national', as opposed to 'European'.

To the mass of primary teachers such internal bickering must have seemed a high irrelevancy. The rank and file would probably have settled for nothing less than the complete rehabilitation of SNI. In any case they were more worried about the cost of living. They were not at all grateful for the meagre salary rises granted them,[95] despite the fact that in August 1943 a further increase gave them a basic scale of 16,000 – 32,000F a year, to which was added a supplement of 4,000F. Even the members of the new associations resented the way they had been treated since the armistice: the school of the past, they said, was neither to be condemned nor restored, but '. . .we are right to remain attached to it . . . we ask that the primary teacher be humiliated no longer'.[96] But one critic, Lemonnier, writing in the collaborationist periodical, *L'École de demain,* slating teachers incidentally as 'attentistes', Gaullist, and anti-German, deplored 'the persistence of post-1870 ideas in the hearts of primary teachers'.[97] His estimate of their mood was probably accurate. Other former members of the pre-war unions, disregarding the new associations, were beginning to regroup clandestinely. Georges Lapierre became secretary-general of the reconstituted SNI, operating illegally and continuing to publish secretly *L'École liberatrice,* the periodical he had founded in 1929. In 1942 the efforts of Vichy to regiment teachers in the new associations must have seemed a red herring to most teachers.

With Bonnard at the ministry, a hornet's nest was stirred up for teachers, after the comparative quiet of Carcopino's tenure of office. One collaborationist teacher hoped that the minister would put an end to the 'persecutions', as he put it, that had occurred, 'Carcopino regnante'.[98] Others took the opportunity to sum up the situation somewhat differently. Two teachers wrote anonymously to Bonnard declaring that Laval's return to power had turned them against Pétain and, as for him, their new chief, 'Veuillez agréer, Monsieur le Ministre, l'assurance de notre profond mépris.'[99] One bewildered teacher, dismissed for his masonic activities in the distant past, plaintively protested that out of a staff of thirty-three colleagues, thirty-one were Gaullists, two were indifferent, and he alone, now out of a job, was devoted to Bonnard and the 'new Europe'.[100] Bonnard's staff received threatening letters: one, a former teacher at the Lycée Claude-Bernard, was assured that his ex-pupils had taken note of his Nazi eulogies and that, like 'tous les amis de la Bochie', he could expect short shrift at the Liberation.[101]

Bonnard favoured teachers who were members of the Déatiste and Doriotiste collaborationist parties in Paris. Déat, as an ex-philosophy teacher, prided himself on his contacts with the teaching profession. In December 1942 he set up within his party, the Rassemblement National Populaire, a Union de l'Enseignement, open to all those educationists 'who wished to contribute to French revival and the building of European socialism'.[102] A parallel may be drawn with the NS-Lehrerbund within the Nazi party. The Union was led by Ludovic Zoretti and backed by Léon Eméry and the writer Jean Giono. Zoretti's career resembles that of others who threw in their lot with the Nazis.[103] An ex-Normalien, a mechanics professor at the faculty of Caen, he had founded the Institut Technique de Normandie and the pre-war Syndicat de l'Enseignement des Second et Troisième Degrés, for secondary and higher-education teachers. A Socialist, he had at one time supported the Compagnons de l'Université Nouvelle in their efforts to achieve a more democratic education system. Dismissed by Vichy in 1940, he had joined up with Déat. Since he had also been secretary-general of the Fédération Générale de l'Enseignement, to which most teachers' unions had belonged, he had extremely wide contacts. It was perhaps this that impelled Bonnard to reinstate him in 1944, when the minister asked him to set up a Université de Travail, where both employers and workers would be trained together. The scheme came to nothing. After the war Zoretti was sentenced to seven years in a labour camp, where he died. The wartime Union de l'Enseignement had in the meantime achieved little. It fed the minister with denunciations, particularly of academy inspectors suspected of sabotaging the teachers' associations or the call-up of teachers for compulsory labour service. The Germans used the Union as a convenient propaganda vehicle.

At first, however, few teachers were involved in the ideological battle and most remained neutral as regards the war. If they taught their charges 'the Marshal's song', it was often with tongue in cheek. They largely approved of Carcopino's order of 'no politics in school'. His desire for 'neutrality' was so strictly interpreted that one headmaster even forbade the reading out of Pétain's famous 'messages' to the class.[104] When Bonnard came, this policy changed. On the pretext that a State 'doctrine' for young people should be taught, as in the youth movements, the collaborationists passed to the attack, as one or two minor instances illustrate. They denounced a teacher who was studying with his pupils Jules Romains's *Visite aux Américains,* although in fairness to them it must be said that the teacher was also advocating that the class should improve its English by listening to the BBC.[105] They pressed claims for the teaching of German in schools and universities. They suspected English language clubs, for, they alleged, their purpose was 'surely not to condemn the conduct of the Anglo-Saxons nor to hasten the coming of the new Europe. . . We know the wicked part played by English teachers for many years as more or less conscious agents of England.'[106] Charges of Gaullism against teachers became increasingly frequent, particularly in Northern France, where they caused alarm to the Occupation authorities.[107] The director of the regional sports centre at Roubaix noted that the young primary teachers who came on his courses were 'all imbued with the Gaullist spirit which reigns in our region'.[108] But generally the development of teachers from an attitude of 'attentisme' to the conviction of an Allied victory was slow – perhaps with good reason.

Secondary teachers were not subject to the same suspicion and close surveillance as their primary colleagues. Simone de Beauvoir claims that she and Sartre, both philosophy teachers, were free to teach what they liked,[109] although she was later forced to resign. Vichy threatened to close the hostel for older pupils that the pair ran jointly, on the grounds that their charges were sleeping together.[110] Lablénie, later to play a leading part with teachers in the Resistance, also says that he spoke his mind without restraint to his pupils at the Lycée Janson de Sailly, although the class included the sons of two Vichy ministers. He openly mocked racialism and authoritarianism, sympathized with his Jewish pupils, and read *Tartuffe,* although the play was banned, with his pupils. At one stage he and his pupils even planned to kidnap Bonnard, who lived in the Avenue Mozart, near the school.[111] When in 1942 the exhibition, 'Bolshevism against Europe', was mounted in Paris, teachers in his school forbade their pupils to visit it. Teachers and parents generally appear to have been unsympathetic to this gigantic anti-Communist propaganda effort, since it was visited by only 6,200 pupils in all.[112] When teachers arrived at the 'Montoire room' in the exhibition, where the famous photograph of Hitler with Pétain was displayed, they hustled their charges through quickly before they could take in the scene.[113] Although a comparatively more relaxed atmosphere prevailed in State secondary schools this did not prevent a rush to teach at such private schools as the Collège Cévenol[114] or in French *lycées* abroad, although Vichy ensured that these posts overseas were reserved for those loyal to the regime.

The greater surveillance of primary teachers is borne out by the study of prefects' reports from September 1941 to March 1942.[115] About one-third of these monthly reviews state that their morale is good or otherwise report favourably upon them. The remaining reports reflect very varying views. After a year of 'purges' teachers were still being punished. The prefect of the Finistère noted laconically that he had been obliged to send one teacher to a 'concentration camp' (*sic*) for a few days; another merited dismissal for having attended a Breton autonomist rally. From the occupied part of the Jura the 'scandalous immunity' of local primary teachers from sanctions was noted, a particular example of which occurred when a former Communist teacher, posted away from his village as a punishment, had threatened the local mayor with a revolver. A number of departments, particularly the Nord, reported that Communist teachers were lying low and biding their time. In November 1941 a special police investigation in the Vendée had resulted in forty-one teachers being sent packing. From the Vosges it was reported that, although outwardly compliant, the teachers remained 'Republican and secular'. Some reports verge on the ludicrous: in the Morbihan a woman teacher had been jailed for putting out her tongue at a German, a charge she vigorously denied. Although secondary teachers are mentioned much less frequently, they are often characterized as Anglophiles, Gaullists, and 'attentistes'. Confused, outwardly conforming, but inwardly 'of the same conviction still', the majority of all teachers, as this first stage of the Occupation drew to a close, probably reflected accurately public attitudes as a whole. The shock of defeat had been surmounted, but it was felt that a happy issue to the war was still a very distant contingency.

Bonnard's sea-change in policy, seeking to win over the teachers, was undoubtedly concerted with Laval. In the past the propaganda addressed to them had been merely aimed at converting them to Pétainism: in particular primary-school inspectors harangued newcomers to the profession and paid particular attention to the teaching of civic education. The initial thrust of change had been social as much as political. Now, with Bonnard, it was the political purpose of propaganda that was paramount, no longer to encompass the Révolution Nationale but subtly to convert the teachers to the idea of a German-dominated 'New Order' in Europe. The methods used were ingenious. The recruitment to the ministry of former SNI activists was only a beginning. The strategy was to avoid flamboyant gestures of holding out the olive branch, since this would merely arouse scepticism, as well as fuelling the hostility of those who felt that teachers had not yet been punished enough for their past 'misdeeds'. On the contrary, a first step was to involve them in seemingly innocuous acts 'which flatter their amour-propre, make play of their self-sacrifice, engage their spirit of loyalty'.[116] On Joan of Arc Day, for instance, it should be the teacher who was invited to recite publicly a 'Crédo à la patrie'. By tiny gestures their sense of self-importance, among adults as well as children, could be fostered – after all, this was how in the past their Republicanism had been nurtured. On the national scale Bonnard fired the opening shot in his campaign: by July 1942 thirty-five teachers had been rehabilitated.[117] At Lille he publicly proclaimed that teachers had *not* been responsible for the defeat. In August he followed this up by making a 'Forgive and forget' broadcast : 'Your former opinions are of no interest to me,' the minister magnanimously and mendaciously declared.[118]

This policy of conciliation was also adopted by Pétain. In September 1942 the Marshal presided over an 'Education Day' for teachers at Vichy. He recalled that as a young officer he had considered himself the 'teacher' of his soldiers. Later, at the École de Guerre, he had exercised as an instructor a more traditional teaching function. Now he spoke, he declared, 'as a primary teacher', one of themselves, 'resolved to restore to their function the dignity that befits it'.[119] Laval likewise paid his tribute. At a dinner the same evening he recollected that in a pre-war secret session of the Chamber of Deputies he had praised the primary teachers for helping him 'to become what I am', whilst castigating the unpatriotic among their number.[120]

Bonnard also held out a number of small inducements. By equating the 'brevet supérieur', the normal teaching qualification, with the baccalaureate, he enabled those primary teachers who lived near a university to enrol part time for a degree. The director of secondary education was not enthusiastic about this concession but agreed that 'the demagogic effect will be excellent'.[121] The universities became alarmed. The Paris Faculty of Letters enquired whether the dispensation opened the way to study for a secondary teaching qualification ('licence d'enseignement') or merely for a general degree ('licence libre'). The question was solved when Bonnard, worried by the increase in student numbers, instituted in 1943 a special entrance examination, as an additional hurdle for those wishing to enter the Faculty of Letters. This double-dealing enraged Albertini, of Déat's Rassemblement National Populaire, who threatened to expose the minister's duplicity in *L'Œuvre.*[122] Despite this, Jolly, the director of primary education, upon his return from a tour of inspection reported that the exemption from the baccalaureate, the promised salary increases, and the suspension of the unpopular law requiring women teachers to retire at fifty had convinced teachers that the ministry had suffered a genuine change of heart. But, he added, whilst they approved of Pétain they remained hostile to collaboration, 'without bothering about the contradiction between the two attitudes'.[123] This was not quite what Bonnard had hoped to hear.

The minister wanted his own propaganda platform. In January 1943 he therefore launched a Bulletin de l'Enseignement Primaire, which, starting with an initial credit of 470,000F, had a circulation of 80,000.[124] Bonnard himself wrote articles for it in delicate prose, in which he assured teachers that by collaborating they would remain 'faithful to the idea of peace and justice they had served in former days' – a rather dubious reference to their former pacifism – and would thereby 'create a new type of Frenchman'. Even with this new vehicle for his proselytizing, the minister found his task an uphill one. A young primary teacher, a docker's son, leftish in his politics but clearly *persona grata* with authority, brutally pointed out the obstacles that had to be surmounted. Some people complained, he wrote, that teachers' lack of enthusiasm for the Révolution Nationale displayed the 'lukewarmness of faceless, over-scrupulous public servants'. But these same complainants were the very ones who had 'tried everything to castrate us' (*sic*). In the past many primary teachers had gone Communist (in the margin of the document someone has written, '2,000 out of 120,000') with the result that 'A vile campaign was mounted. A scapegoat was sought. In France the Jew scarcely fits the bill. The priest has become a tough nut to crack. But the primary teacher, although he's already had his turn, is still ripe for it. . . And we felt sweeping through our school, held responsible for the disaster, the wind blowing from the bishop's palace.'[125] Bitterness, distrust of the regime, anticlericalism: these sentiments still dominated most primary teachers.

Nevertheless, Bonnard continued in his efforts to win their favour. He was quick to take advantage of any opportunity to praise them. After the bombing of Rouen in May 1944 he particularly commended a group of young teachers in training who had acquitted themselves well in the rescue operations: 'I shall seize with pleasure every occasion to point out to the nation the services and the merit of teachers, who in general continue to be full of excellent qualities, and particularly the primary teachers, whose zeal and devotion remain untiring.' (C. of May 10, 1944.) Only after the Allied invasion does a sour note begin to creep in. When teachers applied for time off to remove their family from the danger zone he commented acidly, 'Too many Frenchmen persist in wishing to follow their habitual routine, despite the fact that the world is turned upside down.' (C. of June 17, 1944.) There could be no summer holidays for teachers in 1944, because of 'the effort demanded from everyone'.

Vichy's general policy of trying to revitalize the Révolution Nationale, distinctly moribund in 1942, through the teachers, and Bonnard's particular variant of the policy which sought to enlist support for building a Nazi Europe both failed. The more astute teachers realized that they were being manipulated. As one clandestine tract proclaimed, 'Labour in vain, M. Bonnard': teachers would not be cajoled by flattery and 'the crusade against reason would fail'. Jean Magister (*sic*) continued, 'We are not going to pass into the service of a new Europe.' Although Resistance exploits lie outside the scope of this work, it is relevant to note that, just as the new conciliatory policy got under way, from mid-August to November 1942 a steep rise occurred in the number of primary teachers arrested.[126]

From Algiers, after the liberation of North Africa, teachers were warned of the consequences of collaborating with the Germans. Capitant, de Gaulle's Commissioner for Education, suspended all teachers in North Africa who, after January 1, 1941 had been members of such collaborationist organizations as Doriot's PPF, the Groupe Collaboration, the Légion Tricolore, or the Phalange Africaine, or those who after January 1, 1942 had held office in the Légion des Combattants.[127] In the event the 'épuration' commissions set up in metropolitan France after the Liberation had only to deal with 4,800 cases concerning those employed in education. Of these, 1,515 were exonerated and a further 368 received only a minor punishment. More severe penalties were imposed on 1,168 persons, including 6 rectors, 33 inspectors, 116 school principals, and 272 secondary and 552 primary teachers.[128] Since in 1940 there were 14,487 secondary teachers, the proportion of those found guilty of any offence was under two per cent.[129] Likewise, since there were 154,502 primary teachers, the proportion of these was under half of one per cent. With the exception of a few 'lost leaders', on the whole the teaching body turned a deaf ear to the blandishments both of the Germans and their minions.

In March 1944 a document probably originating in Pétain's office, entitled, 'Current questions in primary teacher circles', noted that the attractions of being a primary teacher had considerably diminished. Relations between primary teachers and the Légion des Combattants had improved, but the quarrel between them and Catholics had intensified.[130] These straws in the wind may indicate that the teachers had fully recovered their nerve after the cataclysmic experience of 1940 and had stood firm against a regime whose main features were repugnant to them.

Chapter V

The Regimentation of Youth

In 1939 probably less than 15 per cent of young people aged between fourteen and twenty belonged to a youth movement. In the 1930s the various youth organizations, from the bodies belonging to the Association Catholique de la Jeunesse Française (ACJF) or its Protestant counterpart, to the various branches of scouting and the different political groupings, had failed to capture the mass of young people. During the slump it was the young that had been hardest hit by unemployment: in 1934 Bertrand de Jouvenel estimated that no less than half of the six million young people aged between 15 and 24 were unemployed. He had suggested expanding training centres, youth clubs, and sports facilities.[1] After the collapse of 1940, when mass youth unemployment was a distinct possibility – in the event it failed to materialize – such amenities became available.

The feeling that something must be done for youth was deep-seated. There was a consciousness that youth lacked dynamism. It was this that impelled Baudouin to include the younger generation in his commination of France:

> You have witnessed the defeat. Never forget its causes. France was beaten because it lacked a soul; because it had no consciousness of its strength, of its greatness and its mission, because Frenchmen had lost a sense of national community and were exhausting themselves in the class struggle. Youth lived without ardour, discouraged before it acted. As it was refused its chance, it no longer even cherished the desire to demand one. It fled from risk and shrank from effort. It was sad and paralysed.[2]

The question was: How could the energies of the young be harnessed to the task of restoring French greatness? It is possible that the idea of a special ministry for youth sprang from Baudouin and his friends. Before the war, in the Catholic *Revue des jeunes,*[3] he had called for a new 'chivalry', under resolute leadership, to defend Western civilization and preserve France from dictatorship and anarchy. The periodical in which his appeal was published was edited by Garric and Forestier. Garric, a university teacher, after the First World War had founded the Équipes Sociales, which comprised students and young workers who came together to study social questions. The ideas that were sparked off foreshadowed the Révolution Nationale. Father Forestier had founded the Rover Scout movement, which had flourished in some 'grandes écoles'. As chaplain-general to the Scouts de France and a faithful follower of Pétain, he was to play an important role in the 're-education' of French youth, particularly after he had also been appointed chaplain to Vichy's first youth organization, the Chantiers de la Jeunesse. Also among Baudouin's friends were several civil servants with scouting connections, among them Henri Dhavernas, an inspector of finance, who was to become the first leader ('Chef Compagnon') of the other new Vichy youth movement, the Compagnons de France. Scouting also had links with the army. General de La Porte du Theil was a one-time scout commissioner for the Île-de-France. He had become a scoutmaster in 1928 when he found that the scout troop his children belonged to, Saint-Sulpice in Paris, had no one to lead it. A friend of Pétain, he became the head of the Chantiers de la Jeunesse, the civilian movement which took in young men as conscripts for a period of eight months. Another General, Lafont, became Chief Scout. Other scouts close to Baudouin included Pierre Schaeffer, the first director of another Vichy innovation, Radio-Jeunesse, and Pierre Goutet, who became the first director for youth in the ministry for family and youth set up in 1940. Weygand and other General Staff officers believed that youth movements might be a surrogate for military service. None, however, believed in a single, monolithic movement on Nazi lines.

Paternalism towards youth – the more acceptable face of authoritarianism – was the dominant attitude of those closest to Pétain. They took as their example Marshal Lyautey, whose ideal of 'the social role of the officer', conceived of as being the educator of his men, because the period of military service completed the conscript's schooling, was widely canvassed. Garric and the first Vichy secretary-general for youth, Georges Lamirand, had become close intimates of Lyautey before he died in 1934. Lamirand had served in both World Wars. He was an engineer, a graduate of the École des Arts et Métiers, and before taking up his post on September 27, 1940 had been a director of Renault. In 1925, in his capacity as an industrialist, he had published a book in palpable imitation of Lyautey – indeed Lyautey had written a preface to it – entitled *Le Rôle social de l'ingénieur,* in which he had urged his fellow-industrialists to exert a paternal and educative influence over their workers. Described by some as a 'beau garçon' and hail-fellow-well-met,[4] he made a great impression on Pétain. Hence his selection for the post. His views were shared by one of his associates, Louis Garrone, a devout Catholic and former teacher connected with the well-known École des Roches at Verneuil, which was run on the lines of an English public school. Garrone joined the new secretariat for youth (SGJ) as a senior official.

Immediately after the defeat youth affairs had got off to a difficult start. In July 1940 a former right-wing deputy and supporter of Col. de la Rocque's Croix de Feu, Ybarnégaray, had been appointed to the dual office of secretary of state for the family and youth. President of the national pelota association, this Basque sportsman had enlisted also the services of his friend, Jean Borotra, the world tennis champion, who, as will be seen, was to serve Vichy well in the fostering of sport. A member of Reynaud's government, Ybarnégaray had supported Pétain in his decision to ask for an armistice. None the less, his appointment to the new secretariat was a curious appointment for Pétain to make, for Ybarnégaray had been de Gaulle's friend for many years. In the government reshuffle of September 1940 the ministry of family and youth had been split, Ybarnégaray had been dismissed, along with other former 'parliamentarians', but Borotra had stayed on. Youth affairs had then been placed in the charge of Lamirand, who was at first subordinate to the ministry of education; from November 1, 1940 the SGJ had been transferred to the office of Laval, as Vice-President of the Council, before returning to the nominal charge of the ministry of education on January 8, 1941. Although Lamirand survived these changes, such uncertain beginnings affected greatly the efficiency of the SGJ.

Meanwhile, however, the determination to 'revitalize' youth was common to a closely knit caucus of intellectuals, industrialists, army officers, and civil servants, all strong Catholics or at least sympathetic to religion, all disenchanted at the time with democracy. The group had the ear of Pétain and was initially powerful enough to counterbalance the two other main contenders for influence over youth: Massis and the Maurrassians, more inclined to the Fascist model, and the far more sinister group of Paris collaborationists, whose beliefs moved steadily towards out-and-out Nazism. Within this quadrilateral of forces – because the ACJF was also a strong influence – youth was pulled in different directions.

The one 'doctrine' – the word was fashionable at Vichy – all held in common was that youth sould be 'encadré', interpreted to postulate hierarchical leadership, strong discipline, and regimentation.[5] In Paris Déat represented this doctrine in its most extreme form: he wanted a 'jeunesse unique', a single organization for all young people within a one-party state, and even proposed party work-camps for them, from early childhood to adulthood, 'as in Italy and Germany'.[6]

Lamirand's assignment was more modest, although very wide-ranging. His mission was to oversee, either directly or indirectly, the moral, social, civic, and vocational training of young people over school age. These tasks, with the exception of vocational training, he delegated to Garrone. Garrone was also responsible for running the special new training schools for leaders, the 'écoles des cadres' – the term 'leaders' schools' was deliberately avoided as smacking too much of Nazism. He had also to liaise with existing youth movements and head a new regional and local network of youth services. This network grew rapidly:[7] by September 1941 twenty-three regional delegates had been appointed, together with 173 local delegates, usually honorary, whose numbers had increased to 1,200 by 1943. Over the other function of the SGJ, vocational training, there was a continual problem of what prefects described as 'a regrettable duality of services'.[8] Such training, originally intended for the young unemployed, was at first organized by the SGJ in centres and workshop schools, but in 1942 was for a while assimilated into the ministry's directorate for technical education, which also functioned in the same field. This overlap was typical of the causes of friction that arose between the educational professionals, the rector and the academy inspector, and the newly-appointed amateurs, the youth delegates drawn often from the non-educational field, who had the privilege of reporting directly to the prefect instead of going through the educational hierarchy. Such ambiguities of function were never really resolved and the SGJ remained badly administered to the end.

In order to carry out its supervisory functions the SGJ had the power to bestow recognition upon youth movements. Approval procedures were worked out at a meeting held in June 1941 at Uriage attended by representatives of all the principal movements. The granting of 'agrément', as the procedure was known, carried with it eligibility for a subsidy. Initially it was also seen as an expedient to eliminate German interference and patronage of those youth movements the occupation forces favoured. To qualify for 'agrément' a movement had to provide training – sporting, patriotic, and moral – on the lines of the Révolution Nationale, had to be hierarchically organized, and see that its leaders received training in the 'écoles des cadres'. At first recognition was granted only to well-established non-political organizations such as those run by the Church or the scouts, or official ones such as the Compagnons de France, but under Bonnard collaborationist organizations also received a subsidy.

How youth movements developed under Vichy cannot be understood without reference to the very different 'mentors' who controlled them. Lamirand was content to delegate his functions, conceiving his role largely as that of a propagandist for the regime, and a 'stimulator'. He therefore spent much of his time travelling the country and making speeches. In May 1942 this semi-political role was challenged by Georges Pelorson, one of the more curious characters that the regime threw up, who was appointed by Bonnard as Lamirand's deputy – he was already working in the SGJ, in charge of youth propaganda. An ex-Normalien,

Pelorson had a pre-war connection with Dublin. In 1928 Samuel Beckett, the Franco-Irish writer, after graduating in modern languages at Trinity College, had been appointed on a reciprocal arrangement as English 'lecteur' at the École Normale Supérieure. It so happened that Pelorson was the sole English specialist of that year. Beckett dispensed English lessons to his solitary pupil in the cafés of Montparnasse, where Pelorson frequented some of the surrealist poets. In 1929 Pelorson in turn was appointed French 'lecteur' at Trinity College, to which a year later Beckett returned as a lecturer, and the two met almost daily to dine, drink whiskey, and read Proust together. Pelorson produced for the modern-languages club a sketch by Beckett entitled 'Le Kid', a pastiche of Le Cid. Pelorson returned to France and, after Beckett returned to Paris in 1937, the two were in touch. Their paths then diverged. Beckett remained in France during the war and eventually, through a teacher, joined the Resistance group 'Étoile', based on the Lycée Buffon, and in 1945 was awarded the Croix de Guerre for his intelligence work.[9] From 1935 onwards Pelorson had been running a progressive private school. He had also founded a review, *Volontés.* In 1940 he had become a prisoner of war but had somehow secured his release. Early in 1941 he had published a book, *De l'enfant à la nation,* and had been appointed to the SGJ. Conceded by Pétain's entourage to be 'a young writer of talent', he was disliked and mistrusted.[10] His anticlericalism and his literary capacity probably induced Bonnard to promote him to be Lamirand's deputy. His politics led him to become critical of Vichy's youth policy.

A more complete contrast to Lamirand, a strong Catholic, owing his first loyalty to Pétain, neutralist in politics, could not be imagined. Moreover, after November 1942 Lamirand became markedly anti-German. After the whole of France had been occupied, the SGJ addressed a meeting of regional youth delegates, calling for them to rally round the Marshal, who was now a prisoner in all but name. As for the fate of France, the rumours of German–Russian peace talks and the cooler Spanish attitude towards the Axis meant, he declared, that the Laval government was the last before the appointment of a Gauleiter.[11] Doubtless at Pétain's wish, Lamirand clung on to office until March 1943, but his eventual replacement was inevitable. His successor was Félix Olivier-Martin, a professor of administrative law who in 1941 had been among those considered for the Paris rectorship.[12] Politically he was inclined to de la Rocque's Parti Social Français. He was held to be mildly anti-German. Brilliant and cultured, he was dubbed 'peu sérieux, peu pratique', disliking effort and incapable of leadership, according to a report of Pétain's 'cabinet militaire'.[13] When Olivier-Martin was appointed, Pelorson was dismissed and the post of deputy was not filled. By then Pelorson had become unpopular with the permanent officials of the ministry and even more so with Pétain's entourage, who disliked his rabid, tendentious speeches.

In January 1944 Olivier-Martin was in his turn replaced by Gaït, an ex-Normalien, a journalist by profession, then deputy director of Bonnard's 'cabinet'.[14] Gaït, who fell in with what Bonnard wanted, declared that his aim was to make youth affairs 'more modest, more serious, less ostentatious and more effective',[15] perhaps an oblique reference to Pelorson's flamboyance. He survived in office until the Liberation, concentrating largely upon what still passed for moral and civic training, but by then his department exercised little real influence.

As well as controlling the SGJ, the ministry of education was responsible for other agencies connected with young people's welfare. To promote sport and physical fitness Jean Borotra, at Pétain's invitation, had collaborated with Ybarnégàray to set up a Commissariat Général for 'General Education' and Sport (to give it its eventual title). In September 1940 this had also passed under the control of the ministry of education and Borotra had acquired the additional task of looking after sport and physical education in schools, as well as certain other alleged 'character-training' activities ('General Education'). Both Borotra and his successor, Col. Pascot, asserted as much as possible their independence from the ministry.[16]

Neither did the ministry's yoke rest easy upon the two secular youth organizations that Vichy created. The Compagnons de France was set up in 1940 to take in young people under twenty who had been uprooted from their homes or who were unemployed. With Baudouin's encouragement, Dhavernas registered it as an association under the law of 1901 at Lapalisse (Allier) on July 25, 1940. It aimed to 'regenerate' youth and also to help in the task of reconstruction. The stages through which the movement passed, which ended with its then leader joining the Resistance, are described elsewhere.[17] Whereas the Compagnons was a voluntary organization, the Chantiers de la Jeunesse, although civilian in character, was compulsory for young men of military age and was plainly intended to replace conscription. Also engaged upon civilian tasks demanding hard, physical work, the purpose of the organization was not to provide a pool of cheap labour but to inculcate in youth a sense of moral and civic responsibility. Formally constituted on July 31, 1940, it came for a while under the aegis of the ministry of education. The difficult and dangerous history of the Chantiers, in the course of which its head, General de La Porte du Theil, was deported to Germany, is also told elsewhere.[18] With their usual, justifiable suspiciousness, the Germans forbade both the Compagnons and the Chantiers in the occupied zone.

Control of the other youth movements was exercised obliquely by the ministry of education, through the SGJ, although its position was challenged by propaganda sections of the ministry of information, which also had an interest in youth. These youth movements, whether connected with the Church, such as the ACJF, or whether secular, such as those that were directly linked to political parties, held many different contending 'mystiques', to use another vogue word.

The Catholics were particularly concerned to maintain the autonomy of the ACJF. Their great fear was that a single State-controlled youth movement, a 'jeunesse unique', would be set up. If such a monopoly were established and a totalitarian ideology such as Nazism got a firm hold on youth, Christianity in France itself would be placed in jeopardy. As it was, their own youth movements, federated in the ACJF and the scouts, were numerically the strongest and represented a well-disciplined and organized body of young people capable of defending the Church. Thus they opposed any moves towards unification and even, to some degree, of standardization. When Lamirand proposed a 'Charte de la Jeunesse', which contained clauses stipulating that every young person should belong to *some* youth movement and perform some form of civic service for twenty days a year, they came out against it. The ACJF called the proposals 'une gendarmerie de la jeunesse'. By December 1940, however, the first attempts of the collaborationists to popularize the concept of a 'jeunesse unique' had been successfully resisted and Pétain himself had declared against it.

The hierarchy's attitude to movements other than their own was one of courteous acceptance, but they remained on the alert. They mistrusted particularly political movements such as Déat's Jeunesses Populaires. The comparatively neutral Équipes Nationales, which did useful work in air-raids, was viewed warily, because at one time Pelorson seemed to have ambitions to build up the organization into a monolithic movement. Towards the Auberges de la Jeunesse they were implacably hostile because of the alleged tolerance of immorality in hostels by the leaders. In the countryside they feared that the Corporation Paysanne, set up by a law of December 2, 1940 to organize farmers and farm workers, would claim exclusive rights over the 'jeunes ruraux'. The Church claimed that family rights, which it should control, should take precedence over any rights deriving from an occupation. In the event this danger was not very great, because many of the leaders of the Corporation Paysanne were former members of the Jeunesse Agricole Chrétienne (JAC), affiliated to the ACJF. On June 3, 1942 the Jeunesse Paysanne, the youth organization of the Corporation, signed an agreement with the JAC setting out how both organizations would co-operate by jointly establishing youth centres and 'foyers ruraux'. The bishops were jealous of any movement that would infringe upon Church rights and privileges.

Catholic youth leaders were allowed to take a key role in the secular youth movements because it was hoped that they would bring about conversions. But they were warned that they functioned as secular leaders who happened to be Catholic ('en Catholique') rather than specifically as Catholics ('en tant que Catholique'). Even this concession was grudging: the Bishop of Viviers (*La Croix*, April 16, 1941) warned against too active a participation by Catholics in secular movements. Others agreed that the ACJF could join in youth rallies, but stipulated that the separate identity of the Catholic movements should always be stressed. The threat of a 'jeunesse unique' was revived from time to time, despite two formal statements of the Assembly of Cardinals and Archbishops, on February 6, 1941 and again on July 24, the last one of which affirmed, 'Jeunesse unie?. . .Oui!. . . Jeunesse unique? . . .Non!'[19]

Fortunately for the Catholics, it was logical for the Germans also to be against a 'jeunesse unique', despite the pleas of the collaborationists. On the principle of 'divide and rule', Abetz, the German ambassador, reported to Berlin in late 1940 that it was imperative to maintain the existing variety of movements. The semi-military style of the Compagnons and the Chantiers had prompted the ban on them in the occupied zone. The fear was that youngsters would take the road to 'dissidence' and end up in London with de Gaulle. On the other hand, they were ultra-suspicious of Catholic movements, which, despite the official ban in the Northern zone, managed to carry on a semi-legal and restricted activity. Young Catholics, the Germans felt, might become 'the conscience of youth' and also join the Resistance. They particularly disliked the Jeunesse Ouvrière Chrétienne (JOC) which operated efficiently, especially in Northern France, where it had always been strongest, and later, completely illegally, in Germany itself, when young Frenchmen were sent there on forced labour. The JOC were, so to speak, the 'Communists of Catholicism', inasmuch as they operated through 'cells', had clear-cut beliefs, and sedulously cultivated their contacts with the working class. Scouts were also regarded with suspicion. A group caught playing a tracking game occasioned a strong remonstrance from the Germans to the prefect of the Nord, hinting that such activities might be construed as a form of military training.[20] An intriguing report from the Abwehr in September 1943 reported that scout troops were being run under cover names such as the 'Amis de St-Michel' and were very well organized on the coast, 'particularly in Normandy [where they]... intend to act as an auxiliary and reception organisation upon any proposed English landing'.[21] By contrast, the Germans considered the overtly collaborationist youth movements as harmless, to be used for propaganda purposes as and when they thought fit. They were wary of the operations of the SGJ in their zone. In May 1941 they discovered that youth centres had been established in it without their knowledge and insisted that permission must be sought for any new ones.[22] The order went out that close surveillance be kept on Lamirand, whose propaganda tours, like Borotra's sporting engagements, took him into the occupied territories, even as far as Nancy, to see whether these were a cloak for anti-German activities.[23] A paramount concern of German policy was to see that French youth did not get out of hand and endanger the safety of the occupation forces. Whilst maintaining a vigilant watch they were therefore well content to let Vichy get on with the difficult task of controlling young people.

They looked to Bonnard, when he arrived at the ministry, to curb the Pétainist influence of Lamirand. The new minister sought to impose upon youth political beliefs that went far beyond the precepts of the Révolution Nationale. The kindred spirits that he appointed to his 'cabinet', mainly former left-wingers, seconded his efforts to steer French youth towards collaboration. (Serge Jeanneret, whose sympathies were much more to the right, resigned in mid-1942 because of what he described as the lack of revolutionary spirit that prevailed, reproaching Bonnard with reluctance to implement his principles.[24]) Apart from Pelorson, one of Bonnard's right-hand men for youth matters was Bousquet, who styled himself nationalist, socialist and 'European'. A Paris *lycée* teacher, he had started a school-pupils' movement, Les Jeunes du Maréchal[25], and in October 1941 had become the head of the national 'leadership school' in the northern zone, located at La Chapelle-en-Serval, an appointment that met with the approval of the Occupation authorities because, they said, 'it corresponded to the German interest'.[26] Despite being deemed 'suspect' by Pétain's staff, by June 1942 Bousquet had been appointed to the rank of inspector general. His colleagues now included the collaborationist ex-members of SNI. By September 1943 Georges, the Corsican from Bastia and suspected Resistance agent, had joined this hand-picked group of pro-Germans. On the other side were ranged Lamirand, de La Porte du Theil, and some of the top ministry officials. Education and youth matters illustrate how varied and divided the Vichy regime was.

The detailed history and ultimate fate of the various Vichy youth organizations is given in Part III. In March 1942, however, the regime thought it a suitable moment to draw up a balance sheet of success and failure as regards its policies for children and young people. With hindsight, the time seems singularly appropriate: the Révolution Nationale had almost run its course and, after a summer and autumn of agonizing reappraisal, youth was to enter upon its period of greatest trial. The medium for policy review chosen was the youth commission of the Conseil National, whose proceedings highlight not only the shortcomings of the regime but also the diversity of opinion within France.

The Conseil National had been established by a law of January 22, 1941 to act as a consultative body pending the promulgation of a new constitution, when the plenary powers granted to Pétain by the National Assembly would cease. The brief of the Conseil was limited, inasmuch as it could discuss only those matters referred to it by the Marshal. But, because ministers could take part in its deliberations, it might well have developed into an assembly of notables. However, it was inhibited from the beginning, since an applicatory decree of March 22, 1941 stipulated that it should work only in commissions, which limited its advisory role still further. Members of the Conseil were designated by Pétain. There were 188 in all, of whom no less than seventy-eight had been deputies or senators. The rest were experts in a particular field or were chosen because of the past services they had rendered to France. Seven commissions in all were set up. It was intended that their work should be preparatory to drawing up a new constitution. The commissions were: (1) study of the constitution – the most important one; (2) administrative reorganization; (3) municipal law; (4) general information; (5) youth; (6) economic organization; (7) study of the Paris region.

The youth commission met only once, from March 5–12, 1942, holding ten sessions in all. It was presided over by Gidel, rector of the university of Paris, and comprised sixteen Conseillers Nationaux and nine other representatives of national life. Others could be summoned to give evidence.[27]

Much thought was given in Pétain's entourage as to what line the Marshal should be recommended to take in his opening address to the commission.[28] His 'cabinet' attempted to predict what attitudes various people would adopt. Thus they expected that Pucheu, then minister of the interior, would attack the SGJ for its 'boy scout', 'churchy' ('calotin') mentality. Pucheu was a technocrat, an ex-member of Doriot's PPF who had become a Germanophile, despite his later change of colours. A similar line was predicted for Gaston Bergery, who, as a senator in 1939, had voted against the granting of war credits to the government and who in 1940 had advocated the integration of France into a German-dominated Europe. On the other hand, Lamirand, they considered, would combat any 'totalitarian intentions'. In this he would be supported by the Maurrassian, Henri Massis, who was one of those called upon to advise Pétain on youth matters, and Mgr Beaussart, the Church representative. Pétain's staff were anxious for the Marshal not only to condemn any 'totalitarian tendencies' but also the 'conscientious objections' voiced by the École des Cadres at Uriage and 'the friends of Marc Sangnier', the Christian democrat who had founded the Sillon movement early in the century. The reference here is to Dunoyer de Segonzac, the director of Uriage, who was accustomed to speak his mind freely, and to Emmanuel Mounier, the editor of the Catholic review, *Esprit,* and his colleagues, whose brand of Catholicism was more social and, although not democratic, hardly authoritarian. His staff hoped that Pétain would steer a course between these extremes.[29]

In the event Pétain's charge to the commission remained politically neutral and he did not allude specifically to either camp. His speech contained little new. He saw the upbringing of youth as the task of the 'natural communities' in society; the role fell to the family, spiritual bodies, and occupational organizations, with the State exercising a protective function, co-ordinating and overseeing its activities, but imposing its own 'doctrine' for civic education. Once more the Marshal came out against a 'jeunesse unique', although he did want young people to be united. He wanted the 'generation gap' to be bridged. The education system could be improved by utilizing the findings of the human sciences – this was perhaps a reference to the work of the new institute founded by Alexis Carrel, which had recently been subsidized, and to the new 'psycho-pedagogical' institute set up at Lyons.[30] Cavalierly disregarding the fact that he had supplied the commission with the answers already, the Marshal left its members with two main questions to ponder: to whom does youth belong? What was the place of youth in the nation? The debates that followed revolved round these two questions but were certainly not devoted exclusively to them.

In view of the membership of the commission, this was perhaps understandable. Its key members were: Carcopino; Bonnard, on the verge of supplanting Carcopino as minister; General de La Porte du Theil, representing the Chantiers de la Jeunesse; General Lafont, representing the scouts; Mgr Beaussart, representing the Catholic Church; Pastor Boegner president of the Fédération Protestante de France; Gidel, the chairman; François-Poncet, a one-time ambassador to Berlin; Le Cour Grandmaison, vice-president of the Société d'Éducation et d'Enseignement; Dorgères, of the Corporation Paysanne; Pernot, a senator and member of the Comité consultatif de la Famille française; and Valentin, director of the ex-serviceman's organization, the Légion des Combattants. The oldest member was Lafont (b.1874), and the youngest Valentin (b.1909). Those actually of the generation under discussion were conspicuous by their absence.

Pétain's address was followed by a report of Lamirand, giving a very full account of the activities of the SGJ since its inception.[31] In its first phase, in spite of covert hostility, both the Chantiers de la Jeunesse and the Compagnons de France had been established, with the latter recruiting 6,000 members in two months. A second phase, covering the first half of 1941, had been a difficult one. The Chantiers had suffered from mediocre leaders, poor living conditions, and consequently low morale, so much so that if he (Lamirand) had not convinced Pétain otherwise the Marshal would have yielded to public opinion and disbanded the organization. On the credit side, the creation on December 2, 1940 of a section to deal with youth unemployment had met with success. Lamirand admitted that his initial organization had been defective, but this was perhaps to be expected, in view of the difficult conditions. On the other hand, even now organization was unsatisfactory. Reforms which had given greater autonomy to the Chantiers de la Jeunesse, and transferrred to ministry of education officials his duties for vocational training had not been to his liking, because he had been left with a purely residual role, one of being largely responsible for social, moral, and civic training. He was gratified that by a recent law (L. of February 27, 1942) his powers and functions had been re-enlarged, despite, he added cryptically, a clash of personal ambitions and rivalries.

His over-all evaluation of the first sixteen months of activity by the SGJ was pessimistic. He estimated that 40 per cent of young people remained physically and morally unable to cope with life; in urban areas the proportion was as high as 65 per cent. The spirit of unhealthy pleasure continued to dominate youth, enjoyment financed by easy pickings made on the black market; in rural areas young men drank too much; too many girls were of easy virtue, because prostitution flourished. What was the remedy? First, he considered that families, schools, and employers should be faced with their obligations. Thus industry must take in hand the training of young employees. The various other agencies responsible must become more involved: the ministry of the interior, for young refugees; the ministry for the family, for young people's camps ('colonies de vacances'); the ministry of education, for assistance to students; the ministry of information should create a healthier moral climate by exerting a stricter control over the press and entertainment. More instructors were required to train youth, but the instructors themselves required training. This was the task of the new 'leadership schools', whose staff had originally been drawn from regular officers on 'Armistice leave' (i.e., temporarily retired), demobilized engineers and lawyers. Now the three national 'écoles des cadres' set up at Uriage and La

Chapelle-en-Serval for men, and at Écully for women, were training departmental youth delegates as well as instructors for other 'écoles des cadres' and ran information courses for present and future administrators, such as Polytechniciens. Nineteen regional schools, nine of which were located in the occupied zone, trained subordinate cadres and ran courses for those considered to be key personnel, such as primary teachers, army officers, clergy, industrialists, and students. Eight specialized schools existed for those working in youth centres. Other schools were reserved for the Compagnons de France, the Jeunesse Ouvrière Chrétienne, 'Parents Aubergistes' (housefathers and housemothers for youth hostels), and vocational-training instructors. To date some 16,000 key youth personnel, including 6,000 from the occupied zone, had passed through one or other of these schools.

Lamirand conceived of three different 'communities' in which youth might be organized. Within the educational community there were movements such as the Jeunes du Maréchal, for schoolchildren, and the Corporation des Étudiants, for students. Within the occupational community about two million youngsters under twenty constituted a segment of the labour force. About a third of these worked in industry and were organized by the 'comités sociaux' established under the Charte du Travail. Rural youth was grouped in the Corporation Paysanne. A third community was that constituted by the youth movements proper, and here there were problems. Some pre-war movements, such as the Auberges de la Jeunesse and those affiliated to political parties had to be purged of undesirables, and this sometimes ran counter to German wishes. This, however, was the purpose of the system of 'agrément'. To date approved movements included the Compagnons, the Scouts, the Auberges de la Jeunesse, and those in the ACJF or recognized by the Conseil Protestant. In the southern zone membership of movements numbered some three million members, usually aged between fourteen and twenty. The number of members in the principal movements was:

Compagnons de France	33,000
Le Scoutisme français[32]	115,000
ACJF	2,300,000
Secular clubs ('patronages laïques')	400,000
Conseil Protestant	30,000
Jeunesse française d'Outremer	15,000
Camarades de la Route (Auberges de la Jeunesse)	2,000
Cadets de la Légion	(no figure given)

In the occupied zone, although youth movements were nominally forbidden, some were 'tolerated', a circumstance, added Lamirand, which 'makes them suspect'. He cited some of the overtly political ones: Bucard's Francistes, Clémenti's Jeune Front (Mouvement National Collectiviste), and Déat's Jeunesses Nationales Populaires.

In addition, the SGJ had set up its own 'maisons des jeunes', single-sex youth clubs where leisure activities, practical service to the community, and moral, social, and civic education courses were organized. Leaders for these were trained at Chamarges (for men) and Saint-Cyran (for women) in special 'écoles des cadres'. The Direction du Travail des Jeunes, responsibility for which had passed directly to the ministry of education, ran two kinds of vocational-training centres: reception centres mounting three-week courses; and apprenticeship centres giving two- or three-year courses, both types managed jointly by committees of employers and workers. To date 608 vocational centres (332 for boys and 276 for girls) had been opened and 83,000 young people (52,500 boys and 30,500 girls) had passed through them.[33]

Despite Lamirand's pessimism, such an array of facts and figures looks impressive, but one can only guess at the reality that lay behind the statistics. One notes that the ACJF was by far the largest organization, and to them must be added a considerable proportion of the scouts, to arrive at the total stake of the Catholics in youth movements. Over such religious groups, apart from the element of compulsory civic education, Lamirand had little control. The mushrooming of 'écoles des cadres' clearly shows that leadership had become a cult. It is also clear, reading between the lines, that, with German connivance, totalitarian groups were continuing the game of politics. And one takes note, despite all the efforts made, of the honest admission of failure.

Mgr Beaussart commented upon Lamirand's report. He raised the question of the Compagnons de France, of whom he was very critical, being particularly concerned that any 'doctrine' taught should not conflict with Christian principles. He felt that the training of cadres had been too improvised. Why, he asked, had not teachers been used: 'Some had had their failings – but who had not? They should be trusted.'

Pucheu, perhaps the most important participant in the commission's work, took up the question of the use of teachers.[34] He asserted that adults were not capable of modifying their attitudes sufficiently and particularly doubted the capacity of teachers to do so. Secondary teachers, for example, 'had been trained in such an atmosphere of individualism and even of anarchy that one would encounter a wall of incomprehension'. It was, he hinted, incumbent upon the ministry of education to deal with what he termed the 'political problem' within education. Meanwhile, since neither parents nor the school were up to the task of training the rising generation, it was the duty of the youth organizations to do so.

Carcopino brushed aside all reference to the secondary teachers but did staunchly defend the primary teachers.[35] We have no right', he declared, to a remarkable chorus of hear-hears, 'to say that the primary teachers are the cause of the defeat and were the corrupters of the régime; on the contrary, it was the régime which rotted the healthiest sectors of the nation'. Teachers were now beginning to play a more prominent role with young people. A thousand primary teachers were already running post-school compulsory courses in agriculture for boys, and similar classes in housecraft were being organized for girls. A law on apprenticeship was being worked out. Thus, with his customary sense of practicalities Carcopino adroitly skirted round the 'political problem' alluded to by Pucheu.

Pelorson, still only in charge of propaganda at the SGJ, painted a sombre picture of young people in the occupied zone, from his point of view.[36] Youth, aided and abetted by its teachers, refused to accept the Révolution Nationale. Under a cloak of ostensible 'neutrality' both school and university were hostile – an oblique reference to Carcopino's ban on politics in educational institutions. In class-rooms Pétain's portrait was either absent, or displayed lacerated and bespattered with ink. Posters of the Marshal's 'messages' had suffered the same fate. In Paris *lycées* clandestine news-sheets, such as *La Jeune Nation Française,* circulated freely. There was even opposition at the top. When he had addressed a meeting of senior education administrators at Rennes they had failed to applaud his mention of Pétain and cries of 'Vive de Gaulle' had even been heard. It had taken him six months to procure the dismissal of the rector of Caen, a 'notorious Gaullist'. Turning to young workers, he noted that they were at best indifferent, or openly opposed to the regime. Delegates of the Jeunesse Ouvrière Chrétienne had refused to give him their co-operation, which he considered surprising, since the SGJ had been dubbed 'clerico-reactionary'. For all this he (Pelorson) proposed radical policies. A prime object must be to demonstrate that the Révolution Nationale was neither 'militant clericalism' nor 'muttering clericalism' nor 'employer paternalism' – a sally here at Lamirand, perhaps – but a genuine revolution, based not so much on sacrifice as on the material advantages that might emerge from it – the nature of these was not specified. This would make mass propaganda attractive to the young. (Bonnard, on the verge of becoming minister, applauded this tirade.) What was required, concluded Pelorson, was equality of opportunity.

Predictably, Mgr Beaussart construed Pelorson's remarks as an attack on the Church. If the state of young people was deplorable, he retorted, this was explicable because for almost two years it had been drummed into them that France as a nation was sunk. As for the 'clerico-reactionary' image, the Church would even be prepared to sacrifice its own youth movements if the interests of the Révolution Nationale would be better served. (This rather rash statement would certainly not have been supported by the ACA, which regarded the ACJF as 'the apple of its eye'.) Since Pelorson had spoken only of the occupied zone, where confessional organizations had only a half-life, this offer was somewhat gratuitous.

Pucheu intervened once more to back up Pelorson's estimate of the 'lamentable' state of youth. When Gidel claimed that anti-Pétain incidents were now rare in Paris schools, Pucheu retorted that, although the situation might have improved, in the *lycée* his own children attended they were still a daily occurrence and 'a pupil still cannot wear [the francisque] without running a risk'.

Two of the directors of the national 'écoles des cadres' were questioned about their work – Dunoyer de Segonzac, for Uriage, and Bousquet, for La Chapelle-en-Serval.[37] De Segonzac declared that there was a misconception: Uriage's prime purpose was not to train leaders but to identify those suitable for training as such. Unfortunately, he said, most of those who had gone through the course possessed 'little force of character and lacked courage'. Some were not even above petty thieving at Uriage. Pastor Boegner's intervention, to say how impressed Protestants had been by Uriage, was a lone voice. Bonnard, sarcastic and hostile, commented that de Segonzac might have a 'knightly soul' but his school lacked a doctrine, which the State should supply. Bergery wanted greater political direction of the school. Massis went further and exclaimed that the political tendency of Uriage was clear: it was under the influence of Mounier and was Gaullist, so that 'there a scandal exists which can no longer be tolerated'.[38] Bousquet was then called to report on La Chapelle-en-Serval[39] and distinguished himself by greeting the commission with a Nazi salute.[40] His 'doctrine', he asserted, was clearly in line with the Révolution Nationale. He underscored Pelorson's plea for equality of opportunity by complaining that his courses could only be attended by those without family responsibilities, the very young, or the very rich, since there was no indemnity for loss of earnings.

The report on the Compagnons de France, given by Commandant Tournemire, who had succeeded Dhavernas as the head of the movement,[41] was largely factual. Of the two kinds of membership, Compagnons de Chantier (full time) and Compagnons de Cité (part time), numbers in the first category had risen from 500 in October 1940 to 6,000 in December, but had since dwindled as young refugees had been able to return home. But the figures had now become more stable, because vacant places had been filled by young unemployed, although not all of these were of high quality. The second category, the part-time Compagnons de Cité, had risen from 14,000 in May 1941 to 25,500 in January 1942. They carried out civic and social work and followed similar courses.

Bergery then attacked the Compagnons. He waxed indignant that the movement's news-sheet, Le Chef Compagnon,[42] had given sympathetic publicity to Bernanos, just after the writer had insulted Pétain on the London radio. The movement had also published an allegation that in November 1941 the Marshal had dismissed Weygand under duress and had been compelled to send a cordial message to the French volunteers fighting in the Légion Antibolchévique on the Eastern Front. A recent circular issued by the Compagnons had attempted to draw distinctions, far-reaching in their implications, on the duty of obedience, maintaining that as *subjects* men should obey the government, even 'although it may not be free', but that when conscience dictated otherwise, rebellion was legitimate. Tournemire retorted that he had recently published a statement making clear his own political neutrality. Bonnard then attacked him, but from a different viewpoint: three of the six 'écoles des cadres' run by the movement, he alleged, had been closed as redundant: why had this shortfall not induced the Compagnons to wind themselves up? The tussle between Bonnard and Tournemire was renewed after Bonnard had become minister of education.

Massis, who had been appointed a member of the commission of the Conseil National dealing with the new constitution, was requested to state whether any part of the draft document dealt with youth. He could only quote a general clause which ran: 'The State directs the spiritual upbringing of the nation. It recognises the eternal truth and the great moral certainties . . . it protects them.'[43] Father Forestier, the scouts' chaplain-general, extolled the virtues of scouting[44] and was supported by François, commissioner of the (secular) Éclaireurs de France, who volunteered the surprising statistic that 60 per cent of his scoutmasters were primary teachers.[45] De La Porte du Theil put forward a similar figure for the Chantiers de la Jeunesse: two out of three primary teachers called up for service eventually were appointed leaders.[46] Luc, the ministry's director of technical education, reported on progress in vocational training: in 1941 321 youth centres under his aegis had given accelerated training courses to 30,644 youngsters.[47] Borotra summed up the efforts he had made in sport and physical education.[48] By the time the hearings were over the commission had a very complete picture of Vichy's efforts for young people.

The main argument that went on in the commission was an organizational one. Despite Pétain's opening remarks, the question of a 'jeunesse unique' was raised. Bonnard, without directly contradicting the Marshal, asked rhetorically how best young people could be politically integrated into the State[49] and hinted that this could best be done through a single movement. Pelorson obviously shared this view. Roy, secretary of the Fédération des Métaux, and Bergery were even blunter, wanting a 'mouvement unique' functioning in both zones.[50] Bergery attacked any idea that the Church could provide the basis for a single movement. The fact that most of the centres for unemployed youth that existed in the northern zone were run by Catholic 'patronages' was a potential cause of anticlericalism. He felt that the Compagnons also were unsuitable as a nucleus for a national movement. Yet he considered that one sole youth movement enjoying a monopoly was essential to realize that egalitarian, classless Socialism that already prevailed in Germany and which was also the ultimate solution for France. This was harking back to the declaration made on July 10, 1940 by Bergery in the National Assembly, and backed by Déat, Scapini, and Vallat, among others, advocating a 'new order' which would be authoritarian, national, and social and not based upon social class.[51] Bergery, who inclined more to Déat's RNP, also took the opportunity to attack Doriot, whose periodical, *Jeunesse,* which circulated mainly in the occupied zone, was receiving a subsidy, he claimed, of 80,000F a month from Vichy funds. Needing 250,000F a month in all, it milked the rest of what it needed from the Secours National, or, since the publication had a 'clearly Hitlerian conception', from German sources. Having condemned the three types of existing youth movements – confessional, official, and political – , Bergery nevertheless compromised by saying that since Pétain had set his face against a 'jeunesse unique' he would settle for *compulsory* membership of any *one* organization.

Valentin, director of the Légion des Combattants, proposed a solution in which the Légion would institute a compulsory *residual* youth movement for the 85 per cent of young people who did not already belong to one.[52] He admitted that in departments where groups of 'Jeunesses Légionnaires' had been started the experiment had not worked, but pointed to Algeria, where 20,000, the majority of young French people living there, had been enrolled as 'cadets' and cadettes' of the Légion. Valentin's suggestion was of course impracticable because the Légion was also a forbidden movement in the occupied zone.

Other voices in the commission were raised against both a single movement and compulsion. Pastor Boegner, defending confessional movements generally, disclaimed any intention on the part of the Church to 'take over' all young people. He added ecumenically that if anticlericalism did exist this 'does not arise in any way from the action of the French hierarchy, which moreover is itself anticlerical', a well-worn cliché of the day which, according to the official account, was greeted with 'smiles'.[53] Reverting to the question of social class, Carcopino thought that a fusion of social classes was possible already through the scouts, the Compagnons, compulsory rural service, as well as through sport.[54] Mgr Beaussart, who clearly felt once more that the Church was on the defensive, admitted that the Catholic youth movements of ACJF operated according to a class system: the Jeunesse Ouvrière Chrétienne and the Jeunesse Étudiante Chrétienne, for example, functioned in different worlds, but this was a social reality that had to be recognized.[55] Although the Chantiers de la Jeunesse was a compulsory movement, albeit only for young men of a certain age, General de La Porte du Theil came out in favour of pluralism and voluntarism. Support was also given by Le Cour Grandmaison and Pernot, who as a member of the Comité consultatif de la Famille française, saw a 'jeunesse unique' as encroaching on parental rights.[56]

There was, however, unanimity that movements should

have a strongly national character. Massis argued that they could express a common purpose through their courses in civics. To encourage social mixing de La Porte du Theil wanted exchanges between the cadres of the various youth movements and between these and other institutions such as the schools, the Army, the colonial service, and the professions. General Verneau, representing the war ministry, was enthusiastic about this proposal: it is apparent that there was a strong military interest in the way in which youth should be organized.[57]

Dorgères, leader of the Corporation Paysanne, put forward a very different form of organization, proposing that young people should be grouped by occupation.[58] In the Corporation the 'jeunesses corporatives paysannes' already included 60 per cent of all young agricultural workers and they were allowed to function freely in both zones. In one year 1,500 youth leaders had been trained. The committees of the various agricultural 'syndicats' within the Corporation each included one youth representative. Such a corporative system had not only the great advantage of representing a worker through his occupation, but also whole families, since, if the father joined, all his dependants automatically became members. Bergery objected to Dorgères's proposal on the grounds that within movements organized by occupation social-class structures would be perpetuated.[59] Dorgères did concede that the occupational approach might give rise to new forms of the class struggle, such as rivalry between young agricultural and industrial workers.

Another problem debated by the commission was how far youth should be permitted to undertake political action. Dorgères favoured such involvement because, he somewhat unexpectedly declared, 'The collapse of the German armies will perhaps pose tomorrow formidable problems of internal order.'[60] Pucheu, Bergery, and Roy were also in favour of youth being involved in this way. François-Poncet wanted action to be limited to the rather innocuous rural civic service, as did Pastor Boegner, although he did admit that an élite might need to assume a more positive political role. Mgr Beaussart remained non-commital, but Pernot thought that incitement to political action might be imprudent. De La

Porte du Theil shared this view, arguing the immaturity of youth: the end result might be to produce 'bully-boys' ('bagarreurs'), such as happened before the war.[61] The shocking history later of the Milice, who were drawn considerably from the ranks of the young, was to prove the general's point.

In its final session the commission formulated ten recommendations, which formed the basis upon which Pétain's 'cabinet' eventually made a summary of the proceedings.[62] This résumé confirmed that the principle of a 'jeunesse unie', but not 'unique', had been agreed, although some uniformity should be arrived at through leaders undergoing a similar training. The plurality of movements should reflect 'les grands courants de la pensée française'. The question of the grouping of youth by occupation was left for Pétain to decide. Although the commission had set its face against a single movement, it was noted that Bergery, Roy, and Bonnard hoped that one day complete unification would be possible. The summary commented that the Marshal condemned any organization that might rekindle class rivalries, but was equally against any totalitarian movement that might be set up to remove class barriers. Youth might be grouped by occupation for compulsory vocational training but moral, civic, and social education could be left to youth movements to which they also belonged. The principle of some form of compulsory civic service was accepted. The commission believed that if agricultural assistance, as given in the 'service civique rural' proved a success, it might one day lead to 'cohorts mobilised in the service of the Révolution Nationale'. Gidel, the summary solemnly records with a touch of bathos, was willing for his students to be put to farm work, but insisted that they be adequately shod!

The summary notes that the two main 'leadership schools' came in for criticism. Uriage was charged with lack of positive political direction, with fostering extreme individualism, and promoting 'a democratic spirit contrary to the Principles of the Community'. La Chapelle-en-Serval was accused of being 'much more oriented to immediate political propaganda and subject to totalitarian influences'. Both schools needed a unified teaching doctrine, which should be embodied in a 'leadership manual' based on Pétain's messages and writings. Since the upbringing of the young was a co-operative effort shared by the family, the school, Church, youth and vocational organizations, as well as other 'spiritual communities' of the nation, over-all responsibility should be entrusted to a single ministry for education, youth, sport, and the family. (A later document excluded the family from such a massive administrative machine.)

The youth commission of the Conseil National cannot be dismissed as a mere propaganda exercise – the complete record of its deliberations was never published and the contemporary press contained only fragments of what was discussed. Its proceedings give a valuable insight into the way that youth was faring after twenty months of the new regime. More generally, it also illustrates that the Vichy phenomenon was never homogeneous and consistent, but always fluctuating and riven by internal dissensions. The commission included the sincere and the misguided, as well as the hypocritical who sought personal advantage. The various – incompatible – strands of political thinking – socialism, totalitarianism, egalitarianism, nationalism, and traditionalism, but not liberal democracy – are unsuccessfully woven together. On the one hand there is an attempt to install Fascism or worse, on the other a striving to preserve the time-honoured and Christian values. The report shows how a polarization was occurring, separating those who wanted to enmesh youth in a Nazi-style ideology from the more moderate. At the same time it reveals that the mobilization of youth in the Révolution Nationale had been a failure.[63] It must have been evident to more perceptive men like Carcopino that pipe-dreams for the future must await the peace. That peace, it was becoming increasingly clear, would not necessarily be a German one. Thus so-called practical projects such as 'doctrinal' handbooks for youth leaders were derisory. Against the background of an imminent intensification of the war, grandiose plans for the future of French youth, who in any case had not been consulted, were patently unrealizable.

Part II

Morality, Culture, and National Identity

Chapter VI

'Moral Reformation'

How greatly did France stand in need of moral regeneration in 1940? Posed in the context of Nazi and Fascist excesses the question is derisory. Yet one of the strangest phenomena of the period immediately after the defeat was the imperative felt by many Frenchmen to beat their breast and condemn their generation root and branch. As the war continued, however, a reaction set in. Some began to question the good faith of Vichy in its advocacy of moral change, arguing that a reform aimed at youth was merely a step towards the instauration of a totalitarian regime. The Resistance always suspected such a moral reformation of the young, for the very reason that the idea had caught hold of France when the Germans were seemingly victorious. Others such as Mounier and the Personalists, Salièges, Archbishop of Toulouse, and certain Catholic youth groups shared a reluctance to do penance, although in general the hierarchy improved the shining hour, urging the mass of Frenchmen to acknowledge their sinfulness. Yet, to read some fulminations of the Establishment, there is no doubt that a few, however misguided, were sincere. Administrators were prominent among them. Typical is one outburst by Pelletier, prefect of the Somme, opening a new Law School of Picardy at Amiens in November 1941.[1] France had been beaten, he declared,

> because it was insufficiently prepared; because for twenty years material values had prevailed over moral ones; because easy profit had become the rule and effort the exception; because detestable politics and its train of lies had penetrated everywhere; because authority had grown feeble and those who exercised it were often the most unworthy to do so; because the legislative power overflowed into the executive sphere; because liberty had meant licence and excluded needful discipline; because the word equality had lost all meaning in the face of the privileges that had grown up; because the word fraternity went uncomfortably with ever-increasing divisions; because the dissolvent of internationalism, of which communism was the most detestable form, sapped

the nation's foundations; because, in a word, one could no longer think French; because, finally, we had no leader.

And the prefect concluded this harangue before the assembled students by adjuring them to follow Pétain 'without discussion' and citing the by now ritual injunction that 'the young . . . must learn again how to obey and how to discipline themselves'.

Such severity of language was common at the time. Was this a case of the fathers visiting their sins upon the children? Pétain and Weygand, at any rate, did not hesitate to draw up an indictment against a whole nation. The octogenarian head of state condemned an individualism which was 'at the origin of the evils through which we almost perished'.[2] Weygand stigmatized 'the spirit of pleasure and permissiveness' ('facilité').[3] Lamirand followed his master's voice; in Paris in 1941 he spelt out what was expected of youth: 'Young people . . . it is in the name of the Marshal that I come among you; I come to bring you his instructions. The time is no longer one for mincing matters, the time is for orders, the time is one for leaders to command and troops to obey. What I bring to you are orders. The language in which I shall address you will be that of the Leader ['Chef'], a stern language.'[4] Lesser lights took their cue from above. The army followed its commanders. A certain Colonel du J——— 'contributed', as he put it, to the study of youth problems by preparing a paper for Pétain[5] in which he castigated the physical and moral slovenliness of youth; students affected Bohemian ways, working-class youth lacked manners; in both idealism was lacking, authority scorned; self-respect, energy, enthusiasm, and initiative were singularly absent; young people were beset by lassitude. Educationists joined in the chorus, with local academy inspectors lecturing the young. Thus in 1940, opening the new school year at Grenoble, the inspector accused youth of being 'too free', too infected with 'the spirit of fraud, cheating and the art of 'fixing things' ('système D'); henceforth – the litany recurs – the first lesson must be obedience, the second, service. Other contemporary moralizers, with the Church well to the fore, damned pre-war youth as egotistic and debauched. Peyrade, whose frequent sermonizing of the youth was a feature of *La Croix*, wrote, in a 'langue musclée' the flavour of which can only be conveyed in French, a homily for New Year's Day, 1941 on 'The Search for Effort':[6]

L'époque de moindre effort est révolue. Nous ne voulons plus voir traîner dans les rues de nos villes des jeunes gens aux démarches alanguies, aux tenues mollement débraillées, au langage tristement vulgaire. Nous ne pouvons plus supporter ces petits crevés dont l'unique ambition était de se lever tard, de s'asseoir au café, de céder à tous les désirs troublés et de se coucher tard, satisfaits d'une journée creuse. Un romancier de l'immoralité, qui, nous l'espérons bien, n'aura plus de lecteurs, en leur apprenant que "tout plaisir est bon à prendre", les mettait sur la voie des défaites. Le pays, pour être sauvé, a besoin d'hommes audacieux et réalisateurs. Notre jeunesse a l'ambition de les lui préparer. Rien ne s'obtient que par l'effort.

(The era of least effort is over. We no longer desire to see hanging about our city streets young men sloppy in their bearing, slack and slovenly in their behaviour, sadly vulgar in their talk. We can no longer suffer those young fops whose sole ambition was to rise late, install themselves in a cafe, allow free rein to their confused desires and take themselves off to bed late, content with their empty day. A novelist of immorality, who, we hope, will no longer have any readers, set them on the road to defeat by teaching them that "every pleasure was good to be taken". Our country, to be saved, needs bold men capable of achieving something. Our youth aspires to train them for her. Nothing is obtained without effort.)

The reference to Gide is significant. Already on July 9, 1940 *Le Temps* had led the attack in an article entitled 'Jeunesse de France'. Gide's *Le Traité de Narcisse* and *L'Immoraliste* came in for special condemnation. An entry by Gide in his *Journal* (July 16, 1940) shows how he reacted to the charge that he had been the exemplar for a whole 'regrettable school, moulding an arrogant and decadent generation'. Both the works mentioned, he pointed out, had been written before 1914 and yet their readers, young and old, had fought bravely in the First World War. Therefore, he concluded, his influence had been exaggerated.[7] Other detractors nevertheless kept up the attack. The Protestant René Gillouin, Pétain's educational advisor in the early days, reproached his lapsed co-religionist for having portrayed the family as a social prison.[8] Guéhenno, a fellow-writer and also a *lycée* teacher, noted in his diary (April 19, 1941) how his pupils wrote essays lauding Proust and Gide, 'those masters almost entirely turned in upon themselves, so weak, so feminine, so vain'.[9] Gide's detractors accused him of advocating freedom from all intellectual, moral, and religious constraints. Thus when Gide planned to lecture at Nice in May 1941 on the Belgian poet, Henri Michaux, another artist whose work might be represented as a flight from reality, he was rebuked by the local section of the Légion des Combattants, led by Darnand:

> It is scarcely acceptable at a time when the Marshal wishes to foster in French youth the spirit of sacrifice to see step on to the lecture platform one of the men who has made himself the triumphant champion of the spirit of pleasure. . . The refrains of Nathanael must have weighed as heavily in the balance as many political intrigues. So we ask you, M. Gide, to let Nathanael be forgotten, him and all his family. . .[10]

Gide cancelled his lecture. About this time he may well have been reflecting on his own moral position, for he also, like Baudouin, had thumbed through Renan's *Réforme intellectuelle et morale.*

Even French exiles in London spoke of the need for reform: Raymond Aron described the teaching of patriotism as a subject sadly neglected in the schools of the Third Republic. For Vichy, youth was an alibi for the unsuccessful past, along with schoolteachers, Jews, freemasons, and foreigners. But for Frenchmen everywhere youth was, paradoxically, also the hope of the future.

What form should re-education take? Déat urged totalitarian indoctrination, aping Nazi methods. Among the writers, Brasillach also postulated an 'obligatory ideology'.[11] Other collaborationist intellectuals, such as Chateaubriant and the poet Bazan, recommended the German example. Sicard considered that 'French youth must be brought back, by every means and by force if necessary, to the elementary forces which make up our country: land, blood and race.'[12] Maurice Bardèche wanted youth to be cast in a heroic mould, but with a taste for brutality,[13] a Spartan rather than an Athenian ideal. This went too far for Maurrassians, as Massis was to make clear after the war: 'It was against a certain ideology for youth, however, that was adopted immediately after the disaster by the pro-Hitlerites and collaborationists, it was against that mystique, merely copied from the Hitler

Youth, against which we had first to revolt. We had not to become barbarians again, but to find ourselves once more.'[14] Others, however, saw this return to barbarism as the way of salvation. Henry de Montherlant conceived the German victory as the defeat of Christianity. In his collection of essays, *Le Solstice de juin,* published in October 1941 and at first banned by the Germans in their zone, he wrote: 'The victory of the solar wheel [the swastika] is not only the victory of the sun, of paganism. It is the victory of the solar principle, which is that *everything moves on* [the wheel comes full circle]. Today I see the triumph of the principle in which I am steeped, which I have sung and which I feel governs my life.' This principle, one of power and energy, was closely linked to Nazism. It was connected with manliness, whereas Christianity was a 'female' religion, which Europe must break with for a long time. About youth, like many others, Montherlant pontificates: young people, oblivious that Vichy is exploiting them for its own ends, revel in the vulgar, the sensational, and the over-sentimental, whereas virility should be their ideal.[15] Such a view of Christianity plainly clashes with that of those who saw the German onslaught on the Soviet Union as a latter-day crusade, as did many Catholics and otherwise lukewarm Christians. Bonnard, perhaps speaking with tongue in cheek, commended the anti-Bolshevik exhibition in Paris to teachers as an opportunity 'to inspire in their pupils respect for Christian civilization', and to hold up the Soviet Union as 'a striking example of the spectacle of the aberrations and suffering into which a country that despises moral values may be dragged'.[16] At least none of the differing advocates of moral regeneration wanted youth to remain neutral. In this they were right: circumstances eventually imposed the necessity of choice where ideological arguments failed to convince.

Few of these self-appointed mentors of moral reformation exonerated youth from blame for the national plight. Yet many ordinary people must have thought as did the obscure industrialist, chairman of an association for vocational education in the Rhône, who spoke to pupils at a prizegiving in July 1941: 'I shall not speak of our misfortunes. You know them and are not responsible for them. It is not your generation which took as its slogan, "Don't worry", that foolish motto which has done us so much harm. . .' He continued, making the obligatory obeisance to Pétain: 'In the storm the captain on the bridge is better placed than the passengers to decide,' but went on to quote Fichte, lecturing to his Berlin students after Jena:

To allow a nation that has fallen to raise itself up again, the education of a new youth is the sole remedy. . . We have been beaten. Do you wish us to be despised as well? It is up to us to decide. The armed struggle is over, but just as soon as we wish there will begin a new struggle for principles, morals and character. A faithful devotion to our country, the love of duty, public and private virtues, this is the image that we must show today to those who occupy our country, so that the memory of it will remain with them when they depart.[17]

Few there were who spoke so positively to youth during the Occupation.

Instead the rather uninspiring formula of 'Work, Family and Country' was trotted out on every conceivable occasion. In *Là Croix* Peyrade prissily epitomized the censorious attitude towards the young:

Il ne s'agit plus d'être spirituel, léger, libertin, railleur, sceptique et folâtre, en voilà assez. . . Dieu, la nature, le travail, le mariage, l'amour, l'enfant – tout cela est sérieux, très sérieux, et se dresse devant toi.

(No longer must there be question of being witty, light, libertine, mocking, sceptical, and whimsical – that's enough. . . God, nature, work, marriage, love, children – all that is serious, very serious, and looms ahead of you.[18]

Service and obedience became obsessions. Chevalier urged youth to follow the Carthusian monks in practising the latter virtue. A practical way to inculcate the necessary discipline, he believed, was to have pupils move around the school in military fashion, a strange reversion to Napoleonic practice. Obedience was necessary, said one critic, because 'the Frenchman is a facile person, inclined to talk big and to mock, an undisciplined carper, inclined to jib'.[19] Such attitudes were appealing to the military, who saw in service and devotion to duty the highest ideal. 'Never look to your personal interest', enjoined General de La Porte du Theil. Youth must be encouraged to accept responsibility; those called to lead must have a strong taste for action, danger, and boldness, rather than be satisfied with an office desk (*Le Temps*, April 30, 1942). In different ways men such as Borotra and Dunoyer de Segonzac were in deadly earnest in seeking to inculcate the public and private virtues. Against the hypocrisy of some must be opposed the moral seriousness of others who rallied at the beginning to the Vichy regime.

Postulating an almost Carlylean view of history, the cult was for heroes. The special niche accorded to Pétain has already been considered; those accorded to Joan of Arc and Péguy will be considered later. *La Croix* (January 26–7, 1941) proposed as examples other patriots: Saint Louis, Bayard ('le chevalier sans peur et sans reproche'), Turenne, Montcalm, de Foucauld, the Catholic missionary and explorer, and de Bournazal, the French officer-hero of Morocco. In the State youth movements groups called themselves after such men. One notes the sprinkling of military warriors and pre-Revolutionary figures, the lack of 'Republican' heroes. A lunatic fringe carried the cult to extremes. The Atlantis movement, as it was known, sought to revive for youth the medieval ideals of chivalry – not those of the Teutonic knights –, to create a new 'European élite'. The vogue was for military valour. As early as 1934 Pétain had urged all children to learn about the battle of the Marne, which for him was '*gloire* in all that is most noble, most virile, most brilliant, most pure'.[20] Alas, in 1940 there had been no miracle of the Marne.

Christianity, or at the least belief in Christian values, was held to lie at the root of moral teaching. Chevalier had tried to promote the one, Carcopino the other. Even Maurras fell into line: 'The moral question is a religious one. That's the great truth,' he declared.[21] But such teaching yielded little lasting result. In 1946 the headmaster of one of the largest schools in France commented unfavourably on its ethos, contrasting it with that of English schools.[22] During the Occupation, however, *Le Temps* had not such a high esteem for what went on across the Channel. Pondering on how professional ethics could be instilled into future lawyers, doctors and teachers, it attacked a proposal originating in the university at Lyons that there should be a special mark for moral and civic sense, tartly remarking that the idea smacked too much of English universities, and that England had not been too successful![23]

Any new constitution, according to Massis, would refer to the State's role in national spiritual and moral training.[24] The youth commission of the Conseil National had wanted a systematic programme in this respect.[25] In the event, responsibility should be shared: the family was to be the principal moral educator, but the State had a duty to protect the young from moral danger. It was in this protective role that Vichy justified its control of the media.

The press, books, radio, and cinema were alleged in the past to have played a significant part in undermining morals. Crouzet had insisted on the bad example that society had set for youth since 'the spectacle of the desire for unrestrained pleasure. . . [was] a living denial of moral teaching'.[26] Between the wars, some asserted, literary success had often been founded on 'pure pornography' and 'unhealthy literature' had deliberately been placed before the young.[27] Maurras, almost exactly Gide's contemporary, even warned against the Romantics, to whom should be preferred Mistral and classical writers.[28] Literary works of the eighteenth century came in for special obloquy. One mother wrote to Pétain complaining that her daughter, a student, was obliged to study the most licentious works of the Enlightenment – Voltaire's *Contes,* Rousseau's *La Nouvelle Héloïse,* even Laclos's *Les Liaisons dangereuses;* why not, she asked despairingly, Blum's infamous treatise on marriage?[29]

From literature to children's comics, nothing escaped the propagandists for a new 'moral order'. In 1939 an astounding total of three million copies of children's comics were sold weekly, at a time when the total child population (aged 5–14) was only five million. During the Occupation the number of titles available steadily diminished until in the occupied zone none was left. *La Croix* especially criticized comics which dealt with kidnapping, or retailed adventures devoid of any moral lesson. The Transatlantic provenance of the comic made it suspect. One writer was heartened that Marion, minister of information, had decided to 'clean up' in September 1941 and finished his article on a triumphant note, '*Tarzan, Jumbo* and *Aventures* are suspended from today.'[30]

He must therefore have been somewhat upset when, in January 1943, a new and different kind of comic, *Le Téméraire,* was launched for children. Its hero, Marc le Téméraire, is an exemplary collaborationist, helping the police to track down 'terrorists' and eventually going off to fight on the Eastern Front. The comic strips (*sic*) showed scenes of Jews torturing and butchering children; the accompanying text extolled the superiority of the Aryan race.[31] This 'journal de la jeunesse moderne', as it styled itself, had its own club, 'Le Cercle des Téméraires', modelled on the lines of the Hitler Youth, at whose meetings Nazi films were shown. With an initial print run of 100,000 copies the comic clearly had German backing and typified the new morality with a vengeance.

If 'moral reformation' could be encompassed by propaganda the most effective instrument would be the film show, since it became easily the most popular form of wartime entertainment. The number of admissions to the cinema rose from 224.8 millions a year in 1941 to 245 millions in 1944.[32] Perhaps 3½ million adults and 1½ million young people visited the 4,000 cinemas of France once a week. This huge attendance was not looked upon favourably in all quarters. Mgr Beaussart, charged with looking after Catholic educational interests, condemned the cinema for its 'vulgarity'.[33] Another critic, labelling it 'the night school of the simple', commented that since in the past the film villain had triumphed too often, this reversal of values may have contributed to the moral breakdown of France.[34] Films, however, remained a prime attraction for the young: they satisfied a desire to escape from harsh reality, fostered a feeling of solidarity because in the cinema they were with their own generation, and were even attractive because of the warmth of the auditorium.

The Germans used the screen skilfully as a medium of their own propaganda. Already in 1940 they showed to audiences still stunned by their military might a series of news-reels on the blitzkrieg in Poland. Three German films in particular, all dubbed in French, enjoyed very long 'first runs' in Paris and were screened in the large provincial cities. In September 1941 they put on in Paris *President*

Kruger, an epic of Boer resistance to their hated English oppressors, which incidentally depicted an alcoholic, withered Queen Victoria emptying a whisky bottle hidden behind her throne. It was followed by *Jude Süss*, a violently anti-Semitic film, which played to packed houses, although in some southern cities it was hissed by students. (When this occurred, as it sometimes did during the showing of German news-reels, the house lights were turned up and vigilante squads kept watch.) The third film was *Hitlerjunge Quex*, made in 1933 but first shown in Paris in March 1942. This panegyric of Nazi youth was particularly taken up by collaborationist organizations for showing to young Frenchmen. The Légion des Volontaires Français contre le Bolchévisme screened it at Christmas as a treat for the children of prisoners of war; the Rassemblement National Populaire showed it to 1,000 young people at Orleans; Costantini's Ligue Française put it on at Dijon, exhorting its youth to follow the example of the Hitler Youth.[35]

The Vichy ministry of information also used films extensively, its products sometimes going beyond propaganda for the Révolution Nationale to verge on out-and-out collaborationism.[36] This markedly pro-German stance may be attributed to the character of those responsible for Vichy 'information'. The first head, Paul Marion, ex-Communist, ex-Doriotist, had turned to Fascism in 1939. He was succeeded in 1944 by Philippe Henriot, who, from being a right-wing Catholic before the war (when he had been prominent in advocating aid to confessional schools) turned to collaborationism because of his hatred of Communism. The themes of the films financed by the ministry are therefore predictable. Thus *Français, vous avez la mémoire courte* (1942) presented a picture of the growth of Communism against a background of forty years of French history but went beyond this to approve of Hitler's pre-war struggles with the Marxists. The film was shown to parties of schoolchildren at the exhibition, 'Le Bolchévisme contre l'Europe'. In *Forces occultes* (1943) the alleged role of freemasonry, in particular of the Grand Orient, in provoking the declaration of war in 1939 was depicted. A third target was the Jews. After Pearl Harbor *La Libre Amérique* (1942) set out to demonstrate how Jews manipulated the leading strings of American policy. Later in the year, after Jews in the occupied zone had been obliged to wear the Star of David, there appeared *Le Péril juif* and *Les Corrupteurs*, both extremely anti-Semitic and showing Jews as the corrupters of the young. The latter film showed how American movies, made by Jews, led a young Frenchman into crime; how a young girl, at the insistence of a Jewish film producer, was forced into prostitution; and how Jewish bankers brought about the ruin of many modest 'rentiers'. Other 'thèmes d'actualité' screened included a view of the soldierly life led by the LVF in the German-occupied territories of the East ('Fort Cambronne': *sic*) and the delights enjoyed by young Frenchmen working in German (*Travailleurs de France*). In addition the ministry produced a number of cartoons, some heavily ironic in tone, such as the series featuring 'Monsieur Girouette', whose views change like a weathercock with Gaullist and Communist propaganda, and in 'Nimbus libéré', where the notorious professor, listening in to the BBC, is rejoicing in the Allied victories when an Allied bomb falls upon his house. Such productions show how far collaborationists had penetrated the Vichy propaganda services, which had special sections for youth and even infiltrated the Chantiers de la Jeunesse.

On the whole French commercial film-makers contented themselves with turning out 'escapist' productions or ones that mildly extolled the virtues of Pétain's France, with occasional excursions into moralizing which were not always felicitous. The first of such films, Marcel Pagnol's *La Fille du puisatier* was made in 1940 but not screened until 1941. As an example of how films were vetted by interested bodies, the following appraisal of the film by the very Catholic Association du Cinéma Familial is quoted: 'Principal elements: *good:* patriotism, perseverance in work, the bearing of adversity, faithfulness to friends and fiancée, filial devotion; *bad*: seduction, an illegitimate birth presented as normal. Good triumphs over evil despite the seduction scene, which is taken very far. Coarse dialogues ('dialogues gaulois'). Note the appeal of Marshal Pétain for unity.'[37] At the Liberation the film was apparently reissued, but with Pétain's Armistice appeal of 1940 replaced by de Gaulle's call to continue the struggle! Another very popular film was *Le Corbeau.* The title is the pseudonym used by an anonymous letter-writer to denounce the scandals of a small provincial town. This caused the Gestapo to intervene, because by implication the film denounced 'poison-pen' missives, at a time when such denunciation procedures were much appreciated by that arm of repression. From time to time a film might be interpreted as obliquely lauding Nazism. In *L'Éternel Retour* Jean Marais is depicted as the young, dominating, fair-haired, Aryan type, supported by a no less flaxen-haired and Germanic-looking Madeleine Sologne, in a modern version of the Tristan and Isolde legend. After the war, when the film was shown in London, English critics wrote that 'Jean Marais, with the fair hair of an avenging angel and in jackboots more resembles a Wagnerian hero or an S.S. man than a medieval knight.' Other films lauded the Révolution Nationale: *Le Voile bleu* tells the story of a widow who devotes her life entirely to the education of those young people who are destined to become the future élites. *La Nuit merveilleuse,* so admired by Pétain that he requested it be shown him at Christmas, recounts a modern version of the birth in a stable, with the three wise men represented by a student, a sailor, and a Senegalese.

Occasionally, however, the audience read allusions to the Resistance into films. In *Pontcarral, colonel d'Empire* (1942) an ex-officer of Napoleon replies proudly to a judge: 'Sous un tel régime, monsieur, c'est un honneur que d'être condamné.' In the last reel the Army of Africa is shown marching off with band playing and colours flying, a scene which brought the audience to its feet, applauding wildly. *L'Assassinat du Père Noel* features a beautiful girl (France?) who dreams of the Prince Charming (de Gaulle?) who will one day awaken her. In *Les Visiteurs du soir* (1942) the Devil scourges Anne, turned into a statue but still a living creature: is this the symbol of Hitler's fruitless struggle against a France that continues to resist him?[38] Some thought so at the time.

Remonstrances preaching collaboration, homilies laced with moralizing, covert references to freedom: there is no way of assessing how much the 220 full-length and 400 short films, some of them superb technical productions, produced in France during the Occupation influenced their most assiduous audience, the young. From personal conversation after the Liberation, the present writer believes that Zarah Leander, the singer who supplanted Marlene Dietrich in popular favour, or Marika Rökk, the dancer, impressed young Frenchmen more than any overt or covert propaganda on celluloid. In any case towards the end young men stayed away from the cinema, where they were too easy a target for German raids searching for recruits for forced labour. From April 1942 the Germans established themselves as sole censors in their own zone and even banned the Catholic practice of publishing locally weekly lists of films that the Church recommended or prohibited its flock from seeing.[39] Altogether nothing regarding the cinema escaped the vigilance of those two mentors of youthful morals, Vichy gerontocracy and Nazi nihilism.

If the most faithful audience of the cinema was the young, probably only the young intellectuals and students among them frequented the theatre during the Occupation. No detailed analysis can be attempted here, but young theatregoers must have found it difficult to interpret any contemporary message they gleaned from plays. Anouilh's *Antigone* may be construed as an apologia for the Resistance or as a defence of collaboration, although it is arguable that the heroine wins at least a moral victory over Créon, whose collaboration may be ascribed to reasons of State. Sartre's *Huis Clos*, with its slogan, 'Hell is other people', may be viewed either as a story of a 'ménage à trois' or, at a loftier level, as an indictment of Fascism. On the other hand, his *Les Mouches* is more clearly a reaction against the 'mea-culpism' of the times. Occasionally youth may have applauded 'mots' that the playwright may (or may not) have intended, such as the celebrated line in Montherlant's *La Reine morte*, 'En prison se trouve la fleur du royaume.' They may have been impressed – if they took the trouble to see the play – by the great hopes expressed as to the future of youth in Simmer and Bertheau's *Le Grand Rayon* (1942). They would certainly have recognized their younger brothers in Roger Ferdinand's *Les J-3*, a group of older *lycée* pupils more anxious to trade in cigarettes and silk stockings than to get down to the study of philosophy. In 1942, according to Le Boterf,[40] they applauded heartily when, in 'La Rabouilleuse' the chorus sang the refrain of 'Veillons au salut de l'Empire':

> Si le despotisme conspire
> Vengeons la France et ses lois,
> Liberté! Liberté!

Young people were bidden to follow Pétain's example and lead an upright life. Yet sexual vice and the disease that flowed from it were widespread: the wartime casualties of promiscuity threatened to rival those of the battlefield. The Church's reaction was to redouble its measures of prudishness. Even the otherwise liberal Archbishop Salièges insisted that sport – and fashion as well – required strict supervision, lest 'the way lie open for nudity' and all that implied.[41] The Church forbade mixed sports meetings. Gerlier even banned all mixed gatherings of young people, adding avuncularly, 'If we [the hierarchy] ask for a few sacrifices, they must be accepted with a good heart.'[42] The Archbishop of Auch thought it useful to lay down strict rules for any theatrical performances: a show should be divided into two parts, the one for boys, the other for girls. Males should vacate the backstage area before females were allowed in to change; the sketches presented must be morally irreproachable; where boys played girls' parts (and vice versa) this must be done 'with delicacy'.[43] The Church recommended that social gatherings should be single-sex, and not even bring together young men and children. According to the Bishop of Viviers, where Catholic and secular organizations met jointly, as sometimes occurred, the same rules of segregation must apply 'for co-operation does not mean promiscuity', said the bishop, using the word precisely.[44]

Concern at sexual immorality came as well from other quarters. Professors warned young men against succumbing to 'unhealthy temptations' that led to venereal disease as well as to tuberculosis, that other scourge of wartime France. Young women were exhorted to seek out healthy husbands, 'for the future of the race', a precept half-way towards the teaching of 'Rassenkunde'.[45] Such entreaties were linked to the population problem. Bertier, of the well-known private school, the École des Roches, advocated scrupulous sexual conduct but strongly urged young people to have children, for one should never forget that 'the innumerable army of empty cradles prepared the way to defeat'.[46] Bonnard himself waxed eloquent in his own impeccable prose about the relationship that should exist between the sexes. In a message to youth organizations for Joan of Arc Day, 1942, he rose to lyrical heights. Joan, he declared, was respected by her rude soldiery. Likewise, 'Young men of a reinvigorated France, you must always show respect for girls, who are the new springtime of France.' Their former promiscuity must be abjured, as they began to share with girls

> une camaraderie franche et gaie, sans pruderie et sans équivoque, qui exclut toute familiarité interlope et qui ne permet d'autre amour que celui qui unira loyalement des époux.

> (a frank and cheerful comradeship, neither prudish nor equivocal, which excludes any ambiguous familiarity, allowing only the kind of love that will unite faithfully husband and wife.)[47]

It was in these terms that the misogynist bachelor preached the moral rules beyond his power to follow.

Doubtless youth reacted with mixed feelings to such lofty sentiments. Bonnard dispatched a circular on the same subject to the schools, designed for teachers only, but whose gist was to be conveyed to pupils. A teacher who was a close acquaintance of Bonnard informed the minister that he had nevertheless read out the complete text to his class of fifteen-year-olds. Some of the pupils were delighted, others taken aback by the uncompromising nature of the message. As for the rest, 'enraged despondency but apprehension of the remaining third, poisoned by the English radio, by parents, friends and teachers, although not one had dared to protest. Meanwhile the first group clapped a round of applause, which I interrupted merely to say, "Is it not French? Is it not frank?".'[48] Girls came in for a particular kind of homilies: they were urged not to 'give way' to their boy-friends before the latter left for forced labour in Germany. Whether such abundant moralizing on sexual matters was heeded is difficult to say. The evidence would seem to point to its having little effect. On October 4, 1941 the prefect of the Nord reported that in the department there were 65,000 young unemployed who were 'demoralized'. The boys engaged in homosexual practices, the girls in clandestine prostitution. A special VD service for girls aged between 14–16 had had to be set up in Lille. On New Year's Day, 1941, at Hazebrouck 61 girls were pregnant by German soldiers; at Estaires there were 81. On December 26, 1941 the prefect of the Charente-Maritime reported that young girls were conducting themselves shamelessly with German troops and that 'un sérieux redressement est à faire'.[49] But the situation was probably no better and no worse than elsewhere among the fighting nations.

One outlet for enjoyment was denied young Frenchmen. Dancing, particularly upon Sundays, had been the rage among young people before the war, but after the Occupation was banned both by Vichy and the Germans. The Germans were wary because such gatherings of young people might cause unrest. Vichy had other reasons: dancing was held to be indecorous when so many Frenchmen had been killed or were languishing in prisoner-of-war camps; it would encourage fraternization with German soldiers; it might promote promiscuity. In any case, 'le bal' was associated with the dissolute, pleasure-seeking Third Republic. Nevertheless, in early 1942 the prohibition began to be flouted. Cardinal Gerlier noted with regret that even some Christian families were infringing the ban, which he deplored because 'among all the different forms of recreation, dancing is the one that expresses joy most fully'. There was too much misery abroad and, he added in a reference to the Germans, it was wrong 'to dance under the gaze of those who observe us'.[50]

Those ever-present 'observers' had lifted the ban in the occupied zone for their own troops by mid-1941 but had left the decision regarding French civilians to the Vichy authorities for 'if [they], in spite of the disgraceful defeat of their country, wish to dance, it is in the German interest not to prevent their so doing'.[51] Since Vichy continued the prohibition, many private dancing schools, which were allowed, sprang up to circumvent the ban. Learning ballet and ballroom dancing was suddenly found to be a very popular activity. Measures were therefore taken to control the schools by imposing stringent conditions: not more than fifteen couples per session were allowed to take part; enrolments had to be for at least five sessions; apart from the dancers, only parents could be present; the sole musical accompaniment must be a piano or a gramophone; no drinks whatsoever could be served; advertising of classes was forbidden.[52]

The high fees demanded by the schools limited their clientele and frequently they were patronized by middle-class 'zazous', the contemporary equivalent of the 'teddy-boys' and their partners. Descriptions of this gilded youth vary. Simone de Beauvoir terms them rebels against the Révolution Nationale, wearing long hair 'à la mode d'Oxford' (*sic*), sporting umbrellas (which Chamberlain had brought into vogue in France), and generally comporting themselves in an anarchic, Anglophile fashion.[53] But a character in the best novel of the Occupation, Jean Dutourd's *Au bon beurre*, condemns them more succinctly as 'snotty-nosed brats'.[54] They affected an outlandish garb: the young men wore dirty drape suits with 'drainpipe' trousers under their sheepskin-lined jackets and brilliantined liberally their long hair, the girls favoured roll-collar sweaters with short skirts and wooden platform shoes, sported dark glasses with big lenses, put on heavy make-up, and went bareheaded to show off their dyed hair, set off by a lock of a different hue. The 'zazous' used English expressions, read American literature, and delighted in crooning, in the style of Johnny Hess, 'Je suis swing, dadoudadou/ Dadou la. . .oua. . .oua.'[55]

Jazz presented a problem to the 'purs et durs' of the Révolution Nationale. Attempts were made to give this 'judéo-négro-américain' music a respectable European pedigree. Not that this worried French youth overmuch. In Paris young people flocked to the big cinemas such as the Normandie and the Moulin-Rouge to hear the latest 'combos' perform before the main film. The 'Swing-Swing-Club-Breton' (*sic*) of Nantes demanded that Radio-Paris broadcast jazz in which the traditional Breton 'bombarde' replaced the clarinet, an original kind of regionalism. Django Reinhardt, king of French jazz during the Occupation, installed at Pigalle, competed for popularity among young people with Pétain.[56]

The Marshal himself preferred to preside over music of a more traditional kind, accompanied by the ballet dancing of Serge Lifar.

But the 'ploutocrato-zazous', the exponents of jazz, were not held in esteem by the extreme collaborationists. Vauquelin, of the Jeunesses Populaires Françaises, held them to be 'the victory of democratic besottedness and Jewish degeneracy . . . the product of twenty years of Anglo-Saxon snobbery on the part of decadents . . . the proof . . . of the physical and moral degradation of a section of our young people'. Vauquelin's squads of bully-boys were ordered to 'get them'.[57] Thus on June 14, 1942 the squads carried out raids at Neuilly, in the Quartier Latin, and on the Champs-Élysées, cropping the hair of any 'zazous' they could find.[58] The police joined in the hunt as well.

Youth will none the less be served. Thus, as the war dragged on, the ban on dancing was increasingly disregarded and the 'bals clandestins' flourished.[59] In the countryside the Jeunesse Agricole Chrétienne reported in 1943 that dancing was going on in almost every canton of the Rhône, not only in isolated barns and remote houses, but even in the small towns.[60] In Paris students danced in bars off the Boul' Mich' and 'la jeunesse dorée' in more sleazy establishments near the Étoile. Dancing, jazz, outlandish dress became marks of a veritable counter-culture of youth, one which differed from that of the Resistance because it was effete, but nevertheless anti-killjoy, anti-prudish, and, in the final analysis, pro-Allied.

The 'new order' also sought regeneration by instilling in youth the virtues of honesty and probity. General de La Porte du Theil confessed that he had been deeply shocked by the lack of backbone shown by the army in 1940, which was for him symptomatic of 'the dreadful decadence of France'.[61] In the Chantiers de la Jeunesse he was deeply distressed to find that untruthfulness persisted: men wrote home complaining that their rations were insufficient, at a time when their food was better than that of the civilian population, in order to receive parcels from home. They gave any pretext to get leave. The good general urged their comrades to send such liars to Coventry.[62] And at a lower level dishonesty was also rife. Pétain was deeply concerned at the cheating that went on in schools. Broadcasting in 1941 at the beginning of the school year[63] he commended the 'Leagues of Fairness' ('ligues de loyauté') started in some schools as part of 'the struggle against cribbing'. His message was reinforced by a poster campaign.[64] At the same time the semi-political pupil movement, Les Jeunes du Maréchal, made one of its aims the revival in schools of a sense of honour.[65] Somewhat paradoxically, one of its chosen means was the encouragement, akin to the practice in nineteenth-century Jesuit colleges, of 'sneaking' on class-mates. This habit of talebearing was relatively innocuous until it was enlarged to reporting on anti-German or anti-Vichy activities.[66] But even outside school such denunciation was encouraged. In a periodical for countryfolk André Bettencourt, writing a column for young people, declared: 'The young in every village must be the agents of the Marshal. I would willingly call them the police of the Révolution [Nationale]. It is perhaps a sad thing to ask youth to undertake this inquisitorial task...' but 'When it is necessary to accuse someone for the general good, no friendship must enter into it. There is one's duty: denunciation . . . Don't let's compromise with the devil!'[67]

Such misplaced efforts to install an 'honour code' were naturally doomed to failure in a situation where cheating and lying in order to hoodwink the Germans had almost become a patriotic duty. Some critics of contemporary morals regarded such conduct as merely the continuation of pre-war practices. The *Cahiers d'Uriage,* emanating from an institution whose head, Dunoyer de Segonzac, had at least the saving grace of sincerity in advocating the old-fashioned virtues, noted despondently in 1942: 'In the former France everybody cheated: the schoolboy copied in the baccalaureate, the butcher deceived by giving short weight, the citizen diddled the tax man; recent efforts do not seem to have changed this state of affairs.'[68] Certainly the campaign for honesty in the schools was notoriously unsuccessful. The headmaster of a Marseilles school with some 2,300 pupils admitted in 1941 that cheating, forging signatures, and truancy went on unabated despite all 'the admonitions to the young'.[69] In 1942–3 seven cases of cribbing in examinations were detected in the Bouches-du-Rhône, 'despite the message of the Marshal to the schoolchildren of France'.[70] (Jeanneret asserted that children cheated because syllabuses were too encyclopedic and over-factual.[71]) The most glaring scandal occurred in 1942 when baccalaureate questions were 'leaked' and openly hawked in Paris, Marseilles, Toulouse, and Dijon.[72] One commentator wryly remarked that there would have been no takers if parents had not provided their children with the wherewithal to buy the questions.[73] In 1944 an indignant Admiral Platon, the ex-minister for the colonies, reported to Bonnard the name of a primary teacher at Bergerac who had helped a candidate for the *lycée* in the examination room, writing to the minister, 'A minor matter . . . but great is its value as a symptom of the general rottenness and power to corrupt of a notable section of the teaching profession.'[74] This preoccupation in high places with trivialities is perhaps the most extraordinary facet of the matter. As for youth, it could be argued that it had seen through the hypocrisy of its elders, forced to prevaricate in order to exist: war brings its own moral devaluations, which schools are powerless to check.

Not unexpectedly, petty crime of all kinds flourished among the young. The special causes of juvenile delinquency are easy to identify: the abdication of conventional morality among adults; the lack of schooling, or truancy from school; the absence of the father, detained as a prisoner or working in Germany.[75] Undernourishment, which was at its worst among the ten to fourteen age group, and the desire for easy money led to youngsters trading on the black market. This encouraged wrongdoing. At Lille children pillaged coal wharfs and food warehouses, so much so that in 1944, after the schools were partially closed, the municipality urged that they should be reopened to keep pupils out of mischief.[76] Criminality was not restricted to the poor; Pétain singled out for special condemnation middle-class traffickers who attended the *lycée*.[77] In Monaco, rationed as in France, schoolgirls of the bourgeoisie carried on a thriving trade in bread tickets.[78] A pupil of the Lycée Janson de Sailly, located in a select area of Paris, used his ingenuity by collecting silver teaspoons from a nearby café and selling them to a film company, which needed silver to process its films.[79] There were, as one contemporary observer sardonically noted, four categories of youth: the 'zazous', the indifferent, the 'engagés' – whether for the Révolution Nationale or for de Gaulle – and '. . . those very well brought up young people who contented themselves with operating on the black market, along with their excellent parents'.[80] Although the poor traded in goods from sheer necessity, others also did so to enliven the boredom of a rather drab existence. The most adept pupils dealt in tobacco, chocolate, alcohol, and soap. Schoolgirls of fourteen exchanged for lipstick the vitamin biscuits they had received free in school. One Marseilles pupil of fourteen, when ordered to turn out his pockets, was found to have on him ten thousand francs. On one occasion a whole class was made to disgorge: the total sum in cash amounted to 300,000F. Marcel Aymé, in his novel, *Le Chemin des écoliers,* puts the income of his sixteen-year-old hero, Antoine Michaud, at 30,000F a month, 'earned' on the black market whilst he is preparing for the baccalaureate; on this he keeps a mistress.[81] The satire may not have been too overdrawn. Some young men who had just left school also found themselves earning very high wages working for the Todt Organization. Legitimate or illegitimate, such high earnings led easily to crime among young people.

The war bred psychological disturbances on the grand scale. Children in their early teens would appropriate bicycles, lamps, and rucksacks and run away from home so as 'to live like the Maquis'. They lived on thefts from abandoned buildings. In any case, towards the end, when an atmosphere almost of civil war prevailed, youngsters, taking their example from their elders, thought it no crime to commit acts of violence and banditry. The zoning of the country contributed to 'le vagabondage' – youngsters wandering aimlessly far from home. In 1944 in Paris alone 654 minors were brought before the courts as having no fixed abode; many of the girls had become street-walkers. The steepest rise in crime occurred in the big cities. Already in the second half of 1940 the juvenile court of the Seine had convicted double the number of offenders it had done a year earlier.[82] By late

1941 more than half the thefts in Beauvais were committed by young people under twenty.[83] At Lyons by March 1942 juvenile delinquency had more than quadrupled since 1939.[84] By far the commonest offence for both boys and girls was theft: in Paris in 1944 69 per cent of all minors were convicted for this offence.

The following table shows the national incidence of juvenile delinquency for selected years, for minors aged between 8–18.[85]

	1938	1940	1941	1942	1943	1944	1945
No of delinquents convicted	13,310	15,933	30,912	34,775	30,362	22,404	17,530
Percentage of girls convicted	13.0	16.8	16.2	17.6	17.3	19.9	16.8
Delinquency-rate per 1000	1.94	2.38	4.66	5.31	4.68	3.51	2.79

In a longer time series, making allowance for the size of the age cohort and with the index of 1913 = 100, the coefficient of progression in the development of juvenile delinquency for the years 1938–45 is:

(1913 = 100)

1938	1940	1941	1942	1943	1944	1945
111	140	302	333	289	178	119

The figurès far exceed those for the First World War. They take no account of the much greater number brought before the courts but not formally convicted. In any case the juvenile delinquency-rate shows only the tip of the iceberg. Henri Wallon, the eminent psychologist associated with the post-war Langevin–Wallon Plan for educational reform, estimated that perhaps two million children suffered some form of psychological damage because of the war.

Vichy was well aware of the problem at the time. To its credit, the regime realized the promise nevertheless of a minister of justice in 1937 that there would be no more children's prisons.[86] A law of June 27, 1942 substituted the concept of re-education for the idea of repressive punishment. The old 'colonies pénitentiaires' had already been renamed 'instituts d'éducation surveillée'. Regional associations for the protection of young people were set up, first under the control of Admiral Platon and then under Dr

Grasset, minister of the family and health. Training schools were set up to produce new personnel to look after new centres which young men such as Georges Bessis, later deported, pioneered at Ker-Goat in Brittany.[87] For a while cadres of the Compagnons de France took over the staffing of the young prisoners' wing at Lyons prison. Another law of July 22, 1942 instituted children's courts and the concept of probation ('liberte surveillée'). It decreed that children under thirteen were not legally responsible for their actions to any court.[88] Although these humane measures could only be partially implemented because of wartime conditions they laid the basis for post-war reform.

The basic question remains: how far did the moral doctrines of the Révolution Nationale therefore succeed in winning even the nominal allegiance of the young? The success of the various youth movements will be considered elsewhere, although it must be remembered that these did not touch the lives of more than one young person in six at the most. Those who became delinquent represent the failures of Vichy policy. So, in a very different sense, do those who turned to the Resistance. At the other extreme, the minority who opted for collaboration rejected what they considered the milk-and-water pabulum served up as 'moral renewal'. Vauquelin urged his Jeunesses Populaires to be tough and violent, affecting dash and haughtiness of manner: 'We must know how to strike. It matters little if we are hated; let us be content at the outset if a small number like us and the remainder fear us.'[89] Such language was hardly moral or in accordance with the spirit of national unity that Pétain desired. The Révolution Nationale, once its initial impact had been blunted by the continuance of the war, evoked no high level of commitment among the young, not even among those who adhered to the new State or Catholic youth movements, which from the summer of 1942 progressively distanced themselves from Vichy and all its works.

Belief in the possibility of a successful, Vichy-inspired 'moral renaissance' had begun to decline much earlier. More intelligent young people had seen through the farcical nature of such a revival. Micheline Bood, an adolescent schoolgirl, wrote in her diary for February 18, 1941: Nothing has changed, in spite of the so-called "moral revival". The same things are done as before, only they are done more hypocritically.' A month later she added: 'God, how fed up I am with school and the Révolution Nationale.'[90] In early 1942 prefects were reporting that bourgeois youth had not felt the impact of the defeat and did not realize the plight in which France found itself. Working-class youth, at first hit by unemployment, had suffered more from the situation but displayed no inclination to help: 'Filled with bitterness and rancour, youth gives way to the need to forget its sorrows, which is unfortunately only too understandable.' Thus wrote Carles, the prefect of the Nord department, adding that school-children, for ever truanting off to the cinema or dipping their fingers into café tills, followed their elder brothers in lacking any moral sense.[91] Even those young men who lived in the southern zone and had not suffered the rigours of the German occupation were apathetic. In August 1942 a local branch of the association of ex-members of the Chantiers de la Jeunesse characterized young men as '. . . of an unimaginable inertia. No guts. Don't care about politics. What they want is the return of dancing and apéritifs, and above all no military service or service in the Chantiers.'[92] Youth was gripped in the dreariness of wartime. There were few occasions for jollity; even at Christmas and New Year public festivities were held to be unseemly.

A year after the Liberation a school headmaster testified to the immediate post-war mood of the young people in his care:[93]

> I wrote in 1945: Politeness is out of fashion and even if the majority know the rules it is hardly practised. Since the hot weather began appearance is, to say the least, neglected. Minds are scarcely interested in solving problems or formulating thoughts, but are too often employed in escaping from the constraints that any rule imposes. The older boys think of dancing or the cinema. They may recognise the value and necessity of rules, but nonetheless try to evade them. I feel that there is no free consent to discipline, but a spirit of total independence as soon as their personality develops. Efforts are made only because of tests and competitive examinations and not at all because of education or culture, interest in which is only minimal. I fear that all this is merely the manifestation of a mentality in the family which, at table or in private conversation, continually emphasises the disorder in society and the ease with which money can be made when one has a little

> know-how (which can be acquired anywhere but in the classroom).
> Many years must pass before there can be a remedy for this sickness, which springs from wars that have upset the minds of parents and children; [there must be] a long period of peace and firm discipline, whether the latter is freely accepted or not.

This is eloquent testimony to the failure of Vichy's moral revival, the causes of which were both social and individual. If youth learnt morality better by example than by precept, with a few distinguished exceptions example among the Vichy leaders was singularly lacking. If war could sometimes engender great courage and devotion among the young – as indeed it did not infrequently in wartime France – it also bred less desirable qualities. Instinctively young people felt that in appealing to them to mend their ways, their elders were seeking to foist the blame of defeat in part upon the wrong shoulders. In any case they surmised correctly that Vichy, and all its works and 'doctrines', were ephemeral and thus dismissed them.

Chapter VII

'General Education', Sport and Health

Historically physical education in France has had national and military overtones and been linked to anti-German and even pro-English sentiments.[1] After 1870 the cry was raised that Frenchmen had gone soft and flabby and for a while gymnastics became a cult. Voices were raised advocating that physical training and games be introduced into the *lycée* curriculum, particularly soccer and rugby, in order to balance intellectual 'over-pressure' ('le surménage'). The English public school had long been held up as an example by those educationists who recalled Montalembert's assertion that Waterloo had been won on the playing fields of Eton. Thus by 1900 four periods of the school week had been allocated to physical education, although under the Third Republic lack of facilities made this largely a 'paper reform'. Baron Coubertin, founder of the modern Olympic games and a noted Anglophile, had favoured the physical hardening of youth. This went hand in hand with military training, so much so that even in the pacifist 1930s amateur rifle clubs attracted government subsidies. Thus it was to be expected that in 1940 the Germans viewed renewed French interest in sport and the outdoor life as a threat, particularly since it was the very instrument that they themselves had used to foster national sentiment and military prowess, the indispensable ingredients of revanchism. Nor can there be any doubt that some of those at Vichy who were enthusiastic for sport and games had revenge in mind.

After the defeat it was fashionable to say that schooling in the past had been too bookish, the emphasis being on 'instruction' rather than 'education' more broadly conceived. To remedy this, 'general education' was introduced, a portmanteau term which included the familiar Vichy ingredients of civic, social, and moral education, but also artistic activities, physical training, and games. 'General education' as a principle was adopted at all levels of the education system and in youth movements. The wider concept of education that evolved, which included a component of physical well-being, survived the regime, perhaps more as a principle than because of its being implemented.

Bertier, headmaster of the private École des Roches, modelled on the English public school, had rallied to the new regime. He deplored the fact that before the war at school prizegivings the winners of sports awards would be greeted with derision.[2] Even so, in the 1930s attitudes towards sport had been changing. Interest had been growing among a wider public, although it was reflected more in spectatorship than in participation. Money had been spent more on building stadiums than on setting up sports facilities for more people to use. In 1939 France possessed only 400 swimming-pools and 100 cycling-tracks.[3]

Vichy policies for sport and leisure were in many respects a continuation of those begun by the Front Populaire. In 1936 Blum had appointed three under-secretaries of state, under the ministry of health, one for physical education, one for the protection of children, and one for the organization of sport and leisure. The last post, destined to become the most important, was held by Léo Lagrange, the Socialist deputy for the Nord, in every respect an exceptional politician, who became in fact, if not in name, the first 'minister of leisure'. The legislation regarding the 'congés payés', two weeks' paid holiday for every worker each year, gave him his chance. For the first time the working class were able to get to know their own country: cheap travel, reduced hotel prices in the Alps and on the Riviera, camping provision, and many other recreational facilities were made available. In 1937 Lagrange arranged for 200,000 children to spend a holiday in the 'colonies de vacances'. The aim was to show that a democratic society could offer leisure and sports facilities every bit as good as those of totalitarian societies such as Nazi Germany, with its 'Kraft durch Freude' organization.

When the Chautemps administration replaced Blum in June 1937, Jean Zay, with Lagrange's agreement, took his department under the wing of the ministry of education. For ten months the two worked harmoniously together.

Lagrange believed that sport should be open to all Frenchmen, and not just to an élite, an idea also shared later by Borotra. Thus Lagrange set up for schools a Brevet Sportif Populaire, which in 1937 was successfully taken by some 400,000 youngsters. This comprised simple tests of physical fitness and was eventually integrated with the primary-school leaving-certificate. Vichy's Brevet Sportif National – a mere change of adjective – was an imitation, without acknowledgement, of Lagrange's innovation. With Zay's support Lagrange also strengthened the organization of sport in the armed forces, set up an Office du Sport Universitaire, and created a Comité Interministériel des Loisirs to promote leisure activities of all kinds. A Comité National des Fédérations Sportives was entrusted with the task of applying the principles laid down by a Conseil Supérieur des Sports. Youth hostelling was encouraged: between June and December 1936 the number of hostels was more than doubled, reaching 500. Meanwhile, in his 1938 reforms Jean Zay had attempted to introduce into schools a daily half-hour of physical education and had envisaged setting up regional physical-training institutes for teachers.[4] Some effort had been made to provide equipment and Zay claimed that by 1939 sports facilities were available in twenty-nine departments.[5] The war had halted further progress. During the war also it was a great loss to politics when Lagrange, a strong patriot as well as a committed Socialist, was killed, the only minister to die in battle. Vichy was perhaps embarrassed to acknowledge its debt to him because, with Blum, he had been accused, as one of the architects of the social measures of the Popular Front, of promoting that 'espirit de jouissance et de facilité' that the exponents of the Révolution Nationale so roundly condemned. The Church's attitude was similar: Cardinal Gerlier declared, 'Whilst our neighbours were working we were dreaming up how to organize our leisure.'[6]

Within three days of Pétain being granted full powers Borotra had been appointed to his new post in charge of physical education and sport in the ministry of family and youth run by Ybarnégaray. In the autumn the new department had been transferred to the ministry of education and he had assumed responsibility for 'general education', physical education and sport in schools. This did not please some educational administrators, who did not welcome the intervention of the world ex-tennis champion. But Borotra took up where Lagrange had left off. He drew a direct connection between physical fitness and the defeat. He pointed out that in Germany the proportion of medically unfit conscripts had fallen from 25 per cent in 1913 to 17 per cent in 1938, whereas in France over the same period it had risen from 25 to 33 per cent. Fitness flourished in Germany because it possessed 50,000 sports-fields and 20,000 of its schools had facilities for sports, whereas in France opportunities were abysmally limited.[7]

Borotra's sincerity and single-mindedness were beyond question. The man chosen to revitalize French sport, politically to the right, had an impeccable record of patriotism. Characterized by contemporaries as 'elegant and gentlemanly',[8] 'bold, passionate and charming',[9] he was then in his early forties. A graduate of the Polytechnique, a veteran of both World Wars, a petroleum engineer by profession, he cherished his amateur status in sport. Not surprisingly, his appointment was not welcomed by the Germans nor the Germanophiles. The collaborationist RNP accused him of having been a fanatically proclerical member of de la Rocque's Parti Social Français and also of being a 'determined Gaullist'.[10] That he was not at all reconciled to the defeat was certain. Carcopino, with whom Borotra had mostly to deal during his term of appointment, says bluntly that the sports champion cherished hopes of military revenge.[11] The Germans watched closely to see whether the Commissariat Général for sport would take on a military character. Nor were their forebodings disappointed. In early 1941 they discovered with dismay that twelve out of the thirty-four inspectors and sports delegates for the occupied zone were ex-regular officers. (From the professions given of the others it may also be deduced that these were also at least reserve officers.)[12] De Brinon was forthwith ordered to report monthly to the Germans on the Commissariat's activities and to list the postings of its top personnel, with details of their former employment. The Occupation authorities feared that Borotra's frequent appearances at sports rallies round the country might provide the occasion for Gaullist demonstrations,[13] so much so that they obstructed his movement by holding up his travel permits and even by quartering troops in the stadiums themselves.

Meanwhile the German Embassy set about collecting evidence of the Commissioner's anti-German sentiments. They quickly concluded that he was 'england- und judenfreundlich'. They wrongly alleged that he was married to an Englishwoman, the daughter of an Austrian Jew, and that his sister had married an Englishman suspected of working for the British Secret Service. They noted that before the war Borotra had served on the committee of the influential Association France–Grande Bretagne.[14] Despite this, they could not find a pretext for ousting him until Laval returned to power in 1942, when he was accused of making a speech in which he had alluded to 'the resumption of the struggle' ('la reprise du combat').[15] Borotra resigned with reluctance, declaring, 'It will be the honour of my life to have been the first head of this organisation.'[16] Having enjoined loyalty to his successor, Col. Pascot, who had served under him,[17] he retired into relative obscurity. In November 1942 he attempted to escape to North Africa – in 1940 already he had been within a hair's breadth of fleeing to join de Gaulle in London – but was caught and deported to Germany. The fact that he survived the war at all may be because his former tennis partner, the King of Sweden, let it be known to the Germans that he was interested in Borotra's fate.[18] If de Gaulle represents one way in which Frenchmen in 1940 interpreted duty and honour, Borotra represents another, equally worthy of esteem.

For a while it became fashionable in France to speak of 'renewal' through physical education, with which some – not Borotra – associated the rather un-French concept of race.[19] Pétain and Weygand had stressed before the war the need for physical fitness.[20] It was a theme to which the Marshal constantly returned. Sport would give back not only health, but also courage and discipline. General de La Porte du Theil, as head of the Chantiers de la Jeunesse, backed up the Marshal.[21] For him, physical culture and manliness went together. An outdoor life, where both at work and play the body was exposed to the elements, elevated man spiritually. The bearing of discomfort was part of the hardening process: the general spoke approvingly of 'the harsh discipline of cold water'.[22] Games were the instrument to strengthen the moral fibre of youth, particularly, in the view of the general, if they were of a kind that necessitated reflection as well as physical prowess. Swimming was good, life-saving exercises were even better. Through team sports the young would learn the virtue of co-operation and the sacrifice of self, for individualism was a cardinal sin for the Vichy moralists. Sport was a schooling of the will, one that fostered group loyalties and broke down class barriers. Such ideas of masculinity, competitiveness, the conquest of difficulty, and the subordination of self to others are in an educational tradition that dates back at least to Rousseau and had been encouraged by nineteenth-century public-school headmasters. In Germany, before the Nazis came, Kurt Hahn was their protagonist. In Vichy France they found intellectual backing through Alexis Carrel, whose research institute was financed by the new regime to investigate the connections between biology and psychology and whose book, *Man the Unknown,* although dating from 1935, was later to win international acclaim. 'Plus est en vous' might not have been an unacceptable motto for the times, but ideas were exaggerated and perverted to wrong ends. To ascribe to sport, as Pascot, Borotra's successor did, the inculcation of such virtues as the ideal of service to the community, for example, was extravagant and counter-productive.[23] Some at Vichy regarded the sports arena as a convenient device to distract the young from politics, as a latter-day 'panem et circenses'. Certainly for the youngster who had a taste for games and the outdoor life the regime offered exciting opportunities. But in the latter years of the Occupation sport was subtly associated by collaborationists with Nazi ideals. Bonnard, speaking at the Sorbonne on the fiftieth anniversary of the modern Olympic games, referred to the Berlin meeting of 1936, linking sporting and military prowess and invoking the memory of those fallen in Russia fighting for the new 'European order'.

In 1940 Borotra, however, set about his task in a different spirit, perhaps basing his ideas of physical fitness on the

Germans, but drawing his inspiration from the English for character-building. The Commissioner believed that the academic subjects in school must go hand in hand with 'the disciplines of action': sport, handicraft, musical, and eurhythmic activities. Sport could be used as a means of regeneration, provided that it was practised rather than merely watched, and some proficiency could be attained by everybody. Borotra saw the logical consequence of this as amateurism, so that as many as possible could compete. The former amateur player at Wimbledon also shunned professionalism because it was associated with financial gain, whereas sport should be 'chivalrous and disinterested'.[24] He declared that 'shamateurism' ('l'amateurisme marron') was 'the principal cause of the moral weakness noted in recent years in some sporting circles and of the disrepute into which certain sports had fallen'.[25] Thus over a period of three years he aimed to phase out most professionalism in sport. Temporarily professional boxing and pelota would continue; in cycling only 300 licensed professionals would be allowed to race; in football, only twenty-two teams allowed to play.[26]

Meanwhile young people had to be motivated to take up sport. The Brevet National Sportif, instituted in 1941, was a great success, like its predecessor, Lagrange's Brevet Sportif Populaire. In the first year there were over 94,000 candidates for the qualification in the Paris academy alone, although, disappointingly, only 28 per cent were girls.[27] Only youngsters who had passed the diploma were allowed to compete at sports rallies.[28] At such contests an 'Athlete's Oath' was sworn. The first such ceremony took place at a mass gymnastic display in Paris in 1941 at the Parc des Princes, when the contestants made a solemn pledge: 'I promise on my honour to practise sport disinterestedly, with discipline and fairness, so as to become a better person and to serve my country better.'[29] Similar ceremonies were held yearly in each department and thousands of youngsters swore the oath before the local prefect. Sometimes the grand march that preceded the competition[30] gave rise to comparisons with Nazi youth rallies, although Borotra had in mind the Greek rather than the Nazi ideal. Another innovation was the introduction of a series of tests to be taken as part of school examinations. In the baccalaureate such tests, which ranged from running to weight-lifting, remained optional, although those that passed them received bonus points. In 1941 already half of all candidates took the tests.[31] In 1942 a compulsory test was reintroduced into the primary leaving-certificate. Such examinations in physical education survived the war.

Another significant innovation into schools was 'general education'. In schools by 1941,[32] in universities by a year later, a wide range of relevant activities had got under way. In primary education, apart from PE and games, which theoretically accounted for five hours a week, there was also an hour of choral singing and half an hour of practical hygiene and first aid, as well as moral and civic education. Carcopino commended the measures as an instrument for training 'robust and well-balanced men'.[33] 'General education' was conceived of as the remedy for the state of France. That condition was summed up by Col. Pascot: 'The France of 1939 was an unhealthy France, physically weary and exhausted.' The collapse had been 'above all a physical defeat': 'we have been – and we still are every day – beaten in our bodies.'[34]

A massive training programme for cadres and teachers of 'general education' was started, but here Borotra encountered a set-back. He wanted 10,000 cadres to train the teachers. The appeal went out for volunteers, particularly, it was stressed, if they had had experience of *English* education.[35] On the eve of his dismissal, however, Borotra had succeeded in recruiting only 2,000 cadres. He had nevertheless established two national and fifteen regional training centres, which, in their first full year of operation, took in, on short courses, 20,000 out of some 140,000 primary teachers. In secondary schools specialist teachers were appointed, although other teachers had also to be pressed in to help. For the first time what today would be called a system of 'pastoral care' was introduced into French schools. Class teachers taught civics, organized social-service activities, co-ordinated school work, and liaised with parents and school medical officers.[36] By 1944 3,000 teachers of 'general education' were functioning in secondary schools, as well as ninety in higher education. Although results can only be described as mediocre, this emphasis on character-building and physical well-being, in addition to intellectual training, marked a change in educational attitudes.

Such an effort required an organization commensurate to the task. The Commissariat Général quickly took on its own ethos, which had strong military overtones. As with some of the new youth service and movements, the Commissariat was seen as a cover for evading the Armistice terms by employing Army officers on what was clearly obliquely related to military service. Borotra was himself a reserve officer. His successor, Col. Pascot, claimed later that the war ministry connived with Borotra in recruiting him (Pascot) and a fellow colonel, Maisonneuve, into key posts, and other officers into subordinate posts.[37] The military presence made it easy to reorganize sport in the hierarchical and authoritarian style advocated in youth matters. The control exerted by the Commissariat was nevertheless indirect. Like a single youth movement, the idea of a single sports body was also rejected. But steps were taken to eliminate sports organizations too closely associated with the Republican regime. This entailed the abolition of the Ligue de l'Enseignement, which had run flourishing sports sections for young people, and the Fédération sportive et gymnique du Travail. The Church managed to frustrate the attempt to dissolve its popular Fédération Sportive Catholique.[38] Like other national advisory bodies, the Conseil Supérieur de l'Éducation Physique was dissolved, but replaced by a revitalized national sports committee. At local level advisory committees on 'general' and physical education were set up, whose members had to be vetted as politically acceptable. Correspondents were appointed in every commune to oversee all sporting activities, right down to the humble 'boule'.[39]

A law of December 20, 1940, which became known as the 'Sports Charter', grouped all sports clubs into federations, one for each of the main sports. It was only after vetting that clubs were allowed to declare themselves as associations under the 1901 law. Prefects instigated enquiries into the past record of officials and mayors had to certify that the clubs were non-political[40] – although this stipulation had also been written into the statutes of many pre-war clubs. The national sports committee (Comité National des Sports) acted as an 'umbrella' for the federations, forty-four of which existed by 1943, comprising some 30,000 sports clubs with three million members. A rump of about 3,000 similar bodies, such as the Catholic Union des Patronages, whose purpose was of course only partly sporting, remained outside the federations.

The Germans showed their dislike for this flurry of organization by holding up publication of the Sports Charter in the *Journal officiel* for three months after Pétain had signed it.[41] Furthermore, they insisted on approving the statutes of all sports clubs in the occupied zone. Occasionally, however, they acted with incredible naivety. Thus in the free zone they tolerated the continuance of rifle clubs,[42] which in the past had been used for pre-military training, and did not stop the use of all large-bore guns until 1942.[43] Some clubs, 3,500 of which still nominally existed in 1945, were under the misapprehension that they functioned under the terms of a circular dating from 1930 and submitted applications for official approval to the French military authorities,[44] which in turn used them, as it did also the Scouts and the Légion des Combattants, as sources for recruitment to the small standing force the Germans still permitted the French.[45] The Germans did not even ban gliding until December 1942. In 1941 the SGJ had convened a meeting of all aeronautical clubs in the free zone in order to inform them about 'the possibilities opened up by non-powered flight to train sporting . . . young people'.[46] A Centre Supérieur de Vol was set up at the Montagne Noire, near Toulouse. By 1942 an organization had been established, from national down to local level, to put on courses in gliding. Some enthusiasts were even keen to make glider construction and training part of school activities.[47]

To provide general sporting facilities was a most urgent task. After threatening resignation if he did not get his way,[48] in 1940 Borotra obtained a massive credit of 1,900 million francs, of which 1,580 millions were earmarked for capital expenditure.[49] Playing-fields, swimming-pools, and sports centres should be set up, he maintained, in every commune, for the general use of the population as well as for schoolchildren. Subsidies could be granted.[50] Even in 1943, when shortages were much more acute, credits to the tune of 838 million francs were still being allocated for 'general education' and sport.[51]

Since prime responsibility fell upon the communes the first step was to convince local mayors and their councils that such facilities were needed. The ministry of the interior sent out a suitably dramatic circular:

> The essential condition for a lasting and profound revival of our country is the reform of the education of young Frenchmen. This reform will consist essentially in making it possible for young people to participate in outdoor exercise, as well as intellectual activities, to strengthen their bodies and their character... With this aim in view a field of physical training and games must be made available for every school.[52]

Communes agreeing to provide facilities would receive a land grant of 60 per cent of the cost, and be reimbursed 80 per cent of the expense of converting it into a small sports complex. The matter was deemed so urgent in 1940 that communes were exhorted not to wait until credits had been authorized, but to start work immediately. Pupils, working under the supervision of an engineer, might even help provide some of the manual labour.

In some areas what followed was worthy of Clochemerle. Some mayors espoused sport with enthusiasm, seeing the provision of facilities as something of a status symbol for their commune.[53] But in many villages resistance was encountered. The attitudes displayed not only reveal something of life in Vichy France but also how officials, parents, and teachers conceived of schooling. Primary-school inspectors reported that teachers feared the hostile reaction of parents if sports programmes were implemented, since they thought schools were not the places for gymnastics, but for hard intellectual slog. Female teachers declared their total incapacity to supervise games in any shape or form.[54] Rural communes complained that their children had enough exercise already: they walked long distances to school, worked in the fields when lessons were over, and played enough games on Thursdays and Sundays. What more exercise did they need? The mayor of Bersac (Hautes-Alpes) wrote to the prefect: 'Thirteen pupils walk roughly three kilometres to get to school. Then because of the bread shortage, many go home at eleven to eat, which means twice there and back, some ten to twelve kilometres. To force these children now to play games will mean that they get even more tired.'[55] The mayor of Saléon reported that the commune had not any use for a sports-field: at present there were only three pupils in the school, two over eleven and one aged six; soon only one would be left.[56] Mayors of communes in mountainous regions injected a note of realism into the proposals: 'What's the use of buying a lot of land covered with snow and therefore unusable for most of the months of the school year?' In any case, land near the school was often the best agricultural tillage, far too valuable to be used for sport. One commune built on rocky ground proposed an alternative: 'We thought about buying a ball and adapting the school playground, although it is only small (6 metres by 8 metres, roughly), as an export field [*sic:* 'terrain d'export', for: 'terrain de sport'].'[57] Another mayor suggested that it would be nonsensical to provide facilities for the seven different schools in the commune, each located in a different hamlet.[58] Another commune merely forwarded the minutes of the council meeting, which read: 'The council esteems it unnecessary for these pupils to be pestered by physical education.' (The last phrase had been underlined in blue pencil at the prefecture.)[59] Such a point-blank refusal represented the true feelings of many local worthies. Many rural communes were hostile: the prefect of the Landes reported in December 1941 that only thirty-nine out of 229 communes had bothered to apply for a sports subsidy.[60] Parents protested that in any case children had neither the appropriate clothes nor footwear for games.[61] The most compliant communes were those where Vichy had deposed the elected representatives and appointed a 'délégation' to take their place.

A cogent argument against sport was the sheer expense. A modest sports installation would cost 126,000F,[62] of which a small commune would have to find 25,000F, the remainder being met by a government subsidy. More ambitious installations comprised a running-track, an obstacle course, volley- and basketball-pitches, changing-rooms and showers, and could accommodate up to fifty pupils at a time. From the Vosges, a war-devastated area, the prefect reported bluntly that the population favoured houses more than sports facilities.[63] In any case, as the war continued, sports equipment became less easily obtainable. There was an air of cloud-cuckoo-land about the whole scheme and the Paris collaborationists, taking their cue from the Germans, derided it.

Col. 'Jep' Pascot, Borotra's successor, who had been appointed on April 18, 1942, nevertheless persisted. He was very much an independent spirit, so much so that he refused to reply to any letters addressed to him that were not signed personally by the minister of education: he did not deal with subordinates.[64] Already responsible for 'general education' and sports – a task which brought more than one brush with the academic authorities – he also allocated sports subsidies to the various youth organizations and clubs that had been recognized, which gave him considerable powers of patronage. As a former rugby-international scrum-half, he was particularly fanatical about games. He did not prove so rigorous regarding amateurism as had been his predecessor, allowing greater freedom to professional boxing and cycling. But he insisted that the professionals should compete only at week-ends and spend the time otherwise in training the young.[65] Flying in the face of the medical advice and despite the severer food rationing, he opposed the cut-back in time devoted to sport in schools. He complained when he took over that in some cases the time allocation had been reduced to two hours a week, a situation worse than the time allotted in any programmes prescribed since 1902.[66] In his view, food shortages meant that children needed more open-air exercise, not less. His other ideas were sometimes just as bizarre. When the Germans began to round up young men at sports meetings for forced labour in Germany he protested in wounded terms: 'We have made of the stadium the place for national meetings imbued with the spirit of the community. By the ceremony of the Athlete's Oath we have endowed it with a sacred character.' Therefore, he concluded, for the Germans to raid it would be as sacrilegious as raiding a church![67]

Following a sports policy that can only be described as one

of 'caporalisation',[68] Pascot came near to imposing the monolithic organization earlier rejected by Pétain and Borotra. He opposed any request for sports clubs to function outside the federations system and even reacted hostilely to direct requests from the Marshal, such as when Pétain asked him to allow de la Rocque's Union des Sociétés de Préparation et d'Éducation sportive to operate.[69] Sport organized for young people by the Légion des Combattants was also frowned upon because it lay outside his control.[70] But his authoritarian attitude won the approval of some collaborationists, who continued to dislike his subordinates.

Physical culture, as distinct from games, became very popular for a while. The method used was known as 'Hébertisme', named after a Lieutenant Hébert, who had worked it out in 1906 and applied it during the First World War. Used extensively in the Compagnons de France and the Chantiers de la Jeunesse, the method consisted of a series of exercises divided into ten basic groups: walking, swimming, running, jumping, crawling, climbing, balancing, throwing, lifting, and self-defence. In centres for the unemployed and in apprentice-training workshops young people devoted six hours of their forty-five hour week to physical exercise.[71] This was seen as a vital element in moral regeneration. Precision, order, speed in carrying out orders, perfect turn-out – all these were conceived of as part of the training of the will and the development of character. Borotra had even floated the idea[72] of introducing a mark for 'moral worth' into the schools, to be awarded for 'right thinking', sociability, courage, and will-power, but the suggestion was coolly received. Not unnaturally, parents asked who would evaluate first those responsible for awarding the mark. The proposal was dropped.

The cult of physical fitness in a nation they had written off as decadent continued to alarm the Germans. When the Commissariat Général wanted to encourage ski-training in mountainous regions they were vigilant: an internal memorandum that circulated at German headquarters in Paris was endorsed: 'By giving instruction in skiing will not interests other than sporting ones [sc. military ones] be pursued?'[73]

Eventually the programme of 'general education', sport,

and games sparked off criticism among Frenchmen as well, but for different reasons. The ministry of family and health passed on some caustic comments it had received.[74] These criticized the time wasted in travelling from schools to sports stadiums, the poor organization, and the shortage of equipment. Head teachers and parents were sceptical, it seems, whether the kind of oblique moral education given through sport was a very efficient means of training. Why not, they said, teach directly such concepts as honour, loyalty, obedience, team spirit, and social solidarity? Teachers of 'general education' confessed themselves often baffled to know what they should be doing – and enquired why they got no extra pay for their work! In *Le Temps* there was an intellectual backlash. 'General education', it was argued, should be more akin to Plato's gymnastics.[75] Competitiveness should be played down. In the past the young Frenchman had too often been a mere 'bête à concours'; it was surely wrong now to turn him into a 'bête à performances sportives'. Although there was nothing wrong with physical training, competitive games and athletic competitions were to be deprecated. A mandarin class of intellectuals should not be replaced by a sporting one: 'Let us not forget the intellect . . . it is towards mental supremacy that we must bend all our efforts, without at all neglecting physical education.' On three further occasions in 1942 the newspaper returned to the charge, arguing that French greatness derived from the mind, that 'the reign of muscle is not desirable, nor will handsome athletic brutes be able to accomplish the intellectual and moral restoration of our country'.[76] Carles, the prefect of the Nord, spoke out in similar terms, declaring that 'the reaction against what it has been agreed to call the excesses of intellectualism should not risk going beyond what is reasonable'.[77] Another critic reflected that in any case 'the generation of the defeat had sacrificed generously to the gods of the stadium'.[78] Even Pétain conceded that sport, if carried to excess, might lead to 'a certain intellectual impoverishment'.[79]

The Church was least enthusiastic over this new cult of the body. Some Catholic schools did not even introduce physical education at all, and the prefect of the Vendée, where their schools educated the majority of pupils, urged that they should be made to do so.[80] Many bourgeois parents who had patronized State schools moved their children to Catholic ones, precisely because they thought time would not be wasted on non-academic subjects. The bishops worried lest sports attire should offend standards of modesty. The case of novice nuns who had to take PE tests in order to qualify as teachers was raised. Exercises unbecoming to females, solemnly declared the bishop of Viviers,[81] should be avoided; in mixed schools neither sex should see the other disporting itself. Indeed, the archbishop of Bourges added later, 'the natural method used, in which young males display themselves almost naked, offends decorum and shocks our Christian souls', for such young men might be seen by girls and 'we know the inmost mind of adolescents'. As for girls, he concluded primly, 'physical exercises do not become womenkind'.[82] Catholic youth clubs, urged to co-operate with their secular counterparts in sport, felt difficulties, because for them sport was only one facet of upbringing, which could not be isolated from others.[83] Some of the sporting fraternity hinted in turn that Catholic reluctance to co-operate might lead to a recrudescence of anticlericalism.

Resistance elements in France and overseas reacted ambivalently to Vichy's sports policy.[84] They rejected utterly any kind of 'general' or physical education that smacked of Nazism.[85] The Algiers government declared null and void the Vichy laws on sport (Ordinance of October 2, 1943); it nevertheless set up its own youth and sports service within the Commissariat for the Interior, a service which was later transferred to the education authorities. Although the idea of 'general education' survived the war, its debt to Léo Lagrange and Jean Zay must not be forgotten.

What practical outcomes emerged from Vichy policy? Sports facilities certainly improved. After the war Pascot claimed that he had been responsible for equipping completely 1,000 sports installations for schools and for putting another 1,000 into working order.[86] Swimming was popularized: in 1940 there had been only twenty-three swimming-pools of competition standard in France; by early 1944 the number had risen to 460.[87] Health initially improved, but this improvement was soon counterbalanced by the effects of food shortages. The standard of fitness of those who served in the Chantiers de la Jeunesse gives some indication of the initial improvement. Of those discharged from the first contingent in 1941 some 93 per cent had put on at least 3–9 kg in weight. All had improved their chest expansion.[88] There were social benefits as well. Villages reported that the 'intransigence' of young peasants to sport had completely vanished[89] and that it had helped in slowing down the flight from the countryside to the towns.[90] For a while the number of participants in sport increased.[91] Between 1940 and 1941 the athletics federation alone increased its membership from 90,365 to 208,425.[92] Fabre-Luce, perhaps writing with tongue in cheek, even reported that in the *lycée* of Cannes better physical education had resulted in fewer pupils being punished and in more passing the baccalaureate![93]

The more general impact of sport is difficult to assess. The pious hope that on the sports-field all ideological and political differences would be forgotten was not borne out by events.[94] Attitudes were difficult to change. Some teachers avoided giving PT lessons by taking their children for a walk instead.[95] As for 'general education', one headmaster in Aix reported that he had been unable to introduce it before mid-1942 because not a single teacher was willing to teach it.[96] (As for sports equipment, he caustically remarked that he had been pressing for this since 1935 and by 1942 had still received none.) The headmaster of one of the largest *lycées* in France stated in 1946 that his school still lacked any sports facilities.[97] In the Pas-de-Calais area in 1966, twenty years after the war, there was only one sports-ground for every eleven schools and one gymnasium for every 10,000 pupils.[98]

Sport was another grandiose undertaking of Vichy mainly for the benefit of youth. It failed because regimentation in sport proved unacceptable; because living conditions were too precarious to generate much enthusiasm for strenuous pastimes; because equipment and qualified teachers were not available. Moreover, the Germans were hostile and parents were reluctant to regard physical education as a major aspect of schooling. Sport as a form of moral education or as an instrument of national unity and regeneration was a thesis difficult to accept.

Physical and moral well-being was of course inextricably linked to health, particularly as the sheer struggle for survival began to erode moral standards. When the hard winter of 1940–1 set in, France was already suffering from food shortages that threatened the nation's health. The British blockade affected supplies so drastically that at one point Pétain contemplated appealing to the Pope to bring in food convoyed under the Vatican flag or that of the Knights of St. John. The situation was exacerbated because the Occupation troops were living off the land and France had become one vast larder for the Reich. In March 1941 the British lifted the embargo they had imposed and granted 'navicerts' to American ships bound for French Mediterranean ports, including Algeria. The Rockefeller Foundation began shipping condensed milk and vitamins for French children.[99] On April 7 Admiral Leahy, the American ambassador, welcomed the American ship *Exmouth* bringing a relief cargo. Pétain conveyed his thanks to Howard Kershner, the head of the Quaker Relief Committee. By the late spring American Quakers were able to provide in the South a meal for children in eight cities and to distribute 10,000 pints of milk a day.[100] These measures were of course insufficient. Young people from poor families, defined at the time as those existing on an income of less than 1,500F a month, had to make do with 1,460 calories a day as against the 2,080 calories which it was calculated were still being consumed by middle-class children. In the first half of 1941 it was estimated that 40 per cent of adolescents aged between twelve and nineteen had lost three kilogrammes in weight.[101] Pressure grew to rescind the extended physical-education and sports programme and also to lighten the academic load in schools. Some Catholic colleges gave up compulsory attendance of their pupils at early morning mass in order to let them sleep longer. In early 1941 a national health survey, covering forty departments, was made on behalf of the Secours National by a neutral, Dr Reh, director of the Geneva Institute of Hygiene. His conclusion, which came as no surprise, was that southern France was hardest hit: 18,000 children under fourteen drank no milk at all; two departments, with 129,500 children, did not get enough bread to eat; another department, with a child population of 138,000, lacked meat; fruit and fats were almost unobtainable. Children from the occupied zone also showed serious signs of malnutrition: sent to recuperate in Switzerland, they were found to be 4.6 kilogrammes below normal weight and 8.4 centimetres below normal height.[102] By 1942 a case was made for students also to receive the more generous J-3 ration card issued to adolescents.[103] In Lyons candidates for a law examination received an extra dole of 250 grammes of dried vegetables, jam, and flour products.[104] In Nancy a medical check resulted in students being allocated rations of cheese biscuits.[105] There was grumbling at the inequities of the rationing system. Young unemployed doing manual work in the Compagnons de France lived on 1,750 calories a day, whereas those called up for service in the Chantiers de la Jeunesse were allowed 2,603 calories, which included a pound of potatoes and half a litre of wine a day.[106] The statistics of undernourishment aroused cries of alarm, particularly at a time when the Secours National was receiving reports from Greece that hunger was rife and hundreds of emaciated corpses lay unburied.

Children in certain industrial areas suffered most. In the 'forbidden zone' opposite the English coast, where bombs were a daily hazard and movement was severely restricted, the food situation was desperate, because the inhabitants were not allowed to forage for provisions outside the narrow coastal strip bounded by the Colme Canal. An inspector, after visiting classes in Calais and Dunkirk, where he saw thin, hollow-eyed children who had just spent the night in an air-raid shelter, was so moved that he wrote a personal letter to Bonnard urging that they be given extra rations and sent on holiday to a safe area.[107] In large conurbations the food problem was alleviated by the establishment of canteens, started either by the Secours National or by private initiative. Just before the Liberation thirty-three canteens were operating in the Somme department, subsidized to the tune of 700,000F a year.[108] Efforts were made in school to supplement children's diet; for a while 50 grammes of bread a day was doled out to each child in class, but eventually this had to be restricted to children lunching at school.[109] In Roubaix, where 120 nursery and primary schools were attended by 24,000 children, 9,600 meals a day were provided, two-thirds of which were free.[110] In the Seine department the Association Franco-Européenne, a collaborationist organization, prepared free meals each day for children of prisoners of war.[111] By 1941 a hundred canteens were functioning in Lyons, catering for 15,000 pupils; for four francs, reduced to one franc for the very poor, pupils received a bowl of soup, a helping of vegetables occasionally supplemented by meat, and a dessert.[112] In Marseilles 12,000 pupils were catered for each day in 149 canteens.[113] In the occupied zone alone, by 1941 the Secours National was servicing 3,700 school canteens. So that children should not waste bread or feed it to animals, teachers were instructed to give a dictation which began, 'Bread is the sacred food, the essential food for all Frenchmen.'[114] Parents were obliged to buy a daily half-pint of milk for their children at school, but this soon became unavailable.[115] Babies received preferential treatment. In the Lille area, where a nineteenth-century charity, L'Œuvre de la Goutte du Lait, distributed free milk, the infantile mortality-rate actually fell slightly from 7.43 per hundred in 1943 to 6.69 per hundred in 1944,[116] although the figure was still excessive. Schoolchildren also received cheese biscuits in class from the Secours National, strictly rationed in number according to age,[117] although one Paris pupil complained that a good half of the school's allocation was wolfed by the teachers![118] Sometimes these biscuits were so hard that the children used them as castanets. Occasionally raspberry-flavoured vitamin tablets and vitaminized chocolate, reeking of fish, would be distributed.[119] Unfortunately, despite the efforts of the Secours National, welfare was insufficiently co-ordinated, which led to disparities. In any case the numerous artificial territorial divisions that the Germans had established within France, not to mention their appropriation of food stocks, prevented young people from receiving their fair share.

Alcohol consumption was at first a legitimate cause of

disquiet to the new Moral Order. Before the war excessive drinking had been a problem in France, which had led the world with a yearly consumption of 176 litres of wine and 20 litres of 100 per cent proof alcohol per head. In 1940 there was one establishment selling alcohol for every eighty Frenchmen. In neighbouring Switzerland it was one for every 770 inhabitants.[120] Immediately after the Armistice Ybarnégaray, as minister for the family and youth, took steps to reduce consumption. Opposed by the powerful lobby of the Confédération des Boissons,[121] his measures received strong backing from the Catholics, who saw alcoholism as the wrecker of family life, and believed young people must practise moderation and weaker vessels total abstinence.[122] Aperitifs, now limited in strength to under 16° proof, were proscribed for teenagers.[123] Prefects were empowered to close cafés and wine merchants sited near to schools and youth camps.[124] More positively, a move was made to improve the water-supply to villages, where wine had often been the sole drink readily available to thirsty young labourers. Despite this, excessive drinking continued among young people. In early 1942 medical checks in the Eure-et-Loir revealed that children from the Perche region were physically retarded because of alcoholism. A survey showed that, depending on the areas, between 25–40 per cent of children downed a nip of 'berluche', a spirit distilled from cider, before setting off for school; at midday they repeated the dose. Doctors were enlisted to give talks in schools explaining the evils of strong liquor, but, as one authority put it, it was 'yet another case where parents need to be educated before their children'.[125] Eventually the shortage of alcoholic drinks, at least in urban areas, partially solved the problem. The same danger was not perceived for smoking, although some units of the Compagnons de France did ban it for the under-eighteens.[126]

The general state of health of young people continued to arouse misgivings. In 1939 roughly one-third of those called up had been graded below A1 medically and 19 per cent had been immediately discharged,[127] a proportion which undoubtedly included some younger men. The Chantiers de la Jeunesse were not so exacting as regards physical standards as the armed forces, yet the figures for three successive call-ups show that an alarming percentage of young men were not even capable of performing this form of civilian service:[128]

Date of call-up	Nos. called up	Nos. unfit	Per cent unfit
March 1941	47,508	2,902	6.1
July 1941	35,765	2,007	5.6
November 1941	52,278	2,536	4.9

The Chief Scout, General Lafont, was shocked by the 'deplorable physical condition' of 5,000 scouts he inspected at Marseilles.[129] Young workers felt particularly the strain of wartime living. In early 1944 a group of ninety youths petitioned the mayor of Saint-Dizier (Haute-Marne), asking for the vocational courses they followed to be given in working hours, 'as the law prescribed'. Their work, 'often monotonous and wearing', occupied them for 8–9 hours a day and then, on three evenings a week, they had to attend evening classes until 9.30 p.m. Afterwards they had to walk long distances home because they either lacked bicycles or the tyres to ride them.[130] They had no time for sport and ate insufficient food. The outcome of this new 'cahier de doléance' is not known, but it illustrates the state of war-weariness of working-class youth on the eve of the Liberation.

Organizations did their best to counter this extreme fatigue. Vichy subsidized various activities such as 'colonies de vacances' for children and youth camps run by scouts, youth organizations, and the Auberges de la Jeunesse. Rest centres were started in safe areas for young people who had suffered in the bombing. Special efforts were made to give children a break. In the summer of 1941 two hundred and fifty teenagers were sent to recuperate in Morocco.[131] The Swiss, with their customary humanitarianism, received many such groups of children. In 1940 they had opened their borders to 800 young war victims.[132] The Red Cross had a plan to evacuate children to Sweden for two years, using the French School in Stockholm in which to educate them.[133] Such international ventures could of course touch only the surface of the problem. In France, as in England, 'the evacuee' was a familiar sight. In the summer of 1942, when the air raids on Brest were severe, a plan was made to evacuate all children to Lyons for the duration.[134] The Légion des Combattants, operating only in the southern zone, had already provided holidays for 25,000 children from the bombed areas of the North when in 1942 it was asked by Pétain to receive a further 100,000. An appeal to its members, presented as 'a crusade for childhood', produced the desired result.[135] Secours National, as the voluntary organization through which, as in the First World War, relief of all kinds was channelled, was very active: in the Nord department alone it organized 90 camps for 40,000 children and 108 'colonies de vacances'.[136] Such examples of generous action and mutual solidarity were frequent in wartime France.

Apart from undernourishment and the dangers of war, there were other threats to the health of the young. A constant risk was tuberculosis, which was the largest single cause of death among the 15–19 age group:[137]

Incidence of death from TB, 15–19 age group
Selected years

	1940	1941	1942	1944	1945
Total number of deaths from all causes	9,645	8,304	8,163	14,594ˣ	7,558
Deaths from TB	3,207	3,613	3,580	2,387	1,987
Per cent dying from TB	33	44	44	16	26

ˣFor 1944 this includes 8,741 male deaths, presumably a figure inflated because of war causes. The 1940 figures also show a slightly disproportionate number of male deaths, doubtless also because they include war casualties.

In 1942 a Paris medical professor reported that students were abandoning their studies because of anaemia, general exhaustion, and lack of food, but above all because of tuberculosis, which was rapidly on the increase.[138] Two years later the SGJ, warning of the 'serious decline in health of young people', particularly stressed the virulent recrudescence of tuberculosis, although from the figures shown above this does not appear to have resulted in so many deaths as in previous years.[139]

There was also a fear of minor and major epidemics. The ministry of education, commenting on the fact that lice had been found on pupils in towns, warned families to be on their guard against these potential typhus-carriers. Boys in whose hair the bug was found would be shorn immediately; after three warnings girls found to be infested would suffer the same treatment.[140] The real cause was recognized to be insanitary home conditions. Another scourge was polio. It was a disease that struck terror even into the Germans. In 1943 they refused to recruit young men coming from departments where polio had broken out for forced labour in Germany.[141] There was also a perpetual struggle against venereal disease. Already in 1941 the Institut Prophylactique in Paris had pleaded for more funds to fight syphilis, since 'to continue to allow young people to pass on a disease which strikes down more than a fifth [*sic*] of the population is to destroy the race and ruin hopes for the family'.[142] Syphilis is a progressive disease from which death ensues in later life, yet in 1941 six young people under twenty-four died of it, and in 1942 another thirteen.[143] The battle the institute was fighting was certainly a desperate one, because two and a half years later it reported that the number of people infected in the Paris area had trebled between 1939–42.[144] The handmaiden of venereal disease was prostitution, in which young girls solicited for food. In Beauvais, within the space of three months, twenty-three girls under the age of eighteen had received their first warning under a law that dated back to 1908.[145] Three such warnings entailed their being placed in an institution under care, but before these warnings could be given many must have passed the crucial age and been obliged to carry the 'carte spéciale'.

Vitamin deficiencies were a contributory factor in the deterioration in child health. In a poor quarter of Montpellier fifteen children aged between 10–13 were given a retinal sensitivity test: three had slight and eleven major vitamin deficiencies. Only one of the group, a butcher's son, proved entirely normal. In the schools of Cap Breton (Landes), 329 children were weighed regularly for seven months. The weight of 35 per cent remained stationary or even decreased, a very abnormal phenomenon in a growing child. In one school a growth in height of eight centimetres had been accompanied by a weight increase of only two kilogrammes. Girls suffered weight loss more than boys.[146] Dr Reh, the Swiss specialist, summed up the over-all health situation of the young. Mortality- and morbidity-rates had risen because resistance to infection had been undermined. There had been a recrudescence of rickets and skin diseases among the very young, whereas their older brothers and sisters suffered from thinness and extreme tiredness. Reh advised avoidance of physical exertion and even a ban on public sport. He quoted a description[147] by another neutral observer of working-class living conditions:

> . . . family of seven children. Filthy hovel. Nine people sleep in a single damp room. As the result of an accident the father has only one kidney; the health of the whole family is failing. Twice a week cabbages and turnips are distributed to the most needy. . .
> Everywhere else can be seen only yellow faces, drawn features, hollow eyes and cheeks; the sight of the children tugs at one's heartstrings; women and children go barefoot. . . [the men] are down at heel and their trousers are in rags.

The effects of such deprivation did not cease instantly with the coming of peace. During the immediate post-war years more than one school principal remarked on the tiny stature and general puniness of his younger pupils.[148]

One salutary outcome of this enforced preoccupation with health was the establishment of an embryo health service for the young. In Marseilles the employment of full-time school medical officers had been mooted in 1940.[149] The ministry of education encouraged this local initiative and suggested that a ratio of one doctor to 600 pupils would be appropriate. By August 1943 regular medical inspections were compulsory for all young people under eighteen if they were pupils, students, or members of the Compagnons de France. The law also applied to private institutions.[150] In primary schools medical inspection was free. If numbers are any criterion, the scheme was a success. Whereas in November 1941 only two departments had established a school medical service, covering 670,000 children (12 per cent of the school population), two years later the number had grown to seventy-five departments, covering 4,500,000 pupils (80 per cent).[151] The youth commission of the Conseil National had recommended obligatory checks on young people. In his prison cell, however, Jean Zay must have ironized over Vichy's discovery of preventive medicine for students, since the new measures followed closely his own decree-law of 1939, which had been inspired by the initiative taken in some universities.[152]

As the war dragged on and hardships multiplied it was recognized that the physical pressure on children must be reduced. Already at the end of 1940 the education authorities for Paris had prescribed twenty minutes' rest for all pupils after lunch.[153] They had also declared – presumably with ministerial authority – that 'instructions will be given to baccalaureate examiners to adjust their legitimate requirements to the necessities of the hour', which was interpreted to mean that leniency would be shown in marking. A year later the ministry advised pupils to avoid over-strenuous exercise and recommended that they should not work after the evening meal. Parents were informed that, even for young people over school age, nine hours' sleep was advisable.[154] In the occupied zone schools eventually delayed opening until nine o'clock.[155] This was also because Paris followed German time, which meant that the winter mornings were dark as well as cold.

The sympathy and generosity of the French adult went out to children. The work of the many relief organizations that sought to improve their lot must not be underestimated, despite the mixed motives that inspired some of them. Vichy's aim of improving juvenile health, just as that of broadening the scope of education, was not without merit. But what was lacking was a sense of realism, the recognition that the means available were inadequate for the task. So long as a German presence endured on French soil it could not be otherwise.

Chapter VIII

Cultural 'Revisionism'

Modern political change is often accompanied by attempts to reverse or revise cultural patterns. The Occupation authorities in Paris and the regime in Vichy were no exceptions, although their actions were more negative than positive both in intention and in effect. The most obvious means of changing cultural trends was by censoring the printed word. The Germans sought to suppress books by 'undesirables' such as Jews, writers of enemy nationality, and other authors unfavourable to the Reich, particularly if these works might fall into the hands of the young. The action of the Révolution Nationale overlapped: a ban was placed on works by Jews, freemasons, authors held to be hostile or 'immoral', and those closely identified with the defunct Republican regime or the doctrines of 'internationalism' and Communism. In both cases the purpose of the rigorous cultural censorship that was imposed was ultimately political. It was an ill wind that blows nobody any good: such a massive purge meant that publishers, although they had to withdraw many titles, profited, at least until paper stocks ran low, by printing new books or 'bowdlerised' editions of the old ones.

The Germans wasted no time in instituting this cultural 'Verbesserung' ('improvement') of the French. In Lille the local commander peremptorily ordered the university to withdraw 'anti-German' books from its library.[1] Remarkably, however, the first German official ordinance on the subject merely banned four books.[2] This first German measure, of August 30, 1940, applicable only in the occupied zone, prohibited the books for 'the insulting and unjustified remarks against the German people and its Army'. The penalty for flouting the prohibition was a year's imprisonment. They quickly added thirty more books to the tally. From this developed the notorious 'Liste Otto',[3] in which were included a motley group of authors: German refugee writers found a place alongside Maurois, Malraux, Bainville, and Aragon;

pro-Vichy authors such as Massis and Claudel were listed along with more collaborationist ones, such as Henry Bordeaux. To this first catalogue of names the Syndicat des Éditeurs, representing 140 publishers, mainly located in Paris, wrote a sycophantic preamble:

> Desirous of contributing to the creation of a more healthy atmosphere, French publishers have decided to withdraw from sale the books which have systematically poisoned. . . [French] public opinion: in particular we have singled out the publications of political refugees and Jewish writers who, betraying the hospitality France had granted them, have unscrupulously promoted a war from which they hope to gain advantage for their own selfish ends.[4]

The Germans were naturally delighted with this Paris initiative. The 'Liste Otto' was progressively lengthened so that by May 1943, when a third – bilingual – edition of it appeared, it contained 700 authors, together with an appendix which proscribed 600 French authors of Jewish origin.[5] The Germans also forbade translations of English works, save for the classics, all Polish works, and also all books about Jews, unless they were of a scientific nature.

In a document setting out German demands on France Abetz formally stipulated the banning of all history and German-language textbooks that appeared anti-German.[6] The aim was to make the French more receptive to German culture. Thus Dr Rilke and Dr Reiprich, of the 'Kultur und Schule' group attached to the German High Command in Paris, began a systematic appraisal of books used in French schools.[7] In November 1940 the French proposed a mixed Franco-German commission to scrutinize the books, although it is not known whether this commission ever functioned.[8] However, by the end of the year the Germans considered the purge to be almost complete.[9] Abetz reported that eighteen history textbooks should be forbidden forthwith and 115 rewritten. The actual banning was done by the ministry of education, although the Germans reserved the right to authorize new, revised editions. Eventually French publishers submitted all proposals for textbooks to the ministry beforehand,[10] which referred doubtful cases to the Germans. German interest was sustained. Thus in early 1942 they expressed concern that what they deemed books with an anti-German bias were coming on to the market.[11] Their suspicions were aroused again in 1943, when paper shortage had curtailed the publication of new or acceptable editions of textbooks, with the result that the previously banned ones had gradually drifted back into use.[12]

From their viewpoint the Germans discovered that not even the works of recent ministers of education were beyond reproach. Rivaud, a German scholar and a Maurrassian who had never really abandoned his anti-German feelings, was promptly banned. The German military commander in Bordeaux[13] judged it necessary to draw his superiors' attention to a passage in Chevalier's works on Descartes: 'If our ancestors, from the Crusades to the soldiers of Napoleon, have dreamt of conquering the world, this did not occur, as it did with the Boche, in order to enslave and exploit it, but to enlighten and liberate it.' The use of the term 'Boche', like 'Hun' and 'barbarian', never failed to provoke German wrath. A most glaring example of this was when they came across an illustration in a French history book which depicted a cart with a *swastika* on its side, and which bore the caption: 'The Huns pillage a Gallo-Roman villa'.[14] They were also ultra-sensitive to references to the Treaty of Versailles and 'war guilt'. Any discussion of Alsace-Lorraine and even of Richelieu's policy, which had led to the conquests in Alsace, had to be expunged.[15]

Films used in schools likewise came under German scrutiny. They were up in arms in 1942 when a luckless primary teacher showed a film containing shots of a *Soviet* school.[16] The Commission Française pour le Film d'Enseignement, set up in 1935, was hastily reconstituted. Rejuvenated as a Commission du Cinéma, it launched an ambitious programme to build up a repertory of 700 new films over a five-year period. The Germans took on the thankless task of reviewing the 447 films the Commission already had in stock, but eventually the Filmprüfstelle in Paris forbade only thirty-four.[17]

Vichy's own supporters had been quick to demand the revision of school-books. In August 1940 *Le Temps*[18] accused the Third Republic of allowing books that were dogmatic, error-ridden, sinning by omission as well as by commission, imbued with an 'aggressive ideology', and heedless of moral and patriotic values. It made an appeal for 'the spirit of the Révolution Nationale . . . to enter the pages of books destined to shape future generations'. Past control of textbooks was criticized. The approval and adoption of textbooks had been left by the ministry to the teachers' unions, operating through local committees. This had meant that many such books used in school were partial, pro-Republican, and anticlerical. Thus in 1940 a new procedure, providing for the annual review of books, was devised. A central commission appointed by the minister, composed of teachers, inspectors, and other interested parties, would vet proposals forwarded by local primary inspectors and teachers, but these would already have been pruned as they came up through the various echelons of the educational hierarchy. Furthermore, a decree of December 13, 1940 gave the local academy inspector the power to ban any book he thought fit.

When schools reopened in 1940, however, no procedures had been devised and there was a flood of enquiries as to which books were to be permitted. Sometimes the Germans took the law into their own hands. One German NCO simply went to the village school and ripped out offending pages from a book concerning the Franco-Prussian War and the First World War, although the work had not been officially banned.[19] It was a local bookseller who informed the academy inspector at Nancy that banned books were being used within his jurisdiction.[20] Confusion was compounded when it was decreed that school libraries should also be purged of 'tendentious and immoral' works.[21] Some academy inspectors acted with extreme circumspection, requiring specific permission to be obtained for each new acquisition. In the Vaucluse school principals had to write an appraisal of each proposed accession and certify that it was not partisan nor belonging to 'la littérature légère'.[22] In the academy of Grenoble not only were 'political' authors prohibited, but also anticlericals such as Buisson, salacious writers such as de Sade, and 'dissidents' such as Bernanos; the Duchess of Atholl was proscribed because she had supported the Spanish Republicans. Yet in the department of the Hautes-Alpes in November 1940 a list of books authorized for use in schools included one on ethics by Buisson and several by Jewish authors.[23] The process of control was only gradually enforceable. On a first list of twenty-five banned works it was noticeable that many were published by the publishing house of SUDEL, in which the SNI had a financial interest. Chevalier surpassed himself by banning an arithmetic book![24]

School-book censorship caused endless muddle. Catholic schools had to be brought into the censorship arrangements, which was difficult. Concessions had eventually to be made because of the paper shortage. Baccalaureate examining-boards were eventually notified that the use of certain 'old' textbooks would be tolerated for the duration, but that teachers were warned to make any necessary excisions.[25] The Germans continued to pry round schools and found books in use that they deemed unsuitable, although not officially banned.[26] Works appeared in new, censored editions, but steps had not been taken to amend the 'Liste Otto', which had rather cavalierly condemned all editions of all works by certain authors – 'omnia opera, in odium auctoris', to use the language of the Catholic Index.[27] Since some new editions were identical in format and cover to the old it was often difficult to distinguish the banned from the unbanned. In 1943 control became virtually ineffective when it was conceded that in the same class a variety of textbooks – provided they were not banned – would be tolerated.[28] Difficulties arose when some books prohibited by Chevalier because of their sectarian or 'internationalist' views were reinstated by Carcopino.[29] To be absolutely sure that he was complying with the regulations the teacher had to abandon the use of all books in his class.

In schools history was naturally the subject in which cultural 'revisionism' was, according to Vichy, most needed. The lobbying for a different presentation of the past in schools, youth centres, youth movements, and 'leadership schools' was a reaction against alleged past Republican bias. The new tendency particularly opposed the former lauding of democracy and the Revolution of 1789. Instead, Maurras wanted a rehabilitation of the monarchy and feudalism.[30] His preference went to Fustel de Coulanges, the great historian of the 'ancien régime', because he had exploded certain 'myths', such as the racial antinomy of the Germanic barbarians and the Gallo-Romans, as well as pointing out the thread of anti-national sentiment that ran through the French Revolution.[31] Serge Jeanneret, in 1940 a leading light in the Cercle Fustel de Coulanges, asserted that 'The essential preoccupation of history teaching in the primary school was in fact to blacken the old monarchy and extol the political institutions that arose from the movement of 1789.'[32] Thus the picture of the Revolution had been deliberately falsified so as to prove to 'the people' that everything good sprang from it.[33] He cited a manual that portrayed life before and after 1789. The pre-1789 picture in the textbook showed a cottage, a peasant walking at night alongside a cart, carrying a stick, in a valley illuminated by torches. After the Revolution the peasant was depicted living in a stone house lit by electricity and travelling by bicycle or train. Likewise institutions such as the Church had been vilified as intolerant and oppressive, as exemplified in the way in which Galileo, the St. Bartholomew massacre, and the Wars of Religion had been presented.[34] According to *Le Temps*, secularism and democracy had been so extolled that only a fervent Republican was held to be patriotic.[35]

The revival of national pride was the leitmotiv of the initial Vichy reform of history teaching. Primary teachers were instructed (C. of October 10, 1940) to stress the persistent effort that had been made under all regimes to maintain the greatness of France. Thus the eighteenth-century Philosophes, the Revolution, and Republican policies were not to be stressed to the exclusion of all else. Since publishers had declared their willingness to reorientate textbooks in the spirit of the Révolution Nationale, these should contain, for example, maps showing how various kings had been 'the assemblers of French territories',[36] although, as d'Ormesson prudently remarked in *Le Figaro*, there might well be difficulty in finding men of 'integrity' to write such manuals.[37] Daniel-Rops declared his view that there had been many omissions in the past: in the 1937 baccalaureate he had interrogated twenty-six candidates and only one had been able to give the date of the martyrdom of Joan of Arc or cite a single achievement of Louis XIV.[38] Maurras attacked those textbooks which placed 'love' – his term – of the League of Nations above love of France. He even condemned Brunschvicg's edition of Pascal because he had cited one of the 'Pensées' to justify the principle of arbitration in international disputes.[39] The Légion des Combattants joined in the discussion, solemnly listing as one of its aims the banning of 'bad' history textbooks.[40] The previously much-used textbooks of Malet-Isaac were particularly anathematized, although covertly they continued to be used.[41] One history teacher advised his pupils to hide one such former textbook away carefully at home, so that secretly the truth could be passed on to posterity: France would be occupied by the Germans for a long time to come and 'one might expect for several generations a systematic falsification of history teaching'.[42] To what extent the character of history teaching really changed because of the Vichy measures is an open question.[43] Jeanneret complained that in the primary school it was still taught as a panegyric of democracy, a state of affairs still approved by visiting inspectors; it was he also who accused the inspector appointed to head the text-book revision commission of being a freemason.[44] On the other hand, one who interpreted the cult of nationalism in a rather original way was General de Lattre de Tassigny: after the Armistice he gave lectures to his young soldiers on such figures as Vercingétorix, the leader of the Gauls against the Roman invader.[45] Even before the war Pétain had pleaded for a more 'national' kind of history, arguing that young conscripts were ignorant of the past glories of France.[46] Now he was doubly served.

In announcing his own major reform of history syllabuses Carcopino had undoubtedly a difficult course to steer. In the Instructions that accompanied the reform he struck a conciliatory note. The Revolution of 1789 must be viewed as merely confirming a trend towards a more just society. 'All generations have accepted the same duty and lived out the same hopes, with the same faith in the destiny of our country.'[47] Since, after the annulment of the Chevalier measures, religion would no longer figure in the programme, in the primary school history would take its place to a certain extent by demonstrating the place of the Christian tradition in the past.[48] As Le Roy had put forward in his plan for educational reform, history would be taught in two phases: in the early years, when facts are easily absorbed, the chronology of events would be taught; later, the secondary pupil would study the evolution of ideas and the development of civilization.[49] Thus at sixteen he would be capable of tackling a synthesizing study of five great eras of civilization, as exemplified in the history of Greece, Rome, the Middle Ages, the Renaissance, and 'Le Grand Siècle'. By stressing the social and economic, rather than the political aspects, and by emphasizing the French seventeenth century, the minister adroitly side-stepped some causes of dissension, so much so that even Catholic opinion was mollified. At last, wrote *La Croix,* the distortions of the past would be rectified and the young would acquire 'an exact, complete knowledge of our country'.[50]

History to redress the errors of the past, to stimulate patriotism, and to raise national morale: such were the ostensible motives for the reform. Anatole de Monzie, a former minister of education, considered that the changes would administer a 'therapeutic shock', restoring to despondent young Frenchmen their 'élan vital'.[51] Great therefore was his dismay to learn later that the time devoted to history was to be reduced so that more could be devoted to sport. Bluntly he wrote: 'I would simply recall that after Jena Germany did not employ physical training instructors as the mentors of its thought and summoned up its history to summon up enthusiasm. The example is worth recalling.'[52] But he had forgotten that in Prussia alongside Fichte had stood the good Turnvater Jahn.

The teaching of languages was also discussed, but with somewhat less fervour than history. Advocates of the ancient languages had evoked Bergson's arguments in their support, and Le Roy had wanted the education of an élite to be firmly grounded on the classics. Maurras praised Latin and Greek because they stimulated mental flexibility and assisted the mastery of the mother tongue.[53] Not only did they remain the hallmark of the high culture, but they possessed intrinsic 'moral worth' and had value as 'mental gymnastics'. The

Church was sympathetic: after all, its Jesuit colleges had long used the study of Greece and Rome to teach morals, sedulously neglecting their pagan aspects. Carcopino had taken note of these pleadings, but had decided that the classics should not be unduly emphasized in secondary education. Other views were more extreme: the Cercle Fustel de Coulanges even urged that all future primary teachers should learn classics.[54]

The debate regarding modern languages was less impassioned. Maurras wanted to see the Romance tongues achieve parity with English and German in schools.[55] Teachers had been prejudiced against them, he asserted, because of Fascism in Italy and the dominant position of Catholicism in Spain. Regarding Spanish, political considerations entered into the discussion. Pétain, whose ideas on government, on regionalism, and on a hierarchical social order in which the Church played a substantial role, had been strengthened by his ambassadorship to Franco immediately before the war, had much sympathy with 'Hispanidad'. It had been rumoured that the Caudillo had even invited Chevalier before the war to reorganize the Spanish education system. The neutral stance that Franco was able to adopt during the war was envied and it was held that links with Spain should be strengthened. One upshot of this was Bonnard's decision in July 1943 (C. of July 16) to increase the number of teaching posts for Spanish, with the object, he said, of reinforcing intellectual ties.

On the other hand the Germans were interested solely in promoting their own language. Carcopino had stipulated that in secondary school English or German should be compulsory, but in fact most pupils continued to opt for English. Hard-line collaborationists kept watch to see that wherever possible the option to choose either of the two languages was observed.[56] In April 1941 the Germans registered a minor victory when the ministry appointed a second inspector general for German – English already had two. With the teaching of German to adults the Germans also had some success. In May 1941 they noted that 6,000 Parisians had registered for courses at the German Institute.[57] On the other hand, when the Institute opened a centre in Besançon and recruited students for German courses the prefect reported that the clientele was comprised of mainly shop girls and waitresses'.[58]

A different facet of cultural 'revisionism' was Vichy's drive to restore the diversity of provincial life, perhaps because it was in keeping with a semi-feudal, pre-1789, even medieval vision of France. For the first time since the Revolution France was divided into regions which in their boundaries corresponded to the ancient provinces, and regional prefects were appointed in 1941. These regions were grouped according to geography and local affinities. Pétain, doubtless with the Spanish example in mind, regarded the regional prefects as the precursors of future provincial governors. One must remember that the right had always been hostile to the form of centralized government which had emerged from 1789. Abetz believed that it was to the Germans' advantage to promote the regionalist trend and in late 1940 urged Berlin to bring pressure to bear in this respect upon the French.[59] But Pétain needed no convincing. He held that people, by becoming attached to 'la petite patrie', the locality where they lived and worked, would thereby develop naturally a love for France itself. In 1939 the peasants still constituted the largest social group and it was hoped that by fostering local attachments a stop might be put to the growing exodus from the countryside. It might even encourage something else which the Marshal wished: the return of town-dwellers to the soil, 'the land which does not lie', as he himself expressed it.

These ideas had an educational corollary. Provincial loyalties should be fostered in various ways. Ripert, himself a Provençal, wished to encourage school visits to local places of interest, so that pupils might get to know better 'le petit pays' where they lived: a start might be made by a visit to the local war memorial. Teachers should study the local dialect, so as to be able to explain the origin of local place-names and to point out comparisons between standard French and the local speech. They should encourage interest in authors writing in the local dialect. Enthusiasts waxed lyrical over the use of patois by children, claiming that it was 'noble, human, beautiful and enriching'.[60] By presenting a more attractive side of country life, by making the school the hub of modest cultural and intellectual interests for adults as well as children, the village teacher served to promote the rural community, knowledge of which was 'the first form of patriotism'.[61] Local history and geography were also taught and textbooks such as Pierre Morel's *Petite Histoire du Languedoc* were written. Carcopino strongly favoured such regional studies, dismissing the criticism of the Lorraine writer Jacques de Lacretelle that such an approach to education was potentially destructive of national unity.[62] He even envisaged truly regional universities, with chairs in local history as a first step to full regional-study courses. Such provincialism was also encouraged in the youth movements, where local songs, folklore, and customs were revived. Young people displayed the badge of their province on their uniform and paraded under its banner. Localism was seen as an important element in civic education.

If such regional sentiments were too much encouraged, however, there was a risk of stimulating separatism. In Brittany and Flanders, as will be seen, the danger was already present. On the other hand 'Occitanisme' had no such centrifugal tendency, since it merely sought to preserve the use of the 'langue d'oc' over a large area of the Midi whilst preserving the best Occitan traditions. The movement was supported by right-wing intellectuals, the 'bourgeoisie bien pensante', and numerous learned societies.[63] It had been taken up enthusiastically by the Maurrassians. Maurras, a Provençal like Ripert, was keen that young people should study the works of Mistral (1830–1914), the great poet of Provence, and the Felibrige movement which in the mid-nineteenth century had done much to revive local customs and folklore and had campaigned for the study in schools of Provençal language and history. This aim was also that of Maurras, for he believed that 'Mistral and Mistralisme' could contribute to the moral regeneration of France.[64] It was a belief that appealed to Pétain who, on the one hundred and tenth anniversary of Mistral's birth, was persuaded to pronounce an eulogy on the poet of 'the cult of altars, homes and tombs', particularly lauding his great patriotism.[65]

The movement for the teaching of Occitan in schools, started by Jean Bonnafous between the wars, had been revived in September 1940, when a congress of 'occitanistes' at Arles had urged that voluntary school lessons in the language should be made available and that an optional paper might be offered in the baccalaureate, as well as calling for the establishment of chairs of Occitan in universities.[66] Thus by a C. of October 9, 1940 Ripert gave permission for local studies to be introduced into primary schools, although at the time Pétain, despite pressure from the Maurrassians at Vichy, was reluctant to go further. Later, however, Carcopino (A. of December 24, 1941) authorized the teaching of regional languages in school, for one and a half hours a week, to those who wished. As a Latin scholar the minister was particularly enthusiastic about Occitan: echoing Jules Simon, he saw it as 'a kind of Latin of the people, a Latin which, far from being an obstacle to the teaching of French, will serve it like a brother'.[67] One notes how Carcopino based his argument on the strictly educational level, avoiding any political or moral overtones. A later circular (of March 13, 1942) instructs teachers to highlight the grammar and specific vocabulary of the local patois and looked forward to when textbooks would even be written in the local dialect.

Groups for the study of Occitan were also started in the youth movements. The language enjoyed a particular vogue in the Chantiers de la Jeunesse; one detachment even changed the title of its news-sheet to 'Remountaren' ('Nous remonterons'). A clandestine Resistance publication circulating in the Marseilles area was named 'Lou Mestre d'Escole' ('Le maître d'école'). If Vichy had been able to realize its project of creating provincial councils, each headed by a governor, local language would doubtless have played an important part, although as Spanish experience later proved, the results might not have been entirely favourable.

It may be that the very provincialism of Vichy, which remained to the end the seat of government, sustained this decentralizing tendency. The contrast with the Third Republic is striking. That regime had abhorred all centrifugal forces and had insisted upon the teaching of the national rather than the local culture. The unity of the 'hexagon', of which the common tongue was the most important symbol, had been impressed upon children from the time they began school. Thus it could be argued that Vichy's provincialist policy played into the hands of the separatists and their covert German supporters. In a post-war, Nazi-dominated Europe the 'master race' hoped to preside over the destinies of a France dismembered, the rump of which would form a nation of peasants and helots whose function would be to provide food, luxuries, and pleasure for their conquerors. It may be argued that Vichy was playing a more subtle game, although a dangerous one. By conceding a measure of cultural autonomy the regime deflated the extravagant claims of the few but strident separatists and rallied moderate opinion to it by a policy of regionalism. It is a fact that nowhere was youth won over to any significant degree to support of separatist movements. Even in Alsace, where the pressures were almost overwhelming, the evidence is that young people remained profoundly attached to France.

There is also the reverse of the coin. Vichy exalted truly national figures whose fame transcended provincial boundaries. War engenders hero-worship, of which Pétain and de Gaulle are striking examples, although the shield and the sword each claimed to represent commanded divided loyalties. Two other national heroes, however, Charles Péguy, and Péguy's own heroine, Joan of Arc, inspired both the young who endured their lot and the young who resisted and, within that Resistance, both Catholic and secularist – 'celui qui croyait au Ciel et celui qui n'y croyait pas'. Before the war Péguy had already been something of a cult figure in Catholic youth organizations. Inevitably in 1940 he was taken over by the Révolution Nationale. The poet of Joan of Arc, his work extols the soil of France and its Catholic heritage, particularly that fertile plain of the Beauce over which broods Notre Dame de Chartres. The men of Vichy recalled that he had died a hero's death in 1914, perishing on the battlefield of the Marne like some French Rupert Brooke. But they conveniently forgot that Péguy had also expounded the virtues of Socialism, had championed the cause of Dreyfus, and had fallen fighting those same Germans to whom at Montoire Pétain had extended the hand of collaboration.

Even here distinctions must be drawn. At Vichy in 1940 the Catholic movement closest to Péguy's ideas was Mounier's 'Personnalisme', which was particularly attractive to students and young intellectuals and, as will be seen, greatly influenced the École des Cadres of Uriage. Rejecting totalitarian ideals, which demand the abdication of the individuality, in favour of a doctrine of personal responsibility, Mounier was at first listened to approvingly in some Vichy circles. He had the advantage of having been for a time Chevalier's pupil, having studied philosophy under him. The link with Péguy was continued through Chevalier, whose master, Bergson, had been highly esteemed by the Catholic poet. Mounier advocated the establishment of a moderate Christian economic and social order which had some affinities with Péguy's own conception of society; he had consequently adopted the motto that had appeared on the first *Cahier de la quinzaine* in 1900: 'The social revolution will be moral or it will not be'. Within the Compagnons and the Chantiers, as at Uriage, Péguy's works became recommended reading. The young read his poetry avidly and interest was aroused among a wide public. In October 1940 Daniel Halévy republished his study of *Charles Péguy et les Cahiers de la quinzaine*. André Rousseaux published a three-volume work entitled, *Le Prophète Péguy*. Later on the Légion des Combattants reprinted Péguy's *Notre jeunesse*. Contingents 'passing out' from the Chantiers named themselves 'promotions Péguy'. Nor had the Révolution Nationale the monopoly. Robert Debré, the eminent paediatrician who distinguished himself in the Resistance, despite his Jewish background acknowledged his debt to Péguy.[68] The clandestine Éditions de Minuit published a volume entitled, *Péguy-Péri*, in which, to show the affinities, are presented extracts from Péguy's writings and those of the Communist Gabriel Péri, shot as a hostage by the Germans in December 1941.[69] Throughout the Occupation Péguy remained a significant influence, particularly among Catholic students and in Catholic youth movements.

The other, even more symbolic, national hero honoured

during the war by all Frenchmen everywhere, was Joan of Arc. For Free Frenchmen the Cross of Lorraine became the hope of a liberated France. Within France the saint became the prototype of sacrifice. On her feast day in May schools and youth organizations were instructed to remember her premature death and her example. But this commemoration was ambiguously interpreted: for some it was the fact that she had died at the hands of the English that was significant: for others it was that she had freed French soil from the foreign invader.

In May 1941, the first anniversary of St. Joan after the defeat, Carcopino issued instructions that the occasion was to be commemorated. Astutely 'neutral' as usual, he asked young people to use the occasion to make some particular gesture of appreciation towards their mother.[70] This conveniently avoided the more contentious patriotic aspect. In the southern zone Catholics celebrated the feast day with unusual fervour. At a mass in Lyons Cardinal Gerlier appealed to youth to 'have courage, to march behind Joan, not to tremble in the face of effort'.[71] At Pau eight hundred children performed a cantata in her honour and scenes from Péguy's 'Jeanne d'Arc' were enacted in the cathedral. At Limoges 15,000 young people filed past her statue. But if Catholics exalted her saintly example, the sentiment in some State schools was different. Before processions set out for church pupils stealthily showed one another, concealed under their coat lapels, 'the Franco-British colours'.[72]

In 1942 also the saint's day was variously interpreted. Bonnard's message to schools and youth organizations alluded to English guilt for her martyrdom. Whereas Joan had only a weak Dauphin to sustain her, modern youth had Pétain, and 'French boys and girls must all be behind the greatest Frenchman.'[73] The chaplain of the *lycée* at Vichy, Father Soras, adopted a more subtle line. Preaching in Lyons before Lamirand, he reminded his youthful congregation that the situation in 1942 was not unlike that in Joan's day: then too France had been three-quarters occupied, but the saint had liberated her country.[74] It might have been interpreted as a call to arms.

The cult of heroes leads to emulation and imitation, but

excessive hero-worship eventually stultifies action. The Vichy regime was guilty of the latter. Like most gerontocracies, it was also guilty of harking back to a dead past: the years since the great Revolution, nor the great Revolution itself, could not simply be obliterated from the French cultural heritage. Culturally the much lesser Révolution Nationale was an attempt to put the clock back, to play a confidence trick upon the young, in a word, to prevent France, in de Gaulle's memorable phrase, from 'rejoining its century'. As such it was doomed to failure.

Chapter IX

Young France: 'Une et indivisible'?

What national identity would have remained to young Frenchmen in the event of a German victory? It is now clear that a German-dominated Europe, if all Nazi plans had been realized, might have meant the dismemberment of France and the loss of nationality for many of those born within the 1939 frontiers of the country.

In 1940 many plans were circulating for carving up French territory: they revolved round a number of options, including the incorporation of Northern and Eastern France into a Greater German Reich, the establishment of a State of Burgundy, and the integration of French Flanders with Belgium and Holland as Reich Protectorates or vassal states.[1] Hitler particularly ordered Stuckart, Secretary of State in the German ministry of the interior, to make a study of the future western frontier of Germany. Stuckart proposed the incorporation into the Reich of all those areas of Northern and Eastern France 'which belong not to the West, but to Central Europe, on historical, political, ethnographic or other special grounds'.[2] Hitler's own view was that Germany should have territory permanently on the Channel coast. Thus the frontier would run from the mouth of the Somme through the northern extremity of the Paris Basin and Champagne to Argonne, bending south across Burgundy, to include Franche-Comté, and ending at the Lake of Geneva.[3] On June 19, 1940 the German General Staff, located at Goering's HQ, drew up a document entitled, 'General Plans for Political Developments', which made similar proposals.[4] The SS wanted to create an SS state of Burgundy stretching from the Atlantic to the Mediterranean, comprising Picardy (including Amiens), Artois, Hainault, Luxemburg, Champagne (including Reims and Troyes), Lorraine, the 'free county (Franche Comté) and duchy of Luxemburg', Dauphiné, and Provence,[5] thus truncating much of Belgium as well as France. Spieser, the Alsatian separatist, wanted the new

Reich frontier to stop just short of Lyons and then run diagonally across France to the coast at the mouth of the Somme. In this way Alsace would no longer be a German outpost on the Western marches, but part of the German 'heartland'.[6]

The divisions made in the Armistice of 1940 (see map) must therefore be seen as a first step towards the dismantlement of France. The agreement stipulated that the unoccupied or 'free zone' (usually referred to as the 'southern zone'), would comprise only approximately one-third of French territory. The occupied zone would include all the area north and west of a line drawn from Geneva, Dôle, Châlons-sur-Saône, Paray-le-Monial, Moulins, and Vierzon; from there the line turned south, skirting Tours to the East, taking in Poitiers, Angoulême, Bordeaux, and Mont-de-Marsan and reaching the Spanish frontier just east of Saint-Jean Pied-de-Port. In addition, the Italians, who had claimed Nice, Corsica, and Savoy before the war, occupied small frontier strips in the Alps and, for a while, after the total occupation of France in November 1942, a much larger zone to the east of the Rhône, but excluding the river delta. Moreover, within their occupation zone the Germans made further significant divisions. Alsace and parts of Lorraine – the three departments of the Bas-Rhin, the Haut-Rhin, and the Moselle – were annexed *de facto* to the Reich and from July 24, 1940 the Vosges became, as they were in 1914, the new eastern frontier. The Pas-de-Calais and the Nord were placed under the jurisdiction of the German High Command in Brussels, and for a while were virtually cut off from Paris. For a whole year the Somme became as strictly controlled a boundary as that between the two main zones. Furthermore, the coastal strip of these two departments, which faced England, to a depth of between 20–30 km. became a 'prohibited area' ('Sperrgebiet') or 'red zone' within which all movement was strictly controlled. By 1942 this 'red zone' had been extended south from the Somme as far as the Spanish frontier. Moreover, within the occupied zone a further division was made which was extremely relevant to plans for dismembering France. A 'North–East Line' ('Nord–Ost Linie', sometimes also termed the 'Schwarze

Map of occupied France
Source: H. Michel, *La Seconde Guerre mondiale*, Presses Universitaires de France, Paris, 1968.

Linie' or the 'Führer-Linie') marked out a 'reserved zone' ('zone réservée') running from the line of the Somme and the Aisne and continuing south to the west of Bar-le-Duc to Dôle. Within this 'reserved zone' was yet another zone, a 'forbidden zone', comprising all territory as far east as Mézières. The 'Nord–Ost Linie' would seem to have been a key boundary from many viewpoints. The German military transport chief, General Gherke, described it to Berthelot, then the Vichy communications minister, in 1940 as 'Die Auffangslinie de Flüchtlinge', the 'stop-line' for refugees wishing to return north and east of it. Gherke explained it away by claiming that in the area food and transport were difficult. Berthelot, a railways expert by profession, noted that within it the French railway system was controlled from Brussels.[7]

Such a patchwork quilt of divisions, major and minor, corresponded to political aspirations as well as military necessity. The Germans did not forget that during the French occupation of the Rhineland after the First World War the French had encouraged Rhenish separatism. Now in Alsace-Lorraine the political ambitions of the autonomists turned integrationists (into the German Reich) were in the process of being realized; in Brittany and Flanders the hopes of a handful of autonomists were miraculously revived. In these two latter provinces the Germans followed their usual 'thorn in the side' policy: they allowed the separatists to harass Vichy, but not unduly, since they considered the survival of the regime served a purpose in waging the war against the Allies. Nevertheless, the existence of such manifold divisions created great difficulties, in particular for young people, for, depending upon the degree of German support or promotion of centrifugal tendencies, the Vichy writ ran strongly, weakly, or not at all on their behalf. Until November 1942, when the Germans occupied all France – and even afterwards, for the Germans continued to distinguish to some extent between the southern zone and what they termed the 'operational zone' – the edicts of Vichy were more closely observed where there was no German presence. Elsewhere local German commanders, as well as the high commands in Paris or Brussels, intervened freely in matters affecting the young.

A small but significant step was taken in 1940 when a semi-official German enterprise, known first as 'Ostland', and then, perhaps more ominously, as 'Reichsland', took over agriculture in the north-east of France, particularly in the frontier department of the Ardennes. Whole communes were simply occupied by Volksdeutsche, peasant farmers from the new eastern territories occupied by the Germans. The French had evacuated the area at the time of the invasion. Now the Germans forbade evacuees to return; if they evaded the controls and did get back they were forced to work as hired labourers on their own land. Other foreign workers from the eastern marches of the expanded Reich and from Eastern Europe were also brought in. A French source gives a figure of 5,000 Polish settlers.[8] Patently the aim was to create a German colony.

If German plans for the establishment of a Burgundian–Lotharingian state had been realized, Besançon (Ge. Bisanz) would have been an appropriate capital. The town was on its guard against all such moves. Thus when the indefatigable Dr Epting, director of the German Institute in Paris, projected an institute in Besançon (as he did also in Rennes, Nantes, Angers, and Dijon) the rector reported to the ministry of education that he contemplated taking countermeasures to reinforce French culture in the area. In the summer of 1940, he wrote, the German commander had told him that the Reich would annex Franche-Comté. Although he had now been given assurances that this plan had been abandoned, he was clearly taking no chances.[9]

The sealing-off of the Pas-de-Calais and the Nord from France and their rule by General von Falkenhausen from Brussels had followed upon the Armistice. On June 24, 1940 the Germans had forbidden the removal of goods either north to Belgium or south to the rest of France.[10] On September 15 they ordered all customs posts on the Franco-Belgian border to be closed and all frontier control to cease.[11] It was alleged that this measure was taken 'on superior orders'. After French protests that this would mean Belgian despoliation of their food stocks, the order was withdrawn after three days. To the south, for more than a year the Somme acted as a demarcation line for the transfer across it of goods, information, and people, particularly civil servants. Complete surveillance of this river line was only withdrawn in December 1941 because of the shortage of German troops.[12] Within the area even the collaborationist newspapers were banned. Vichy legislation was often ignored or overridden by the Occupation authorities. The first Vichy protest was nevertheless not made to the German Armistice Commission at Wiesbaden until October 20, 1940. The Germans were particularly slow in giving permission for refugees to return, especially if they were concerned with education. By June 1941 only about half the teachers had taken up again the posts they had held in 1939,[13] although the total includes some who were prisoners of war.

The Germans felt particularly at home in Northern France. There were even family ties from the First World War. Thus General von Falkenhausen, who ruled over Northern France from Brussels, was the nephew of von Bissing, governor of the Western-occupied territories during the previous occupation. Likewise General Baron, the Oberfeldkommandant of Roubaix, was the nephew of the previous holder of that office in 1914. Other, non-personal and non-military, reasons for this 'régime d'exception' are not hard to discover. The fact that de Gaulle was a native of Lille and that the Northern French were traditionally pro-British was held to necessitate a closer supervision of the population. Nor did the Germans forget that in the First World War Lille had thrown up a handful of Flemish separatists. How far this second wave of occupiers really believed the area to be substantially different from the rest of France is difficult to say. Certainly von Falkenhausen did: in 1943 he wrote, 'The territory between Dunkirk and Bailleul (Flemish: Belle) belongs, as far as its population is concerned, entirely to "Flemingdom".'[14] As the separatists would put it, 'Franks, Flemings, Frisians are first names, German is the family name.' Nazi 'Geopolitiker' dreamt of a Low German ('dietsch', 'thiois') state, blood brother to the Reich, embracing the Netherlands and Belgian and French Flanders.

Before the war the two areas of Northern France where minorities at least understood, even if not all could speak, the West Flanders dialect of Flemish were the 'Westhoek' and the districts surrounding Lille. The 'Westhoek' included the north-west corner of France, particularly the area extending south down the coast from Bray-Dunes to Dunkirk and even to Gravelines. Those quarters of Lille and in its vicinity where Belgian immigrants had settled comprised the other main linguistic concentration. Local separatists envisaged none the less a greater 'French' Flanders than this, bounded by the North Sea, the Somme, and the Scheldt. Within this larger region they distinguished three zones. The first, where the language was spoken, comprised the 'taalgebied'. The second, which included Flemish Artois and the districts round Calais (Kales) and Boulogne (Bonen), was the 'volksgebied', ethnically and culturally Flemish. Lastly there were the southern marches of 'Flemingdom', which constituted the 'grensland' or frontier area. Thus it was no accident that the Germans set the course of the Somme as the southern and western limit of the 'forbidden zone'.

To understand the potential threat that faced the youth of Northern France it is necessary to go back in history. Since the Middle Ages the valley of the Lys had been the dividing-line between spoken French and Flemish. In the mid-nineteenth century most of the 'arrondissement' of Dunkirk and that half of the 'arrondissement' of Hazebrouck contiguous to it were still Flemish-speaking areas.[15] In the early years of the Third Republic the clergy gave their sermons and instructed the children in the catechism in Flemish. Some continued to do so even after this was forbidden by a decree of 1890, refusing to admit to First Communion those children who could not recite and explain the catechism in the language.[16] When Boulanger stood in 1888 for election at Dunkirk his posters ended bilingually but patriotically: 'Vive la patrie. Leve het vaderland.' But his Flemish-speaking supporters put up a poster which declared: 'Flemish, that's what we are, not French. We have no other fatherland than Flanders.'[17] André Malraux's grandfather, a Dunkirk shipowner who died in 1909, spoke Flemish in preference to French. The primary teacher at the close of the nineteenth century had attempted to stamp out Flemish – or rather its West Flanders dialect – by forbidding his pupils to speak the language, even at playtime, and by meticulously correcting the numerous Flemish usages of Northern French. Compulsory schooling, as well as industrialization and the posting-in of civil servants from outside the area, had hastened the disappearance of the indigenous language, yet in 1940 as many as 150,000 people, mainly in rural areas, may still have been using Flemish as their everyday speech.[18] Abbé Lemire, the much-loved and patriotic deputy for Hazebrouck, had pleaded on three occasions, in 1902, 1910, and 1919, in the Chamber of Deputies, for permission to be given for Flemish to be taught in schools. It was not until 1926, and then only in secondary schools, that this was allowed.[19]

Meanwhile literary regionalism had been kept alive, first by the publication of the bilingual periodical, *Le Beffroi de Flandre* (1919–28). From 1923 onwards there had been published as well *De Vlaemsche Stemme in Vrankryk* (*sic:* regional spelling). In 1929 *De Torenwachter* succeeded both periodicals, eventually combining with another journal which started in the same year, *Le Lion de Flandres.* In the same period a new movement, the Vlaamsch Verbond van Frankrijk (the Flemish League of France) had sprung up in 1924. Like many Flemish autonomist movements on the other side of the frontier, it had clerical connections. Its founder, Abbé Gantois, who often published articles under more Flemish-sounding names such as Jooris-Max Gheerland and H. van Bieleveld, supported by other separatists such as Canon Looten and Justin Blanckaert, set as his initial goal the defence of the Flemish language and culture in France and the fight against intervention by the central government.[20]

The Vlaamsch Verbond van Frankrijk gained renewed strength by the foundation of similar movements in Belgium. In 1931 Joris van Severen founded the rigidly authoritarian Verdinaso. (Verbond van Dietse Nationalen. Solidariteit voor geheel Nederland: League of Low German Nationalists. Solidarity for the whole of the Netherlands), which had intellectual analogies with Maurras's Action Française.[21] The ideal of Verdinaso was a state associated with Germany, made up of what later became Benelux. By 1937 Gantois supported the ideal for French Flanders and called himself 'dietsch', 'thiois'. Even closer to his views was the Belgian Vlaamsch Nationaal Verbond (VNV), founded in 1931 by Staf de Clercq, with its proud slogan, 'All voor Vlaanderen, Vlaanderen voor Christus'.[22] Yet a third movement that influenced Gantois was Léon Degrelle's French-speaking Rexistes (Rex = Christus Rex), which was strongly authoritarian and had firm links with the Association Catholique de la Jeunesse belge. In 1941 the VNV opened an office in Lille and supporters of De Clercq and Degrelle, mainly Belgians or of Belgian origin, made themselves known to Gantois.

Already in December 1940 Gantois had submitted a memorandum to Hitler in which he argued for 'southern Flanders' to be part of a 'Dietschland': 'We are Low Germans and we want to return to the Reich.'[23] His followers, mainly intellectuals or Belgian Flemings who had resided for many years in France, reviled the France of Latin culture, now condemned the anti-German sentiments of Maurras and extolled the Nordic race to which they claimed to belong. They received support from north of the frontier. A significant move was made in 1941 by Borms, a Belgian 'activist' who had lent his name to Flemish separatism during the First World War. He set up for 'southern Flanders' an association called Zannekin, named after a Flemish folk hero. Its purpose was to work for a 'dietsch' state. He claimed that there were 120,000 (*sic*) Belgian Flemings living in Northern France and demanded that special schools should be set up to preserve the 'Flemishness' of their children and prevent their absorption into the French community. Zannekin would run the schools. In October 1942 the Belgian authorities,. who had been asked to subsidize the venture, rejected a proposal for the first school to be established in Lille, but declared a readiness, at some future date, to consider setting up a Belgian State school there (on the model of the German 'Auslandsschulen'). Despite this rebuff Zannekin gave out that the Belgian authorities had granted it a subsidy of 217,000 Belgian francs to support a school and appealed for further funds. But the proposal ran into the sand.

Zannekin also wanted to 'colonise' Northern France with Flemish immigrants. It particularly wanted Flemish teachers, peasants, civil servants, and priests to emigrate there and for land to be systematically bought up by the Flemings. This chimed well with the policy of Staf de Clercq, which was a Flemish version of 'Lebensraum'. France had a declining population, Belgian Flanders an increasing one. Thus the remaining French should be persuaded to move out and make room for Flemings to build a 'dietsch' state. These proposals were, however, too specific for the Germans, whose aim was to exploit the industry of Northern France without causing unrest. The upshot was that by the end of March 1941 the Germans forbade any further mention of such a state or of the Flemish 'need' for 'Lebensraum'.[24]

This did not mean, however, that they were not prepared to keep 'dietsch' sentiments alive, in readiness for the peace, in small ways. Radio Lille not only relayed the Flemish programmes of Radio Brussels, to which it became linked as Radio-Zender Brussel–Rijsel (Lille), but also stepped up its own broadcasts in the language. In January 1941 Abbé Gantois was given permission to resume publication in Roubaix ('Roobeke') of his periodical, *Le Lion de Flandres –De Torenwachter (The Lion of Flanders–The Belfry Look-out).* This occasionally printed ingenious propaganda in the form of children's stories in Flemish by a certain van de Meule, a Christian Brother.[25] The magazine exhorted parents to band together to teach their children Flemish, because this would have 'a snowball effect'.[26]

Since December 1941, when Vichy had authorized the teaching of regional languages in school for one and a half hours a week, on a voluntary basis, no action had been taken as regards Flemish. The German Oberfeldkommandant raised the matter with Carles, the regional prefect of Lille, stressing that the Germans attached great importance to the matter and the maximum use should be made of the opportunity provided.[27] The prefect referred it to Vichy, fearing, he said, that German pressure regarding Flemish was 'likely to have repercussions on the mind of the population'.[28] He contemplated fobbing off the Germans by replying that there had been no demand from parents to have classes arranged, but eventually offered the excuse to the Germans that the primary teachers either did not know Flemish or knew it insufficiently well to teach it.[29] Locally the matter was not allowed to rest. It was raised at the annual congress of the Vlaamsch Verbond van Frankrijk in the summer of 1942. At that gathering, which was distinguished by the singing of the Wilhelmus and the Vlaamsche Leeuw, one speaker declared that the bastion of Flemish remained 'the place where the catechism was taught'.[30] Official reluctance to pander to any Flemish aspirations was again shown when Vichy authorized the singing of regional songs in school; the local authorities informed the ministry that no suitable anthology of regional songs in Flemish existed, an assertion indignantly refuted by the Flamingants.[31]

The youth section of Gantois's movement, the Zuid Vlaamsch Jeugd (South Flemish Youth), consisted mainly of adult members' children. Numerically it was insignificant: its meetings – for singing, folk dancing, and excursions – hardly ever attracted more than fifty youngsters, many of whom were of Belgian nationality. One excursion made by the youth group, in May 1943, was to commemorate the third anniversary of the death of the Verdinaso leader, Joris van Severen, handed over by the Belgian Sûreté to the French and shot by them, together with his friend, Jan Rijkoort, on May 25, 1940. A ceremony held around his grave at Abbeville, attended by the South Flemish Youth in uniform and marked by Nazi salutes, caused a local scandal because of the insults that were proffered to the French army. Other activities included the publication of a journal, *Jeunes de Flandres,* which lauded anti-French attitudes, characterizing young Frenchmen as 'sloppy layabouts whose only thought is to go out dancing'.[32] Little wonder that the Germans, whose policy was one of 'divide and rule', thought it profitable to subsidize this tiny, aberrant, 'French' youth movement.

By 1943, when public opinion in the region was convinced that Germany could not win the war, the Vlaamsch Nationaal Verbond had muted its aspirations to separate from France. A few extremists, however, did not give up. Young Frenchmen underwent courses at the Waffen SS training school at Antwerp. The aim was to have at least 1,500 pass through this school, which not only gave military instruction but also put on cultural and political indoctrination courses conducted by notorious Flamingants. A police superintendent reporting on this to his superiors wrote: '. . . the idea of attaching French Flanders to the Germanic bloc is not abandoned . . . this contingency subsists and would be realised with the complicity of Frenchmen who gravitate round the Flemish League of France, if the nightmare that Germany is suffering on the Eastern Front were to be dispelled.'[33] A leading light behind the training scheme was a Dr Q—— of Douai, a former member of Taittinger's Jeunesses Patriotes, an eccentric racialist who went round measuring the skulls of local schoolchildren and students, presumably for proof of their 'Nordicity'. Although associated with the Flemish separatists, he also played the 'Wallonia' card. He promised former members of the Jeunesses Patriotes good jobs after the war if they would support his idea of a new state comprising Wallonia and the two Northern departments.[34]

A final move regarding French Flanders came in 1944, when the Belgian collaborators had fled to Germany before the Allied advance. Two provisional 'governments' were set up there for Belgium, the one under van de Wiele, the head of another Belgian Flemish movement, De Vlag, and the other under Degrelle, the Rexist leader. Van de Wiele said that after a German victory southern Flanders (Northern France) would be one of the twelve 'gouwen' ('Gaue') of a new Dutch-speaking state.

The Germans also sponsored in Northern France another, potentially much more dangerous, movement. In early 1942 there was set up at Douai the Volksdeutsche Sprachgemeinschaft Nordfrankreich (the 'German-language Community of Northern France').[35] Its membership comprised mainly Poles who had settled in the area. Most of these, whether they originated in pre-1914 German Poland or not, had worked in the Ruhr or Upper Silesia until 1921, when they had been obliged to opt for German or Polish nationality. At the time many had emigrated to Northern France. Now those who joined the new 'German-language Community' sought to obtain or recover German nationality and the material advantages this might confer. One estimate gave the association a membership of 25,000 (half the total Polish community living in Northern France) but this figure was probably exaggerated.

Nevertheless both the Germans and the French took the movement extremely seriously. German encouragement, through funds and other means, was given through the office of a Reichskommissar SS responsible, according to the title of his office, for 'the strengthening of Germanicism in the area of the Military Commander in France'. At the same time the Germans restricted the teaching of the Polish language, which had been allowed in French schools as a voluntary option. The prefect was informed that such teaching could only be continued for children whose parents had specifically requested it before 1942, and lists of those in question had to be submitted to the Germans.[36] The more thoughtful members of the Polish community of course realized that their sons might be lured into the German forces – in fact some enlistments into the Wehrmacht, the Waffen SS, and the NSKK (Transport Corps) did occur. The French, for their part, were dismayed that children of those whom they had considered always to be Polish, or even French, were being enticed by food to attend German language classes in a local château.[37] The sub-prefect of Douai reported that

> This propaganda is to be compared to that . . . with Flemish and autonomist leanings and it is to be feared that at a given moment Germany may say that Northern France comprises many Germanic people (Flemings, German Poles and now Ukrainians, who have recently arrived to work in the mines, although they are not miners), so that a referendum may be demanded.
>
> It is also to be feared that one day hands may be laid on the mining companies on the grounds that the miners are mainly Germans.
>
> This state of affairs worries many personages that are aware of it.[38]

The young, potential 'Volksdeutsche' continued nevertheless to be courted by the Germans. Special holiday camps, each run by a German 'Führerin' and housed in sumptuous country residences were set up. One report says that eight hundred boys and girls were dispatched to Hitler Youth camps in Germany, so that on their return they could pass on the training and indoctrination they had received. Buildings were even requisitioned for the schooling of the new élites and a few teachers arrived from Germany.[39]

German efforts to promote separatism in Northern France, perhaps as a countervailing force to pro-Allied sentiments, eventually grew half-hearted. At the beginning of the Occupation they had been more intense. The German military authorities in Paris had even vetoed the appointment of a new academy inspector at Laon to replace one whom the French considered to be inefficient because, they said, '. . . the placing of a more efficient academy inspector beyond the North–East Line can only serve to maintain French culture'.[40] Locally the French feared total annexation, the creation of an enlarged Flemish or Dutch-speaking state, or of a Lotharingian one.[41] For any such project to succeed, the winning over of youth was vital. On the whole, despite the efforts to embroil young people in separatist or anti-French activities, only a tiny minority became involved. Indeed there is evidence to support the view that the number of young people deported from the region to Germany for resisting the occupying authorities was unusually high, which gives an indication of the will to oppose German attempts to divide them from France.[42]

Another threat to French unity was posed by the parallel case of Brittany. As in Flanders the Breton autonomist movement had nineteenth-century roots and had been associated with the preservation of an indigenous language. In Lower Brittany confessional education had been deeply entrenched and resistance to the centripetal and secularizing educational reforms of the Third Republic had been fierce. The Breton language was seen in Paris as a mark of particularism, so much so that the anticlerical ministry of Combes had banned preaching in the vernacular. In Upper Brittany (the strip of land that extends across the neck of the peninsula) Breton had given way to French more quickly, since there the Revolutionary law of 1794 decreeing a school for every commune had been more effectively implemented.[43]

If Breton autonomism had a fairly long history, it came to the fore in the 1930s with the activities of a secret nationalist society, the Gwenn na Du – the 'White and Black' of the Breton flag. This organization had carried out bombing attacks, the most daring one having been directed against the prefecture of the Finistère. Moreover, slightly earlier, in 1927 the latest in a series of 'nationalist' parties, the Parti

Autonomiste Breton, had been set up by two figures who were to loom large during the war, Mordrel and Debauvais. The party's initial aim was federalism. The periodical *Breiz Atao* (Brittany for ever) became its spokesman, as it evolved more towards separatism. Since the party's opposition to war with Germany was well known, in 1939 Mordrel and Debauvais fled to the Reich. On the flimsy pretext that the Bretons were an oppressed racial minority, some half-hearted German backing for autonomy really began with the invasion.[44] On July 6, 1940, in a bid to take over power, Debauvais returned to Rennes with 600 Breton prisoners of war whom the Germans had released. In the event his Breton 'army' turned against him and joined a counter-demonstration. Debauvais had to ask for German protection. Nevertheless at Pontivy a so-called Breton National Council was formed.[45] The creation of this body was reported in a garbled German news-agency message which gave rise to rumours that an autonomous state was about to be set up and that for the five Breton departments the Germans had appointed a military governor independent of the High Command in Paris. Such rumours were reinforced by another 'canard' that the Germans, as a gesture of goodwill, intended to release all Breton prisoners of war and were considering a former deputy from the Lorient area as the head of an eventual autonomous regime. It was also rumoured that the Duc de Rohan had first been offered this post, but had declined.

In reality, German support for the Breton separatists was very muted. So long as the war against Britain continued, von Ribbentrop did not wish to provoke Vichy antagonism where there was not immediate advantage.[46] Local support for the autonomists was in any case extremely marginal. The Church excommunicated some of its leaders. The so-called 'national council' faded away. Another nationalist party, the Parti National Breton, headed by Raymond Delaporte, although a party 'tolerated' by the Germans, was never promoted to their 'approved' category,[47] and they gave it scant support. For three million Bretons, if they had wished it, the crucial hour for independence was past, at least until a German victory.

Breton sentiment, although not autonomist, was regionalist. This did not at all contradict Vichy's policy. Thus the regime was in no way ill-disposed when, in November 1940, the Union Régionaliste Bretonne and the Association Bretonne advanced claims 'on behalf of the province of Brittany' for a regional assembly and for the recognition of its linguistic and cultural rights.[48] The linguistic issue was particularly pressed: a request was made for the compulsory teaching of Breton in the primary schools of Lower Brittany.

The demand for the teaching of Breton had been one of the planks of the pre-war Breiz Atao movement. In 1934 an association named Ar Brezoneg er Skol had been founded to achieve this objective. In 1936 Trémentin, a Breton deputy, had introduced a bill to allow bilingualism in rural primary schools where Breton was normally spoken, with optional courses in urban areas and in secondary schools. Jean Zay, however, was opposed to any such concessions to educational regionalism.[49] Already in 1936 the Bishop of Quimper had made Breton a compulsory subject in the Catholic schools of his diocese. Another movement of similar name, Ar Brezoneg er Skoliau, had been founded by Delaporte in 1937 to promote the language in all the confessional schools of the province. By the outbreak of the war most of the elected leaders in the five Breton departments and their communes advocated teaching the language to all schoolchildren.[50]

The measure of December 1941 which had allowed regional languages to be taught in primary schools did not satisfy enthusiasts such as Yann Fouéré, editor of *La Bretagne* and a former sub-prefect at Morlaix. Fouéré, although not an autonomist, pressed his friend Mouraille, then Bonnard's 'chef de cabinet', to persuade the minister to extend this concession to secondary schools. He accused Souriau, the eminent French literary scholar, then rector of Rennes, of dragging his feet on the linguistic issue, and wanted Bonnard to give a subsidy to Ar Brezoneg er Skol.[51] Whether this request reflected popular demand is open to question: in February 1942 the prefect of Finistère reported that only one parent had asked for optional courses in Breton in the primary school.[52] Nevertheless, the language issue was kept alive throughout the war. In 1941 a group of writers undertook the harmonization of the main Breton dialects as a necessary preliminary to the production of Breton textbooks. For some reason the group was held to be too collaborationist and was supplanted by another, who produced a different standardized orthography. From 1942 onwards a school at Plestin (Côtes-du-Nord) undertook experimentally to teach all subjects in Breton. In 1944 the academy of Rennes requested that there should be an optional test of Breton in the baccalaureate.[53] The advance of the language was temporarily halted at the end of the war, although the Deixonne Law of 1951 eventually allowed it again to be taught as an option.[54]

The positive attitude of Vichy towards Breton culture was illustrated when, in March 1941, Carcopino announced his intention of allowing Breton history to be taught in schools and appointed a six-man commission to draw up guidelines for a textbook. The chair of Breton history at Rennes, vacant since 1894, was filled by the appointment of Pocquet du Haut-Jussé. In 1942 a test of Breton history and geography was introduced into the primary leaving-certificate. In 1943 a summer school was held at Ploërmel (Morbihan) to train primary teachers in the teaching of Breton regional studies.[55] Such steps took the wind out of the autonomists' sails. If autonomists were teachers, the authorities tried to transfer them out of the province, although on at least one occasion the Germans forbade the removal of an activist teacher.[56] Delaporte's Parti National Breton established links with Doriot's Parti Populaire Français and became less militantly 'bretonnisant'. At one stage Doriot suggested that the youth movements of the two parties should merge. By 1943 the Doriotistes had set up a commission which eventually published a brochure[57] demanding some autonomy for Brittany and respect for cultural rights. Such manœuvrings found little support among the bulk of the population. Nor were they well-disposed towards the Germans, except for a small minority. However, a few young Bretons, led by Le Coz, who went under the name of Laisné, broke away from the Parti National Breton and, under the name of the 'Milice Perrot', ended up as a military unit fighting under German command.[58]

In general, however, Vichy went some way towards meeting moderate demands. The first regional prefect of the province, Jean Quenette, appointed by Darlan, adopted a liberal policy. He established a regional committee which elaborated a draft statute providing at a later date for a regional assembly in which Breton would be recognized as an official language. In this case, through a prudent set of educational and other measures, Vichy successfully defused a situation that was potentially dangerous for French unity.

The case of Alsace-Lorraine aroused different feelings among Germans, although, with the exception of the brief interlude from 1870–1918, the territories had been French since the seventeenth century. Their return to France had been welcomed in 1918 by the local population. It had been the 'schools question' that had been the immediate cause of some local ill-will being manifested towards French policy. At first the Republic had respected the Concordat and had allowed State schools in Alsace-Lorraine to continue to be denominational. When in 1924 Herriot had announced that the law on the separation of Church and State was to be applied this had aroused such a storm of protest that, after reference to the Conseil d'État, Paris had given way and maintained the status quo. Nevertheless, from then onwards small minority groups had raised demands for some degree of autonomy, some with the covert aim of eventually reintegrating the provinces into the Reich. In 1926 the Elsass-Lothringisches Heimatbund had been founded, followed a year later by the Autonomische Landespartei, the work of Karl Roos, eventually executed in 1940 by the French as a traitor. A further development was the setting-up by Bickler, a Strasburg lawyer, of the Elsass-Lothringische Jungmannschaft, which developed from being a youth organization into a Nazi-type political party recruited, among others, from former members of the 'Studentenkorps' of the one-time Kaiser-Wilhelm university of Strasburg, who sought reunification with Germany. At the same time a close friend of Bickler's, Friedrich Spieser, started the Wanderbund Erwin-von-Steinbach, on the lines of the Wandervogel, the German youth organization. The rise of Nazism alienated most Alsatians completely from such organizations, which were officially outlawed by Daladier in 1939. Meanwhile across the Rhine, Robert Ernst, an Alsatian in exile who had opted for Germany in 1918, had founded the Bund der Elsass-Lothringer im Reich. There were also sections for Alsace-Lorraine students in the 'Studentenkorps' of most German universities and at Frankfurt University there had been set up an academic institute for the study of Alsace-Lorraine affairs. Official Germany covertly backed all such anti-French organizations, whilst declaring in a 'good neighbour' treaty signed with France in December 1938 that it had irrevocably abandoned all claim to the provinces.

In 1940 the situation changed dramatically. Although the Armistice applicable to the whole of France in its 1939 frontiers contained no specific reference to Alsace-Lorraine, the Germans immediately set about installing their own civil administration in the departments of the Haut-Rhin, the Bas-Rhin, and the Moselle – those parts of Alsace and Lorraine which had reverted to France in 1918. The legitimacy of French jurisdiction prompted Vichy to maintain, although with diminishing insistence, muted opposition to Germanization of the area. According to Weygand no less than 112 protests were registered with the Germans,[59] but secrecy was maintained for fear that public expostulation would aggravate the lot of the inhabitants, although refugees from the area made known their discontent regarding this policy at Vichy. This had no effect upon the Germans, who maintained their vigilance even in small matters. Thus, for example, French publishers were not allowed to show the disputed provinces as part of France on maps in textbooks for use in schools.[60] No Vichy minister was allowed to visit the region, although Lamirand did once get as far as Nancy, once more a French frontier city.[61]

Within Alsace and Lorraine Germanization proceeded swiftly, accompanied by the introduction of Nazi institutions.[62] All outward vestiges of French rule had to disappear. From July 29, 1940 the use of French was forbidden. All inscriptions in French had to be removed, street-names were changed, family names, if markedly French, were Germanized, as were even the very inscriptions on gravestones. French flags had to be torn up. The wearing of the beret was forbidden. Kléber's statue was removed from its square in Strasburg. The action of eradicating all traces of Frenchness was carried out with German thoroughness. In June 1940 the new Gauleiter in Lorraine had ordered the teachers of Metz to instruct their pupils immediately in the singing of the first verse of 'Deutschland über alles' and of the so-called 'Niederländisches Dankgebet', the hymn of thanksgiving.[63]

Young people, whether they had escaped to the southern zone or remained behind in the enlarged Gau of Baden, into which Alsace was incorporated, or the newly constituted Westmark, into which the annexed part of Lorraine, together with Luxemburg, was incorporated, were soon directly affected by the new regime. In Colmar Robert Ernst, who had returned from Germany to be the advisor to the new Gauleiter and Oberstadtkommissar (burgomaster) of Strasburg, founded, on June 20, 1940, the Elsässischer Hilfsdienst, which on March 22, 1941 became the Alsatian section of the Nazi Party. Also in June 1940 there was set up in Strasburg a Deutsche Volksjugend, renamed on September 8, 1940 the Hitlerjugend (Hitler Youth). Its first members were drawn from the Elsass-Lothringische Jungmannschaft and the Wanderbund Erwin-von-Steinbach. By the end of August 1940 all French youth organizations in Alsace had been dissolved; Lorraine followed suit shortly afterwards.[64] By January 1941 there were 8,141 Hitler-Youth members in the 'Kreis' (canton) of Zabern (Saverne) alone. Bullying and blackmail, particularly if the father were a civil servant, were used on families to get children to join. On Hitler's fifty-second birthday a special drive for recruitment was made in Metz. From 1941 onwards only boys and girls belonging to the Hitler Youth (HJ: for boys) or the female equivalent, the Bund Deutscher Mädel (BDM), were allowed to enter secondary schools. On January 2, 1942 a law making membership of a youth organization compulsory for all young people aged between 10–18 was introduced into Alsace from Germany, where it had been applied since 1936. The Germans claimed that 70 per cent of these age groups did already belong to either the HJ or BDM (for 14–18-year-olds), or the Jungvolk or Jungmädelbund for

10–14-year-olds.[65] For boys the movement was seen as a preparation for military service: special sections – transport, air, naval, signals – were instituted in the HJ. At twelve youngsters underwent rifle and machine-gun practice. At fourteen they had to attend a month's military-training course in camp. By 1943 fourteen-year-olds were manning anti-aircraft guns, thus releasing soldiers for service in Russia.[66]

Youth was subjected to a constant barrage of propaganda. Occasionally, however, this misfired. Taken from school to see the German film, *Victory in the West*, pupils applauded heartily when French troops were shown entering Belgium.[67] But the Germans persevered. Their aim was to train youth as fanatical Nazis: this meant withdrawing young people as much as possible from parental or religious influences. Thus the HJ held three meetings a week, with the Sunday one deliberately timed to coincide with Church services.[68] But this Nazi regimentation of youth made no lasting impression: as one commentator remarked, at the Liberation 'the whole Hitlerian edifice crumbled as quickly as it had been imposed'.[69]

The most dramatic change for the young, the schools, and public life in general, was the switch to High German as the official, and sole, language. In schools it naturally became the sole medium of instruction. For five years no French at all, even as a foreign language, would be taught in school. Pupils caught speaking French were severely punished. In a move to eliminate dialect, the German *Schriftsprache* was introduced into teacher-training institutions. A drive to teach High German to adults, undertaken by the *Deutsches Volksbildungswerk*, was so successful that by the end of 1940 some 1,000 courses followed by 25,000 students were running in Alsatian towns and villages.[70] Schools, public libraries, and even private homes were 'purged' of French books. At the winter solstice ('Sonnewendefeier') Hitler Youth lit a great bonfire on the crest of the Vosges, consigning to the flames as many French books as they could lay hands on, as well as German translations of such notoriously anti-German works as Bazin's *Les Oberlé* and Barrès's *Colette Baudoche*.[71]

Schools formally reopened in October 1940 and by then

Hitler's portrait had replaced the crucifix in the classrooms. The entirely confessional institutions, such as the 400-year-old Protestant Gymnasium (*lycée*) of Strasburg, remained closed. At Metz, however, the old grammar school, where von Ribbentrop had been educated, did reopen. Some schools were able to function only in half-day sessions, because of the teacher shortage.[72] The confessional or semi-confessional character of schools, which dated back to the Napoleonic Concordat and which neither the Germans in 1870 nor the French in 1924 had succeeded in changing, remained a problem for the Nazis, who wanted to diminish the influence of the Church. In 1940 Bürckel, the new Gauleiter of the Westmark, which included Lorraine, wrote to Goering urging that the 'schools question' be settled once and for all by a Diktat aligning schools with those of the Reich: a clean break with the past should be made.[73] The outcome was that Hitler unilaterally declared that the Concordat was no longer binding in the newly annexed territories. Schools were allowed to retain religion as a subject on the timetable, but otherwise they would be secularized. Orders such as the 1,500-strong Sisters of Ribeauvillé were no longer allowed to teach. Religious instruction became obligatory only up to school-leaving age and after that age pupils did not even require parental permission to give it up. Religious-instruction lessons were placed at the end of the morning or afternoon sessions, so that it was made more attractive for pupils to persuade their parents to let them opt out, as was also possible. Moreover, eventually 'opting-in' was required: parents had to apply within the first two weeks of the school year for their children to receive religious instruction. It says much for the piety of Alsatians that very few pupils failed to attend the lessons, despite the difficulties placed in their path. Even these lessons had to end with the obligatory 'Heil Hitler' from the teacher, to which the more insubordinate pupils responded in rhyming phrase, 'Zwei Liter', adding *sotto voce,* 'Und sechs Gläser' (Two litres – and six glasses). Every effort was made to traduce the faith of the young: children were taught in school to sing such edifying couplets as:

> Wir wollen nicht mehr Christen sein
> Denn Jesus war ein Juden Schwein.
> (We no longer wish to be Christians,
> for Jesus was a Jewish swine.)[74]

At the same time school structures were changed to conform to the German tripartite model of Volksschule (primary school), Mittelschule (intermediate school), and Höhere Schulen (secondary schools). The innovation that most shocked the largely Catholic population of Alsace was the introduction of coeducation into the Volksschule. Protestants and Catholics alike were also incensed at the mixing of the denominations in the same school.

A new, German aim was adopted for schooling: it had been laid down by Rust, the Reich Education Minister on December 15,1939, as the training of the young to work for 'Führer and People'. In Alsace the Baden syllabuses of 1939 were brought into use. In them it was decreed that the content of education should reflect a 'warlike mentality' ('wehrgeistiges Prinzip'). German lessons in the primary school should deal with the national heroes, those endowed with the characteristics of the Nordic type, such as honour, will-power, sense of duty, and loyalty to one's kith and kin. To update Alsatian children's knowledge of German Dr Karl Probst wrote a special textbook, *Deutsches Denken. Deutsche Sprache,* in which a whole section was devoted to new German word-formations such as 'curtain of fire', 'shock troops', 'convoy', 'flamethrower'. In history and geography the emphasis should be on the period spanned by Bismarck and Hitler and on the threat to the Reich because of its geographical position, as a 'people without space', 'ein Volk ohne Raum'. In both history and biology the ethos was one of dominance and racism.

A special school for training future élites, known by its acronym as a Napola (National-politische Erziehungsanstalt), was set up at Rouffach in 1941, on the model of the thirty other Napolas scattered all over Germany. It would appear that other types of special schooling, such as the Adolf-Hitler-Schulen run by the HJ and also intended for élites, were not available in Alsace, but suitable pupils were sent across the Rhine to institutions in Baden.[75] In Alsace teacher-training colleges, where the pupils wore HJ uniforms, were set up at Colmar (for boys) and at Célestat (Schlettstadt) (for girls), but the overwhelming majority of the pupils were from Baden and not from Alsace. Meanwhile, as will be seen, the French 'écoles normales' of Alsace continued to function in exile in the southern zone.

One major problem facing Schmitthenner, appointed by the civil administration as head of the department of education, was what to do with the teachers of Alsace. Finally they were dispatched on re-education ('Umschulung') courses: primary teachers were sent to 'Gauschulen' on Lake Constance, secondary teachers just across the Rhine to Karlsruhe and Freiburg. Those teachers trained before 1918, during the previous period of German rule, had only to stay six weeks. Younger ones, trained by the French during the inter-war period, had to stay up to six months and then, instead of returning immediately to Alsace, spent some time teaching in schools of the 'Altreich' in order to become thoroughly familiar with the German system and to learn how to use the curriculum to promote Nazism. The retraining courses comprised lectures on how to teach German, history, and geography, which were compulsory for all teachers, and the rehearsing of German Volkslieder and the Party repertoire of songs. Before teachers could be returned to Alsace the approval of the local Nazi-party branch had to be given; in many cases this was denied and Alsatian teachers were forced to remain in Germany to teach, their places being taken by Germans.[76]

These measures caused a crisis of conscience for many teachers, still loyal in their hearts to France. Their dilemma was heightened when they were obliged to swear an oath of allegiance to Hitler and Germany, the most extreme form of which ran:

> I am resolved to remain active in the service of the Führer and National-Socialist Germany . . . The Führer has wiped out the shameful *Diktat* of Versailles after a gigantic struggle, reconquering German Alsace for the Reich. I endorse the return of my homeland to the Reich and will unconditionally and cheerfully fulfil the task entrusted to me as a German teacher and a servant of the State. As such I acknowledge that I must accomplish my duty to the Reich wherever there is need, in accordance with the principles of the National Socialist Reich. I will

therefore unreservedly fulfil the mission entrusted to me, wherever I may be placed.[77]

Such apostasy to the French cause gave rise to much heart-searching. Eighty primary teachers smuggled a message asking for instructions about the oath to the rector of the academy of Strasburg, in exile at Périgueux. The reply came back that they should subscribe to the declaration but continue to serve the interests of France. If sent away to Germany they should make good their escape. By August 1941 about thirty had done so.[78] For teachers in Alsace the final link with France had been severed when the Syndicat National des Instituteurs, along with all other unions, had been dissolved and they had been obliged to join the Nazi teachers' union, the NS-Lehrerbund. It is understandable that at the Liberation the most difficult cases of collaboration to decide were those that concerned Alsace-Lorraine. On the whole leniency prevailed. Even those teachers who had joined the Nazi Party itself – and great pressure was put on them to do so – were usually not dealt with severely, provided that the step had been deferred as long as possible.[79]

In higher education the break was even more drastic. Since the university of Strasburg had been evacuated to Clermont-Ferrand, this left a gap the Germans were not slow to fill. They announced that they would reinstall the old Wilhelmine Reichs-Universität Strassburg. In the words of the Alsatian-born and anti-French historian, Ernst Anrich, the city would become, after having once been 'a gate of invasion for the Western mind', 'the salient of a great defence against Western thinking' and 'a point of illumination [for German culture]'.[80] A former rector of Bonn, Karl Schmitt, was appointed to head the reconstituted Kaiser-Wilhelm Universität. The traditional Catholic and Protestant theology faculties which, exceptionally, had survived under French rule, were not restarted, on the specious grounds that religious needs were already met in nearby Freiburg and Heidelberg.[81] This decision did much to discredit in advance the new institution among the still devoutly religious local population. It was ironical that the father of Anrich, appointed the new dean of the Philosophical Faculty, had once held the chair of ecclesiastical history in the university.

The university was solemnly opened by Rust, the Reich education minister, in November 1941, in the presence of all the other German university rectors. It had been intended to recruit an academic staff of 129, but this number was eventually reduced. Not a single member of the old French university was re-engaged, and the only full professor of Alsatian origin was Anrich himself. The faculties were heavily slanted towards Nazi ideology. In the philosophical faculty the emphasis was on 'Germanistik', strongly tinctured with totalitarian ideology. In law it was not the rational nature of jurisprudence but 'the people's feeling for law' ('völkisches Rechtsempfinden') that was stressed,[82] which was the negation of legality as it is normally understood. In science prominence was given to the Nazi form of biology. The largest faculty was medicine. Its infamous 'research' interests are well known. It was here that Haagen performed his wicked experiments on victims taken from the Struthof concentration camp and Hirst, anatomist extraordinary, built up a collection of Jewish skulls in order to facilitate 'racial comparisons'. Perhaps it is little wonder that, despite running extension courses and receiving enthusiastic support from Ernst, burgomaster of Strasburg, the university attracted little local support and hardly reached one thousand students, of whom half were in the medical faculty.

Measures to nazify the older young people could not in the end succeed without military-style coercion. A first step in this direction was taken when compulsory labour service ('Reichsarbeitsdienst') was introduced for all young people, male and female, aged between seventeen and twenty-five for a period lasting nine months. In November 1941 the first contingent of about a thousand entrained for manual labour on the other side of the Rhine. One such convoy, defying the presence of German officers, departed to the singing of the 'Marseillaise'. Military service proper was still to come, although in October 1940 voluntary recruiting offices for the Waffen SS had been opened in Alsace and by June 1941 young men were being accepted as volunteers into the Wehrmacht. Ernst claimed that by 1942 the number of recruits volunteering had risen to 2,700 in all.[83] To swell the ranks of 'volunteers' pressure was sometimes put on their families, some of whom were even threatened with deportation.[84] As in the rest of France, a few young men enlisted in order to take part in the 'Crusade against Bolshevism', exhorted to do so by Bacher, a Strasburg schools inspector, and Georg, a local student leader.[85] Secondary-school pupils who did so were exempted from the school-leaving examination and were granted immediate officer rank.[86] In May 1942 Hitler decreed the call-up of those of the 1922 'class' who had completed their labour service and had shown themselves to be reliable. Argument arose as to how this measure of compulsion could be applied. To avoid complications in international law, conscripts had to be given full German nationality. The Wehrmacht, supported by Wagner, the Gauleiter of Alsace, had misgivings as to the loyalty of those press-ganged in this way.[87] In general, however, the Party chiefs saw it as an ideal way of assimilating young 'Volksdeutsche'. Eventually they got their way and on August 25, 1942 general conscription was formally introduced into Alsace. Four days later it was announced that Lorraine was following suit. The call-up initially affected the 'classes' of 1920–4, although it was progressively extended to include all those born between 1908 and 1927. The announcement raised a storm of muted protest. By November 11, 1942 some 12,000 young men had fled to France proper or to Switzerland to avoid service. Many conscripts left their Alsatian villages as a group, according to one source, marching to the station under the French flag and singing French songs. Some donned their old French army uniforms to report at the German barracks.[88] Care was taken to distribute these recruits of dubious loyalty throughout the Wehrmacht rather than to concentrate them in local units. In September 1944 Hitler had ordered the call-up of the last reserve, the 'Volkssturm', which included boys of sixteen; on October 25, 1944 this measure was extended to Alsace. In all 200,000 Alsace-Lorrainers were mobilized, 25,000 were killed, 22,000 were reported missing, and 10,000 badly wounded. French youth, illegally mobilized in the service of the enemy, paid its toll on the Eastern Front.

The weakness of Vichy's reaction to these arbitrary

measures remains inexplicable. In 1941 the French delegation to the Armistice Commission had warned Vichy 'that the strong vitality emanating from National Socialism can appeal to youth'. It reported that in Alsace-Lorraine at the time youngsters were throwing themselves into 'the delights of generously organised sport' and a few were volunteering for the SS.[89] After the German announcement of conscription Laval did make a protest to Abetz in September 1942,[90] and the frequency of French protests increased as the Allied invasion drew near. But the Germans paid no heed and even arrested French deserters from the German army in the southern zone, theoretically free from their direct control.

In their turn the Germans complained about the continued existence of the institutions of Alsace-Lorraine in the southern zone, and the freedom of movement that Alsace-Lorrainers enjoyed there. Those whom they were now willing to accept as their own nationals but who remained outside their clutches posed a threat to them. The threat was sometimes a real one, as witness what one young Lorrainer, a soldier serving in the Vichy Armistice Army, wrote to *Algrange en exil,* a Lorraine news-sheet published in the southern zone: '. . . .for a young man who has done his military service, served in the war and been taken prisoner, what finer thing is there than to remain a soldier [after release] and facilitate our return?'[91] All German attempts to stifle such sentiments of 'revanche' were unsuccessful.

A particular bone of contention was in fact the position of Alsace-Lorrainers serving, like the soldier mentioned, either in the Armistice Army or in the Chantiers de la Jeunesse. In late 1940 the French armistice delegation at Wiesbaden received a number of German demands that such young men should be discharged and repatriated. General Doyen merely replied that, since they were Frenchmen, there was nothing abnormal about their situation. German armistice-control commissions visiting camps in the southern zone made a special point of questioning men from Alsace-Lorraine. This gave rise to a number of incidents. They claimed, for instance, that 150 youths in this category were being held against their will in the Chantiers camp in the forest of Tronçais (Allier), having been deprived of their clothes and demobilization papers. Similar cases of camps near Pau were cited.[92] At first the French maintained a firm line and told General von Stülpnagel that the Germans had no standing in the matter. As a result of political pressure, however, there was a shift in policy. After a meeting in November 1940 presided over by Pétain and attended by Laval and other interested ministers, it was agreed that a blind eye would be turned to the desertion of Alsace-Lorrainers from Chantiers camps. Indeed their escape was made easier by posting them to camps located near the demarcation line. Shortly afterwards General Doyen informed the Germans that those who wished to return home would be discharged. Lists would be furnished so that the Germans could strike off any who belonged to families whom the Germans had already expelled from Alsace-Lorraine as being pro-French. Of the 4,000 men serving at the time in the Chantiers de la Jeunesse who were affected, only half requested to be included in the list.[93]

As regards those who had actually volunteered to serve in the Armistice Army, Pétain at first proved more intractable. Von Stülpnagel claimed to have received hundreds of letters from wives and parents pleading for the return of their menfolk. In January 1941 the French finally agreed to release all those who wished to return home. Again, only about half, out of a total of 3,500, expressed a desire to do so. Even for these, when it came to making practical arrangements, the French dragged their feet. The Germans complained that seven special trains, due to bring back about 4,500 discharged from the Chantiers and the Army, arrived in the occupied zone with only 700 men on board. Even after the French had released the classes of 1938 and 1939, in August 1941, the Germans alleged that some 2,000 Alsace-Lorrainers remained in the Army, having been provided with false papers to conceal their identity. The Germans were particularly perturbed that until November 1942, when the Armistice Army was virtually disbanded, Alsatian units survived. The 152nd Infantry Regiment traced its lineage back to the 'régiment d'Alsace' of 1794. A half-brigade of riflemen wore insignia of Alsace and paraded colours which displayed the arms of Alsatian towns.[94]

On strictly educational matters Vichy arrangements

regarding Alsace-Lorraine were a thorn in the Germans' side. At Périgueux the academy of Strasburg and at Clermont-Ferrand the university of Strasburg carried on in exile under their rector, Terracher, until the Germans directly intervened in 1943. Terracher was resolutely anti-German. He was not an Alsatian. He had made his career abroad and then served in succession as rector of Dijon and then Bordeaux before being appointed to Strasburg in 1938. Pétain held him in high esteem. At one stage the Marshal had offered to make him minister, but Terracher had declined, saying that he wished to continue as rector of the academy in exile. He had nevertheless accepted first the post of director of secondary education and then secretary-general in the ministry whilst still continuing as rector of Strasburg.[95] His promotion under Chevalier to be the top civil servant in the ministry may have sparked off a peremptory German ultimatum three days later for the immediate return of all Alsace-Lorraine teachers, for the Germans regarded him with great hostility and made repeated attempts to oust him.[96]

A number of teacher-training institutions had been evacuated with their pupils to the Dordogne and there were many other pupils from Alsace-Lorraine in the southern zone. The tide of refugees, adults, and children, from the annexed territories, originally put at 400,000, had receded to about a quarter of that number by the end of 1940.[97] Nevertheless, at first some 800 primary teachers had been evacuated and 400 classes for refugee children had been started, scattered throughout the southern zone. In the Vaucluse the prefect thought it necessary to issue instructions that they were to be well treated and not mocked for 'their accent, customs or beliefs'. The local academy inspector appended an instruction that the local children should be given, as part of moral instruction, lessons on the duties owed to refugees.[98] The number of primary teachers fluctuated, but by the Liberation they had increased to 3,000, made up of those that had escaped, some 400 monoglot French speakers expelled by the Germans from Lorraine, and about the same number of teaching nuns unable to exercise their calling, as well as those that had not returned originally. This sizeable nucleus of an *émigré* community gave the Germans cause for concern.

Thus in September 1940 the Occupation authorities made a first demand for the return home of Alsace-Lorrainers training to be primary teachers.[99] This demand remaining unanswered, they sent a detailed list of institutions and pupils: the Catholic teacher-training colleges for the Bas-Rhin, normally located at Obernai (Oberenheim), with 40 boys, evacuated to Solignac (Haute-Vienne), and the one normally located at Strasburg, with 40 girls, evacuated to Périgueux (Dordogne); the Catholic colleges for the Haut-Rhin, normally located at Colmar, with 160 boys, evacuated to Aiguillon (Lot-et-Garonne), and at Célestat (Schlettstadt), with 120 girls, evacuated to Bergerac (Dordogne); and the two Protestant teacher-training colleges for Alsace, with a total of 100 pupils, boys and girls. They alleged that the trainees were being subjected to 'frenzied propaganda' not to return home. By December 1940 German patience was exhausted and they resorted to bluff. It was then that, three days after his appointment as minister, Chevalier was telephoned by Abetz in the early hours of the morning and called upon to deliver up 'all education personnel' to the Germans within twenty-four hours. Otherwise the Germans would invade the southern zone![100] To his credit – and this was mentioned in his favour at his trial after the war – Chevalier called the bluff, refused to comply, and was backed by Pétain.[101] The sledge-hammer threatened by the Germans to crack a nutshell may have also been employed because of their general suspicion and dislike of Chevalier. They were clearly irritated also when the French offered salary inducements to persuade refugee teachers not to return home.[102] In June 1942 they publicly announced that those Alsace-Lorrainers who failed to return home within a month would forfeit all their property. Paradoxically, they did not use force to compel them to return after the total occupation of France.[103]

From Alsace a special envoy, Ministerialrat Kraft, who had for a while been in charge of secondary education in Alsace after the annexation, was sent to Paris to negotiate the return of people, material, and 'cultural objects' to Alsace-Lorraine. Kraft informed de Brinon that 'according to the Armistice agreement the German government has the right to demand the return of people and material to their Alsatian homeland by the speediest possible means'.[104] Many parents wanted news of their children: accordingly he demanded a nominal roll of Strasburg students now studying at Clermont-Ferrand and elsewhere, newly qualified Alsatian teachers now assigned to posts in France, and pupil teachers in training. At the same time the French university authorities should hand over the dossiers of some 500 Alsatian students who had now transferred to German universities and those of 610 secondary teachers now teaching in France, although domiciled in Alsace. Vichy replied that it would only give up the files if those concerned agreed. (In June 1942 a request from the Lorraine authorities for 143 dossiers of teachers was answered in the same vein.) Rather naively, Kraft also planned to administer a questionnaire to the teachers about their attitudes. The real purpose was apparent when teachers were asked to subscribe to a declaration in the questionnaire which ran, 'The Führer has given Alsace back to the Reich. I subscribe to the return of my homeland to the Reich and will fulfil my duty as a German educationist.' Teachers who signed the statement, which was similar to the one teachers in Alsace itself had had to make, were asked to accept repatriation and to serve anywhere in Germany.

Chevalier (C. of January 22, 1941) had already conceded that students could return home if they wished, even although they might have contracted to serve the State, for example, as a teacher, for a fixed period of years, as was usual. He asked that those who did *not* wish to return home should sign a declaration to that effect. The rector of Besançon pointed out that this might provoke German reprisals on their families, and the declaration was dropped. When Carcopino succeeded Chevalier he gave Terracher *carte blanche* to 'act according to your mind and conscience so as to safeguard French interests'.[105] Kraft was thereupon promptly rebuffed: neither teachers nor pupils would be compelled to leave the southern zone. As for older school pupils, even if their parents in Alsace had requested their return, Terracher declared that he would act according to two statutes, one French, the other German. The French legal text merely stated that fathers had no right to instruct children over sixteen when they should (or should not) use their passport to leave the country; the German text stated simply that over the age of fifteen a child owed no absolute duty of obedience to his parents. A French inter-ministerial commission for Alsace-Lorraine affairs confirmed these rights.[106] The Germans continued their protests, but in practice accepted the situation. Kraft had better success with the 'cultural objects' whose return he had demanded, such as the Treasure of Strasburg Cathedral, but recouped little material belonging to the Alsatian training colleges: Terracher fobbed him off with fifty dilapidated beds!

Within France German policy regarding Alsace-Lorrainers was erratic. Sometimes local German commanders made impossible demands, such as ordering French teachers to instruct refugee pupils in German, disregarding the fact that they did not know the language.[107] In summer 1941, presumably in the hope of luring some to stay, they allowed pupils from Alsace-Lorraine, as well as some from the Low Countries, to return home for a holiday. In 1942 the French sought entry and exit permits for visits by 150 pupils to Alsace and by 120 to Lorraine. This time the request was refused on the grounds that 'internal traffic' in Germany was too heavy, although permits would be granted for the one-way trip.[108]

Even after the invasion of the southern zone Périgueux continued to be a rallying-point for young Alsatians. Deserters from the German army were passed on to the Resistance by teachers, sometimes after they had winkled out *agents-provocateurs* planted by the Germans. In 1943 a 'maquis Alsace-Lorraine', with a nucleus of a score of primary teachers, was constituted. The number of refugee primary teachers grew, and all continued to draw their salaries.[109] Little wonder that Kraft, the frustrated envoy, reported, 'Terracher is the greatest opponent of Franco-German entente and should be removed from the government (*sic*) as soon as possible.'[110]

A further threat to young Alsace-Lorrainers came in early 1943 when Vichy called up the first contingents of young Frenchmen to work in Germany. Terracher persuaded Laval to exempt them, since if they returned beyond the Vosges they would immediately be conscripted into the Wehrmacht.[111]

General de La Porte du Theil similarly protected those discharged 'jeunes' of the Chantiers de la Jeunesse who did not wish to return home.[112]

After the creation of their own Reichs-Universität in Strasburg the Germans were constantly irritated by the continued existence of the University of Strasburg in exile. Himmler regarded its 500 students at Clermont-Ferrand as a security threat[113] and was anxious that they should return home to swell the numbers of the new university, in which the SS had a strong interest. On the other hand the German Foreign Office and Wagner, the Gauleiter of Alsace, believed that it would be better if the students were coaxed back rather than coerced. Abetz did his best to stifle the activity of the university in exile, even trying to persuade Vichy to ban its publications and to invalidate its diplomas. Finally alleged Resistance activity in the university gave the German hardliners the pretext to act. A student, G___ M___, denounced some of his fellows and the teaching staff for 'terrorism', espionage, use of false papers, and anti-German propaganda, charges that the university later refuted. However, the SS got its way and on November 25, 1943 German troops stormed the university precincts, in so doing killing M. Callomp, a professor of Greek who also held a chair at the Collège de France, and also two students.[114] Eighty-six students and staff were held for questioning; only sixty of these belonged to the university of Strasburg (the buildings were shared with the university of Clermont-Ferrand) and of these only thirty-eight were natives of Alsace-Lorraine; seventeen were of military age. This led Vichy to believe that the raid might not necessarily have been directed against students from the annexed territories.[115] By February 1944 those not released had been shipped via the staging camp at Compiègne to concentration camps in Germany. When the Americans entered Buchenwald they found alive a group of nineteen professors and students. With characteristic opportunism the Nazis confiscated the university records, appropriated some equipment, and undertook 'racial investigations' of 107 students, among whom they gratifyingly found 39 with 'biologically valuable blood'.[116] It would appear that Vichy made no protest at the raid until August 3, 1944.[117]

Nevertheless, the raid soon became widely known. It inspired Aragon to write his poem, 'Chant de l'université de Strasbourg'. A Resistance news-sheet, *Étoiles,* associated with the Éditions de Minuit, condemned these 'new crimes against the spirit'.[118] A Paris student group, L'Union des Étudiants Patriotes, circulated a tract about the raid, a copy of which fell into Gidel's hands and eventually reached Bonnard. They also clandestinely laid a wreath on the Sorbonne war memorial in memory of the dead students.

The Germans had hoped by their action to bring about the closure of the university. However, Vichy merely arranged for its dispersal to supposedly safe areas.[119] It was agreed that the Catholic theological faculty should move to Angers, the Protestant one to Aix-en-Provence; medicine should be relocated at Bordeaux. The other faculties were also dispersed. Terracher, now stripped of his posts, was to be succeeded as rector by Forster, dean of the medical faculty.

The refusal, ineffective as were the actions taken, to acknowledge that the youth of Alsace-Lorraine were lost to France is perhaps the most striking example in educational matters where German persistence was opposed by French unwillingness to yield.[120] Only the likes of Bonnard would appear to have accepted the fact of annexation. For having declared that one day a France that included Metz and Strasburg would be restored in its entirety a history teacher at the Lycée Louis-le-Grand was banished by the minister to the provinces.[121] This contrasts with his predecessors, Chevalier and Carcopino, who had given way as little as possible to German pressure. Perhaps the continued will to resist German exactions came from Pétain himself. Unlike the facile compliance that characterized so many acts of Vichy *vis-à-vis* the conqueror of 1940, in this matter subterfuge and Fabian tactics were the order of the day.

On the other hand the public silence that Vichy maintained over the regimentation of youth in the Eastern departments can only be described as an error of the first magnitude. What the Germans did patently infringed the Armistice agreement. The conscription of young Frenchmen into the German and armed forces blatantly contravened the Hague Convention (cf. Art. 45 of the Annexe of Convention IV, 1907). Neutral opinion, such as was left, might have been mobilized against such infractions of international law. Jean Zay, from his prison cell, reported hearing the band of the local group of the Chantiers de la Jeunesse playing 'Vous n'aurez pas l'Alsace et la Lorraine.'[122] This was an almost universal sentiment shared by Frenchmen everywhere.

If Germany had won the war, France, as has been seen, might have ceased to exist as a great nation-state. Young people, both the few misled into supporting separatist dreams and those that would have suffered the consequences, would have been the principal losers. The actors in this potential drama of dismemberment were few in number, but they foreshadow what might well have become reality.

Part III

Youth in Step. Trials and Tribulations

Chapter X

The Compagnons de France

The first new official youth movement to spring up after the defeat was the Compagnons de France. The idea arose from a committee of youth movements that a young Inspecteur des Finances, Henri Dhavernas, had set up in Paris, styled the Comité Jeunesse de France,[1] immediately after the Armistice. Dhavernas was a graduate of 'Sciences Po.', a Scout who for a while had been acting chief commissioner for the (Catholic) Scouts de France. Having spent his boyhood in the United States, he was bilingual. Medically unfit, he had not served in the 1940 campaign. After the collapse he had been struck by the enforced idleness of teenagers, vegetating either in refugee camps or at home through lack of employment. Meanwhile, because so many men were prisoners of war, the harvest lay rotting in the fields. With the powerful backing of Baudouin and the practical assistance of Catholic fellow-scouts such as Goutet and Father Forestier, Jean Gastambide, the head of the Protestant Scouts, and men such as Fraisse from the Jeunesse Ouvrière Chrétienne, he had registered the movement already as an association in July 1940. It was intended to cater for young men in their teens and to be an 'assembly of young Frenchmen wishing to join in the material and moral reconstruction of the nation by offering aid to the auxiliary services for refugees and prisoners and in general to all efforts at initiative or undertakings which might associate young men with service to their country'.

Given immediate official financial support and promised cadres from existing youth organizations, Dhavernas organized the first Compagnons' camp, from August 1–4, 1940 at Randan, near Vichy. Forty-five members of other youth movements, twenty-five of whom were secular and twenty confessional representatives, came together. They included Gortais, at the time secretary-general of the ACJF, and Andegond, the head of the Jeunesses Socialistes. They drew up the 'Charte de Randan' approving the Compagnons, stressing patriotic duty and the need to shape the personality and deepen the personal convictions of the young, and agreeing to provide cadres – one such was the future General Huet, a leader of the Vercors Maquis. The name 'Compagnons' had been chosen to signify the 'compagnonnage' of the medieval journeyman. The code of conduct was to be a veritable catalogue of the scouting virtues, epitomized in the maxim, 'Fight to be a man'. Initially the leaders were anti-capitalist and anti-liberal democracy, and thus anti-Gaullist, since the leader in London would undoubtedly restore democracy. On the other hand, they abhorred any form of totalitarianism. The promotion of a 'community spirit' was to be the ideal. A ritual quickly evolved. The Chef Compagnon's command, 'A moi, Compagnons!' evoked from the Compagnons the response, 'France!'. At 'colours ceremonies' a solemn salute, sometimes kneeling, was given. The Germans, suspicious of all 'regeneration' movements for youth, promptly forbade the movement in the occupied zone.

The organization was medieval, with units, in ascending order of size, ranging from 'Cités', 'Baillages', 'Commanderies', 'Pays', up to 'Provinces'. Recruits joined as 'apprentices', being admitted after a month's probation to the status of a fully fledged 'journeyman'. A military-style dark blue uniform was worn: beret, blue shirt (on which was sewn the movement's emblem, the 'coq gaulois'), shorts, or ski trousers.[2] Other features were military: there was a salute, which unfortunately resembled the Nazi greeting; absolute obedience and respect for rank was the rule, save off duty. The 'doctrine' upon this last matter was clear: it was 'the relationship between him who can only row and him who can steer; from superior to inferior this is called "legitimate authority", from inferior to superior, obedience, love and fidelity'.[3] Such a military regime was undoubtedly designed to keep potentially rebellious youth on a tight rein, although the immediate purpose was to employ them on socially useful tasks. Companies of some fifty men were placed at the disposal of services for water, forestry, bridges, and highways. The work was very varied, from land and flood reclamation to grape harvesting, sports-field construction work, and help to refugees. In 1940 pay was fixed at 20–25F a day.[4] Some projects were unusual. Thus in the Lyons area the Compagnons ran thirteen restaurants – the 'Relais du Coq'. Another interesting initiative sprang from a group of young musicians at Lyons, who founded the Compagnons de la Musique, became affiliated to the movement, and eventually developed into the celebrated Compagnons de la Chanson. Great efforts were made to interest youngsters in cultural activities such as singing, popular art, and drama, although there was a strong emphasis on physical fitness. In the camps the daily routine was strict: 6.30 Reveille, 7.15 breakfast, 7.30 PE ('Hébertisme'), 8.00 inspection, 8.15 'colours' ceremony and short 'pep talk', 8.30–noon work, 12.15 lunch, 13.30–16.30 work, 16.45 snack, clean-up, laundry, make-and-mend, 17.30 sport or vocational training, 18.15 talk by the leader (an expansion of the topic broached at the morning parade), 18.30 educational classes, 19.15 dinner, 20.00 entertainment. The time-honoured principle of keeping young people so busy that they had no time for mischief was never better observed.

The Compagnons de Chantier, as the full-time members of the movement were known, eventually dwindled in numbers, as refugees returned home, but were partially replaced by the young unemployed. At the same time, another branch of the movement, the Compagnons de Cité, composed of part-time members only, developed. A parallel but not very successful girls' movement – women had been represented at the first camp at Randan – the Compagnes de France, was started in 1942. Eventually the Compagnons de Cité became much the larger group. By January 1941 there were 6,770 Compagnons de Chantier and 11,497 Compagnons de Cité, with 1,726 cadres, half of whom were volunteers.[5] Numbers rose to their peak in 1943, when there were 29,000 Compagnons in all, of whom only 3,562, housed in 90 centres, were full time.[6] At the end of that year the then leader, Commandant de Tournemire, estimated their number at 30,000, with 1,500 cadres, 810 of whom were salaried.[7] The size of membership is important when one weighs later charges of lavish and extravagant expenditure. As compared with Catholic youth or Scout organizations the Compagnons were small fry as a movement. Yet, because they were one of the two movements that were officially inspired and directly controlled, they were closely scrutinized.

What kind of volunteers were attracted to the movement? Initially the Compagnons de Chantier, consisting of the young unemployed, attracted much unfavourable comment, such as, 'real bad eggs escaped from reformatory schools'.[8] By 1942 a spate of complaints about the Compagnons in general was streaming in, some coming from within the movement itself.[9] One report ran: 'Fifty out of sixty Compagnons here are for de Gaulle. They say: 'Pétain's O.K., but the "traitor" is better!' Another member, however, noted: 'The group carries on in a way that I detest. Several Jews have got in, some as leaders.' (Jews were expelled from the movement only in May 1942.) Yet another member declared that 'in the Compagnons it's not very interesting because one doesn't learn much, and, what's more, one becomes more of a layabout than a worker'. An outside observer described them as 'idle fellows, badly looked after, badly fed, not to mention the Compagnons' "exploits" – thefts, burglaries, etc. . . They couldn't care less.' Another described them as an undisciplined bunch who went about singing the 'Internationale', 'Ça ira', and the 'Carmagnole', and mocking at religious processions.[10] Some such reports emanated from circles at Vichy who were seeking at the time to discredit the movement.

The Compagnons were in fact attacked on all sides. Marcel Glass, writing in *Je suis partout,* is typical of the attitude of the Paris press in asking: 'By what miracle can one hope to transform into a revolutionary body a movement which includes 90 per cent who are awaiting events ('attentistes'), revanchists and pure Gaullists?'[11] Rival organizations of collaborationist persuasion, such as the Francistes, the Jeunesses Populaires Françaises, and the Jeunes de l'Europe Nouvelle, alternately derided and envied the movement. The Francistes accused the Compagnons' leaders, not without justification, of aiding and abetting defaulters from compulsory labour service in Germany.[12] When the movement was finally wound up the *Franciste* (5.2.44) chortled at the demise of that 'joke in poor taste ['fumisterie'] . . . the so-called Compagnons movement'. The Jeunes de l'Europe Nouvelle accused the Compagnons in North Africa of siding with the 'dissidents'. This reproach was also not unjustified because de Tournemire, by then leader of the Compagnons, was pro-Giraud and disowned Dupeyron, his Chef Compagnon in Tunisia, who remained loyal to Vichy.[13] For the Action Française Admiral Auphan led the opposition to the Compagnons.[14] Catholics were also unfavourable to the movement, for different reasons. At the beginning their fear was that, despite the co-operation of various Catholic youth leaders, it might become a totalitarian State movement. Thus for Pierre Limagne, of *La Croix*, it was, as he wrote in his diary for August 15, 1940, 'a new youth movement of a fairly disturbing official kind'.[15] More extremist elements claimed later that it had been 'invaded by Jewish elements', who had infiltrated it through the drama groups it organized. Compagnons were accused of obliterating Doriotist slogans on walls but leaving intact those extolling the RAF and de Gaulle, and of destroying Axis publications on news-stands.[16] Within the SGJ the department dealing with youth unemployment reported in March 1941 that the movement attracted only poverty-stricken youth, was 'essentially . . . Statist in inspiration and tendency and has, during these latter months, taken on habits of independence in which it has appeared as a little state within the State'.[17] On the other hand, other factions at Vichy labelled the movement as being too Christian Democrat in its ethos.

Mounier, editor of *Esprit*, the Catholic review of independent tendencies, complained about the 'inflation' in the number of Catholic youth leaders associated with the Compagnons[18] and confided his fear to Mgr Guerry that it was indeed the precursor of a totalitarian youth organization, a misgiving that the secretary of the Assembly of Cardinals and Archbishops shared. He seems, however, to have quickly changed his mind, for in October 1940 he wrote: 'At Vichy "Youth" (the ministry [*sic*] and the Compagnons) is certainly what is best there, although somewhat short on ideas, but with clear-cut and sane intentions',[19] and in March 1941 he wrote in his diary that his initial mistrust had been allayed, at least temporarily.[20] His reservations arose in part from a hearty dislike of the leadership of the Compagnons, whom he saw as men of boundless ambition, trimming their sails to the prevailing wind. Whilst some had dreamt of making of the Compagnons a great youth movement, others, Mounier hinted obscurely, saw in it only 'a crossroads with posts for observation and surveillance'.[21] Nevertheless he agreed to contribute a weekly article to the movement's news-sheet, *Compagnons,* edited at the time by one of the former contributors to *Esprit,* Jean Mazé,[22] who later went over to the collaborationists. A fellow-writer for *Compagnons* at the time was Pierre Courtade, a future leader writer on *L'Humanité.*[23]

The tumultuous history of the Compagnons can be traced with reference to its periodical and to its leaders. Dhavernas, its founder and first leader, started with the advantage of Baudouin's backing as well as being the son of one of Chevalier's best friends.[24] This did not deter Chevalier, however, when minister, from criticizing the movement and threatening in early 1941 to disband it. To some extent the authorities were to blame for its shortcomings. Dhavernas had been told when he had started to expect later up to 500,000 unemployed youths in the movement. He began modestly enough by setting up facilities for half that number. In the event unemployment did not occur on the scale expected and young refugees had been able to return home; the Chantiers de la Jeunesse had taken away from recruitment to the Compagnons young men of military age. Yet, despite the shortfall in numbers, between October 1940 and January 1941 the movement received the enormous sum of 19 million francs in subsidies, in addition to an initial sum of 6.1 million francs handed over personally to Dhavernas by Baudouin.[25]

An inquiry was opened by the ministry of finance as to how these sums had been spent. This purported to have established[26] that immediately after the Armistice the Compagnons had acquired without authority foodstuffs to the value of 51 million francs (whether these were ever paid for is not clear) and spent another 15 millions on transport. The 'leadership schools' that the movement had started lacked a coherent training programme and were ill-attended, yet produced a 60 per cent failure rate in the courses they ran. The schools were not subject to any outside control and were extravagant: so far as could be ascertained from their very insufficient accounting procedures, 115F per head per day was spent on courses. Despite this contemporary indictment, after the war Chevalier,[27] who as the minister ultimately responsible for youth matters must have known the true state of affairs, deliberately refrained at his trial from accusing Dhavernas of financial malpractice or malfeasance. Somewhat obscurely, the ex-minister merely stated that he had been forced to dismiss the Chef Compagnon because he had not taken steps to legalize the movement and that his attention had been drawn to this by Paul Fontaine, a naval aide-de-camp to Admiral Darlan, who was also a leader in the Compagnons.[28] Since the movement had certainly been legally registered as an association under the law of 1901 one is puzzled to know to what Chevalier may have been referring. False rumours started about a journey that Dhavernas made to Paris in December 1940 to sit for examinations connected with his permanent employment as an Inspecteur des Finances. A conspiracy was mounted against him to allege that whilst there he had contacted Laval, who had recently been ousted from the Vichy government, Abetz, Doriot, and Déat, whose preference for a single youth movement of a totalitarian nature was well known. Who was behind such rumours is not known, but there was clearly a patent attempt to get rid of him. After his dismissal Dhavernas forwarded documents to his friend and fellow-Inspecteur des Finances, Du Moulin de Labarthète, of Pétain's 'cabinet', which demonstrated that he had made no such contacts.[29] Chevalier did state later that at the time he had rejected a German demand for Dhavernas's reinstatement.[30] That the Germans backed Dhavernas is incredible in view of another accusation made against him, that he had surrounded himself with Jews, Anglophiles, and former Communists.[31]

That Dhavernas had been the innocent victim of a power struggle became apparent in the events that followed his dismissal. In the leadership crisis that followed, which lasted until May 1941, an attempt was made to bring the Compagnons closer to the German camp. Paul Marion, who in

March had assumed charge of the ministry of information, proposed as leader Armand Petitjean, an ex-Normalien with links with the collaborationist writer Drieu La Rochelle, a candidature supported by Pucheu and others. In the event the general assembly of the Compagnons implicitly rejected collaborationist tendencies when it elected the candidate supported by Lamirand and some of the youth organizations,[32] Commandant de Tournemire, on May 18, 1941 as the new Chef Compagnon.

The new leader was a career army officer, who had been trained at Saint-Cyr, had entered the cavalry, had been the youngest ever to reach the rank of captain in France, and had passed through the École de Guerre. After the armistice he had worked in Paris for a while helping in the youth employment service. After the anti-German student demonstrations of November 11, 1940 Lamirand had asked him to attempt to restore working relationships with the Germans and in this he had been successful. Known and liked by Lyautey, de Tournemire was a great admirer also of Giraud, under whom he had served in North Africa. In view of later developments, this fact has some significance. He saw his new role as principally in the field of civic and vocational education, got Pétain to declare that that was his mission, and obtained equipment, some from the army, and funds from the Marshal. He also borrowed cadres from other youth movements.[33] Pétain let it be known that, under its new leader, the Compagnons enjoyed his full confidence. De Tournemire managed to secure his independence from the ministry's director of technical education, Luc, whom he disliked because 'his spirit is incompatible with the Révolution Nationale'.[34] By August the slate had been swept clean and de Tournemire was able to assume effective command.

Those who had opposed his appointment, particularly Marion and Pucheu, did not accept defeat lying down. They fired off a barrage of criticism of the movement for its alleged ineffectiveness. Petitjean, the unsuccessful candidate for the leadership, resigned from the movement, as did his friend Mazé, who became as violent a detractor of the Compagnons as he had once been a supporter of them.[35] For him now the SGJ was 'the last place where the Révolution

Nationale was to be made' and, he declared: 'I want to be part of a really revolutionary body. The sentence, "The Compagnons movement is against nobody" is unacceptable. "Une fleur au chapeau, à la bouche une chanson" [a popular Compagnons song] is all very well, but it's not enough. A knife in one's belt, if necessary, to fight.' This bellicosity, needless to say, was not directed against the Germans. Mazé joined Marion at the ministry of information and lobbied vociferously for a 'jeunesse unique', a demand which was renewed about this time.

Meanwhile de Tournemire's very independent line manifested itself in the periodical *Compagnons,* the official organ of the movement, no longer edited by Mazé. Already in May 1941, before de Tournemire had officially taken over, the periodical had been critical of Weygand's dismissal and of the Franco-German agreements regarding Syria. In March 1942, when de Tournemire was summoned to appear before the youth commission of the Conseil National, he was strongly criticized by Bergery and others for the freedom with which the periodical expressed itself on matters political. He disregarded the implicit warnings that were then handed to him and adverse reports on the publication continued to flow into Vichy. One such report[36] systematically reviewed the contents of nine issues published in August and September 1942. An article had been published commenting sarcastically on the Relève – the release of prisoners of war in exchange for French workers volunteering to work in Germany – which stated: ' "Wanted: 100,000 volunteers" – to help the peasants of France.' In no issue did the Révolution Nationale merit a favourable mention, nor did any Vichy leader save Pétain. There was no propaganda against the Jews or freemasons. Instead, there was extensive criticism of rationing, the ineptitude of local officialdom, and the high cost of living. Political articles stressed a France renowned for liberty and justice and omitted any reference to the value of authority and a hierarchical social order. Exaggerated sympathy was shown for the huge numbers of Germans dying on the Eastern Front, in order to insinuate that a German victory was impossible. A report on a mass pilgrimage to Puy on the Feast of the Assumption drew special attention to the statue of the Virgin of *Strasburg.* An article devoted to Madagascar did not even mention the British attack on the island. Over the period a score of films were reviewed, including nine American ones, which enabled reference to be made, as the critical report put it, to the 'neo-American Charles Boyer'. Yet another report to the SGJ[37] dealt particularly with the issue of November 21, 1942 in which the events of North Africa did not even rate a mention, although American Flying Fortresses were referred to flatteringly as 'giants of the air'. An editorial by André Fabre contained these lines pregnant with double meaning:

> Are we not driven to remind ourselves that today there exists a certain form of courage:
> – the courage to say nothing;
> – the courage not to give way to the temptation of futile actions and words;
> – the courage to hold on in spite of everything;
> – the courage to be simply and humbly reasonable;
> – the courage to be simply realist in order to safeguard the future,

Three weeks later a third report[38] quoted an article that had appeared under the title, 'L'Enfant, ami public No. 1'. It began: 'In these times of universal perversion, in which those values most commonly acknowledged among men are denied, struck down and overturned by the idolizers of Race, Power and Blood, there remains to us one consolation and hope: the gentle and clear gaze of a little child.' The originator of the report on the article remarks on the 'clumsiness' of the allusions to Germany where, 'much more than in democratic [*sic*] France, they can appreciate "the gentle and clear gaze of a little child" '. Two of the three reports cited were made to Pelorson, then Lamirand's deputy, and found their way to Bonnard. The periodical was closed down. Its barbed comments in a France now totally occupied were unacceptable both to the Germans and to the 'new men' allied to them, who were coming increasingly to the fore in the government. They determined now to oust de Tournemire in his turn, depite his professed total commitment to Pétain and the friends he had among the Marshal's entourage.

Pétain had attended the second anniversary of the foundation of the Compagnons held at Randan in the summer of

1942, when an oak had been planted in the clearing where the movement had originated. The Marshal had been presented with a bag containing soil from every region of France and the Empire, to symbolize French unity. The event was also notable for a singular commemoration of the first Compagnon caught in anti-German activities. André Noël, a 'chef de commanderie', had been shot by the Occupation authorities at Besançon on November 29, 1941 for spying for the French Deuxième Bureau.[39] In his honour the flag was lowered to half-mast. It may not be a coincidence that de Tournemire and Georges Lamarque, a secondary-school teacher who was one of his trusted lieutenants, made their first contact with the Resistance about this time. For many of the movement's leaders the watershed of allegiance to the regime was reached in November 1942, when the government failed to react to the German invasion of the southern zone. Some of the rank and file of the Compagnons, on the other hand, did demonstrate: at Cojarc and Agen they reacted by singing defiantly, 'Vous n'aurez pas l'Alsace et la Lorraine'. It was a prelude to what was to follow.

Already in 1940 certain measures of Vichy, particularly the first restrictions on the Jews, had 'disgusted' – the word is Mounier's[40] – some Compagnons. (On the other hand, according to one source, thirteen Compagnons, all supporters of Doriot, had been arrested in August 1941 for blowing up the synagogue at Vichy.)[41] After November 1942 de Tournemire continued for a few months to give his allegiance to Pétain and, because of his confidence in the Marshal, accepted the Laval administration. The introduction of compulsory labour service in Germany for young men in February 1943 was bitterly resented by many Compagnon leaders, who protected defaulters by enrolling them in the movement, as they also did young Jews, under false identities.[42] One leader, Maurice Thiard, even lectured to an audience at Poligny which included Vichy officials on how to evade this new burden laid on youth; the officials walked out of the meeting, but the speaker was not arrested. Meanwhile adverse reports on the Compagnons began to pour in to the Sûreté Nationale.[43] In Provence a Compagnon was caught gathering information regarding German troops and installations. From the Eastern Pyrenees came information that the Compagnons were printing illegal tracts and some members had already gone over to the Resistance: a ski camp run by the Compagnons in the mountains was being used as a staging-post to escape through Spain and join de Gaulle. (Already in the winter of 1940–1 it had been alleged that some Compagnons, using contacts in Cannes, had departed to join the Free French.) The Sûreté was told that Gaullist cells had been formed within the movement itself and that some of the leaders had fought for the Republicans in the Spanish civil war – a fact that de Tournemire himself confirmed.

Despite their uncertain loyalty, the Compagnons continued to receive favoured financial treatment. Subsidies paid out or budgeted (it is not clear which) for the various movements in 1942 showed that they received the lion's share of subsidies:[44]

Compagnons	30,030,000F
Le Scoutisme français	16,280,594F
ACJF (Catholic youth movements)	2,740,850F
Jeunesse française d'Outremer	2,500,000F
Camarades de la Route	1,110,000F
Compagnes de France	230,000F
Other movements.	2,656,035F
Total	55,547,479F

The Compagnons thus got 54 per cent of the budget for youth movements, excluding the Chantiers. In 1943 the budget estimates[45] allocated 65 million francs to the Compagnons, but the total allocation to youth movements was estimated at 137 millions, so that its proportion fell to 47 per cent.

It was finance that was the immediate cause of de Tournemire's downfall, just as it had been of his predecessor. Bonnard was clearly set to find a pretext to dismiss him. In January 1943 Lamirand had responded to a request from the minister to carry out a thorough appraisal of the Compagnons.[46] He reported that de Tournemire's personal devotion to Pétain and his loyalty to the Laval government appeared to be unassailable. In August 1942 the Chef Compagnon had personally pledged his loyalty to Laval in an interview with the head of the government. Lamirand had himself interviewed de Tournemire, who had assured him that the Compagnons believed in authority, discipline, a hierarchical order, and the promotion of community welfare and justice – in short, they accepted 'the basic principles of the État Français'. The SGJ nevertheless wanted to investigate the movement further, particularly its political affinities. The outcome of such an enquiry might well be the disbandment of the movement or, more favourably, some reorganization of it, with the elimination of the more undesirable elements, and eventually increased financial support.

Ironically, it was financial matters that triggered off a fuller public inquiry, which ended in March 1943. In 1941 investigators known as Commissaires du Pouvoir had been appointed to hunt out abuses in public institutions. One such Commissaire, Bernon, charged with looking into the financial affairs of the Compagnons, submitted a very alarming report.[47] Despite the budgeted figure of some thirty million francs, he alleged that in 1942 no less than sixty-three millions had been handed over to the movement, without any official control. This sum was exorbitant, particularly when under eight hundred cadres were actually salaried employees. De Tournemire was required by Pétain himself to reply in writing to the charge.[48] The Chef Compagnon made a detailed rebuttal[49] of the accusation by the Commissaire du Pouvoir that there had been 'a shameless waste of public money'. He claimed that the SGJ exercised control over the movement and that ever since the previous inquiry, initiated by Chevalier and continued by Carcopino, the ministry of education itself had scrutinized the movement's accounts. The Chef Compagnon asserted that the investigation had confused the finances of the Compagnons with those of an entirely different organization with a similar name, the Compagnons du Devoir du Tour de France. He admitted that Pétain's 'cabinet civil' had handed five million francs over to him personally but he had been told at the same time that 'he was accountable for it to his conscience alone'. The explanations appear insufficient, but it is probable that, such was the way in which the monies were handled, whether direct from the public purse or in the form of 'secret funds' disbursed by some ministry or other agency, de Tournemire had little idea of how the movement's finances were appropriated – or misappropriated. He also dealt with another section of the

Commissaire's report which had accused the Compagnons of being hostile to government policy. The report alleged that all flags in their camps had been flown at half-mast after the total occupation of France. In fact, replied de Tournemire, they had been flying at that position ever since July 27, 1942, following upon Pétain's visit to Randan: he had ordered this, as the movement's leader, to continue 'until France had been refashioned according to the Marshal's principles'. He denied a lesser allegation: in his office there was not displayed solely Weygand's picture, but also a large one of Pétain.

His attempt at justification was not accepted, because the witch-hunt continued. In the autumn of 1943 de Tournemire was on the run. By then Lamirand had been replaced as SGJ by Col. Olivier-Martin and Bonnard had ordered the suspension of all credits to the Compagnons retroactively from October 1, 1943.[50] In effect, this meant that the fourth quarter of the yearly subsidy would not be paid over, although sums from it had already been committed. De Tournemire got in touch with Dr Ménétrel who, both as private secretary and personal physician to Pétain, exerted increasing influence over his octogenarian patient. The style of the note, dispatched through an intermediary to whom de Tournemire beseeched Ménétrel to listen, reveals that the two knew each other well. It ran:[51]

> Dear Doc ('toubib'),
> I should like to come and see you but it is difficult because there are really too many people taking an interest in me. . . And yet I should be glad to ask you for some advice in order to save a show ('boutique') to which for over two years I have given myself wholeheartedly. . .

This 'cri de cœur' proving abortive, it was followed by another, this time in the form of an appeal to Laval.[52] De Tournemire claimed that the hostile reports on the Compagnons had been started by rival movements (he doubtless had the collaborationist youth organizations in mind). He acknowledged that he might be personally unacceptable to Laval's government because of his connections with Giraud, whom he continued to admire despite his having gone over to the Allies. He refused to compromise by toadying to the

Germans. His own beliefs were summed up in the phrase, 'independence and French pride'. So long, however, as Pétain continued to underwrite it, he accepted Laval's foreign policy – presumably he meant the policy towards the Germans. He realized that the cadres of the Compagnons had very diverse political backgrounds – implying that some might legitimately be the object of government suspicion. He appealed for protection for some contingents of the Compagnons who had been attacked by the Maquis and concluded by asking Laval to release the subsidy that had been withheld and to provide for the movement in the budget estimates for 1944. The document betrays de Tournemire's political naivety and how little he realized that Laval, no less than Bonnard, was now committed to a German victory.

Since the plea inevitably fell on deaf ears, on November 29, 1943 de Tournemire made a last, desperate appeal to Pétain himself.[53] He had fled from his headquarters, he said, to escape the German police, a fact which, according to Laval's government, created a 'new element' ('fait nouveau') in the position. At the beginning of November he claimed that he had extracted a promise from Laval to release the frozen credits, but this had now been cancelled on the grounds that it would displease the Germans, particularly as de Tournemire himself was now 'insaisissable'. Yet, the Chef Compagnon argued, the funds could have been paid perfectly legally to Paul Weber, his deputy. This would have enabled the movement to continue to function, which he desperately wanted. He also wanted to continue as leader and took the opportunity to reaffirm his personal loyalty to Pétain. He realized, however, that German intervention would inevitably mean disbandment. If this were to happen he would try to keep the Compagnons loyal but, he added, with the hint of a threat, 'I fear there might be many who . . . might adopt a subversive attitude or one hostile to all legal authority.'

His last card was nevertheless played in vain. In the New Year police, aided by the Milice, raided the Compagnons' headquarters at Lyons, Marseilles, and Toulouse. On January 21, 1944 a decree was published in the *Journal officiel* dissolving the movement. Dr Kunze, in charge of youth affairs at the German embassy, declared, with a distinct lack of elegance, that he would 'have the "hide" of Commandant de Tournemire'.[54] But the ex-Chef Compagnon had already taken to the Maquis. In the spring of 1944 he met in Paris Dunoyer de Segonzac, the former head of the 'école des cadres' at Uriage, who had also joined the Resistance when his institution had been closed down. De Segonzac noted that de Tournemire was pro-Giraud and pro-American, whilst he was for de Gaulle. Part of de Tournemire's dilemma arose because he did not support the Free French, whom he considered disloyal, and yet his hero, Giraud, had 'defected' to the Allies and formed an alliance with the Gaullists. He was followed into the Resistance by many Compagnons, one group of which was actually responsible for warning London of the imminence of attack by the V1 and V2 bombs.

What was the significance of the Compagnons movement? The initial aspect of welfare, whereby the movement provided food and shelter for young refugees and unemployed, was not the most significant facet of its activities. But the impact of the movement on the larger category of part-timers grouped as the Compagnons de Cité, with the accent on community service, is difficult to assess. Despite the involvement of Catholics, at the outset the Church, for reasons associated with its fear of a 'jeunesse unique', was at best lukewarm, and some Protestants were overtly hostile.[55] The Paris collaborationists and an extremist clique associated with the Vichy regime, failing to take over the movement, then sought to destroy it. Eventually Pétain, either through lack of authority or through having lost faith in the movement, withdrew his support. The combined pressures of the Germans, Laval, and Bonnard succeeded in overtoppling de Tournemire but by then it was too late to do anything save wind up yet another Vichy youth experiment that had failed. The saga of the leadership throws an interesting light on the way the regime operated, such as, for example, the incredible ease with which large sums of money were disbursed without public accountability. It also illustrates the disunity of Vichy and the power struggles that continued throughout the war. Pétain's support for a long time of one who remained a staunch admirer of Giraud also reveals something about the view that the Marshal held of his contemporary. De Tournemire himself represents a kind of 'third force', neither for de Gaulle nor for the Germans but standing, in the Maurrassian phrase (but not in the Maurrassian context), for 'La France seule'. Youth, as ever, was caught in the cross-fire of conflicting interests, although in the end de Tournemire gave a clear lead as to where the path of duty and honour led.

Chapter XI

The Chantiers de la Jeunesse

The other principal youth organization that arose from the Vichy regime was the Chantiers de la Jeunesse. On the eve of the North-Africa landings, in October 1942, a British Foreign Office memorandum appraised this organization as 'the most important influence at work on young Frenchmen', noting that the movement was 'reported to be strongly anti-German and of high morale'.[1] What therefore were the aims and activities of the Chantiers and how important was it, if at all, in bringing French youth over to the Allied side?

The men originally incorporated into the Chantiers de la Jeunesse were young conscripts, many of whom had been called to the colours only a few days before the Armistice in 1940. By its terms the Germans had forbidden military service and ordered the disbandment of all forces save a small army of 100,000 men needed to maintain internal order. Since demobilization could only be gradual it meant that the youngest serving would be the last to go. Some 92,000 young men were in this category,[2] many of whom had lost their parents, were now homeless, or could not return immediately to where they lived. Two senior officers were particularly concerned about their plight. One was General de Lattre de Tassigny, who took steps immediately after the defeat to organize the young soldiers under his command.[3] As military commander of the Puy-de-Dôme he set up a work camp at Opme, near Clermont-Ferrand, where he brought together a hundred conscripts of the 1940 class, some prisoners of war who had been freed or escaped, men from his own 14th Infantry Regiments, and students from Strasburg evacuated to the area. This deliberately heterogeneous group was set to rebuild the village under the supervision of skilled craftsmen. Sport and physical exercise, accompanied by talks from the general, completed the opportunity for young men of vastly differing backgrounds to work and play together. This improvised unit was later taken under the wing of the Chantiers de la Jeunesse.

De Lattre de Tassigny was not chosen to command the new organization. His subsequent career, when he offered a brief resistance to the Germans as they marched into the southern zone, was imprisoned but escaped to return to France with the Liberation Army, demonstrates an independence of character hardly likely to appeal to those who held power at Vichy. Instead, the choice fell upon General de La Porte du Theil, admirably qualified because he was familiar with both the military and the scouting traditions. A former commander in the field of the 40th Division, then at the head of the Seventh Corps, this 'vieux paysan à béret et fortes moustaches'[4] gave absolute loyalty to Pétain. Indeed, when he was finally arrested by the Germans in 1944 a German general, Alexander von Neubronn, declared that the Marshal had lost 'one of his most sincere collaborators'.[5] Even before the installation of the Vichy regime General Colson, then minister of war, had given him *carte blanche* to do what he liked with the youngest conscripts. De La Porte du Theil had perceived the possibility of combining scouting ideals with a semi-military form of service to replace conscription. He submitted a proposal to Weygand, who by then combined the posts of minister of defence and commander-in-chief,[6] suggesting this kind of service for young men when they reached the age of twenty. It would be a means of mixing all social classes together, but in camps, where 'on vit en communauté', rather than in barracks, where 'on vit en promiscuité'. Anxious that such an organization should escape the direct control of the German Armistice Commission, the general proposed that the movement should be headed by a commissioner-general, be grouped by provinces, and be attached to a civilian ministry rather than to the military. Numbers might rise to as many as 250,000 a year and include a permanent staff made up as follows: 300 higher cadres, equivalent to field officers; 3,000 junior cadres, equivalent to captains and lieutenants; 2,000 subordinate ranks, equivalent to sergeants; and 200 doctors and 800 nursing and welfare staff. Two call-ups a year would give an effective service of five months for each contingent. The first call-up would normally take place in mid-January; work in the Chantiers would extend from February to the beginning of July, thus releasing agricultural workers in time for the harvest. The second call-up, in mid-July, would include industrial workers, as well as students, who would thus lose only one term of their studies. Although Weygand was asked to reply to this proposal only by October, in the event it was approved almost immediately and forwarded on August 30, 1940 to the ministry of family and youth. A provisional commissariat-général was established at Clermont-Ferrand and a document set out the rationale of the new movement.[7] It was described as being 'exclusive of any considerations of a political or military nature', although, as things turned out, this must be open to question. Although those called up would work, the purpose was not utilitarian: the aim was training – 'manly training', because through physical exertion was created a predisposition to moral development, and also direct moral training, effected through the 'cult of honour' and through living together. De La Porte du Theil was known for his strong moral principles based on his religious convictions. He affirmed a political agnosticism, declaring that his own 'doctrine' was to have none,[8] although it would seem that he favoured a neutral France based on a new social order.[9] Thus he wanted the Chantiers to be apolitical, with a sole loyalty to Pétain and to France.[10]

The nucleus of the Chantiers was formed on the basis of a law of July 30, 1940 'relative to the retention in youth groupings of young men called up on June 8 and 9, 1940'. Their status was demilitarized and they were called upon to serve for a further period of six months. The law applied only to the southern zone.[11] The recruits, called 'Jeunes de France', eventually shortened to 'Jeunes', were taught the motto of the movement was to be 'Toujours prêts!' – a palpable imitation of the scouts. They were organized roughly as de La Porte du Theil had envisaged. Men were grouped in squads of twelve ('équipes', originally termed, as in the scouts, 'patrouilles'), which the general considered to be 'the corner stone' of the Chantiers. Each squad had a leader ('chef d'équipe') of the same age as his men. Ten such squads constituted a group, with its own camp, under a group leader ('chef de groupe') a few years older. Camps were deliberately sited far from large towns in remote spots. Ten to a dozen groups constituted a 'groupement' of up to 2,000 men, who included a special group providing ancillary services such as was provided in the army by a headquarters company. For example, 'Groupement 37', known as 'Groupement Bayard', had as its permanent staff a commissioner-commandant who was aided by four deputy and five assistant commissioners, one Protestant and two Catholic chaplains, three doctors, a dentist, and a pharmacist, and who had under his command 1,700 men. 'Groupements' were attached to one of half a dozen regions, under a regional commissioner whose headquarters were respectively at Lyons, Clermont-Ferrand, Toulouse, Montpellier, Marseilles and Algiers, all incidentally headquarters-towns of army-corps regions. Each 'groupement' chose a famous Frenchman as its patron, usually military, medieval, or Catholic heroes; the omission of Revolutionary or republican figures was notable. The headquarters of the Chantiers were finally established at Châtel-Guyon (Puy-de-Dôme).

After the residual contingent of military conscripts, it was arranged that other call-ups would follow. A law of January 18, 1941 fixed the period of service at eight months and made provision for postponements. Penalties for non-compliance – up to five years' imprisonment and a fine of 1,000F – were as severe as had been those for evasion of military service. The measure applied to Algeria and other parts of the overseas Empire where Chantiers could possibly be started and it was hoped to extend it to the occupied zone. A law of the same date placed the Chantiers under the SGJ, although in April 1941 this arrangement was modified so that for a while it became a separate department of the ministry of education, being on a par with the SGJ, the Secrétariat Général de l'Instruction Publique, concerned with educational institutions proper, and the Commissariat Général à l'Éducation Générale et aux Sports. Thus, for a while, under Carcopino's ministry General de La Porte du Theil, Lamirand, Terracher, and Borotra presided together over the four key divisions of the ministry, all to a greater or lesser degree either 'neutralist' or opposed to a German victory.

Provision was also made to extend on a day-to-day basis

the service of up to 8 per cent of the total strength of the Chantiers and to recruit up to 7 per cent of volunteers from the occupied zone, where the Germans had forbidden the movement. A naval Chantier was started, reserved for pupils of the École Navale and of navigation schools, merchant-navy apprentices, and 'inscrits maritimes'. Frenchmen living outside France or the Empire were exempt from service. In July 1942 Jews were excluded from the movement. A law of February 16, 1942 also exempted those who had worked at least one year in Germany. As for conscripts, daily pay was fixed at minimal rates: 1F.50 for a 'Jeune', double for his squad leader. By March 1942 there was a permanent staff of 4,040. This included 163 chaplains, who were mainly Jesuits. Father Forestier, chaplain-general of the Catholic scouts, fulfilled the same function for the Chantiers.

What was the 'doctrine', in Vichy jargon, in which the 'Jeunes' were to be instructed?[12] It did not differ substantially from that which the Révolution Nationale laid down for schools, although in the Chantiers it was probably more applied. The first principle of moral training was the appeal to the individual's sense of honour. Personal honour, based on self-respect, was the ideal, although few could achieve it completely, whereas the honour of the group, particularly that of the small entity of the squad, could be safeguarded by all. Both within and between squads emulation should be fostered, although there should be no attempt to rank individuals in an order of merit. The sacrifice of self for the common good would train character, develop responsibility and a sense of duty to others, breeding fraternity. Such fraternity was considered of prime importance. It would be encouraged by the evening relaxation around the camp fire, under the group leader, when each would examine his conscience and minds would be uplifted. At the close the men should disperse in silence.

'Manly training' ('formation virile') stimulated moral training. It entailed work and exercise in the open air for half the waking hours, a hygiene of exposing the body to air, sun, and water. Exercise should always be simple and vigorous, on the lines of 'Hébertisme', capable of being performed by everybody. Games should be educative. An outdoor life, in contact with nature and subjected to the buffeting of the elements, would elevate and harden men, enabling them to bear discomfort. Discipline must be freely accepted, punishment borne without complaint. But General de La Porte du Theil acknowledged that recruits were in bad physical condition. He was concerned to discover that some newcomers had been excused all physical exercise because of their poor state of health, but at the same time, he declared, 'We must prevent them becoming clapped out' – 'Il faut éviter des claquages'. In point of fact deaths were extremely rare. The problem was to find a gradated series of exercises for the less strong, since physical and moral development went hand in hand.[13] The general pinned his hopes on the new generation of physical-training instructors emerging from the national training school that had been set up at Hyères. Meanwhile the more energetic sports must be available only to those already of a reasonable standard of fitness. By dint of one route march a week he hoped that by the end of his service the 'Jeune' would be able to walk some thirty kilometres without giving up. The ideal was perfect physical fitness. Like the rest of the 'doctrine', however, this was unrealistic in the circumstances of war.

Social mixing was another such ideal. De La Porte du Theil was particularly worried about the university students, whom he rated as physical weaklings, lacking manual skills, leading a bourgeois, cosseted existence, brought up by families who had opted out of their duties to the community. Yet students and young workers, as had been attempted in the pre-war Équipes Sociales, had somehow to be brought together. The students, whilst theoretically assenting to associating with those less privileged than themselves, in practice did not mix and held a disdainful opinion of some of their fellows. The general recalled one student who wrote of his life in the Chantiers: 'The group leader is good for the lunatic asylum. Squad leaders are onetime potmen and butchers, who maltreat us and drink all day long.'[14] He dismissed such grumblings but was well aware that students regretted the interruption to their studies and considered manual labour a waste of time. More radical elements at

Vichy were resolved that the Chantiers should be used as an instrument of social engineering. Pelorson, whilst deputy to Lamirand, wanted complete equality of treatment. Thus students would not be allowed to postpone their period of service, because this would vitiate social mixing, 'one of the most important aspects of the Chantiers'.[15] He was in favour of retaining the Chantiers because, if not called upon to serve, students would become mere 'attentistes'. At the other end of the political spectrum some, but not all, Catholics, were in favour of different social classes of youth getting to know each other better.[16] Certainly de La Porte du Theil believed that leadership qualities were not the prerogative of any one social stratum, although he accepted that students, as intellectuals, would have a key role in shaping the new France.[17]

As regards civic education, the 'doctrine' of the Chantiers was simple. It should be based on the community ideal.[18] The Révolution Nationale should be explained by leaders as being founded on the paramountcy of the 'natural communities' of the family, occupation, and the State, which represented the welfare of all. Leaders were instructed to show how this concept complemented the ideas expounded in the new Charte du Travail, with which many new recruits might be expected to be familiar.

The 'Jeunes' certainly lived out the 'doctrine' in a very strenuous fashion. One-third of the day was given over to hard physical labour, another third to physical exercise, educational activities, meals, or leisure. The remaining third was spent in hard-won sleep. A day's activities could be punishing. On December 28, 1940 the Groupement Bayard paraded at 6 a.m., with the temperature at −6 °C., and took off on a route march of twenty kilometres, stopping only for a snack and a 'vin chaud' and arriving back at 1 p.m.[19] Manual labour at the beginning was particularly arduous because everything had to be improvised: lacking stores and tools, the 'Jeunes' had to build their own camps, helped only by mules whose fodder was often the bread ration issued to their drovers, and sometimes having to manhandle felled trees on icebound slopes angled at over 45°. Since forest land was one of the few natural assets that the southern zone possessed in abundance, tree-felling and charcoal-burning in ovens that had to be maintained night and day were standard activities. Other strenuous tasks included road-building. Although the work accomplished had economic benefit, this was not its main purpose, which was, as one 'chef' summed it up, 'to make you better, hard-working, joyful and physically and morally strong'. Although the French peasant was no stranger to hard work, a philosophy of labour as a redemptive force is one more associated with Puritanism and Calvinism than with Catholicism and the Latin countries. General de La Porte du Theil, himself a 'fils du terroir', believed in the saving grace of work for French youth.

Education in the Chantiers had academic, cultural, and vocational aims. First, deficiencies in schooling had to be remedied. A group of primary teachers who had just completed their service in the Chantiers maintained that many 'Jeunes' were less knowledgeable and used their brains less than the twelve-year-olds they normally taught.[20] Recruits were therefore encouraged to take classes and pass the primary leaving-certificate. Others indulged in simple cultural activities such as choral singing, country dancing, and regional folklore. These pursuits merged naturally with civic education. Visits to local monuments were arranged and outside speakers were invited. Thus a peasant might explain the working of the Corporation Paysanne in the locality, an industrial worker how the 'comité social' set up in his factory under the Charte du Travail operated, or the secretary to the local mayor how the communal administration functioned. Artisanal activities, from the installation of electrical wiring to the making of clogs and Christmas toys, were also taught. Instruction in more technical processes was given in larger workshops and on the Chantiers' own farms. The stress was less on the activities than on the concomitant learning. Thus the manipulation of tools was designed to develop skill, order, precision, dexterity, and the ability to foresee practical difficulties. One aim was to teach the logic of manual operations ('le Froissartage') and to instil a spirit of initiative and inventiveness in work. The whole procedure has some affinities with Marx's elaboration of the polytechnical principle in education. Students who had never worked with their hands before would, for example, acquire a proper respect for the dexterity of the manual worker. Such an ambitious educational programme required considerable resources, supplied by a special section for education located at Châtel-Guyon, although the working-out of the programme was left firmly in local hands. In this respect the leadership offered by the Chantiers differed fundamentally from that in the Nazi youth groups or the German compulsory labour service ('Reichsarbeitsdienst') to which it bore superficial resemblances: within the parameters set, subordinates in the Chantiers had complete freedom to tackle tasks as they thought fit.

The very remoteness and smallness of the camps made the educational programme more attractive to the rank and file. Apart from normal leave, none could leave the campsite without special permission and even outsiders were only allowed in on business. At first no radio, cinema shows, or newspapers were allowed, apart from a locally produced information bulletin. The ethos was that of a strictly regulated community. Careful attention was paid to detail. Thus, to promote the community spirit, accommodation had not to be in tents or makeshift shacks. Winter quarters, hutments rather than chalets, had to be built. Work on Sunday was forbidden. Men must not be employed as casual labour on farms, but on national projects, for 'A man must not get the justifiable feeling that what he is doing in the Chantiers he might just as well be doing at home for his own benefit, particularly when his own field is lying fallow and he is ploughing that of another.'[21] Scrupulous cleanliness had to be observed: stripped to the waist, the men washed every morning in cold water. 'This discipline of cold water is harsh . . . but it is an integral part of the life that we require in the Chantiers.'[22] Even beards were regulated: 'Jeunes' were forbidden to grow the 'ear-to-ear' variety, because it made them resemble 'seasoned campers'.

These and similar instructions, which give the flavour of the Chantiers, appeared in the weekly bulletins or in special instructions put out for leaders by de La Porte du Theil. They epitomize the 'wisdom' of a commander to his subordinates, paternal, familiar, sometimes severe, but always tinged with sympathy and even affection. Such publications deal with routine matters that came to light as the general made the rounds of the various groups. Yet as the weeks go by one senses in the bulletins an increasing mild despair at the possibility of ever changing anything permanently, which contrasts with the initial optimism.

The general affirmed his own confidence in youth: '. . . one has never the right to doubt a man who has not failed you up to yet, particularly if he is only twenty. [To do so] is the best way to close the gateway of his soul to you for ever. What is needed is not to repeat to people that you have confidence in them, but to demonstrate it.'[23] But, went on the general, if trust is betrayed punishment must be severe and immediate, entailing '. . . instant and merciless repression of all the bad characters, and it is natural that in the times in which we live, with the education they have received and the examples that have been set before them, many of our young men will, alas, have gone to the bad'.[24] 'Chefs' are reminded that they have the power to sentence a man to two months' imprisonment. Individualism was the great enemy: 'We almost died from an excess of individualism . . . We have seen where that led us: France crumbled easily, with a rapidity that disconcerted even its enemies.'[25]

Already in October 1940 a long-term programme of moral instruction had been mapped out in the weekly bulletin.[26] It dealt with a veritable catalogue of virtues, from honour to heroism. History was impressed into the teaching of ethics, using a biographical approach. Two model programmes were set out. The first included Vercingétorix and the resistance of Gaul – an ambiguous example, as has been seen in the case of General de Lattre de Tassigny –, Charlemagne, Joan of Arc, Louis XIV, Napoleon, Pasteur, Lyautey, and Pétain. The other is similar, but gives a passing mention to 1789 whilst continuing to omit all reference to the Third Republic. Such anti-republicanism was sometimes carried to ludicrous extremes: one 'chef' argued that the Tricolour was not the invention of the Revolutionaries but had been part of the habit worn by St-Louis and the twelfth-century order of Trinitaires, who had the singularly appropriate mission of the redemption of captives![27]

Moralizing was a popular pastime of Vichy and the

Chantiers followed the fashion. Robert Aron quotes from a Chantiers text that summarizes the all-embracing nature of moral education:[28]

> Moral education occurs at the morning colours ceremony;
> Moral education occurs during daytime work, well-organised, stimulated by the leader, never entailing weariness or exhaustion, but labour at which one sings;
> Moral education occurs when one unravels some technical problem in the workshop or at manual work round the camp fire;
> Moral education occurs when one is teaching the illiterate to read, preparing men for the primary leaving certificate, teaching by giving short talks on history, geography and a thousand other subjects;
> Moral education occurs at the campfire when the squad and its leader are yarning together;
> Moral education takes place in the galley, in the tailor's shop or at the shoe repairer's, at food or clothing store, in the garden, in the stable or garage, when on the march, on visits or excursions.

Even the type of plays mounted by the amateur companies in the Chantiers conveyed moral fervour, such as one such piece, 'Échec à la Nuit', located in Greece, which held up Sparta as an example of a state 'powerful through having kept its young people free from corruption'.[29] Moral fibre would be the mark of the new Frenchman. When Gillouin, Pétain's Protestant friend who later escaped to Switzerland, passed on to de La Porte du Theil a parent's protest that camp life was too hard, the general retorted firmly: 'It's not by mollycoddling children, as has plainly been done in this case and, alas, in so many other French families, that character is forged . . . And it was a few tens of thousands of young men of this kind that we had to put up against hundreds of thousands of young Germans.'[30] Even with some exaggeration, the general never ceased to hold up the past as a horrendous lesson. If the Marshal's orders sometimes seemed harsh, it was because they ran counter to the old habits of 'laziness, egoism and cowardice'. Occasionally moral exhortation touched lyrical heights: in *La Croix* 'Chef' Jacques Plénay enjoined those who had passed through the Chantiers 'to cultivate the "clear gaze", that gaze through which one may read your soul, and for this there is but one means: be pure . . . be a man, strong and virile . . . be French'.[31]

Religion was held to be a personal affair, but chaplains were numerous in the Chantiers, acting as general counsellors as well as spiritual directors. Officially their task was to teach a morality based upon Christianity, but one not specifically denominational. Those who served as cadres had to accept as a minimum that there was a 'natural morality' which corresponded to the Christian ethic. Although Mounier's personalist doctrine had not the influence that it had at Uriage, his periodical, *Esprit,* was recommended and widely read in the Chantiers.[32] De La Porte du Theil believed that, so long as France remained a Christian nation, youth must be educated in the Christian tradition, for he was personally convinced, as he put it, that 'one cannot make a society without God'.[33]

A feature of the life of the Chantiers was the stress placed on solemn ceremony and pageantry, particularly since it revolved round Pétain. On the movement's first anniversary the Marshal presented it with new colours and, flanked by the Commissioner-General, Lamirand, and Carcopino, attended mass at the church of St-Louis in Vichy. The head of State was also wont to visit frequently Chantiers' camps, to be greeted with a resounding 'Vive le Maréchal' and later dispatched with a fervent 'Ce n'est qu'un Au Revoir'. The many local news-sheets of the Chantiers, redolent of Baden-Powell ideology and Kipling's 'If', echoed the adulation after such visitations by publishing eulogies in verse:

> Grand Ancien, je voudrais pouvoir m'agenouiller
> Simplement, comme on fait devant la Sainte Image,
> A tes pieds.[34]
>
> (Venerable one, I would that I were able to kneel
> Simply, as one does before the Holy Image,
> At your feet.)

or:

> . . . vous qui venez
> Ainsi qu'un envoyé de Dieu,
> Sauver la France bien-aimée . . .
> Oh! vous dont la vieillesse
> Égale en sa noblesse
> De Jeanne d'Arc la jeunesse.[35]
>
> (. . . you who come as an envoy from God
> To save beloved France . . .
> O you whose age
> Matches in its nobility
> The youthfulness of Joan of Arc.)

Eventually in these pastiches of Péguy and similar encomiums, the Vichy censors clamped down and gave instructions that the Marshal's longevity should no longer be mentioned. But not only Pétain, but every Vichy celebrity from Darlan to Bonnard would appear to have made at least one ritual visit to a Chantiers' camp, although it is said that when Bonnard visited the headquarters in Châtel-Guyon in May 1942 General de La Porte du Theil gave orders that the Tricolour should not be flown.

For the second anniversary of the Chantiers the Groupement No. 1 (Groupement 'Maréchal Pétain'), joined by the Légion des Combattants and others from youth movements, staged a great spectacle in the forest of Tronçais near Vichy.[36] Plays on the first evening were followed by a torchlight retreat. The next day, after a solemn 'colours' ceremony, wreaths were laid on the war memorial and a march past was followed by mass. In the afternoon a ceremony was held at the foot of the oak previously dedicated to Pétain, sports were held, and a concert given. An evening aquatic show was followed by a mock stag hunt. Finally, as bugles sounded the 'Bonsoir de l'Équipage', the colours were lowered and the ceremony closed with the 'Marseillaise'. Such solemnities were frequent. Fabre-Luce recalls another such occasion at Challes,[37] where around the camp-fire of each group the evening roll-call was held, with each man answering by repeating the group motto, such as: 'Face up!' or, 'Straight to the goal!'. Finally 6,000 'Jeunes' ran to the central flagstaff and linked arms. Some occasions held greater significance than others. Thus in 1941, on All Souls' Day, a few days before Armistice Day, when all commemoration was forbidden, the Chantiers everywhere were ordered to parade at the local war memorial.[38] Passing-out parades before demobilization were also special events. Those leaving would go down on one knee and, with arm outstretched towards the flag, swear to continue to serve France. General de La Porte du Theil would send a paternal message of farewell: 'I have loved you all as my children, you who are of the same age as my own.'[39] The poignancy of such ceremonies in defeated France could not have been entirely lost on youth.

De La Porte du Theil well realized that the success of the

movement he created would depend upon the quality of the leadership. The most senior leaders were army officers – in June 1942 they numbered 163 out of 165.[40] Younger leaders were cadet officers, some drawn from the artillery school the general had once commanded. Although such military links were therefore strong, the army recruiting staff who campaigned in the Chantiers camps for volunteers did not meet with much success. The lowest level of cadres were promoted from the rank and file, for the general believed that advancement should not be on intellect alone. Whether this made a difference and encouraged the recruitment of leaders from other social classes is questionable, because on one leadership training course, out of eighty-one trainees, half were students, seminarists, and primary teachers.[41] In any case high standards were set. The general's subordinates had to demonstrate their unselfishness, for, he said, if the number of altruists had diminished before the war, 'the fault was to be ascribed to the general lowering of morality, the frenzy of pleasure and egoism which had gripped the country'. Abnegation demanding a sense of mission, an 'apostolate', was particularly required of the squad leader, who had to set an example by placing first the moral and material welfare of his men, participating in all their activities – and outshining them in all – and ensuring that in leisure hours they were kept happy and occupied. Especially important was the evening 'veillée' round the camp-fire, where the 'chef' had to foster comradeship and a family atmosphere. There should be talk about the day's happenings and plans for the morrow, games, sing-songs, recitations, and do-it-yourself activities. Such a leader 'does not make speeches, he knows how to listen, to understand, to refute if necessary, gently to guide others'. But the leader must remain an individual: 'For nothing in the world', wrote the general, 'would I wish leaders all to be cast in the same mould. All initiatives must be respected and even boldly developed.'[42] He held such diversity to be essential because, 'although there is not a people in the world more homogeneous than ours, regionalism rightly understood has its good points'.[43] Once again the difference in leadership style from that in totalitarian countries is stressed.

The first contingent of the Chantiers returned to civilian life in January 1941. Call-ups followed regularly until late 1943, although first reports regarding the movement had been so damning that in late 1940 Pétain had considered abandoning the experiment and was only dissuaded by the insistence of de La Porte du Theil. This was despite a report from one 'groupement' which was very adverse, but which, when it arrived in October 1940, he had thought it his duty to pass on to the Marshal.[44] It spelt out very precisely the state of the 'Jeunes', who had had to cope with very great material disadvantages. They even found leisure pursuits difficult, although some did like sport and music, if it were playing the harmonica or the accordion rather than choral singing; but few were used to reading. They found camp-fires uninspiring and 'colours' ceremonies unimportant. They appreciated the role of the Chantiers in rebuilding France but did not want to participate themselves in that task. After their release the experience in the Chantiers would be quickly forgotten. Any real loyalty to France was non-existent. The defeat had changed young men very little. They still lacked will-power and enthusiasm; their dominant trait was passivity and a liking for humdrum routine; they were 'grousers', lacking personal discipline and any moral discrimination. On the credit side, however, they had learnt to appreciate frankness and seriousness and had acquired a sense of comradeship. Luckily the general was able to follow up this pessimistic appraisal with a more optimistic one when the first contingent was discharged.[45] He noted how deplorable morale had been at the beginning, how frequent had been the complaints of the bourgeoisie that 'it was scandalous that a boy coming from a good family should mingle with working-class lads and be set to such manual tasks as cutting down trees or building roads'. Now, he declared, the patriotism of the 'Jeunes' shone through, so much so that 'almost all these men, if required to, would accept the supreme sacrifice'. About one in ten had become really actively militant for the Révolution Nationale. At last the social classes had come together. Individually the men had learnt self-control. Physically there had been an outstanding improvement. Veneral disease had been decimated. Although there was still some illness, the sickness-rate was down to 1.31 per 1,000 per day, the mortality-rate overall to 0.69 per 1,000; 72 per cent of 'Jeunes' had put on weight, and 15 per cent had gained more than 5 kilogrammes. The general was confident that, although 'the radical and definitive change in youth' had not yet been effected, a start had been made and the Chantiers were viable.

Not all shared the Commissioner-General's optimistic satisfaction. Some felt that in the movement there was not enough stress upon intellectual activities, the self-same reproach that had been levelled at education. The charge was answered by a 'chef' writing in *Jeunesse. . .France*:[46] although the camps were sited far from 'artificial and unhealthy' town life this did not mean that the mind must atrophy; in particular, leaders must remain mentally alert, for 'it would be to misunderstand the Chantiers if one reduced them to a reaction against intellectualism'. Another complaint made was that the movement was too non-political, so much so that Marion, the minister of information, set up a special propaganda section within the Chantiers which, despite de La Porte du Theil's protests, was allowed to function. The new section disclaimed any intention of becoming 'partisans of portmanteau slogans and soft-syrup propaganda',[47] although these were what was contained in the special news-sheet it issued for the 'Jeunes', whose circulation had reached 200,000 by the end of 1942.

Non-official comment was often hostile. When one unit arrived in the neighbourhood the local newspaper bluntly stated: 'The hordes . . . have arrived' and advised farmers to bolt their doors.[48] The collaborationist press in Paris complained vigorously against the Chantiers. In early 1941 the Doriotist weekly, *Jeunesse. . .Organe de la génération 40,* headlined an article, 'Un scandale qui doit cesser: chantiers de jeunesse, chantiers d'illusions', and condemned the deplorable conditions and the atmosphere of 'caporalisme'.[49] Déat was another persistent sniper at the movement, criticizing the leaders for not being up to their task and for using ridiculous means: 'It's not by the methods to which they resort – songs, marching in step, childish round-singing, all the little ways used successfully in the nursery school . . .

that they will succeed.'[50] Even Catholics, who had played such a prominent part in backing the movement, blew hot and cold. Thus Pierre Limagne, political leader-writer of *La Croix,* wrote in December 1940 in his diary: 'New from a youth camp. At this season the "boarders" are most often idle and bored; no enthusiasm, indeed the very opposite.'[51] Rumblings of discontent also continued within the movement. The prefect of the Allier reported in November 1941 that 'Jeunes' were grumbling that they were not being used rationally and that the country dwellers among them complained that they would be more productively employed at home.[52] In 1942 a war-ministry report noted that those called up were obsessed by food, the longing to go home, and a determination to avoid work; leave was granted in preference to those who could bring back something valuable from home, such as food, car oil, and even nails![53]

Complaints against the cadres, and particularly the quality of the junior leaders, were frequent. Limagne ascribed this to the over-hasty enlistment as permanent staff of former army personnel, when what was required was a complete break from the barrack-room mentality.[54] At least one former 'Jeune' criticized the mediocrity of his leaders, who lacked enthusiasm and any spirit of self-denial.[55] De La Porte du Theil was scandalized when he heard that some squad leaders did not even bother to get up in the morning for the 'colours' ceremony but sent their deputies instead.[56] The general meted out some forthright criticisms. There was a great need for submission to authority, he wrote, for 'I have always been struck by the state of perpetual disobedience in which French youth has lived.'[57] Women should be treated with great courtesy; he clearly feared that the recruitment of female nurses might lead to unsavoury incidents, and insisted that they be accorded respect, 'a respect that has been lost and we must restore. I know well that many women forfeited it through their own fault, but it is not for us to judge the issue.'[58] He criticized the unbridled language used by the men, adding – and one wonders whether the flattering reference is to Britain – 'I do not wish . . . to make the comparison with a certain great people whose proverbial discretion is today [June 1942] giving the world so striking a lesson.'[59] He exhorted young men to shun neglectfulness and idleness, 'which, it must be said, have greatly increased in recent years'.[60] The general's forthrightness was echoed by some of his subordinates. The deputy commander of one unit published a monumental telling-off in the camp news-sheet: 'This is for you and nobody in particular' ('Ceci s'adresse à vous et à personne en particulier'). Its burden was: You don't want the Révolution Nationale, because you wear your beret on the right when it should be worn on the left. You don't button up your tunic jacket. You don't salute your leaders. Your talk is rough. You're always grousing. Why this scruffiness and laziness? asks the despairing 'chef': 'It is because you're those little Frenchmen of before the war, because you are the sons of your fathers.'[61] And on this gratuitous insult to the previous generation this singular tirade closed. But this was in 1942, when morale in the Chantiers had clearly degenerated. A year before, writing about Pétain's Christmas message, another leader elsewhere had been able to hope that in a few months 'Youth . . . that Youth which the "grontic men" [*sic:* Pétain was *not* intended] of a rotten regime called out to march past in ridiculous Red carnivals, with hatred on its lips, will have been restored to its rightful place: the first in the service of the nation'.[62] For the rise from the nadir of despair to the apogee of hope and the swift relapse into despair two years, from the Armistice to June 1942, sufficed.

In an astute move de La Porte du Theil had started in June 1941 an Association des Anciens des Chantiers (ADAC). Aware at the outset that his intentions would be evaluated adversely, he hastily made a disclaimer: 'There is nothing about it [ADAC] which can embarrass anyone or awaken anxieties.'[63] The new association was not constituted 'for some kind of purpose not known'. Former 'Jeunes' were invited, not forced to join. Some might think the general protested too much. He sought to allay the fears of parents who saw membership as enlistment in a kind of military reserve, not wishing 'to give the impression that we are keeping our "Jeunes" in a state of permanent mobilization, which is incorrect'.[64] The 80–90 per cent of those discharged honourably from the Chantiers with a certificate of 'ability and morality' were eligible to put on the green beret, tie, and badge of ADAC, which constituted its sole uniform. Declared as an association under the law of 1901, with Carcopino's approval, its statutes stated that the aim was 'to prolong and develop. . . the instruction given and the practices observed in the Chantiers'. Members of ADAC were at first encouraged to join other youth organizations as well and take a prominent part in them, although in November 1943 the collaborationist group Jeunes de l'Europe Nouvelle reported to Laval that ADAC members were then forbidden to join other organizations.[65]

The activities of the new association appeared innocuous enough.[66] Assembled at local level by communes or cantons, they were grouped by departments. Meetings consisted of artistic, cultural, and sporting activities, and study groups; camps were organized, charities assisted, and civic ceremonies arranged; the local branch acted as a mutual employment agency. Growth was rapid: from ten sections in January 1942 they numbered 1,500 sections by April and 2,000 by September. How ADAC members felt about politics is not clear. In August 1942 the ADAC commissioner for Provence reported the 'patriotic sentiments' of members as being good on the whole, although this might bear different interpretations.[67] In September an ADAC news-sheet published an article by 'Un Ancien de Valence' in which he asked his former comrades pertinently, 'Do you believe that France can liberate herself if all her sons forget the demarcation line, her prisoners and her dead?'[68] This rhetorical question assumes that young men did not accept the status quo unreservedly. In Lyons, for example, the ADAC branch was in touch with the Resistance.[69]

How did the Germans view the Chantiers in general? In a report to Ribbentrop Abetz congratulated himself on having nipped in the bud a single youth movement as well as on having prevented the generals from assuming key posts in those movements which had been started. This leaves the Chantiers out of account. The generals, Abetz went on, had been anxious to take over such positions before the return of the prisoners of war, who would undoubtedly come back as strong pacifists and thus put paid to France ever again becoming a world power.[70] Against this must be weighed de La Porte du Theil's assertion at Abetz's post-war trial that he had nevertheless partially armed the Chantiers and could have fielded forty divisions against the Germans if he had had the opportunity.[71] The Germans certainly did their best to sabotage the Chantiers. Only very grudgingly did they eventually allow 37,000 of the first contingent of the Chantiers, the conscripts of June 1940, to return home to the occupied zone after demobilization. 'Jeunes' who were Jews or who lived in the 'reserved zone' were not allowed to cross the demarcation line.[72] In March 1942 the Germans eventually allowed permanent cadres of the Chantiers to go on leave to the occupied zone, but stringent conditions were imposed on the six hundred who availed themselves of this concession.[73] In January 1944 Chantiers units stationed near the Mediterranean coast were ordered to withdraw inland.[74] Déat's proposed successor in 1944 to the Chantiers, a Service National de la Jeunesse, was vetoed by the Germans mainly because they feared any disciplined body of young Frenchmen. By then they had good reason to do so.

Vichy's intentions in setting up the Chantiers were doubtless mixed, although it is difficult to accept that the General Staff, which supported the idea, had no military purpose in mind. Paxton, however, states categorically that the Chantiers were never intended by anybody to become clandestine military units.[75] Delage takes the opposite view when, writing after the war, he claims that the real purpose was to constitute a 'reserve of combattants'.[76] Weygand allegedly told de La Porte du Theil to 'work so that they may be an army, but above all do it clandestinely so as not to attract attention'.[77] De La Porte du Theil claims that in 1941 Pétain instructed him to 'make me an army again, because I will need it'.[78] Certainly some of the Chantiers were motivated to fight, because the movement became a haven for all who fell foul of the Germans, whether escaping prisoners of war, Alsace-Lorrainers, men on the Gestapo 'wanted list', or defaulters from compulsory labour service in Germany. Mgr Ruch, the Bishop of Strasburg in exile, even went so far as to congratulate de La Porte du Theil for pulling the wool over the Germans' eyes.[79] Military material was concealed in some camps. There were contacts with General Leclerc in North Africa through Leclerc's brother, Commissioner de Hauteclocque of the Chantiers. After November 1942 a leading member of the Chantiers very close to de La Porte du Theil, Antoine de Courson, an ex-officer, warned his groups to be ready for any eventuality.[80] As for ADAC, according to Delage its real purpose was to keep track of ex-members of the Chantiers and 'constitute reserves in case of mobilization'.[81] ADAC was officially dissolved, on German instructions, by a law of March 14, 1944, but the law was slow to be implemented. Carcopino, who believed that de La Porte du Theil, no less than Borotra, was out for military revenge,[82] confirmed after the war that he had assented to the formation of ADAC in order that mobilizable units could be got together.[83] Schweizer, the leader of the collaborationist Jeunes de l'Europe Nouvelle, reported to Laval in the late autumn of 1943 that in the Chantiers, where there was fear of imminent disbandment, men had been given new equipment and clothing, including ski boots and mountaineering rucksacks, all of which had to be packed ready by their bedside in case of emergency, that they had received back their civilian clothes, and that the 'Jeunes' were being incited to join defaulters from compulsory labour service in Germany.[84] Despite all assertions to the contrary, there is much circumstantial evidence that the Chantiers did indeed have a military purpose.

However, it is likely that the strength of that purpose varied considerably with the Chantiers' leaders. Thus, for example, the prospect of insurrection may have been strong in the minds of a group of ex-air-force officers attached to the directorate of civil aviation when they appealed for youngsters to volunteer for a Chantiers' group to be named 'Jeunesse et Montagne'. Priority in recruitment was given to those associated with or interested in aviation. Volunteers, clad in dark blue air-force uniform but without military insignia, were sent off for training in mountaineering and skiing to remote camps at Pralognan-la-Valoise and Montroc-le-Planet. Someone at Vichy was clearly interested in keeping such units out of the limelight because, when like other Chantiers units they wanted to start their own news-sheet, *Le Roc*, this was forbidden.[85] It is inconceivable that such units could have been started without the blessing of the French General Staff.

It is nevertheless disappointing that, despite its covert military objective, so little active resistance emerged from the Chantiers directly in the end. The last phase in the existence of the organization began in March 1943 when orders were first given that the 'Jeunes' were to be progressively incorporated into the STO and shipped off to Germany or to work in France for the Nazi military machine. Their reactions and the working-out of this ultimate constraint on an organization that was never pro-German are discussed elsewhere. What General de La Porte du Theil felt about this radical distortion of his original purpose is difficult to ascertain. In a message to ADAC the Commissioner-General tried to rationalize the need for the law calling up for the STO the classes of 1940–2, which included many ex-members of the Chantiers as well as those at present serving. He recalled Russian successes and the 'threat to Europe' these represented. In asking his Anciens to understand and obey the general added, 'but one is not asking from you any demonstration of enthusiasm'.[86] About this time members of the Chantiers may have been subjected to threats from either the Resistance or the Milice because on August 27, 1943 a rather curious law promulgated by Vichy stipulated sanctions against anyone who 'offered outrage by word, gesture or threat to any member of the Chantiers de la Jeunesse in the exercise of his functions or by reason of his status'. It is probable that incitement of the 'Jeunes' to 'dissidence' may have motivated this measure. Certainly their discipline and loyalty to their leader had deteriorated. Another law of October 28, 1943 prescribed severe penalties for those 'Jeunes' who disobeyed orders: prolongation of service, posting to the Chantiers' penal company, or even prison. Clearly the organization was at breaking-point; for the Commissioner-General himself the end was also in sight.

At the end of 1943 Pétain had quarrelled with Laval and had attempted to oust the latter's cronies from the government, including Bonnard, whom the Marshal had wished to replace by de La Porte du Theil as minister of education.[87] The reluctance of the Chantiers to co-operate in finding men for the STO, the reports flowing in to the Germans that their camps were becoming recruiting grounds for the Resistance, the general's unswerving loyalty to Pétain and his disregard of Laval, his 'neutralist' stance – all these factors made the Occupation authorities decide that the time had come to rid themselves of this somewhat stubborn Frenchman. The immediate pretext was a chance remark made by the general at Pétain's table, overheard by a waiter in German pay and duly passed on to the Gestapo, to the effect that the Germans on the Eastern Front were finished.[88] Abetz notified Laval that de La Porte du Theil, together with General Laure, Pétain's faithful friend, and Bouthillier, were to be deported to Germany. On January 5, 1944 the Commissioner-General was arrested, a few days after his post as head of the Chantiers had been officially abolished.[89] A law of January 19, 1944 set up a directorate-general to run the rump of the movement, whose sole purpose became to act as a labour reserve for the Germans. Although Vichy did not formally dissolve the Chantiers until June 10, 1944 the process of dismemberment by assigning the 'Jeunes' to forced labour was carried through in early 1944.

The Chantiers remained to the very last a cause of concern to Vichy. A report as late as July 28, 1944, based on postal intercepts, paints a graphic picture of the life of those still left in the camps.[90] The arrest of their leader had thrown the movement into disarray, made worse by the fact that many other cadres had then decamped. Those left behind adopted an 'attentiste' attitude, hanging around with nothing to do. They had little food: one Sunday lunch consisted of an artichoke and half a pound of potatoes. Yet, despite deplorable conditions, their unanimous resolve was not to be bundled off to Germany: 'We do not want to fall into *their* clutches.'

Dissolution of the Chantiers by Vichy was not enough for the Germans, who promulgated their own ordinance disbanding the movement on June 15, 1944. It was followed by yet another decree, this time by the Algiers authorities, on July 5. Even this was not enough, because on December 13, 1944 the organization was again officially dissolved by a decree of the provisional government. On October 6, 1944 the minister of education had sent out a circular to the Commissaires de la République – the provisional prefects – reasserting his control over the Chantiers, requiring returns to be made of personnel and equipment, and ordering a purge to be undertaken of the movement's cadres without delay.[91] Interestingly, the regional commissions charged with this task comprised six members of whom two had to be members or ex-members of the Chantiers themselves. This was an oblique acknowledgement that, in its way, the organization had also striven for the cause of France. It was also some vindication of General de La Porte du Theil, whose views, although misguided from the Gaullist viewpoint, had been motivated by a true patriotism. He, and many of his colleagues, were sincere in their belief in 'neutralism'. The policy proving in the long run untenable, many opted as individuals for resistance to the Germans. As for the youth they led, were they, as de Launay claims, 'safeguarded and protected'?[92] The answer can only be negative: rather they were sacrificed on the altar of Vichy's political expediency and of Germany's dream of hegemony.

Chapter XII

Leadership Schools

'Leadership schools' (écoles des cadres') became an important instrument for training young people and others who, in their turn, would be directly concerned with training youth, as well as 'indoctrinating' those in key positions in national life. In them those destined for positions of responsibility would be physically hardened, intellectually indoctrinated, and receive the civic and moral education necessary for their task. If this was the rationale of the schools, the reality was sometimes otherwise. At Uriage, in the southern zone, the national 'école des cadres supérieurs' maintained high standards of probity and preached a loyalty exclusively to France and, – but not to the end, – to Pétain. Its counterpart in the occupied zone, the 'école des cadres' at La Chapelle-en-Serval (Oise) took on a different, totalitarian ethos. Between these extremes there were many variations.

By March 1941 some sixty such 'leadership schools' were functioning,[1] only about half of which were directly under the control of the SGJ. The latter controlled twenty-one schools in the southern zone, as well as eight in the occupied zone.[2] They fell into three categories. Three were national, training in the main higher cadres: Uriage and, for girls, Écully-les-Lyon in the south, La Chapelle-en-Serval in the north. Twelve were regional – ten for men and two for women, with two more for women projected – providing courses for youth leaders at a lower level and for a more general clientele: students, primary teachers, industrial and agricultural workers, and military personnel. By March 1942 one hundred and forty courses had been mounted.[3] There were also ten specialized schools, five in each zone. These trained PE instructors, teachers of 'general education' ('éducation générale'), wardens for youth vocational-training centres and hostels, and 'housefathers' for the recreational youth hostels (Auberges de la Jeunesse). (A new movement, Les Camarades de la Route, formed to win over former

Ajistes to the Révolution Nationale, sent future 'housefathers' on the courses). The rest of the 'écoles des cadres' were run by other ministries, the youth movements themselves, and other organizations, political and military. By April 1942 the Chantiers de la Jeunesse, for example, had set up five schools of its own, after its first group of leaders had been trained at Uriage.[4] By early 1944 the Légion des Combattants had one national and six regional schools, where four-day courses in political and civic education were given. The Légion's schools had great success: in 1943 3,000 attended their courses, over half of whom were primary teachers, many of whom attended the special school at Allevard which gave courses in civic education particularly designed for them.[5] All such schools were postulated on the unproven conviction that the defeat had been due to lack of leadership and that 'leadership qualities' could be developed through careful training.

This concept of leadership, however, was occasionally interpreted in totalitarian terms, as was the case at the 'école des cadres' of La Chapelle-en-Serval, which acquired an unsavoury reputation. Sited on confiscated Jewish property, it ran courses that lasted only a few days, although there were a few also lasting six months. Its most notorious director was Bousquet, the Paris schoolteacher whom Bonnard had appointed to his staff after he had successfully founded a youth organization, Les Jeunes du Maréchal, in the Lycée Voltaire, and who had distinguished himself, when called to give evidence before the youth commission of the Conseil National, by giving the Nazi salute. Local inhabitants had been shocked when, in palpable imitation of the pre-war German labour service ('Reicharbeitsdienst'), the guard at the school was mounted by men equipped with spades. Bonnard explained this away to Laval, perhaps with tongue in cheek, by saying that it was a way of honouring agriculture![6] Attenders on courses acquired an unsavoury reputation. They were accused of petty thieving and scrounging. A Church dignitary visiting the school at Easter 1942 was scandalized to hear the distant strains of the 'Internationale' arising in the grounds from a group of primary teachers on a course. There was also trouble with the staff.

In June 1942 Pétain was informed that Bousquet had dismissed a number of his subordinates, one because he was accused of not being a 'Hitlérien'. When the member of staff defended himself by saying that he was 'un fasciste français' he was told by Bousquet that that was not good enough: only 'Hitlériens' were wanted.[7] This astonishing director of the school was also charged with maligning Pétain for landing the French in their present mess. When, finally, a new director was appointed he reported that the institution was 'in an absolutely indescribable administrative state'.[8]

After Bousquet's departure the school's discipline was tightened up, but in 1943 it attracted the Germans' attention when it publicized in the occupied zone a course to recruit forty new youth delegates.[9] This got to the ears of Stülpnagel, the German commander; as a result the SS police chief, Knochen, wrote to de Brinon ordering that all future appointments as regional or department youth delegates must be submitted for German approval. By then the occasional long course that was run at La Chapelle-en-Serval included not only law but also courses in political science and 'the philosophy of action', which included 'questions of race and heredity'.[10]

Near to this singular 'école des cadres' it was proposed to run a 'collège des jeunes chefs'.[11] Plainly modelled on the German Adolf-Hitler-Schulen, the purpose was to take in youngsters of sixteen and give them an intensive eight-year course, thereby 'to provide for the country, each year from 1948 onwards, young revolutionary leaders to serve in youth movements, in diplomacy and other branches of the administration'. Whether it would be a substitute for the 'grandes écoles' was not made clear. The course would include a military training 'compatible with our situation', political education, a spell 'preparing for a command', and another period in the colonies. There would be a hierarchy of ranks: the recruit would be styled a 'novice'; after his first 'promise' – one notes the monastic or scouting connotation – he would be promoted to 'page', before going on to become a 'squire' and, on passing out, attaining the rank of 'chevalier'. Like other training schemes, there was a harking back to medievalism, as if to compensate for the bleak present. Initial publicity for the new institution attracted 2,000 provisional enrolments, but there is no record of whether this 'junior leaders' school' did eventually open. The Germans are likely to have frowned upon the plan.

In the southern zone a rival school to Uriage[12] was founded near Vichy at Mayet-de-Montagne in October 1941 by Paul Marion, whose ideas were also cast in the totalitarian mould. Run by the ministry of information and, perhaps because Pucheu also had a hand in its creation, it was designed to train not only propaganda officials but also civil servants for the ministry of the interior. An anonymous report reaching Pétain's staff painted a disturbing picture of the school in the winter of 1941–2.[13] Real training, it would seem, was minimal, and the classes mounted were more remarkable for their rhetoric than for their content. Students on the courses were encouraged to denounce each other. Politically the courses were to the Left – many students were former supporters of the Front Populaire or even Communists. Anticlericalism was a dominant theme, and the SGJ, because of its Catholic bias, was constantly vilified. The director of the school, G____, had written (*Idées* No. 2, December 1941) that the leaders of the Vichy youth movements were 'seeking to make of every Frenchman a little Jesus'. The atmosphere in the school was alleged to be oriented to the class struggle, anti-employer, ultra-collaborationist, anti-Légion, anti-English and violently anti-Gaullist, favouring Nazi ideas, and imbued with a mystique of 'Eurafrique' – the youth movement Jeunesse Française d'Outremer was highly esteemed. There could be little in the report that did not make depressing reading for Pétain and Lamirand. The school was clearly intended to counterbalance the vastly different ethos of Uriage.

The creation of an 'école des cadres' at Uriage was the work of Captain Pierre Dunoyer de Segonzac, a regular cavalry officer. At thirty-four the defeat had deprived him of his profession. Catholic and aristocratic, he also viewed the collapse as a failure of leadership, with youth badly led, or led not at all. Through Commandant de la Chapelle, one of Ybarnégaray's staff, he received the authorization on August 12, 1940 to set up a school. At Vichy he was already highly esteemed.[14] The school was first installed in a château near

Gannat, but the accessibility to Vichy, with its atmosphere of intrigue, and the regime's manifest desire to keep the school on a tight rein, quickly proved intolerable.[15] Nevertheless a first course was run for 140 junior officers, baptized symbolically the 'promotion nouvelle France'. They were to form the first cadres of the newly constituted Chantiers de la Jeunesse,[16] although de Segonzac was pleased to sever this brief connection with de La Porte du Theil, whom he considered too dependent on Vichy.

He was also glad to move the school in October 1940 to Uriage, near Grenoble, into a castle associated with Bayard. Perched amid forests and fields overlooked by the snow-capped peaks of the Belledonne, the castle was splendidly isolated from the world. Such a setting, in an all-male society, favoured a Spartan, military-style existence, in which the essential element was comradeship. The ideal type that emerged was the clean-cut, clear-eyed, strong-willed, muscular, young man. It was not quite the type that Vichy would have preferred, for the reverse of the medal was non-compliance and the refusal to accept the defeat. Lamirand blamed the geographical remoteness of the school as one reason why the principles the school professed eventually were so much out of tune with those held at Vichy.[17] Nevertheless, perhaps some 4,000 men passed through it before it was closed down.

What kind of colleagues did de Segonzac gather round him to run the school? As with the Chantiers and the Compagnons, the nucleus consisted of young officers, a dozen instructors in all, a civilian PE teacher, Roger Vuillemin, and Father Naurois, who became the first chaplain. The deputy director was Eric d'Alançon, a particularly dedicated personality, strongly Catholic, and so austere in his personal life style that he was termed the 'soldier-monk'. D'Alançon was the course director, heading a team of instructors, each of whom looked after a group of students – an 'équipe', which was the basic unit for all activities. A director of studies ran another team concerned with the intellectual training of the students attending courses. Artistic and practical activities were also catered for. Later, instructors were drawn from civilian life: teachers, actors, sportsmen, trade unionists, and others. One of the more notable was Hubert Beuve-Méry, the future editor of *Le Monde,* director before the war of the Institut Français in Prague and also a journalist, who had resigned from *Le Temps* because of its stance on the Munich agreement. Among such men the defeat still rankled and Naurois and Beuve-Méry, in particular, were very outspoken in their anti-German sentiments, particularly after the 'handshake of Montoire'.

Uriage catered not only for future youth leaders, but also for those who occupied positions where they could influence others, from priests to schoolteachers, 'men who would constitute the structure of the France of tomorrow'.[18] Some undoubtedly thought also that the school had a quasi-military purpose. De Segonzac disagreed with the orthodox Vichy view that the military leaders were not to blame for the collapse. On the contrary, the men had been badly led. During the 1920s, visiting the Rhineland, he had seen at close quarters the incipient Nazi organizations, and contrasted the comportment of German youth with that of his own men in 1940, who preferred listening to Tino Rossi records to more worthwhile pursuits. Both officers and men had lost the will to fight. Wladimir d'Ormesson also saw Uriage as an effort to remedy the shortcomings of young reserve officers on whom rank had been bestowed for intellectual ability rather than because of their capacity to command. De Segonzac was particularly scathing about students under the Third Republic: 'Our universities were peopled by young students, future champions of the intelligence, but meanwhile champions of long and greasy hair, generally skinny, spotty and slovenly.'[19] Many young men who passed through Uriage felt that its real object was 'to breathe a new spirit into the army and prepare it . . . for the struggle to come'.[20] Thus if the school had been founded in response to a national challenge, that challenge, in the last resort, was conceived to be a military one.

The standard course lasted three weeks, although there was one that lasted as long as six months as well as a number of 'information sessions' lasting only a few days. Between sixty and 120 men attended the standard course and much had to be compressed into a short time. The first week was taken up with settling into a strenuous pattern of physical exercise, manual work, and intellectual study. The second was given over to the problems of youth and the last to an exposition and discussion of the 'doctrine' of Uriage. Activities proceeded briskly from 7 a.m. to 10 p.m., with manual tasks, sports, and games alternating with lectures, discussion, study-groups, and various artisan activities. Visits were made to farms, factories, and apprenticeship centres. Environmental studies – what became popular in French schools in the 1950s as 'l'étude du milieu' – were much favoured. Students would talk about their jobs. The general routine was much as in the Chantiers or the Compagnons, with the evening 'veillée' ending the day, which always terminated with a period of silent reflection before dispersal for the night.

The intellectual component of the course was provided by lectures, seminars, and study-groups. Mounier spoke on a variety of topics, such as 'La fin du bourgeois français'.[21] Guest lecturers included Mgr Bruno de Solages (until, like Mounier, he was forbidden); Chevalier; the President of the Senate, Jeanneney; the Jesuit Father Dillard; the economist, Robert Mossé; the diplomat François-Poncet; Mounier's collaborator on *Esprit,* Jean Lacroix; the Catholic sociologist, Chombart de Lauwe; and Mgr Guerry, who outlined the Church's attitude to social problems. Professors were invited from nearby Grenoble, as were industrialists, engineers, trade unionists, clergy, and higher civil servants. Standards were high, and it was in the quality of its intellectual contribution that Uriage was most notable. No topics were barred and both lecturers and audience were encouraged to express their views freely. Some whom Vichy might have liked to see invited were not. When Doriot was proposed, de Segonzac agreed but warned that on the day Doriot came he would be absent. The PPF leader never came. Darlan did not wait for an invitation but descended on Uriage in the summer of 1941, shocking his listeners not so much by his assertion of his 'neutralism' but by the coarseness with which he expressed it: 'J'emmerde l'Angleterre, je me fouts de l'Allemagne.'[22] Colloquia brought together such widely differing personalities as Mounier and Massis. Claudel came to

Uriage for a reading of his 'Jeanne au Bûcher'. Study-groups concentrated on a wide variety of themes: 'travail, famille, patrie', youth movements, personality, leadership, capitalism, European civilization, the army's role, 'social' Christianity, and educational reform. The books of Proudhon, Maurras, or Péguy were studied in depth, as were excerpts from the works of Teilhard de Chardin. Occasionally a whole week would be given over to the study of one topic such as 'character'. For this a dossier would be handed out, containing extracts from Pétain's 'Messages', passages from Vigny's *Servitude et grandeur militaires,* information on such figures as Lyautey, and study-notes and suggestions for further reading. At the evening 'veillée' linked to this topic there might be a satirical miming of 'l'homme-swing', the French teddy-boy of the 1940s, or the recital in chorus of the ever popular Kipling's 'If'. Individual work connected with the theme might include the designing of posters or the writing of articles on it. Each study-group would have to come up with some suggestion for action, ranging from the relatively trivial injunction, 'Don't smoke while you're studying', to 'Getting over the false respect for others which inhibits one from hissing some scandalous film showing in the town nearby' (was *Jud Süss* intended, one wonders?), or 'Protesting against the public profanation of certain values'.[23]

How did participants receive such a programme? There were a few hostile reactions. One attender on a course in September 1941 commented adversely on the course as being so contentious that he thought Uriage might almost be termed 'a Gaullist school'.[24] A year later another hostile participant from the occupied zone was likewise even more carping. He complained that Franco-German collaboration was barely mentioned and that when it was the lecturer merely said that that was a matter for the government. He was also told that Nazification had to be resisted and that national unity could only be achieved when the Germans had been driven out. Positive political indoctrination, in the sense that he understood it, was non-existent. Instead there was only the exposition of a moral ideal, which was hardly sufficient to bring about the Révolution Nationale. All in all, he concluded, 'If there had been Gaullists or Communists amongst us, they would hardly have had occasion to perceive that they had set off on the wrong track.'[25]

De Segonzac himself was beginning to change direction. He had started as a patriot, a Catholic, and a monarchist. In setting up Uriage he had thought that the patriotism of others interested in youth – Lamirand, Borotra, de La Porte du Theil, Weygand, to say nothing of Pétain himself – was sufficient guarantee that French interests would always remain the paramount concern. Now he was more unsure. His Catholicism ran more deeply than that of the normal army officer and had not been undermined. But the attitudes he had begun with, élitist and authoritarian, which had derived from the Action Française – Massis held a watching brief over Uriage for the SGJ – were beginning to change. By the end of 1940 he had discarded his original vision of a new France based on monarchism and syndicalism as unworkable and had thrown in his lot with Mounier and Beuve-Méry. Maurrassianism, which still maintained its watchword of 'La France seule', its anti-Semitism, and anti-English character, was beginning to play down its anti-Germanism, which had once been its main plank. Thus Mounier's personalist philosophy gradually became the basic doctrine of Uriage.

Mounier had come into contact with the school through Jean Lacroix, who was a friend of Father Naurois, the first chaplain. Despite his own strong religious faith, the form of personalist philosophy that Mounier had evolved had given him in some Catholic circles the reputation of being something of an 'enfant terrible'.[26] The basic tenet that the spiritual element in life should be predominant and the view that the person, although significant in his own right, acquired greater meaning through social relationships expressed in service to others, did not clash with orthodoxy.[27] The condemnation of individualism that was implied was also very much in accord with Vichy 'doctrine'. It was in its potential political implications that the philosophy became less acceptable. Personalism held that, whilst materialism in all its forms was to be condemned, so also was capitalism, because it represented the triumph of egotistical individualism. Totalitarianism was equally unacceptable because it was essentially negative and denied the creative freedom of man. In any case the State was meant for man, not man for the State. Since bourgeois capitalist democracy was also to be rejected, being too inhuman and self-seeking, some kind of socialist structure for society should be evolved. The essentially revolutionary nature of Mounier's doctrines is thus revealed: as well as a moral and psychological sea change in the individual a complete economic and social restructuring of the community is necessary. This goes much farther than the Révolution Nationale and the legislation that it enacted, such as the Charte du Travail, had envisaged.

Mounier was more politically sophisticated than de Segonzac, more aware of Vichy's inner contradictions, more willing to expose them. Thus he quickly fell foul of Massis, who had seen his influence at Uriage decrease. Although he was allowed to resume publication of *Esprit* in November 1940, he soon became *persona non grata* to ruling Catholic circles at Vichy. He quarrelled with Chevalier, his old philosophy teacher, over the question of subsidies to Catholic schools. From December 1940 his connection with Uriage became even closer, because he approved of the independent position it maintained and its categorical rejection of collaboration as a 'French alternative'. In April 1941 Vichy forbade him to lecture at Uriage, although the ban was later lifted at de Segonzac's insistence; but he was forbidden to participate in the study-groups that formed an important teaching instrument within the school. Official opposition to him hardened even more when in June 1941 *Esprit* attacked the showing of the film *Jud Süss*. The following month Mounier's doctrines were assailed in the *Action française* as being contrary to the Révolution Nationale.[28] In August *Esprit* was finally banned. In January 1942 Mounier was arrested, suspected of contacts with Combat, the Resistance movement. The fact that Frenay, its future leader, who had been commissioned at the same time as de Segonzac, had visited Uriage secretly on the very same day as Darlan, did not come to light.[29] Despite Mounier's imprisonment his influence survived: as a confidential note to Pétain remarked, 'Uriage is still dominated by the doctrine of a man at present in prison for conspiracy.'[30] Mounier always felt gratified at the impact his views had made on the school. To his friend and collaborator, Étienne Borne, he wrote in 1941: 'Because we did not withdraw into our tents, we have known real pockets of health, "corners of France truly free", the Ecole d'Uriage, Jeune France.'[31] Late in 1942 Mounier, physically very weak after having been on a hunger strike, was released from prison. So far as is known, he did not renew his contacts with the school before it was finally disbanded in December 1942.

Mounier's postulate of 'the primacy of the spiritual' was understood at Uriage in conjunction with two others: the cult of honour and service to one's country. On these three premisses it was hoped that a different life style would emerge for 'l'homme nouveau', one in keeping with the twentieth century. At the beginning de Segonzac saw no conflict between these premisses and those on which the Révolution Nationale was founded, although how they would be interpreted was vital. De Segonzac hoped that the new life-style might internalize some of Vichy's professed values: the willing acceptance of discipline and an altruism that would reconcile warring social groups and promote fraternity between them. His own 'doctrine' accepted the principle of authority, but he believed that this authority should be exercised by an élite with a difference, one forming part of a spiritual community based on transcendental values and giving service to others. The theory of leadership that he worked out postulated therefore that the leader derived his rights from the nature of the task assigned to the group he led: thus he was neither a mere executant, as in a democracy, but neither did he have any divine right to command. Gilles Ferry has summed up the purpose of Uriage as not so much to train leaders as to train them to do their job. By living at the school they would become aware of the ties that bind a superior to his subordinates and learn how the group functions best. The community must not be conceived of as a collection of individuals, but as a group of persons, which implies relationship with others.[32] The life-style, the new synthesis of humanism that would arise, would be based on the cultivation of the virtues, indeed on the cultivation of the most difficult ones, such as purity, self-sacrifice, and chivalrous conduct. The prototype was Péguy, the Christian, the patriot, and the Socialist.

That such a Utopian doctrine for youth could be expounded after a lost war is in itself astounding. The very imprecision of the ideas gave rise to a charge of mystification, but perhaps vagueness was necessary for such an ideal to be ecumenical, as was wished. Since the spiritual basis of life gave rise to common values, it was one that Catholics, Protestants, Jews, and those of other faiths or of none could share in, and did. Ecumenicalism was put into practice: Lochard, a Protestant pastor, and Father Fraisse, a Jesuit, served happily together on the staff of instructors. Members of youth organizations, including the notoriously secularist youth-hostel movement, atheistic trade unionists, and Socialists found common ground with Christians.

However, in 1942 there was at the school a shift away from moral self-improvement and the study of economic and social problems was more emphasized. This was in part in response to the needs of industrialists, managers, and workers who now came increasingly on the courses and were eager to discuss the working-out, for example, of the Charte du Travail. This was a different audience, but one capable of exerting great influence over the young. De Segonzac used the opportunity to concentrate upon the perennial conflict between employer and employed.[33] He attacked the lack of leadership on both sides, but blamed in part the modern operating conditions in industry: the large-scale enterprise, mechanization, and automation had widened the gulf between the factory-owner and his men.

Social and economic questions inevitably led on to politics. De Segonzac had always insisted on complete autonomy, the freedom of instructors and instructed to follow the argument wherever it led. Increasingly the orthodoxy of Vichy was left behind; this development was viewed with great alarm.[34] Even the doctrine of obedience, which had been preached unremittingly to youth since 1940, was challenged: conscience became the supreme arbiter of action. Uriage instructors not only condemned pre-war democracy, but also spoke out freely against any and every totalitarian doctrine. The sole hierarchy should be of merit: status acquired solely through birth was no longer acceptable. Father Naurois, who had known pre-war Germany well, repeatedly warned against the evils of Nazism, until eventually his outspokenness resulted in his dismissal, at Vichy's insistence. Students on the course were encouraged to speak their mind about unpleasant experiences they had suffered at German hands. Beuve-Méry was just as unrelenting in exposing the shortcomings of the government. The fortnightly publication of Uriage, *Jeunesse . . . France,* reflected the evolution in ideas, becoming progressively lukewarm towards Pétain's policies and more overtly anti-German. De Segonzac had never concealed his views. In the winter of 1941, after lecturing at Grenoble University, when he had expressed his hope for a British victory, he had received a warning from the prefecture. In the beginning his loyalty to Pétain had been unquestioning – although this did not necessarily extend to the Marshal's government. He was convinced that Pétain was secretly working towards resistance to the Germans, even against the wishes of his closest collaborators. If the Marshal could not stomach Gaullism it was because, like many at Uriage, he could not forgive Mers-el-Kébir, Dakar, and Syria. A few days before Joan of Arc Day in 1941 de Segonzac broadcast on Radio-Jeunesse, emphasizing Joan's military achievements.[35] About Pétain he had this to say: 'Thanks to [the Marshal] our community will rise in strength ['surgira avec force': the meaning seems deliberately ambiguous] as soon as there are in France a sufficient number of true men to constitute it. At Uriage we are seeking to work towards this.'[36] From mid-1941 de Segonzac had no hesitation at conniving at covert acts of resistance, such as procuring false papers for Jews, helping escapees and those who wished to cross the demarcation line illegally. Weygand's dismissal in November 1941 came as a severe blow to him, as it did to Commandant de Tournemire of the Compagnons. He had nourished the hope that in North Africa, with the secret support of Pétain, Weygand had been making ready an army of liberation. Despite this set-back to his expectations, de Segonzac's moment of decision had not yet come.

Any military hopes on his part were always conditioned by his view that France could not achieve its former greatness until it had operated a spiritual renewal. An important part of the work at Uriage was seen to be the investigation into how this could be effected. A 'Bureau d'études permanent' was set up to carry out research into the question and also to provide documentation for use on the courses. It was from this group that Mounier had been banned. The range of its investigations was very wide, from studying the effect of such allegedly deterministic mechanisms as heredity and the findings of psychoanalysis on social problems to making analyses of the political situation. Its political interest was strengthened when the team was reinforced in 1942 by Paul Reuter and Gilbert Gadoffre. Even when Uriage had been dissolved the 'Bureau' continued to work clandestinely. In the Château de Murinais where cadres were then trained for the Resistance and not for the Révolution Nationale, the group embarked on the elaboration of what was described as a '*Summa* of the twentieth century', a new humanism that would synthesize and reconcile the work of Marx, Nietzsche, and Péguy[37] and form the basis of a post-war revolution in France. The enterprise was halted and all the documents destroyed when the SS and the Milice raided the castle in December 1943, but work was continued in the Maquis, resulting in the publication in 1945 of Gadoffre's *Vers le style du XXe siècle.*

An important development was the foundation in 1941 of an association of all those who had been through Uriage. The Équipe Nationale d'Uriage, similar in conception to ADAC (of the Chantiers de la Jeunesse), was however much more influential because many members now occupied key positions, particularly those concerned with youth. Members pledged themselves to follow the life-style they had learnt at Uriage. Vichy saw the association as a further attempt by de Segonzac to free himself from its control. Suspicions were later justified because after 1942 many of the 'Anciens' belonging to the Équipe Nationale joined their leader in the Maquis.

Some Catholics disliked the new association because they thought it would further weaken their own youth movements. The hierarchy remained hesitant about Uriage in general. Gerlier feared that the extreme tolerance of the school would be detrimental to Catholics who passed through it. The Association Catholique de la Jeunesse Française saw Uriage as a rival, since they considered social change as well as evangelism was part of their own mission. The Jacistes and Jocistes within the movement, more inclined to Christian Democrat views, were rather reserved regarding Uriage. Those Catholic students associated with *Cahiers de notre jeunesse* thought the school concentrated too little upon the shape of the new institutions necessary for national renewal and the laws and customs that would regulate the new community: it was 'as if only good intentions were necessary to create a harmonious unity'.[38] But the students were not at all hostile to Uriage. On the other hand Father Forestier, influential among Catholics because he was Chaplain-General of both the scouts and the Chantiers, deemed it necessary to warn against 'neutrality' in the leadership schools and cited the catch-phrase of Pétain, 'Puisque la vie n'est pas neutre . . .'[39] But this was to misunderstand the kind of commitment that was developing at Uriage. De Segonzac came in for criticism because of the abstruse nature of his theories: 'This gives rise to a terrible rigmarole and, what is worse, to a "personalism" inspired by Mounier which the latter was able to teach with impunity at Uriage until an order . . . arrived to put a stop to this scandal.'[40]

Lamirand and one of his close collaborators, Garrone, were not pleased when they saw the institution which commanded most influence eluding their control. They worried at the kind of teaching that went on in the school, but felt that it would be wise to avoid open conflict, since this would alienate at least a part of the Christian opinion on which they relied for support. It was of course the political implications of personalism that disturbed them. After the dismissal of Father Naurois they would have liked his replacement to be a middle-of-the-roader, someone 'entirely in line with the thinking of the Marshal, equidistant from the "Totals" (sc. "totalitarians") and the democrats'.[41] They did not get their way because Father Maydieu, who was appointed, became a firm supporter of de Segonzac's ideas. Nevertheless, Lamirand backed Uriage as long as he could, despite the fact that this endangered his own position. Darlan, during his period as head of government, was plainly out of sympathy with Uriage but had tried to change it. Thus, after visiting the school, which up to then had been open only to volunteers, he decreed that all entrants to the Grands Corps d'État should pass through the school. Unfortunately a rift in the lute soon developed, because the admiral planted informers to report on the school's activities. One, a naval officer, was uncovered and promptly shown the door by de Segonzac.[42] Uriage nevertheless struggled on until the return of Laval, when the storm-clouds over the school grew blacker. Bonnard and Pelorson were totally out of sympathy with its aims and although de Segonzac saw Laval personally at least twice, efforts to achieve an understanding failed. The end was not far off.

The path that de Segonzac had followed, from independence to nonconformism, although Lamirand acknowledged that his personal loyalty to Pétain was unquestioning,[43] ended finally in dissidence. After the North-African landings no other course was possible. A little later other army officers, de Tournemire and de La Porte du Theil, to name only two concerned with youth, also failed to reconcile their concept of honour and service to France with that of those who time-served at Vichy from November 1942 onwards, when Pétain had become a 'roi fainéant', lacking the power or the will to influence events. Even then Lamirand made a last desperate intervention on de Segonzac's behalf: he wrote to Bonnard urging that it would be wrong to close down Uriage and dismiss its head.[44] It would seem that before the North-African landings the minister had had it in mind to post him back to the ministry of war or exile him to the Sahara! However, at Christmastide 1942 de Segonzac addressed the last course, which included Gilbert Dru and Jean-Marie Domenach, the Catholic students who had been leading lights in the Cahiers de Notre Jeunesse, now closed down, and who eventually joined the Resistance. His theme was on the right of disobedience, in certain circumstances, of those placed under orders. A warrant was issued for de Segonzac's arrest, but he and many of his collaborators had already fled to the Maquis. The action against Uriage led to the temporary closure of other 'écoles des cadres', because of the number of staff resigning in sympathy, in the case of one school in what Vichy termed, 'a collective and irrational resignation'.[45]

The Château de Murinais at Saint-Marcellin, where a clandestine Uriage was reconstituted for a while, was not far from the Vercors. De Segonzac had previously been wary of Resistance networks, considering them precipitate, imprudent, and over-political. He had kept his distance from the Gaullists in London, although he did think that with all such men 'One was among good Frenchmen'. In clandestinity he did not lose this basic mistrust.[46] A visit to Algiers at the beginning of 1944 did nothing to reassure him, although he did eventually pledge nominal allegiance to de Gaulle. His own Maquis of the Tarn was a free corps consisting of Catholics, Protestants, and Jews, including many Jewish scouts who had been through Uriage and other former students. At the invasion he joined up with de Lattre's army and continued with it to Germany, resuming, perhaps disappointingly for French youth, his duties as a regular officer, and ending up as a general.

What concrete results emerged from Uriage? The school trained many who were to achieve influence in post-war France, although they were not to reach the very highest positions. In publishing and the intellectual field they were particularly strong – Beuve-Méry at *Le Monde*, Domenach as editor of *Esprit*. At least one, Gilles Ferry, achieved eminence in the educational field. Indeed, in pedagogy the Uriage methods of study-group and seminar became very popular. The evolution of 'éducation populaire' with which Dumazedier and Cacérès, two former associates of Uriage, were prominently connected, is another example of the school's pedagogical influence. The creation of the 'Maisons des Jeunes' also owes something to Uriage.

The Uriage experiment cannot therefore be considered merely as a return to medievalism, the search, in a romantic setting, for an impossible ideal. Nor was it the French counterpart to the Nazi 'Ordenburg' in which a new Aryan élite were to be trained to rule a European 'New Order'. Rather must it be seen as a serious attempt to discover a 'via media', a new form of society appropriate to the modern world, but based on virtue. Such an unsophisticated conception does not lack nobility but Uriage is the 'history of an alternative Vichy'[47] that might have been. For de Segonzac to opt in

1940 as he did was, as his friend, Charles d'Aragon wrote, 'a striking error of appreciation'.[48] In the circumstances of the defeat any such institution founded to encompass the moral reconstruction of France was doomed from the outset. Uriage in clandestinity exemplified this: the spiritual revolution it sought could only be accomplished after France was liberated.

Chapter XIII

Other Youth Organizations

The Chantiers and the Compagnons, the Catholic and scouting organizations, represent respectively the main official and unofficial youth movements that flourished in wartime France. Apart from these, however, there were a score of others, semi-official or private, which also achieved some national status. All paid lip-service to the Révolution Nationale and its educative mission for the young, but interpreted their own role differently. A few, principally those that existed under the aegis of political parties, had existed before the war. Others were formed specifically to promote collaboration with Germany; for them Nazism was the ideal, with its doctrines of right is might, of anti-Bolshevism, anti-Semitism, and anti-freemasonry, and the devaluation of the Christian ethic. Some of these championed 'Europeanism', a 'new order' in which France would be the senior but subordinate partner in a German-dominated Continent. Others were more 'maréchaliste', preferring Pétain to Laval. One or two were concerned with cultural or leisure activities, or became auxiliaries of the social services. Those that toed the German line nursed ambitions to become that 'jeunesse unique' of the French state that Vichy had consistently rejected. Their leaders, particularly if the movements were political, may have drawn a parallel with the eve of the Nazi 'Machtübernahme' of 1933, with Pétain cast in the role of Hindenburg and they as latter-day Hitlers. But the influence of all such movements can only be a matter for conjecture. What is certain is that the Catholic movements and the scouting movement remained more effective than all the rest. If before the war only one French youth in seven had been attached to a movement, it is likely that by the Liberation, after a dramatic increase from 1940–2, this proportion had not changed significantly. It is even more probable that the number active in the Resistance movements (which lie outside this study) at that time was considerably greater.

One entity, although not a youth organization in any technical sense, represented an official grouping of young men of considerable importance and was to be found in Germany. It consisted of the large number of cadet officers whom the Germans had captured in 1940. At French request, 3,500 of these were assembled in 1941 at the camp of Stablack in East Prussia. They were placed under the command of General D———, a French officer who combined an enthusiasm for Pétain with apologetics for Nazism. Like other officer-prisoner camps the new camp soon became a hotbed of propaganda for the Révolution Nationale. There was a daily 'quart d'heure Pétain' in which a young cadet officer had to explain to his comrades some aspect of Vichy policy. Since all other news and views were censored this was a not inefficient method of indoctrinating those whom Vichy hoped would constitute an important element in the élites of the new France. Only as the war dragged on did disillusionment set in.[1]

Youth movements affiliated to political parties or organizations 'approved' or 'tolerated' – it will be recalled that the Germans distinguished between the two categories – by the Occupation authorities were most active in the northern zone. Provided they played the German game, they were seen as a useful weapon to divide Frenchmen and to use as a threat against the Vichy regime. The Germans cared little for the political ambitions of these movements: whether France, Italy, or any other power would have a share in future German power must await the peace. The Germans saw their cause advanced when they and the movements shared common enemies: religion, the Jews, secret societies, de Gaulle. By playing off one group against another the Germans could prevent the emergence of a single youth movement, a contingency they abhorred as much as Pétain. In their blindness in not realizing that they were pawns whom the Germans used, the collaborationist leaders displayed the self-same naïvety of which they frequently accused the SGJ.[2]

If one omits the small Ligue Française set up by Costantini, a very ill man by the Liberation, Clémenti's Parti Collectiviste Français was the earliest political party to attract attention after the defeat. The party had been founded in 1934 and later this former sports journalist linked to it a para-military group, the Garde Française, which included the Jeune Front, a section for youths aged sixteen to twenty. After the Armistice the Garde Française had installed its headquarters in a shop on the Champs-Élysées, commandeered from its absent owner. From this base in August 1940 it attempted to storm the offices of the secularist wing of the Auberges de la Jeunesse, which had been strongly identified with the defunct regime. The youth section, which had close links with the anti-Semite newspaper *Au Pilori,* contented itself with damaging the property of freemasons and Jews. On Armistice Day, 1940, however, it had been an incident with a hostile crowd gathered outside the movement's headquarters which had sparked off the anti-German demonstration that followed and which eventually led to the closure for a few weeks of the University of Paris. A few days later, on November 17, 1940, at Dijon younger party members had also clashed with students there, which led to the Germans temporarily also closing that university and banning the movement. After this brief flurry of activity the youth section of Clémenti's party, never very strong, dropped out of the limelight.[3]

Of greater significance were the Jeunesses Nationales Populaires (JNP), the youth section of Déat's Rassemblement National Populaire (RNP), set up in 1941 by Roland Silly, a former Socialist syndicalist. The speeches of Déat, Silly, and Albertini, the secretary-general of the RNP who retained his interest in youth from the days when he had been a leading light in the Jeunesses Socialistes, reveal the kind of France that was proposed for the rising generation.[4] Under a single leader, State and party would be one in a new Europe neither capitalist nor Communist, not rooted in the individual, but 'communautaire'.[5] A social hierarchy would arise no longer founded on wealth or blue blood, but in which youth would have to know its place. Although young people were magnanimously exonerated from responsibility for the past, nevertheless 'one does not possess every right because one is twenty years old'.[6] They owed a duty to their leader, because he knew best. Congresses or courses at the party's own 'leadership school' were occasions for attacks on Vichy youth policy, which was thought to be too much under the thumb of the Church: holiday camps and 'theatrical evenings with rosewater' were not a satisfactory diet for the young. The Christian mystique, said Albertini at the JNP congress in 1943, had nothing to offer French youth. He launched into a systematic diatribe against those at Vichy who had held responsibility for youth since the defeat.[7] Firstly, there was a succession of unsuitable ministers of education. Rivaud was slated as a notorious Germanophobe whose pre-war book, *Le Relèvement de l'Allemagne,* demonstrated his deep-seated hatred of Germany. His successor, Mireaux, was a director of *Le Temps* who represented only the Comité des Forges and the conservative upper bourgeoisie. Ripert was noteworthy only for his incompetence. Chevalier was characterized as a lecturer on Bergson who spoke only about Chevalier, a fiercely anti-syndicalist, clerical reactionary. Carcopino was written off as a mere *attentiste.* Bonnard, although endowed with great intelligence, had found the path to reform obstructed. Those with responsibility for youth affairs were also inept. Ybernégaray was a reactionary clerical, Lamirand an 'immobile' whose sole asset was that he looked a young forty-five and showed up well in shorts! Pelorson had not been given the chance he deserved. Olivier-Martin, a former member of de la Rocque's PSF, had done nothing but intrigue after being promoted from the directorship of the 'leadership school' of La Chapelle-en-Serval (he had succeeded Bousquet), where he had lectured on how to behave in a society drawing-room! On the whole, youth matters at Vichy had fallen into the hands of 'idle sons of the bourgeoisie' and 'pious girls'.[8] Under an authoritarian regime, where personalities perhaps count for more than in a democracy, such comments are not without interest and perhaps not without a grain of truth.

Such a torrent of invective did not inhibit the JNP from applying for massive subsidies from the regime it so freely attacked. For the last quarter of 1943 alone a sum of 1.8 million francs was requested and for 1944 a bid was made for 10 million francs, of which 4.2 million francs were destined for 'propaganda'.[9] The rank and file of the JNP, some of whom were former members of the Faucons Rouges or came from strongly syndicalist families,[10] followed their leaders in affecting a national and socialist mystique not unacceptable to Bonnard and his coterie. Thus requests for large subsidies did not fall on deaf ears.

The other main political movement, Doriot's Parti Populaire Français (PPF), which the ex-Communist had founded in 1936, had as its youth arm the Jeunesses Populaires Françaises (JPF), which emerged in May 1942 from the fusion of the Union Populaire de la Jeunesse Française (UPJF), (the Doriotist youth movement which before the war had counted for a while Maurice Duverger, the future political editor of *Le Monde,* among its leaders) with the Jeunesses Impériales and six other minor youth movements. The PPF claimed to be the only 'revolutionary' party operating both in the whole of France and in the Empire. The JPF, which boasted it was 'the strongest organisation of French youth', had Doriot as its honorary president, but effective control was exercised by Vauquelin des Yvesteaux, his right-wing, aristocratic henchman.[11] Its 'doctrine', save for the 'imperial' dimension, appears to differ little from that of the rival JNP – anti-Semitic, anti-Communist, anti-masonic, anti-capitalist, favouring collaboration and a 'jeunesse unique'. It carried racialism to such extremes that in May 1942 the movement's higher cadres agreed to submit to racial and heredity checks before they married.[12] Its expansionist views led it to claim for the French Empire Mauritius, Canada, and the French-speaking areas of Belgium and Switzerland.[13] Vauquelin was fond of expounding his views of how youth should develop. Boys must be brought up to be hard, rough, violent, and proud.[14] Girls belonging to the movement were enjoined not to ape the American female, 'an ironing board who smokes and drinks', but to 'create for the nation' not only flesh and blood but also 'spirit', because 'the collapse of France, it must be said, was in great part the collapse of French women'.[15] Newly married couples should therefore be assisted to set up home and start families. Young peasants should be given land to till and enjoy, 'to "disport" themselves, as Rabelais said, before the English had stolen the word from us'.[16] Youth should think big and be involved in large-scale projects such as the construction of a canal to link the Mediterranean and the Atlantic. An 'Imperial Labour Service' should replace the former military service. An official racial policy was essential, for 'the earth, blood and race are the three elementary forces of our country'.[17]

How far such a policy was attractive to youth is uncertain. In most such youth movements attendance, if not membership, fluctuated according to German military fortunes. Police reports in the Lille area in 1943 show that the JPF meetings were attended by only a score of members. Even Vauquelin failed to draw an audience: in January 1944 he spoke in Lille to only fifteen young people.[18] By July the PPF, which, said the report, was universally abhorred, had ceased all activity in the area, save for a group of a dozen young men, housed in German barracks, who continued to work for the Propaganda-Staffel.[19]

In the Nord department there also sprang up a branch of Eugène Deloncle's Mouvement Social Révolutionnaire (MSR), which had for a while been closely linked to Déat's RNP. By December 1941 the MSR in the Lille area had completely ousted the RNP membership and comprised a group of young people under twenty-five who were of every political complexion, from Royalists to out-and-out Nazis, all of whom were detested locally. From the Nazi element arose a small youth movement, which probably functioned only in the Lille area, which called itself the Jeunesses Nationales Socialistes and also acted as an arm of the Propaganda-Staffel until its leader was found to be embezzling funds.[20]

The other main political grouping, Bucard's Franciste movement, had its headquarters at Aix-en-Provence and modelled itself more on Italian or Spanish Fascism than on Nazism. Bucard had fought bravely in both World Wars, being wounded three times and receiving eleven citations. He had first founded his Blue Shirts in 1933. The Parti Franciste had been banned by Blum but revived under a new guise. In 1941 it reappeared once more, styling itself the 'French fascist movement'.[21] It wanted a corporate State governed by a leader assisted by a Directory – such references to the Revolutionary tradition are frequent – with ministers as executives and an enlarged Conseil d'État to act as an advisory body on legislation.[22] Property rights, but not hereditary ones, would be preserved but, 'a bloody Revolution? . . . Yes, if the people's interest requires it.'[23] For the rest, it shared the same shibboleths as the other collaborationist parties.

Its youth movement, the Jeunesses Francistes, was headed first by Claude Planson, a fervent advocate of the Révolution Nationale, and then in 1944 by Robert Poïrimoo. It comprised 'cadets', 'avant-gardes' (the older boys), and 'guides' (girls). Its ambitious programme of civic education included topics such as capitalism, Marxism, Judaism, and Freemasonry, supplemented by 'general culture' which included geopolitics and 'the philosophy of history' and, for girls, housecraft and mothercraft. But the reality was somewhat different from this impressive abstract schema. In Lille it could mean weekday evenings spent in fencing, swimming, and a sing-song, followed by a week-end excursion to a local park.[24] Not all activities, however, were so innocuous. Occasionally the Jeunes Francistes took the law into their own hands, such as when they threatened the mayor of Marcq-en-Baroeul (Nord) at pistol-point unless he removed the bust of Marianne from his 'mairie'.[25] Towards the end of the Occupation punch-ups with 'zazous' and armed affrays with 'terrorists' were not infrequent.[26] On July 4, 1944 Bucard was arrested and accused of trying to rob a Jew's flat and jewellery shop, as well as killing a policeman,[27] but released after the intervention of Abetz. As a leader he would appear to have been a bad organizer; according to one report in July 1943 five million francs had been spent on a meeting at the Vel' d'Hiver which had turned out to be a monumental fiasco despite the fact that 'M. Bucard avait groupé des jeunes gens et des jeunes filles en quantité industrielle.'[28]

In fact, the Jeunesses Francistes seemed to have an unassuageable need for money. Belatedly, they received the 'agrément' of the SGJ in December 1942 and immediately dispatched the ritual message to Bonnard, their new Maecenas, expressing their grateful 'devotion'. The movement then set about angling for the retrospective payment of a sum to cover the cost of holiday camps it had run before receiving official approval.[29] Thus in 1943 it received a total sum of

1.25 million francs, despite legal objections raised by the ministry of finance. In March 1944 it submitted a bid for a subsidy of six million francs, renewing its demand in June and pleading for one million francs to be paid over on the nail in order to bail out ('dépanner') the movement. By then, however, Franciste youth was not merely in financial disarray but concerned for its own safety. Some members had sought a 'safe' haven by enlisting in the Milice or the Waffen SS; a few more prudent ones had opted for the safer Premier Régiment de France, the rump of the French army originally allowed under the Armistice.[30] In Lille, however, not a single member had responded to Bucard's appeal to join the Milice.[31] Nor when they were ordered from the North to Paris to assist refugees from the invasion area had a single member obeyed. The Lille police reported that they had slunk off home, blaming their leaders bitterly for the plight they found themselves in.[32] The halcyon days when they had proudly paraded down the Champs-Élysées were past.[33] Not that the movement in Lille had ever had much success: already in June 1943 the police were reporting how much this 'paramilitary formation', as it was described, was detested by the local population.[34]

One non-party but extremely politically biased movement also spawned its own youth organization. The successor to the pre-war Comité France–Allemagne was the Groupe Collaboration – the 'Groupement des énergies françaises pour l'unité continentale'. Founded in late 1940 under the presidency of the writer and journalist Alphonse de Chateaubriant, its founding committee included Bonnard, Baudrillart, and Drieu La Rochelle. A year after its foundation in Paris it was authorized in the southern zone also. It attracted many notables, including de Brinon. Its grand design was to further cultural, artistic, and scientific collaboration with Germany in a new European order, but it was not above taking on more menial tasks, such as denouncing fellow-Frenchmen. Weiland, its director-general, passed on to Bonnard a number of letters received from parents who complained that their children were being victimized by their schoolteachers because of their pro-German sympathies.

The junior branch of the movement, known as Jeunes de

l'Europe Nouvelle, had been founded by Marc Augier, who had been at one time a member of Léo Lagrange's 'cabinet'. Its leadership passed to Jacques Schweizer, a young and brilliant lawyer, a former president of the Jeunesses Patriotes, who boasted that it was based on National Socialism and a 'European France': 'Our two youths [French and German]', wrote Schweizer, 'yesterday confronting each other, tomorrow shoulder to shoulder, will be able to build a world worthy both of Germany and France'.[35] As a youth movement it does not seem to have made much headway until late 1942, but it eventually opened up twenty-seven centres all over France and ran its own periodical; its Paris centre became especially a meeting-place for 'young Europeans'.[36] The Germans blew hot and cold regarding the organization. Thus de Brinon and Abetz had considered it to be the appropriate body to liaise with a Union of European Youth set up under German auspices in September 1942 in Vienna, at a meeting to which had been invited youth from those nations officially fighting with the Germans on the Eastern Front.[37] These included nine nations from Western Europe, but not France, because the LVF was a private association. When he learnt that Baldur von Schirach was organizing a second meeting, Pelorson discreetly enquired whether France might be represented this time, but was rebuffed by von Ribbentrop.[38]

Laval nevertheless gave the movement his support when it put in a request for a subsidy.[39] In his submission Schweizer described its activities. To achieve its purpose of getting to know young people, from students to workers, from other European countries, it ran courses of political indoctrination and had set up its own 'leadership school'. It had its own protection group to keep order at meetings, some of which were attended by members of the Waffen SS, and at lectures given by officers of the (renegade) Vlassov army or under the auspices of the Comité Anti-Bolchévique. Its female members corresponded with Frenchmen fighting in Russia, particularly with the wounded and those without relatives. Many former members of the movement were in fact now also serving on the Eastern Front or working as civilians in Germany. On the anniversary of the return in 1940 of the remains of the Aiglon to the Invalides the movement had co-operated with others in organizing an all-night vigil over the sarcophagus, although they were 'disgusted' to discover later that Jewish scouts had also participated in the ceremony. They were vigilant in denouncing the Chantiers for opening its cadres to young Jews. They had not hesitated to accuse General de La Porte du Theil of links with the Maquis after 'terrorists' had been caught wearing uniforms suspiciously like those worn by the 'Jeunes' of the Chantiers. After drawing an idyllic picture of total collaboration with Germany, Schweizer referred to 'the courageous action of M. Abel Bonnard' – what action is unspecified – and coolly requested a subsidy of four million francs for 1944.

The movement ran propaganda film-shows at which the appearance of Hitler on the screen would be greeted with enthusiastic applause. Performances were rounded off with the singing of Nazi marching songs. One report in May 1944 of such a film-show commented approvingly: 'It is consoling to see that not all Paris youth is 'zazou' or a [STO] defaulter.'[40] But in the same month a different comment came from the Lille police, who reported that however much the movement might wish to expand locally the organizers 'will certainly not succeed in jolting young people out of their indifference and apathy, particularly for any movement that extols Franco-German collaboration'.[41]

None of the political youth movements mentioned enjoyed a large membership: numbers in each probably fluctuated between 3,000 and 6,000 at the most.[42] For instance, there were 2,000 Jeunes Francistes at the end of 1942 and 6,000 in 1944, although by March 1944 there were only ninety members in all the five sections that theoretically existed in the Lille area. Wild claims of membership were made by the movements themselves. But all this is small beer to the figure of 85,455 Young Communists reported in 1937.[43] Yet, because they were doled out high subsidies, were able to use the media for propaganda, and were generally favoured by Laval and the Germans, in 1942 and 1943 these movements wielded a power disproportionate to their numbers.

The ephemeral nature of the smaller youth organizations

committed to collaboration means that their number cannot be exactly ascertained. In the occupied zone they had to obtain German approval, or at least tolerance; to expand anywhere they had to obtain funds, either by subsidy or from 'secret' funds administered by the Germans or by other government agencies, such as the ministry of information, if the ministry of education was not forthcoming. Often such movements were eccentric. Thus the 'Cellules Françaises', whose head, Villemain, had ambitions of creating an 'ideal chivalry', aimed at producing the future leaders of a national socialist France, a kind of Iron Guard, rallying the ranks of 'hesitant Catholics' to the cause.[44] Bonnard thought this enterprise sufficiently promising to ask the Germans to recognize it, despite its numbering only 500 members, because these were distinguished by their quality and 'as in the present circumstances the unification of French youth has not been possible, it seems good to support movements of this kind by allowing them to exist'.[45] The movement does not appear to have prospered, because in 1943 Villemain, then working for the Institut des Questions Juives, wrote asking for a subsidy for another youth movement, 'Les Cordées', which he claimed was racist, national, socialist – and Christian.[46] Bonnard's alacrity in supporting such scatter-brained movements is further evidence of his commitment to Nazi ideology and of how far removed he was from the neutralist elements in his ministry, and particularly in the SGJ.

A much more significant movement, because it was based on the schools and thus had a potentially large following, was Les Jeunes du Maréchal. Its significance was enhanced because it was in a sense under the personal patronage of Pétain, since he permitted it to function under his aegis. Its rapid evolution towards full-blown collaboration was consequently viewed with alarm by the more moderate elements at Vichy. Les Jeunes du Maréchal was started in November 1940 at the Lycée Voltaire in Paris by Bousquet, described by a Resistance source as 'a young teacher hard up for a doctorate',[47] who, it will be recalled, was made director for a while of the national 'leadership school' of La Chapelle-en-Serval and eventually became one of Bonnard's staff.[48] The movement originated in the top *lycée* classes preparing for the 'grandes écoles':

the pupils – already of an age to be university students – had been unsettled by the defeat and, according to Bousquet, had talked of nothing but politics. He endeavoured to turn their thoughts in different directions. Eventually they agreed to appoint a 'class leader' whose task was to enforce discipline, to liaise with the school authorities, and to punish by fines those who persisted in political discussion, swore, or 'ragged' in class. The embryo movement spread to nearby schools. It had achieved some recognition when Lamirand visited the school in July 1941 and it had been allowed to form a guard of honour. By September Bousquet had obtained Pétain's blessing, but full official recognition from Gidel, the rector of Paris, came only after members of the movement had rendered signal service in the air raids of March 1942. Despite some expansion the movement complained that it was still 'looked upon unfavourably by school heads who are not all greatly committed to the Révolution Nationale'. It began to diversify its activities, working, for example, with the ministry of information in 'the struggle against Gaullism and Communism'. In May 1942 Bonnard not only authorized sections to be started in any school, but also in youth centres and higher education. A circular of June 9 authorized it to establish 'corporative centres' in schools to co-operate leisure activities. Three membership categories were recognized: 'cadets' (10–14), 'jeunes' (14–17), and 'gardes' (17–21).

By the autumn of 1942 Bousquet was working on Bonnard's staff and able to devote more time to the movement, D____, the headmaster of the Lycée Voltaire, was appointed the national organizer of the 'corporative centres' in schools. The instructions he issued[49] prescribed the Hitler-style salute; a khaki uniform should be worn, which should bear the national and local badges. Out of uniform the badge, a red 'francisque' on a white background, should be displayed. During school breaks unarmed drill should be practised. The movement would be responsible for organizing the 'colours' ceremonies in schools and for acting as stewards at school functions. Members had to practise 'frankness and fairness', as the Marshal had prescribed, ensure that teachers were obeyed, and be responsible for seeing that the Marshal's portrait and any propaganda were prominently posted up. School sections should volunteer for social and civic service in the community. Bousquet perceived that his movement was unique because it functioned in a place where the attendance of young people was obligatory yet in an environment that was familiar, and where, for example, some 140,000 primary teachers might be recruited as section organizers. In this, however, he was over-optimistic: only 2,647 teachers volunteered to attend training courses for the cadres of the movement.[50] Preaching a French and 'European' Socialism, the movement might in time become the nucleus of a 'jeunesse unique'. It was even suggested that Hitler Youth centres and SS camps in Germany should be visited in order to study how best this might be accomplished.[51]

Despite the fact that sections might be started in all schools, propagandists for the movement claimed that they were meeting with a hostile reception. At the Lycée Condorcet one speaker had addressed the school section on 'English aggression' in Madagascar and had heard the headmaster comment at the end of his talk that, although the British would never hand back the island, neither would the Germans have done if they had conquered it. Subsequently the complainant received a note signed 'Pupils of Condorcet' but plainly written by an adult: 'Now give us a talk on Indo-China and Alsace-Lorraine.'[52] Occasionally the movement was met with derision: when the 'Jeunes' paraded through Compiègne singing 'Maréchal, nous voilà' – a new kind of national anthem – they were jeered.[53] Pétain's entourage became alarmed at the extremism of the movement's leaders. They considered 'dangerous' Bousquet's plan for extending recruitment to the southern zone and to those above school age. It went beyond what the Marshal had personally sanctioned; moreover, 'the personality of M. Bousquet justifies all kinds of fears'.[54] Catholics were apprehensive that the movement would become a carbon copy of the Hitler Youth and import into France the anti-religious ideas of Baldur von Schirach, the Reich youth leader.[55]

The later history of the movement is unedifying. By September 1942, because of internal squabbles,[56] its leadership was in a state of crisis, so much so that Bousquet proposed to resign in favour of Pelorson, a move that the German Embassy strongly supported.[57] In December eight leaders whose dismissal had been secured by the SGJ angrily announced their intention of enlisting in the Wehrmacht. Villemain, founder of the Cellules Françaises, wrote to Bonnard and volunteered to resolve the crisis by taking over the leadership and creating an élite corps of 'SS Pioneers' within the movement, adding optimistically, 'et de ces pionniers nous ferions monter les chevaliers'.[58] At Vichy alarm was expressed at the propaganda the Germans would make out of the incident; the conclusion was reached that since 'young traitors' had 'torpedoed' the movement there was no alternative but to disband it.[59] However, it lingered on for several months. The inspector general for youth noted in his report for 1942–3 that the movement had 'made itself conspicuous by rowdy, unfruitful activity', that it had 'gone downhill very rapidly through the fault of its leaders . . . more possessed by ambition than by scruples', who had used it for their own political ends.[60] The decision to wind up the movement was finally taken in May 1943 after the revelation that some of the rank and file had been denouncing their teachers, and sometimes their parents, to the authorities.[61] Official indignation was aroused after the disbandment when it was learnt that former members who had volunteered for work in Germany had paraded through Berlin in their uniform and received a gala welcome.[62] Once again, however, Pétain had succeeded in extricating himself from total commitment to a Nazi youth ideology. The strength with which that ideology had been held in the Jeunes du Maréchal can be gauged from the fact that, with the exception of one centre at Lyons, unlike both the Chantiers and Compagnons, the movement had not been penetrated by the Resistance.[63]

Other less radical movements were more calculated to appeal to those closest to Pétain. One such was the Jeunesse de France et d'Outremer (JFOM), founded in Marseilles in October 1940 by an ex-air-force officer, Lt. Pugibet, with the assistance of Roger de Saivre, who was later to become a member of the Marshal's staff specializing in educational questions.[64] At its first congress, held in October 1941, it passed resolutions condemning Gaullism and 'les internationales d'or et du sang'. This orientation of the movement, which made a special effort to recruit young workers, is amplified in its 'ten points of doctrine',[65] summarized as follows: 'The revolutionary New Order will be national, social, integral, European . . . The new man will be positive, integrated, community-oriented, enthusiastic . . .' Apart from the usual gamut of youth activities, the movement also busied itself with propaganda of an apparently novel kind. An ex-Compagnon reported:

> The essential activity of the JFOM consists in mouthing negative slogans on the lines of, 'Down with de Gaulle', or worse, 'Jews out'. I have seen a group of JFOM march on to the Place Masséna [in Nice], stop in front of the largest café in the locality, drink a toast to the Marshal before the gawping onlookers, and set off again in good order, serene and satisfied with the fine revolutionary task they had accomplished.[66]

Nevertheless, for a while the JFOM enjoyed the support both of Darnand and of the Légion des Combattants, and claimed a membership of 14,000 boys over 14, 3,000 under that age, and 6,000 girls. Deeply concerned with the defence of the Navy and the Empire, it became increasingly anti-British as the colonies 'defected' to the Allied cause. After the total occupation of France it continued to operate, but on a reduced scale. In the closing stages of the war a number of its members joined the Milice.[67]

Strangely, the movement most favoured by Pétain, the Légion des Combattants, was never able to develop a successful youth section. The Jeune Légion, although Lamirand spoke publicly in its favour in December 1940,[68] never became widespread in the southern zone. Yet its aim was the purest Vichy orthodoxy: to educate children in the doctrines of the Révolution Nationale.[69] Its bulletin, *Jeune Légion,* published articles on all the familiar themes, from Gaullism to Communism.[70] But the failure of the movement was due in part to its leadership. According to one Vichy source,[71] its head, X———Y———, was known as 'the raving leader' ('le chef à lier', presumably on the analogy of 'le fou à lier', 'the raving madman'). The subsequent defection of Valentin, the head of the Légion as a whole, may have been a contributory factor. Nor was the study programme for the Jeune Légion encouraging, based as it was on 'our disasters, the lessons to be drawn from them, the conditions for revival'. Since serious recruitment was late in starting, such a basis may not have appealed so much in 1942 as in 1940, when beating the breast – and particularly the breast of youth – was temporarily a national obsession.

Another movement, the Équipes et Cadres de la France Nouvelle: Jeunes Dracs (*sic*), was started at Vichy[72] in early 1941 by Georges Riond, an official in the SGJ.[73] It revived a pre-war non-confessional religious movement but was oriented to the training of young leaders of high spiritual and moral calibre. Its faintly ridiculous subsidiary aim was 'to convince young men that youth constitutes a stage in their future mission as fathers of large families', a reflection of official concern with depopulation. For a membership given as 36,000 its impact was remarkably feeble. A similar pre-war movement, revived with the personal blessing of Pétain, who even contributed an article to its periodical,[74] was the Fédération des Cercles Jeune France, started originally in 1936 by the philosopher Jean Rivain. It also had a strong moral purpose and operated mainly among students, using study-groups. It claimed to have foreshadowed many doctrines of the Révolution Nationale, seeking to combat individualism, sensualism, an over-critical and over-analytical approach to life, verbosity, 'facilité et légèreté', intellectual narcissism, formalism, mechanism, and materialism – a formidable inventory of the vices to which the intellectual is prone.

The Jeunesses Paysannes was a movement whose orientation was specifically based upon an occupation.[75] The aim of the 'greenshirts', as they were known even before the war, when their membership already numbered 40,000, was to help agricultural workers. Their leader, Dorgères, felt, as regards his young members, that the SGJ, which he styled 'les Alliés démocrates', was more of a hindrance than a help.[76] He complained bitterly that his movement, which had branches in 1,054 communes, had had only 240,000F in subsidies up to July 1943,[77] despite the fact that by the end of 1942 60 per cent of young land workers were enrolled in it.

Other movements were based on leisure activities such as youth hostelling. One such, the Auberges de la Jeunesse, had had a long history, since the 'mouvement ajiste' proper went back to 1918.[78] In 1930 the confessional Ligue Française pour les Auberges de la Jeunesse had been founded by the Catholic politician Marc Sangnier, who had also been the inspirer of the embryo Christian Democrat movement grouped around Le Sillon. In 1933 the secularist Centre Laïque des Auberges de la Jeunesse had been set up by Marc Augier, who had subsequently become a member of Léo Lagrange's 'cabinet', when in the years immediately before the war the latter had been under-secretary of state for sport and leisure. Under Lagrange's patronage the 'mouvement ajiste' had flourished, particularly when the branch of youth hostelling set up by Augier had received powerful support from the Ligue de l'Enseignement and the Confédération Générale du Travail. (Augier's subsequent career demonstrates how decisively the war changed the lives of some public men. In 1940 he had been associated with an ephemeral attempt to create a united Front de la Jeunesse. By 1941 he had become an extreme collaborationist. After founding the Jeunes de l'Europe Nouvelle, the youth section of the Groupe Collaboration, he had joined the LVF and fought on the Russian front, ending up in 1944 as the political officer of the ill-starred Charlemagne Division. Under the pseudonym of Saint-Loup he wrote lurid, highly romanticized novels of his experiences, such as *Les Volontaires* (on the LVF) and *Les Hérétiques* (on the French Waffen SS). He escaped to exile in Argentina, but returned to France in 1953.) Lagrange had wanted to unite the two opposing wings of the Auberges de la Jeunesse, but had been frustrated by the outbreak of war. Augier had nevertheless had under his wing a movement accommodating 60,000 young people a year and owning 900 hostels. Many of these were damaged in the 1940 campaign. In the occupied zone the secularist branch of the Auberges was banned by the Germans. Vichy wanted the movement to become an arm of the Révolution Nationale and in the spring of 1941 steps were taken to revive it in the southern zone. Its role would be to act as a service agency for the other youth organizations, providing accommodation and other facilities.[79] Vichy was nevertheless very suspicious of the political reliability of those connected with the movement.[80]

In August 1941 a group of former 'ajistes' met at Uriage to reconstitute the movement on a different basis. However, it reasserted the democratic nature of the movement, its non-racial stance, and its approval of mixed hostels – this last was unacceptable to Catholics. A technical 'umbrella' association, the Camarades de la Route, was established, which numbered 10,000 members by the autumn of 1942. Headquarters were established for the Auberges at Valence. The movement adopted a strongly educative note, planning to use the hostels as centres for local environmental studies, arts and crafts, and folklore.[81] This may have been because they were placed under the direction of an educationist, Luc Bonnet, and because teachers were strongly represented on the management committee as well as locally: twenty out of thirty-five department representatives in the southern zone were associated with the teaching profession. The movement also declared its determination to work towards 'eliminating the antinomies between the social classes'.[82] But Vichy's political suspicions of the movement proved justified. Eventually Marc Sangnier, the founder of the Catholic wing of the Auberges, whose part in the refounding of the movement is not known, together with 250 'Ajistes', was imprisoned for Resistance activities and on August 15, 1943 the movement was formally wound up by Vichy.

Other outdoor organizations did not wish to be outshone as regenerators of youth. Thus Les Campeurs Français felt impelled to spell out its aims: 'Physically, morally and intellectually we wish to equip our young people for the hard struggles that await it. From them will arise men and women worthy of the oldest French traditions.' That this declaration[83] of the movement strikes a cheerfully ambiguous note may be ascribed to its being made in the spring of 1944.

A cultural and leisure movement of very high quality was Jeune-France, which had close associations with Emmanuel Mounier. Through popular art, folk music, and drama it aimed to give young people an aesthetic education. Started in January 1941 by Pierre Schaeffer, then a broadcasting engineer,[84] it received the backing not only of writers such as Mounier but also musicians such as Daniel Lesur and Henri Baraud.[85] Mounier was especially enthusiastic, even envisaging the kind of Maisons de la Culture set up after the war by Malraux. Accused of Resistance activities, however, he was forced to relinquish the post that he had taken with Jeune-France in September 1941.

Indeed the Maîtrises Jeune-France collaborated only half-heartedly with the regime. Mounier recounts how some of its Gaullist members walked through a village at night chanting 'Vive de Gaulle', to which the local gendarme luckily turned a deaf ear.[86] There was a strong patriotic note running through the movement. For Christmas 1940 the Maîtrises composed a song for French youth entitled 'Le Chant de la Fidélité', to be sung by a group linking hands as for Auld Lang Syne. At one point, however, the circle thus formed would be broken, to represent those absent. To the tune of Auld Lang Syne ('Le Chant des Adieux') the following words would be sung:

> Joignons nos joies, nos peines,/ Joignons nos mains,/ Joignons à notre chaîne/ Ceux qui sont restés loin./ Sur leurs mains invisibles/ Nos doigts serrés,/ Autour des places vides,/ Notre fidélité,/ Noël des Séparés./ Au-delà des frontières,/ des barbelés,/ Sont nos sœurs et nos frères,/ Nos fils, nos fiancés./ Qu'ils forment aussi la chaîne,/ Nos bien aimés./ Ils sentiront fidèles/ Nos mains à leurs poignées,/ Noël des Séparés.[87]

> (Let us link our joys, our sorrows, let us link our hands, let us link to our chain those who remain far distant. On their invisible hands, our fingers clutched, around the empty places, our faithfulness, Christmas of the Separated. Beyond the frontiers and the barbed wire are our sisters and our brothers, our sons, our fiancés. Let them too form the chain, our beloved ones. They will feel us faithful, our hands on their wrists, Christmas of the Separated.)

The poignancy for youth in such an act, as they thought of those who had joined de Gaulle or who mouldered in German prison camps, must not be underestimated. But the song also contains a note of defiance. Thus it was perhaps inevitable that Jeune-France, the most creative of all the youth movements, could not last long: on June 11, 1942 it was officially dissolved.

As air raids intensified youth organizations began to

play an increasing civic role, assisting in rescue operations after the bombings, helping the bombed-out and the evacuees, and acting as messengers for essential services. The ministry of education had authorized (C. of August 8, 1941) branches of the Junior Red Cross to be started in schools, mainly *lycées,* and until it was forbidden, many youngsters had served with their elders on some particularly dangerous jobs.[88] The need for such services led to the creation of one other official organization, the Équipes Nationales (not to be confused with the Équipes et Cadres de la France Nouvelle), whose mission was 'to share in the protection of the population against the incidents of war'.[89] Although set up in late 1941 or early 1942,[90] this organization did not begin effectively to function until 1943, when heavy demands were made upon its services, particularly in the northern zone, where it was strongest. Headed by Rabaud, an inspector general, the movement operated directly under the SGJ, working in close co-operation with the Défense Passive, the Red Cross, and the Secours National. Youths between fourteen and twenty-five were enrolled either as 'cadets', 'pioneers', or 'volunteers', depending upon age.[91] There were special sections for girls. At first voluntary, it eventually became compulsory (under the 'requisitioning' law of July 11, 1938) for all those over eighteen, who were not otherwise engaged on war work. Towards the end compulsion seems to have been applied even below this minimum age.[92] Thus Bonnard wrote to rectors (C. of April 20, 1944) commending the action of the academy inspector of Rouen during recent air attacks for placing at the prefect's disposal all pupils old enough to be of use and exhorted the rectors 'to be inspired by this example'.[93] At least one academy inspector was prompted to enquire whether this meant that all children should be enrolled willy-nilly in the Équipes Nationales.[94]

Even with this organization, however, there were political overtones. The catholicity of its membership gave a last chance to the proponents of a 'jeunesse unique'. It was for this reason that Pelorson, so long as he remained in the SGJ, manœuvred to keep the movement under his direct control; to a colleague whom he suspected of trying to interfere he wrote brusquely: '[Re] . . . the matter of the Équipes Nationales. That matter is my thing'. (His underlining.)[95] So much jockeying went on for power over the movement that in February 1943 Rabaud, who was nominally in charge, threatened to resign if Pelorson did not stop interfering.[96] Since members of any youth organization or none were free to join the Équipes either collectively or as individuals, whoever ran them had the nucleus of a very strong power base.[97] Local sections were also charged with carrying out the usual activities of youth movements. The study programme included, curiously enough (although the emblem of the movement was the Celtic cross), particular stress upon the Celtic heritage as an important part of French 'spiritual values'.[98] Rabaud himself had political ambitions, wanting the movement to 'habituate young people to think and live the New Order' and at last bridge the gap between the social classes.[99] Such aspirations were a cause of concern to Pétain's entourage[100] but matters grew worse when, in March 1944, Tartarin, a strong collaborationist, supplanted Rabaud.[101] At local level, however, neither the leadership nor the members were necessarily pro-German.[102] Indeed Déat stigmatized the rank and file as 'avowed Gaullists' and placed them on a par with the Secours National, described as 'attentiste' and 'clerical' if not Gaullist, and the Red Cross, characterized as the 'aristocracy of Gaullism'.[103] And towards the end even the top leaders of the Équipes Nationales were no longer trusted by the Germans.[104]

Whatever their political allegiance, however, – and some were too young to have any clearly formed views – the Équipes carried out their duties courageously during the Allied bombings,[105] particularly when the attacks intensified. The movement was particularly commended after the raid on Boulogne-Billancourt on April 4, 1943. Bonnard issued instructions (C. of April 24, 1944) that since the Équipes had been heavily involved during the air raids they should not be placed at a disadvantage in school 'compared with those of their classmates who have not had the same courage'. Those who had acquitted themselves particularly well were to have their school records endorsed accordingly and examiners were instructed to take this into account.[106] One sign of the value attached to the Équipes Nationales was that at the Liberation they were not dissolved but developed into the Service Civique de la Jeunesse, which later combined with the Communist-inspired Union de la Jeunesse Républicaine.[107]

The movements described by no means exhaust the list of those that flickered ephemerally across the Vichy stage.[108] Some, such as the military-style Jeune Garde Française[109] (by then new names were difficult to invent) or a Service des Unités de Jeunes Travailleurs,[110] proposed as an auxiliary police force, either faded away rapidly or never got beyond the drawing-board. All attempts to co-ordinate the great variety of initiatives seem to have been abortive. One difficulty was the number of small, local organizations that flourished for a time. Thus the Jeunes Français de Flandre-Artois, started with the help of Northern industrialists, never had more than 200 members.[111] Despite the meeting of the principal youth organizations at Uriage in June 1941, where a common declaration of aims had been agreed, no great co-ordination was ever achieved.[112] A Rassemblement National des Jeunesses Françaises, mooted by a certain Marcel Gillou, also got nowhere.[113] Occasionally efforts made to group together a number of similar movements were successful. Thus the Ligue des Jeunes de France et de l'Empire, headed by X. Pasquier, linked together a dozen organizations, including the Jeunesse de France et d'Outremer.[114] Towards the end youth organizations did get together in joint congresses but by then these had become mere propaganda exercises to further the German war effort. Thus in April 1944 a rally was held in Paris on the theme, 'The military duty of French youth in the present war', whose purpose was to recruit for the LVF.[115]

If unity was ruled out, neither was complete unification of youth organizations round a common purpose achieved. Part of the blame for this must fall upon the SGJ which became increasingly weak and ineffectual, so much so that it was eventually downgraded in January 1944 to a Commissariat Général for Youth headed by the faithful Gaït. The SGJ doled out subsidies, sometimes even illegally, often lavishly, even to those who attacked it, without proper accountability. For much of the later period there was scarcely veiled hostility between Bonnard and the permanent officials, with the notorious exception of Pelorson. Whereas Bonnard strained every nerve for a German victory, Lamirand and Olivier-Martin were 'attentiste' and, although scarcely democratic, by no means held totalitarian views. Within each movement and even between movements professing the same aims there was a wide spectrum of political beliefs. The increasing collaborationism of government was reflected in the appointments made to the later youth movements such as the Équipes Nationales, where the leaders were far more favourable to the Germans than the rank and file or the coterie round Pétain, which remained in splendid isolation from the battle for the mind of youth which was taking place. All in all, it is not surprising that, despite the huge sums spent on propaganda and despite occasional coercion, French youth in the main stayed indifferent to the blandishments with which it was wooed.

It is therefore all the more tragic to tell the story of the unhappy few who carried their faith in Germany to the ultimate step of fighting its battles. They comprised a few idealists, who believed sufficiently in the German cause to risk their lives for it, and others, such as many in the Milice, who, setting out with patriotic intent to defend what they conceived to be the cause of France, found themselves drawn progressively into the vortex of armed collaboration. They did not constitute a movement as such, but since many – perhaps the majority – were young, they require mention in any study of French youth in wartime.

The history of the Milice is also that of Joseph Darnand, gallant soldier of two World Wars, but a man of Fascist tendencies and limited intellect.[116] His officers were a mixed bag of Pétainists, collaborationists, and every other hue of right-wing politics, but it was young men who comprised the other ranks of the Milice. The Milice had its origins in the strongly patriotic and Pétainist Légion des Combattants, within which were first set up 'protection groups' and then a 'Service d'Ordre Légionnaire' (SOL). From these developed the Milice. Like the Légion, the SOL was first reserved for ex-servicemen, but eventually opened its ranks to youngsters who had seen no military service but who favoured a tough Révolution Nationale to shake up the older generation. As such, it became a kind of 'ginger group' which attracted the young bourgeoisie and students. Their fond parents regarded the SOL benevolently almost as another kind of boy scouts, perhaps a little over-brutal and over-politicized. But they reasoned, what harm could it do their sons, when its fanaticism manifested itself as a patriotism steeped in deep loyalty to the Marshal?[117] Such extremism, however, made the average Légion member uneasy when the SOL took a collaborationist turn, expressed in 1942 by many joining the LVF to fight on the Eastern Front. The allied invasion of North Africa marked a watershed, when Darnand called upon young men to join an 'Imperial Legion'[118] later renamed, with Spartan and Spanish overtones, the 'Phalange Africaine'. The creation of the Milice marked the point of no return.

The Milice was formally set up in January 1943 at the direct request of Hitler, when Laval was invited to form an auxiliary police to maintain internal order. The SOL was transferred to the new organization, which was headed by Laval himself, with Darnand as secretary-general. Its official purpose was stated to be the comparatively innocuous one of 'participating publicly in the life of the country and invigorating it politically by watchful action and propaganda'.[119] Yet the gamma symbol, the badge of the new organization, was to become almost as hated as the swastika. At the inauguration ceremony those who wore it were referred to by Bonnard as 'the ardent youth of France'. These were 'Young men from the bourgeoisie, students, adolescents; many of these youngesters are not even twenty; they did not fight in the war; they come from traditionalist families; daddy was at Verdun; daddy admires the Marshal; daddy praises the martial qualities of the Germans, which serves to enhance the merit of the veteran of Verdun.'[120] J.-L. Curtis, in his novel, *Les Justes Causes,* draws a true-to-life picture of the typical militiaman. The snivelling Garrigou, captured at the Liberation by the FFI, had been a fervent Pétainist in his teens, when he had been attracted to the collaborationist writers and the scurrilous pro-German press. At school he had unsuccessfully denounced his English teacher for Gaullism, who in retaliation had made him read aloud to the class one of Kipling's patriotic poems. At sixteen he had donned the blue shirt of the PPF and been promptly sent to Coventry by his class-mates. At eighteen, after the baccalaureate, he had joined the Milice, convinced that he was participating in a great crusade, but the reality turned out to be otherwise.[121]

The Milice's bourgeois character did not at first appeal to the working-class youth, who was not impressed by its initial conservative and persistent anti-Communist philosophy. Nor did it attract youth from the other youth movements in the southern zone: when the 'Jeunesse de France et d'Outremer' was, at the leaders' request, formally merged with the Milice, only one in ten of the movement's original members joined. In its higher echelons the Milice was aristocratic. After Dunoyer de Segonzac had taken to the Maquis, Bayard's castle at Uriage was taken over as an 'école des cadres' for future officers of the Milice. Commanded first by a French-speaking Acadian, the very Catholic and Royalist de la Noüe du Vair, and then by another Maurrassian, Giaume, the courses were attended by scions of the *haute bourgeoisie,* organized in platoons of thirty, young men aged between eighteen and twenty-five recruited directly from the *lycée* or the university.

Within the Milice there was also created a corps of 'francs-gardes'. Mainly full time, as distinct from the part-time militiaman, this unit was designed to form an élite. In fact it turned out to be the very opposite. Made up of young ruffians, hoodlums, and even crooks, some on the run from compulsory labour service in Germany, the 'francs-gardes' were to become the infamous adepts of cruelty.

By autumn 1943 the Milice claimed 29,000 members of both sexes,[122] but of these only some 10,000 participated actively in semi-military and policing activities. The indispensability to the Germans of such an auxiliary organization is shown in a secret 'plan de redressement français' submitted to Hitler on September 17, 1943 by Darnand, Déat, Luchaire, and two lesser lights. They estimated that the number of defaulters from compulsory labour service was 160,000 (not all of course young men), of whom half had taken to the Maquis. Darnand saw the development of the Milice as a strong force to combat them: it would recruit from all pro-German groups and act as a selection agency for cadres to lead a new conscript army of Frenchmen which would be placed at the disposal of the Reich. In return he and his fellow-planners sought ministerial office in a re-formed Laval administration.

Darnand's personal aspirations were fulfilled. On December 30, 1943 he was appointed to the government as 'secretary-general for the maintenance of order', in charge of the Milice and all police forces, responsible only to Laval in his role as minister of the interior. The Milice was eventually authorized to operate as an armed force in the northern as well as the southern zone. A law of January 20, 1944 instituted summary court-martials to mete out immediate 'justice' and instant punishment; there began a reign of terror, led by the scum of the Milice, the 'francs-gardes', who had by June 1944 increased their number fivefold to 5,000 men. Meanwhile many of the bourgeoisie, the 'fils à papa', had taken fright and dropped out of the Milice.

The savagery that accompanied the massive 'anti-terrorist' sweeps, often with the Milice and the Germans collaborating, was appalling. In Tulle young militiamen not above twenty poured acid over wounds that they had inflicted on the face of their tortured victim. Reciprocally, at Voiron a group of technical teachers and their pupils butchered four militiamen, also slaughtering in the process an old lady of eighty-two and a baby of eighteen months. The Milice were not tender with the perpetrators of this incident. When caught they were tortured, then executed in the presence of their fellow-pupils, who, for good measure, were then deported to Germany. An horrific climax was reached at the time of the invasion, when all 'francs-gardes' were fully mobilized and began to rival the SS in their ruthlessness.

The ultimate destiny of the Milice is linked to that of the other young men who had donned German uniform to join the 'Crusade against Bolshevism' in Russia. Among those tacitly supporting Germany, Spain had sent an official contingent, the 'Blue Division'. Among other near neighbours of France the Dutch Quislings had supplied a Division Nederland and the Belgians not only the two Flemish SS Legions, Flandria and Langemarck, but also a Division Wallonie, led by the Rexist Degrelle, whose ambition was to head a Burgundian State after the war. The French equivalent, the Légion des Volontaires Francais contre le Bolchévisme (LVF), had been hastily constituted, with a first contingent entraining to the East in August 1941, eager to be present at the then anticipated final defeat of the Russians.

The LVF was highly politicized, inasmuch as it drew its recruits from the younger members of the PPF, which merits pride of place because Doriot was the only political leader actually to serve on the Eastern Front, the RNP, and the MSR. The differing political views within the LVF gave rise to endless bickering, particularly because the volunteers included a few ex-Socialists and ex-Communists who were allowed to join and 'redeem' their political past. For the rest, enlistment attracted a few young idealists, the unemployed, and ex-criminals. The youthfulness of those recruited is evidenced by the fact that in one period, the first fortnight of 1942, 239 men enlisted, of whom 105 were aged between eighteen and twenty-two.[123] In the first three years of its existence the LVF attracted only 13,400 volunteers, of whom only 5,800 were actually enrolled: 4,600 were rejected as unfit and another 3,000 turned down because of their criminal record. Moreover, of the final 5,800 3,000 had been recruited in the first three months of the Légion's existence. By January 1943 numbers had dropped to 3,205, of whom a mere 2,702 were actually in Russia or Poland.[124] By August 1944, of the total enrolled, only 2,200 were left: 2,400 had been discharged, 400 had been killed, and 800 had deserted.[125] Thus, despite the huge propaganda campaign mounted in its favour, the LVF had little attraction for French youth. The force was also militarily ineffectual, being relegated by the Wehrmacht mainly to warding off attacks of the Russian partisans behind the front line. Although Pétain had sent the Légion a grandiloquent and misjudged message saying that it was upholding a portion of French honour, a more general view was expressed by Hassler, the

Alsatian-born French general, who wrote to Vichy explaining why he had refused an offer to command the force: 'So long as Germany occupies a large part of our territory, it cannot appeal to the great mass of Frenchmen, and, in particular, to young people.'[126] Apart from a few initial imprudences, Vichy moved slowly in giving the LVF any official status whatsoever. Starting merely as an association under the law of 1901, it did however eventually acquire the much rarer status of being 'reconnu d'utilité publique'. In 1942 it suffered a set-back when Vichy planned to set up its own Légion Tricolore, as a fully blown official unit on equal footing with those of Germany's 'allies', but it was the Germans themselves that set their face against this plan.

In late 1944 the LVF was compulsorily incorporated into a (French) Brigade Charlemagne. On the whole its members did not accept this willingly, because it meant they became part of the Waffen SS and donned its black uniform. In particular, some former Jocistes had conscience scruples, but were finally convinced by the unit's chaplain, Mgr de Mayol de Lupé, the aristocratic, ageing, pro-Nazi soldier-priest, who was fanatically anti-Bolshevik.[127] Some waverers allowed themselves to be reassured by the fact that their leaders, men such as Col. Puaud, the Légion commander, and Commandant Bridoux, the son of the Vichy war minister, seemed sufficient guarantee of patriotism.

The other main element in the Brigade Charlemagne was the SS Brigade No.7 (Frankreich), also a unit of the Waffen SS. A Vichy decree of July 1943 had authorized Frenchmen to join this new élite unit. In March 1944 recruiting for it was stepped up and a number of recruiting rallies were held – Degrelle, for example, addressed a huge rally of collaborationists in the Palais de Chaillot. Eventually some 3,000 men, of an average age of twenty, were recruited from the PPF, the RNP, and the Francistes and dispatched for training at Sennheim in Alsace and at Neweklau in the Czech Protectorate.

A few young Frenchmen had also been attracted to other more specialized units more directly part of the German war machine.[128] The Wehrmacht recruited Frenchmen to serve in a unit known as 'Technische Nothilfe' ('technical emergency aid'), for instant repair work in communications and the public services. From the summer of 1942 Frenchmen had been eligible to join the NSKK, the Nazi transport corps. From April 1943 Flak (anti-aircraft) units composed of Frenchmen, wearing French uniform, had been in action against Allied aircraft. The Todt Organisation enrolled special 'protection squads', who, after a training period at Saint-Cloud (La Celle) were dispatched, ostensibly for guard duties, to the Atlantic Wall, to the Reich, to the Baltic States, or Norway, where they were later converted into full fighting units. From February 1944 onwards the German navy, with Vichy approval, began recruiting Bretons, Normans, and 'Flemings' of the 'circonscriptions maritimes' for service in minesweepers, motor torpedo-boats, and even submarines. Assembled at Caen, many were then sent on to Alsace for practical and 'political' training, whence, forced to discard their beribboned German naval caps and to become infantrymen, they joined up with other Frenchmen and eventually fought in the East. Moreover, a number of Frenchmen also served in the so-called 'special units' – the Jagd-Verbände – such as that commanded by Skorzeny, the rescuer of Mussolini.

To these Frenchmen already irrevocably committed to the Nazi cause were joined, when in August 1944 the great retreat sounded, those of the Milice who had succeeded in reaching Struthof, their rallying-point in Alsace. Despite Darnand's promise that they would never leave France, on September 21, 1944 they crossed the Rhine into Germany.[129] Some were only just past their sixteenth birthday. To a sprinkling of rather bewildered younsters were added a number of political fanatics and rogues. Those from the occupied zone were determinedly collaborationist and Fascist, whereas those from the southern zone were often monarchist and Catholic, such as Jean de Vaugelas, dismissed from the French Army before the war because of racialism, who had gone on from the Chantiers de la Jeunesse to command for a while the Milice training-school at Uriage. All had taken an oath to die for France, if necessary, as their song, 'Le Chant des Cohortes', reminded them:

A genoux, nous fîmes le serment,
Miliciens, de mourir en chantant,
S'il le faut, pour la nouvelle France.
Amoureux de gloire et de grandeur,
Tous unis par la même ferveur,
Nous jurons de refaire la France:
A genoux, nous fîmes ce serment.

(On bended knee we, the Militiamen, made the oath to die with a song on our lips, if necessary, for the new France, Loving glory and greatness, all of us united in the same fervour, we swear to rebuild France: on bended knee, we made this oath.)

Anxious for glory and greatness they might be, but it was for a Greater Germany rather than a 'new France' for which they were to die. Some escaped their fate when they reached their new staging-post at Ulm by becoming civilian workers in German factories, but 2,500 out of the 4,000 that got thus far were eventually drafted into the Waffen SS.[130]

Milice, LVF, and other Frenchmen caught up in the German débâcle – the framework of reference for the word had changed – were eventually incorporated into the French Brigade Charlemagne, raised in February 1945 to the status, but not to the strength, of a full division. The backbone of the new unit was the former LVF and the former Brigade Frankreich, each of which constituted the nucleus of an infantry regiment. The Miliciens were distributed between these two units – all save eleven, led by André Brillant, a youth of twenty, who refused to don German uniform.[131] Within the new Division Charlemagne there was even a 'youth section', which formed part of the 'honour company' and consisted entirely of under-eighteens – some were even youngsters of sixteen.[132] The Division, thrown into the breach when the Soviet armies reached the German border, incurred terrible losses. In April 1945 a decimated rump of about 800 men was still fighting in the streets of Berlin: 'Honour is my loyalty', the motto of the Waffen SS, could not be taken further. But to these young Frenchmen who fought on the losing side little quarter was shown. The Milice, because it drifted almost unwittingly into its final position, is perhaps the most piteous example of how war can lead the young to the abyss: the simple-minded group with the boy-scout mentality that had started out with the very patriotic Légion des Combattants had developed into a horde of young barbarians. They are only worthy of mention because they constituted such a tiny minority of French youth, as contrasted with the many who from the total occupation of France to the Liberation, threw in their more uncertain lot with the Resistance or the Gaullist forces.

Chapter XIV

Youth and Forced Labour in Germany

From 1942 onwards harsh obligations began to be laid upon young people. One such burden, which eventually affected the majority of young men aged between eighteen and twenty-four, was conscription for industrial work in Germany. The Service du Travail Obligatoire (STO) was a compulsory form of labour service which, coming into fullest operation in the closing stages of the Occupation, changed radically the lives of young Frenchmen. This chapter analyses its impact upon them, and particularly upon three groups: young Catholics and Protestants, university students, and the 'Jeunes' of the Chantiers de la Jeunesse. Membership of these three categories often overlapped: for example, the most articulate young Catholics were also students. With Christians it was a moral reason that motivated resistance to the STO; with students and the 'Jeunes' of the Chantiers, to put it no higher, it was the sheer futility of a task which they perceived to be neither in the best interests of France nor of themselves. Thus all groups shared in common a will to protest, a refusal to submit to coercion.

Already by early 1942 the war against the Soviet Union had begun to tax German manpower and factories in the Reich were suffering from labour shortages. Military manpower needs were supplemented by the troops of puppet allies and foreign mercenaries raised by Nazi sympathizers were serving on the Eastern Front, although the French contingent, the LVF, never achieved the wholehearted acceptance of the Wehrmacht. But these reinforcements did not suffice and, as more Germans were sucked into the military machine, foreigners, including French civilians and prisoners of war, were required to replace them in German industries. In France itself, at the Nazi behest, labour was also concentrated in firms working for the German war effort. Later, when the threat of an Allied invasion became more urgent, Frenchmen were impressed into the Todt

Organisation to build the coastal defences of the Atlantic 'Westwall'. Such measures of constraint weighed heaviest upon younger men. Their consequences for organized youth, whether Catholics, students, or serving in the Chantiers, were particularly traumatic. Young Frenchmen were forced to opt: for a German victory, as they were exhorted to do by Laval and Bonnard; for resigned submission to constraint, as Pétain urged, backed by 'neutralist' Vichyites and many of the Catholic hierarchy; or for the Resistance, the ultimate act of rebellion. No matter the course of action selected, this imperative of choice entailed far-reaching personal consequences.

On March 21, 1942 Hitler had appointed Sauckel, the former Gauleiter of Thuringia, an early Nazi party member who had been a prisoner of war in France in 1914, as his 'plenipotentiary' in the occupied territories for the recruitment and employment of surplus manpower. His task was to mobilize, if necessary by force, foreign workers for German factories, a mission that earned this rather disreputable Nazi the unenviable title of 'the slavetrader of Europe'. An ordinance (Anordnung No. 4 of May 7, 1942), applicable to all German-occupied countries in the West, gave a cloak of legality to Sauckel's transactions. At first in France only volunteers for work in Germany were canvassed. In the summer of 1942 Laval, after declaring his wish for a German victory, struck a bargain which he thought would earn him some cheap popularity with his compatriots. For every three *skilled* workers that volunteered, one French prisoner of war would be returned home. Thus the notorious campaign for the 'Relève' was instituted. In reality the complete terms of the bargain were even less advantageous. Laval undertook to recruit 400,000 workers, of whom only 150,000 would be skilled workers. Thus only some 50,000 prisoners at the most would be released. But there is a grain of truth in the assertion of Masson, Commissioner-General for Prisoners, that 'a different policy from that of prime minister Laval would not have prevented the workers for leaving, it would only have prevented the prisoners from returning home'.[1] In other words, it was claimed that Laval was striking a bargain where the Germans had no need to bargain, just as he did by sacrificing foreign Jews in order to save French ones. The average Vichy official probably shared the view of the prefect of the Vaucluse that it was an edict to which France must submit because it had been conquered.[2] And, as he added, in other countries the operation had been carried out by different methods.

After the total occupation of France Sauckel extended the scope of the ordinance accordingly, although his recruiting offices had already been allowed to operate in the south. His insatiable demands became increasingly threatening. As Hemmen, the German minister in Paris put it, the mere announcement in the press of the Gauleiter's impending visit was 'sufficient to see for days on end hundreds of young men scurrying to the various Paris stations with their little suitcases'.[3] Laval sought to retain the initiative by promulgating a law of September 4, 1942 which decreed complete direction of labour 'in the higher interest of the nation'. Men aged between eighteen and fifty and women between twenty-one and thirty-five could, with certain exceptions, be directed to work anywhere. For youngsters under twenty the SGJ set up a special volunteer organization, the Jeunes Ouvriers Français Travaillant en Allemagne (JOFTA). After an accelerated training course in France these young workers would leave in units, under the discipline of their own leaders. But by January 1943, after a brief period of apprenticeship, only 110 young men had been dispatched to Germany by JOFTA; in addition, 400 were following a similar course in Germany and another 1,000 in France.[4] This was a meagre harvest, but in 1944 JOFTA, whose name had been changed to the Service Encadré du Travail, still continued to recruit volunteers. Volunteer status was presumed to give some choice of location and type of employment, on a one-year renewable contract,[5] although in the event these advantages were seldom realized. In general, however, if press hand-outs are to be believed – and all figures are to be treated with extreme caution because they are so conflicting – 247,000 men of all ages, including 145,000 skilled workers, had volunteered.[6] Germany was also able to call upon the services of 932,000 remaining French prisoners of war, some of whom were given civilian status to work in Germany.

In February 1943 the final German débâcle at Stalingrad, coupled with the increasing vulnerability of the Atlantic coastline, led Hitler to decree the mobilization of all Nazi-occupied Europe. It was, as Jäckel puts it, 'the hour of birth of total war'.[7] Sauckel set a new manpower quota for France: half a million men, of whom half, including 145,000 skilled workers, must leave France by mid-March 1943.[8] Laval realized that his voluntaryist policy had failed: such a number of volunteers could not be mustered in the time. He bowed to the inevitable, and decided that the time had come to introduce measures of compulsion. By the law of February 16, 1943 registration for the STO was decreed for the military classes of 1940, 1941, and 1942, young men aged between twenty and twenty-two. Service was to be for two years, although students would be liable to service in Germany for only one year. Exemptions were granted to coal-face workers, agricultural workers, police, railwaymen, and a few other essential categories; certain 'military' categories were only liable to work for the Germans in France. Sauckel stuck to his impossible deadline and quotas were fixed by department. By the end of March 77,000 of those called up under the STO law were already in Germany.[9] Pétain did not object to the principle of compulsion, although he did complain when a few young men under twenty were called up, presumably by mistake.[10] Publicly Vichy put a bold face on things: the government maintained that only one in seven of those called up would go to Germany, the balance being found from volunteers.[11] When there were clear indications that the total of half a million men would not be reached, either through volunteers or pressed men, Sauckel angrily decreed that Laval would have to find from then on 100,000 a month. Laval responded by extending the STO obligation to the remainder of the 1939 class who had not served in the war and dispatched to Germany immediately all students serving in the Chantiers de la Jeunesse.[12] Eventually the target laid down for the first quarter, reduced to 250,000 men, was met, but between April and mid-October only a further 180,000 left for Germany, although another 60,000 had been called up for service in France. Measures against defaulters were stiffened: a stringent law of June 11, 1943 prescribed administrative internment for those who failed to register, as well as a heavy fine; employees who failed to ensure the registration of their employees were also liable to penalties. But it was all to little avail.

The upshot was that in the later summer and autumn of 1943 Laval was subjected to extreme German pressure, so much so that on August 18 the regional prefects were summoned to Vichy to review the situation. After the meeting a press communiqué[13] stated that Laval had:

> expressed his will to complete rapidly the operations concerning the departure of young workers for Germany, in accordance with undertakings previously given. No failure of duty can be tolerated in any field. Swift and energetic measures must revive to consciousness of their duty too many young men who have let themselves be carried along without realising exactly what is the cause they are called upon to serve.

That the situation did not improve can be deduced from an unpublished account[14] of another meeting of regional prefects called in September, presided over by Laval and attended by Bichelonne, minister of industrial production, Bonnafous, minister of food, and Cathala, minister of finance, at which the serious shortfall in numbers was again discussed. It was announced that Sauckel had demanded a second contingent of 200,000 men by July 1, but only 150,000 had been forthcoming. In the month intervening since the last meeting only another 10,000 men had been scraped together. Yet statistics showed that the young men eligible for call-up alone numbered about 795,000. These could be enumerated as follows:

Granted deferment: coal-face workers	61,000
Deferment whilst working for the Germans in France	55,000
Exemptions: farmworkers and medically unfit	322,000
Defaulters or presumed defaulters	200,000
Available for STO	170,000
	808,000

(The discrepancy betweeen the two totals given, one of 795,000 and the other of 808,000, is not explained.)

Discussion at the meeting naturally revolved round the 200,000 defaulters ('réfractaires'), some 54 per cent of those who could be available for service. Various explanations were offered as to their whereabouts. It was evident that large numbers were in hiding or had taken to the Maquis. Indeed, it was reported that in some mountainous areas the 'maquisards' already had armed superiority over the police. In the Finistère and the Morbihan between 14,000–16,000 defaulters were roaming the countryside in gangs. In the Rhône department some 4,800 checks had been carried out by the police since July, but these had yielded only 483 defaulters, of whom a mere 125 had since left for Germany. A Breton bishop had written personally to all seminarists in his diocese appealing to them to obey their call-up summons, but only 56 had responded. Laval raised the question of what should be done with young Jews. It was decided that all French Jews aged between twenty and thirty should be set to work in firms in France working for the Todt Organisation and that all foreign Jews, with the exception of the Swiss and the Portuguese, should be repatriated. This provoked some statistics from the representative of the Seine department: of 5,460 Jews called up for the STO in his department, only 462 had complied with the summons, and of these 248 were found unfit; thus no less than 4,998 were defaulters. Of these 795 had since been arrested by the Germans; it was known that 2,043 had decamped 'without leaving a forwarding address'! Finally Laval outlined to the meeting the reasons he would advance to Sauckel for not having met the quota. For three departments he could say that the responsibility lay with the Germans themselves, because polio had broken out and they refused to accept recruits from those areas. Likewise, in the departments of the Somme and the Oise, and in the Rouen district, the local German authorities had depleted the stock of men available by requisitioning those aged between eighteen and forty-five to work for them on the spot. Furthermore, in those French factories already working for the German military machine (the *S-Betriebe: Schutz-* or *Speer-Betriebe)* it was the Germans themselves who had refused to release the young men. But it was realized that these pretexts, although accounting for a few thousand men, would not be sufficient to appease the Germans, particularly when they discovered that over half of those immediately eligible were in any case defaulters.

German fury was indeed exacerbated. On January 15, 1944 Sauckel made the exorbitant demand for a further one million men,[15] to be dispatched to Germany at the rate of 90,000 a month throughout the year, as well as the call-up of a further one million to work on coastal defences. Pétain was shocked, but powerless to react. Laval protested that such a mobilization of manpower embracing the whole of the nation's youth would precipitate the flight to the Maquis, to German as well as French detriment, since more Occupation troops would be required to maintain order. Eventually Abetz persuaded Sauckel to reduce his first demand to an initial 270,000 men, to be sent in equal batches in March, April, and May, after which the position would be reviewed. Laval and his ministers nevertheless met on February 5 and agreed that it would be impossible to raise more than 100,000 men by the end of May. By then Speer, a Nazi technocrat more rational than a Party bully like Sauckel, had intervened and agreed with Bichelonne on a more feasible plan of action. First, it was decided that the labour force, numbering some 723,000, employed in the 3,301 French firms designated as *S-Betriebe*, should be totally exempt from service in Germany. Second, mixed Franco-German 'combing-out commissions' ('commissions de peignage') should go the rounds of the other French firms and conscript non-essential workers. Meanwhile liability to the STO had been theoretically extended to all men aged between eighteen and sixty (up to the age of forty-five they could be sent to Germany), subject to certain exceptions; likewise all single women or women with no children aged between eighteen and forty-five became liable, with the proviso that women under twenty-five should be placed in employment from which they could return home every evening (L. of February 1, 1944). In the circulars[16] instituting the 'combing-out commissions' the government justified such drastic measures by asking for 'understanding of the present necessities of the European struggle', thus identifying itself more closely with the German cause than previously. It also declared its intention of calling up foreigners first, although it had to find substitutes for those who had absconded whilst on leave from the STO in Germany, and reaffirmed its resolve to lay its hands on malingerers ('oisifs').

All such measures naturally extended to the whole labour force, although it is likely that they bore down heaviest upon the younger generation. How many the new drive for recruitment produced is not certain. Between mid-January 1944 and the Liberation it may have yielded as few as 11,000, and of these 5,000 were volunteers.[17] Meanwhile the call-up had been extended to the 1943 class, ostensibly only for work in France, although in practice many were dispatched to Germany.[18] On the day of the Allied invasion, June 6, 1944, Sauckel instructed Laval to decree by 10 a.m. the immediate call-up of the 1944 class, who had already been registered. This fiat was ignored or evaded, although a few days later Laval did make an order 'requisitioning' in their present employment all men over eighteen. However, on June 23 he sent a confidential telegram to prefects authorizing them to cease all call-ups for the STO. In July, in still occupied Lille, the German Werbestelle, the recruiting office for forced labour, was burnt down by patriotic Frenchmen.[19] It had been located in the appropriately named Rue Négrier!

From their first demands in the summer of 1942 the Germans, at a rough estimate, had asked for over two million workers. The number that actually left for Germany is difficult to determine, partly because of the number of prisoners of war already in the Reich to whom the Germans gave civilian status. Henri Michel puts the figure of those working in Germany at the end of 1943 at 600,000 and esteems that half of these were aged between eighteen and twenty-four.[20] Homze, for the same period, calculates that there were 456,000 workers plus 197,000 'civilianized' ex-prisoners of war. Father Rhodain, Chaplain-General for the prisoners and those working in Germany, calculates that by the end of 1943 the total was one million.[21] Bertrand, the last secretary-general of the Vichy ministry of education, stated that in May 1944 the total was 1,800,000.[22] Such totals show a step-by-step progression. It is therefore somewhat incredible when Tracou, of Pétain's staff, put the 1944 figure at only 640,000 and asserted that since some 710,000 prisoners of war had been released for various reasons, there were fewer Frenchmen in Germany in 1944 than in 1940.[23] But at least 60,000 of those impressed into the German labour force were destined never to see France again.

French workers in Germany were the responsibility of Bruneton, appointed as Commissioner-General, although Bonnard, as minister of education responsible for youth affairs, claimed control over all the younger workers and appointed a *lycée* teacher of German, Meyer, to represent his interests. The quarrel as to who should exercise control over young people in Germany is of little interest save for the fact that General de La Porte du Theil also manœuvred at the time to have one of his Chantiers leaders, Commissioner Marbeaud, appointed to look after the young.[24] If he had succeeded matters might have taken a different turn.

The stout-hearted general was one of many Vichy officials that the Germans were now convinced were playing a double game. That there was connivance at eluding the STO there can be no doubt. Within the ministry of labour itself a group of civil servants under Jean Isméolari set up a special section to *prevent* departures to Germany, unbeknown to their political superiors. The section set up a 'commission d'appel' (which the Germans mistakenly interpreted as 'call-up service', but which the section intended as an 'appeal service' *against* call-up), which issued hundreds of official exemptions from service.[25] Indeed the whole country seemed intent on aiding and abetting defaulters. Near the Swiss border matters were relatively simple: at Annemasse 800 were eligible for call-up, 150 actually registered, and in the end a dozen left. On March 15, 1943 the *Journal de Genève* stated that 90 per cent of those eligible in the 'arrondissement' of Thonon had made good their escape over the frontier. In the Nord department, out of 62,700 registered in the 1940 and 1941 classes, no less than 38,000 procured forged exemption certificates and another 20 per cent managed to register as miners or agricultural workers and thereby be exempted.[26] In December 1943 a count in the Vaucluse showed 1,394 eligible for call-up; 895 did not even bother to register and of the 499 remaining, 147 were declared unfit,[27] making the final departure rate only 20 per cent. In rural areas the evasion rate was particularly high: Finistère 90 per cent; Côtes-du-Nord 95.5 per cent; Puy-de-Dôme 99 per cent.[28] By April 1944, in the whole of Normandy some 14,000 had left for Germany, but an almost equal number were defaulters.[29] Doctors co-operated by issuing as many certificates of unfitness as they dared, even faking X-ray photographs, until the Germans announced that unfitness declared on these grounds must also be agreed by a German doctor.[30] After the general law of September 1942 on the direction of labour many young men, anticipating future developments, joined the Armistice Army, the token force of 100,000 men allowed Vichy by the Germans to reinforce the police and which up to then had been so undermannned that it had had to accept recruits aged seventeen and a half. Their immunity, however, had been short-lived, because after the invasion of the southern zone the Germans had ordered the disbandment of the army. A later expedient to avoid service was to join Darnand's Milice, whose final sinister mission was to hunt down defaulters from the STO.[31]

Protests against the call-up were made all over France. Trains departed for Germany with young men singing the 'Marseillaise' or the 'Internationale', giving a clenched-fist salute and shouting, 'Down with Hitler'.[32] One such leave-taking was obstructed by mothers, wives, and girl-friends lying down on the rails, whereupon all but twenty workers on the train decamped.[33] Seminarists from Evreux, assembled as a group under Father Bergey, the former deputy from the Gironde, boarded the train for Ratisbon, but at the first stop all but two took to their heels.[34] The Germans carried out man-hunts unremittingly, particularly at football grounds, cinemas, and places of entertainment, so much so that Col. Pascot, as Commissioner for Sport, complained to Bonnard, the Germans, and the ministry of labour about the round-ups.[35] In Marseilles evaders who were caught were given half an hour to prepare[36] before being conducted to the notorious transit centre near the Gare St-Charles to await transportation. In a raid near Besançon thirty-nine out of seventy campers were caught after a day's chase and were dispatched to Germany without even being allowed to contact their families.[37] Protests gave rise to fantastic rumours. In Dôle[38] in March 1943 the story spread that disturbances had broken out in several large cities and that a number of young men had been killed. At Salins (Jura) young men awaiting medical examination were harangued and urged to refuse to comply with the call-up by a demobilized sailor. There were cries of 'Vive de Gaulle! On les aura' (sc. 'les Boches'). The incident went virtually unpunished.

A few 'hard-liners' among Vichy officials tried every expedient to harass defaulters.[39] It was suggested that a fine of up to 10,000F should be imposed upon their parents. To catch those who had not registered young men were required to present themselves in person at the food office in order to draw new ration books. Any young man who had for any reason to prove his identity – and this had to be done even to obtain a permit to buy a new bicycle tyre – had at the same time to show that his papers were in order regarding the STO.

The total occupation of France had brought about a hardening of French sentiments against the Germans, but it was not until the introduction of complusory labour service that the younger generation had to make a deliberate choice. Apart from a few fanatical collaborationists and some seminarists and likeminded persons inspired with sacrificial missionary zeal, there was none that accepted departure to Germany gladly. For young men, therefore, since 'neutralism' was no longer an option, the STO marked a watershed in their lives. How three organized groups of young people, Catholics, students, and the 'Jeunes' of the Chantiers de la Jeunesse fared in this situation must now be considered.

The Church's official attitude cannot be understood without recalling how it viewed Vichy and the German occupier generally. Initially the hierarchy would seem to have recognized the complete legitimacy of the Vichy government. Although later it took to referring more to the 'pouvoir établi', avoiding the expression 'autorité légitime', in any case this was a distinction without a practical difference because, so long as the inner life of the Church and the conscience of the faithful were not troubled, Catholics had a duty of obedience to the authorities. It was a matter of indifference that Vichy exercised a despotic form of government, since the Church had traditionally accommodated itself to many forms of political rule. The flaw in this argument is that Vichy exerted effective control over only one-third of French territory and from November 1942 had become a puppet regime almost entirely subject to the will of the occupying forces. As for the Germans, the bishops felt broadly satisfied that they had managed to establish a fragile *modus vivendi* with them, particularly regarding youth. So long as Pétain remained nominally at the helm but enjoined collaboration with the local German authorities, the Church felt justified in maintaining a fairly neutralist posture, intervening only when its vital interests were threatened, such as when a local German commander took action against Catholic youth movements. By 1943, however, such a passive stance was difficult to maintain, and bishops feared that young Catholics would divide into opposing camps, the one engaged in the Resistance, the other in 'the crusade against Bolshevism'.

The crisis came with the STO laws. By then, barring miracles – and there were rumours of terrible new weapons – it was accepted that the Germans had little or no hope of an outright victory. This being so, it was also tacitly acknowledged that the Vichy regime would not survive after the peace. The hierarchy could not retreat into silence when the Catholic bourgeoisie, among whom had been numbered many fervent supporters of Pétain, protested indignantly at their sons being snatched from them. It was plain that the STO laws were German-inspired. The hitherto simple formula of obedience to the Marshal and reasonable compliance with German demands was difficult to sustain.

The Church's reaction nevertheless took time to crystallize. Its supreme body, the Assembly of Cardinals and Archbishops (ACA), presided over by Cardinal Liénart, met only twice a year and since the defeat had been obliged to convene separately in the two zones. Thus its first pronouncement on the principle of compulsory labour service did not come until February 1943, a few days before the law calling up certain military classes. In the southern zone the ACA communiqué referred to 'working class homes' – the bourgeoisie till then had hardly been affected – 'subjected to a harsh separation' and declared that the Church 'was moved at the assaults on the natural rights of the family which, in this domain, are yet again the painful consequences of the war and the defeat'.[40] Eluding the Vichy censorship, the periodical

Jeunesse ouvrière managed to publish this statement. After the promulgation of the conscription law, on March 7 five bishops of the Besançon Province caused to be read in church a denunciation of the manner in which the STO measures were being enforced, which, they considered, was appropriate only to criminals sentenced to legal deportation.[41] The censors clamped down on this protest. A week later a letter from the French hierarchy was read at mass which dealt ostensibly with the proposed dedication of France to the Virgin Mary but which referred obliquely to the STO laws: 'If the human person is subject to duties . . . it has at the same time rights which no power here below can assail.' Unfortunately this forthright and unambiguous statement was not elucidated further.

The general law of September 1942 had theoretically made young women also liable to call-up, a liability which the Church could not accept. Liénart's attention was drawn to a case at Lille where it was alleged that female hospital staff had been bullied into signing a contract to work in Germany. The cardinal protested vigorously, affirming that it would place the women in moral danger. The Germans gave way and rescinded the contract but not before the local Feldkommandantur had expressed pained surprise regarding the so-called 'moral danger' which, it maintained, was no greater than in France.[42] The case probably provoked the Church's declaration that 'we cannot suppose for one moment that one day one will proceed to the call up of female labour . . . [It would be] a threat to the life of the country, to the dignity of women'. The hierarchy conveniently ignored the fact that thousands of women had already *volunteered* for work in Germany. The matter was taken so seriously that Pastor Boegner, of the Fédération Protestante, was asked by both the Catholic and Protestant youth movements to intervene directly with Pétain and obtained the Marshal's personal assurance that there was no intention of conscripting girls for work in Germany.[43] After the law of February 1, 1944 which applied direction of labour to females aged between eighteen and forty-five the Church again signified its opposition (Declaration of ACA, February 19, 1944). This prompted Déat to write a sarcastic article entitled 'Inutiles réticences', published in *L'Œuvre* on March 9: for the first time, he sneered, young ladies of the bourgeoisie were to be forced to go out to work; did not they realize that, through want of money, working-class girls had been doing so for a long time? Further anxiety arose in April 1944 when the rumour circulated that the Germans had demanded that 130,000 young women be dispatched to Germany;[44] so strong was this canard that at least one prefect urged that the fears of families should be allayed.[45]

On the other hand, for young men the situation had become urgent and for young Catholics particularly provoked a crisis of conscience. How this situation further developed may be traced by studying the pronouncements of Cardinal Liénart, because the course that he advocated was that finally adopted by the ACA. In Northern France, heavily industrialized and densely populated, the Germans had hoped to recruit a valuable supply of young, skilled labour. It was therefore a key area, where young Catholics looked to the cardinal for a lead. What did conscience dictate? The Germans feared they knew already how Liénart would react on this score,[46] for in October 1941 he had addressed a secret pastoral letter to his clergy, a copy of which had fallen into German hands. Its gist was: the Church is no vassal of the civil power, although it must submit to it; yet 'one has also the right to express reservations about this or that measure of government', although it would be 'unwise' to make known one's reservations about collaboration with Germany 'except in case of necessity'.

That hour of necessity had surely come. On March 5, 1943 the cardinal spoke on the STO at a 'Journée spirituelle des Jeunes', attended by some 4,000 young people, in St. Martin's church at Roubaix.[47] His message was, it seems, full of ambiguity. Nevertheless the collaborationist press of Northern France proclaimed in banner headlines that Liénart had declared: let us accept compulsory labour service: it would be cowardice to evade it. Even *La Croix* (March 20, 1943), normally more circumspect, put a similar gloss upon his words. The cardinal's injunction, snatched from its context, set off an avalanche of protest, so much so that he resolved to make his position plainer. Thus, on the following Sunday he spoke at a similar meeting, this time 7,000 strong, held in the great St. Maurice church in Lille. He began by acknowledging that he had a duty to speak, but voiced his resentment at the distorted version of his previous remarks published in newspapers which gave him no right of reply. He had *not* declared that the STO was a patriotic duty in order to fight the Bolsheviks, nor had he alluded to Joan of Arc in order to stir up anti-English sentiments. He did not subscribe to anti-German propaganda which viewed working in Germany as wicked, but neither did he support anti-Bolshevik propaganda which claimed that such labour was helping to encompass the defeat of Russia. Both viewpoints were tainted with hatred and therefore unacceptable to true Christians. Moreover, the battle of ideas could not be won by feats of arms. It was true that the burden placed upon young Frenchmen by the occupier violated individual liberty, family rights, and the legitimate demands of patriotism. But youth should possess enough greatness of spirit not to demean itself by hatred. The solution he put forward, he declared, was different, but one in accordance with Christian freedom.

Thus his answer to this question of conscience was:

> I do not say that it is a duty of conscience to accept compulsory labour service. No, because there are at stake demands that go beyond the limits of our legitimate obligations. One may therefore evade it without sin. Moreover, I have not to advise you to comply. We are under constraint. But then I say to you: if you are obliged to leave, you will demonstrate a truly national and social spirit by adopting the attitude I am about to point out to you. . . . Under a fine cloak of patriotism which very inadequately conceals selfish feelings, should the ones that are the most adroit get away with it and let the whole burden of the thankless task fall upon the smallest and the weakest? For after all, whether we wish it or no, the one called upon to go who does not do so causes another to go in his place. Would it not, on the contrary, be finer if, in a spirit of social and national unity, each one nobly shouldered his share of the common ordeal? . . . (There is an apostolic task to be pursued.) There remains the love of Christ. I know the miracles of which He is capable. Thanks to Him, I have seen young Catholics leave, not as vanquished but as victors. Yonder they feel themselves responsible for all their brothers and, as true militants of Catholic Action, they bring the strength of their friendship and the succour of their religious faith to the mass of those thrown, without any other moral support, into a depressing ordeal. They also are there against their will, but the love of Christ sustains and inspires them . . . let us admire them unreservedly and imitate them if this is one day the situation in which we find ourselves.

On this note, after once more performing a careful balancing act, the cardinal finished his admonitions.

He repeated his advice in other nearby towns[48] and some 18,000 copies of his words were distributed until the Germans forbade it. But among young Catholics the ambiguity remained. Some Catholic dignitaries, such as Dutoit, bishop of Arras (who was forbidden to resume his episcopal ministrations after the war) interpreted the remarks as requiring submission. Even within the same diocese Catholic attitudes could diverge totally: Mgr Caillot, bishop of Grenoble, enjoined youth to comply, but at the same time one of his senior clergy, Father Grouès, was encouraging young men to flee to the Maquis, himself helping to set up a Resistance group in the Chartreuse. The perplexity of young Catholics was great. Those who thought it a patriotic duty to refuse their labour were comforted by the thought that the cardinal esteemed it 'no sin' to do so. Others, perhaps no less moved by patriotism, saw their path of duty lying in abnegation and acceptance. Doubtless other less noble sentiments entered into individual decisions: fear for themselves or for their families if they refused; or fear that, with the war winding slowly to a close, they would find themselves both morally and physically on the wrong side of the Allied lines. They realized, as surely Liénart must have done, that the alternative to shipment to Germany was nevertheless separation from home and family, hiding from the Gestapo or its French minions. The only certainty that emerged was that for the first time disobedience to the orders of Vichy had not been condemned. The ACA, meeting on April 6–7, 1943 as a single entity for the first time since the Occupation, endorsed Liénart's attitude, disregarding theological advice on the question which it had previously requested from Father Lebreton. His theological advice, more clear-cut than that of his hierarchical superiors, became known all the same. It was: if Germany is waging an unjust war it is wrong to help it. Thus Aquinas's doctrine and Péguy's proud caveat, 'Pourvu que ce fût dans une juste guerre', came to the aid of perplexed young Frenchmen.

The formal Letter embodying the line taken by the ACA was published on May 9. It was not very forceful in tone. It did indeed deplore the STO and its excesses, particularly regretting that priests were not allowed by the Germans to accompany young workers to Germany. But young Catholics who submitted to the law should do so in a spirit of Christian charity:[49] 'Subjected to constraint, a constraint that the government is attempting to make more humane, but which does not constitute for them [young Catholics] an obligation of conscience, if they wish to be strong they will give their ordeal all its redemptive value, they will be the mainstay of their brothers.'[50] Despite this rather milk-and-water declaration, Guerry, who became the post-war apologist for Catholic actions and attitudes during the Occupation, points out that the letter is significant because for the first time the Church in France had voiced a conscientious objection to a civil law. The fact remains that bishops in German-occupied territory elsewhere spoke out in far less muted voice against the STO.

The collaborationist press had been furious at Liénart's statement. On May 27 *Au Pilori* claimed that the cardinal had 'received a bouquet' from Radio Moscow a few days earlier for his words. The Catholic press gave a mixed reception to the ACA declaration. The collaborationist *Voix françaises,* of Bordeaux, which had links with Cardinal Baudrillart, approved it. The more influential *La Croix* only covertly opposed it. On the whole matter of the STO the seventy-eight diocesan bulletins which in 1943 still continued to appear largely confined themselves to the facts: sixty-three merely published the official instructions of Father Rhodain, chaplain-general to those working in Germany; in five bulletins the bishops enjoined submission to the law; three ignored the subject completely; the rest urged prudence.

Meanwhile Protestants had also been reflecting on what their action should be. Finally the Fédération Protestante Française had issued a statement on April 14 which, read a fortnight later in all Protestant churches, was more forthright than the (later) Catholic one: 'There is an insuperable opposition between the Gospel . . . and any conception of man or society which leads one to treat work as a commodity that one has a right to buy or requisition at will.' Thus for young

Protestants the moral choice was easy and they were encouraged by their pastors to take to the Maquis to avoid the STO.[51]

A key issue was how Catholic youth movements would react to the ACA declaration. When it came, that reaction was largely unfavourable. It is true that the Rover Scouts, without even waiting for the statement, had urged submission: '. . . in the face of the inevitable . . . such will be your service, for which you have chosen neither the place nor the conditions'.[52] However, Mgr Saliège, Archbishop of Toulouse, on May 24, 1943 dispatched a defiant message to a group of scouts leaving for Germany:[53] 'However humiliated France is today, sustain your hope with pride. Our cause was just, you can never be told this enough.' A more complete text of his message, whose authenticity cannot be guaranteed, was couched in even stronger terms and was published some months later (September 10, 1943) in the Swiss *Courrier de Genève:* 'You are leaving for Germany . . . One can bend to a law without giving inner acceptance to it. *Our cause was just,* you can never be told this enough. If *through our own fault* we have lost the war, the justice of our cause remains entire.'[54] The archbishop went on to urge the scouts to look behind the appearances in Germany, a country which had used technology in the service of armed force and sacrificed the individual and the family to a mission of world conquest. These were brave words to utter in the France of 1943, so much so that later Mgr Saliège was threatened with deportation to Germany, which he was only spared because of infirmity.

One group which took an even stronger line was composed mainly of members of the ACJF with a strong interest in social questions who had started, in imitation of Péguy, the *Cahiers de notre jeunesse.* The periodical had already fallen foul of the Vichy censorship when it had reminded the authorities that 'Communism was not the only doctrine condemned by Pius XI in March 1937' (*Cahiers,* March 17, 1943). For this it had been suspended for two months. When it reappeared in June 1943, in a special double issue, its editorial plainly referred to the STO. Headed: 'Resigned? NO' [in capitals], it proclaimed that it would 'be a grave error to legitimize by alleged claims of God certain orders given by men which at bottom are no more than expressions of cowardice . . .' and ended 'We are unwilling to believe that the "soldiers of truth" [i.e. Christians] can agree to lend their hands to the works of the Devil. We are not resigned and, if it is not permitted us to do more, we shall at least have the courage to say NO.' For this brave confession of faith the periodical was closed down for good. In the event, many of their number 'were permitted to do more'. One of the most well known, Jean Domenach, fought with the Uriage Resistance group under Dunoyer de Segonzac in the Massif Central. Gilbert Dru, the secretary-general of the *Cahiers,* was shot by the Germans for engaging in Resistance activities. As Gortais, the secretary-general of the ACJF and first editor of the *Cahiers,* wrote presciently in the *Cahier* of November 1941, anticipating the Archbishop of Toulouse, 'What we must reproach ourselves with is our weakness, not the cause we had wished to defend.' In the final analysis this band of courageous young men overcame that weakness.[55]

Although the Fédération des Etudiants Catholiques was inclined to submit to the STO, the ACJF as a whole was not.[56] On March 6, 1943 the federal council of the ACJF met at Avignon and registered its protest. This went unpublicized, save in *Messages,* the journal of the Jeunesse Étudiante Chrétienne, which was immediately banned by Vichy.[57] Nine days later Christian students had the opportunity to make known their views to fellow-students, when the National Council of Students met at Lyons. At the meeting the Catholic and Protestant representatives were most vociferous in their opposition and finally crystallized student attitudes towards the STO. The report of Brunereau,[58] the Vichy official in charge of student propaganda who attended the meeting, is devastating in its frankness.

He described to Vichy how the labour laws had 'revolted Catholic and Protestant students', who considered them cowardly and almost tantamount to treason. They would have much preferred young people to have been rounded up directly by the Germans without any French connivance. As Christian student leaders they would not recommend their comrades to comply with the law, but would leave the matter to the individual conscience. Meanwhile, they refused to co-operate with the authorities in any way. Thus they rejected an official suggestion that students should follow a special training course before being sent to Germany, because this would merely work to the advantage of the Germans and would moreover entail students being called up before the due date – September 1943. The only form of labour service that students could willingly accept was the Service Civique Rural, the form of agricultural service which in any case had been compulsory for most young people under twenty not otherwise employed since 1942. Brunereau predicted that student leaders would simply urge their members to join the Maquis – as indeed many did later, forming the Jeunes Chrétiens Combattants.

The sole concession Catholic student leaders were prepared to make was that, as had been suggested, Catholic students forced to go to Germany should live in special hostels. But they were opposed to any form of 'political training' for those chosen to be hostel wardens. Their 'training' as Frenchmen and Christians would suffice: 'that of a man [Laval?] who hands his country over to the enemy' was completely unacceptable. They again reaffirmed that it was to the honour of France that it had declared war on Germany. After the defeat it would have been more honourable if it had fallen into the plight of Belgium or Poland. After this blatant insult to the Vichy government the student leaders concluded: 'There can be no question of a revival of France before Nazi Germany is crushed, and all our efforts must be strained to defeat it, even at the price of compromises.'

How Vichy reacted to this attitude of total hostility is not known. Brunereau's report must surely have reached German eyes and confirmed yet again their deep mistrust of young French Catholics and of the Church. Brunereau proposed as reprisal that official recognition should be withdrawn from Catholic youth movements. He pointed out that other student organizations represented at the meeting, including the Catholic scouts, had been more accommodating.

But young Catholic opinion had now crystallized. The upshot was that the diocesan committees of the ACJF received in June 1943 from the secretariat a 'note d'information'[59] which rationally demolished the arguments for compliance with the STO legislation. It contained the texts of four declarations by the Catholic hierarchy which absolved, as they saw it, young people from obedience to the law, leaving the decision to their own conscience: the Letter of the ACA of May 9; the speech of Liénart at Lille on March 15; a Letter of the Belgian bishops of March 15; and one of the Dutch bishops of February 15. A statement of principle followed:

> Before altruism, before an apostolate role [in Germany], before social and national solidarity, must be placed *justice:* what is good, what is evil? What is just and what is injust? It is only after this question has been resolved – and if we esteem ourselves free in conscience to choose between several solutions – that, for example, we can ask ourselves: 'Where does it seem to me that my apostolate role would be most fruitful?' For a question of conscience must not be resolved by questions regarding usefulness conceived in a supernatural sense.

There was then set out a systematic refutation of arguments advanced in favour of compliance:

(1) The argument that it would be wrong to let other young people go to Germany alone, bereft of spiritual support, is invalid, because young workers have done everything, even to the extent of going on strike, in order *not* to go: they do not expect others to accompany them.

(2) The argument that if *you* do not go another will have to take your place can be countered with: 'What then is to be done? To refuse this injustice and to help my neighbour also to refuse.'

(3) The argument that young Catholics must go in order to exercise an apostolate mission in Germany is likewise untenable. Young Catholics are already there and doubtless others will follow. Those who counsel compliance are oblivious of the dangers run by those who go: 'They leave as conquerors but will they not return as renegades?'

(4) The argument that the defeat of Germany would mean the downfall of European civilization and the installation of Bolshevism, it is pointed out, had no weight with Cardinal Liénart nor with the Belgian bishops.

This reasoned rejection had been worked out by Catholic theologians such as Father Riquet, all of whom were later officially rebuked, with *La Croix* (October 4, 1943) reporting an ACA statement that the hierarchy alone 'had responsibility for the direction of consciences'. Needless to say, the students' position was adopted by the clandestine *Cahiers du témoignage chrétien* (No. 7 of July 1943), which strongly upheld 'the duty to resist'. Indeed this final break with Vichy by young Catholics may also be reckoned as something of a landmark in the history of French Catholicism. Never again could the bishops' authority be accepted blindly and without question.

There was, however, real concern at the lack of spiritual and pastoral care for those Catholics already in Germany. In January 1942, when the latter were still few in number, the Church had requested permission to send chaplains. The Germans sat on this request for a year before turning it down. The result was that in January 1943 Cardinal Suhard, as Archbishop of Paris, decided to allow priests to go clandestinely to Germany, after they had ostensibly volunteered as workers. Just before conscription for young men was introduced he made one last appeal to Laval to intervene:[60] 'Families very appropriately remark to us that to leave these young people without the spiritual ministrations to which they are accustomed is to leave them defenceless in the face of every kind of propaganda, even Communist propaganda.' In all twenty-five priests left clandestinely, only two eluding the Gestapo and with three in the end dying in concentration camps.[61] Their ranks were swollen by others: young seminarists called up and hastily ordained before leaving for Germany; priests caught in German round-ups in France; priests who were prisoners of war and who opted for the status of civilian worker in Germany. There were at least 275 in all.[62] The clandestine priests were the forerunners of the post-war worker-priest movement – the book, *France, Pays de Mission?*, which gave rise to the concept had just been published.

Among the first priests to leave was Father Bousquet, who conceived of his mission as having a threefold purpose: to react against Nazi ideas; to open a dialogue with young Germans; and to combat the influence of young, fanatical Doriotistes who were ardent volunteers for the STO and some of whom already held key posts in the organization in

Germany. From the outset such priests were backed by the semi-clandestine Jeunesse Ouvrière Chrétienne (JOC), which before the war was over had established some 1,000 'cells' in 400 German towns, grouping 10,000 members.[63] (Their use of the Communist 'cell' is typical, because they successfully adopted many of the Communist techniques in their organization.) The JOC particularly strove to replace collaborationists as *Vertrauensmänner* in the various camps, although the official Délégation Générale des Travailleurs Français en Allemagne showed a preference for Doriotistes and Francistes in these influential local posts. The Germans were aware that the JOC activities also included, besides the running of welfare services, assistance to those in concentration camps and the organization of an escape network. As a reprisal they made the situation difficult for the JOC in France by closing down the movement's Paris headquarters and placing under arrest its secretary-general, Father Guérin. Repression began in earnest, however, in January 1944 when Himmler ordered the expulsion of 3,000 seminarists at that time working in Germany; after the Allied invasion this developed into a veritable man-hunt directed against Jocistes and the worker-priests.[64] The activities of these young 'social Catholics', not least of which was the 'mission' they saw as having to fulfil in Germany, were one influential factor in determining French attitudes to the Church after the war.

All students had at first been exempt (by a decree of September 19, 1942) from the general law on the direction of labour, a dispensation which pleased their bourgeois parents. Others, however, saw in student status a means of evading the provisions of the law, so that it was eventually stipulated that the first registration as a student should take place not more than two years after passing the baccalaureate (decree of October 29, 1942). Local difficulties with German Kommandanturen led also to the need for a definition of who was a student. Eventually it was decided that a 'student' was anyone enrolled in an institution of higher education, preparing for the 'grandes écoles', training to be a teacher, or a candidate for either part of the baccalaureate.[65] This did not, however, solve the difficulty. After the call-up of February

1943 rectors bombarded the ministry of education with telegrams protesting that the local Occupation authorities were insisting that students and pupils in the relevant age groups should be called up immediately.[66] The situation was particularly tense in the academies of Dijon and of Besançon, where forty pupils of a Pontarlier school had even been issued with travel documents for Germany. Eventually Vichy regained control of procedures and decreed that, as from September 1, 1943, students in the relevant groups would be called up to do one year's STO in Germany followed by one year's civic service in France (decree of February 24, 1943). Postponements would be granted where necessary.

These measures needed further clarification. For example, it was not certain whether they applied to private schools, which supplied more than half the candidates for the baccalaureate. This was eventually resolved in their favour. Another problem concerned the 'capacité en droit', a minor law qualification acquired after study at university, although the course could be entered without the baccalaureate. Numbers enrolling on the course had risen steeply from 900 in 1941 to over 4,000 in 1942, after the law of September 1942 on the direction of labour. The course for future notaries was in a similar position. Eventually it was decided that only second-year students, i.e. those enrolled before the law was passed, could claim deferment. Many other marginal situations arose. Were, for example, students of the picturesquely named École des Cuirs et Peaux provisionally exempt from call-up? There were also manifest injustices. White-collar workers also enrolled as students were eligible for deferment but primary teachers studying part time for a degree were not. Students of the famous École Nationale d'Horlogerie at Besançon were promised that they would work as precision instrument-makers at Nuremberg, with time off for study, but found themselves employed as unskilled labourers.[67]

One final anomaly of the law had been remedied when the STO obligation had been extended to those born in the last quarter of 1919 – that section of the class of 1939 who had not been called up in the war.

Under the call-up of 1943 some 32,000 students appeared to be eventually eligible for service,[68] distributed as in the accompanying table.

Call-up class	Students of technical schools and similar institutions	Faculties of science and similar institutions	Faculties of law, letters, and similar institutions	Teacher-training institutions
1942	3,100	2,300	7,000	500
1941	2,489	1,800	5,600	350
1940	1,899	1,400	4,400	150
1939 (last quarter)	389	200	400	---
Totals	7,877	5,700	17,400	1,000

In July 1943 Laval decided that, of this total of some 32,000 students, about half should be sent to Germany as soon as their deferment had expired. None of the 1942 class would go, with the exception of students in medicine and pharmacy. Medical students of the earlier years would be employed only in France.[69] The medical students of the 1942 class who did leave for Germany found that they were employed as mere nursing orderlies.[70] They may have been earmarked to be a reserve of semi-trained personnel to deal with air-raid casualties because at Lille, for example, before they left they were given an intensive first-aid course as well as instruction in the treatment of venereal disease.[71] For reasons perhaps connected with scientific research some physics and chemistry students were assigned to work in German universities.[72] The other categories of students were promised that they would leave in groups and be found work suitable for their intellectual ability, a promise that was not kept.[73] Jewish students were liable only for call-up for agricultural work in the department in which they lived.[74]

The Germans were markedly displeased that students benefited from any deferment and at one stage threatened strong measures.[75] They subjected them to particular harassment. Thus at Clermont-Ferrand medical examinations for call-up were inconveniently fixed to take place between the final written and oral examinations, identity cards were confiscated, and students had to apply daily for ration coupons, to prevent them making a run for it as soon as their examinations were over.[76] In February 1944 when men and even schoolboys of sixteen were being corralled willy-nilly for work in Germany or in France, many student deferments were arbitrarily cancelled.[77] At Montpellier, where students had to sit their final examinations in early spring because of the fear of a Mediterranean invasion, the local Feldkommandantur rounded up students immediately afterwards for immediate shipment to Germany, but the ministry of education eventually persuaded the Germans to release them until the date of call-up for students in the other universities.

Great bitterness was aroused among students who had already left for Germany, and among parents, when an amnesty was announced for defaulters who reported for service by the end of 1943 – a deadline later extended until April 1944 –[78] and it was intimated that those who did report would be called upon only to work in France.[79] The number of defaulting students had been large. The Germans were enraged to learn in mid-September 1943 that, of the 15,000 students whom Laval had envisaged dispatching to Germany immediately their postponement had expired, only 4,200 had left. Vichy officials, some now openly hostile to Laval, eventually became accomplices in student evasion. Pierre Mauriac, brother of the famous writer, dean of the Toulouse medical faculty and a one-time staunch supporter of the regime, opened the new academic year in 1943 with a speech in which he was careful to distinguish between loyalty to the Marshal and loyalty to the government.[80] In the minds of some officials there was a suspicion that Pétain was in reality opposed to the STO and they acted accordingly. Instances of covert help to students were numerous. In Lille both the State and the Catholic universities refused to hand over the lists of students.[81] Officials neglected to stamp the status of students regarding STO on their student cards, although the law prescribed this; in the spring of 1944 it was proposed that officials caught in this omission should be summarily dismissed.[82] Completed STO forms were stolen from the Sorbonne by a Resistance organization and returned by post to the students concerned. Former ministers of education came to the rescue of students and others. Ripert, now dean of the Paris law faculty, enrolled pseudo-students under false names, antedating their enrolment so that they would escape immediate liability for service.[83] He also hid students and allowed candidates whose papers were not in order to sit for examinations. Chevalier, at the university of Grenoble, claimed to have given out false student identity cards. (But at his post-war trial he was accused of denouncing evaders.[84] To Ménétrel, Pétain's private secretary, he wrote that he had effected a 'magnifique redressement' in his university and re-established 'order', so much so that all students who had been called up had complied with the order and one, already a qualified doctor, had even told him: 'I remembered your command: "Obey!" '[85]) Carcopino, back in his old post as director of the École Normale Supérieure, secured postponement for his students taking the 'agrégation' and then immediately after the examination had them appointed to teaching posts in Paris *lycées* or taken on as mechanics at the Renault works, which gave them a further respite.[86] Admiral Abrial, minister for the navy, claimed to have secured exemption of young sailors, land-based since the Toulon scuttlings, and to have protected student cadets of the École Navale.[87] Even Bonnard boasted later of having helped students of the École des Beaux-Arts by making them museum attendants, a reserved occupation![88]

However, Bonnard was far more zealous in hunting out students than shielding them. Regarding the STO as the ultimate means of sustaining Germany and thus protecting France from Communism, he claimed that service in Germany would strengthen Franco-German *rapprochement* and toughen the sinews of French society.[89] As president of the newly formed Conseil Supérieur du STO he even appealed to students to respond enthusiastically to the call-up.[90] In fact, at his post-war trial the gravest charges against him concerned the STO. On the other hand, it could be argued that, with the exception of Bonnard and those such as Déat and Darnard who later acquired ministerial rank, the government's attitude towards the labour service was equivocal. On Laval's behalf it has been maintained that he adopted Fabian tactics for as long as possible. This can at present be neither proved nor disproved. Certainly the enforced exodus of students, the future intellectual élites of France, drawn mainly from a class that had supported the regime from the beginning, could well be reckoned to be a national disaster.

The disgruntlement of the student body as a whole was expressed at the annual congress of the Union Nationale des Étudiants, held in the spring of 1943 at La Chapelle-en-Vercors (Drôme). Some strongly worded proposals were sent to Bonnard,[91] calling for the study rights of those to be called up to be safeguarded and opposing the putting forward of the date of the yearly examinations in order to facilitate an early call-up, as well as insisting that students leaving for Germany should be found appropriate work. The congress seemed to be under the impression that only those in the former occupied zone would be called up. Belatedly Bonnard acknowledged the strength of student feeling and put forward concessions. In the early summer of 1944 he envisaged that students in Germany[92] could renew their university registration by post; those taking examinations would benefit from a lower pass-mark of 40 per cent rather than the normal fifty per cent; they would be exempted from fees. He also wanted to dispense candidates for some civil-service posts and for some of the postgraduate 'grandes écoles' from the necessity of having a university degree before entry, but in this he was opposed by Bichelonne who, as minister of production, had responsibility for some of the institutions concerned. Bonnard countered this opposition by declaring that he did not want those returning from Germany to become 'old students', because higher education already contained too many beyond the normal student age.[93] Needless to say, none of these panic-stricken concessions were realized.

Meyer, Bonnard's representative in Germany, sent back some brutally frank reports[94] on how young people and students were faring there. By mid-September 1943 he had managed to contact only 1,200 students, but described their situation as 'not brilliant'. They were working a fourteen-hour day, if two hours for travelling were included, and had therefore no energy left for study or leisure pursuits. Health facilities were poor, and medical students who might have been employed as medical auxiliaries were now being used as gardeners or labourers. In any case those who reported sick were likely to be treated as malingerers. They lacked reading material (Bonnard responded to this by immediately sending off 10,000 books for them).[95] On Sundays, their one day of leisure, they were restricted in travel to the particular *Gau* in which they were stationed; the result was that few links with German students could be forged. Meyer had been disappointed to find that only ten out of twenty posts as assistant in German universities had been taken up by French students. Another report made in June 1944 did say that the students' living conditions had improved somewhat, but that they remained bitter and hostile,[96] particularly since their tour of duty in Germany had been extended from one year to two and promises to give them time off for study had not been fulfilled. There was envy because some students had been released by their German employers after one year only and had been allowed to return home.[97] It was the usual tale of muddle and confusion.[98]

In all, perhaps only 6,000 out of the 15,000 students promised did actually go to Germany. Nevertheless the figures show[99] that between July and December 1943 the total of all university students, including those liable to call-up, declined sharply:

	Number of students			
	31.7.43	31.12.43	Decrease	Percentage decrease.
Men	69,194	46,524	22,670	32.8
Women	33,537	28,815	5,322	14,1
Total	102,731	75,339	27,392	26.7

Within all faculties save medicine, which registered an increase of 7.3 per cent, a marked falling-off of numbers of at least 29 per cent was apparent. The STO and other factors had taken their toll. Some male students had seen the writing on the wall and had taken to the Maquis; others had been drafted to agricultural, industrial, or defence work within France; and a very few had joined the Milice or volunteered for service on the Eastern Front. Harassed on all sides, those on whom Pétain and de La Porte du Theil had counted to lead a 'new France', were by now in a state of frustration and bewilderment.

How the average young man fared regarding compulsory labour service can be studied by considering the fortunes of the 'Jeunes' serving in the Chantiers de la Jeunesse. The other youth movement, the Compagnons de France, because it concerned a younger age group, was little affected by the call-up, save for its permanent cadres. To the latter, Compagnons headquarters addressed a message with a faintly ambiguous ring to it: 'You must leave France . . . No use bewailing it . . . During this difficult period strengthen your pride in being French . . . More than ever there is question of "France and her sons".'[100]

In the Chantiers de la Jeunesse, however, there were some 32,500 young Frenchmen, principally those called up in November 1942, who were potentially liable for compulsory labour service. According to General de La Porte du Theil, without consulting Pétain, Laval, or himself as head of the movement, Weinmann, the French Commissioner for the STO, agreed to make available to the Germans some 15,000 youngsters of the Chantiers by May 1, 1943.[101] The German plan was that when those serving in the Chantiers reached the end of their service they should not be released, so that 18,000 would be shipped directly to Germany and another 6,000 sent to factories in France.[102] The general complained bitterly that such a procedure would cause him to lose all credibility with his men. Already at the last call-up for the Chantiers one-third had not answered the summons; in the canton of Thonon, for example, out of twenty-four liable for service, not one had put in an appearance. De La Porte du Theil was less able than previously to act autonomously because, by a law of March 5, 1943, the Chantiers had been placed under the direct authority of Laval. Reluctantly, therefore he fell in with the initial German plan.

His compliance is nevertheless puzzling. It may be ascribed to his personal devotion to Pétain or the oath of loyalty he had taken – the Marshal, after all, had not openly contested the principle of the STO but had merely complained to

Bichelonne when cases of youngsters under twenty being called up had been brought to his notice.[103] It may also be due to the great importance de La Porte du Theil still attached to the Chantiers. In November 1942, for example, he had been by chance in North Africa at the time of the Allied landings. Although he may have been aware that his subordinate, Van Hecke, the head of the Chantiers in Algeria, had been one of the 'Group of Five' that had collaborated with the Americans to bring North Africa back into the war, he nevertheless returned to metropolitan France rather than cast in his lot with the Allies. He may also have thought that the growing number of those who had passed through the Chantiers and joined ADAC, its association of 'Anciens' might have a part to play in the future invasion of France. He was certainly aware that in early 1943 the Germans were seeking to close down the Chantiers completely. He may therefore have judged it expedient, in order to save the movement, to play along with the Germans and to sacrifice some 'Jeunes' for the sake of the many others.

Whatever the motivation, the upshot was that the first draft of 5,000 men left for Germany at the end of May 1943 without any home leave, poorly equipped, and in a flurry of confusion. De La Porte du Theil sent them a message in which he tried to justify their precipitate departure: 'What you bring is not your person, reduced to a servile state, but your labour. And that the government has a right to demand in any circumstance, but even more so in the circumstances of the war through which we are now living.'[104] Others did not share his view. The commandant of one transit camp through which the drafts passed, found that one hundred and fifty had absconded but was so incensed at the general plight of the men that he refused to allow police to patrol the camp, openly condemned what was virtual deportation, and cited the Declaration of the Rights of Man, which, he said, affirmed that in certain cases insurrection was the most sacred of all duties.[105] The movement had come a long way from the Révolution Nationale and the duty of obedience preached in 1941. Other cadres in the Chantiers also connived at escapes. De La Porte du Theil waxed indignant at their disobedience to orders and required four chaplains and thirteen 'chefs' to resign. In some contingents absentees numbered more than half the total – in Groupement 23 (Languedoc) it reached three-quarters.[106] The general commented gloomily: 'Alas, the French state is bordering on total collapse. If we do not check its downhill course we shall be lost. Thus there can be no longer time for indulgence, which in its leaders becomes an error.'[107] The force of the remark was doubtless not lost upon the Germans.

There was worse to come. Sauckel instructed von Nidda, the German consul at Vichy, to press for further drafts from the Chantiers in the autumn. The Wehrmacht, wanting 30,000 more men for the factories, on August 9, 1943 ordered the immediate transfer of 4,000 from the Chantiers. This time de La Porte du Theil refused to comply and told Laval that he would prefer the Chantiers to be wound up rather than submit. Sauckel instructed von Nidda to exert pressure upon the general. During a heated argument between the two the general told the consul that Germany was on the verge of defeat and that his 'Jeunes' were ready to go over to the Resistance. The Germans feared that they had gone too far and that Laval might be forced to resign. They therefore withdrew their demand for the time being and agreed that they would require no further drafts from the Chantiers until 1944.[108] De La Porte du Theil thereupon released some 'Jeunes' before their time had expired, leaving them free to decide whether to obey any future call to leave for Germany when it might come.[109]

Those that went to Germany were very disaffected. Meyer, Bonnard's representative, reported that among the Chantiers' leaders that accompanied their men 'a not inconsiderable percentage inclined to Gaullism',[110] although, ironically, some of these leaders were later assembled together in Germany and sent off to Sigmaringen to join Pétain and the rump of the Laval government at the end of the war. Complaints of bad treatment and mis-employment of the 'Jeunes' were frequent and de La Porte du Theil acknowledged that they were well founded: his own son, an agricultural student, was doing navvying work alongside Russian prisoners of war.[111] In some ways the 'Jeunes' sent to work in France in Todt Organisation camps suffered a worse fate than those that left for Germany. At one such camp on the Breton coast they were harangued on arrival by a French officer wearing the uniform of the LVF, on the virtues of being 'pioneers of French national-socialism'. After initially trying to win over these reluctant workers the Germans resorted to harsh treatment and severe punishment. They left for work at 5.45 a.m. and did not return to camp until 8 p.m. Guarded by sentries and hemmed in by barbed wire, they shared appalling conditions with men of many different nationalities.[112] When the Allies invaded it was difficult to discover those who were there of their own free will and those who were pressed men.

By August 1943 it would appear that 16,372 'Jeunes' had left for Germany, out of the 18,000 the Germans demanded; 3,748 were working for the Germans in France, out of the 6,000 demanded; 6,916 of the 1942 class were 'absent irregularly'; and 4,900 coal-face workers and farm workers had been released.[113] The class of 1943, when called up, should have been set to work in France, but this practice was not always followed. In early 1944 the Germans announced that Frenchmen of seventeen and upwards might serve as auxiliaries in the German navy.[114]

Morale among the 'Jeunes' that remained was mercurial. They feared total disbandment of the Chantiers and immediate transportation to Germany. By the summer of 1943 any spirit of discipline that the Chantiers might have inculcated had been dissipated. In certain of their camps the gendarmes patrolled, giving them the feeling that they were mere cattle awaiting shipment ('bétail à livrer').[115] Eventually, however, a mood almost of resignation set in, so that even the number of escapers diminished, perhaps because the Germans threatened reprisals on their families. In the autumn the Germans began searches themselves of the camps and there were renewed fears of disbandment. Not all 'Jeunes', however, accepted their situation passively. One young Alsace-Lorrainer expressed, in a letter addressed to de La Porte du Theil (doubtless before making good his escape), his sentiments in no uncertain terms towards those whom he did not hesitate to call 'les Boches': 'You are not unaware of what the occupying power is scheming: it is the deportation of French youth so that its best elements will be paralysed to act at the not far distant hour of revenge. We are only awaiting the day when we shall put on French uniform, which by then will have found its true colour and its true glory.'[116]

By then Laval had recognized that de La Porte du Theil was no longer acceptable to the Germans. His arrest and subsequent deportation, which have been described elsewhere, were the signal for many more 'Jeunes' to take to the Maquis.[117]

Those still remaining at Châtel-Guyon, Chantiers headquarters, were stunned at the loss of their leader. When the government floated a proposal to create a new type of two-year labour service for youth, the Chantiers staff reacted in a letter to Pétain which began plaintively, 'The Chantiers de la Jeunesse having been deprived of their leader . . .' but nevertheless went on to suggest how they might co-operate in the new service.[118] At local level leaders were more rebellious, urging their charges to desert[119] as the date of the Allied invasion approached. Meanwhile effective power in the Chantiers had passed to one of the commissioners, Tartarin, who had been in Tunisia during the Allied landings. Whilst the Chantiers in North Africa had generally gone over *en masse* to the Allies, the group commanded by Tartarin had not; thus a section of ADAC in Tunisia had even built landing-strips for German aeroplanes. In January 1944 Tartarin was against the 'Jeunes' being assigned to the Todt Organisation, because he foresaw dangers in this for the Germans.[120] They might defect to the Resistance or become even more anti-German. Pro-Gaullist elements, he argued, were in favour of a merger of the Chantiers with the Todt Organisation because it would cast the Germans in the discreditable role of slave-drivers. He wanted the character of the movement to change in a different way. He was willing to lead the Chantiers in actively assisting the Germans in France whilst continuing to give a form of civic education – doubtless one that would be pro-German. The movement would be under the vigilant scrutiny of 'political inspectors' and numbers could be increased quickly by February 1944. He claimed that his plan had the blessing of Laval and Abetz, so that through it would emerge 'the embryo of a true single youth movement which would embrace all others and would orientate them in a predetermined political direction and towards civic action'. In the event, Tartarin's ideas proved unacceptable. An industrialist, Loubet, was appointed nominal head of the Chantiers, although Tartarin continued to direct the movement behind the scenes.

Déat had been scornful in the past of the Chantiers. Now, as secretary-general for the utilization of manpower, responsible to Bichelonne as minister of industrial production, he was anxious to use the organization as the nucleus of a superior labour force. This new development had been foreshadowed already in November 1943 when some of those called up had been placed in factories. Known as 'jeunes bleus' – young blue-collared workers –, they lived and worked in units under discipline. Others called up at the same time became known in contrast as 'jeunes verts' – the Chantiers uniform was green – and were set to work partly in industry, partly in agriculture. At the request of the German Armistice Commission the status of all those engaged in industry was converted into that of 'jeunes bleus'. By a law of February 1, 1944 the duration of service in this new form of the Chantiers was raised from eight months to two years. Meanwhile the Commissariat Général of the Chantiers had become a directorate of the ministry of labour (law of January 19, 1944). The transformation of the Chantiers from a movement whose primary role was educative to a utilitarian purpose was complete.

The ground was now cleared for Vichy to propose a new 'Service de la Jeunesse au Travail', to include all young men of the classes of 1943 and 1944 not already in essential employment, serving in the Milice, or fighting with the LVF. The purpose of this new form of service proposed was somewhat obscure. Laval is alleged to have wanted to prevent more young people being packed off to Germany: entertaining the Chantiers leaders to lunch in 1944 he remarked, 'As for the Germans, I don't care about their ideology. I am continually striving to cut down their demands.'[121] Even if this were true, he can only be said to have failed miserably – and in the craft of statesmanship failure is just as reprehensible as deception. Likewise it is alleged that Déat had a similar aim in mind:[122] in his suggested new organization young men would serve their first year in France. Déat had been working on his plan with Canon Duhamel, the new chaplain-general of the Chantiers. On the other hand it has been suggested that Déat wanted to pursue a diametrically opposite course: younger men should be sent to Germany to replace those already working there, in a kind of 'relève de la Relève'.[123] In his proposed new service, whilst there would not be 'political inspectors', cadres would be required to supervise their charges both physically and morally out of working hours in order 'to prevent pernicious or anti-governmental influences working upon young people'. Thus the diligent hierarchy of the ant-heap, based upon the ethic of work for the conquerors, would be imposed upon young Frenchmen. The high aim with which the Chantiers had started out had become debased beyond recognition.

However, Déat's proposal for a refurbished youth labour service, with a new-style uniformed force under para-military discipline, proved unacceptable to the Germans. 'For certain reasons', they said, 'not least of which is the general situation', the Chantiers had to be disbanded by mid-June 1944.[124] But, whether as 'jeunes bleus' or 'jeunes verts', young workers must continue in their employment. If they continued to wear uniform – some by then had no other clothing – it must be without insignia. Their leaders should be enrolled in 'the forces of order'. Certain of their vehicles should be handed over to the Milice, but the bulk should be turned over to the Todt Organisation. That organization would take on any remaining 'Jeunes' not already placed; they would be assembled in so-called 'Centuries of France', under a German foreman. (Déat claimed that he delayed shipping young men off to the Todt units located on the coast until after the Allied landings, when it became impossible.) Clearly the Germans feared to the very end that, even without their leader, the Chantiers might start an armed uprising. The movement was officially disbanded in June and all departures for Germany ceased just after the invasion. Thus ended a movement born in idealism from the ashes of a defeat, which had evolved into a modern form of slavery for the young.

The picture of young people under conscription of labour is one of progressive deterioration.[125] Postal intercepts for April 1943 show that young people working in Germany still compared their living conditions and rations favourably with those in France. Worse than their ten-hour working day were the horrors of bombing. But by June 1943 conditions had deteriorated dramatically. A terse Vichy report read: 'Relève et service obligatoire. La situation est de plus en plus effroyable.'[126] Yet 'ces messieurs', as one official 'Note' describes the Germans, were insatiable for more men. In July it was reported that the impossibility of keeping clean had led to the outbreak of epidemics in French camps.[127] There was bitterness about the 'fils à papa' then just leaving school and walking into reserved jobs in France, which 'is going to exacerbate dissension among the different working classes'.[128] By September it was reported that those workers coming on leave from Germany and vanishing into the blue were increasing in number.[129] The Germans were indignant that even in 1944 there could still be seen in France 'muscular young men who are doing nothing (there are some in every social class) who mainly live off the black market and do well out of it, hanging noisily round bars and cafés'. Sauckel was so incensed that he had film shots taken of cafés on the Champs-Élysées to prove French youth was idling whilst German youngsters were sacrificing their lives on the Eastern Front. He hoped the films would induce Hitler to take sterner measures against the French.[130]

In April 1944 the French authorities set out for the Germans a document giving the distribution of the French male labour force.[131] Out of a total of 7.5 millions 1.8 million were working in Germany either as prisoners of war or as STO workers; 3.2 millions were engaged in agriculture in France; 1.3 million were working in factories designated as 'Speer-Betriebe' or for the Todt Organisation in France; 1.2 million were employed as civil servants, in the liberal professions, or in commerce. Any further call-up of labour, they considered, would have catastrophic consequences.

In any case, for the young, who were the main victims of the German demand for manpower, the catastrophe was a reality. But in the end, despite the invocation of Pétain, despite the exhortations of the hierarchy, few young Frenchmen accepted the German yoke willingly. Whether Christian or lacking any religious commitment, whether part of a privileged student élite or underprivileged young workers, they and the various youth movements through which many passed, evolved from acquiescence to passive or active revolt. The role of helot forced upon them by the Germans left them no other choice.

Chapter XV

Conclusions

Those Frenchmen who influenced the destinies of youth between July 10, 1940 and August 21, 1944 were by no means at one on the policy to adopt. As in other domains of national life, in education and youth matters there was not one policy, but several, evolving over time. This is because, as compared with the era of the Third Republic, the spectrum of politics that the Vichy interlude refracted was almost as broad. The shift was to the right, with the traditional hues of red and infra-red rigorously excluded, but the colour gradations were as subtle as the doctrines they represented. These beliefs determined the policies they adopted towards youth.

After the defeat the dominant mode was Maurrassian. Charles Maurras's distinction between the 'pays légal' and the 'pays réel' implied a contrast between an outmoded, dry-as-dust concept of democracy, whose political leaders were profoundly divided by abstract and elusive party ideologies, with a concept of the living community, whose members were linked by common interests at the level of the nation, the commune, the family, and occupation, which represented concrete, substantial realities. Against the mechanistic view of society was set that of the organic, vital body, where village schoolmaster and parish priest presided harmoniously over all the activities of the young. It was to this idyllic, mythical past that the Révolution Nationale sought to return. Schools and youth movements, with the backing of the Church, would be the transmitters of the time-honoured French values, reinforced by the home: work, particularly valuable if it required skill; respect for a God-given social order that cosily excluded such 'universalists' as Communists, freemasons, and Jews. In short: 'Travail, Famille, Patrie'. But for a fallen people such as the French in 1940 to return to the garden Paradise, repentance was first necessary. The 'evils' of Republicanism, which stretched back episodically for a century and a half, must be excised. Surrogate scapegoats were found: not only the 'universalists', but also the teachers and the youth of France. Once scourged and purified of the sins their elders had committed, the young would become the hope of a new France. They would be worthy to take over a 'mon-archic', traditionalist form of society, culturally 'revised' and spiritually renewed. It was of course an impossible dream: 1789 had been – and in 1940 the swastika flew over the Chamber of Deputies.

The key role that could be played by youth was recognized by all concerned, whether German or French. Pétainism merely continued a youth cult which had begun with the rise of totalitarian youth movements after the First World War. Before 1914 the young had not bulked large in national affairs. Nazi and Fascist youth movements had inspired imitators in France between the wars; it was inevitable that they should continue to do so during the Occupation. The potential, the sheer physical vitality of the young – and brute force is at the heart of authoritarian regimes – gave the rising generation a major role to play. The old, the middle-aged, and even those who had fought in 1940 were content to see Pétain, the embodiment of gerontocracy, exalted whilst seeking to regiment those whose only real title to future power was their very inexperience and the fact, unacknowledged at the time, that they were the only segment of the nation who had not been a party to the defeat. The paradox of maturity's reliance upon youth was never better illustrated.

Youth itself had been stunned by the collapse of France. In Paris on Armistice Day 1940 a few bold spirits had reacted against the German presence, but among the majority the vicissitudes of the war for a long while afterwards did not encourage further reaction. The extension of the conflict to the Soviet Union helped to effect a first crystallization of attitudes round Pétain, collaboration, or the Resistance. Many young people remained bewildered. In early 1942 a young man, after a visit to the occupied zone, expressed views not untypical of his contemporaries. In the North, he declared they were either committed Gaullists or pro-German. They were not committed Frenchmen, as Pétain wanted them to be. For him Gaullism was impossible, because, although among those in London there were some brave men, those who exiled themselves in 1940 had taken refuge in flight and allied themselves to a country which was fighting for the survival of capitalism. Young people remembered Mers-el-Kébir, Dakar, and Damascus and could not accept that Frenchmen should kill each other. Britain remained the traditional enemy. On the other hand, it was difficult to align oneself with the opposite camp. Collaboration was a principle acceptable to young people when it was applied universally. When it related exclusively to Germany and Italy then 'we must all the same be told a little more precisely what is asked from us and what we are offered'.

Laval's return to power meant a further crystallization of attitudes among young people. By then they had grasped the significance of America's entry into the war. In 1942 the Allied landings in North Africa and the defence of Stalingrad had strengthened their belief that Germany was not invincible. The turn of the tide in Russia and the victory in North Africa convinced them that the total German victory desired by Laval was not possible. De Gaulle gained in popularity and began to look an alternative to Pétain. By February 1943, when the massive deportation of young men to Germany began, most were certain that Hitler could not even force a compromise peace. The evolution in young people's thinking was gradual: only slowly did they grow aware of the choice that circumstances were forcing upon them. Finally, neutralism and 'attentisme' became an impossible option.

Vichy policy likewise developed. At the beginning, all shades of opinion agreed that youth had to be regimented ('mise au pas') and the educational system reformed. But regimentation had many different connotations. For Lamirand it meant a pluralism of youth movements, whose common denominator lay in moral and civic education, defined in practice as a traditional view of morality, the disciplined acceptance of Christian values, the cult of patriotism, and the recognition of social duties. For the collaborationists regimentation had a different meaning. It meant embracing the moral law of the jungle, where might was right; it meant

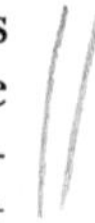

a patriotism that was stridently nationalistic, save when it came to recognizing the paramount status of Germany in a new European order; it meant a fight to the death against Communism, a rejection of the 'Anglo-Saxon' scheme of political and social values. The instrument of such a political philosophy would be a 'jeunesse unique', a single, totalitarian youth movement. On the other hand, in the more protected world of the school, where the collaborationists never gained a foothold in the only place where it mattered, the classroom itself, moral and civic education was also variously interpreted. The hard core of teachers probably continued to teach a 'sociological morality', allegedly Durkheimian in character; others accepted the obliquely Christian and more overtly patriotic tenor of the Carcopino reforms. The Catholics sought to go farther and to reinforce the specifically Christian basis for moral education, as well as to interpret other school subjects such as history in the light of their view of Christianity.

If the teachers remained the least affected of all the interest groups as regards change, some of those who ran the youth movements, particularly the military men, evolved with their charges. Some in their heart of hearts, and among them must be numbered de La Porte du Theil and Borotra, a reserve officer, may have always thought that victory could be snatched from the jaws of defeat. The fact that officers held leading positions in the SGJ and in the various youth organizations must have impressed young people. Gliding, skiing, hard physical training under arduous conditions were activities highly relevant to future military service, as the Germans were quick to see. Young people had seen Weygand imprisoned by the Germans and Giraud, de Lattre de Tassigny, even Darlan (the latter more by a conjuncture of circumstances than by volition) pass over to the Allied camp. Some of their immediate leaders had emulated them: Borotra, who had however been caught, de Segonzac, de Tournemire. They must also have realized the significance of de La Porte du Theil's deportation. The progression of their leaders from neutralism to active anti-German sentiments – if not always to being pro-Allied – was patent. Moreover, first in London, then Algiers, and finally in France itself, the voice of armed resistance increasingly impinged upon their consciousness. Example was infectious.

Until the departure of Lamirand, however, the SGJ aligned itself with Pétain, although orthodoxy fought a hard battle with such men as Pelorson and Bonnard. In any case the 'doctrine' that the SGJ put out was ill-defined; hence its many interpretations. It relied too much on precept, too little on practice. An ounce of pragmatism would have been worth a pound of theory, and 'primum vivere, deinde philosophari' might have been a more fitting maxim. Too many of the ideas floated were redolent of the boy-scout mentality or a milksop view of youth entirely inappropriate for the most ruthless war being waged. The collaborationists scoffed not only at the SGJ, but also at the Compagnons and the Chantiers movements which likewise exhibited a certain simple-mindedness. Apart from Uriage, which had its own originality, there was the lack of any intellectual component to the Révolution Nationale, save for slogans. Even the cult of physical fitness was carried to extremes. The military men doubtless saw in it an instrument for the training of the will. But physical prowess and brute strength were no substitute in a total war for tanks, heavy artillery, bombers, and fighter planes. Moreover, there was too much 'caporalisme', too much deference to the hierarchical principle; despite de La Porte du Theil's encouragement of initiative, too little was done to foster this spirit. Instead there was an insistence on obedience and discipline, which, in the circumstances gave rise to much heart-searching among the more thoughtful. Young people noted that not a single leader, not even Mounier, had a good word to say for democracy. The cult of 'leadership', appropriate in an army from which the democratic principle is excluded, was eventually rejected by young people. Inevitably they broke free and eventually even discarded their loyalty to Pétain, which had constantly been dinned into them as being the touchstone of patriotism. As between conscience and submission to a somewhat dubious lawful authority, ultimately conscience prevailed, as youth saw injustice heaped upon injustice.

The SGJ sought swift action and quick results in its policy towards youth, but unfortunately these were not forthcoming.

Even the most idealistic at Vichy, after the first flush of enthusiasm, realized by the spring of 1942 that change was not easy to accomplish. Youth was in the process of being 'corrupted' by the material conditions of war, as were its elders – cheating the Germans, for example, became almost a form of patriotism. Circumstances, one of which was the continual presence of the Occupation troops, who made their own demands, engendered a different view of moral standards than that given out by the SGJ or the Church. With the invasion of the southern zone the vestigial belief in the possibility of 'reforming' French youth faded. The hardships of total war, bombing, food shortages, and forced labour dominated the lives of young people. Those that could react did so by joining the Resistance or leaving France to join de Gaulle. A small minority indulged in the counter-culture of an extravagant life-style which mocked their mentors. The idealists, with their jejune moral precepts and hurrah-patriotism, had failed. It was the turn now of the opportunists, men like Bonnard whose personal commitment could only be justified by a German victory, however impossible that appeared. The Révolution Nationale had turned sour.

Whereas the school continued to function with a surprising degree of effectiveness in the circumstances – Carcopino had accepted that Rome could not be built in a day and had initiated a policy of gradualism – the mechanisms for controlling the youth organizations did not run so smoothly. The SGJ was amateurish in its methods; the criticism of the Paris press was not unjustified. It did not succeed in imposing one 'doctrine' on a plurality of movements. It could not be otherwise when the most effective youth enterprises, such as those directed by de La Porte du Theil and Dunoyer de Segonzac, were run as independent fiefdoms, as indeed was the special domain of sport and 'general education' that Borotra had carved out. Catholic youth movements kept their distance from the SGJ, accepting subsidies but maintaining a strict autonomy. The collaborationist youth movements demanded subsidies but bit the hand that fed them. In any case the SGJ was very vulnerable. Constant squabbling went on within its ranks; its own internal structures were not definitively fixed until the beginning of 1942; it was not its own master but subject to the ministry of education; there was a disunity regarding fundamentals that manifested itself all too frequently. All these factors militated against the success of what was one of the most ambitious innovations of the Vichy regime.

The only 'doctrine' that could satisfy the collaborationists was a totalitarian one, mainly the neo-Nazism of Déat (to which was joined his neo-Socialism) but also a neo-Fascism on the Italian model, particularly after the renaissance of Bucard's Francistes. Under the cloak of 'Europeanism' the collaborationists advocated the submission of youth to the German will. The socialist component in collaborationism was also important because, when linked to extreme nationalism, it resembled Nazism like a brother. It had also significant educational overtones regarding equality, which were never worked out; Carcopino's measures were dismissed as an inadequate sop to equality of opportunity. This also accounts for Pelorson's view that the Chantiers must continue to exist because they brought about a compulsory social levelling of youth. To align France with the 'New Order' youth was a most valuable pawn in the game.

Another interest group consisted of the Germans. A constant throughout was their suspicion of young people, the movements to which they belonged, and their mentors, whether youth leaders or teachers. They wanted no 'regeneration' of French youth, whether physical, moral, or patriotic. They were opposed to a 'jeunesse unique', realizing how youth, monolithically organized under determined leaders, could be turned against them. They had memories of the French occupation of the Rhineland in the 1920s, when former German officers, covertly linked with the reduced forces of the Reichswehr, had constituted youth groups with the ultimate aim of resisting the occupying forces. The leading role played by military men in French youth organizations strengthened their deepest fears. The German aim was to keep youth divided and quiescent. Through Bonnard and Pelorson they wished to have men appointed, both in education and in the youth movements, who would obey their wishes. Part of the Germans' implacable hostility to the Church derived from the fact that Catholic youth organizations, more powerful than any created by Vichy, eluded their control.

That other interest group, the Church, at first pursued its ends with single-mindedness. In 1940 it thought its chance had come. It sought, and obtained, subsidies for its schools, and thus created a valuable precedent for later years. It sought, and failed, to reassert its influence over the education of all children. It sought, and had only partial success, to enforce its own strict moral code upon the young. Its youth organizations, a thorn in the German side, were one of the chief bulwarks against the installation of a 'jeunesse unique'. On the other hand, it can be maintained that the lead that the hierarchy gave to youth was insufficient. At a time when a social response was required to the wickedness of Hitlerism the Catholic was told to search his individual conscience. In education they belittled the ideals of 1789 and the achievements of the Republican school system. But the hierarchy is not the entire 'company of the faithful'. Among the rank-and-file Catholics many, such as the Jocistes in Germany or those in the Resistance, redeemed the errors of their bishops and pastors.

In the narrowly educational field, the effects of Vichy reforms – particularly those of Carcopino – were more enduring, although the impetus given before the war by Jean Zay must not be forgotten. However, the concept of education was enlarged from that of 'instruction' to an acknowledgement that it required the development of the whole man. There was a deliberate attempt to upgrade and generalize technical education as well. Such measures were not entirely unacceptable, for Vichyites, Gaullists, and the Resistance all realized the need for reform. There was also an equally unanimous acknowledgement that civic education had been unduly neglected. But in other domains, such as the teaching of history or the education of girls, Vichy efforts to put the clock back failed. Despite the propaganda of Bonnard, teachers, once they had recovered from the shock of being stigmatized as responsible for the defeat, continued to teach as they had always done. In the end the fabric of the education system was not permanently damaged by the war.

The Vichy regime, perhaps like all authoritarian institutions, was one of personalities. Some, like Bonnard, whom Pétain maintained in office from March 1942 until the Liberation, remain enigmas. Others, such as Lamirand were well-meaning, but did not realize fully how much circumstances were against them. The military leaders of youth (if this is a legitimate classification) reacted in the only way they knew. There were as many responses to the situation as there were leaders. This accounts for the complexity and diversity of the Vichy phenomenon. In the end, however, their lasting effect upon French youth was negligible. Despite the extreme pressures at the end of the war, the majority of young people, like the majority of their mentors and counsellors, were not converted to the German camp. From passive acceptance of their lot they passed to passive resistance and finally, for many, to active resistance.

Appendix I

The Student Demonstration of Armistice Day, 1940

The demonstration by students and pupils in Paris on Armistice Day 1940 has been described by many authors, a few of whom are listed below. So far as is known, however, no official German account has ever been published. The account which follows is taken from AN AJ 40.565 – Angelegenheiten der Akademien – Generalakte. File: Beiakte zu VKult. 421: Demonstrationen am 11. November 1940. The subsequent unrest at Dijon is described in AN AJ.40.563. Allg. Angelegenheiten d.frz.Bildungswesens – Sammelakten – Bd. I.

The German records, which were compiled by the Gruppe 'Kultur und Schule' attached to the German High Command in Paris, state that a German order of 29.10.40 forbade all demonstrations or ceremonies whatsoever on November 11, 1940. Tension was already building up beforehand. Pupils of the Lycée Louis-le-Grand had been shouting insults at German soldiers as they passed by in lorries. Minor outbursts had occurred in Paris cinemas. Finally, on Armistice Day itself a German medical student – a soldier – arrived at the École de Médicine to find that classes had been cancelled and that an atmosphere of excitement prevailed. 'Vive de Gaulle' had been written on a blackboard.

During the morning ten students – the word seems to be used to describe both school pupils and students – were arrested. In the afternoon the French police removed from the Clémenceau memorial on the Champs-Élysées a number of bunches of flowers bedecked with tricolour ribbons. By about 5 p.m., when afternoon school was over, both pupils and students were roaming the streets. A crowd of young people estimated at between 500–1,000 found their way to the Arc de Triomphe blocked by the French police. The Geheimfeldpolizei (the German military security police) decided that German military assistance was required. A detachment of German infantry was sent and tried to disperse the crowd into the side-streets leading off the Champs-Élysées. A Frenchman fired a shot. A German lieutenant gave the order to fire back and four Frenchmen were wounded. Members of the Paris unit of the Propaganda-Staffel emerged from a building they occupied on the Champs-Élysées and made a number of arrests. By 6 p.m. the demonstration was over. It had lasted only an hour.

It would appear that the German military security police did not even know that the French police had received special instructions on how to deal with any demonstrations that might occur. Their head claimed that the French police were to blame for not having acted earlier and more energetically. On the other hand the head of the German military administration for Paris (Chef des Militärverwaltungsbezirks) thought that the Germans should not have interfered because the French police could have dealt with the situation. A political evaluation of the incident by the Germans was that the average Frenchman considered the action of the young people irresponsible – some even boxed their ears: 'horror and consternation' ('Entsetzen und Bestürzung') were the typical reaction. The population at large feared that reprisals would be taken; the university feared not only reprisals against the students, which were to be expected, but also against educational institutions.

By November 13, 1940 some sixty-three 'Hochschulen' (the Germans used the word not only to describe the 'grandes écoles' but also other institutions of higher education) had been closed. By November 17 the five university faculties had been shut down, as well as twenty-four other 'Hochschulen'. There were 143 people under arrest: 19 students, 93 pupils (this probably included pupils of student age preparing for the 'grandes écoles' in *lycée* classes), and 31 people drawn from a wide variety of occupations. School pupils had all been warned by their teachers not to demonstrate. Only one teacher, René Baudouin, a science teacher at the Lyceé Lakanal, had been arrested. Demonstrations were also feared for November 21 – a Thursday, when pupils did not attend school, and a large number of preventive arrests were made on that day, mainly of students and pupils aged between fifteen and twenty-one. Only one arrest was confirmed; the rest of the young people were released between 10 p.m. and 11 p.m. (Report of Paris Police to the Chef des Militärverwaltungsbezirks, Paris, 22.11.40.) On November 30 the German High Command decided that all young people under eighteen could be released; the fortnight they had spent in prison was sufficient punishment. Some of the others might face a German court-martial or spend two months in a work camp set up specially for them. (Later the Germans decided that two school pupils, Guy Le Bras and Paul Jean Laurent, should be tried for having distributed anti-German tracts. Baudouin, the teacher, should also go on trial because, although he had not actually demonstrated, he had declared his intention of doing so. Also due to appear before a court-martial were Gérard Huet, an actor, because he had stirred up others, and a mason, Ménand, because he had resisted arrest.) It was also agreed, although the decision was not made known to the French at the time, that educational institutions should be allowed to reopen on January 1, 1941, and the French authorities would be notified that any further manifestations would be met with Draconian measures.

On December 2, 1940 the Germans granted Carcopino, then acting rector of Paris, an interview. He was accompanied by two inspectors general, Lavelle and Roy, who acted as interpreters. Carcopino stated that on the list of arrests he had received there were only nineteen students from the 'grandes écoles' ('Hochschüler') and consequently the closure of these was bitterly resented ('sehr bitter empfunden'). He had also taken the opportunity at the interview of asking for the release of Langevin, the scientist, whom he described as a dreamer ('Phantast'). Although he (Carcopino) had never shared Langevin's (Communist) views, he was aged sixty-nine, enjoyed an international reputation, and, if the Germans released him, the minister of education proposed to dismiss him.

A letter signed personally by Abetz (German Embassy, Paris, 6.12.40.) to von Stülpnagel urged that when the ban on the reopening of French educational institutions was lifted the Germans should demand the dismissal of all Jewish teachers in higher education and of any others who in the past had been 'outspokenly anti-German'. This demand of Abetz was not followed up, although the Germans did ask for the 'loyal enforcement' of the anti-Semitic laws. They were particularly worried by the fact that Jews taught at the École des Sciences Politiques, where they could exert political influence.

All educational institutions were eventually allowed to reopen on December 20, but since this meant that they would close again practically immediately until the New Year, the advancement of the date from January 1 (which the Germans had already decided upon) meant that there was little change in practice. On December 23 the obligation that had been imposed on students living in the Paris area to report daily to the police was lifted. The Germans were allegedly warned by ex-servicemen's associations that another student demonstration was planned to take place over Christmas and the New Year, when the Germans would be off their guard. This came to nothing.

The charge against Huet, the actor, was dropped. Other names cropped up in the charges. An architect, Schoelcher, was first accused of attacking a German soldier, a charge that would carry the death penalty, but was plainly later charged with a lesser offence, because he received a one-year prison sentence only. Raynoldy, a mechanic, and Thibouville, a hotel worker, were at first accused of jeering at German soldiers, a minor offence, but it is not clear whether they were ever tried. On the other hand, two girl students, Mlles Tager and Mottini, each got three months' jail, Le Bras and Laurent six months each, Baudouin, the teacher, one year, and the unfortunate mason, Ménand (his name is also spelt Menant), three years. Carcopino had intervened before the trial on Baudouin's behalf, alleging that the teacher was a depressive neurasthenic, subject to fits of extreme agitation, and that the minister had already dismissed him. After the sentence had been passed on Baudouin Carcopino again put in a plea for clemency for him, on grounds of ill health.

The 'Lageberichte' ('situation reports') of the Gruppe Kultur und Schule attached to the German High Command report that after the closure of the University of Paris, some of its students had returned home to Dijon and had caused trouble there, so that the University of Dijon had also been closed ('Lagebericht' of 18–24.11.40.) A later report recognized that the disturbances at Dijon had not been directed against the Germans, but at Clémenti's Parti Français National-collectiviste, outside whose headquarters in Dijon the students had demonstrated. It is not stated whether the students who took part were from Paris or Dijon.

Reference is made to the incidents of Armistice Day, 1940, their origins and consequences, in the following:

Aragon *(Le Témoin des martyrs), Témoignages. Le Crime contre l'esprit.* Éditions de Minuit, 1944. (First published clandestinely), 10–12.

R. Langeron, *Paris, juin '40,* 1946, 181–97. (The account of the former Prefect of Police.)

J. Guéhenno, *Journal des années noires, 1940–1944,* 1947, 54.

J. Carcopino, *Souvenirs de sept ans, 1937–1944,* 1953, 198–226.

Vice-Admiral Fernet, *Aux côtés du Maréchal Pétain. Souvenirs, 1940–1944,* 1953, 89.

Robert Aron, *Histoire de Vichy,* 1954, 70–1. (Unreliable on this matter.)

P. Bourget and C. Lacretelle, *Sur les murs de Paris, 1940–44,* 1959, 38–40.

F. Grenier, *C'était ainsi,* 1959, 99–100. (Unreliable. Grenier, like the BBC French service in 1940, claims that some students were killed.)

A. Voguet, 'Souvenirs de l'année universitaire, 1940–1941', *La Pensée,* 89, January–February 1960, 23–4.

R. Josse, 'La naissance de la résistance étudiante à Paris et la manifestation du 11 novembre 1940', *Revue d'histoire de la Deuxième Guerre Mondiale,* 47, July 1962, 8–29. (The most reliable account.)

P. Bourget, *Histoires secrètes de l'Occupation,* T.i., Le Joug, 1970, 218–35.

Vercors (Jean Bruller), *La Bataille du silence.* Souvenirs de Minuit, 1967, 150.

Freda Knight, *The French Resistance,* London, 1975, 70–1.

Official reference is made in:

La Délégation française auprès de la commission allemande d'Armistice, Vol. ii, 1950, 446–8.

The following relevant documents are held at the Comité d'histoire de la Deuxième Guerre Mondiale, Paris:

Circular of rector of Paris to *lycée* head teachers, 14.11.40

Circular of Carcopino, rector *ad interim,* to *lycée* head teachers, 14.11.40. (*sic*).

Circular of Carcopino, rector *ad interim,* to *lycée* head teachers, 19.11.40.

Discours de distribution des prix, Lycée Voltaire, Paris, July 1945.

Appendix II

The Growth of Catholic Education

The table below shows the percentage increase in pupils in private elementary education between December 1, 1939 and December 1, 1943. It therefore shows the gain in numbers of pupils, expressed as a percentage, in private elementary schools, which were mainly Catholic, as between the first year of the war, when subsidies were not paid and the last academic year of the Occupation in which subsidies were paid.

The table has been calculated from statistics of pupil numbers given in: *France. Annuaire statistique,* Vol. 56, *1940–1945,* Paris, 1946, 44 and 45. The statistics relate to the first day of December in each year.

For the Ille-et-Vilaine identical figures were shown for 1942 and 1943. This may be due to a clerical or printer's error. Owing to the Allied invasion of Corsica, figures for 1943 were not available. No statistics were available either for the three annexed departments of the Moselle, the Bas-Rhin, and the Haut-Rhin. For the Vosges the figures for 1943 were also not available.

In all the eighty-seven departments where full or partial figures were available, an increase was shown, *with the exception of the Somme,* where a slight decrease was shown.

Percentage of pupils in private elementary education by department

Department	1939	1940	1941	1942	1943	Increase: 1939–43
1. Ain	14.0	13.0	14.1	14.6	15.3	1.3
2. Aisne	2.6	2.5	3.6	4.2	4.4	1.8
3. Allier	8.6	8.9	10.7	11.1	11.1	2.5
4. Alpes (Basses)	5.3	6.1	6.5	7.9	7.9	2.6
5. Alpes (Hautes)	5.5	5.5	6.2	8.0	8.6	3.1
6. Alpes-Maritimes	8.8	9.4	11.4	13.6	13.7	4.9
7. Ardèche	41.7	42.4	44.7	46.5	48.0	6.3
8. Ardennes	1.9	n.a	4.0	4.9	5.3	3.4
9. Ariège	8.2	7.8	8.8	8.1	9.0	0.8
10. Aube	4.4	5.1	7.2	7.5	6.8	2.4
11. Aude	5.6	5.4	6.5	7.3	8.0	2.4
12. Aveyron	35.5	36.7	39.3	40.9	42.8	7.3
13. Belfort	7.7	8.6	9.6	11.0	11.3	3.6
14. Bouches-du-Rhône	10.9	11.5	14.5	16.4	19.5	8.6
15. Calvados	13.3	12.8	14.0	14.9	15.7	2.4
16. Cantal	16.7	15.8	16.9	18.0	19.2	2.5
17. Charente	7.8	6.8	7.6	7.9	8.1	0.3
18. Charente-Maritime	5.5	6.1	7.3	7.5	7.2	1.7
19. Cher	6.2	7.0	7.4	6.3	10.1	3.9

Department	1939	1940	1941	1942	1943	Increase: 1939–43
20. Corrèze	8.7	9.5	9.3	10.4	10.6	1.9
21. Corse	2.9	2.6	2.9	3.1	n.a	0.2 (1939–42)
22. Côte-d'Or	5.9	6.0	6.8	6.7	6.9	1.0
23. Côtes-du-Nord	34.7	34.7	39.5	38.4	41.4	6.7
24. Creuse	2.7	2.9	3.3	4.5	4.3	1.6
25. Dordogne	6.0	6.6	7.3	8.2	9.2	3.2
26. Doubs	9.6	9.6	9.6	11.1	11.6	2.0
27. Drôme	14.1	14.9	16.3	18.0	18.0	3.9
28. Eure	10.1	8.7	10.2	10.8	10.9	0.8
29. Eure-et-Loir	8.7	7.8	9.6	10.3	12.2	3.5
30. Finistère	40.2	41.5	46.5	48.0	49.1	8.9
31. Gard	18.3	19.3	20.5	22.1	23.3	5.0
32. Garonne (Haute)	10.4	11.5	11.9	14.3	15.2	4.8
33. Gers	8.5	8.8	10.3	10.2	9.4	0.9
34. Gironde	9.9	10.4	11.2	12.5	14.6	4.7
35. Hérault	14.3	14.7	15.1	19.2	21.6	7.3
36. Ille-et-Vilaine	56.3	58.7	60.7	62.3	62.3	6.0
37. Indre	8.4	7.2	9.6	9.5	11.1	2.7
38. Indre-et-Loire	14.6	13.9	13.4	17.6	18.6	4.0
39. Isère	15.0	15.7	17.0	18.2	18.3	3.3
40. Jura	9.3	9.2	9.8	10.6	10.4	1.1
41. Landes	8.4	7.8	8.7	9.9	10.0	1.6
42. Loir-et-Cher	12.9	12.4	13.0	13.5	14.2	1.3
43. Loire	32.2	n.a	34.6	35.9	38.0	5.8
44. Loire (Haute)	34.4	27.8	44.3	41.8	42.2	7.8
45. Loire-Inférieure	52.4	54.2	57.8	62.1	71.1	18.7
46. Loiret	12.3	13.2	12.6	14.1	14.4	2.1
47. Lot	14.0	14.4	15.7	16.3	16.9	2.9
48. Lot-et-Garonne	11.0	11.8	12.9	13.7	14.6	3.6
49. Lozère	31.3	31.5	33.0	35.7	37.1	5.8
50. Maine-et-Loire	54.6	56.8	58.6	60.2	60.2	5.6
51. Manche	15.4	14.8	16.6	18.1	17.8	2.4
52. Marne	8.8	9.7	12.1	13.2	13.2	4.4
53. Marne (Haute)	6.6	6.2	7.7	8.6	8.2	1.6
54. Mayenne	42.4	42.8	44.4	46.9	46.6	4.2
55. Meurthe-et-Moselle	6.5	6.6	8.3	9.2	8.8	2.3
56. Meuse	4.2	3.8	5.9	6.4	5.7	1.5
57. Morbihan	56.8	59.1	62.3	65.1	68.3	11.5
58. Moselle	n.a	n.a	n.a	n.a	n.a	n.a
59. Nièvre	9.6	10.8	12.0	12.8	12.7	3.1
60. Nord	20.8	22.0	24.1	25.2	28.3	7.5
61. Oise	5.6	4.7	5.9	6.4	7.2	1.6
62. Orne	19.3	19.5	20.4	21.5	22.2	2.9
63. Pas-de-Calais	21.6	20.2	22.2	23.2	22.5	0.9
64. Puy-de-Dôme	23.1	23.4	25.8	27.3	27.5	4.4
65. Pyrénées(Basses)	16.5	n.a	17.5	20.7	20.8	4.3
66. Pyrénées (Hautes)	10.8	12.5	14.0	14.0	16.8	6.0
67. Pyrénées-Orientales	4.4	4.7	4.8	6.1	8.2	3.8
68. Rhin (Bas)	n.a	n.a	n.a	n.a	n.a	n.a
69. Rhin (Haut)	n.a	n.a	n.a	n.a	n.a	n.a
70. Rhône	23.7	26.5	28.2	30.3	34.7	11.0
71. Saône (Haute)	5.0	5.2	7.2	8.1	8.2	3.2

Department	1939	1940	1941	1942	1943	Increase: 1939–43
72. Saône-et-Loire	16.4	16.6	17.8	19.6	18.1	1.7
73. Sarthe	18.8	18.4	19.3	19.9	20.1	1.3
74. Savoie	9.0	10.0	10.7	12.9	11.0	2.0
75. Savoie (Haute)	14.6	14.9	21.0	18.6	18.5	3.9
76. Seine	9.8	8.1	13.4	16.6	20.3	10.5
77. Seine-Inférieure	9.7	9.7	11.3	12.6	13.7	4.0
78. Seine-et-Marne	5.8	4.4	5.6	7.4	8.3	2.5
79. Seine-et-Oise	8.1	8.3	10.4	12.6	14.7	6.6
80. Sèvres (Deux)	24.5	24.0	27.0	28.3	28.7	4.2
81. Somme	5.6	3.7	4.9	5.5	5.3	–0.3 (Decrease)
82. Tarn	22.7	23.9	25.0	26.1	27.7	5.0
83. Tarn-et-Garonne	18.1	18.7	19.1	23.6	24.5	6.4
84. Var	6.0	6.6	7.3	6.4	7.8	.2.8
85. Vaucluse	17.0	17.5	18.2	19.6	20.6	3.6
86. Vendée	57.8	56.1	59.5	62.3	62.4	4.6
87. Vienne	14.6	14.4	19.8	16.4	17.1	2.5
88. Vienne (Haute)	8.0	8.4	9.6	11.0	11.7	3.7
89. Vosges	9.6	8.7	11.5	10.8	n.a	1.2 (1939–42)
90. Yonne	6.6	6.1	7.0	6.7	8.2	1.6
Totals (87 Departments)	17.7	18.4	19.9	21.3	22.6	4.9

Bibliographical Note

I. *Unpublished sources*

The official archives of the Vichy regime remain closed to researchers. However, the writer obtained special permission to consult some seventy boxes of archival material at the Archives Nationales. These comprised the following:

(1) *Papers coming from the 'cabinet' of Abel Bonnard*

F.17. 13336 General papers.
F. 17. 13337 to 13341 Personal activities of the minister.
F.17. 13342 Minister's correspondence, 1942.
F.17. 13343 Notes of Mouraille, 'chef du cabinet'; and correspondence, 1942.
F.17. 13344 Correspondence of Neret, personal secretary of the minister, 1942. A–R.
F.17. 13345 Ibid. S–Z.
F.17. 13346 to 13349 Minister's correspondence, 1943–4.
F.17. 13350 to 13352 Correspondence of Georges and Neret, 1943–4.
F.17. 13353 and 13354 Various correspondence.
F.17. 13356 and 13357 Correspondence and other papers relating to education.
F.17. 13363 Secondary education.
F.17. 13364 Primary education.
F.17. 13365 Technical education; private education.
F.17. 13366 and 13367 General commissariat for youth [1944].

(2) *Papers of M. Roy* [Inspector general attached to de Brinon's staff]

F.17. 13373 Memoranda and general instructions, October 1940 – July 1944. Correspondence 1941–3 of the Délégation Générale. Correspondence, September 1940 – July 1944, with German High Command, Paris.
F.17. 13375 Circulars to prefects, rectors, etc.
F.17. 13376 Monthly reports of prefects (extracts): September 1941–March 1942.
F.17. 13377 Reports of educational institutions, April 1941–December 1943. Monthly reports for the Délégation Générale, April 1941–May 1943.
F.17. 13378 School textbooks.
F.17. 13379 Alsace affairs: Kraft files (1940–1); correspondence (1940–4).
F.17. 13380 Various matters.

F.17. 13381 Various matters, including General Commissariat for Sport: correspondence, 1941–4; reports to the minister, 1943–4.
F.17. 13382 and 13383 STO. Students.
F.17. 13390 Liaison with private education. Teachers' unions, 1942–4.

(3) *Inventory of the Archives of the 'Cabinet' of the Head of State*

AG II 14 PP 13 Personal papers of Marshal Pétain.
AG II 27 SG 7 Archives of the Secretariat-General.
AG II 75 SP 2 Archives of Ménétrel: Letters from Bonnard, Vichy, 1941; Borotra, n.p., 1942 (?); Carcopino, Vichy, 1941; Chevalier, Cérilly, 1943; Delage, Vichy, 1943; Guerry, Cambrai, 1942.
AG II 76 SP 3 Archives of Ménétrel: Letters from Roussy, Paris, n.d.; Tournemire, n.p., 1943.
AG II 78 SP 5 Archives of Ménétrel: various medical matters, including some concerning education.
AG II 79 SP 6 Archives of Ménétrel: 'Dossiers intéressants: Dr Bernard Ménétrel'. Youth matters and organization of SGJ.
AG II 80 SP 7 Archives of Ménétrel: 'Dossiers intéressants: Dr Bernard Ménétrel'. Documents on 'éducation générale'; on the Révolution Nationale, by Pelorson.
AG II 81 SP 8 Archives of Goudard [primary teacher attached to the Private Secretariat headed by Ménétrel]. One file on STO.
AG II 440 CC 3 Archives of 'cabinet civil'. File on 'Jeunesse'.
AG II 459 CC 34 do. File entitled: 'Transmissions No. 2' on education, Chantiers de la Jeunesse, sport, and youth.
AG II 461 CC 36 Archives of 'cabinet civil'. File entitled 'Intérieur, no. 2': A: STO.
AG II 495 CC 78 Archives of 'cabinet civil'. File entitled: 'Éducation nationale'.
AG II 497 CC 79 Archives of 'cabinet civil'. Youth—family—health.
AG II 542 CC 139 Archives of 'cabinet civil'. Jardel file.
AG II 543 CC 141 Archives of 'cabinet civil'. Various matters.
AG II 570 CC 175 Archives of 'cabinet civil'. Education and youth.
AG II 604 CM 18 Archives of 'cabinet militaire'. File on Légion des Combattants. G: 'Jeune Légion'.
AG II 607 CM 21 Archives of 'cabinet militaire'. Various matters.
AG II 609 CM 25 Archives of 'cabinet militaire'. File of Commandant Féat.
AG II 613 CM 30 Archives of 'cabinet militaire'. Féat—Pétain file.

(4) *Inventory of the Archives of the Conseil National (Dossier 'Admiral Darlan')*

AG II 650	'Huitième Commission du Conseil National: étude des questions de jeunesse, session du 5 au 12 mars 1942.'
AG II 654	Files entitled: 'Archives. Documents': 304 'Éducation Nationale'. 308 'Jeunesse'.
AG II 659	Documentation of the general secretariat of the Head of State. 117 Sports.

(5) *Chantiers de la Jeunesse*

AJ 39 1	General documents.
AJ 39 49	Correspondence with the ministry; relations with the army.
AJ 39 77	State of mind and morale of the Chantiers, November 1940 – October 1943.
AJ 39 108	Situation of Alsace-Lorrainers, September 1940.
AJ 39 128	General situation, April–December 1941.
AJ 39 129	Ibid. January–June 1942.
AJ 39 130	Ibid. July–November 1942.
AJ 39 131	Ibid. December 1942–November 1943.
AJ 39 135	Meetings of regional commissioners.
AJ 39 174	The Chantiers de la Jeunesse and the STO.
AJ 39 175	Ibid. (cont.)
AJ 39 177	Various matters, including the 'events of 19.11.42 and their consequences for the Chantiers'.
AJ 39 179	Various documents concerning the disbandment of the Chantiers before the Liberation.
AJ 39 276	Various documents.

(6) *German documents* (German references follow each entry)

AJ 40 555	Gruppe Kultur und Schule: VKult 400 K1; V400K1; V400K2.
AJ 40 556	Appointments: 400K2; STO, December 1942–July 1944: 402 AK3.
AJ 40 557	SGJ, 1940–4, K4 16; Chantiers de la Jeunesse, 1942–4, 403 ChK 4 15; Commissariat aux Sports, 1940–May 1941, 404/1 K4 17; General Observations on political behaviour of students and university professors, November 1940–December 1943, 405 K4 21.
AJ 40 558	Report on school books, 1944, K126; Censorship of school books: Liste Otto, K.127.
AJ 40 559	Censorship of school books, 407B K6 27.
AJ 40 560	Ibid. I–Z, 1940–4, K9 29.

AJ 40 563	Various matters, 1940–4, 409 K40; Report on activity of Gruppe 4, 410K 41; Reform of education 1941–2, 411/I K 43.
AJ 40 565	General observations on the 'académies', 1940, 420 K57; teaching of German in the Channel Islands (February–October 1943), 420 A K58; academic affairs in the territories newly occupied (December 1943–July 1944), 420 N K59; various matters concerning the 'académie' of Paris (August 1940–December 1942), 421 K51; demonstration and manifestation of 11.11.40, 421/463 K90.
AJ 40 566	Various matters.
AJ 40 567	Organization of French students.
AJ 40 568	'Grandes écoles' not controlled by the ministry of education.

At the Archives Départmentales du Nord, Lille, the writer was also given special permission to consult eighty-five smaller packages of documents provisionally classified under the series R (Guerre, 1939–45).

He was also allowed to consult, without special permission, a limited number of original documents, a number of printed official documents, such as the local Bulletin de l'enseignement primaire and instructions to mayors from the prefects, as well as a number of printed ephemeral documents of the Vichy period at the following Archives Départementales:

Ardèche (Privas); Bouches-du-Rhône (Marseilles); Calvados (Caen); Drôme (Valence); Hautes-Alpes (Gap); Haute-Marne (Chaumont); Jura (Lons-le-Saunier); Maine-et-Loire (Angers); Morbihan (Vannes); Somme (Amiens); Vaucluse (Avignon).

Original documents were also available for consultation at the Bibliothèque Emmanuel Mounier and the Centre de Documentation Juive Contemporaine, Paris.

A number of oral testimonies were also collected, in particular one from a former primary-school teacher and a local historian, M. Fernand Guériff, of Saint-Nazaire.

The Comité d'histoire de la Deuxième Guerre Mondiale, Paris, also made available a number of unpublished oral testimonies, as well as a wealth of typescript or roneoed sources.

II *Published sources*

It would be otiose to list the books and articles mentioned in the notes to each chapter. At present there is no publication that deals exclusively with education and youth during the Vichy period. For a running bibliography the general reader is advised to consult the general list that appears in successive numbers of the *Revue d'histoire de la Deuxième Guerre Mondiale.* A special number of that review, No. 56 (October 1964), entitled 'Vichy et la Jeunesse', gives an excellent general conspectus. Other relevant articles have also appeared from time to time.

Among official sources the *Journal officiel* is indispensable, as is also the *Gazette du palais* for the period of the Occupation. The papers of the French delegation to the Armistice Commission, published as: *Délégation française auprès de la Commission allemande d'Armistice. Recueil de documents publié par le gouvernement français,* 5 vols., 1947–59, has a certain amount concerning youth movements. The trials of Pétain *(Le Procès du Maréchal Pétain. Compte-rendu sténographique,* 2 vols., 1945) and of Bonnard and Chevalier (available in part in roneoed form only) also give useful information.

Both Chevalier and Bonnard have published articles in *Ecrits de Paris* (J. Chevalier, 'Un témoignage direct sur deux points d'histoire', 19.7.53, 83–7, and A. Bonnard, 'Témoignage', May 1960, 22–9.) But the monumental work by Jérôme Carcopino, *Souvenirs de sept ans, 1937–1944,* 1953, although really to be classed as memoirs, is indispensable.

Other useful memoirs are: J. Zay, *Souvenirs et solitude,* 1945; J. Guéhenno, *Journal des années noires (1940–1944);* L. Planté, *'Au 110 Rue de Grenelle': souvenirs, scènes, et aspects du ministère de l'Instruction publique – Éducation nationale, 1920–1944,* 1967; and Micheline Bood, *Les Années doubles. Journal d'une lycéenne sous l'Occupation,* 1974. Whilst these relate directly to education and youth, other memoirs contain many valuable references.

The flavour of the period as regards education and youth can be discerned in such works as: S. Jeanneret, *La Vérité sur les instituteurs,* Paris, 1942; H. Bourgin, *L'École nationale,* Paris, 1942; G. Bertier, *Une mystique pour les jeunes Français,* Toulouse–Paris, 1944. The many journals (such as: *Jeunesse . . . Organe de la génération 40,* or: *Cahiers de notre jeunesse,* to name two extremes), political pamphlets, and brochures of many kinds that were published relating to youth, likewise convey the atmosphere of the times.

Among general books the following may be mentioned: Fondation Nationale des Sciences Politiques, *Le Gouvernement de Vichy, 1940–1942,* 1972, which contains a paper by Aline Coutrot, 'Quelques aspects de la politique de la jeunesse', 265–84; Robert Aron, *Histoire de Vichy, 1940–1944,* 1953; J. Duquesne, *Les Catholiques français sous l'Occupation,* 1966; R. Griffiths, *Marshal Pétain,* London, 1970; Mgr Guerry, *L'Église catholique en France sous l'Occupation,* 1947; Hoover Institute, *La Vie de la France sous l'Occupation, 1940–1944,* 3 vols., 1957; R. O. Paxton, *Vichy France: Old Guard and New Order,* New York, 1972; P. Arnoult *et al., La France sous l'Occupation,* 1959, which contains a paper by A. Rosier, 'L'Université et la Révolution Nationale'.

The writer also consulted the following national and local newspapers, not all of which were published throughout the Occupation: *Action française; Cherbourg-Eclair* (Cherbourg); *La Croix; Le Phare* (Nantes); *Le Figaro; Le Progrès de la Somme* (Amiens); *Le Temps,* as well as odd numbers of a few others.

Notes

I. NEW BEGINNINGS

1. Quoted in J. Vidalenc, *L'Exode de mai–juin 1940,* 1957, 381.
2. H. Amouroux, *La Grande Histoire des Français sous l'Occupation,* Vol. i., *Le Peuple du désastre, 1939–1940,* 1976, 398–401. Amouroux cites a number of pathetic cases of missing children. For a realistic description of the 'exodus' cf. the flight of Sarah and her child Pablo in: J.-P. Sartre, *La Mort dans l'âme,* 1949 (Livre de Poche), 17–30.
3. Vidalenc, op. cit. 34.
4. Ibid. 183.
5. H. Becquart, *Au temps du silence. De Bordeaux à Vichy,* Paris, 1945, 15.
6. AD du Nord, Lille, R.1052 – Enseignement. The small number of students that arrived at Le Touquet stayed there until the end of June. Cf. Letter from the acting rector, the dean of the law faculty, to the Prefect of the Nord, Le Touquet, June 15, 1940.
7. In 1940 the present writer received a letter from a medical student, a girl of nineteen, who normally lived in Lille. Her case is perhaps typical of the disarray and confusion that reigned. She had taken flight with her mother, a widow of the First World War. They reached Cosne-sur-Loire by car. She then went off to Dijon to take her medical examinations. The return journey to Cosne took two days by train. On Sunday, June 16 she wrote saying that she had had to leave Cosne the previous day because the bridges over the Loire were to be blown up. She interrupted her letter: 'Excusez-moi, je dois partir de *suite* – c'est urgent!' On Monday evening she resumed her letter-writting. They had run out of petrol and were as far as the department of Cher. She had just heard that Pétain had asked for an armistice:

   > 'We are desolate and in despair. I cannot tell you in a letter what I feel at this moment, nor the state of mind of our soldiers and of the inhabitants. I cannot succeed in realising our situation. It still seems to me that this capitulation is impossible. . . . Doubtless the English have made grave mistakes that France – alas! – is paying for at this moment. We too have committed some in recent years. It is the whole people which is suffering today in all that it holds most dear. This war is the story of a great betrayal against which the bravery of our valiant soldiers struggled in vain. What is going to become of us? . . . I am afraid. I do not want to fall under the German yoke and yet we are expecting them at any moment in the region where I now am.'

   The letter, from Anne-Marie D___, now a doctor, was finally sent from Dun-sur-Auron (Cher), postmarked June 17, 1940 and received by the present writer on August 9, 1940. One notes the theme of betrayal, presumably by the politicians of the Third Republic, the belief that France is paying for British errors, and the fear of German rule.
8. Vidalenc, op. cit. 252.
9. Ibid. 253.
10. Ibid. 239.

11. J.-P. Azéma, *De Munich à la Libération, 1938–1944,* 1979, 62.
12. M. Leblond, *Redressement,* n.d., n.p., 85, cited in: Vidalenc, op. cit. 364.
13. P.-H. Simon, *La France à la recherche d'une conscience,* n.d., n.p., 166–7, cited in: Vidalenc, op. cit. 365.
14. Col. Carles, 'La "Corniche" de Montpellier', 1939 à 1942, *RHDGM,* 112, October 1978, 16.
15. Becquart, op. cit. 260–1.
16. For information on the Cercle Fustel de Coulanges and for other background information I am greatly indebted to: J. A. D. Long, 'The French Right and Education: The Theory and Practice of Vichy Education Policy, 1940–1944', Unpublished D.Phil. thesis, Oxford, 1976.
17. Henri Boegner, a teacher from Mulhouse, must not be confused with Pastor Marc Boegner, the French Protestant leader whom Pétain appointed a member of the Conseil National, whose task was to draw up a new Constitution.
18. Henri Boegner had made the same point in his: *L'Éducation et l'idée de la Patrie,* 1936.
19. Cf. H. Amouroux, *Pétain avant Vichy,* 1967, 193–4. For a general conspectus on Pétain's ideas on youth and education, cf. also: R. Griffiths, *Marshal Pétain,* London, 1970, *passim.*
20. Gen. Neissel, 'Les Chantiers de la Jeunesse', *Revue des deux mondes,* December 15, 1941, 470.
21. F. Alengry, *Principes généraux de la philosophie sociale et politique du Maréchal Pétain,* Paris, 1943, 77–8.
22. T. Zeldin, *France 1848–1945,* Vol. i, *Ambition, Love and Politics,* Oxford, 1973, 564–5.
23. G. Miller, *Les Pousse-au-jouir du maréchal Pétain,* 1975, 85–6.
24. For a summary cf. O. Wormser, *Les Origines doctrinales de la 'Révolution Nationale', Vichy, 10 juillet 1940–31 mars 1941,* 1971, 112 et seq.
25. Pétain, *Paroles aux Français: Messages et écrits, 1934–1941,* Lyons, 1941, 7.
26. Ibid. 224.
27. Ibid. 226.
28. Ibid. 229.
29. Quoted in Paul (Admiral) Auphan, *Histoire élémentaire de Vichy,* 1971, 101.
30. Gen. Weygand, *Mémoires,* Vol. iii, 1950, 298–9.
31. 'Exposé des motifs' on the plan for reform of the Constitution, quoted in: *Les Questions actuelles. L'Enseignement en France (juillet 1940–octobre 1941),* Paris, n.d. [1942?], 7.
32. P. Baudouin, *Neuf mois au gouvernement: avril – décembre 1940,* 1948, 214–15. Renan's book, *La Réforme intellectuelle et morale,* appeared in 1871.
33. R. Gillouin, *J'étais l'ami du Marechal Pétain,* 1966, 22–3. In February 1934 Gillouin had demonstrated with the Nationalists. A talented man of letters, he wrote some of Pétain's early speeches. For a few hours or a few days – accounts vary – he was secretary-general in the ministry of education, a new post, but was dismissed by Ripert. Disliked by Laval as an alleged Anglophile and crypto-Gaullist, he had to flee to Switzerland in 1942.
34. H. R. Kedward, *Resistance in Vichy France,* Oxford, 1978, 197 et seq.
35. J.-P. Cointet, 'Marcel Déat et le parti unique (Été 1940)', *RHDGM,* 91, July 1973.

36. R. Silly and G. Albertini, *Pour sauver notre avenir,* Paris, 1943, 27.
37. For an analysis of the ideology of the Révolution Nationale cf. Robert Aron's essay, 'Qu'est-ce que le Pétainisme?' in his: *Dossiers de la Seconde Guerre Mondiale,* 1976, 157–169.
38. R. Descouens, *La Vie du Marechal Pétain racontée aux enfants de France,* Nice, 1941, quoted in: Azéma, op. cit. 104.
39. Jean-Noel Jeanneney (ed.), *Jules Jeanneney, Journal politique, septembre 1939–juillet 1942,* 1972, 469, n.168.
40. H. Cole, *Laval,* London, 1963, 125. Ménétrel was an extreme right winger, and very condemnatory of the Resistance. From November 1942 onwards, however, he also became very anti-German. Regulating access to Pétain, he 'manipulated' the Marshal.
41. Azéma, op. cit. 78. Cf. also: *La Croix,* 2.2.41 and 5.2.41.
42. *Le Temps,* February 21, 1941.
43. Ministerial instructions, December 7, 1940, quoted in: Bulletin départemental de l'instruction primaire, Académie d'Aix, Avignon, January 1941.
44. J. Guéhenno, *Aventures de l'esprit,* 1954, 173.
45. *La Croix,* November 18, 1941.
46. G. Pailhès, *Rouen et sa région pendant la guerre, 1939–1945,* Rouen, 1948, 109.
47. A. Fabre-Luce, *Journal de la France, 1939–1944,* Geneva, 1946, 389.
48. Paul (*sic*), 'La lettre au Maréchal', *L'Élan. Organe régional des jeunesses communistes de la Drôme,* Valence, 21, November 10, 1944.
49. Bulletin départemental de l'enseignement primaire, Hautes-Alpes (Gap), 2, 1941.
50. *Action française,* May 6, 1941.
51. *La Croix,* January 18, 1941.
52. AN F.17.13377 Rapports mensuels ayant servi à la rédaction du rapport général définitif de l'éducation nationale. Rapport mensuel no. 3 [March] 1941.
53. AN AJ 40 557 (German files). Note of May 12, 1941, 'An die Gruppe 8Vju im Hause' [i.e., to the Group, 'Kultur und Schule', Hotel Majestic, Paris].
54. The epithet is that of Raymond Aron, *De l'Armistice à l'insurrection nationale,* 1945, 37.
55. L. Planté, 'Au 110 Rue de Grenelle', *Souvenirs, 1920–1944,* 1967, 250–2.
56. Becquart, op. cit. 240–1.
57. This pleased the army. At the beginning of the century the war minister had enlisted freemasons to spy upon army officers, observing whether they went to mass and whether they sent their children to Catholic schools. The freemasons compiled their famous 'fiches de délation'. Cf. D. Brogan, *The Development of Modern France, 1870–1939,* London, revd. edition, 1967, 382.
58. Raymond Aron, op. cit. 37.
59. Quoted in: *Le Temps,* November 29, 1940.
60. For the German account of the Armistice Day (1940) student demonstration in Paris, cf. Appendix I.
61. Fabre-Luce, op. cit. 315.
62. H. du Moulin de Labarthète, *Le Temps des illusions. Souvenirs, juillet 1940–avril 1942,* Geneva, 1946, 68–9. The author was director of Pétain's 'cabinet civil' until the return to power of Laval in April 1942, when he went to Switzerland. An Inspecteur des Finances, he had tried unsuccessfully to enter Parliament as a right-wing candidate. Sacked by the Front

Populaire government in 1936, he had become, like Baudouin, a director of the Banque d'Indochine. When Pétain had been made ambassador to Madrid he had been appointed his financial attaché. A one-time protégé of Reynaud, he tended to back Pétain in any action where the Marshal resisted the Germans.

63. Robert Aron, *Histoire de Vichy,* 1954, 329.
64. *Le Procès du Maréchal Pétain, Compte-rendu sténographique,* 1945, Vol. i, 547.
65. Chevalier was taken up by Prof. Henry Miers, Waynflete Professor of Mineralogy at Oxford from 1895–1908. M. W. Porter, *The Diary of Henry Alexander Miers, 1858–1942,* Oxford, 1973, records (p. 16): 'A pupil rather out of the ordinary came to Sir Henry' and quotes from the professor's diary: 'Dec. 1903. Chevalier began to work in my laboratory this term. A young Frenchman at Oxford with a philosophical scholarship from Paris, he was studying religious movements in England (especially Wales just then); I took him to hear César Franck's music at the Musical Club. He wanted to know something about scientific work but could not get admission to any Laboratory in France or England because he had no grounding in Physics or Chemistry. I took him straight up to my laboratory to do *research* work. He worked with me for nearly two years, published 2 papers on crystallization. Later he became Professor of Philosophy at Grenoble and we always remained fast friends.'

    Marshal Pétain kept up friendly relations with Chevalier after his removal from the post of minister of education. Cf. AN AG II 459. Copy of a letter from Pétain to Chevalier, August 12, 1941. Chevalier, then minister for health and family, fell ill in the summer of 1941. He put in a medical certificate and asked for a month's leave. The Marshal, in a kindly worded letter which began, 'Mon cher ami', told him to take three months off and to give up his ministry, because he was obviously suffering from a year's overwork. They would meet at Cérilly, Chevalier's home, in November. Chevalier recuperated at Evian and then resumed his post at Grenoble.
66. Alain Darlan, *L'Amiral Darlan parle,* 1952, 281–2.
67. J. Berthelot, *Sur les rails du pouvoir (1938–1942),* 1968, 145.
68. J. Carcopino, *Souvenirs de sept ans (1937–1944),* 1953, 271.
69. CDJC, Paris, Carton CDXCV, Lagebericht (German military 'sitrep'), April 1941 and Carton LXXVIII, 90.
70. Marie Granet, *Le Journal 'Défense de la France',* 1961, 52.
71. The text of Carcopino's broadcast is given in: *L'Information universitaire,* March 22, 1941.
72. Long, op. cit. 195, quotes the *Journal officiel* for April 2, 1941 giving the outcome of this final 'purge' of education personnel:
    - 3 dismissals for 'absence illégale du territoire'.
    - 13 fresh retirements or 'relèvements des fonctions' under the law of July 17, 1940.
    - 10 definitive repostings or retirements of those already suspended under the same law.
    - 63 other cases of personnel against whom action had been taken by previous ministers finally resolved.

    After April 2, 1941 Carcopino compulsorily retired 24 other teachers and reposted 5 academy inspectors.
73. Quoted in: *Les Questions actuelles* (cf. Note (31)), 52.
74. Their report is to be found in: AN F.17.13380.

75. Statement made by Carcopino, September 3, 1941, reported in: *La Croix,* September 4, 1941.
76. AN F.17.13380. 'Note pour M. Roy, I–G'. (attached to de Brinon's staff in Paris) from: Direction de l'enseignement secondaire, September 6, 1941. The circulars of July 28, 1925 and September 29, 1934 allowed places in the special preparatory classes attached to *lycées* to be filled by pupils from other primary schools.
77. Carcopino, op. cit. 412.
78. AN AJ 40.557. Report of the Prefect of Police, Paris, for May 11, 1942.
79. AN F.17.13364. 'Rapport sur le niveau des études dans les classes de 6è et les résultats qu'a donnés l'institution du DEPP', n.d., n.p. [early 1943].
80. AN F.17.13364. 'Résultats définitifs du DEPP à Paris' [1942?].
81. AN F.17.13364. 'Effectifs des lycées et anciens collèges classiques au 5.11.41 et au 5.12.42', Direction de l'enseignement secondaire, January 30, 1943.
82. AN F.17.13364. 'Réunion du 25 janvier 1943. Suppression du DEPP'.
83. Carcopino, op. cit. 419–20.
84. The fees for tuition in a provincial *lycée* varied from 648–864F a year, depending on the grade. Carcopino, op. cit. 412–17 discusses the reintroduction of fees. Cf. also his speech of September 3, 1941, reported in: *Les Documents français,* 3 (9). September 1941.
85. E. Maillard, 'La réforme de l'enseignement', *RHDGM,* 56, October 1964, 64.
86. For example, in maintaining the right of the senior academics to elect the vice-president of the Conseil de l'Université, the supreme internal body.
87. AN AG II 459. 'Questions des élections au Collège de France'.
88. Ibid., Letter dated Vichy, July 11, 1941.
89. Ibid., Letter dated Vichy, July 17, 1941.
90. Quoted in: Carcopino, op. cit. pp. 688–93 contain an account of how the ex-minister was treated.

II. DECLINE AND FALL OF THE 'NEW ORDER'

1. H. du Moulin de Labarthète, *Le Temps des illusions. Souvenirs, juillet 1940 –avril 1942*, Geneva, 1946, 250.
2. Robert Aron, *Histoire de Vichy,* 1954, 496.
3. Louise Weiss, *La Résurrection du Chevalier, juin 1940–août 1944. Mémoires d'une Européenne,* 1974, 247.
4. L. Planté, *'Au 110 Rue de Grenelle'. Souvenirs, 1920–1944,* 1967, 331.
5. J. Zay, *Souvenirs et solitude,* 1945, 259.
6. A. Mallet, *Pierre Laval.* Vol. i. *Des années obscures à la disgrâce du 13 décembre 1940,* 1955, 337.
7. Mallet, op. cit. Vol. ii. *De la reconquête du pouvoir à l'exécution,* 1955, 32, 43.
8. Planté, loc. cit.
9. AN AJ. 40.557. Extract from German translation of the weekly report of the Paris Prefect of Police, 11.5.42.
10. Du Moulin de Labarthète, op. cit. 246 and 150–1.
11. Bonnard, at a press conference, May 1942, quoted in: F. Alengry, *Principes généraux de la philosophie sociale et politique du Maréchal Pétain,* Paris, 1943, 108 et seq. Cf. also an article by Bonnard in the Doriotist paper, *Jeunesse . . . Organe de la génération'40,* 33, 10.8.41.
12. AN AG II 609. 'Rapport sur l'Enseignement technique', n.d., unsigned, submitted to Pétain's 'cabinet'.

13. AN F.17.13345. Note of Néret, to Luc, dated 25.10.43.
14. C. signed by Luc, director of technical education and youth employment, to prefects, Paris, 2.1.42.
15. C. letter from Délégué départemental de la jeunesse, Lons-le-Saunier, 13.2.41.
16. AN F.17.13366. Report of the Inspector General for Youth, for 1942–3. Cf. also AN. F.17.13366, 'Note sur les questions relatives au Travail des Jeunes', n.d. This shows that by 1944 this figure had risen to 85,000. Boys outnumbered girls in the centres by two to one.
17. AN F.17.13381. Note from Pelorson, deputy secretary-general for youth, to Bonnard, 5.12.42.
18. Cf. AN.F.17.13365. Report headed: 'Les disciplines de culture scientifique. Esquisse d'un lycée technique,' attached to a letter addressed to Bonnard from M. B___, a teacher at the École des Arts et Métiers at Aix, dated Marseilles, 22.9.42.
19. AN F.17.13347. Letter from Abbé Gouget, chairman of the organization of Chefs d'Établissement de l'Enseignement Libre, to Bonnard, Paris, 17.3.43.
20. AN F.17.13344. Note from Luc to Bonnard, Paris, 18.12.42.
21. AN F.17.13337. Letter from Laval's office to Bonnard, Paris, 4.7.44.
22. AN F.17.13337. Letter from Bonnard to Déat, Paris, 29.7.44.
23. There are two accounts. Bonnard gave a statement in Madrid in 1955 which was published in: Hoover Institute, *La Vie de la France sous l'Occupation, 1940–1944,* Paris, 1957, Vol. ii, 869–72. There is also an article by him entitled, 'Témoignage', *Écrits de Paris,* May 1960, 22–9.
24. A. Rosier, 'L'Université et la Révolution Nationale', in: P. Arnoult *et al., La France sous l'Occupation,* 1959, 129.
25. Zay, op. cit. 130. An indictment of Bonnard is given in the roneoed printed record of his trial, Fascicules 1–5, March 1960.
26. D. of 2.12.41., *Journal officiel de la France libre,* 20.1.42.
27. P. Nicolle, *Cinquante mois d'Armistice. Vichy, 2 juillet 1940–26 août 1944. Journal d'un témoin,* 1947, Vol. i, 502.
28. Quoted in: H. Michel and B. Mirkine Guetzévitch (eds.), *Les Idées politiques et sociales de la Résistance (Documents clandestins, 1940–1944),* 1954, 217.
29. H. Michel, *Les Courants de pensée de la Résistance,* 1962, 177.
30. Cf. R. Blanc and F. Potton [both males], 'Culture et la vocation féminine', *Cahiers de notre jeunesse,* 11, July–August 1942, 17–20.
31. *Bulletin de l'enseignement primaire,* Hautes-Alpes (Gap), No. 1 of 1941.
32. J. Ernest-Charles, 'Ces bachelières', *Le Temps,* 20.10.40.
33. AD de la Haute-Marne, Chaumont, T.122. Enseignement technique. Réunions du comité, 1937–1944. Letter from Directeur Départemental du Ravitaillement général to Prefect, 30.12.43. Cf. also: AN AG II 570. If over thirty-five, teachers with five years' experience were granted the qualification without examination. The law of 18.3.42 required all housecraft teachers to have diplomas, but an A. of 6.9.42 allowed dispensations up to 1.10.43.
34. AN F.17.13347. Bonnard to Renaudin, Commissioner General for the family, 3.6.44.
35. The information in this paragraph is contained in: Ministère de l'Éducation Nationale, IPN, Académie de Lille, *Annales du Centre départemental de la Documentation Pédagogique de la Somme. A la Recherche du passé. V. Les Misères de la guerre, 1939–1945. Témoignages d'enfants,* Amiens, 1964.

36. The information in this paragraph comes from: AN F.17.13364. 'Inspection de l'Enseignement primaire. Conférences pédagogiques des Écoles maternelles, Marseille, le 10 décembre 1943'. The document is signed: A. R____, Inspectrice 17.12.43.
37. Micheline Bood, *Les Années doubles. Journal d'une lycéenne sous l'Occupation*, présenté par Jacques Labib, 1974, *passim*.
38. J. Guéhenno, *Journal des années noires, 1940–1944*, 1947, 82 and 90.
39. Ibid. 120.
40. Ibid. 11.
41. La Lettre de la France Libre, Forces Françaises Libres. Service de Presse et d'Information, London, roneoed, 6.2.41.
42. AN F.17.13343. Letter from Mouraille to Commissariat Général for Sport, 10.10.42. For playing the record the English teacher at the Lycée Cours de Vincennes had merely been reprimanded.
43. AN F.17.13373. 'Note pour M. L'Inspecteur Général Roy', n.d., concerning the head of a Bordeaux school who got his pupils to sing the tune. His punishment was transfer to another post outside the department.
44. H. Michel, *Vichy, Année '40*, 1966, 420.
45. AN F.17.13381. Message from ministry to the rectors in the occupied zone, 8.11.41. Since the commemoration could not be held later than 9.11.41 the notice was impossibly short.
46. AN F.17.13346. Letter from Bonnard to Academy Inspector, Gironde, 17.6.44 in reply to his report.
47. Anon., 'Sous le signe du Maréchal. Mois de mai, mois des jeunes', *L'Action jurassienne* (weekly), Dôle, 31.5.41.
48. C. of 15.10.41.
49. e.g. the 'Rapport annuel de l'École Primaire Supérieure de garçons d'Aix-en-Provence' for 1.7.42 showed that pupils had collected, among a variety of articles, 255 kg. of chestnuts in November 1941 and 10 kg. of clothes for North Africa.
50. Cf. L'Enseignement de la démographie' (leading article), *Le Temps*, 23.4.42. and C. of 16.11.43.
51. AN F.17 Ter. 299 contains a series of documents for lessons on demography, which were not to be omitted even if pupils were preparing for the 'grandes écoles'.
52. AN AG II 650 (40), Neuvième Commission du Conseil National. 3è Commission d'Information générale, session du 25 mars au 1 avril 1942.
53. C. of ministry of education to Prefects, n.d.
54. AN F.17.13380. 'Note concernant la défense passive', Directeur de l'enseignement primaire to rectors, 21.6.43. The file also contains circulars of 15.5.42, 8.6.42, and 8.2.43 dealing with defence precautions.
55. C. of Prefect of the Vaucluse (Avignon), 21.10.41.
56. Note of the academy inspector in: Bulletin départemental de l'enseignement primaire, Hautes-Alpes (Gap), March 1941.
57. Cf. Note (56). Bulletin of May/June 1942.
58. P. Bourget and C. Lacretelle, *Sur les murs de Paris, 1940–1944*, 1959, 120. Cf. also: *Le Temps*, 18.9.42.
59. AN F.17.13347. Bonnard's reply to the ministry of information is on an undated copy and may therefore not have been sent.
60. AN F.17.13336, 'Service de Monsieur Roy'.
61. AN F.17.13379, 'Note sur les réquisitions des locaux scolaires', 3.11.42.
62. AN F.17.13379, 'Pourcentage des locaux scolaires réquisitionnés par académie et par ordre d'enseignement à la date du 25.10.42'.

63. These evaluations of personalities connected with education are given in: AN AJ 40.556. Angelegenheiten d. Sekretariat d'État à l'Éducation Nationale et à la Jeunesse. Band II: VKult. 402. April 1941.
64. AN F.17.13379. Copy of letter from Delwig, Head of the Rennes office of the Propaganda-Abteilung in France, to Galletier, Rector of Rennes, 13.3.41.
65. AN F.17.13379. Letter from de Brinon to ministry of education, Paris, 1.4.41.
66. AN F.17.13379.
67. J. Carcopino. Souvenirs de sept ans (1937–1944), 1953, 242.
68. Bulletin de l'enseignement du 1er degré et de l'éducation post-scolaire du Calvados, Caen, No. 3 of 1943.
69. AD du Nord, Lille, R.301. Report of academy inspector, 21.10.41.
70. AN F.17.13379. Report of academy inspector, Eure, Évreux, 12.6.41 to Rector, academy of Caen.
71. AN AJ 40.557. Letter from Propaganda-Abteilung, Paris, 22.8.41 to Dr Best, Verwaltungsstab, Hôtel Majestic, Paris.
72. AN F.17.13379. 'Note pour Monsieur le Ministre', from the 'Cabinet du Ministre', n.d. [April 1944?]
73. AN AJ 40.557. Letter from: Chef des Militärverwaltungsbezirks C (North-East France) to German High Command in Paris, Dijon, 18.4.41 and teleprint (Meldung No. 36) from Dijon, 25.5.41 to Propaganda-Abteilung, Paris.
74. AN AJ 40.557. Bonnard wrote an apology to the Germans on 20.7.42.
75. AN F.17.13379. The head of a boys' school at Montbard wrote to the academy inspector of the Côte d'Or protesting against the ban.
76. AN AJ 40.557. German translation of weekly report of the Paris Prefect of Police, 20.4.42.
77. AN F.17.13376. Monthly report of the prefect of the Morbihan, 1.4.42.
78. AN du Nord, Lille, R.301. Report on incident by prefect to de Brinon, Lille, 18.6.43.
79. AN AJ 40557. Draft circular by Dr Dahnke, ref. Vkult 429/449, May 1941, and note on 'Gaullist propaganda in Paris schools', ref. VKult 405, Gruppe 4, Paris, 24.7.41. The final version was sent out to all German forces on 30.7.41.
80. The list of 'crimes' is culled from: AN F.17.13377, 'Rapports mensuels pour la Délégation générale du Gouvernement français, avril 1941 – mai 1943'.
81. AN F.17.13346. 'Liste des arrestations qui nous ont été communiquées' (25.7.43 – 25.8.43).
82. H. Gayot, *Charente-Maritime, 1940–1945. Occupation, résistance, libération,* La Rochelle, n.d., 158.
83. Cf. P. Héraclès, *La Loi nazie en France. Préface et commentaires de Robert Aron,* n.d.
84. *Recueil des Actes administratifs de la Préfecture de la Somme,* Amiens, 568 and 745.
85. H. Amouroux, *La Grande Histoire des Français sous l'Occupation,* vol. iii, *Les Beaux Jours des collabos, juin 1941–juin 1942,* 1978, 101.
86. O. Abetz, Pétain et les Allemands. Mémorandum d'Abetz sur les rapports franco-allemands. 1948, 53 (Telegram of Abetz, No. 1556 of 18.12.40).
87. AN AJ 40.556. Note of Dr Dahnke, of the group 'Kultur und Schule' to Dr Storz, Kriegsverwaltungsabteilungschef, German High Command in Paris, Paris, 7.2.41.
88. *Le Temps,* 18.7.40, announced that in the Southern zone the baccalaureate examinations, which would also be open to refugees, would take place between July 26–30.
89. R. d'Harcourt, 'Baccalauréat et Résolutions', *La Croix,* 1.7.41.

90. Announced in: *La Croix*, 14–15.5.42.
91. Ripert's letter appeared in: *Le Temps*, 18.9.42. A first leader, 'Le Baccalauréat', appeared on 22.9.42 and a sequel the following day.
92. AN F.17.13346. Letter from Bonnard to Audra, dean of the faculty of Letters, Lille, 24.6.43.
93. AN F.17.13347. Quoted in a press communiqué of *Inter-France*, 28.6.44, Supplement No. 1, article headed, 'Une charte de l'intelligence'.
94. AD du Nord, Lille, R.330 A. of Prefect concerning the 'rentrée', 18.10.43.
95. *Le Phare*, Nantes, 5.10.43 and 29.10.43.
96. Instructions relatives à l'enseignement secondaire pendant l'année scolaire, 1943–1944, n.d., n.p., published by the ministry of education.
97. *Le Progrès de la Somme*, Amiens, 25.2.44.
98. AN F.17.13347. Note to ministry of education from ministry of labour, Paris, 12.5.44.
99. AN F.17.13346. Letter from the headmaster of the École Nationale, Egletons (Corrèze), 7.6.44 to Director of technical education, Paris.
100. Figures given in: AN AJ 40.563 (German file).
101. AN AJ 40.563, File headed: 412R, Räumung der Universitäten', document entitled, 'Frage der Evakuierung der im Küstensicherungsgebiet liegenden Universitäten', n.p., 28.2.44.
102. AN F.17.13380, 'Note pour Monsieur le Ministre, Paris, 19.2.44'. The Germans merely stated that they did not want the bother of the surveillance of 3,409 students.
103. AN F.17.13348. The agenda is drawn up in Bonnard's own hand.
104. AN F.17.13348. Letter from Commissioner General for the family, 27.3.44, to Bonnard.
105. AN F.17.13337. Note in Bonnard's own hand: 'Choses à dire aux journalistes', Paris, 31.5.44.
106. AN F.17.13347. Sheet marked in Bonnard's own hand, Madame L.', 20.4.44. Appended to it is a: 'Horoscope particulier de H' (identity unknown), full of incomprehensible allusions. Bonnard's alleged credulity is attested to by many stories that went the rounds at the time.
107. AN F.17.13346. Message from Inspector B____, Caen, 29.6.44. A further message was received on 3.7.44.
108. AN F.17.13346. Message from Bonnard to rector of Caen, Jean Mercier, 5.7.44.
109. AN F.17.13380. 'Remarques au sujet de l'ajournement des Concours', Paris, 25.5.44 , in a file marked: 'Note remise à M. Auer le 25.5., à M. Reiprich le 26.6'.
110. Bonnard at a press conference, 9. 3. 44, quoted in: *Le Progrès de la Somme*, Amiens, 11.3.44.
111. AN F.17.1337. 'Alertes et examens', 25.4.44. Detailed instructions are given: examination rooms are to be located near air raid shelters, with candidates split up into small groups; during an alert all should take cover, but volunteer invigilators should remain to ensure the security of the examination rooms. In the shelters no talking between candidates was allowed.
112. AD du Nord, Lille, R.871. Note dated 23.6.44.
113. *Le Progrès de la Somme*, Amiens, 26.5.44.
114. AN F.17.13347. Letter from Gidel to Bonnard, Paris, 12.6.44.
115. AN F.17.13346. 'Note pour les candidats qui se sont présentés aux épreuves du baccalauréat dans les centres de l'Académie de Caen', drawn up by: Direction de l'Enseignement supérieur, 2è Bureau, Paris, 5.8.44.

116. *Le Progrès de la Somme*, Amiens, 19.8.44.
117. The diary is in: AN F.17.1336.
118. Other, unidentified names also appear in the diary for this time: Massol, Sarmeur, Maigret (*sic*), Birman (?), B. Ajam (Benjamin ?).
119. AN F.17.13337.
120. J. Tracou, *Le Maréchal aux Liens. Le Temps du Sacrifice*, 1948, 415. Cf. also: Planté, op. cit. 348–9 and the record of Bonnard's trial. (Cf. Note (25)).
121. Robert Aron, op. cit. 711.
122. Ibid. 720.

III. THE CHURCH AND EDUCATION

1. R. Rémond, *Les Catholiques, le communisme et les crises, 1929–1939*, 1960, 227 *et passim*.
2. This is Pucheu's characterization of Suhard. For Pucheu Liénart represents the 'evangelizing Church' and Gerlier the 'fighting Church'. Cf. P. Pucheu, *Ma vie*, 1948, 288–9.
3. J. Duquesne, *Les Catholiques français sous l'Occupation*, 1966, 35 et seq.
4. Quoted in: J. Cornec, *Laïcité*, 1965, 157.
5. Cf. A. Latreille and A. Siegfried, *Les Forces religieuses et la vie politique. Le Catholicisme et le Protestantisme*, Cahiers de la Fondation Nationale des Sciences Politiques, No. 23, 1951, 206–11.
6. Notice sur la vie et les travaux du Pasteur Marc Boegner (1881–1970), par M. Oscar Cullmann, Membre de l'Académie, lue dans la séance du mardi 28 mai 1974. (Académie des Sciences morales et politiques.)

   The Fédération Protestante co-ordinated all its youth movements into a Conseil Protestant de la Jeunesse. Boegner, like the Catholics, was opposed to one single youth movement for everybody. Cf. *Les Églises protestantes pendant la guerre et l'Occupation. Actes de l'Assemblée Générale du Protestantisme Français, 22–26 octobre 1945*, 1946.
7. Quoted in: G. Combes, 'L'Esprit public en Haute-Loire de 1940 à 1942', *RHDGM*, 85, January 1972, 57.
8. Cf. 'Les projets de réforme de l'enseignement devant la conscience catholique', *La Nouvelle Revue des jeunes*, iii, 1931.

   J. E. Talbott, *The Politics of Educational Reform in France, 1918–1940*, Princeton, NJ, 1969, 192–7, describes the activities of the Lille group, which included a number of teachers at the Catholic faculty ('la Catho'), including P.-H. Simon, the eminent literary critic.
9. Cf. *Institut National de la Statistique et des Études Économiques. Statistique générale de la France. Annuaire statistique*, 1958, Paris, 1961. Combining Tableau VII, 58, and Tableau X, 60, the following table shows the relative proportions of pupils in public and private (mainly Catholic) secondary education in 1939 and in subsequent years. This shows clearly how Catholic secondary education increased during the Occupation years.

Year	*Percentage secondary education*		*Total*
	Public	*Private*	
1939	60	40	100
1940	58	42	100
1941	52	48	100
1942	47	53	100

Year	*Percentage secondary education*		*Total*
	Public	*Private*	
1943	55	45	100
1944	n.a.	n.a.	–
1945	55	45	100
1946	57	43	100
1947	57	43	100

10. Cf. J. Cotereau, 'L'Église a-t-elle collaboré?' (Brochure), Série, 'Problèmes actuels', May 1946, No. 6, 5.
11. P. Baudouin, *Neuf mois au gouvernement. Avril – décembre 1940*, 1948, 253.
12. Cf. Pétain's articles in the *Revue des deux mondes,* August and September 1940.
13. Duquesne, op. cit. 17.
14. ibid. 11.
15. Baudouin, op. cit. 246.
16. Duquesne, op. cit. 27.
17. O. Wormser, *Les Origines doctrinales de la 'Révolution Nationale'.* Vichy, *10 Juillet 1940–31 mars 1941,* 1971, 117.
18. H. Du Moulin de Labarthète, *Le Temps des illusions, Souvenirs, juillet 1940–avril 1942,* Geneva, 1946, 301.
19. Duquesne, op. cit. 46.
20. 'Déclaration des cardinaux et archevêques réunis à Paris sur l'attitude à l'égard du pouvoir établi et les vertus à promouvoir', 15.1.41., quoted in: A. Deroo, *L'Épiscopat français dans la mêlée de son temps, 1930–1954,* 1955, 78. The distinction should be noted between 'pouvoir établi' and 'autorité légitime', the stronger phrase. The declaration is doubtlessly cautiously framed in this respect.
21. Duquesne, op. cit. 41.
22. Quoted in: Cornec, op. cit. 154–5.
23. AN F.17.13376. Report of prefect for the Pas-de-Calais, 3.3.42.
24. AN AG II 459. Letter from Chanoine Polimann to Pétain, Bar-le-Duc, 13.5.41.
25. The circulars, dated 15.4.41 and 18.7.41, were issued by Darlan in his capacity as minister of the interior. The second circular left the matter to the discretion of the municipal council.
26. AN AG II 459. Letter to the ministry of education from Pétain's 'cabinet civil', Vichy, 31.5.41. The letter affirms that Pétain himself had ruled on this point.
27. AN F.17.13364. A note, no heading, date, or place, in Bonnard's handwriting, attached to a paper headed: 'Csl. [Conseil] du 2 mai 1943, 11 présents'. The note relates to a meeting of all academy inspectors, in Paris for the annual national scholarship awards, at which they had been invited to report their problems. One raised concerns the display of the crucifix.
28. L. Planté, 'L'enseignement de la morale à l'école primaire', *Écrits de Paris,* January 1957, 45–6.
29. The text of Lefas's paper is given in: AN AG II 609. File CM 25 A: 'Questions religieuses'.
30. A. of 23.2.23.
31. It has not been possible to identify this commentary. Jeanneret gives the authors as Gay and Mortreux and refers to p. 38. Cf. S. Jeanneret, *La Vérité sur les instituteurs,* Paris, 1942, 173.

32. J. Chevalier, 'Un témoignage direct sur deux points d'histoire', *Écrits de Paris,* 19.7.53., 84.
33. *Les Questions actuelles. L'Enseignement en France (juillet 1940–octobre 1941), Documents officiels et textes administratifs,* Paris, n.d. [1942?], 123.
34. Quoted in: J. Jeanneney, *Journal politique, septembre 1939–juillet 1942.* Edited by Jean-Noel Jeanneney, 1972, 472.
35. J. Carcopino, *Souvenirs de sept ans, 1937–1944,* 1953, 271 and 288.
36. Chevalier, op. cit. 85.
37. The source of the quotation is not known. It is given in: Louise Weiss, *La Résurrection du Chevalier [no connection], juin 1940–août 1941. Mémoires d'une Européenne,* 1974, 246 note.
38. P. Limagne, *Éphémérides de quatre années tragiques, 1940–1941, Vol. i. De Bordeaux à Bir-Hakeim,* Paris, 1945, 90.
39. AN F.17.13342. Letter to Bonnard from the parish priest of Saint-Sauveur-les-Amiens, near Ailly-sur-Somme, 2.7.42. The priest said that Paris primary teachers visited museums on Thursdays with their pupils so that they would not attend catechism.
40. Carcopino, op. cit. 303.
41. *La Croix,* 13.11.41.
42. Referred to in: AN AG II 609. In File CM 25A is a folder headed: ' "Documents relatifs à la suppression du nom de Dieu dans les programmes scolaires". (Réforme Carcopino, mars 1941.) 8 Pièces'. A note says: 'M. Carcopino, by modifying the new programmes, has caused God no longer to figure in any official text – programme or Instructions – so that if an action came before the Conseil d'État brought by a primary teacher claiming the right to pronounce the name of God in school, it would be dismissed. The French school, since March 12, is officially atheist.' The writer of the note concludes that a circular must be issued to reaffirm that the school has a spiritual, deist basis.
43. AN AG II 609. Letter from Pétain's 'cabinet militaire' to the ministry of education, Vichy, 5.5.41.
44. Carcopino, op. cit. 306.
45. Limagne, op. cit. 138.
46. Duquesne, op. cit. 93.
47. AN AG II 607. File CM 21E: 'Éducation Nationale et Jeunesse'.
48. Ibid. Letter from General Castelnau to Pétain, Toulouse, 2.4.41.
49. AN AJ. 40.563. File: Beiakte zu VKult., Bd.I. August 1940 – .
50. Mgr Guerry, *L'Église catholique en France sous l'Occupation,* 1947, 247.
51. AN AG II 650. File: Huitième Commission du Conseil National. Études des questions de jeunesse. Session du 5 au 12 mars 1942. Pucheu testified to the commission at its eighth session (10.3.42., p.m.) and this phrase appears in the 'compte-rendu analytique' of the session.
52. Carcopino, op. cit. 310.
53. *Esprit,* Lyons, February 1941, No. 97, 237.
54. E. Mounier, Œuvres, Vol. iv. *Recueils posthumes. Correspondance,* 1963, 686–7. Cf. also: M. Winock, *Histoire politique de la revue 'Esprit', 1930–1950,* 1975, 229.
55. Mgr Guerry, op. cit. 338.
56. AN F.17.13390. Letter from Carcopino to the Bishop of Limoges, ref. I/3039/OPVC, 19.10.41. *La Croix* (5.11.41) reported that the bishop had written to Carcopino on 16.10.41 asking whether, in isolated hamlets far from the local church, the school could be used for religious instruction – or even in the towns, when it was very cold. The prelate added that the

'new France' did not want the discrimination once shown by 'the meanderings of the Herriot school bus which, in the mountains, would only pick up children attending the State school from isolated hamlets, whilst the youngsters from the confessional school trudged long distances through the snow and ice'. Carcopino gave permission for the school to be used in isolated hamlets. Regarding the general problem of unheated churches he urged the bishop to use the sacristy only.

57. AN F.17.13380. Letter from prefect of the Doubs, Besançon, 7.11.41, to the Délégué du Ministère de l'Intérieur auprès de la Délégation Générale dans les Territoires occupés, Paris.
58. AN F.17.13390. Letter from Bishop of Limoges to Bonnard, Limoges, 21.10.43.
59. Cf. Note (42).
60. AN F.17.13365. 'Création d'un service d'aumônerie dans les instituts de formation professionnelle'. M. R___, a history teacher at the Lycée Rollin, fowarded a petition from his former student teachers at Pau stressing that future primary teachers needed some religious connection. The petition was supported by the directorate of primary education.
61. AN F.17.13337. 'Note sur l'affaire de l'aumônier du Collège moderne de jeunes filles de Nice', Paris, 26.6.44.
62. AN F.17.13348. Letter from the Bishop of Saint-Brieuc and Tréguier to Bonnard, 7.2.44. Bonnard replied on 15.2.44 that the matter had been taken up with the rector of the academy of Rennes.
63. AN F.17.13346. Letter from Bishop of Autun, Autun, 2.3.43, to Bonnard, to which are attached two memoranda from two officials of the ministry.
64. Oral testimony and letter from M. F. Guériff, Saint-Nazaire, 15.6.76. For an interesting background to life in Saint-Nazaire during the war, cf. F. Guériff, *Saint-Nazaire sous l'Occupation allemande,* Éditions des Paludiers, La Baule, 1971.
65. AN AG II 570. 'Les Écoles concurrentes et l'unité nationale', by Mlle de la B___, Loire-Inférieure.
66. AD du Nord, Lille, R.539. 1941. Situation religieuse. Enseignement. M. Guéry [*sic*].
67. Guerry, op. cit. 325.
68. AD du Nord, Lille, R.539. 'Situation religieuse dans le Département du Nord'. Note pour Monsieur le Préfet, Lille, 19.8.41, from the Chef de la 3ième Division, Préfecture. Cf. also AD du Nord, Lille, R.1582.
69. AD du Nord, Lille, R.1582.
70. AN F.17.13390. Letter of 8.6.42.
71. Cotereau, op. cit. 13.
72. Y. Bouthillier, *Le Drame de Vichy,* 1950, Vol. ii, 355.
73. Jeanneney, op. cit. xv., Diary for 5.9.40.
74. Mornet, *Quatre ans à rayer de notre histoire,* 1949, 89.
75. *Esprit,* March–April 1949. No. devoted to: 'Propositions de la paix scolaire'. 375.
76. Carcopino, op. cit. 301 et seq. Cf. also AN F.17.13365. Louis Garrone had left the SGJ and had been appointed as inspector general for private education. In a report dated Vichy, 10.6.42 to Terracher, the secretary-general of the ministry, it was stated that the abolition of the single Caisse for both State and private schools was 'to avoid struggles for influence. . . and also the repugnance that might be felt by a possible donor anxious to know how his money was to be used'.
77. AN AG II 459. Letter from 'cabinet civil' of Pétain to Bonnard, Vichy, 8.8.42. The rest of the correspondence that passed on this issue is in the same file.

78. For example, the prefect of the Maine-et-Loire in October 1940 had authorized a free distribution of coal to both State and private schools. Cf. *La Croix,* 9.1.41.
79. AN F.17.13376. Report of prefect of the Seine-Inférieure, 14.10.41.
80. Carcopino, op. cit. 320 et seq.
81. AN AG II 570. File: 'Plan de réformes de l'Education Nationale (documentation)'.
82. Cotereau, op. cit. 14.
83. AN F.17.13346. 'Note sur le détachement de professeurs dans l'enseignement libre', Paris, 3.7.44.
84. AN AG II 654. 'Notes au sujet des difficultés financières de l'enseignement privé', by Abbé H. R___, 11.2.41.
85. AN AG II 613. 'Note sur l'enseignement dans l'Ouest', by M. de la F___, n.d.
86. Bouthillier, op. cit. 353.
87. AN AG II 27 SG 7. File SG 7E, marked 'Enseignement', contains details of the Lille initiative.
88. Carcopino, op. cit. 317.
89. AN AG II 459. Copy of letter from Pétain to Carcopino, Vichy, 18.7.41.
90. Carcopino, op. cit. 319.
91. Quoted in: Guerry, op. cit. 321.
92. Carcopino, op. cit. 321.
93. 'Exposé des motifs' of the law, published in: *Journal officiel,* (Z.O), 9.11.41.
94. E. Maillard, 'La réforme de l'enseignement', *RHDGM,* 56, October 1964, Numéro spécial: Vichy et la Jeunesse, 49.
95. Pucheu, op. cit. 285 et seq.
96. Guerry, op. cit. 320.
97. AN F.17.13376. Report of prefect of the Gironde, 4.10.41.
98. Duquesne, op. cit. 99.
99. Du Moulin de Labarthète, op. cit. 302, cites Bayet but does not accept his assertion.
100. Duquesne, op. cit. 106.
101. AN F.17.13376. Report of prefect of the Aube, 8.10.41.
102. Ibid. Report of prefect of the Côte d'Or, 4.11.41.
103. AN F.17.13365. 'Note sur l'enseignement libre', 15.10.42.
104. AN F.17.13364. 'Note pour M. le Ministre', 15.5.42. The note says that at the end of the school year it would be helpful to let State teachers know that the State education system was not going to be replaced by the confessional one.
105. AN F.17.13342. Letter forwarded to ministry by Déat. from *L'Œuvre.* sent by Mme B___ C___, Estrées-St-Denis, Oise.
106. AN F.17.13365. Roneoed document: 'Statut de l'Enseignement libre et Droits familiaux', signed, 'Pour les APEL de la zone libre', by the president, Jean Tournassus, 7 rue Childebert, Lyons.
107. Cf. AN AG II 609. 'L'enseignement privé', Vichy, 17.4.43.
108. Carcopino, op. cit. 332, quotes: *La Semaine religieuse,* Paris, 6.12.41.
109. AD du Nord, Lille, R.536. Letter from Liénart, Évêché de Lille, 22.11.41. to regional prefect, and letter from regional prefect, Lille, 21.10.41. to ministry of interior. Paris.
110. AN F.17.13376. Report of prefect of the Morbihan, 1.3.42.
111. Cf. Note (103).
112. AD de la Haute-Marne, Chaumont, T. 38. 'Subventions aux écoles privées, 1941–1944'.

113. AN F.17.13365. Report by inspector general D___, deputy director of secondary education, to Bonnard, 18.6.42.
114. Cf. Note (107). Eventually three-monthly payments ('tranches') in arrears were authorized. The first payment, in December, could be made on the prefect's authority, whether or not the budget had been finally agreed. Cf. AN F.17.13390. File: Enseignement libre, JL 1.
115. Cf. Note (27).
116. AN F.17.13365. Letter from Mgr Aubry, president of the Comité National de l'Enseignement Libre, Paris, 24.9.43, to Pétain.
117. AN F.17.13337. Note: 'Objet: Réunion des préfets', Cabinet du ministre, Vichy, 16.1.42.
118. Cf. Note (76). Report of Garrone.
119. AN F.17.13365. A printed document headed: 'Diocèse de Lyon. Direction de l'Enseignement, septembre 1942. Barême diocésaine de traitements pour les maîtres des écoles libres subventionnées'. This gives annual salaries as follows:

    Religious: nuns: 12,960F; men: 14,160F (country), 15,360F (towns of over 5,000 inhabitants).

    Other teaching personnel: Salaries range, for teachers in training, from 11,700F to 17,760F, for the 'première classe', reached after 27 years. Lodging, heating, and lighting are provided. The area of residence and number in the family gave additional allowances. Thus a man with 27 years' service, having six children and living in Marseilles, but receiving a living-out allowance, might receive 33,760F.
120. Cf. Table of increase in Catholic primary education by department given in Appendix II.
121. Cf. Note (76). Report of Garrone. Despite the abrupt stoppage of subsidies in 1945, Catholic primary education continued to flourish. In 1950 in the Ille-et-Vilaine, the Morbihan, the Maine-et-Loire, and the Vendée a majority of pupils still attended Catholic schools; in the Finistère, the Côtes-du-Nord, the Mayenne, and the Loire-Inférieure the proportion varied between 30–50 per cent; to the south, in the Haute-Loire, the Ardèche, the Lozère, and the Aveyron, the same proportion also held good. (Cf. also Note (122) below, article by Chatelain.)
122. AN F.17.13365. 'Statistiques des élèves dans l'enseignement public et l'enseignement privé' [1941]. See also Note (9). For the 1950 statistics cf. A. Chatelain, 'Pour une géographie sociologique de l'éducation et de la laïcité', Annales VII, 1952, 332–6.
123. AN F.17.13380.
124. AN F.17.13390. File: Enseignement libre, JL 1. Increases over 1942–3 showed: Maine-et-Loire, from 23,816,760F to 26,625,835F; Morbihan, 20,277,511F to 22,024,866F; Ardèche, 9,805,000F to 13,470,000F.
125. AN F.17.13390. File: Enseignement libre, JL 1. 'Note' dated 22.1.44.
126. AN AG II 609. Copy of letter (writer not indicated) to A___ H___, Bureau de Documentation, 34, rue des Fosses, Lille, 16.2.43, Lille.
127. AN AG II 570. 'Examen critique de la loi No. 964 du 4 août 1942 relative à la délivrance des diplômes professionnels'.
128. AN AG II 459. Letter from Liénart to director of technical education, ministry of education, 14.11.42.
129. AN AG II 459. In May 1941 the Institut Catholique had requested permission to style itself a university, a title forbidden to Catholic institutions since the early days of the Third Republic. AN AG II 495.
130. AN AF.17.13365. 'Note sur la subvention aux Universités libres', 16.5.44.

131. AN F.17.13346. Letter from the rector of the Institut Catholique, Paris, 3.3.43.
132. AN F.17.13342. Letter from rector of the 'Université Catholique de l'Ouest', Angers, 24.11.42, to Bonnard in which Pétain is styled, 'Le vénéré chef de l'État', and Laval, 'l'éminent chef de son gouvernement'.
133. AN AG II 495. 'Attribution aux Facultés de Théologie protestante de Paris et de Montpellier d'une part sur la subvention exceptionnelle à l'enseignement supérieur libre (loi du 31 décembre 1942)', Vichy, 30.1.43.
134. Cf. Note (130).
135. AN F.17.13365. 'Note pour . . . le Ministre, Paris, 1.2.43. from C____, inspector general.
136. AN F.17.13346. Letter from Bonnard to Donati, regional prefect at Angers, 27.7.44.
137. AN AG II 570. 'Répercussions des propos anticléricaux du Ministre de l'Éducation Nationale', June 1942.
138. AN F.17.13344. Letter to Bonnard from the Bishop of Chartres, Chartres, 19.4.42.
139. R. Brasillach, *Une génération dans l'orage. Mémoires. Notre avant-guerre. Journal d'un homme occupé,* 1968, 438. Collaborationists were strongly opposed as to the appropriateness of subsidies to Catholic education. Some, like Déat, were utterly opposed. Others, like Philippe Henriot, who became Laval's minister of information, or Xavier Vallat, the first Vichy 'commissioner for Jewish questions', were committed Catholics, who before the war had spoken out in favour of subsidies.
140. Robert Aron, *De Gaulle before Paris. The Liberation of France, June–August 1944,* tr. by Humphrey Hare, London, 1962, 50.
141. G.-M. Garrone, *Le Secret d'une vie engagée: Mgr Guerry d'après ses carnets intimes,* 1971, 91.
142. G. Cogniot, 'Les subventions à l'enseignement confessionnel', *La Pensée,* nouvelle série, No. 3, avril–mai–juin 1945, 93.
143. Duquesne, op. cit. 451–2.
144. Procès-verbal des séances du Conseil-Général de la Loire-Inférieure, Séance du 28 novembre 1945, Nantes.
145. Procès-verbaux des déliberations du Conseil-Général, deuxième session, 1945 (Maine-et-Loire), Angers.

IV THE SCHOOL TEACHERS

1. J. Delperrié de Bayac, *Histoire du Front Populaire,* 1972, 171.
2. Ibid., 350–1. Cf. also: G. Duveau, *Les Instituteurs,* 1958, 171. In P. Nicolle, *Cinquante mois d'Armistice. Vichy, 2 juillet 1940–26 août 1944. Journal d'un témoin,* 1947, 94, it is reported that Delmas visited Vichy on 20.9.40. This visit enraged Pétain. It would seem that the visit took place just after the last meeting of the governing committee of SNI, after Delmas had taken up his teaching post again. At the meeting Delmas announced his intention of going to Vichy to contact René Belin, another former trade-union militant, whom Pétain had just appointed as labour minister. Despite his cool reception at Vichy, Delmas professed his loyalty to the Marshal. (Cf. P. Delanoue, *Les Enseignants. La Lutte syndicale du Front Populaire à la Libération,* 1973, 85 and 221.)
3. P. Ory, *Les Collaborateurs, 1940–1945,* 1976, 29.
4. Quoted in: P. Crouzet, *L'Enseignement, est-il responsable de la défaite?* Toulouse–Paris, 1943, 46.

5. AN AG II 14. Papiers personnels du Maréchal Pétain. Green file labelled: L'École. Letter to Pétain (signature unreadable) from the director of L'Instituteur National, 23.12.38, in which he thanks him for the interview granted him on 22.12.38.
6. J. Giono, *Triomphe de la vie,* 1942, 29.
7. C. Serre (ed.), Commission sur les événements survenus en France de 1933 à 1945 (Report to National Assembly No. 2344 of 1947). Première Partie: Les Événements du 7 mars 1936, 1951, Annexes to Chapter II of 'Documents sur l'état de l'armée française au 7 mars 1936'. Annexe No. 6, 'Valeur des officiers de réserve', 113.
8. J. C. Cairns, 'Along the Road back to France, 1940', *American Historical Review,* April 1959, 586–7.
9. General Gamelin, *Servir, 1946–1947,* Vol. i, 357 and Vol. iii, 425.
10. R. Denux, *Le Drame d'enseigner,* Paris, 1944, 94.
11. General Sir Edward Spears, *Assignment to catastrophe,* London, 1954, Vol. ii, 84.
12. R. Paxton, *Vichy France: Old Guard and New Order, 1940–1944,* New York, 1972, 37.
13. J. Duquesne, *Les Catholiques français sous l'Occupation,* 1966, 27.
14. Serge Jeanneret, *La Vérité sur les instituteurs,* Paris 1942, 6–12.
15. Ibid. 24.
16. R. Saint-Serge, 'La Vérité sur les Instituteurs', (*sic*), *L'Action jurassienne,* Dôle, 15.11.41. (The similarity of names and titles with Note (14) causes one to wonder whether Jeanneret, writing under a pseudonym, was the real author of this article.)
17. The two provincial newspapers mentioned are quoted in: B. Montergnole, *La Presse grenobloise de la Libération, 1944–1952,* Grenoble, 1974, 19.
18. Leading article, 'Dignité de la Fonction Publique', *Le Temps,* 18.11.40.
19. A. V. Jacquet, 'Pour la rénovation de l'École', *Le Temps,* 14.11.40.
20. Ripert at a press conference reported in: *Le Temps,* 1.12.40.
21. The figures are those of Delmas, who attended a colloquium on Daladier. Cf. R. Rémond and J. Bourdin (eds.), *Édouard Daladier, chef de gouvernement,* 1977, 201. Other participants at the colloquium gave, by area, the following numbers of teachers who went on strike:
    Nord: 'a few' (153).
    Isère: No teachers in higher or secondary education struck. The local branch of SNI countermanded instructions to strike given to primary teachers and ordered its members to supervise, but not to teach their pupils. Even this instruction was followed by less than 2 per cent of teachers (164).
    Bouches-du-Rhône: in Marseilles 9.7 per cent of primary teachers struck, but not more than 3 per cent in the department as a whole (174).
    Cantal: Out of 968 primary teachers, 130 (13 per cent) struck.
    Haute-Loire: Out of 1,100 teachers 54 (5 per cent) struck.
    Allier: Out of 1,335 teachers 290 (22 per cent) struck (183, et seq.).
22. G. Lamirand, Messages à la Jeunesse', *Les Cahiers français* [Paris, 1941?], 11.
23. C. of 6.12.41, quoted in Crouzet, op. cit. 35.
24. Crouzet, op. cit. 66–73.
25. F. Dexmier, 'Pour une éducation nationale: aux instituteurs français', Limoges [1943] (Pamphlet in: AN F.17.13346). In the First World War 35,817 primary teachers had been mobilized, of whom 8,119 (23 per cent) had been killed (cf. Delanoue, op. cit. 28).
26. Denux, op. cit. 104.

27. Crouzet, op. cit. *passim*. Cf. also an article written by him in: *Le Temps*, 31.10.40.
28. The influence of the French sociologists, led by Durkheim, on education in the Third Republic has still to be assessed.
29. C. Maurras, *Chronique des jours d'épreuve*, Lyons, 1941, 239 and 245.
30. AN F.17.13346. 'Note sur l'enseignement officiel de la sociologie'. Durkheim had held the first chair of sociology in France. In 1940 there were four chairs, two in Paris, one in Bordeaux, and one in Strasburg. It was alleged that their influence was disproportionately large; that the École des Hautes Études had been constructed 'on a sociological basis'; that the École Normale Supérieure had been dominated by 'a sociological spirit', as had philosophy and history at the Sorbonne. The usual charge was made that sociology was not a discipline but a philosophical doctrine.
31. S. Lukes, Émile Durkheim. An Intellectual Biography. Oxford D.Phil. thesis, 1968. Vol. ii of the thesis contained the full text, hitherto unpublished *in extenso*, of Durkheim's course of lectures, 'De l'enseignement de la morale à l'école primaire', given in Paris in 1903–4.
32. S. Lukes, *Émile Durkheim, his Life and Work. A Historical and Critical Study*, London, 1973, 357, note 45.
33. Two teachers retired from the training colleges of the Ardèche, a 'Red' department, in forty years could recall only two colleagues who were extreme left wing. Cf. E. Reynier and Louise Abrial, *Les Écoles normales primaires de l'Ardèche, 1831–1944 et 1922–1944*, Privas, 1945, 81 et seq. The book is a history of the mens' and the womens' training colleges.
34. AN AG II 570. Letter from an ex-headmaster, P___ J___, to Pétain, n.d.
35. J. Barthélemey, 'Doctrine de l'État', *Le Temps*, 6.8.40.
36. Marcellia Lissorgues, 'Le problème de l'élite', *La Croix*, 26.7.41.
37. J. Cornec, *Laïcité*, 1965, 160. Cornec reports how the Bishop of Quimper and Léon procured the removal of his parents, both teachers and strong secularists. They were later reinstated.
38. L. Planté, *Un grand seigneur de la politique: Anatole de Monzie, 1876–1947*, 1965, 315.
39. J. Zay, *Souvenirs et solitude*, 1945, 261–2.
40. E. Maillard, 'La réforme de l'enseignement', RHDGM, 56, October 1964.
41. L. Maurin, 'Élèves-Maîtres', *Cahiers de notre jeunesse*, Lyons, No. 14, December 1942.
42. AN AG II 570. Paper, n.d., n.p., by B___ (Marne) on the recent reform of teacher training. Cf. also, in the same file, 'Formation des maîtres', Étude No. 66 of 19.5.43 by the Comité d'Études pour la France.
43. AN F.17.13337. Document headed: 'Formation pédagogique des maîtres de l'enseignement secondaire'. (In pencil, probably in Bonnard's handwriting, 'M. Isambert, Institut Pédagogique de Lyon', implying that M. Isambert wrote the document) n.d., n.p.
44. E. Henriot, 'La première classe', *Le Temps*, 4.9.40.
45. AN F.17.13342. Pamphlet on the 'rentrée' at the Lycée de Laval, 30.9.40.
46. Paxton, op. cit. 156, quoting the law of 17.7.40.
47. Vichy punished all civil servants (cf. C. of 8.8.40) who had ordered evacuation without authority, but this was merely a continuation of a procedure that had begun before the collapse.

    On May 26, 1940 Mandel had dismissed eight police superintendents from the Nord department who had given evacuation orders without authority; a few days later several mayors were dismissed for the same reason. On the other hand Mandel promoted Liénart to the rank of Commander of the Légion d'Honneur for his exemplary calm and refusal to budge during the débâcle. (Cf. P. Reynaud, *La France a sauvé l'Europe*, Vol. ii, 1947, 292–3.)

Lesser fry, particularly primary teachers, who were punished after the defeat for deserting their post and who in many cases acted as mayor's secretaries, had merely communicated and obeyed the orders of the local civic authorities.

48. C. of 16.8.40. Cf. also AD du Nord, Lille, R.1585. Report of academy inspector to prefect, 26.11.40. On May 18, 1940 the ministry had authorized all primary teachers in the department to leave their posts.
49. J. A. Faucher and A. Ricker, *Histoire de la franc-maçonnerie en France*, 1967, 304. This book was approved by the Grande Loge de France.
50. J. E. Talbott, *The Politics of Educational Reform in France, 1918–1940*, Princeton, NJ, 1969, 100.
51. Cf. Note (49), 367.
52. P. Chevallier, *Histoire de la franc-maçonnerie française*, Vol. iii, *1877–1944*, 1975. At the end of this book is given a list of prominent freemasons.
53. Simone de Beauvoir, *La Force de l'âge*, 1960, 478.
54. J. Guéhenno, *Journal des années noires, 1940–1944*, 1947, 37. This first declaration was made on 19.9.40. A diary entry for 7.8.41 (p. 137) shows that he had to make the same declaration four times.
55. AN F.17.13344. Letter from A___ R___ to Bonnard, 24.6.42 and letter from the headmaster of the École Primaire Supérieure Jean-Baptiste-Say, n.d.
56. Faucher and Ricker, op. cit. 433. *La Croix* (16.10.41) estimated that there were 50,000 freemasons, of whom 12,000 were 'dignitaries' (office-holders).
57. Paxton, op. cit. 156.
58. AN F.17.13344. Note from the director of primary education to Néret, of Bonnard's 'cabinet', Paris, 25.6.42. The figures apparently relate only to the occupied zone.
59. AD du Nord, Lille, R.1050.
60. AN F.17. bis 172. 'Fonctionnaires relevés de leurs fonctions – israélites – étrangers'.
61. Jeanneret, op. cit. 165, 167–8.
62. Maillard, op. cit.
63. Deposition of M. X___, an inspector general working in the directorate of secondary education at the time, given at Bonnard's trial.
64. Testimony of M. X___, lodged at the Comité d'Histoire de la Deuxième Guerre Mondiale.
65. M. Winock, *Histoire politique de la revue 'Esprit', 1930–1950*, 1975, 229–30.
66. J. Carcopino, *Souvenirs de sept ans*, 1937–1944, 1953, 342–57.
67. Cf. Note (63).
68. Ibid.
69. AN F.17.13376. File of prefects' reports, September 1941–March 1942.
70. Ibid.
71. Ibid.
72. AN F.17.13337. Monthly report of prefect of the Gers, 3.3.42.
73. AN F.17.13364. 'Note sur la situation des instituteurs publics', n.d., n.p. [Paris, 1942?].
74. AN F.17.13364.

75. AN F.17.13364. 'Note sur la situation pécuniaire des instituteurs', n.d., n.p. [autumn 1942?]. The note observed: 'It is understandable that staff are not satisfied.'
76. AN F.17.13348. News-sheet of Inter-France Information headed: 'Note strictement confidentielle et personelle', 21.4.44.
77. AN F.17.13364. Sheet showing in diagrammatic form the many tasks of the primary teachers (1944) and a 'Projet de circulaire', 28.4.44, forbidding outside organizations to ask the primary teachers to give more assistance.
78. AN F.17.13380. Letter from Feldkommandantur (677) V Az Dr D/Z Ve 2a Br.B Nr. 5355, Poitiers, 9.6.41, to the prefect of the Vienne.
79. AN AJ 40.565. File: Angelegenheiten der Akademie Poitiers. 'Note de la Direction de l'Enseignement primaire', for Inspector General Roy, Paris, n.d. [June 1941] and: AN AJ 40.563. Lageberichte ('sitreps') der Gruppe IV. The report for 22–29.6.41 states that the measures against the Colorado beetle had been agreed with the French.
80. AN F.17.13337. Anonymous note to Bonnard, n.d., n.p.
81. Leading article, 'La Petite Cité', *Le Temps,* 3.10.40.
82. AN F.17.13364. 'Note relative à l'application aux institutrices publiques de la loi du 11.10.40 sur le travail féminin', by Jolly, director of primary education.
83. *Délégation française auprès de la Commission allemande de l'Armistice. Recueil de documents publiés par le gouvernement français,* Vol. i, *29.6.40 –29.9.40,* Imprimerie Nationale, 1947, 227. (Compte-rendu No. 20, 6–9 Sept. 1940.)
84. AN F.17.13382. 'Note pour le ministre: les instituteurs et le Service obligatoire du Travail', Paris, 19.3.43.
85. AN F.17.13348. Letter from the Secretary-General for the Labour Force, Paris, 20.3.44. to Bonnard.
Delanoue (cf. Note (2)) gives a different account (pp.148 and 283–5). The number of primary teachers actually leaving for Germany depended upon the attitude of the academy inspectors, about half of whom had been appointed before the war. In the Seine 56 per cent of those teachers eligible (272 out of 486 registered) actually left; in the Marne and the Nord none left at all. By March 1944 replacements for those leaving would be difficult to find. About 1,800 new teachers were emerging from the new style professional training institutes but most were packed off immediately to Germany.
86. M. Chrétien, 'Les associations professionnelles de fonctionnaires', *La Gazette du palais* (ed. G. Moore), 1941, 2è semestre (Vol. ii) 26–32.
87. AN AJ 40.556. Note to Vpol., German Military Commander in France, from Oberkriegsverwaltungsrat Dr Dahnke, Paris, 7.11.41.
88. Delanoue, op. cit. 193–8, gives details of these recruits to Bonnard's staff. His book also has an account (118–39, *passim*) of the part primary teachers played in the Resistance and of the clandestine activity of the former teachers' unions.
89. Delanoue, op. cit. 58.
90. Bulletin of the Association professionnelle des Instituteurs et Institutrices publics de la Drôme, Nos. 1. and 2 (Vacances 1943), 1.10.43.
91. AN AG II 609. 'Affaire Descombes et ses rebondissements'. Descombes, the academy inspector of the Drôme, had been transferred through the manœuvrings of Lavenir, who had succeeded in getting a friend appointed in his place. Reports said the new inspector was acting strangely, trying to start up an anticlerical campaign and working in league with Lavenir in

other ways. One report of 22.7.43 said that he had called Bonnard 'un ami des Boches'.

92. AN F.17.13346. Account of meeting of 29.4.43.
93. AN F.13336. Letter from Marcel Sivé to Bonnard, received 27.8.42.
94. Cf. correspondence in AN AG II 570.
95. AN F.17.13337. Copy of letter, undated, from M. M___ to Inspector General Roy, Paris. In the margin is pencilled: 'We have won nothing from the primary teachers. SNI is trying purely and simply to reconstitute itself; the salary increase has been absorbed without the slightest sign of gratitude.'
96. Cf. Note (90) 'Carnet de notes de l'A.P' ('Association Professionnelle').
97. Quoted in Delanoue, op. cit.200–1.
98. AN F.17.13342. Letter forwarded by Déat to Bonnard from a teacher, M. B.-D., of Provins.
99. AN F.17.13342. Anonymous letter to Bonnard, n.d., n.p., signed: 'X et Y, universitaires'.
100. AN F.17.13342. Letter to Bonnard, 15.6.42, from M. G___, former teacher at the Lycée d'Auxerre.
101. AN F.17.13342. Letter, n.d., n.p. signed: 'C.S.A.L.F.'.
102. Reported in: *Le Phare,* Nantes, 10.9.43.
103. Talbott, op. cit. 59, Note raises the question as to why so many ex-Normaliens became political activists in the Third Republic. The same question might be raised regarding the political activism of ex-Normaliens under Vichy, to cite at random only a few mentioned in the present volume: Brasillach, Carcopino, Chevalier, Déat, Garric, Mireaux, Pelorson, Pucheu, and Zoretti.
104. AN AG II 459. 'Questions pendantes entre le Secrétariat d'État à l'Éducation Nationale et le Cabinet civil' (of Pétain), Vichy, 18.6.41. The 'cabinet civil' had written to Carcopino on 9.7.41 asking for instructions to be issued that Pétain's 'messages' should be read in schools.
105. AD du Nord, Lille, R.2287. Report of rector to prefect, April/May 1943.
106. AN AF.17.13344. Note No. 492. 845.
107. In Northern France pro-British sentiment was constant from the beginning of the Occupation. Cf AN AJ 40.557. Letter from Bezirkschef A. Verw. IIe,O.U. of 8.11.40 to German Military Commander in France, Paris. The report states that the Propagandastaffel Nordwest (Lille–Calais area) notes a pro-British attitude among the primary teachers.
108. AN F.17.13367. Note by the regional delegate of the SGJ, Flandre–Artois, Lille, 18.6.42.
109. Simone de Beauvoir, op. cit. 528.
110. P. Jardin, *La Guerre à neuf ans. Récit.,* 1971, 125.
111. E. Lablénie, *Aspects de la résistance universitaire,* Bordeaux, 1964, 9–15.
112. Delanoue, op. cit. 154.
113. AN F.17.13342. Bonnard's staff received a copy of a statement made by M. D___, the manager of the bookshop at the anti-Bolshevik exhibition, to the organizers, the Comité Anti-Bolchévique. The statement contains a number of allegations criticizing teachers' conduct at the exhibition.
114. Janet Teissier du Cros, *Divided Loyalties: A Scotswoman in Occupied France,* London, 1962, 201.
115. Cf. Note (69).
116. AN F.17.13364. Document headed 'Propagande Instituteurs', n.d.,n.p. [mid-1942].
117. AN F.13364. 'Sanctions révisées à la date du 24.7.42'. In Bonnard's handwriting is written on it: 'Pas un Communiste'. Bonnard showed no leniency to Communists.

118. Broadcast of 28.8.42. Reported in: *Le Temps,* 31.8.42.
119. *Le Temps,* 3.9.42.
120. Typed copy of speech preserved in the De Chambon Collection, Hoover Institution, to which the writer expresses his thanks for permission to quote.
121. AN F.17.13364. 'Équivalence du brevet supérieur et du baccalauréat', Paris, 22.7.42. It was estimated that only 3,000–4,000 primary teachers would be affected by this measure.
122. AN F.17.13345. Letter of Albertini to a member of Bonnard's staff, Paris, 13.10.42.
123. AN F.17.13364. 'Note pour Monsieur le Ministre', Paris, 17.9.42. by Jolly, director of primary education.
124. AN F.17.13364. (*a*) 'Note pour Monsieur le Ministre. Projet de Bulletin National des Instituteurs', Paris. 5.10.42.
 (*b*) 'Bulletin national de l'Enseignement primaire. Objet de sa publication', n.d, n.p.
125. AN F.17.13337. 'Réflexions d'un jeune instituteur "de gauche", fils d'un docker'.
126. AN F.17.13377. Rapports mensuels des ordres d'enseignement et des établissements pour la Délégation Générale du Gouvernement Français (Paris). Report for 15.8.42 – 1.11.42 (*sic*).
127. Announced by the clandestine periodical: *Défense de la France,* No. 43 of 15.1.44. Cited in: Marie Granet, *Le Journal 'Défense de la France',* 1961, 236.
128. X___Y___, 'Épuration administrative', roneoed document held at the Comité d'Histoire de la Deuxième Guerre Mondiale.
129. The number of personnel in secondary education at 31.12.40 is given in AN F.17.13380.
130. AN AG II 459. File: 'Instituteurs'. Document headed: 'Questions qui sont à l'ordre du jour dans les milieux instituteurs'. Pencilled on it: 'Printemps 44 (mars)'. The document gives the following figures to show the decline in recruitment to primary teaching: taking 1939 as 100, by 1943 the index for boys had fallen to 58, for girls to 53. This does not mean that there was a shortage, but merely that quality of recruitment had declined.
 There is also a tally of sanctions taken against primary teachers, but it is unlikely that the figures given are global or definitive. They show:

Dismissals	102
Compulsory retirement	99
Posting to other departments	199
Posting to other schools in the same department	500
Total	900.

V. THE REGIMENTATION OF YOUTH

1. B. de Jouvenel, 'Plan national pour la jeunesse', *La Lutte des jeunes,* Paris, 4.3.34.
2. Message published in: Bulletin de liaison des Compagnons de France, 15.11.40.
3. P. Baudouin, 'Discours à des jeunes qui entrent dans la vie', *Revue des jeunes,* January 1939, cited in: *Églises et chrétiens dans la Deuxième Guerre mondiale. La région Rhône–Alpes. Actes du Colloque de Grenoble,* 1976, publiés sous la direction de Xavier de Montclos, *et al.,* Lyons, 1979, 127. The analysis of relationships between Baudouin and others concerned

with youth at Vichy in 1940 is given in a paper by B. Comte in the Actes, entitled, 'Les Catholiques dans les nouvelles institutions de jeunesse, Vichy, 1940', 125–9.

4. P. Pucheu, *Ma vie,* 1948, 291. After the war proceedings that had been taken against Lamirand were dropped in July 1947. He subsequently became mayor of La Bourboule, where he was a company chairman, and associated with left-wing Gaullist deputies. (Cf. H. Coston, *Dictionnaire des hommes politiques,* Vol. ii, 1972.)
5. A. Basdevant, 'Les services de jeunesse pendant l'Occupation', *RHDGM,* 56, numéro spécial: Vichy et la jeunesse, October 1964, 81. Basdevant's account is the most authoritative.
6. J.-P. Cointet, 'Marcel Déat et le Parti unique (été 1940)', *RHDGM,* 91, July 1973, 19.
7. An overview of the organization can be found in a booklet issued by the SGJ, 'Instruction Générale [*sic*] pour les délégués de la jeunesse', Vichy, 30.4.41, filed in AN AG II 654, File A 308: 'Jeunesse'.
8. AD du Nord, Lille, R.1583. Synthèse des rapports des préfets de la zone occupée, April 1942.
9. Cf. Deidre Bair, *Samuel Beckett,* London, 1978, *Passim.* I am indebted to Mr S. Ó Seanóir, of the library of Trinity College, Dublin, for drawing this book to my attention.
10. Pelorson's career is summarized in: AN F.17.13367. A 'Note' for Pétain in: AN AG II 459, Vichy, 12.5.42 mentions the suspicion held in Pétain's office that Pelorson will take on a political role.
11. The discussion at the meeting was reported to Pelorson. The report (n.d.) is in: AN F.17.13367.
12. AN AJ 40.563 Lagebericht ['sitrep'] of Gruppe IV (Kultur und Schule), 25–31.8.41 to 1–6.9.41.
13. AN AG II 609. Document headed: 'État du Secrétariat Général de la Jeunesse', dated [in pencil] 28.7.43.
14. There is some mystery about the resignation of Olivier-Martin. He may not formally have resigned until 2.6.44. In AN F.17.13347 a letter from him to Bonnard of that date speaks of 'the bitterness of a setback' and the 'differences which may have set us at loggerheads'.
15. AN F.17.13366. Speech of Gaït to the regional youth delegates, 12.1.44.
16. Cf. Chapter VII.
17. Cf. Chapter X.
18. Cf. Chapter XI.
19. J. Duquesne, *Les Catholiques français sous l'Occupation,* 1966, 215.
20. AD du Nord, Lille, R.1915. Letter to Prefect from Oberfeldkommandantur 678 Lille, 14.1.44.
21. CDJC. Carton CDXC IV – 7–8. Report from Abwehrstelle, Bordeaux, Ref: Br. B. Nr. 5301/43G III C 2 to Abwehrleitstelle Frankreich, Paris, dated Bordeaux, 27.9.43.
22. AN AJ 40.557. (German file). Angelegenheiten der Sekretariat (*sic*) Général de la Jeunesse im frz. Unterrichtsministerium. Bd. I V.Kult. 403J. Letter signed for Dr Best, Chef des Verwaltungsstabes, ref. Verw.V.pol. 256.02/2., Paris, 31.5.41, addressed to the SGJ. Cf. also Circular from Verwaltungsstab Abt. Verw. Az.V. pol. 256/02/2, Paris, 31.5.41. to all Feld- and Kreiskommandanten.
23. Ibid., Note, 7.5.41., ref. V Kult. 407, by Dr Dahnke, Verwaltungsstab.
24. AN AG II 570. File: 'Plan de réformes de l'Éducation Nationale (documentation)'. Cf. also: AN AG II 440, 'Note pour M. Jardel', Vichy, 30.6.42.
25. Cf. Chapter XIII.

26. AN AJ 40.557. Aktenzeichen V.Pol. 256/02/4, Paris, 7.12.41.
27. AN AG II 650. File marked: 'Huitième Commission du Conseil National. Étude des questions de jeunesse. Sessions du 5 au 12 mars 1942'. The file contains a list of commission members, a 'synthèse des travaux' of the commission, drawn up by Pétain's 'cabinet civil', and an analysis of each of the sessions of the commission, with annexed documents, including the final recommendations. Subsequent notes in this chapter refer to the various sessions.

    The reference to the youth commission as the *eighth* commission is intriguing. It is usually cited as the *seventh* commission and it is assumed that there were only seven commissions in all. (Cf. Note (28) following, regarding the paper of Rossi-Landi.)

    The commissions listed in the text are given in random order, which does not represent the numeral normally assigned to each.
28. The speech was allegedly written by Massis. Cf. G. Rossi-Landi, 'Le Conseil National', in: *Le Gouvernement de Vichy, 1940–1942,* Fondation Nationale des Sciences Politiques, 1972, 54.
29. AN AG II 440. File CCIIIH Document V/HD., 'Note concernant la session [*sic*: the term is otherwise applied, not as here to the whole meeting, but to the different sittings of the commission] du Conseil National consacrée à la Jeunesse', Vichy, 26.2.42. In this document Mgr Beaussart is referred to as 'Bossard' and Marc Sangnier, the founder of 'Le Sillon', becomes 'Marx Saugnier'.
30. In AN F.17.13337 is a pamphlet headed: 'Cahier de la Fondation Française pour l'étude des problèmes humains. Régent: Dr Alexis Carrel. I. Ce qu'est la Fondation. Ce qu'elle fait', PUF, Paris, 1943. The foundation was set up by a law of 17.11.41. It comprised sixteen teams, each with a speciality. One team was concerned with 'le développement de la jeunesse'. Some work seems to have dealt with race and heredity: there was one team for 'la biologie de la lignée'.

    Although Carrel's institute had the initial backing of Pétain, he would appear to have distanced himself fairly quickly from the Marshal. In AN F.17.13346 is a letter from the Vice-President of the institute – not even from Carrel – to the ministry of education, dated Paris, 29.7.43, refusing an invitation addressed to Carrel to become a member of the Conseil National. Carrel, through his intermediary, did not accept because, he said, he was too busy.
31. Première séance, 5.3.42.
32. In a ceremony at Toulouse on 1.3.42 scouting organizations had just united in a federation named 'Le Scoutisme français'.
33. These figures may be an overstatement. Cf. Chapter II, p. 38.
34. 'Extrait du compte-rendu analytique de la séance du lundi, 9 mars 1942. Audition de M. Pucheu, Ministre de l'Intérieur'. At this session Pucheu, who was an anticlerical, alluded to the measures taken by Carcopino to annul the proclerical ones taken by Chevalier.
35. Huitième séance, 10.3.42. Cf. J. Carcopino, *Souvenirs de sept ans, 1937–1944,* 1953, 520–3. Carcopino states that, despite being minister, he was not consulted before the youth commission of the Conseil National was convened. He offered his resignation but this was not accepted. He was deliberately absent from Vichy for most of the time the commission was meeting. He also states that he expressed dissatisfaction with the 'école des cadres' at La Chapelle-en-Serval, which had been set up in the occupied zone without his knowledge, and, at the same session, his great satisfaction

with the Chantiers de la Jeunesse. He does not mention in his memoirs Pucheu's criticisms of the ministry of education.

36. Cinquième séance, 7.3.42.
37. Troisième séance, 6.3.42.
38. Duquesne, op. cit. 209, reports, without stating his source, that Dunoyer de Segonzac was also taken to task by Lafont and de La Porte du Theil for allowing Mounier's personalism to be the paramount doctrine at Uriage.
39. Troisième séance, 6.3.42.
40. Reported in AN AG II 440. File CCIIIH.
41. Quatrième séance, 7.3.42.
42. Cf. *Le Chef compagnon,* 1.11.41.
43. Deuxième séance, 6.3.42.
44. Quatrième séance, 7.3.42.
45. Ibid.
46. Troisième séance, 6.3.42.
47. Deuxième séance, 6.3.42.
48. Huitième séance, 10.3.42.
49. Quatrième séance, 7.3.42. Bonnard said: '. . . if in the France of yesterday a care for purity inhibited one from preparing a child for political life, which had become a profitable industry or a centre of infection in the nation, one cannot conceive that in the world and in the State which is at present being built children should not be prepared for political life and integrated into the State that they must sustain and nourish'.
50. Cinquième séance, 7.3.42.
51. Bergery may have been an embarrassment, for in 1942 he was eventually packed off to Ankara as ambassador.
52. Huitième séance, 10.3.42.
53. Cinquième séance, 7.3.42.
54. Huitième séance, 10.3.42.
55. Neuvième séance, 11.3.42.
56. Cinquième séance, 7.3.42.
57. Septième séance, 10.3.42.
58. Huitième séance, 10.3.42, and Annexe I to the 'Rapport Général': 'Note sur l'organisation des Jeunesses Paysannes, présentée par M. Dorgères'.
59. Synthèse des travaux. Cf. Note (27).
60. Sixième séance, 9.3.42, and: Huitième séance, 10.3.42.
61. Huitième séance, 10.3.42.
62. Synthèse des travaux. Cf. Note (27).
63. Cf. J. Berthelot, *Sur les rails du pouvoir (1938–1942),* 1968, 254. He reports that by the spring of 1942, 'disappointed, satiated with mediocre speeches, the young are turning their hopes and imagination elsewhere'.

VI. 'MORAL REFORMATION'

1. Recueil des Actes administratifs de la Préfecture de la Somme – Année 1940, Amiens, 1941, 570 et seq.
2. *Revue des deux mondes,* 15.8.40.
3. In a note to Pétain quoted in: P. Baudouin, *Neuf mois au gouvernement, avril–décembre 1940,* 1948, 224.
4. Speech given in Paris by Lamirand in 1941, given in a pamphlet: *France nouvelle, à nous, jeunes. Vers l'unité,* n.d., n.p., probably 1942, lodged in AD du Nord, Lille, 4483.
5. AN AG II 654, 'Contribution à l'étude du problème de la jeunesse en France', by Colonel du J____, 17.4.41.

6. J. Peyrade, 'Recherche de l'Effort', *La Croix*, 1–2.1.41. In order to convey the tone of such injunctions the quotation, like some subsequent ones, is given in the original French, as well as in translation.
7. A. Gide, *Journal, 1939–1942*, 1946, 62–3. Entry for 16.7.40.
8. R. Gillouin, in a preface to: J. Guibal, *La Famille dans la Révolution Nationale, Les Cahiers français*, Clermont, n.d., 2.
9. J. Guéhenno, *Journal des années noires, 1940–1944*, 1947, 106.
10. Quoted in: R. Aron, *Histoire de Vichy, 1940–1944*, 1954, 393–4.
11. R. Brasillach, *Écrit à Fresnes*, 1967, 325.
12. M. Sicard in: *Émancipation Nationale*, quoted in: Mgr Guerry, *L'Église catholique en France sous l'Occupation*, 1947, 149.
13. At the time Bardèche was a young lecturer at the Sorbonne.
14. H. Massis, *Maurras et notre temps*, 1961, 334.
15. H. de Montherlant, *Le Solstice de juin*, Paris, 1941. For this paragraph I am greatly indebted to: J. Cruickshank, *Montherlant*, London, 1964, *passim*.
16. In a circular to schools quoted in: Mornet, *Quatre ans à rayer de notre histoire*, 1949, 168.
17. AD de l'Ardèche, Privas. M.132. 'Cours professionnels: demandes de subventions, 1936–1943'. Copy of the presidential address at a prize-giving organized by the Société d'Enseignement professionnel du Rhône, July 1941.
18. J. Peyrade, 'Notre jeunesse', *La Croix*, 27–8.4.41.
19. H. Bourgin, *L'Ecole nationale*, Paris, 1942, 81.
20. Pétain, speaking at Meaux in 1934, reported in: R. Griffiths, *Marshal Pétain*, London, 1970, 163.
21. C. Maurras, *La Seule France*, Lyons, 1941, 247–8.
22. AD des Bouches-du-Rhône, Marseille, IT bis – 62 – 1. Annual report for 1945–6 of the headmaster of the Lycées Périer and St-Charles, Marseilles.
23. *Le Temps* published a series of articles on 'Le Travail et la Vie universitaires' (*sic*) on 29.5.42, 1.6.42, 3.6.42, and 4.6.42, before discussing the Lyons proposal in a leading article on 26.6.42 and returning to the subject of professional ethics on 21.8.42 in another leading article entitled 'Conscience professionnelle'.
24. AN AG II 650. Huitième Commission du Conseil National. Étude des questions de jeunesse. Session du 5 au 12 mars 1942. Compte-rendu analytique de la 2è séance, 6.3.42.
25. Ibid. Cf. 'Rapport général présenté au nom de la Commission par Georges Pernot. Dispositif des Avis et Vœux'.
26. P. Crouzet, *L'Enseignement, est-il responsable de la défaite?* Toulouse–Paris, 1943, 68.
27. Cf. Article in: *Le Temps*, 9.7.40. Through his books Gide was accused of 'shaping a proud and effervescent generation'.
28. Maurras, op. cit. 245.
29. AN F.17.13365. Letter of Mme B___ of Saint-Marcel, to Pétain, 21.2.43.
30. M. Gabilly, 'Les journées de Vichy: un assainissement qui s'imposait', *La Croix*, 14–15.9.41.
31. AN AG II 81. One parent wrote to Pétain from Reims on 7.6.43 complaining that the comic contained material not fit for his ten-year-old son. Cf. also: P. Ory, *Les Collaborateurs*, 1976, 76–7.
32. For much of the information on the cinema the author is indebted to: J. Daniel, *Guerre et cinéma*, 1972. Attendance figures are given on p.184, n.15. Daniel's book contains also an account of relevant productions shown in France during the period of the 'phoney' war, such as Ryder's, *Après*

Mein Kampf *mes crimes, par Adolf Hitler.* (1939). He also refers to productions made in Hollywood during the war, including Renoir's *This Land is Mine* (1943) *('Vivre libre'),* which depicts the courageous action of a primary teacher in denouncing the Germans and shows him – without acknowledgement to René Bazin's *Les Oberlé* – returning to his class-room to teach a last lesson to his pupils on the Declaration of the Rights of Man before being arrested. Daniel also gives a summary account of the innumerable post-war films on the Occupation and the Resistance. Thus *Au Cœur de l'orage* has some shots of the tumultuous scenes at railway stations that sometimes occurred when young people left for forced labour in Germany. *Le Grand Rendezvous* depicts the Chantiers de la Jeunesse as the training ground for young Resisters. Marcel Ophuls's *Le Chagrin et la pitié* (1969) is in a class by itself. It illustrates that neat classifications of Frenchmen during the Occupation into either Gaullists or Communists, with a small minority only of Pétainists or collaborationists, are far too simplistic. As regards youth, it sheds new light on the Révolution Nationale when Lamirand, SGJ, whose main task was to put over that 'revolution' to the young, allegedly terms it in 1969 'nothing but a slogan'. Cf. *The Sorrow and the Pity. Chronicle of a French City under the German Occupation. Text of the film,* published by Paladin Books, St. Albans, Herts, 1975.

33. Mgr Beaussart also spoke of 'une littérature malsaine'. The expressions were used at the youth commission of the Conseil National. Cf. Note 24. Compte-rendu analytique de la 5è séance, 7.3.42.
34. E. Vuillermoz, 'L'assainissement de l'écran', *Le Temps,* 10.11.40.
35. P. Ory, op. cit. 85. Cf. also: H. Amouroux, *La Grande Histoire des Français sous l'Occupation.* Vol. iii. *Les Beaux Jours des collabos, juin 1941–juin 1942,* 1978, 434.
36. A good analysis of these films is given in: Ory, op. cit. 86–9.
37. [The Catholic] Association du Cinéma familial: Distribution, 1944. Recueil de films autorisés avec scénarios et critiques techniques et morales, Lille, ed. Morel, 1944.
38. H. Le Boterf, *La Vie parisienne sous l'Occupation, 1940–1944.* Vol. i, 1974, 113. The section on the cinema is given on pp. 91–162.
39. Recueil des Actes administratifs de la Préfecture de la Somme – Année 1942, Amiens, 231.
40. Le Boterf, op. cit. 200–1, Cf. also P.-H. Simon, *Histoire de la littérature française contemporaine,* Vol. ii, 1956, 145–96, *passim.*
41. Reported in: *La Croix,* 2.1.42.
42. Ibid. 14.11.41.
43. Ibid, 21.11.41.
44. Ibid. 11.2.42.
45. *L'Action jurassienne,* 22.2.41, Prof. A. Pinard, 'A la jeunesse. Pour l'avenir de la race française', and 10.5.41, Prof. Calmette, 'Aux jeunes gens . . . Contre les tentations malsaines'.
46. G. Bertier, *Une mystique pour les jeunes Français,* Toulouse–Paris, 1944, 90 et seq.
47. *Le Temps,* 12.5.42.
48. AN F.17.13342. Letter to Bonnard dated Paris, 27.6.42.
49. AN F.17.13376. Report of prefect of the Nord, 4.10.41. and ibid., Report of prefect of the Charente-Maritime, 26.12.41.
50. Letter of Cardinal Gerlier to his diocesans, 'Pour la dignité et la fraternité française', quoted in: *Cahiers de notre jeunesse,* Lyons, No.7, February–March 1942.

51. CDJC. Carton CDXCV. Lagebericht ('sitrep') of Group 'Kultur und Schule' for April–May 1941.
52. Recueil des Actes administratifs de la Préfecture de Vaucluse, Avignon. Bulletin administratif des Mairies, Recueil No. 47 of 16.10.43.
53. Simone de Beauvoir, *La Force de l'âge,* 1960, 529.
54. J. Dutourd, *Au bon beurre,* 1952, 79.
55. G. Pailhès , *Rouen et sa région pendant la guerre, 1939–1945,* Rouen, 1948, 106.
56. Le Boterf, op. cit. Vol. i, 323–37 gives some idea of the popularity of jazz at the time.
57. Vauquelin, Discours de fondation des Jeunesses Populaires Françaises, à la Mutualité, le 25 mai 1942 in (brochure): *Les Documents de la jeunesse,* No.1, n.d., n.p.
58. Amouroux, op. cit. 445.
59. For attempts to get rid of the 'bals clandestins', cf. P. Bourget and C. Lacretelle, *Sur les murs de Paris, 1940–1944,* 1959, 77.
60. AN AG II 542, Letter from Jeunesse Agricole Chrétienne, n.d. (1943), n.p., to Pétain's 'cabinet civil'.
61. J. de La Porte du Theil, *Les Chantiers de Jeunesse ont deux ans,* Paris, 1942, weekly bulletin of 19.2.42.
62. Ibid., weekly bulletin of 31.10.40.
63. Broadcast of 13.10.41.
64. There was also the prospect of a trip to Vichy. The Marshal had asked pupils to give fairness and frankness a trial and let him know by Christmas how they were getting on. The senders of the 1,000 best letters (approximately ten per department were chosen) would spend a day at Vichy.
65. Cf. 'Consignes générales pour la constitution d'un groupe de Jeunes du Maréchal. See p. 337.
66. Guéhenno, op. cit. 11 and 231.
67. A. Bettencourt, 'Ohé les Jeunes: Nous dénoncerons', *La Terre française,* 11.10.41.
68. J. Dumazedier, 'Esprit du sport et de l'éducation', *Jeunesse . . . France, Cahiers d'Uriage,* 3è année, No. 30, April 1942.
69. AD des Bouches-du-Rhône, Marseille, IT bis 62–1. Annual report, 1940–1 of the headmaster of the Lycées Périer and St-Charles, Marseilles, 1941, 3.
70. AD des Bouches-du-Rhône, Marseille, IT 5–18, Conseil de l'enseignement primaire, sessions of 18.9.42 and 19.3.43.
71. S. Jeanneret, *La Vérité sur les instituteurs,* Paris, 1942, 26–7.
72. R. Denux, *Le Drame d'enseigner,* Paris, 1944, 129.
73. H. d'Amfreville, 'Rajeunissement de la jeunesse', *Les Cahiers français,* special youth number, Paris, n.d. [1942?], 50–2.
74. AN F.17.13348. Letter from Admiral Platon to Bonnard, Pujols-sur-Dordogne, 28.5.44. Platon, an austere Protestant, believed that France could only be saved by collaborating loyally with Germany.
75. Cf. H. and F. Joubrel, *L'Enfance dite coupable,* 1946, 21–5.
76. AD du Nord, Lille, R. 871. Extrait du Régistre des délibérations du Conseil Municipal, Lille, session of 8.2.44.
77. H. d'Amfreville, loc. cit.
78. Sisley Huddleston, *France: The Tragic Years,* London, 1958, 123.
79. M. Martin du Gard, *Chronique de Vichy, 1940–1944,* 1948, 326–7.
80. J. Le Marchais, 'Une jeunesse sage', *Les Cahiers français.* Cf. Note (73), 58–9.
81. M. Aymé, *Le Chemin des écoliers,* 1946. In a final 'coup' Antoine earns 750,000f. trading in coffins which he has not even seen!

82. M. Clément, 'Recrudescence inquiétante de la criminalité infantile', *Jeunesse . . . Organe de la génération 40,* Paris, No. 10 , 2.3.41.
83. AN F.17.13376. Report of prefect of the Oise, 31.10.41.
84. AN AG II 650. Huitième Commission du Conseil National. Étude des questions de jeunesse. Observations at eighth session, 10.3.42, by Pernot. It was also reported that in Lyons truancy affected one in four school pupils.
85. The two tables are taken from: M. Levade, *La Délinquance des jeunes en France, 1825–1968,* 1972, 2 vols. Volume of tables and graphs, Tableau 15 (Arabic figures) and Tableau XI (Roman figures).
86. H. Gaillac, *Les Maisons de correction, 1830–1945,* 1971, 363 and Joubrel, op. cit. 91 and 94.
87. Joubrel was also a director of this centre. He ascribed the causes of delinquency of those he found there to syphilis and alcoholism among parents, which led to the break-up of the family. Cf. H. Joubrel, *Ker-Goat, Le Salut des enfants perdus,* 1945, 103.
88. Delinquents under 13 constituted 11.1 per cent of the total in 1938. The peak was reached in 1941 with 13.0 per cent.
89. Vauquelin. Cf. Note (57).
90. Micheline Bood, *Les Années doubles. Journal d'une lycéenne sous l'Occupation,* 1974, 83 and 91. Diary entries for 18.2.41 and 23.3.41.
91. AN F.17.13376. Monthly reports of prefect of the Nord dated 2.1.42 and 2.3.42.
92. AN AG II 459. Postal intercept containing: Rapport mensuel de l'Association des Anciens des Chantiers. Canton de Châlus, Haute-Vienne, August 1942 (extracts).
93. AN des Bouches-du-Rhône, Marseille, IT bis 51–58. Annual report of the Collège moderne et technique des garçons, Aix-en-Provence, 20.11.45.

VII. 'GENERAL EDUCATION', SPORT AND HEALTH

1. The author would like to acknowledge his debt to: R. J. Holt, Aspects of the social history of sports in France, 1870–1914, Unpublished Oxford D. Phil thesis, 1977.
2. G. Bertier, *Une mystique pour les jeunes français,* Toulouse–Paris, 1944, 70–1. Bertier eventually joined the Fondation Alexis Carrel as an educational advisor.
3. B. de Jouvenel, *Après la défaite*, Paris, 1941, 102.
4. M. Ruby, *La Vie et l'œuvre de Jean Zay,* 1969, 246 et seq.
5. J. Zay, *Souvenirs et solitude,* Paris, 1945, 146, 243–4.
6. *Semaine religieuse,* Lyons, 27.9.40, reproducing one of Gerlier's sermons.
7. AN AG II 650. Testimony given to the Youth Commission of the Conseil National by Borotra.
8. R. Gillouin, *J'étais l'ami du Maréchal Pétain,* 1966, 180.
9. Y. Bouthillier, *Le Drame de Vichy,* Vol. ii, 1950, 348.
10. R. Silly and G. Albertini, *Pour sauver notre avenir,* Paris, 1943, 18.
11. J. Carcopino, *Souvenirs de sept ans, 1937–1944,* 1953, 290.
12. AN AJ 40.557. Draft letter by KVR (Kulturverwaltungsrat) Dr Dahnke, ref. VKult 407, V.pol.272 to de Brinon, Paris, 3.4.41. Cf. also: ibid. File: Zu Vkult 404. Beiakte zu VKult 404. Tätigkeitsberichte.
13. AN AJ 40.557. File: VKult 404, as above.
14. Details are given in CDJC, Carton LXXVIII – État major [allemand], Hotel Majestic, Paris, 82. Cf. also testimony of Borotra in: Fondation Nationale des Sciences Politiques, *Le Gouvernement de Vichy, 1940–1942,* 1972, 86. In 1940 Borotra was captured and escaped from the

Germans three times. On 27.6.40 he had asked Weygand for permission to be demobilized and leave for England. He was duly demobilized and was about to fly to England to join de Gaulle, when on July 3 he heard of the British attack at Mers-el-Kébir. He felt he could not leave France at that time. A few days later he met Pétain, who invited him to help with youth affairs. Borotra says that one of his grandmothers was English.

15. H. Mavit, 'Education physique et sports', *RHDGM,* 56, October 1964, 96.
16. Quoted in: Bouthillier, op. cit. 349.
17. AN AG II 497, 'Au personnel du Commissariat Général. . . ', Vichy, 20.4.42.
18. AN AG II 75. Ménétrel, as Pétain's private secretary, wrote to Krug von Nidda, the German Minister at Vichy, on 29.7.43, at the request of the King of Sweden, to ask whether the monarch could have news of Borotra.
19. Ripert declared to the press on 30.11.40 that his purpose for youth was 'to raise up a new *race* [writer's italics] through physical exercise and sport'.
20. Cf. *L'Écho de Paris,* 23.7.34 and: *L'Ami du peuple,* 21.1.36, quoted in: R. Griffiths, *Marshal Pétain,* London, 1970, 162–3.
21. J. de La Porte du Theil, *Un an de commandement des Chantiers de la Jeunesse,* Paris, 1941, 18. Cf. Chapter XI.
22. Ibid., Bulletin No.15 of the Chantiers de la Jeunesse, 28.11.40, 95
23. Pascot is quoted in: *Équipes Nationales,* Paris, August 1943.
24. *Le Temps,* 29.7.40.
25. AN AG II 459. The document is a copy of a speech made by Borotra, probably in the autumn of 1940.
26. *Le Temps,* 6.10.40.
27. Mavit, op. cit. 97.
28. *Jeunesse. . . France. Cahiers d'Uriage,* 3è année, No. 30, April 1942, 31.
29. The text is given in: *Stades. Revue mensuelle de l'Éducation Générale et des Sports,* No. 5 of 1944.
30. Cf. proposals for the 1944 'Fête du Serment de l'Athlète', AD de la Haute-Marne, Chaumont, T.120.
31. Mavit, op. cit. 94 and: *La Croix,* 12.9.41.
32. Circulars of 18.11.40, 5.6.41, and 28.7.41.
33. Secrétariat d'État à l'Éducation Nationale et à la Jeunesse, Instructions. Tome Premier. Les Activités d'Éducation générale, June 1941. (Preface by Carcopino.)
34. Press communiqué of Inter-France, No. 50 of 29.2.44. 'L'Éducation générale et le redressement français. L'Œuvre du Colonel Pascot.'
35. Mavit, op. cit. 93.
36. *Les Documents français,* No. 9, September 1941. Number devoted to: 'La réforme de l'enseignement'.
37. Hoover Institute, *La Vie de la France sous l'Occupation, 1940–1944.* Vol. ii, 1957, 875.
38. H. Michel, *Vichy, année '40,* 1968, 128.
39. AD des Hautes-Alpes, Gap, T.1.1062.
40. AD de la Haute-Marne, Chaumont, T.120. Sport-Affaires diverses, 1938–44.
41. *Journal officiel,* 8.4.41. The German consent was finally given on 22.3.41.
42. Recueil des Actes administratifs de la Préfecture des Hautes-Alpes, Gap, mai–août, 1941, 148.
43. C. of ministry of interior to prefects. Section générale de la Police Nationale, 283/Pol.4 of 17.4.42.

44. AD des Hautes-Alpes, Gap, T.1 1057.
45. Ibid. T.1 1057.
46. Le Palonnier ['joystick'], magazine of the Aéroclub de Valence, 'Les Ailes Rhodaniennes', Valence, No.3 of 1941.
47. Ibid. No. 6 of 1941. Curiously, and perhaps significantly, the magazine also printed a translation of Kipling's 'If'.

    The German ban on gliding was imposed on 2.12.42 and Pascot protested in a letter to de Brinon dated 8.12.42, a copy of which is in: AN AJ 40.557, File: VKult 404, Bd II.
48. Mavit, op. cit. 92.
49. L. of 13.11.40.
50. Mavit, op. cit. 100. Mavit states that direct financial aid was given to sport as follows: 1942: 36 million francs; 1943: 64 million francs; 1944: 97 million francs.
51. A. Basdevant, 'Les services de jeunesse pendant l'Occupation', *Revue d'histoire de la Deuxième Guerre Mondiale,* October 1964, 68.
52. Circular No. 144 of ministry of interior, Vichy, 24.9.40.
53. L. Planté, *Au 110 Rue de Grenelle,* 1967, 313.
54. AD des Hautes-Alpes, Gap. Letters of departmental inspectors to academy inspector, Gap, in: T.1.1059, and of academy inspector to prefect, 10.10.40 in: T.1.1059.
55. AD des Hautes-Alpes, Gap, T.1.1060. Letter from mayor of Bersac to prefect, 15.4.41.
56. Ibid. Letter from mayor of Saléon to prefect, 2.1.41.
57. Ibid. Letter from mayor of Saint-Genis to prefect, 6.1.41. The use of the word 'export' is interesting: a campaign had been launched to ban the use of the English borrowing 'sport' and to substitute for it the medieval French word 'desport', which was of course the provenance of the English word.
58. Ibid. Letter from mayor of Des Crottes to prefect, 8.1.41.
59. Ibid. Minutes of meeting of Conseil Municipal of Savournoy, 27.4.41.
60. AN F.17.13376. Cf. various reports of prefects during the autumn of 1941.
61. Ibid. Report of prefect of the Loiret, 3.1.42 and of prefect of the Ille-et-Vilaine, 5.1.42.
62. AD des Hautes-Alpes, Gap, T.1.1063. Leaflet headed, 'A games field in every village and small town'.
63. AN F.17.13376. Report of prefect of the Vosges, 31.1.42.
64. AN F.17.13366 'Note sur le Commissariat Général aux Sports', n.d., n.p., but written after 16.6.44.
65. Speech made at Perpignan by Pascot on 3.5.42, a few days after taking over from Borotra, printed in a brochure, 'Politique et doctrine sportives', Commissariat Général à l'Éducation Nationale et aux Sports, n.d., n.p.
66. A C. of 25.11.40 had laid down the time for 'general education' and P.E. combined to be nine hours a week in schools and three afternoons a week in higher education. A C. of 28.7.41 had reduced the time allocation drastically in schools. Circulars of 3.10.41 and 21.10.41 further reduced the time in schools to 2–3 hours a week and in higher education to one afternoon a week. Further reductions relate to the effects of undernourishment, and were imposed by a C. of 22.6.42.
67. Cf. Note (64).
68. 'Caporalisation' is used by A. Rosier, 'L'université et la Révolution Nationale', in P. Arnoult *et al., La France sous l'Occupation,* 1959, 135.

69. AN AG II 570. Letter from Pascot to Pétain, Vichy, 9.7.43.
70. AN AG II 604. In a letter to Col. Chapuis, a member of Pétain's staff, the head of the Légion in the Haute-Vienne says that the Jeunesses Athlétiques de la Légion, founded in the department in 1941, had been continually opposed by Pascot and he asked Chapuis to intervene.
71. AN F.17.13367. 'La formation générale dans les centres de jeunesse', n.d., n.p.
72. At Lyons in March 1941.
73. The Commissariat Général supplied 250 pairs of skis for use in the schools of the Hautes-Alpes. Cf. Bulletin de l'enseignement primaire. Académie de Grenoble. Département des Hautes-Alpes, Gap, No.1 of 1941, 72. Cf. also: AN AJ 40.557. VKult 404.
74. AN F.17.13381. Letter from Maury, ministry of family and health, to Roy, Délégation générale, Paris, 16.2.42, forwarded to Borotra.
75. *Le Temps,* 2.8.42.
76. *Le Temps,* 21.9.42. For a criticism of Pascot's view that in 'éducation générale' sport should be paramount, cf. *Le Temps,* 19–20.9.42, leading article entitled, 'La Synthèse'.
77. AN F.17.13376. Report of prefect of the Nord, 2.2.42.
78. R. Pernet, 'Action et Inaction de l'École', *Les Cahiers français,* No.3, Paris, n.d. [1942?], 29.
79. Michel, op. cit. 127.
80. AN F.17.13376. Report of prefect of the Vendée, 2.3.42.
81. *La Croix,* 31.10.41.
82. AN F.17.13365. Report of: Directeur de l'Éducation Générale et des Sports, Bourges (Cher), 29.10.43. The query regarding the novice nuns arose from the Mother-General Superior of a Franciscan order. Cf. AN F.17.13365, where her original letter to Bonnard is to be found, and: AN F.17.13381 for his reply.
83. AN F.17.13376. Report of prefect of the Loire-Inférieure, 2.10.41.
84. H. Michel, *Les Courants de pensée de la Résistance,* 1962, 404.
85. E. Lablénie, *Aspects de la résistance universitaire,* Bordeaux, 1964, 21.
86. Hoover Institute, op. cit. Vol. ii, 1957, 877.
87. A. Mallet, *Pierre Laval,* Vol. ii, 1955, 209.
88. Figures are given in: *Remountaren (sic),* monthly news-sheet of Groupement 37 (Bayard) of the Chantiers de la Jeunesse, 11,1942.
89. R. Dumay, 'Jeunesse Paysanne' in: *Les Cahiers français,* special issue devoted to youth, 4/10, Paris [1942?], 30.
90. AN F.17.13376. Report of prefect of the Oise, 30.9.41.
91. Ibid. Report of prefect of the Loir-et-Cher, 1.10.41. The ban on dancing had had the effect of making sport more popular.
92. Mavit, op. cit. 99.
93. A. Fabre-Luce, *Journal de la France,* Geneva, 1946, 382.
94. The mayor of Méricourt (Somme) maintained that the sports facilities provided in his village were little used, despite pressure from the local representative of the Commissariat Général, described by him as a 'camouflaged' regular officer. Cf. the mayor's memoirs: G. Richebé, *Souvenirs de guerre d'un fantassin,* 2nd edition, 1962, Méricourt-L'Abbé, chez l'auteur, 171.
95. The practice was to stop. Cf. Instruction of the academy inspector, 15.10.41 given in: Bulletin départemental de l'enseignement primaire, Aix.
96. Annual report of the: École Primaire Supérieure de Garçons, Aix, 1.7.42, in: AD des Bouches-du-Rhône, Marseilles, IT bis 51–58.

97. Annual report of the: Lycée St-Charles, 1945–1946, Marseilles, in: ibid., IT bis 62–1.
98. P. Ducrocq, L'enseignement primaire dans le Pas-de-Calais depuis la deuxième guerre mondiale (1945–1967), unpublished 'mémoire de maîtrise', Université de Lille III, June 1973, 107.
99. Cf. *Le Procès Pétain. Compte-rendu sténographique,* Vol. ii, Paris, 1945, 698. (Testimony of Chevalier.)
100. AN AG II 75. Press communiqué, 7.2.41.
101. AN AG II 495. Report by the: Institut de Recherches d'Hygiène, Marseilles, 18.10.41 to Pétain, of a survey carried out in February – April 1941.
102. AN AG II 495. 'Appel en faveur de l'Enfance française sous-alimentée', by Prof. Dr Th. Reh, Directeur de l'Institut d'Hygiène de Genève.
103. AN F.17.13345. Letter from M. S___, of Dijon, 27.7.42, to Bonnard. Bonnard replied that negotiations for students to be given a J-3 ration card were already under way.

 Not that the J-3 rations were sufficient. It was calculated that at the beginning of 1942 they amounted only to 1469 calories a day. By the addition of a few unrationed goods occasionally available this could be increased to 1742 calories, whereas it was reckoned that young people aged 14–20 needed at least 2800. By the autumn of 1943 J-3 rations had been further reduced. Cf. AN AG II 495. Notes by the doctors of the Clinique St-Éloi, Montpellier, to the prefect, 21.1.42.

 A report produced by the Institut de Conjoncture (AN AG II 495. 'Rapport No. 9, Situation économique') in November 1941 stated that at one year of age a child received in rations 179 per cent of the *minima vitales.* This dropped to 106 per cent at age 7; at 8 years it stood at 98 per cent (i.e. it fell below minimum requirements); at 15 it was 53 per cent; and at 18 it was 47 per cent. The insufficiency was greatest between the ages 15–22. A fourteen-year-old would need an extra 1,110 calories to achieve the minimum, the eighteen-year-old an additional 1,710 calories. (But there was disagreement as to whether the minimum should be reckoned at 2,400, 2,800, or 3,000 calories.)
104. *Le Temps,* 12.6.42.
105. AN F.17.13376. Report of prefect of the Meurthe-et-Moselle, 1.4.42.
106. AN AG II 607. 'Rapport sur l'alimentation des jeunes . . . présenté à la Commission médicale d'Alimentation . . . le 28 juin 1941'.
107. AN F.17.13342. Letter to Bonnard from M. B___, Inspector general, Paris, 10.5.42.
108. Conseil départemental (*sic*), première session ordinaire de 1944, 6 juin (*sic*), rapport du préfet, Amiens, 1944, 56 and 81.
109. C. of 27.2.41. 'Ration supplémentaire de pain aux enfants des écoles'. The extra ration was limited to school days. It was eaten dry, although some children would bring 'jam' ('moût de raisin') to spread on it. The bread cost 16 centimes a day.
110. L. Detrez and A. Chatelle, *Tragédies en Flandres, 1940–1944,* Lille, 1953, 260. The meal was known as 'la soupe de 4 heures'.
111. AN F.17.13344. 'Note' n.d., n.p.
112. *La Croix,* 11.12.41.
113. AN F.17.13350. Letter from the academy inspector, Marseilles, 4.1.44, to Bonnard.
114. C. of 4.4.42.
115. C. of 2.11.40. 'Distribution du lait dans les établissements scolaires'.

116. Detrez and Chatelle, loc. cit.
117. *Le Progrès de la Somme,* 21–2.11.43.
118. Micheline Bood, *Les Années doubles. Journal d'une lycéenne sous l'Occupation,* 1974, 143.
119. *A la recherche du passé V. Les misères de la guerre, 1939–1945. Témoignages d'enfants. Ministère de l'Éducation Nationale. Annales du Centre départemental de Documentation pédagogique de la Somme,* Amiens, 1964.
120. AN AG II 542. Jardel file.
121. A delegation of the Confédération des Boissons arrived in Vichy on 12.8.40. Cf. P. Nicolle, *Cinquante mois d'Armistice. Vichy, 2 juillet 1940–26 août 1944. Journal d'un témoin,* Vol. i, 1947, 60.
122. Anon ., 'L'alcoolisme, est-il en régression?', *La Croix,* 3.9.41.
123. *Le Temps,* 25.8.40.
124. L. of 4.11.40. 'Débits de boissons à proximité des établissements scolaires'.
125. AN F.17.13376. Report of prefect of the Eure-et-Loir, 3.4.42.
126. R. Millet, 'Dans le Haut-Jura avec les Compagnons de France', *Le Temps,* 2.12.40.
127. AD du Nord, Lille, R. 1913.
128. AN AG II 650. Figures given by General de La Porte du Theil in evidence to the Youth Commission of the Conseil National, eighth session of 10.3.42. (The percentages have been checked and corrected.)
129. Ibid. Evidence given by General Lafont.
130. AD de la Haute-Marne, Chaumont, T.122. Enseignement technique. Réunions du comité, 1937–1944.
131. AD du Jura, Lons-le-Saunier, T.1350. Éducation Nationale – Commissariat à la Jeunesse, 1944.
132. *L'Action jurassienne,* 2.11.40.
133. C. of rector of the academy of Paris to head teachers of *lycées,* 10.3.42.
134. *Le Temps,* 1.7.42.
135. Bulletin d'information corporatives, Nice, 6.7.42.
136. Detrez and Chatelle, op. cit. 259.
137. The table is compiled from:
    – Ministère de la Statistique. Direction de la Statistique Générale. Statistique du Mouvement de la Population, Nouvelle série, T.xix. Années 1940 à 1942. 2è Partie: les Causes du Décès, Paris, 1945. Tables (*sic*) I.

    and – ibid. Nouvelle série, T. xxii, 1949, Tables (*sic*) I.

    By 1945 the TB mortality-rate was less than in 1938, although the rate in 1944 had been above the pre-war figure. Both before and during the war the mortality-rate was highest for the 20–24 age group. The following figures show the mortality for this group, per 100,000 inhabitants, male and female, as compared with the mortality-rate for TB at all ages:

	1936		1941		1942	
	M.	F.	M.	F.	M.	F.
Age group 20–24	144	157	221	188	210	179
All ages M. and F.	120		137		159	

138. AN F.17.13342. Letter from Gidel, rector of the academy of Paris, to Bonnard, 27.6.42. Gidel wanted students to receive at least a T-ration card, as did students of the École Normale Supérieure and Polytechnique. This would give them rations equivalent to those holding a J-3 card.
139. AD du Jura, Lons-le-Saunier, T.1350. Éducation Nationale. Commissariat à la Jeunesse, 1944.
140. C. of 1.4.42. 'Lutte contre les épidémies'.
141. AN AG II 81. 'Réunion des préfets régionaux du mardi 21 septembre [1943]'. The meeting was chaired by Laval.
142. AN AG II 459. Document signed by the Secrétaire Perpétuel de l'Académie des Sciences, and others, 1.8.41.
143. Cf. Note (137). T.xix, loc. cit.
144. AN AG II 497. 'Note pour M. le Maréchal Pétain', from the Institut Prophylactique, Paris, 11.3.43.
145. AN F.17.13376. Report of the prefect of the Oise, 31.10.41. In 1942 22.8 per cent of all children born to mothers under 20 were illegitimate, but in 1939 the proportion had already been 20.5 per cent (Cf. Note (137), T.lvi, 1940–5, 1946, Table 5, p. 30 and p.33)
146. AN AG II 495. Note by the doctors of the Clinique St-Éloi, Montpellier, to the prefect, 21.1.42.
147. Ibid. Typescript dated March 1942, 'L'enfance française et la carence alimentaire'.
148. Annual report of the Collège Moderne et Technique d'Aix-en-Provence, 1945–6, 4.
149. AD des Bouches-du-Rhône, IT 2–5, 'Note' from the Inspecteur de la Santé, Bouches-du-Rhône, in response to a proposal of 9.12.40 from the Délégation Spéciale [replacing the Conseil Municipal] of Marseilles. 'Les idées font long feu': in 1793 Lakanal, Sièyes, and Daunou had presented a draft decree to the Convention proposing a medical examination of all schoolchildren three times a year.
150. L. of 13.8.43.
151. *Stades. Revue mensuelle de l'Éducation Générale et des Sports.* No. 5 of 1944.
152. Zay ironized over many of Vichy's 'discoveries', to use his own term: 'l'orientation scolaire', 'la radio scolaire', 'l'apprentissage obligatoire', 'l'éducation physique et les activités dirigées' [='l'éducation générale'], 'la médecine préventive des étudiants'. Cf. Jean Zay, *Souvenirs et solitude,* 1945, 329–30. (Diary for 29.10.42)
153. Reported in: Information universitaire, No. 997 of 11.1.41.
154. C. of 17.12.41. 'Précautions contre le surménage des enfants'.
155. *La Croix,* 27.10.41. In the southern zone school began at 8.30 a.m.

VIII. CULTURAL 'REVISIONISM'

1. AD du Nord, Lille, R.890. Report of university librarian to rector, 26.8.40.
2. Verordnungsblatt des Oberbefehlhabers in Frankreich (VOBIF), 30.8.40.
3. P. Héraclès (ed.), *La Loi nazie en France* (Préface et commentaire de Robert Aron), 1975. Héraclès cites only two measures taken directly by the Germans against books used in French schools: (*a*) The ordinance of 30.8.40. (*b*) The 'Bekanntmachung' ('avis') of 31.12.40, which extended the first list and developed into the 'Liste Otto'.
4. AN F.17.13378, File: 'Manuels scolaires' contains a pamphlet issued by the Syndicat des Éditeurs, 117 Boulevard St-Germain, Paris, 28.9.40. It quotes the agreement made with the German military authorities: final

responsibility for publication rests with the publisher; publication must not harm the interests or prestige of Germany; works of an author banned in Germany must not be published; the Syndicat des Éditeurs will submit doubtful cases to the Propaganda-Staffel (Gruppe Schriftum); present stocks of books will be reviewed and undesirable works 'weeded out'; in future the Germans will receive two copies of every publication.

5. *Unerwünschte Literatur in Frankreich/Ouvrages littéraires non désirables en France,* Syndicat des Éditeurs, 117 Boulevard St-German, Paris. . . .3 Ergänzte und verbesserte Auflage/Troisième édition, complétée et corrigeé . . . Mit einem Anhang der Namen jüdischer Autoren in französischer Sprache, 10 Mai 1943/ Avec un appendice donnant la liste des auteurs juifs de langue française, 10 mai 1943.
6. O. Abetz, *Pétain et les Allemands. Mémorandum d'Abetz sur les rapports franco-allemands,* 1948, 39.
7. AN AJ 40.563. Lageberichte ('sitreps') d. Gr.4 mit Material von den Bezirkschefs.
8. Ibid. Lagebericht of 18–24.11.40.
9. Ibid. of Dec. 1940–January 1941.
10. Syndicat des Éditeurs. Circular No. 240 of 27.5.42.
11. CDJC, Paris, Carton CDXCV. Lagebericht of February–March 1942.
12. AN AJ 40.563. Lagebericht of July – September 1943.
13. AN AJ 40.560. Letter from Chef des Verwaltungsstabs, Bordeaux, 2.7.41, to Verwaltungsstab, Militärbefehlshaber in Frankreich, Paris. Dr Dahnke of the Gruppe 'Kultur und Schule' replied that only school-books were directly censored; other books, unless specifically mentioned, were published at the publisher's discretion.
14. AN AJ 40.560. The textbook was: A. Lyonnet and P. Besseige, *Petite Histoire de France – Cours élémentaire,* published by Librairie Istra.
15. Mornet, *Quatre ans à rayer de notre histoire,* 1949, 35.
16. AN F.17.13376. Report of prefect of the Doubs, 2.4.42.
17. AN F.17.13378. A letter from the director of the Musée Pédagogique, Paris, 12.1.43 informed Pétain's 'cabinet civil' of the number of films authorized.
18. *Le Temps.* Articles appearing on 24.8.40 and 25.8.40.
19. AN F.17.13379. Prefect of the Côte d'Or, Dijon, in a letter to the Délégation Générale du Gouvernement français, Paris, 28.10.40.
20. AN F.17.13378. Academy inspector, Nancy, to rector, 12.11.40.
21. C. of 7.12.40.
22. Instructions of Academy inspector, Avignon, 'Révision des catalogues des bibliothèques scolaires', Bulletin départemental de l'inspection primaire, Aix, 10.2.41.
23. *Bulletin de l'enseignement primaire,* Academy of Grenoble, Hautes-Alpes (Gap), No. 8 of 1941, 306–7.
24. A. of 3.2.41. The banned book was Weber and Gailly, *Arithmétique,* 2 vols.
25. AN F.17. Ter.299. Letter from G. d'H___, inspector general, to director of secondary education, ministry of education, Paris, 18.6.42.
26. Cf. AN F.17.13378. Letter from the headmistress of the girls' *lycée* at Dijon, to Bonnard, 5.4.44.
27. AN F.17.13378. Letter of academy inspector, Maine-et-Loire, to rector of Angers, 30.3.43.
28. C. of 26.10.43.

29. Carcopino lifted the ban on certain books, maintaining it on others; for example, R. Rolland, *Jean Christophe. La Croix* (22.2.41) stated that some books had been banned by Chevalier for their sectarianism and 'internationalism'.
30. C. Maurras, *La Seule France. Chronique des jours d'épreuve,* Lyons, 1941, 243–4.
31. The book in question was: Fustel de Coulanges, *Histoire des institutions politiques de l'ancienne France, 1875–1892.* This attack on the French Revolution was condemned by the clandestine *l'Université libre,* No.100 of 1.8.44.
32. S. Jeanneret, *La Vérité sur les instituteurs,* Paris, 1942, 82.
33. Ibid. 37. But Jeanneret himself was given to romanticizing history. In: *L'École et l'esprit civique,* Paris, 1943, 27, he gives a 'nationalist catechism' for children to learn by heart. They should know the national holidays—Armistice Day, Joan of Arc Day, and July 14. The last date, he maintained, was not really Bastille Day, but celebrates the Fête de la Fédération, when delegates from the provinces swore devotion to France in the presence of Louis XVI.
34. Ibid. 83.
35. *Le Temps,* Leading articles of 8.4.42, 'L'histoire à l'école' and of 11–12.4.42, 'L'histoire éducatrice'. Cf. also a review by Émile Henriot published by the newspaper of de Monzie's *Pétition pour l'histoire;* also G. Bertier, *Une mystique pour les jeunes Français,* Toulouse–Paris, 1944, 53.
36. *La Croix,* 5.12.41, quoting an article published by Michel Hamelet in *Le Figaro.*
37. Quoted in: *La Croix,* 5.3.42.
38. Letter by Daniel-Rops to: *Le Temps,* 14.8.40.
39. Maurras, op. cit., 251–2.
40. AN AG II 604. Poster headed: 'Les buts révolutionnaires de la Légion des Combattants'.
41. Micheline Bood, *Les Années doubles: journal d'une lycéenne sous l'Occupation,* 1974, 44. In her diary for 9.11.40 she wrote that her teacher had asked the class to buy a history textbook and had hinted that it should be the forbidden one by Isaac. At the Lycée Montaigne, Bordeaux, the same textbook was hidden away by the librarian. (Cf. pamphlet: 'Distribution des prix, 11–12 juillet 1945', Lycée Montaigne, Bordeaux.).
42. G. Benoit-Guyod, *L'Invasion de Paris, 1940–1944. Choses vues sous l'Occupation,* 1962, 109.
43. *Gringoire* (13.11.42) evidently thought that change was possible in certain circumstances. It wrote: 'It is not permissible for the history of France to be taught to young Frenchmen by an Isaac.' (Quoted in: G. Wellers, *L'Étoile jaune à l'heure de Vichy. De Drancy à Auschwitz,* 1973, 95.)
44. Jeanneret, op. cit., 162–3, 168.
45. R. Paxton, *Parades and Politics at Vichy. The French Officer Corps under Marshal Pétain,* Princeton, NJ, 1966, 194 et seq.
46. Speech at Metz, 20.11.38.
47. Quoted in: *La Croix,* 14.4.42.
48. J. Carcopino, *Souvenirs de sept ans, 1937–1944,* 1953, 305.
49. Jean Zay claimed that this had been his intention in the 1938 programmes: upper secondary education should be devoted to 'idées et mœurs'. Cf. his *Souvenirs et solitude,* 1945, 131–2.
50. *La Croix,* 7.1.42.

51. L. Planté, *Un grand seigneur de la politique: Anatole de Monzie, 1876–1947,* 1955, 319–20.
52. Ibid. 319.
53. Maurras, op. cit. 260.
54. Ibid. 241.
55. Ibid. 263.
56. AN F.17.13390. Georges Laprade, of *Les Nouveaux Temps,* forwarded a letter to the ministry of education alleging that in a convent school at Pontoise only English was offered.
57. CDJC, Paris. Carton CDXCV, Lagebericht ('sitrep') of April 1941. The Germans also enthused about the interest in learning German in the Channel Islands, which during their occupation were also governed from Paris. Correspondence shows that the Germans were anxious to procure the release of a paper ration to print dictionaries and grammars for use in schools and in evening classes, and eventually even printed a 'pirate' edition of that staple pre-war German textbook for British children, Macpherson's *Deutsches Leben* (Ginn). Cf. AN AJ 40.565. File: Angelegenheiten der Akademien – Generalakte, which contains a folder, 'Deutscher Unterricht an den Schulen der besetzten Kanalinseln' ('German instruction in the schools of the occupied Channel Islands'). Cf. also AN AJ 40.563.
58. AN F.17.13377. Report of the prefect of the Doubs, 15.6.41 – 1.8.41.
59. H. Amouroux, *La Grande Histoire des Français sous l'Occupation.* Vol. iii. *Les Beaux Jours des collabos. Juin 1941–Juin 1942,* 1978. 104.
60. B. Secret, 'La renaissance du patois', *La Croix,* 4.4.42.
61. Ripert, quoted in: *Les Questions actuelles. Enseignement en France (juillet 1940–octobre 1941). Documents officiels et textes administratifs,* Paris, n.d. [1942], 25.
62. Carcopino, op. cit. 428.
63. R. Nelli, *Histoire du Languedoc,* 1974, 303.
64. Maurras, op. cit. 248.
65. Pétain, *Paroles aux Français. Messages et écrits, 1934–1941,* Lyons, 1941, 219 et seq. ('A propos du 110è anniversaire de Frédéric Mistral').
66. R. Lafont, *La Revendication occitane,* 1974, 222–5.
67. Quoted in: *Action française,* 12.12.41.
68. R. Debré, *L'Honneur de vivre,* 1974, 68.
69. J. Debû-Bridel, *Les Éditions de Minuit. Historique et bibliographie,* 1945, 77.
70. The circulars sent out by Carcopino and Bonnard are held at the Comité d'Histoire de la Deuxième Guerre Mondiale, file: 'Enseignement. Mesures générales. (H.C)'.
71. Reported in: *La Croix,* 13.5.41.
72. P. Limagne, *Éphémérides de quatre années tragiques, 1940–1944,* Vol.i. *De Bordeaux à Bir Hakeim,* 1945, 158.
73. Cf. Note (23).
74. Reported in: *Le Temps,* 11.5.42.

IX. YOUNG FRANCE: 'UNE ET INDIVISIBLE'?

1. In 1363 an 'interim' state of Burgundy, consisting of the Burgundian dukedom, Franche-Comté, Luxemburg, and Flanders had been created as a multilingual and multicultural state.
2. Hans Globke, at the Nuremberg Trials, International Military Tribunal, Vol. 38, Document No. F.513, 218 et seq., quoted in: L. Kettenacker, *Nationalsozialistische Volktumspolitik im Elsass. Studien sur Zeitges-*

chichte, Stuttgart, 1973. The present writer would like to acknowledge his debt in this chapter to Kettenacker's study.

3. Hans Globke, *International Military Tribunal, RF-602,* Vol, 6, 742 et seq.
4. A. Déniel, *Le Mouvement breton, 1919–1945,* 1976, 222 et seq.
5. Kettenacker, op. cit. 109.
6. Ibid. 105–6.
7. J. Berthelot, *Sur les rails du pouvoir (1938–1942),* 1968, 83. Cf. also: *Le Vol des provinces. La Tentative de germanisation des Ardennes.* (La W[irtschafts] O[ber] L[eitung], n.p., Office français d'édition, 1945 (Pamphlet).)
8. AN AG II 543. Letter from Pétain's 'Cabinet' to Laval, Vichy, 26.5.43.
9. AN F.17.13379. Letter from the rector of Besançon to the ministry of education, 5.7.41.
10. AD du Nord, Lille, R.871. Decision of Oberfeldkommandantur 670, MVA II – A – I of 24.6.40.
11. AD du Nord, Lille, R. 431. Letter to prefect from Oberfeldkommandantur 670, Lille, 15.9.40.

    Robert Aron, *Histoire de Vichy,* 1954, 284, states this marks the attachment of the two departments to Brussels.
12. E. Dejonghe, 'Aspects du régime d'occupation dans le Nord et le Pas-de-Calais durant la seconde guerre mondiale', MS of a lecture given on 28.1.71, lodged in the AD du Nord, Lille. A shorter version of this lecture appeared in the *Revue du Nord,* Lille, 209, April–June 1941, 253 et seq.
13. AN F.17.13380. Report to the minister by inspector general F___, 4.6.41 on a special mission he made to the area with inspector general P___.
14. E. Jäckel, *Frankreich in Hitlers Europa*, Stuttgart, 1966, 61–2.
15. E. Coornaert, *La Flandre française de langue flamande,* 1970, map facing p.304.
16. J. M. Mayeur, *Un prêtre démocrate: L'Abbé Lemire, 1853–1928,* 1968, 99–101.
17. E. Weber, *Peasants into Frenchmen, 1870–1914,* London 1977, 100.
18. Coornaert, op. cit. 329. There is no distinctive geographical feature that delimits the linguistic frontier. Even today the 'taalgrens' is only ten miles from Lille and seven from Roubaix at its nearest point.
19. S. B. Clough, *A History of the Flemish Movement in Belgium,* New York, 1930, 278.
20. The Church in Northern France, however, gave Gantois no support. Cardinal Liénart even forbade him to say mass, save for his own personal devotions. Cf. H. Amouroux, *La Grande Histoire des Français sous l'Occupation.* Vol. iii. *Les Beaux Jours des collabos, juin 1941–juin 1942,* 1978, 459, n.55.
21. For the ideas of van Severen, cf. A. de Bruyne, *Joris van Severen. Droom en daad,* Zulte, 1961.
22. Cf. W. C. M. Meyers, 'Les collaborateurs flamands de France et leurs contacts avec les milieux flamingants belges', *Revue du Nord,* April–June, 1978, 337–46.

    For other details of the Belgian movements, cf. M. van Haegendoren, *De Vlaamse Beweging nu en morgen,* Vol. i., *Na honderd dertig jaar,* Hasselt, 1962, 74–75 and *passim.* Cf. also: E. Kossmann, *Oxford History of Europe, 1789–1940, The Low Countries,* Oxford, 1978, 630–49.
23. Cited in: Meyers, op. cit. 339.
24. The southern areas of the 'dietsch' state would include: Wallonia between the Sambre and Meuse; French Hainault as far south as Cambrai; the Lille

area between the Scheldt, the Sacarpe, and the Lys; and the Artois area between the Lys and the Aa. Cf. Meyer, op. cit. 340–3.

25. One such story, 'Praatjes uit 't Kievit-Veld. Het onstaan van Kapellebroek', ('Chats from the lapwing field. The origins of Kapellebroek'), published in *Le Lion de Flandres – De Torenwachter,* January 1941, 49, concerns the building of a dyke and ends with the moral: 'Thus our Flemish ancestors could carry out gigantic tasks. Children, you are the descendants of these heroes! Be proud of your forefathers! Be true to their honourable traditions of freedom and industriousness! And love with all your heart our beautiful Flemish land, through their sweat and toil snatched from the sea's waves.'
26. Leading article, 'Après un an', signed 'Het Vlaamsch Verbond van Frankrijk', *Le Lion de Flandres – De Torenwachter,* January 1942. The same number has also an article, 'Charles de Gaulle réclame l'enseignement du flamand', which begins, 'Oui, mais ce n'est pas celui que vous pensez', but a homonym who in 1870 made a plea for the teaching of regional languages.
27. AN F.17.13380. Letter signed by Dr Müller for Oberfeldkommandantur 670, ref: A/Kult Tgb.2/42, 18.3.42, to the regional prefect, Lille.
28. AN F.17.13380. Letter from regional prefect, Lille, to the prefect, delegate of the ministry of the interior, Paris, 23.3.42.
29. AD du Nord, Lille, R.998. Letter from regional prefect, Lille, to Oberfeldkommandantur 670, dated 17.6.42.
30. Report of the Sixteenth Flemish Congress held in August 1942 in Lille, published in: *Écho du Nord,* 24.8.42. The Wilhelmus was sung as well as the Vlaamsche Leeuw because some extremist movements, such as Verdinaso, wanted a 'dietsch' state stretching from Friesland to the hills of Picardy.
31. *Le Lion de Flandres – De Torenwachter,* October 1941, had a note headed, 'A travers la Flandre et le monde. Dédié à nos abonnés vichyssois', which mentions a collection of songs by Edmond de Coussemaker and complains that instead of these popular songs of Flanders, children are being taught to sing Bizet's 'La Marche des Rois'.
32. E. Dejonghe, 'Un mouvement séparatiste dans le Nord et le Pas-de-Calais sous l'Occupation (1940–1944): Le "Vlaamsch Verbond van Frankrijk" ', *Revue d'histoire moderne et contemporaine,* 17, January – March 1970, 50 et seq.
33. AD du Nord, Lille, R.1292. Letter (secret) from the Commissaire Principal aux Renseignements Généraux, Lille, 31.8.43, to the Directeur des Renseignements Généraux, Vichy.
34. Reports from sub-prefect, Douai, to the prefect, Lille, 9.7.42, and 11.7.42, AD du Nord, Lille, R.2029. Dr Q____ is also mentioned in the later letter cited in Note (33).
35. AD du Nord, Lille, R.1301. Letter from Commissaire Principal aux Renseignements Généraux, Lille, 4.11.43, to Commissaire Divisionnaire du Service régional des Renseignements Généraux.
36. AD du Nord, Lille, R.997 and R.305. Letters from the Oberfeldkommandantur, Lille, to the regional prefect, dated respectively 4.11.42 and 24.5.43.
37. AD du Nord, Lille, R.1262. Document received at the sub-prefecture of Douai, 8.9.42.
38. AD du Nord, Lille, R. 1262. Report by sub-prefect, Douai, to the prefect, Lille, 11.7.42.

Not much is known about Carles, the regional prefect for the Nord. In 1940 he was already installed before the collapse. Cut off from the rest of France, before the Armistice he became a regional prefect 'avant la lettre' in the powers that he exercised. Du Moulin de Labarthète, *Le Temps des illusions. Souvenirs, juillet 1940–avril 1942,* Geneva, 1946, 287, refers to him as 'un très grand fonctionnaire'. It was Carles who was chosen to read aloud the text of the oath sworn to Pétain by the prefects assembled at Vichy on 19.2.42. He would seem to have established a businesslike working relationship with the Germans and also co-operated well with Liénart.

39. E. Dejonghe, op. cit., in Note (12), 18–20.
40. AN AJ 40.565. Memorandum, ref. VKult., by Dr Dahnke, Paris, 16.10.40 headed: 'Versetzung in die Sperrzone' ('Transfer to the forbidden zone').
41. The Germans had patently a sense of history. By the Treaty of Verdun (843) a 'Middle Kingdom' (the 'bowling alley') had been created by Lothair I which extended from the North-Sea coast to Burgundy and beyond.
42. M. Rousseau, 'La répression dans le Nord de 1940 à 1944', *Revue du Nord,* Lille, 51: 203, October–December 1969, 737 (Table IV).
43. For the survival of Breton cf. Jorg Gwegen, *La Langue bretonne face à ses oppresseurs,* Quimper, 1975.
44. Robert Aron, *Histoire de Vichy,* 1954, 101–2.
45. J. Dumont (ed.), *Les Grandes Enigmes de l'Occupation,* Vol. i, n.d. Article by P. Sérant, 'Les minorités ethniques devant l'Occupation'.
46. Déniel, op. cit. 222 et seq.
47. CDJC, Carton CDXCV, Lagebericht ('sitrep') des Militärbefehlhabers in Frankreich, Anlage 32, for December 1941–January 1942.
48. Report in: *Le Phare,* Nantes, 12.1.41.
49. R. Lafont, *La Revendication occitane,* 1974, 223–4.
50. Lafont, loc. cit.
51. AN F.17.13343. Courrier Mouraille, 1942.
52. AN F.17.13376. Report of prefect of the Finistère, February 1942.
53. AN F.17.13346. The rector of Rennes forwarded a request dated 25.1.44 from the Conseil Supérieur of Rennes University to Bonnard.
54. The Deixonne Law allows regional languages – Breton, Basque, Catalan, and Occitan, to which was later added Corsican, – to be taught, but distinguishes these from 'langues allogènes', such as Alsatian and Flemish, which are considered to be dialects of national languages of foreign states. Only the standard variety of such foreign languages may be taught. There is no doubt that the Vichy experience has coloured this discrimination. However, using the local dialect as the point of departure, German is now being taught in Alsatian schools. Flemish enjoys no such dispensation and may well die out completely in French Flanders. The teaching of regional languages is an example of an educational innovation introduced by Vichy and revived after the war.
55. Déniel, op. cit. 280–1 and 285.
56. AN F.17.13377. Monthly report of the 'directeur du cabinet', ministry of education, to de Brinon, for 15.4.41 to 15.5.41. D___, a primary teacher at Saint-Guénolé(Penmarch), a released prisoner of war 'en congé de captivité', was transferred to the Nièvre department for his autonomist activities, but was instructed by the Germans not to obey the order.
57. Pamphlet: 'Le PPF et le problème breton', n.d., n.p. [Paris, 1943?].
58. J.-P. Azéma, *De Munich à la Libération,* 1938–1944, 1979, 229, n.4.
59. Preface by Weygand to: L. Cernay, *Le maréchal Pétain, l'Alsace et la Lorraine. Faits et documents (1940–1944),* 1944, p. v.

60. AN AJ 40.560. On 29.1.41 the Librairie Istra, wanting to reprint a geography textbook, enquired of the Propaganda-Staffel, Abteilung Paris, what changes had to be made.
61. The tour of Lamirand is reported in: *La Croix*, 26.7.41.
62. For details of Germanization cf. M.-J. Bopp, *L'Alsace sous l'Occupation allemande, 1940–1945*, Le Puy, 1945, *passim*.
63. J. Annéser, *Vautours sur la Lorraine. Documents inédits sur l'occupation nazie de la Lorraine, 1940 à 1944*, Metz, 1948, 73.
64. E. Schaeffer, *L'Alsace et la Lorraine (1940–1945). Leur Occupation en droit et en fait*, 1953, 94.
65. P. Cézard, 'L'annexion de fait de l'Alsace et de la Lorraine', *RHDGM*, 5, January 1952, 44.
66. M.-J. Bopp, 'L'enrôlement de force des Alsaciens dans la Wehrmacht et la S.S.', *RHDGM*, 20, October 1955, 35.
67. AD de la Drôme, Valence, BP 124. (Roneoed news-sheet), *Algrange en exil. Bulletin des Lorrains réfugiés, 1941–1943*, edited by Abbé Damant, Loriol, Drôme. Number of 15.9.41.
68. G. Benoit-Guyod, *L'Invasion de Paris (1940–1944). Choses vues sous l'Occupation*, 1962, 132–3, quoting a Resistance leaflet of January 1941.
69. A. Basdevant, 'Les services de jeunesse pendant l'Occupation', *RHDGM*, Numéro spécial, 'Vichy et la Jeunesse', 56, October 1964, 68.
70. Kettenacker, op. cit. 180.
71. Ibid. 170.
72. Bopp, op. cit., in Note (62), 262.
73. Annéser, op. cit. 22 and 82.
74. Marie Granet, *Le Journal 'Défense de la France'*, 1961, 23, quotes from No. 5 of this Resistance journal, n.d. [1941?].
75. Bopp, op. cit., in Note (62), 149, maintains that there were no Adolf-Hitler-Schulen in Alsace, but Cézard, op. cit. 43, states that a parallel school for girls was started at Ottrott.
76. Schaeffer, op. cit. 94.
77. H. Michel, *Vichy, année '40*, 1966, 160–1. Kettenacker, op. cit. 146, states that several forms of oath were used. A less compromising formula (cited 146, n. 117) ran: 'I am conscious that I, as a German civil servant and educationist, may have to serve anywhere in the Reich where the national need requires it, and in the manner which corresponds to the principles of the National-Socialist Reich. I will therefore, without any reservation, fulfil in any place of employment the tasks entrusted to me.'
78. Testimony of M. X___ given 25.8.47 and lodged at the Comité d'Histoire de la Deuxième Guerre Mondiale, Paris.
79. P. Novick, *The Resistance and Vichy*, London, 1968, 89.
80. Kettenacker, op. cit. 186–7. Anrich had left Alsace in 1918. He had taught at the universities of Bonn and Hamburg, had been the national education officer ('Reichsschulungsleiter') for the Nazi students' union, and had set up an organization – the 'Wissenschaftlicher Weststab' – to delineate a new frontier for Germany.
81. R. Ernst, *Rechenschaftsbericht eines Elsässers*, 2nd ed., Berlin, 1954, 325.
82. Kettenacker, op. cit. 188–9.
83. Ernst, op. cit. 351.
84. G. Starckey, *L'Alsacien*, 1957.
85. G.-G. Nonnemacher, *La Grande Honte de l'incorporation de force des Alsaciens-Lorrains . . . dans l'armée allemande*, 2nd ed., Colmar, 1966, 98 et seq.

86. Marie Granet, op. cit. 5.
87. General Warlimont, in the English text of the film scenario, *The Sorrow and the Pity [Le Chagrin et la pitié]*, St. Albans, 1975, 42. Cf. also: Nonnemacher, op. cit. 35.
88. Benoit-Guyod, op. cit. 187.
89. *La Délégation française auprès de la Commission allemande d'Armistice. Recueil de documents publié par le Gouvernement français*, Paris, Vol. iii (1952), 102–3. (Henceforth: *Délégation.)*
90. Jäckel, op. cit. 229 et seq.
91. *Algrange en exil.* (Cf. Note (67)), No. of 15.4.42. The soldier was Stanislas Nawroski.
92. *Délégation*, Vol. ii (1950), 23.
93. *Délégation*, Vol. iii (1952), 267 et seq.
94. R. Paxton, *Parades and Politics at Vichy. The French Officer Corps under Marshal Pétain*, Princeton, NJ, 1966, 102–4.
95. Testimony of X___. Cf. Note (78).
96. AN AJ 40.556. Letter of Dr Dahnke, ref. VKult 401, German High Command in France, Paris, 27.5.41, to Consul-General Schleier, German Embassy, Paris.
97. Testimony of X___. Cf. Note (78).
98. *Bulletin départemental de l'instruction primaire*, Académie d'Aix, September 1940, 257–8.
99. Much of the information that follows is taken from AN F.17.13379. Affaires d'Alsace. Dossiers Kraft, 1940–1. Correspondance 1940–4.
100. Robert Aron, op. cit. 343.
101. *Le Procès du Maréchal Pétain. Compte-rendu sténographique*, Vol. ii, 1945, 699.
102. *Délégation*, Vol. ii, 1950, 22.
103. There is some doubt about the total number of institutions involved, as well as the number of people. In: *Le Procès du Maréchal Pétain*, loc. cit., the total number of refugee teachers, teachers in training, and pupils is given as 1,200. Giorney Bolton, *Pétain*, London, 1957, 150, gives the same figure. In his testimony X___ (Cf. Note (78)) speaks of *seven* teacher-training colleges being evacuated. This may be because of double counting because of the different French and German names for the same location. X___ mentions that one out of 120 pupils originally from Sélestat, four out of 80 from Colmar, and two out of 120 from Obernai returned home. The documents in AN F.17.13379 used by the present writer give different figures for the number of teacher-training institutions and pupils involved. Kraft, the Alsatian envoy sent to ask for the return of people and property, mentions in a letter to de Brinon, dated 1.3.41 and written in Paris (in AN F.17.13379), the following institutions: Obernai (evacuated to Solignac), Colmar (at Aiguillon), and Strasburg (at Périgueux). These institutions were for boys. He also mentions girls' teacher-training colleges: that of Strasburg (at Périgueux) and that of Célestat (at Bergerac).
104. AN F.17.13379. Cf. previous note.
105. Testimony of X___. Cf. Note (78).
106. Decision of 10.10.42, cited in: AN F.17.13379. File O–Alsace, 1940–1944.
107. AN AJ 40.563. The Délegation Générale in Paris raised the case of interference by a local German commander near Angers in the affairs of a refugee school with Dr Best, of the group 'Kultur und Schule', on 29.8.40.
108. AN F.17.13379. Correspondence exchanged between inspector general Roy, attached to de Brinon in Paris, on behalf of the ministry of education, and the German embassy, in letters of 25.6.42 and 6.7.42 respectively.

109. Testimony of X___. Cf. Note (78).
110. Ibid.
111. Ibid.
112. Evidence of Professor X___, Lyons, at post-war trial of Chevalier.
113. Kettenacker, op. cit. 192.
114. AN F.17.13347. Gidel, rector of Paris, enclosed a Resistance tract in a letter to Bonnard dated 15.12.43. The tract gives an account of the raid. Bopp., op. cit. 160, gives the name of the professor killed in the raid as Coulon. Elsewhere the name is given as Collomp.
115. AN F.17.13348. An account of the raid, the fate of the people involved, and the conclusions to be drawn from it are given in a document dated 18.4.44, Vichy: 'Note sur l'opération de police entreprise le 25 novembre 1943 à l'université de Strasbourg à Clermont-Ferrand'.
116. Kettenacker, op. cit. 194.
117. Cernay, op. cit. 29. In the tract referred to in Note (114) the Paris Resistance group, L'Union des Étudiants Patriotes, claimed that *all* Alsatian students were arrested, including Dean Froster [Forster?], who had deserted from the German to the French forces in the First World War. It also asserted that students from the University of Oslo (*sic*), who had also resisted the Nazis, had been deported to Germany. Lavenir, then serving on Bonnard's staff, alleged at Bonnard's trial that the immediate cause of the raid was the killing of a German officer by the students. When the Germans raided the university, according to Lavenir, they shot a number of students and staff and took twenty hostages who were sentenced to life imprisonment.
118. C. Bellanger, *et al., Histoire générale de la presse française,* 1975, Vol. iv, 130.
119. AN F.17.13348. 'Note pour Monsieur le Ministre sur la dispersion de l'Académie de Strasbourg', signed P___, Paris, 17.1.44.
120. Kraft, whose other negotiations had been unsuccessful, did succeed in obtaining from Bonnard not only the Treasure of Strasburg Cathedral, but also the historical archives of the Haut-Rhin, the notarial archives of Alsace, and the archives and library of the St. Thomas Chapter of Strasburg, all of which had been in French hands and for whose safe custody the ministry of education was responsible. Cf. AN F.17.13373 and AN F.17.13379. Whereas Carcopino had tried to fob Kraft off, when Laval returned to power he intervened personally in his capacity as minister of foreign affairs, promising Kraft most of what he wanted, including equipment belonging to the privately owned École de Chimie de Mulhouse. Laval wrote to Kraft (Cf. AN F.17.13379. Letter ref: 11.564 Pol., dated Vichy, 21.8.42): '[The French government] esteems that these concessions constitute a complete and definitive settlement of questions relating to the return to Alsace and in Alsace of public property, or related to the public interest...' The indefatigable Kraft, having secured these goods, immediately lodged a further claim.
121. Evidence of M. X___, an inspector general during Bonnard's tenure of office, given at Bonnard's trial after the war.
122. J. Zay, *Souvenirs et solitude,* 1945, 271–2.

X. THE COMPAGNONS DE FRANCE

1. AN AG II 613. 'Comité Jeunesse de France. Organisation de la jeunesse en zone occupée, Historique et critique. Solutions proposées. Octobre 1940.' This committee, set up in Paris 24.7.40, would seem to have been the

earliest attempt to organize youth, although its actions in the occupied zone were stopped by the Germans. Three groups were constituted: Les Jeunes de l'Union Nationale des Combattants; l'Union Populaire de la Jeunesse Française; Les Jeunesses Nationales et Sociales (ex-Jeunesses Patriotes). Probably the suggestion for the Compagnons arose from one to open training centres for the young unemployed.

2. Further details of the movement are given in the standard work by R. Hervet, *Les Compagnons de France,* 1965, from which background information for this chapter has been drawn. Cf. also: H. Amoretti, *Lyon Capitale, 1940–1944,* 1964, *passim.*
3. Maurice Clavel, quoted in: Hervet, op. cit. 136.
4. Bulletin (issues first typed, then roneoed), Marche du Mouvement, Compagnons de France 30.9.40. Issues are conserved in AN AG II 607. The bulletins give further details of the day-to-day life of the movement.
5. AN AG II 440. File CCIIIM: Compagnons de France. 'Raisons du développement des cadres et des installations du mouvement Compagnon', n.d. [spring 1941].
6. AN F.17.13366. Letter from Lamirand to Bonnard, Paris, 28.1.43.
7. AN AG II 609. 'Note au Président Laval établie sur sa demande', by de Tournemire, 12.11.43.
8. P. Amaury, *Les Deux Expériences d'un 'Ministère de l'Information' en France,* 1969, 199.
9. AN F.17.13346. 'Extraits d'interceptions postales relatives aux Compagnons de France'. The intercepts range between January – April 1942.
10. AN F.17.13367. 'Les Compagnons de France à St-Jean-Soleymieux (Loire)', n.d. [summer 1942?] and letter from M___ M___, of the village in question, to Bonnard, 15.8.42.
11. January 1943. Quoted in: H. Amouroux, *La Vie des Français sous l'Occupation,* 1961, Vol. ii, 16, note 2.
12. AN F.17.13349. Letter to Bonnard, 2.11.43, from the Francistes and other collaborationist youth organizations asking for subsidies to be stopped to the Compagnons because the movement was helping 'réfractaires' and passing on funds to them.
13. Pamphlet by: J. Schweizer (head of the Jeunes de l'Europe Nouvelle) reproducing speeches he made at the Second National Congress of his movement, held in Paris, 14.6.43, and at the Regional Congress at Vichy, on 9.1.44. The accusation was made in the second speech (p.37 of pamphlet, n.d., n.p.). The pamphlet is conserved in AN F.17.13348.
14. Hervet, op. cit. 322.
15. P. Limagne, *Éphémérides de quatre années tragiques, 1940–1944.* Vol. i. *De Bordeaux à Bir-Hakeim,* 1945. Diary note for 25.8.40.
16. AN F.17.13346. 'Note sur les Compagnons de France'. The note mentions as taking part in such activities A___ C___, an anti-fascist since 1936, and H___, 'who may be Swedish and has been expelled from the Légion des Combattants'.
17. AN AG II 607. Report made by C___ H___, Commissariat au Chômage des Jeunes, SGJ, Vichy, March 1941.
18. E. Mounier, *Œuvres,* Vol. iv. *Recueils posthumes. Correspondance,* 1963, 674.
19. Ibid., loc. cit.
20. Ibid. 688 and 702.
21. Ibid. 676–7.
22. J. Hellman, 'Emmanuel Mounier: A Catholic Revolutionary at Vichy', *Journal of Contemporary History,* 8:4, October 1973, 11.

23. M. Winock, *Histoire politique de la revue 'Esprit', 1930–1950,* 1975, 223.
24. Chevalier at his trial. Haute Cour de Justice. Audience du 11 mars 1946. p. 15.
25. AN AG II 440. Cf. Note (5). Other sources give the sum as two million francs.
26. AN AG II 440. 'Enquête 1941. Rapport d'ensemble sur les services de jeunesse', n.d.
27. Cf. Note (24).
28. Amaury, op. cit. 199–200.
29. AN AG II 459. File: 'Famille-Santé'. Letter of Dhavernas to Du Moulin de Labarthète, Vichy, 29.5.41.
30. Cf. Note (24).
31. AN AG II 440. 'Note pour le Ministre. Inspecteur Général des Finances. Objet: Activité de M. Dhavernas, Inspecteur des Finances', 13.5.41.
32. Amaury, op. cit. 201.
33. AN AG II 440. Note signed by de Tournemire, 25.6.41: 'Mission du Mouvement Compagnons'. Pétain's reply is dated 30.6.41.
34. Ibid., 'Note pour Monsieur Du Moulin', Vichy, 18.8.41.
35. Amaury, op. cit. 201–2.
36. AN F.17.13346. 'Rapport sur le journal "Compagnons" ', n.d., n.p.
37. Ibid., 'Rapport à M. le Secrétaire-Général Adjoint (SGJ) par H___ C___, Chef de Service de la Formation des Jeunes', Lyons, 26.11.42.
38. Ibid., 'Rapport à M. le Secrétaire-Général Adjoint (SGJ) par J___ D___, Chef du Bureau de Documentation et des Publications, Lyons, 23.12.42.
39. Hervet, op. cit. 199.
40. Mounier, op. cit. 675.
41. Limagne, op. cit. 227.
42. Amoretti, op. cit. 298.
43. AN AG II 440. Note from Sûreté Nationale, Vichy, 5.3.43.
44. AN F.17.13346. 'Subventions'.
45. Ibid., 'Subventions. Crédits demandés pour l'exercice 1943'.
46. AN F.17.13366. Letter from Lamirand to Bonnard, Paris, 28.1.43.
47. AN AG II 440. Report of Bernon, Commissaire du Pouvoir, to Laval, Vichy, 31.3.43.
48. Ibid. Note from 'J. Jardel, Secrétaire-Général du Chef de l'État pour le Secrétaire-Général auprès du Chef du Gouvernement', Vichy, 13.5.43.
49. AG II 543. Tournemire's letter of explanation is dated Vichy, 8.5.43.
50. AN AG II 609. Olivier-Martin, as SGJ, reported to Commandant Féat of Pétain's 'cabinet militaire', in a letter dated 25.10.43, Paris, that he had received the order from Bonnard.
51. AN F.17.13383. Letter dated 31.10.43.
52. AN AG II 609. 'Note au Président Laval établie sur sa demande', signed by de Tournemire, 12.11.43.
53. Ibid. Letter to Pétain dated 29.11.43.
54. Hervet, op. cit. 262, note. According to Hervet (p. 260), Pétain said to the chaplain-general of the Compagnons at Vichy, after de Tournemire's flight. 'What is important is the young people. Tell Tournemire to continue on his course.' Whether this was said when de Tournemire first went into hiding or when he had definitively vanished is not clear.
55. Cf. R. Chapal, 'Vie et témoignage de l'Église réformée d'Aouste-Sallans pendant la guerre, 1939–1945', in: *Églises et chrétiens dans la Deuxième Guerre Mondiale. La Région Rhône-Alpes. Actes du Colloque de Grenoble,* ed. by Xavier de Montclos *et al.,* 1976, 298.

XI. THE CHANTIERS DE LA JEUNESSE

1. Sir Llewellyn Woodward, *British Foreign Policy in the Second World War*, London, 1971, Vol. ii, 306. Cf. also Sisley Huddleston, *Avec le Maréchal*, 1948, 124. Huddleston even states that the Chantiers were pro-British.
2. M. Martin du Gard, *Chronique de Vichy, 1940–1944*, 1948, 204.
3. R. Paxton, *Parades and Politics at Vichy. The French Officer Corps under Marshal Pétain*, Princeton, NJ, 1966, 194.
4. A. Fabre-Luce, *Journal de la France 1939–1944*, Geneva, 1946, 379.
5. General Alexander von Neubronn, 'Als deutscher General bei Pétain', *Vierteljahreshefte fur Zeitgeschichte*, 4 Jg., 1956, 3 Heft/ Juli, Munich, 242–3.
6. AN AG II 613. 'Rapport 30 – 1/Org'.
7. AN AG II 650. 'Dossier de base des groupements de la Jeunesse Française', Commissariat Général des Chantiers, Clermont-Ferrand [August?] 1940.
8. Quoted in: *Le Temps*, 29–30.8.42.
9. R. Paxton, *Vichy France: Old Guard and New Order, 1940–1944*, New York, 1972, 163.
10. J. Duquesne, *Les Catholiques français sous l'Occupation*, 1966, 67. Cf. also: J. de Launay, *La France de Pétain*. 1972, 48. De Launay declares that the Chantiers were revanchist, pro-Pétain, anti-Gaullist, anti-Communist, and against Parliamentary regimes, as well as favouring the Resistance.
11. The most important general sources on the Chantiers are:
   – J. de La Porte du Theil, *Un an de commandement des Chantiers de la Jeunesse*, Paris, 1941.
   – J. de la Porte du Theil, *Les Chantiers de la Jeunesse ont deux ans*, Paris, 1942. (The above two volumes consist mainly of a collection of instructions which appeared regularly in the Bulletin of the Chantiers.)
   – J. Delage, *Espoir de la France. Les Chantiers de la Jeunesse*. Préface du Commissaire Général de La Porte du Theil, Paris, 1942.
   – J. Delage, *Grandeurs et servitudes des Chantiers de Jeunesse*. Préface du Général de La Porte du Theil, 1950. This work has become the standard work on the Chantiers, but is somewhat justificatory after the event.
   – R. Josse, 'Les Chantiers de la Jeunesse', *RHDGM*, 56, October 1964.
   – Marie-Thérèse Chabord, 'Les Archives des Chantiers de la Jeunesse', *La Gazette des Archives*, 81 (nouvelle série), 2è trimestre, Paris, 1973, 85–94.
   – R. Hervet, *Les Chantiers de la Jeunesse*, 1952.
   – R. Vaucher, *Par nous la France . . . ceux des Chantiers de la Jeunesse*, Paris, 1942.
12. De La Porte du Theil, op. cit., 1941, 16–19.
13. Ibid. 246.
14. At a talk given by de La Porte du Theil at the University of Clermont-Ferrand, 23.1.43, reported in: *La Semaine des Chantiers*, Clermont-Ferrand, 18–24 janvier, 1943, Clermont-Ferrand, 1943, 26–7. (Brochure.)
15. AN F.17.13365. 'Note pour M. le Ministre', signed Pelorson, Secrétaire général adjoint [de la Jeunesse], Paris, 26.8.42.
16. J. Peyrade, 'Une amitié française', *La Croix*, 22.3.41.
17. Cf. Commissaire Sallé de la Marnière, 'Comment et dans quelle mesure les Chantiers de la Jeunesse contribuent à la formation de la Jeunesse française', Conférence . . . à la Faculté des Lettres de l'Université de Clermont-Ferrand. le 19 janvier 1943, Toulouse [1943?].

18. 'Les bases doctrinales du nouvel État Français', reprinted in: Bulletin de Chefs. Groupement 33. Le Ventoux, 7.12.42. Available at AD de la Drôme, Valence.
19. *En avant. Journal mensuel du Groupement Bayard* (Groupement 37, Chantiers de la Jeunesse), No. 2 of 10.1.41. Available at AD des Hautes-Alpes, Gap.
20. Cf. Note (17), p. 10.
21. De La Porte du Theil, op. cit., 1941, 97–8. Cynics shared the view that, as J. Galtier-Boissière (*Mon journal pendant l'Occupation,* Paris, 1944, 83) put it: 'Youth camps take young peasants away from their farms to make them listen to sermons advocating the return to nature', given by senior cadres belonging to 'la confrérie de Corydon'.
22. De La Porte du Theil, op. cit., 1941, 95.
23. Ibid. 29.
24. Ibid. 36.
25. Ibid. 82.
26. Ibid. 52 et seq.
27. Cf. Note (19): *En avant,* No. 6 of 15.10.41.
28. Robert Aron, *Histoire de Vichy,* 1954, 238.
29. Programme of: L'Équipe Joye, of the Jeunes de France, who staged the play at Groupement 14 (Die) in 1941.
30. R. Gillouin, *J'étais l'ami du Maréchal Pétain,* 1966, 181–2.
31. J. Plénay, 'En quittant les Chantiers', *La Croix,* 22.1.41.
32. J. W. Hellman, 'Emmanuel Mounier: a Catholic Revolutionary at Vichy', *Journal of Contemporary History,* 8:4, October 1973, 18.
33. Cf. Note (11) : R. Josse, op. cit. 20, note.
34. Capitaine P. Matout, 'Au Chef, à celui qui porte tous nos espoirs', L'Aurore, Bulletin du Groupement de Nyons (Chantiers de la Jeunesse No. 33), No. 2 of 5.10.40. Available at AD de la Drôme, Valence.
35. Cf. Note (19). P. Cauvin, Hommage au Maréchal', *En avant,* No. 5 of 15.9.41.
36. Reported in: *La Croix,* 18.6.42.
37. Fabre-Luce, op. cit. 384.
38. De La Porte du Theil, op. cit., 1942, 212.
39. J. de La Porte du Theil, op. cit., 1941, 124.
40. Paxton, op. cit., 1966, 209.
41. J. Delage, op. cit., 1950, 202.
42. J. de La Porte du Theil, op. cit., 1941, 249.
43. Ibid. 302.
44. AN AG II 613. 'Rapport sur l'état moral des Jeunes du Groupement No.8 (Chatelard)'. The report is written jointly by the commandant and the doctor. In a letter to Pétain enclosing it, dated 7.10.40, Clermont-Ferrand, de La Porte du Theil says that it is 'the starting point'.
45. J. de La Porte du Theil, op. cit., 1941, 158 et seq. 'Extraits du rapport d'ensemble sur la lère série des Chantiers de la Jeunesse', February 1941.
46. Cf. *Action française,* 26.6.41, quoting an article in: *Jeunesse . . . France,* by 'Chef' Dagonet.
47. P. Amaury, *Les Deux Premières Expériences d'un 'Ministère de l'Information' en France,* 1969, 224 et seq.
48. Cited in: J. Delage, op. cit., 1950, 38.
49. *Jeunesse . . . Organe de la génération 40,* 26.1.41.
50. M. Déat, *Jeunesse et Révolution. Conférence à l'école des cadres des Jeunesses Nationales Populaires, avril 1942,* Paris, n.d., 21 (pamphlet).

51. P. Limagne, *Éphémérides de quatre années tragiques, 1940–1944.* Vol. i, *De Bordeaux à Bir-Hakeim,* 1945, 64.
52. AN F.17.13376. Report of prefect of the Allier, November 1941.
53. AN AG II 27. SG 7. 'Synthese sur les Chantiers de la Jeunesse', Vichy, 6.3.42, from war ministry, 'cabinet du ministre, Service civil des Contrôles techniques'.
54. P. Limagne, op. cit., Vol. i, 69.
55. D. Coudroyer, *Équipe. Journal d'un jeune des Chantiers de la Jeunesse,* Grenoble, 1943, 111 et seq.
56. J. de La Porte du Theil, op. cit., 1942, 284.
57. Ibid. 282–3.
58. Ibid. 144.
59. Ibid. 109–10.
60. Ibid. 51.
61. Cf. Note (19). Remountaren (*sic.* – 'Nous remonterons', successor to: En Avant), No. 9 of 15.1.42.
62. Cf. Note (19). 'Chef' Guérard, 'L'Ame des Jeunes: le Maréchal parle aux Jeunes', En Avant, No. 2 of 10.1.41.
63. J. de La Porte du Theil, op. cit., 1942, 157.
64. Ibid. 165.
65. AN F.17.13348. Letter from Jacques Schweizer to Laval, Paris, 25.10.43.
66. An account of the activities of ADAC is given in: Bulletin des Anciens des Chantiers de Jeunesse de la Drôme, April 1942 and June 1942. Isolated issues of this journal are kept at AD de la Drôme, Valence.
67. AD des Bouches-du-Rhône, Marseille, R.1.4224 – Chantiers de Jeunesse. Report to prefect of the Bouches-du-Rhône, 19.9.42 from Commissioner Z___ H___.
68. Cf. Note (66). Article by 'Un Ancien de Valence', 'Pour l'unité française', Bulletin, September 1942.
69. Paxton, op. cit., 1966, 207.
70. O. Abetz, *Pétain et les Allemands.* (Mémorandum d'Abetz sur les rapports franco-allemands), 1948, 85–6.
71. O. Abetz, *Das offene Problem,* Cologne, 1951, 320.
72. *Délégation française auprès de la Commission allemande d'Armistice. Recueil de documents publié par le gouvernement français,* Vol. iv, 1957, 6–7.
73. AN F.17.13381. Letter from de La Porte du Theil to the Militärbefehlshaber in Frankreich, Châtel-Guyon, 17.2.42.

    The same file also contains a letter from inspector general Roy, of the Délégation Générale in Paris, dated 13.10.42, addressed to the Militärbefehlshaber in Frankreich, Verwaltungsrat, Wehrmacht Gruppe Versorgung und Fürsorge, which gives a complete description of the Chantiers' activities.
74. A. Autrand, *Le département de Vaucluse de la défaite à la Libération, mai 1940–25 août 1944,* n.p., éd. Aubanel, 1965, 34.
75. R. Paxton, op. cit., 1966, 206.
76. J. Delage, op. cit., 1950, 101. The tenor of this post-war volume of Delage is that the Chantiers' real or ultimate purpose was resistance to the Germans, but this view seems somewhat exaggerated and *ex post facto.*
77. H. Amouroux, *La Grande Histoire des Français sous l'Occupation,* Vol. ii: *Quarante millions de Pétainistes,* 1976, 362, n.39.
78. Ibid. 362–3.
79. Delage, op. cit., 1950, 101–3.

80. Ibid. 133–4.
81. Ibid. 253.
82. J. Carcopino, *Souvenirs de sept ans, 1937–1944,* 1953, 290.
83. Ibid. 439.
84. AN F.17.13348. Letter from Jacques Schweizer, head of the Jeunes de l'Europe Nouvelle, to Laval, Paris, 25.10.43. The letter, *inter alia,* says: 'You are certainly aware of the state of mind reigning in the Chantiers . . . For my part I am surprised that, at the present time, young men can still be incited, in a fashion so thinly concealed, to join the [STO] defaulters.'
85. H. Amoretti, *Lyon Capitale, 1940–1944,* 1964, 48 et seq. Cf. also: AD des Bouches-du-Rhône, Marseille, R.1.4224. A circular of the ministry of the interior to prefects, dated 22.6.42, informed them that these units were now formally assimilated to the Chantiers. Cf. also: M. Pacaut, 'La vie dans un groupement de jeunesse (novembre 1942–mai 1943)' in: *Mélanges offerts à M. le Doyen André Latreille,* Lyons, 1972. Pacaut asserts that the ex-air-force officers in 'Jeunesse et Montagne' *did* have in mind the purpose of using the 'Jeunes' against the Germans.
86. Quoted in: 'Le Mot du Chef. Message aux Anciens du Général de la Porte du Theil', *L'Aurore,* March 1943 (Cf. Note (34)).
87. Robert Aron, op. cit. 638.
88. A. von Neubronn, op. cit. 242–3.
89. Robert Aron, op. cit. 651–2. Cf. also: J. Tracou, *Le Maréchal aux liens. Le Temps du sacrifice,* 1948, 30.
90. AN AG II 459. 'État d'esprit dans les Chantiers de la Jeunesse à la suite de leur transformation', Vichy, 28.7.44. The report emanated from Laval's office. It appears that by 26.6.44 there were still 4,601 'chefs' of the Chantiers awaiting assignment to employment for the Germans. Cf. AN AJ. 39.175. File B7A: Peignage. Commission de Peignage instituée par circulaires des 9 et 19 février 1944.
91. Circular letter to: MM. les Commissaires de la République, Paris, 6.10.44 from the ministry of education. Available at AD de la Haute-Marne, Chaumont, T.120.
92. J. de Launay, *Le Dossier de Vichy,* 1967, 281.

XII. 'LEADERSHIP SCHOOLS'

1. G. Lamirand, Messages à la Jeunesse, in: *Les Cahiers français,* n.d., n.p., 15. Speech at Jociste Congress at Clermont-Ferrand, 30.3.41.
2. The figures relate to June 1942. They are given in: AN F.17.13367.
3. *Jeunesse. . . France. Cahiers d'Uriage,* 3è année, No. 29, March 1942.
4. Ibid., No. 30, April 1942.
5. AN AG II 604. File: CM 18F. Centrale de Propagande de la Légion et Service des Écoles. 'Activité du service des écoles', Commissariat Légionnaire à la Propagande, Vichy, 8.2.44.
6. AN F.17.13367. 'École des cadres supérieurs de la Chapelle-en-Serval'. Bonnard received a report from Lamirand, submitted by an investigating inspector ('commissaire du pouvoir').
7. AN AG II 609. 'Objet: Renvoi par M. Bousquet d'un professeur de l'École Nationale des Cadres – Attitude à l'égard du Maréchal', June 1942. Bonnard's reply to Laval regarding the school is headed, 'Note en réponse à un rapport du Commissaire du Pouvoir sur l'École des Cadres de la Chapelle-en-Serval.' Cf. Note (6).
   Cf. also: P. Hamp, 'Les maîtres de bagarre', *La France socialiste,* 16.7.42.
8. AN F.17.13344. Letter from F.Olivier-Martin to Bonnard's 'cabinet', 28.9.42. Olivier-Martin took over as director of the school.

9. AN F.17.13366. Letter of Olivier-Martin, now SGJ, to Bonnard 13.11.43. Copy of letter from SS and SD police commander, SS Standartenführer Knochen, to de Brinon, 20.12.43. Copy of 'Message No. 242 pour le président Laval de la part de M. de Brinon', Paris, 12.11.43.
10. AN F.17.13347.
11. J___ R___, director-designate of the Collège de Jeunes Chefs, wrote to Bousquet, then Bonnard's 'directeur du cabinet', on 7.8.42 announcing that the college would open on 5.10.42. AN 17.13366, in which the letter mentioned appears also contains a roneoed document headed 'Le Collège de Jeunes Chefs', n.d., n.p.
12. This was the way it was conceived by Mounier. Cf. E. Mounier, *Œuvres,* Vol. iv, 1963, 718, Entretiens XII, 20.10.41.
13. AN AG II 440. Report on Mayet-de-Montagne, no heading. Gaït, who eventually became the last head of the SGJ, had passed through the school.
14. J. Bourdin, 'Des intellectuels à la recherche d'un style de vie', *Revue française de science politique,* December 1959. For the information in this chapter the following works, written by those who participated in the Uriage experiment, were consulted:

    G. Ferry, *Une expérience de formation des chefs,* 1945.

    B. Cacérès, *L'Espoir au cœur,* 1967.

    G. Gadoffre, *Vers le style du XXè siècle,* 1945.

    P. Dunoyer de Segonzac, *Le Vieux Chef. Mémoires et pages choisies,* 1971.

    Cf. also AN F.17.13366. 'Pour le Maréchal de France, Chef de l'État, strictement confidentiel. Note relative aux changements de personnel nécessaires dans l'administration de la Jeunesse pour mettre en œuvre la réforme proposée', probably early summer 1942, source not known. In this document de Segonzac is praised: 'Il faut affirmer très haut la propreté, la pureté et le courage de M. de Segonzac.'
15. B. Comte, L'Expérience d'Uriage', in X. de Montclos, *et al.* (eds.), *Églises et chrétiens dans la Deuxième Guerre Mondiale. Actes du Colloque de Grenoble,* Lyons, 1978, 252. This article is the most recent account of Uriage and contains much new material.
16. R. Josse, 'L'École des cadres d'Uriage, 1940–1942', *Revue d'histoire de la Deuxième Guerre Mondiale,* 61, January 1966, 55.
17. AN F.17.13367. 'Note confidentielle' from Lamirand to Bonnard, Vichy, 18.11.42.
18. M.-J. Champel, 'L'école des chefs', *La Croix,* 9.7.41.
19. Wladimir d'Ormesson, 'Former des hommes', *Le Figaro,* n.d., quoted in: *La Croix,* 20–1.7.41. Cf. also: (Brochure), 'Réflexions pour de jeunes chefs', n.d., n.p., in the collection entitled: *Le Chef et ses jeunes (1940–1942),* written by de Segonzac and others, including Jean-Marcel Jeanneney, a future minister.
20. Janet Teissier du Cros, *Divided Loyalties: A Scotswoman in Occupied France,* London, 1962, 207.
21. E. Mounier, *Œuvres,* T.iv, 1963, 693. Pp. 693–712 deal with Uriage.
22. P. Limagne, *Éphémérides de quatre années tragiques, 1940–1944.* Vol. i. *De Bordeaux à Bir Hakeim,* 1945, 182.
23. Cf. Note (3), March 1942. Article by 'L'équipe d'études', 'Présentation d'un cahier de cycle'.
24. AN AG II 440. 'Rapport de M. M___ sur son stage du 18 août au 10 septembre 1941'.

25. AN F.17.13367. 'Impressions sur un stage à l'École nationale des cadres d'Uriage du 4 au 10 août 1942'.
26. For an account of Mounier's relationship with Uriage cf. M. Wynock, *Histoire politique de la revue 'Esprit', 1930–1950,* 1975, 220–2.
27. For an account of personalism cf. E. Mounier, *Révolution personnaliste et communautaire,* 1935, and his: *Qu'est-ce que le personnalisme?* 1947. Cf. also F. Copleston, *A History of Philosophy,* Vol. ix. *Maine de Biran to Sartre,* London, 1974, 310–17.
28. P. Boutang, 'M. Emmanuel Mounier contre Barrès', *Action française,* 10.7.41.
29. H. Frenay, *La Nuit finira,* 1973, 220–1.
30. AN F.17.13366. Cf. Note (14).
31. Letter to Borne partially quoted in: Mounier, op. cit. 695. The complete letter is available at the Bibliothèque Emmanuel Mounier.
32. Ferry, op. cit. 17.
33. His views were criticized in a leading article in: *Le Temps,* 'Le problème des cadres', 11.8.42.
34. The change of tack at Uriage was detected about mid-1941. Cf. AN AG II 440. Document with no heading but pencilled on it: 'Esprit d'Uriage' [June 1941?].
35. H. R. Kedward, *Resistance in Vichy France,* Oxford, 1978, 205–6.
36. R. Josse, op. cit. 69.
37. M. Wynock, op. cit. 238.
38. R. Wargnies, 'Les écoles de cadres du régime nouveau', *Cahiers de notre jeunesse,* Lyons, No. 2, July–August 1941.
39. Fr. Forestier, ' "Puisque la vie n'est pas neutre". Note sur l'organisation des Écoles des Cadres', *Revue des jeunes,* 15.12.40.
40. AN F.17.13366. Cf. Note (14).
41. AN AG II 440. 'Note sur le journal "Jeunesse . . . France" de l'École d'Uriage et sur l'utilité de nommer d'urgence un Aumônier à cette école', n.d., n.p. [1941?].
42. Ibid.
43. Cf. Note (17).
44. Ibid.
45. AN F.17.13366. 'Rapport de l'Inspection Générale de la Jeunesse, 1942–1943'.
46. H. Michel and B. Mirkine-Guetzévitch (eds.), *Les Idées politiques et sociales de la Résistance (Documents clandestins, 1940–1944),* 1954, 170, note.
47. The phrase is that of Kedward, op. cit. 209.
48. In a review of de Segonzac's book published in: *Esprit,* February 1972. 312.

XIII. OTHER YOUTH ORGANIZATIONS

1. H. Amouroux, *La Grande Histoire des Français sous l'Occupation.* Vol. ii. *Quarante millions de Pétainistes,* 1976, 328–9.
2. O. Abetz, *Pétain et les Allemands. Mémorandum d'Abetz sur les rapports franco-allemands,* 1948, 40. In his report dated November 11, 1940, 'Demands to be made on France', Abetz mistakenly thought that Vichy was in favour of a single youth movement. This development, he recommended, should be blocked and 'the existing contrasts' maintained.
3. R. Josse, 'La naissance de la résistance étudiante à Paris et la manifestation du 11 novembre 1940', *RHDGM,* 47, July 1962.
   Cf. also: P. Bourget, *Histoires secrètes de l'Occupation,* Vol. i. Le Joug, 1970, 215.

4. (Pamphlet) M. Déat, *Jeunesse et Révolution. Conférence de Marcel Déat a l'École des Cadres des Jeunesses Nationales Populaires,* avril 1942, Paris, n.d., and: R. Silly and G. Albertini, *Pour sauver notre avenir,* Paris, 1943. [Two speeches made by the authors. Albertini's speech is entitled, 'Un grand ministère de la jeunesse'.] P. Ory, *Les Collaborateurs, 1940–1945,* 1976, 113, mentions that even in the heyday of collaboration – June 1941 – the members of the RNP, according to the latest research, may not have exceeded 20,000. For a discussion of the collaborationist parties, cf. J. Plumyène and R. Lasierra, *Les Fascismes français, 1923–1963,* 1963 (*sic*).
5. In 1936 Déat had published a pamphlet entitled, 'Jeunesses d'Europe'.
6. Cf. Note (4), Déat, op. cit. 11.
7. Cf. Note (4), Albertini, *passim.*
8. Cf. Note (4), Albertini, 22.
9. AN F.17.13349. Two letters from Silly to SGJ, both dated 12.11.43, Paris.
10. C. Varennes, *Le Destin de Marcel Déat,* 1948, 154.
11. AD du Nord, Lille, R. 2409. Letter from J___ T___, administrator of the periodical, Jeunesse, to the prefect of the Nord, 19.6.42, Paris, giving a résumé of the history of the JPF.
12. H. Amouroux, op. cit., Vol. iii. *Les Beaux Jours des collabos. Juin 1941–juin 1942,* 1978, 416.
13. R. Hervet, *Les Compagnons de France,* 1965, 156.
14. Vauquelin, *Discours de Fondation des Jeunesses Populaires Françaises, à la Mutualité, le 25 mai 1942. Les Documents de la jeunesse,* No. 1, n.d., n.p., 32.
15. Ibid. 33–4.
16. Ibid. 36.
17. *Jeunesse . . . Organe de la génération 40,* Paris, No. of 22.6.41.
18. AD du Nord, Lille. R. 1274. Reports of Commissaire aux Renseignements Généraux to prefect, for November 1943 and January 1944.
19. Ibid. Report for July 1944.
20. AD du Nord, Lille, R.1275. File: RNP.
21. (Pamphlet) AD du Nord, Lille, 4497/5. 'Nous n'avons aucun goût pour l'esclavage', Discours de Marcel Bucard prononcé au Congrès restreint [occupied zone only] du Francisme à Paris, le 5.10.41.
22. AD du Nord, Lille 4497/1, Sommaire du Francisme, n.d., n.p. (Pamphlet).
23. (Pamphlet), ibid., M. Bucard, 'Mots d'Ordre au Jeunes', Paris (?), 1943 (?), 8. Speech of Bucard to Jeunes Francistes on 15.11.42.
24. AD du Nord, Lille, R. 1284. Report of Commissaire aux Renseignements Généraux to prefect, for April 1944.
25. AD du Nord, Lille, R.301.
26. Information gleaned from odd numbers of: *Le Franciste. Hebdomadaire de la révolution socialiste française,* Paris.
27. Cf. Note (24). Report for July 1944.
28. AN AG II 81. File of G___, attached to Menetrel.
29. AN F.17.13366. Letter from R___ P___, Commissaire Général de la Jeunesse Franciste, to Gaït, Commissaire Général à la Jeunesse, 31.3.44. Cf. also: AN F.17.13366.' Note à Monsieur le Ministre sur les demandes de subvention formulées par les Mouvements de Jeunesse Politique'. Paris, 27.6.44, signed by Gaït.
30. AD du Nord, Lille, R.1284. Report of prefect to Secrétaire-général au Maintien de l'Ordre, Lille, 20.6.44.
31. Cf. Note (18). Report for March 1944.

32. Cf. Note (18). Report for July 1944.
33. Cf. Note (23). The pamphlet shows a photograph of girls in Franciste uniform marching down the Champs-Elysées on the occasion of the tenth congress of Francisme, 1943.
34. Cf. Note (18). Report for June 1943.
From the inventory of youth movements of political parties, all of which flourished before the war, one pre-war group is missing: that of Colonel de la Rocque's Parti Social Français (PSF), the successor to the most important 'Leagues' of the 1930s, the Croix de Feu. The PSF had three million members in 1938. The league's youth movement, Les Fils de Croix de Feu, had been founded in 1932. In the latter years of the Third Republic the PSF had declared its intention of acting as a parliamentary party. De la Rocque had rallied to Pétain after the defeat but in 1942 became disillusioned and contacted the British. His contacts came to light and in 1943 he was deported to Germany.
35. (Pamphlet) J. Schweizer, 'De France-Allemagne à France-Europe', Paris, 1943.
36. Much information about the movement is gleaned from: (Pamphlet) J. Schweizer, 'La jeunesse française est une jeunesse européenne', n.d., n.p., which contains two speeches delivered by Schweizer on 14.6.43 and 9.1.44 at congresses.
37. AN F.17.13343. Note from a member of Bonnard's 'cabinet' to Bonnard, 19.11.42.
38. AN F.17.13367. 'Note pour Monsieur le Ministre', Paris, 8.9.42, and letter from Pelorson to Bonnard, 1.9.42.
39. AN F.17.13348. Letter from Schweizer to the Commissaire Général à la Jeunesse, 26.5.44. At Laval's request, a note on the activities of the Jeunes de l'Europe Nouvelle was enclosed.
40. AN AG II 81. File SP8E. 'RB/SV. Les Jeunesses de l'Europe', 10.5.44.
41. AD du Nord, Lille, R.1291. Communication from the Commissaire Principal aux Renseignements Généraux to Directeur des Renseignements Généraux, ministry of the interior, 30.5.44.
42. AN F.17.13349 contains a collective letter to Bonnard dated 2.11.43, from the leaders of four youth movements. It asks for subsidies to provide uniforms (particularly shirts!) for their members. Numbers are given as follows:

Jeunes de l'Europe Nouvelle	3,000
Jeunesse Franciste	5,000
JPF	3,000
JNP	3,000

AN F.17.13366 contains an undated two-page document with no headings save 'Suite I' and 'Suite II', signed by Schweizer, which has handwritten: 'Effectif [*sic*] au 1er avril 1943: 6,200'.
AD du Nord, Lille, R.1291. (Cf. Note (41)) gives the Lille figures.
43. C. Maurras, *La Seule France, Chronique des jours d'épreuve,* Lyons, 1941, 211, highlights the strength of Communism.
44. AN F.17.13343. Letter from Villemain to Bonnard, Saint-Mandé, 15.12.42. The file also contains a Bulletin intérieur des Cellules Françaises, 3è année, No. 14, October–November 1942. This would imply that the movement was started in 1940.
45. AN F.17.13343. Courier Mouraille, 1942.
46. AN F.17.13349. Letter from Villemain, Saint-Mandé, 17.11.43, to Georges, Bonnard's private secretary.

47. Marie Granet, *Le Journal "Défense de la France"*, 1961, 94. *(Défense de la France,* No. 18, 17.6.42.)
48. AN F.17.13366. Files labelled: Jeunes du Maréchal. Directeur du Cabinet [Bousquet]. The files give a full history of the origins of the movement and its subsequent development.
49. Ibid., 'Consignes pour l'activité des Centres Corporatifs d'Enseignement', signed: D___, Chef National aux Centres Corporatifs.
50. Ibid., 'Message aux Jeunes du Maréchal', signed: J. Bousquet, Vichy, 1.8.42.
51. Ibid., 'Projet de séjour en Allemagne d'un membre des Jeunes du Maréchal', n.d.
52. AN F.17.13342. Letter from C___ to Bonnard, Paris, 27.6.42.
53. A. Poiremeur, *Compiègne, 1939–1945,* Compiègne, 1968, 15.
54. AN AG II 497. 'Objet: Association "Les Jeunes du Maréchal" ', June 1942.
55. AN AG II 570. 'Note à M. le Secrétaire Général sur les "Jeunes du Maréchal" ', Paris, 18.7.42, from C___, Chef du Service de la Formation des Jeunes.
56. AN F.17.13366. Some leaders sought the resignation of L___, deputy secretary-general of 'Les Jeunes du Maréchal', and staged a sit-in at the movement's headquarters. Eventually L___ resigned and was temporarily replaced by Balestre.
57. AN F.17.13367. Letter from Pelorson to Bonnard, 1.9.42.
58. AN F.17.13342. Letter from Villemain to Bonnard, Saint-Mandé, 1.11.42.
59. AN AG II 440. File CC III N. Mouvements de Jeunesse. Divers. 'Note pour Monsieur Jardel', Vichy, 5.12.42.
60. AN F.17.13366. Report of Inspecteur Général de la Jeunesse, 1942–3.
61. A. Basdevant, 'Les services de jeunesse pendant l'Occupation', *RHDGM* 56, October 1964, 82–3.
62. AN AG II 81. File SP 8E. Press teleprint headed: 'Pour Avis No.782: Les Jeunes du Maréchal défilent dans Berlin en uniforme, Berlin, 30.5.43'. At the bottom of the message is written in pencil, 'Les Jeunes du Maréchal est une association *dissoute!* Interdit'.
63. M. Baudot, *L'Opinion publique sous l'Occupation. L'Exemple d'un département français (1939–1945),* 1960, 63.
64. The background to the movement is given in: R. Hervet, *Les Compagnons de France,* 1965, 151, and: P. Amaury, *Les Deux Premières Expériences d'un 'Ministère de l'Information' en France,* 1969, 203.
65. AN AG II 440 contains a roneoed pamphlet headed: 'Présentation du Mouvement "Jeunesse de France et d'Outremer" ', in which the 'doctrine' is expounded.
66. Amaury, op. cit. 203.
67. Basdevant, loc. cit.
68. Lamirand spoke at Toulouse. Cf. *La Croix,* 16.1.41.
69. AN AG II 604. File CM 18G. Jeune Légion. 'Groupe de Jeunes de la Légion', Vichy, 4.11.42.
70. AD de la Drôme, Valence. La Légion drômoise. Bulletin de liaison des Combattants et des Volontaires de la Révolution Nationale, Nos. of 10.11.42, 10.3.43, and 10.6.43.
71. Cf. Note (69).
72. Hervet, op. cit. 157–8.
73. AN AG II 79. File: D.R.A.C. Une organisation de jeunes. The file contains a pamphlet giving details of the movement.
74. C. Bellanger, *et al. Histoire générale de la Presse française.* Vol. iv. *De 1940 à 1958,* 1975, 81. The magazine was entitled: 'L'Unité française',

and Pétain's article, 'De l'union nationale à l'unité française', appeared in the issue of April–June 1941.

75. Cf. also Ch.V, p. 155.
76. AN F.17.13346. Letter to Bonnard from H. Dorgères, Paris, 12.7.43.
77. Ibid. Dorgères asked in future for a subsidy of 50,000F a month.
78. Cf. Emourine and Lamoure, *Histoire des Auberges de Jeunesse en France de 1929 à 1951, Ligue française pour les Auberges de la Jeunesse,* n.d.
79. *Guide des Auberges françaises de la Jeunesse,* 4è édition, 1.3.42, Secrétariat Général de la Jeunesse, Valence (*sic*).
80. AD du Nord, Lille, R.1304 has a copy of a circular issued by the ministry of the interior, dated Vichy, 23.6.41, and labelled 'secret', addressed to prefects, which deals with Communist propaganda. The circular says that in the past the Auberges had been used by the Communist youth organizations. Now that the Auberges de la Jeunesse movement was about to be reconstituted, the new 'umbrella' organization, the Camarades de la Route, should be carefully watched.
81. Cf. Note (79), 17.
82. Cf. Note (79), 82.
83. AD de la Haute-Marne, Chaumont, T.120. 'Circulaire intérieure', n.d., written possibly in spring 1944 by J___ C___, secretary-general of the movement. The Germans allowed night camping in designated spots, provided no uniforms were worn.
84. AN AG II 440. File: Jeune France CC III L. Roneoed report: 'Association Jeune France. Direction des services de maîtrise. Rapport sur les Maîtrises', n.d.
85. M. Wynock, *Histoire politique de la revue 'Esprit', 1930–1950,* 1975, 222.
86. Wynock, op. cit. 223.
87. Quoted in: *Cahiers de notre jeunesse,* Lyons, No. 5 of December 1941.
88. AN F.17.13346. Letter of Bonnard to the Marquis de Mun, President of the French Red Cross, n.d.
89. The 'circulaire mensuelle' of the SGJ for 1.7.43 gives a full description of the Équipes Nationales.
90. A. Basdevant, op. cit., says that the movement was set up at the end of 1941. The report of the Inspecteur Général de la Jeunesse (Cf. Note (60)) implies that it began to function in 1942 but only became an effective organization in 1943.
91. AN F.17.13347. Membership was open to all young people and could be individual or collective (i.e. youth organizations as such operating under the aegis of the Équipes Nationales).
92. AN F.17.13366. C. of 20.4.44.
93. Ibid.
94. Ibid. Letter from J___, academy inspector of the Côte d'Or, Dijon, 6.5.44, to prefect, who forwarded the enquiry to Bonnard.
95. AN F.17.13366. Letter from Pelorson to R___ C___, Chef du service de la formation des jeunes, 15.9.42.
96. AN F.17.13366. Confidential report from Rabaud to SGJ, Paris, 3.2.43.
97. In July 1943 Olivier-Martin considered that the Équipes Nationales were destined to become 'the bond of union of French youth'.
98. The programme is outlined in the circular mentioned in Note (89).
99. AN F.17.13366. Circular letter of Rabaud, Délégué Général des Équipes Nationales to Délégués Régionaux, Paris, 1.2.43.
100. AN AG II 609. 'État du Secrétariat Général de la Jeunesse', 28.7.43.

101. Announced in: *Jeunes Francistes: Informations,* 30.3.44.
102. Basdevant, loc. cit.
103. M. Déat, Les jeunes dans les ruines', *Le National populaire,* 11.9.43.
104. AN F.17.13366. A list gives the name of eight suspects, including that of the movement's representative for the Seine, appointed only in February 1944.
105. Cf. Note (89). The circular mentions nine raids, all in the space of two and a half months, at which the Équipes Nationales had assisted.
106. The circular is given in: AN F.17.13337.
107. Basdevant, loc.cit.
108. H. Coston, 'Partis, Journaux, Hommes Politiques', *Lectures françaises,* Numéro spécial, Décembre 1960, 96 et seq., lists, for example, twenty organizations comprising a 'Jeunesse Maréchaliste', who met in a big rally at the Mutualité building in Paris on 28.6.42 to declare their allegiance to Pétain. They include some not so well-known ones. The list runs: 1. Jeunes de l'Europe Nouvelle 2. Jeunes du Maréchal 3. La Ligue des Jeunes de France et de l'Empire 4. Phalange Féminine Française 5. Jeunes Équipes de Français (Jeunes du MSR) 6. Section spéciale de l'Institut des Questions juives (*sic*) 7. Jeunes du Centre intellectuel d'Expansion française. 8. Jeunesse Ouvrière Française. 9. Jeunes Ailes Françaises 10. Jeunes du Berry 11. Jeunesses Normandes 12. Jeunesse Française d'Outremer. 13. Jeunesses Unitaires 14. Jeunes Amis de *l'Appel* (Costantini's newspaper) 15. Equipes du Bulletin des Jeunes 16. JPF (Vauquelin) 17. Jeunesse Franciste (then led by Planton) 18. JNP (Silly) 19. Le Front de la Jeunesse (constituted in 1940 by Augier) 20. Ligue des Jeunes (then led by J. A. Foëx).
109. AN AG II 570. Private files of Ménétrel.
110. AN F.17.13367. Letter to Bonnard from Col. D___, Chef des Jeunes Travailleurs, 11.8.42.
111. AD du Nord, Lille, R.1914. File: Jeunesse.
112. The declaration is given in: *Cahiers de notre jeunesse,* No. 2, July–August 1941.
113. AN AG II 79. File: Rassemblement National des Jeunesses Françaises: RNJF.
114. AN AG II 640. File: CC III N. Mouvements de jeunesse. Divers. The reconstituted Ligue emerged as a result of the congress held in Paris in June 1942. (Cf. Note (108).)
115. AN F.17.13366. 'Réunion des chefs ou responsables des Groupements de Jeunesse du 28 avril 1944. (Préparation du Congrès du Jeunesse.)'
116. There are many personal accounts of the Milice, but the best history is that of J. Delperrié de Bayac, *Histoire de la Milice, 1918–1945,* 1969, from which the present writer has drawn freely.
117. Ibid. 108.
118. Darnand in a radio speech, 21.11.42.
119. J. Mabire, *Les S.S. français. La Division Charlemagne,* 1974, 117.
120. Delperrié de Bayac, op. cit. 175.
121. J.-L. Curtis, *Les Justes Causes,* Livres de Poche, 1954, 31–7.
122. Delperrié de Bayac, op. cit. 181.
123. H. Amouroux, op. cit., Vol. iii, 277, n.56.
124. Ibid. 307.
125. J. Delarue, *Trafic et crimes sous l'Occupation,* 1968, 225–6.
126. Ibid. 149.
127. Mabire, op. cit. 83.

128. Ibid., 17–25, gives an account of all the various German military or para-military units in which Frenchmen served.
129. Ibid. 117.
130. Ibid. 172.
131. Ibid. 195.
132. Ibid. 230.

XIV. YOUTH AND FORCED LABOUR IN GERMANY

1. AD du Nord, Lille, R.1355. 'Note d'orientation' [for press], No. 47 of 16.7.43.
2. ADd Vaucluse, Avignon. Compte-rendu de la séance d'installation du Conseil départemental [*sic*] de Vaucluse. Speech of prefect, 23.1.43.
3. Cf. E. L. Homze, *Foreign Labour in Nazi Germany*, Princeton, NJ, 1967, 181 et seq.
4. AN F.17.13367. 'Note sur les réquisitions de moins de vingt ans', Paris, 12.3.43, signed by the SGJ.
5. AN AJ 39.175. File B7A. 'Peignage. Commission de peignage instituée par circulaires des 9 et 19 février 1944'.
6. AD du Nord, Lille, R.1355. 'Note d'orientation hebdomadaire', No. 30 of 12.3.43, of Centre d'Information du Travail français en Allemagne.
7. E. Jäckel, *Frankreich in Hitlers Europa,* Stuttgart, 1966, 269 et seq.
8. Cf. Note (6).
9. J. Evrard, *La Déportation des travailleurs français dans le IIIè Reich,* 1972, 77. The present writer is greatly indebted to this book for much valuable information.
10. Evrard, op. cit. 88.
11. Cf. Note (6).
12. Evrard, op. cit. 84–5.
13. AD du Nord, Lille, R.1355. 'Note d'orientation hebdomadaire', No. 51 of 20.8.43, of Centre d'Information du Travail français en Allemagne.
14. AN AG II 81. 'Réunion des préfets régionaux du mardi, 21 septembre' [1943].
15. A. Brissaud, *La Dernière Année de Vichy (1943–1944): de Vichy à la Haute Cour,* 1965, 285.
16. Cf. Note (5). Circulars 4.C.2 of 9.2.44 and 6.T.2 of the Sécretariat Général à la Main d'Œuvre. It was expressly stated that 'peignage' would include students.
17. Homze, op. cit., give different figures. He states that between 1.1.44 and 31.5.44, 32,244 men were recruited.
18. Circular 43/Cam/11 of the Commissariat Interministériel. Cf. Note (5).
19. L. Detrez and A. Chatelle, *Tragédies en Flandres, 1940–1944,* Lille, 1953, 279.
20. H. Michel, 'Aspects politiques de l'occupation de la France par les Allemands (juin 1940–décembre 1944)', *RHDGM,* 54, April 1964, 26–7.
21. Cardinal Suhard, *Vers une Eglise en état de mission.* Introduction, choix et présentation de textes par Olivier de la Brosse, OP, 1965, 89.
22. AN F.17.13367. 'Note pour Monsieur le Ministre', Paris, 13.5.44, signed by Bertrand, secretary-general.
23. J. Tracou, *Le Maréchal aux liens. Le Temps du sacrifice,* 1948, 142. For other estimated final totals cf. Note (131).
24. AN F.17.13346. Correspondance du Ministre, 1943 à 1944.
25. Evrard, op. cit. 128–42.
26. Detrez and Chatelle, op. cit. 232.

27. A. Autrand, *Le Département de Vaucluse de la défaite à la Libération, mai 1940–25 août 1944,* n.p. Éditions Aubanel, 1965, 46.
28. Clandestine Communist news-sheet, *La Terre,* October 1943, allegedly citing prefectoral sources, quoted in: Gordon Wright, *Rural Revolution in France,* Stanford, 1964, 227.
29. M. Baudot, *L'Opinion publique sous l'Occupation. L'Exemple d'un département français, 1939–1945,* 1960, 33.
30. AD du Nord, Lille, R.1405. Letter from the regional director of the STO, Lille, to prefect, 13.7.43.
31. AN AG II 461. 'Synthèses hebdomadaires des contrôles télégraphiques, téléphoniques et postaux' [summaries of telecommunications intercepts]. One 'synthèse', undated but probably spring 1943, mentions that despite the unpopularity of the Milice, many former 'Jeunes' of the Chantiers were joining it in order to evade the STO.
32. AN AG II 609. File CM25B. Questions relatives à l'enseignement. 'Propagande universitaire. Extraits de rapports de mars [1943] des Délégués universitaires [de propagande]'. In pencil: 'Reçu 22.4.43'.
33. Jäckel, op. cit. 271.
34. Baudot, op. cit. 32.
35. AN F.17.13366. Seidel, of the Feldkommandantur, Mont-de-Marsan, had written (ref: Az Fu/Ch, Biarritz, 24.4.44) to the Prefect of the Landes claiming that the French ministry of labour had instructed the French police to carry out raids and arrest defaulters and 'oisifs'. All men born between 1899 and 1923 were to be checked in the presence of German authorities and also to be immediately medically examined. Those who, after these checks had been made, appeared liable for STO service should be detained until put on the train for Germany. Raids should be made on night clubs and sports-grounds, particularly at public holidays. Whether the ministry of labour issued such instructions is not known, but on the assumption that it did, Pascot wrote a letter of protest to that ministry and sent copies to Bonnard and the Germans.
36. Autrand, op. cit. 46.
37. *Le Procès du Maréchal Pétain,* Vol. ii, 1945, 811. Testimony of Donati, a former Vichy prefect.
38. H. Chazelle, *Dôle sous la botte. Journal d'un Dôlois pendant la guerre, 1939–1945,* 2nd edition, 1971, 166 et seq.
39. This harassment met with little success. At Lille in June 1943 5,233 of the 1942 class had been summoned for medical examination but only 1,500 had actually appeared; finally only 968 (18.5 per cent) were actually recruited. Cf. AD du Nord, Lille, R.1411. By the spring of 1944 only one in five at the most of those who came on leave from the STO in Germany returned there on expiry of their leave. Cf. AD du Nord, Lille R.1355, 'Note d'orientation hebdomadaire', No. 76 of 17.3.44 of the Centre d'Information du Travail français en Allemagne.
40. Cf. E. Poulat, *Naissance des prêtres-ouvriers,* 1965, 250 et seq.
41. Ibid.
42. AD du Nord, Lille, R.1408. Letter from Cardinal Liénart to prefect, 13.2.43.
43. *Le Procès du Maréchal Pétain,* Vol. i, 1945, 368. Testimony of Pastor Boegner.
44. AN AG II 81. 'Note confidentielle', 18.4.44.
45. AN F.17.13348. Report of: préfet délégué of the Meurthe-et-Moselle, 1.5.44.

46. AN AJ 40.563 German file: Allg. Angelegenheiten d.frz. Bildungswesens – Sammelakten, Bd. i. [General matters concerning the French educational system – collective files, Vol. i].
47. AD du Nord, Lille, R.2457. Letter enclosing text of a tract circulating in Lille, from Commissaire de Police, Lille, to prefect, 26.3.43.
48. Armentières (24.3.43); Wattrelos (25.3.43); Tourcoing (date not known).
49. A. Deroo, *L'Épiscopat français dans la mêlée de son temps, 1930–1954,* 1955, 95 et seq.
50. Quoted in: Aline Coutrot and F. Dreyfus, *Les Forces religieuses dans la société française,* 1965, 95.
51. *Églises et chrétiens dans la Deuxième Guerre Mondiale. La Région Rhône–Alpes. Actes du Colloque de Grenoble,* 1976, publiés sous la direction de Xavier de Montclos, *et al.*, Lyons, 1978, 238.
52. *La Route,* 1.3.43, quoted in Poulat, op. cit. 256.
53. *Documentation catholique,* Vol. xlii, Col. 217–18, quoted in: Deroo, op. cit. 100.
54. AN AG II 609 contains a copy of the article, which is entitled, 'Fières consignes de l'Archevêque de Toulouse aux jeunes scouts'.
55. Most of the numbers of *Cahiers de notre jeunesse* can be consulted at AD de la Drôme, Valence, AP 492. The archives contain an extensive list of periodicals of the Vichy period.
56. Coutrot and Dreyfus, loc. cit.
57. Poulat, op. cit. 256.
58. AN F.17.13349. Report of Brunereau to Bonnard and others, dated 17.4.43. Cf. also AN AG II 609, 'Réunion du Conseil National des Étudiants à Lyon, le jeudi 16 avril 1943 à 14h.30'. This is a briefer report which has pencilled at the bottom: 'Gaullisme'.
59. Poulat, loc. cit.
60. Suhard, op. cit. 90.
61. Poulat, op. cit. 268.
62. Ibid. Cf. also: A. Chévrier, 'L'Église et le Service du Travail Obligatoire', *Revue du Nord,* Lille, No. 237 (April–June 1978), 424, who gives different figures. There would seem to have been no shortage of priests in Germany at any time. Even in 1944 there were still 2,387 priests who were prisoners of war and 98 priests, including the 20 volunteers, serving in the STO; there were also 249 priests who were former prisoners of war and who were working as civilians.
63. Poulat, op. cit. 274.
64. Poulat, op. cit. 275.
65. Ministry of education circular, 16.12.42.
66. AN F.17.13382. Various documents in file: STO – I: 'Négociations – incidents – listes des établissements donnant droit au sursis'. Even ex-soldiers were being called up, not to mention ballet dancers, despite the protests of the director of the Paris Opera!
67. AN F.17.13382. File: STO – II.
68. AN F.17.13383. 'Statistique approchée des étudiants astreints au STO à la date du 5 juillet 1943'. Cf. also: AN F.17.13382. 'Note au sujet des départs pour l'Allemagne, 15.7.' [1943]. There are discrepancies between the various figures.
69. AN F.17.13382. Circular of Laval (as minister of the interior), 20.6.43, Vichy.
70. AN AG II 81.
71. AD du Nord, Lille, R. 1405.

72. AN F.17.13382. File: STO – II .
73. AN F.17.13383. Telegram C.422 dated 10.7.43 to prefects from Commissariat Général du Service du Travail.
74. AN F.17.13347. Correspondance Bonnard.
75. AN F.17.13382. 'Note pour Monsieur le Ministre', 20.3.43.
76. AN AG II 81. File: SP 8B.
77. AN F.17.13382. Circular 1.148/TM of the Secrétariat Général à la Main d'Œuvre, Paris, 4.2.44. This circular cancelled many deferments, including those of students.
78. AN F.17.13382. Circular M-15 of Commissaire Général de la Main d'Œuvre, 23.10.43.
79. AN F.17.13382. Letter to Pétain's 'cabinet civil', from B___, Maître de Maison, Maison du Droit, Paris, 4.12.43.
80. Quoted in: J. A. D. Long, The French Right and Education: the Theory and Practice of Vichy Education Policy, 1940–1944. Oxford D.Phil. thesis, 1976, 270.
81. Detrez and Chatelle, op. cit. 232.
82. AN F.17.13348 contains a 'projet de circulaire' announcing this, but it is not entirely clear whether the circular was finally promulgated.
83. Robert Aron, *Histoire de Vichy*, 1954, 625.
84. Haute Cour de Justice. Audience du 11 mars 1946. Ministère public contre M. Jacques Chevalier, Fasc. I, 40 and 51.
85. AN AG II 75. Letter to Ménétrel from Chevalier, Cérilly, 14.10.43.
86. Evrard, op. cit. 127.
87. Cf. Note (83).
88. Haute Cour de Justice. Audience du 22 mars 1960. Ministère public contre M. Abel Bonnard, Fasc. I, 59.
89. Speech to French Press at Sorbonne, 5.3.43, quoted in: Long, op. cit. 268.
90. Ministry of education circular, 19.2.43.
91. AN F.17.13349. Letter of G___ B___, President of UNEF, to Bonnard, Vichy, 3.5.43.
92. AN F.17.13382. File: STO – III. 'Note [signed by Bertrand] sur les avantages que le Ministre de l'Education Nationale se propose d' accorder aux étudiants travaillant en Allemagne', Paris, 2.5.44.
93. AN F.13346. Letter of Bonnard to Bichelonne, Paris, 28.7.44. Another letter from Bonnard to Bichelonne, sent earlier, had outlined his proposals. A letter from Bichelonne to Bonnard, dated Paris, 18.7.44, had rejected them.
94. AN F.17.13347. Reports to Bonnard dated 12.11.43 and 10.6.44.
95. AN F.17.13345. Letter from a member of Bonnard's 'cabinet civil' to Bichelonne, dated Paris, 17.11.43.
96. Cf. Note (94). Report of 10.6.44.
97. AN F.17.13382. 'Note [signed by Bertrand, secretary-general] pour Monsieur Roy, Inspecteur Général', Paris, 3.5.44.
98. Meyer's reports were confirmed by many others reaching France. After having an audience with Pétain the parish priest of Sablé wrote on 22.10.43 to the Marshal's 'cabinet civil' stating that young men from his parish working in Germany were complaining of the poor food – potatoes and sauerkraut – the long working hours, the lack of amusement, and the increasing number of VD cases. Cf. AN AG II 609.
99. From documents in: AN F.17.13383. A student census was ordered by a circular dated 18.6.43. There is some discrepancy in the various breakdowns of numbers given.
100. R. Hervet, *Les Compagnons de France,* 1965, 224.

101. AN AG II 542. 'Note pour Monsieur Jardel', Vichy, 22.4.43.
102. AN AJ 39.174. File: G9B. 'Notes émises ou reçues par le Commissariat Général [des Chantiers de la Jeunesse].' The file contains two important documents regarding numbers:

(1) Document headed: 'Récapitulatif des départs au STO à la date du 5 août 1943'.
[The figures given are broadly in line with those given by Evrard, op. cit. 98. The dates in square brackets are taken from Evrard.]

	Reported	*Departed*
"First contingent [30.5.–1.6.43]	5,878	4,986
Second contingent [11.6.–2.7.43]	11,378	9,554
Third contingent [17.7.–28.7.43]	2,655	1,832
General Total	19,911	16,372

Total number of defaulters: 7,148"[*sic*]

(2) Document headed: 'Organisation – Commandement OCA/G.9. Recapitulation' [n.d.]

"I. Numbers in Chantiers available for STO:

'Jeunes' joining in November [1942]	32,000
'Jeunes' of 1942 class, joining March 1943.	500
	32,500

II. Numbers made available:

	Reported	*Departed*
(a) STO: Germany (18,000 required)		
First contingent	5,878	4,986
Second contingent	11,378	9,554
	17,256	14,540

(b) STO: France (6,000 required)

Dispatched 9.7.[43]	2,878
15.7.[43]	870
	3,748

Groups to be dispatched according to demands of local German authorities.

Remaining to report 1,100 [*sic*]

III. Released from Chantiers service:

Farmworkers (classes of 1940 and 1941)	4,400
Miners (coal-face workers)	500
	4,900

IV. Absent irregularly:

	7,148
(of which 232 of 1943 class) [less]	232
	6,916 "

The reference to the 1943 class may show that the document was compiled before that class were formally called up for STO service.
103. Cf. Note (10).
104. Evrard, op. cit. 92.

105. AN AJ 39.175. Report of Commissaire en Chef S___ L___ B___ 'sur les conditions dans lesquelles se sont effectuées les opérations de mise en route des Jeunes, 28 mai–31 juin 1943'.
106. AN AJ 39.174. Letter from General de La Porte du Theil to the secretary-general of the Chef du Gouvernement, Châtel-Guyon, 10.6.43.
107. AN AJ 39.174. 'Note de service' from de La Porte du Theil to the Commissaires Régionaux, Châtel-Guyon, 30.5.43.
108. Evrard, op. cit. 150–1.
109. J. Delage, *Grandeurs et servitudes des Chantiers de Jeunesse,* 1950, 82.
110. AN F.17.13347. Report of Meyer to Bonnard, Paris, 10.6.44.
111. AN AJ 39.175. Note from de La Porte du Theil to the Bureau des Requêtes, Secrétariat Général du Chef du Gouvernement, ref. No. 1562-DA.C.4, dated 19.10.43.
112. AN AG II 543. Report of Association des Anciens des Chantiers, Châtel-Guyon, 9.5.43.
113. Cf. Note (102).
114. Reported in: *Paris-Midi.* 26.2.44.
115. AN AG II 461. Synthèses hebdomadaires des contrôles télégraphiques, téléphoniques et postaux [telecommunications intercepts], January–September 1943.
116. AN AJ 39.174. Letter from F___ G___, law student, Puy-Charlard, Creuse, to General de La Porte du Theil, 15.7.43.
117. J. de Launay, *La France de Pétain,* 1972, 117–18. Cf. also: Delage, op. cit. 82, and Ch. XI, p. 305–6.
118. AN AG II 80. Letter from Commissariat Général à la Jeunesse, Vichy, 27.1.44, to Pétain.
119. AN F.17.13366. Letter from Mlle C___ B___, Paris, n.d. [probably March 1944] to de Brinon, who passed it on to Bonnard (letter, Paris, 8.3.44), complaining that 'chefs de groupements' in the Chantiers were urging 'Jeunes' not to answer the call-up to the STO.
120. AN F.17.13366. 'Note sur l'utilisation des Chantiers de la Jeunesse', 25.1.44.
121. A. Mallet, *Pierre Laval,* 1955, Vol. ii, 208, quoting Gaït, Commissaire Général à la Jeunesse, from 1.1.44 to the end.
122. C. Varennes, *Le Destin de Marcel Déat,* 1948, 188–9. (The works of both Varennes and Mallet should be treated with caution.)
123. AN F.17.13367. 'Papier communiqué par la D.S.A. le 3.3.44 à 17h.30.', signed N___, and emanating from the minister of production. Cf. also: AN AG II 81. File SP 8F – RNP: 'Note confidentielle du 14 avril 1944'.
124. AN AJ 39.175. Note from General Vogl, Wiesbaden, 12.5.44, to the French delegation to the Armistice Commission.
125. AN AG II 81. Dossiers G___, 'attaché au Secrétariat particulier du Chef de l'État'. G___ had been a primary teacher.
126. Ibid. 'Note' of 4.6.43.
127. Ibid., 'Travailleurs en Allemagne', 1.7.43.
128. Ibid., 'Note' of 23.7.43.
129. Ibid., 'Note', Vichy, 17.9.43.
130. Ibid., 'Note', Vichy, 27.1.44.
131. Ibid., 'Note confidentielle du 18 avril 1944'. Evrard, op. cit. 161, gives figures of numbers of Frenchmen in Germany culled from various, unspecified sources:
   – A German source (30.9.44) gave a total of 646,326 (603,762 men and 42,564 women).

– Another German Source – the *Arbeitseinsatzamt* – stated (no date is given) a figure of 852,278 (including prisoners of war given civilian status), of whom 184,562 were volunteers.
– A French source stated that between 1.6.42 and 31.7.44 the total was 766,162. To this had to be added 197,000 prisoners of war given civilian status, making a total of 963,162.

Index